1982

ROMANTICISM
AND THE FORMS
OF RUIN

Romanticism and the Forms of Ruin

*WORDSWORTH, COLERIDGE, AND
MODALITIES OF FRAGMENTATION*

Thomas McFarland

◊♦◊

PRINCETON UNIVERSITY PRESS

PRINCETON, NEW JERSEY

For
Darr Kartychak

                    I have slept
Weeping, and weeping I have waked. My tears
Have flowed as if my body were not such
As others are, and I could never die.

                    The Ruined Cottage

Contents

◊♦◊

Preface

◊ ♦ ◊

In an earlier meditation on Romanticism called *Coleridge and the Pantheist Tradition*, I found occasion to stress the prevalence of systematic concerns in the Romantic epoch. "To understand Coleridge's thought, both in its own structure and in its relationship to the thought of his contemporaries," I said in that work, "it is necessary to refer all its manifestations constantly and explicitly to the systematic unity, the total organism which he, and almost all other thinkers of his era, accepted as the necessary condition of any intellectual activity at all." I there said that "for Coleridge, as for Kant, the architectonic concern was paramount"; I spoke of "the omnipresence of system, whether, as in Hegel, fully enunciated, or, as in Coleridge, merely implied"; and I concluded that "the urge to system is a reflection, in the special realm of philosophy, of a universal concern, the need to harmonize, to tie things together—what we may call the need for reticulation."

Taking the word "reticulation" as the keynote of the book's movement of thought, I urged that "It is, indeed, possible that the whole thrust to unity so characteristic of Romanticism, as opposed to the classifying instinct of the eighteenth century, should be primarily seen—whether we think of the revival of the *coincidentia oppositorum* in minds as different as those of Hamann, Coleridge, Hegel, and Victor Hugo, or whether we think of the rise of pantheism in religion, of synaesthesia in art, of democracy in politics, of system in philosophy, of distinction-dissolving 'progressive Universalpoesie' in literature—as an intensification of the reticulative need."

But the existence of so powerful a need suggests that the situation actually obtaining must be the contrary of unity: that is, one of fragmentation, of things not tied together, not harmonious, not architectonically ordered. The present book explores that contrary situation from multiple perspectives. It thus constitutes an opposite of the earlier meditation; it does so, however, not by way of repudiation, but by way of necessary complement. The relation of this volume to the earlier one may be thought of, to deploy a variety of metaphors, as the reverse of that coin's obverse; or as the turned identity rendered by an act of mirroring; or still again, as the white field reciprocally definitive of the silhouette that we ordinarily refer to the form of the black outline.

I have been helped during the writing of the book by many people, and the recording of my thanks for such kindness is for me the happiest moment in the entire progression of activity that culminates in publication. I want to express my gratitude once again to my teacher, Frederick A. Pottle, whose character and example have been decisive for my development. Margaret Jane Fischer gave me early help of lasting effect. My friends, John Beer, Albert Cook, Stuart Curran, Angus Fletcher, Albert B. Friedman, Richard Haven, and John Hollander, have read portions and versions of the volume at varying stages of its evolution, and the combined resources of their wisdom and enormous learning have been of invaluable aid to me. Flora Levin graciously elucidated for me the nuances of a number of passages of Plato's Greek. My friend, Robert Langbaum, my friend and former colleague, Samuel R. Levin, my friend and present colleague, Samuel Hynes, and most generously and indefatigably, my friend and departmental chairman, A. Walton Litz, have eased my path in vital ways. I find myself continuingly grateful for the benignity and good will of Harold Bloom, Walter Jackson Bate, and L. C. Knights. Kathleen Coburn, whose dedication and scholarship have virtually created the modern field of Coleridge studies, has stood by me patiently—although she doubtless would prefer to see this book follow, rather than precede, the editorial labors I have undertaken for her monumental edition of Coleridge's works.

The help of five people in particular has been essential in meeting the quotidian demands of the book's progress to completion. Marcus Boggs was a constant source of indispensable encouragement. He not only read most of the manuscript and supplied criticism that was always perceptive, but he also suggested many materials for inclusion in the text. Andrea Korval gave me valued assistance in the final preparation of the manuscript for delivery to the press, and she gave me further assistance in the interim stages of proofreading and checking. Joseph Moses maintained a continuing interest in the book's conception and growth, and I often relied on his discernment and critical subtlety. Gail Filion, of the Princeton University Press, undertook the onerous task of copyediting the typescript, and in its course she made many felicitous suggestions on matters of style, format, and emphasis. And Mrs. Arthur Sherwood, of the Princeton University Press, supervised the volume's emergence into print from first to last with exemplary professional skill.

Although all the chapters of the book were composed as parts of the special whole here envisaged, five of them have previously appeared, under the same titles but in each case in less comprehensive versions, in the following places: *Chapter One* ("The Symbiosis of Coleridge and Wordsworth"), in the Coleridge bicentenary issue of *Studies in Romanticism*, XI (1972); *Chapter Two* ("Coleridge's Anxiety"), in *Coleridge's Variety; Bicentenary Studies*, ed. John Beer (London: The Macmillan Company, 1974); *First Landing Place* ("Poetry and the Poem: The Structure of Poetic Content"), in *Literary Theory and Structure; Essays in Honor of William K. Wimsatt*, ed. Frank Brady, John Palmer, and Martin Price (New Haven: Yale University Press, 1973); *Chapter Five* ("A Complex Dialogue: Coleridge's Doctrine of Polarity and Its European Contexts"), in *Reading Coleridge: Approaches and Applications*, ed. Walter B. Crawford (Ithaca, N.Y.: © Cornell University Press, 1979); *Second Landing Place* ("The Place Beyond the Heavens: True Being, Transcendence, and the Symbolic Indication of Wholeness"), in *Boundary 2; A Journal of Postmodern Literature*, ed. Paul Bové, VII (1979).

Lastly, I wish to express my thanks to the John Simon Guggenheim Memorial Foundation and to the American Council of Learned Societies for fellowships that freed me to engage in some of the research upon which the book is founded.

THOMAS MCFARLAND

Key to Brief Titles Cited

◊ ♦ ◊

Brief titles that appear in the notes refer either to full citations occurring shortly before or to the editions listed below.

Allemann
Beda Allemann, *Hölderlin und Heidegger*, second edition (Zurich: Atlantis Verlag, 1954).

Alquié
Ferdinand Alquié, *Philosophie du surréalisme* (Paris: Flammarion, 1955).

Appleyard
J. A. Appleyard, *Coleridge's Philosophy of Literature; The Development of a Concept of Poetry 1791-1819* (Cambridge, Mass.: Harvard University Press, 1965).

Aris
Reinhold Aris, *History of Political Thought in Germany from 1789 to 1815* (London: George Allen & Unwin Ltd., 1936).

Arnold, *Essays*
Matthew Arnold, *Essays in Criticism; Second Series* (London and New York: Macmillan and Co., 1905).

Arnold, *Poems*
The Poetical Works of Matthew Arnold, ed. C. B. Tinker and H. F. Lowry (London, New York, Toronto: Oxford University Press, 1950).

Art of the Lyrical Ballads
Stephen Maxfield Parrish, *The Art of the* Lyrical Ballads (Cambridge, Mass.: Harvard University Press, 1973).

Bachofen
Myth, Religion, and Mother Right: Selected Writings of J. J. Bachofen, trans. Ralph Manheim (Princeton: Princeton University Press, 1967).

Bacon
The Works of Francis Bacon, ed. James Spedding, R. L. Ellis, and D. D. Heath (London, 1857-74), 14 vols. New edition, London, Longmans, 1870.

Barfield
Owen Barfield, *What Coleridge Thought* (Middletown, Conn.: Wesleyan University Press, 1971).

Baudelaire
Baudelaire, *Oeuvres complètes*, ed. Claude Pichois, Bibliothèque de la Pléiade (Paris: Gallimard, 1975-76), 2 vols.

Berdyaev
Nicolas Berdyaev, "Unground and Freedom," in *Six Theosophic Points and Other Writings* by Jacob Boehme, trans. John Rolleston Earle (Ann Arbor: The University of Michigan Press, 1958).

Biographia
Biographia Literaria, by S. T. Coleridge, edited with his aesthetical essays, by J. Shawcross (London: Oxford University Press, 1907), 2 vols.

Blackmur
R. P. Blackmur, *Form and Value in Modern Poetry* (Garden City, New York: Doubleday Anchor Books, 1952).

Blake
The Poetry and Prose of William Blake, ed. David V. Erdman, with commentary by Harold Bloom, third printing, with revisions (Garden City, N.Y.: Doubleday & Company, Inc., 1968).

Blake, *Letters*
The Letters of William Blake, ed. Geoffrey Keynes (Cambridge, Mass.: Harvard University Press, 1970).

Bloch
Ernst Bloch, *Subjekt-Objekt; Erläuterungen zu Hegel* (Berlin: Aufbau-Verlag, 1951).

Bloom
Harold Bloom, *The Visionary Company; A Reading of English Romantic Poetry*, revised and enlarged edition (Ithaca and London: Cornell University Press, 1971).

Boehme
Jakob Boehme, *Sämtliche Schriften*, new facsimile printing of the edition of 1730, ed. Will-Erich Peuckert (Stuttgart: Friedrich Frommann Verlag, 1955-60), 11 vols.

Bollnow
Otto Friedrich Bollnow, *Neue Geborgenheit; Das Problem einer Überwindung des Existentialismus* (Stuttgart: Kohlhammer, 1955).

Borges
Jorge Luis Borges, *A Personal Anthology*, ed. Anthony Kerrigan (New York: Grove Press, 1967).

Bossuet-Leibniz
François Gaquère, *Le Dialogue irénique Bossuet-Leibniz; La réunion des Eglises en échec (1691-1702)* (Paris: Beauchesne, 1966).

Bostetter
Edward E. Bostetter, *The Romantic Ventriloquists; Wordsworth, Coleridge, Keats, Shelley, Byron*, revised edition (Seattle and London: The University of Washington Press, 1975).

Bradley
A. C. Bradley, *Oxford Lectures on Poetry* (London: Macmillan, 1934).

Bruno
Giordano Bruno, *Dialoghi italiani* . . . with notes by Giovanni Gentile, third edition by Giovanni Aquilecchia (Florence: Sansoni, 1958).

Burke, *Reflections*
Edmund Burke, *Reflections on the Revolution in France*, ed. Thomas H. D. Mahoney, The Library of Liberal Arts (Indianapolis and New York: The Bobbs-Merrill Company, Inc., 1955).

Burke's Politics
Burke's Politics; Selected Writings and Speeches of Edmund Burke on Reform, Revolution, and War, ed. Ross J. S. Hoffman and Paul Levack (New York: Alfred A. Knopf, 1970).

Burnet
John Burnet, *Greek Philosophy; Thales to Plato* (London: Macmillan; New York: St. Martin's Press, 1968).

Byron, *Letters*
Byron's Letters & Journals, ed. Leslie A. Marchand (Cambridge, Mass.: Harvard University Press, 1973-   ), 10 vols. to date.

Byron, *Poems*
The Works of Lord Byron . . . Poetry, ed. Ernest Hartley Coleridge (London: John Murray, 1900-1904), 7 vols.

Carlyle
The Works of Thomas Carlyle in Thirty Volumes, Centenary Edition [ed. H. D. Traill] (London: Chapman and Hall Limited, [1896-99]), 30 vols.

Chambers
E. K. Chambers, *Samuel Taylor Coleridge; A Biographical Study* (Oxford: The Clarendon Press, 1950).

Chekhov
Sophie Laffitte, *Chekhov; 1860-1914*, trans. Moura Budberg and Gordon Latta (New York: Charles Scribner's Sons, 1973).

Church and State
Coleridge, *On the Constitution of the Church and State*, ed. John Colmer (London: Routledge & Kegan Paul; Princeton: Princeton University Press, 1976). Volume Ten in *The Collected Works of Samuel Taylor Coleridge*, ed. Kathleen Coburn, Bollingen Series LXXV.

Clare
Selected Poems and Prose of John Clare, chosen and edited by Eric Robinson and Geoffrey Summerfield (London: Oxford University Press, 1967).

Clough
The Poems of Arthur Hugh Clough, second edition, ed. F. L. Mulhauser (Oxford: The Clarendon Press, 1974).

Coleridge, *Complete Works*
The Complete Works of Samuel Taylor Coleridge, ed. W.G.T. Shedd (New York: Harper and Brothers, 1853), 7 vols.

Coleridge, *Poems*
The Complete Poetical Works of Samuel Taylor Coleridge, ed. Ernest Hartley Coleridge (Oxford: The Clarendon Press, 1912), 2 vols.

Collected Letters
Collected Letters of Samuel Taylor Coleridge, ed. Earl Leslie Griggs (Oxford: The Clarendon Press, 1956-71), 6 vols.

Conjectures
[Edward Young], *Conjectures on Original Composition*. In a letter to the Author of Sir Charles Grandison (London: A. Millar and R. and J. Dodsley, 1759).

CPT
Thomas McFarland, *Coleridge and the Pantheist Tradition* (Oxford: The Clarendon Press, 1969).

Croce
Benedetto Croce, *Aesthetic; As Science of Expression and General Linguistic*, trans. Douglas Ainslie (New York: The Noonday Press, 1955).

Cruttwell
Patrick Cruttwell, *The Shakespearean Moment and its Place in the Poetry of the 17th Century* (New York: Columbia University Press, 1970).

Culler
A. Dwight Culler, *The Imperial Intellect; A Study of Newman's Educational Ideal* (New Haven: Yale University Press, 1955).

Danckert
Werner Danckert, *Goethe; der mythische Urgrund seiner Weltschau* (Berlin: Walter de Gruyter & Co., 1951).

Darbishire
Helen Darbishire, *The Poet Wordsworth; The Clark Lectures . . . 1949* (Oxford: The Clarendon Press, 1950).

Darío
Selected Poems of Rubén Darío, trans. Lysander Kemp, prologue by Octavio Paz (Austin: University of Texas Press, 1973).

Darnton
Robert Darnton, *Mesmerism and the End of the Enlightenment in France* (Cambridge, Mass.: Harvard University Press, 1968).

Darwin, *Descent*
Charles Darwin, *The Descent of Man and Selection in Relation to Sex,* second edition, revised and augmented (New York and London: D. Appleton and Company, 1913).

Darwin, *Life*
The Life and Letters of Charles Darwin; Including an Autobiographical Chapter, edited by his son Francis Darwin (New York and London: D. Appleton and Company, 1919), 2 vols.

Darwin, *Origin*
Charles Darwin, *The Origin of Species by Means of Natural Selection; or the Preservation of Favoured Races in the Struggle for Life,* ed. J. W. Burrow (Baltimore: Penguin Books, 1968).

Davie
Donald Davie, *Articulate Energy; An Enquiry into the Syntax of English Poetry* (London: Routledge & Kegan Paul, 1966).

De Quincey
The Collected Writings of Thomas De Quincey, ed. David Masson (Edinburgh: Adam and Charles Black, 1899-90), 14 vols.

Diels-Kranz
Hermann Diels, *Die Fragmente der Vorsokratiker,* sixth edition, ed. Walter Kranz (Dublin/Zurich: Weidmann, 1971), 3 vols.

Dryden
The Poetical Works of Dryden, a new edition, revised and enlarged by George R. Noyes, Cambridge Edition (Cambridge, Mass.: Houghton Mifflin Company, 1950).

Du Bellay
Joachim Du Bellay, *La Deffence et illustration de la langue Francoyse,* ed. Henri Chamard (Paris: Librairie Marcel Didier, 1961).

Early Years
The Letters of William and Dorothy Wordsworth; The Early Years; 1787-1805, ed. Ernest de Selincourt, revised by Chester L. Shaver (Oxford: The Clarendon Press, 1967).

E. A. Robinson
Collected Poems of Edwin Arlington Robinson (New York: The Macmillan Co., 1972).

Eliot, *On Poetry*
T. S. Eliot, *On Poetry and Poets* (New York: Farrar, Straus and Cudahy, 1957).

Eliot, *Poems*
T. S. Eliot, *Collected Poems; 1909-1935* (New York: Harcourt, Brace and Company, 1936).

Eliot, *Use of Poetry*
T. S. Eliot, *The Use of Poetry and the Use of Criticism; Studies in the Relation of Criticism to Poetry in England* (London: Faber and Faber Limited, 1933).

Else
Gerald F. Else, *Aristotle's Poetics; The Argument* (Cambridge, Mass.: Harvard University Press, 1967).

Erasmus Darwin
The Essential Writings of Erasmus Darwin, chosen and edited with a linking commentary by Desmond King-Hele (London: MacGibbon & Kee, 1968).

Erdmann
Johann Edward Erdmann, *A History of Philosophy,* trans. Williston S. Hough, II (London: George Allen and Unwin, Ltd.; New York: The Macmillan Co., 1915).

Essay on Man
Ernst Cassirer, *An Essay on Man; An Introduction to a Philosophy of Human Culture* (New Haven: Yale University Press, 1970).

Fenichel
Otto Fenichel, *The Psychoanalytic Theory of Neurosis* (New York: W. W. Norton & Co., Inc., 1945).

Ferry
David Ferry, *The Limits of Mortality; An Essay on Wordsworth's Major Poems* (Middletown, Conn.: Wesleyan University Press, 1959).

Feuerbach's Werke
Ludwig Feuerbach's sämmtliche Werke (Leipzig: Druck und Verlag von Otto Wigand, 1846-1890), 10 vols.

Field
Barron Field's Memoirs of Wordsworth, ed. Geoffrey Little (Sydney: Sydney University Press, 1975).

Flaubert
Oeuvres complètes de Gustave Flaubert. Correspondance. Nouvelle édition augmentée (Paris: Conard, 1926-33), 9 vols.

Foakes
Coleridge on Shakespeare; The Text of the Lectures of 1811-1812, ed. R. A. Foakes (London: Routledge & Kegan Paul, 1971).

Fogle
Richard Harter Fogle, *The Idea of Coleridge's Criticism* (Berkeley and Los Angeles: The University of California Press, 1962).

Freud
The Standard Edition of the Complete Psychological Works of Sigmund Freud, trans. and ed. James Strachey, Anna Freud et al. (London: The Hogarth Press and The Institute of Psycho-Analysis, 1966-74), 24 vols.

Friedrich Schlegel
Kritische Friedrich-Schlegel-Ausgabe, ed. by Ernst Behler with the assistance of Jean-Jacques Anstett and Hans Eichner (Munich, Paderborn, Vienna: Verlag Ferdinand Schöningh, 1958-   ), 35 vols. when completed.

Friend
Coleridge, *The Friend*, ed. Barbara E. Rooke (London: Routledge & Kegan Paul; Princeton: Princeton University Press, 1969). Volume Four in *The Collected Works of Samuel Taylor Coleridge*, ed. Kathleen Coburn, Bollingen Series LXXV, 2 vols.

Froude
James Anthony Froude, *Thomas Carlyle; A History of his Life in London; 1834-1881*, new edition (London and Bombay: Longmans, Green and Co., 1897), 2 vols.

Fruman
Norman Fruman, *Coleridge, The Damaged Archangel* (New York: George Braziller, 1971).

Garrod
H. W. Garrod, *Wordsworth: Lectures and Essays* (Oxford: The Clarendon Press, 1923).

Gedenkausgabe
Johann Wolfgang Goethe, *Gedenkausgabe der Werke, Briefe und Gespräche*, ed. Ernst Beutler (Zurich: Artemis Verlag, 1948-71), 27 vols.

George
Stefan George; Gesamt-Ausgabe der Werke; Endgültige Fassung (Berlin: Georg Bondi, 1927-34), 18 vols. in 15.

Gesammelte Schriften
Kant's gesammelte Schriften, ed. by the Royal Prussian Academy of Sciences (Berlin: Druck und Verlag von Georg Reimer; continued to the present by Walter de Gruyter & Co., 1902-   ), 31 vols. to date.

Grosart
The Prose Works of William Wordsworth . . . ed. Alexander B. Grosart
(London: Edward Moxon, Son, and Co., 1876), 3 vols.

Gurwitsch
Aron Gurwitsch, *Studies in Phenomenology and Psychology*, trans. Freder-
ick Kersten et al. (Evanston, Ill.: Northwestern University Press, 1966).

Guthrie
W.K.C. Guthrie, *A History of Greek Philosophy* (Cambridge: Cambridge
University Press, 1962-   ), 5 vols. to date.

Haering
Theodor Haering, *Hegel; Sein Wollen und sein Werke. Eine chronologische
Entwicklungsgeschichte der Gedanken und der Sprache Hegels* (Aalen: Scientia
Verlag, 1963), 2 vols.

Hardy
Collected Poems of Thomas Hardy (New York: The Macmillan Company,
1925).

Havelock
Eric Havelock, *The Liberal Temper in Greek Politics* (New Haven and Lon-
don: Yale University Press, 1957).

Haydon
The Diary of Benjamin Robert Haydon, ed. Willard Bissell Pope (Cam-
bridge, Mass.: Harvard University Press, 1960-63), 5 vols.

Haym
Rudolf Haym, *Die romantische Schule. Ein Beitrag zur Geschichte des
deutschen Geistes* (Hildesheim: Georg Olms Verlagsbuchhandlung,
1961).

Hazlitt
The Complete Works of William Hazlitt, ed. P. P. Howe, after the edition of
A. R. Waller and Arnold Glover (London: J. M. Dent and Sons, Ltd.,
1930-34), 21 vols.

Heath
William Heath, *Wordsworth and Coleridge: A Study of their Literary Rela-
tions in 1801-1802* (Oxford: The Clarendon Press, 1970).

Heffernan
James Heffernan, *Wordsworth's Theory of Poetry; The Transforming Imagi-
nation* (Ithaca, N.Y.: Cornell University Press, 1969).

Hegel, *Briefe*
Briefe von und an Hegel, ed. Johannes Hoffmeister (Hamburg: Verlag von
Felix Meiner, 1952-61), 4 vols.

Hegel's Werke
Georg Wilhelm Friedrich Hegel's Werke, Complete Edition by a Group of Friends of the Late Author: Ph[ilipp] Marheineke, J[ohannes] Schulze, Ed[uard] Gans, L[eo]p[old] v[on] Henning, H[einrich] Hotho, K[arl] Michelet, F[riedrich] Förster (Berlin: Duncker und Humblot, 1832-1845), 20 vols.

Heidegger, *Existence and Being*
Martin Heidegger, *Existence and Being*, ed. Werner Brock (Chicago: Henry Regnery Company, 1949).

Heidegger, *Sein und Zeit*
Martin Heidegger, *Sein und Zeit*, seventh unaltered edition (Tübingen: Max Niemeyer Verlag, 1953).

Heidegger, *Vorträge*
Martin Heidegger, *Vorträge und Aufsätze* (Pfullingen: Neske, 1954).

Heidegger, *Wegmarken*
Martin Heidegger, *Wegmarken* (Frankfurt am Main: Vittorio Klostermann, 1967).

Heine
Heinrich Heine, *Die romantische Schule* (Hamburg, 1836).

Hirst
Désirée Hirst, *Hidden Riches; Traditional Symbolism from the Renaissance to Blake* (London: Eyre & Spottiswoode, 1964).

Hölderlin
Hölderlin, *Sämtliche Werke*, Stuttgart Hölderlin Edition, commissioned by the Ministry of Culture of Baden-Württemberg, ed. Friedrich Beissner (Stuttgart: W. Kohlhammer Verlag, 1946-   ), 7 vols. in 12 to date.

Hopkins
The Poems of Gerard Manley Hopkins, fourth edition, ed. W. H. Gardner and N. H. MacKenzie (London: Oxford University Press, 1967).

House
Humphry House, *Coleridge; The Clark Lectures 1951-52* (London: Rupert Hart-Davis, 1962).

Huch
Ricarda Huch, *Die Romantik; Ausbreitung, Blütezeit und Verfall* (Tübingen: Rainer Wunderlich Verlag Hermann Leins, 1951).

Hugo, *Poésies*
Victor Hugo, *Oeuvres poétiques*, ed. Pierre Albouy, Bibliothèque de la Pléiade (Paris: Gallimard, 1964-74), 3 vols.

Hugo, *Théâtre*
Victor Hugo, *Théâtre complet*, ed. Roland Purnal, J.-J. Thierry, and Josette Mélèze, Bibliothèque de la Pléiade (Paris: Gallimard, 1963-64), 2 vols.

Hulme, *Speculations*
T. E. Hulme, *Speculations; Essays on Humanism and the Philosophy of Art*, ed. Herbert Read (London: Routledge & Kegan Paul Ltd., 1949).

Hunt
Leigh Hunt, *Essays and Sketches*, chosen and edited with an introduction by R. Brimeley Johnson (London: Oxford University Press, 1928).

Ideen
Edmund Husserl, *Ideen zu einer reinen Phänomenologie und phänomenologischen Philosophie*, ed. Walter Biemel, i (The Hague: Martinus Nijhoff, 1950).

Ingarden
Roman Ingarden, *The Literary Work of Art; An Investigation on the Borderline of Ontology, Logic, and Theory of Literature*, trans. George G. Grabowicz (Evanston, Ill.: Northwestern University Press, 1973).

Inquiring Spirit
Inquiring Spirit; A New Presentation of Coleridge from his Published and Unpublished Prose Writings, ed. Kathleen Coburn (New York: Pantheon Books, 1951).

Jackson
J. R. de J. Jackson, *Method and Imagination in Coleridge's Criticism* (Cambridge, Mass.: Harvard University Press, 1969).

Jacobi's Werke
Friedrich Heinrich Jacobi's Werke, ed. Friedrich Roth and Friedrich Köppen (Leipzig: bey Gerhard Fleischer, 1812-25), 6 vols. in 7.

Jacobsen
J. P. Jacobsen, *Niels Lyhne*, trans. Hanna Astrup Larsen, third printing (New York: The American-Scandinavian Foundation; London: Oxford University Press, 1947).

Jacobus
Mary Jacobus, *Tradition and Experiment in Wordsworth's* Lyrical Ballads *(1798)* (Oxford: The Clarendon Press, 1976).

Jaspers, *Philosophie*
Karl Jaspers, *Philosophie*, third edition (Berlin, Göttingen, Heidelberg: Springer Verlag, 1956), 3 vols.

Jaspers, *Plato*
Karl Jaspers, *Plato and Augustine*, trans. Ralph Manheim (New York: Harcourt, Brace and World, Inc., 1962).

Jaspers, *Wahrheit*
Karl Jaspers, *Von der Wahrheit* (Munich: R. Piper & Co. Verlag, 1947).

Jonathan Wordsworth
Jonathan Wordsworth, *The Music of Humanity; A Critical Study of Wordsworth's Ruined Cottage; Incorporating Texts from a Manuscript of 1799-1800* (New York and Evanston: Harper & Row, Publishers, 1969).

Jonson
Ben Jonson, ed. C. H. Herford and Percy Simpson (Oxford: The Clarendon Press, 1925-52), 11 vols.

Journals
Journals of Dorothy Wordsworth, ed. Ernest de Selincourt (London: Macmillan, 1970), 2 vols.

Keats Circle
The Keats Circle; Letters and Papers and More Letters and Poems of the Keats Circle, ed. Hyder Edward Rollins, second edition (Cambridge, Mass.: Harvard University Press, 1965), 2 vols.

Keats, *Letters*
The Letters of John Keats, 1814-1821, ed. Hyder Edward Rollins (Cambridge, Mass.: Harvard University Press, 1958), 2 vols.

Keats, *Poems*
The Poetical Works of John Keats, ed. H. W. Garrod, second edition (Oxford: The Clarendon Press, 1958).

Kenner
Hugh Kenner, *The Pound Era* (Berkeley and Los Angeles: The University of California Press, 1971).

Kierkegaard
Søren Kierkegaard, *The Concept of Dread*, trans. Walter Lowrie (Princeton, N.J.: Princeton University Press, 1957).

Kierkegaard, *Journals*
The Journals of Søren Kierkegaard, ed. and trans. Alexander Dru (London: Oxford University Press, 1951).

Kirk and Raven
G. S. Kirk and J. E. Raven, *The Presocratic Philosophers: A Critical History with a Selection of Texts* (Cambridge: Cambridge University Press, 1971).

Kojève
Alexandre Kojève, *Introduction to the Reading of Hegel*, trans. James H. Nichols, Jr. (New York and London: Basic Books, 1969).

Kroner
Richard Kroner, *Von Kant bis Hegel*, second edition (Tübingen: J.C.B. Mohr [Paul Siebeck], 1961), 2 vols. in 1.

Lamb, *Letters*
> *The Letters of Charles Lamb, to which are added those of his sister Mary Lamb*, ed. E. V. Lucas (London: J. M. Dent & Sons Ltd. and Methuen & Co. Ltd., 1935), 3 vols.

Lamb, *Works*
> *The Works of Charles and Mary Lamb*, ed. E. V. Lucas (London: Methuen & Co., 1903-1904), 5 vols.

Langbaum
> Robert Langbaum, *The Poetry of Experience; The Dramatic Monologue in Modern Literary Tradition* (New York: W. W. Norton & Co., Inc., 1963).

Langer
> Susanne K. Langer, *Feeling and Form; A Theory of Art* (New York: Charles Scribner's Sons, 1953).

Later Years
> *The Letters of William and Dorothy Wordsworth; The Later Years*, ed. Ernest de Selincourt (Oxford: The Clarendon Press, 1939), 3 vols.

Lay Sermons
> Samuel Taylor Coleridge, *Lay Sermons*, ed. R. J. White (London: Routledge & Kegan Paul; Princeton: Princeton University Press, 1972). Volume Six in *The Collected Works of Samuel Taylor Coleridge*, ed. Kathleen Coburn, Bollingen Series LXXV.

Leavis, *Pursuit*
> F. R. Leavis, *The Common Pursuit* (London: Chatto & Windus, 1972).

Leavis, *Revaluation*
> F. R. Leavis, *Revaluation; Tradition & Development in English Poetry* (London: Chatto & Windus, 1969).

Leavis, *Sword*
> F. R. Leavis, *Nor Shall my Sword; Discourses on Pluralism, Compassion and Social Hope* (New York: Barnes & Noble Books, 1972).

Lectures 1795
> Samuel Taylor Coleridge, *Lectures 1795 on Politics and Religion*, ed. Lewis Patton and Peter Mann (London: Routledge & Kegan Paul; Princeton: Princeton University Press, 1971). Volume One in *The Collected Works of Samuel Taylor Coleridge*, ed. Kathleen Coburn, Bollingen Series LXXV.

Lefebvre
> Georges Lefebvre, *The French Revolution*, trans. Elizabeth Moss Evanson, John Hall Stewart and James Friguglietti (London: Routledge & Kegan Paul; New York: Columbia University Press, 1962-64), 2 vols.

Leibniz
> *Die philosophischen Schriften von Gottfried Wilhelm Leibniz*, ed. C. J.

Gerhardt (Berlin, 1875-90; facsimile reprint by Georg Olms Verlags-buchhandlung, Hildesheim, 1960-61), 7 vols.

Levinas
Emmanuel Levinas, *Totality and Infinity; An Essay on Exteriority*, trans. Alphonso Lingis (Pittsburgh: Duquesne University Press, 1969).

Lowes
John Livingston Lowes, *The Road to Xanadu; A Study in the Ways of the Imagination* (Boston: Houghton Mifflin Co., 1927).

Mannheim
From Karl Mannheim, ed. Kurt H. Wolff (New York: Oxford University Press, 1971).

Margoliouth
H. M. Margoliouth, *Wordsworth and Coleridge—1795-1834* (London: Oxford University Press, 1955).

Marlowe
The Complete Plays of Christopher Marlowe, ed. Irving Ribner (New York: The Odyssey Press, Inc., 1963).

Marvell
The Poems & Letters of Andrew Marvell, ed. H. M. Margoliouth, second edition (Oxford: The Clarendon Press, 1952), 2 vols.

Marx
Karl Marx, Friedrich Engels, Werke (Berlin: Dietz Verlag, 1961-68), 41 vols. and a *Verzeichnis*.

Medwin
Thomas Medwin, *Journal of the Conversations of Lord Byron* . . . (New York: Wilder & Campbell, 1824).

Michaud
Guy Michaud, *Message poétique du symbolisme* (Paris: Librairie Nizet, 1947).

Michelet
J[ules] Michelet, *Histoire de la révolution française*, second edition, revised and augmented (Paris: Librairie internationale, 1868-69), 6 vols.

Middle Years, I
The Letters of William and Dorothy Wordsworth; The Middle Years; Part One; 1806-1811, ed. Ernest de Selincourt, revised by Mary Moorman (Oxford: The Clarendon Press, 1969).

Middle Years, II
The Letters of William and Dorothy Wordsworth; III; The Middle Years, Part II; 1812-1820, second edition, ed. Ernest de Selincourt, revised by Mary Moorman and Alan G. Hill (Oxford: The Clarendon Press, 1970).

Milton, *Poems*
John Milton, *Paradise Regained, the Minor Poems; and Samson Agonistes*, ed. Merritt Y. Hughes (New York: The Odyssey Press, 1937).

Milton, *Prose*
John Milton, *Prose Selections*, ed. Merritt Y. Hughes (New York: The Odyssey Press, 1947).

Miscellaneous Criticism
Coleridge's Miscellaneous Criticism, ed. T. M. Raysor (London: Constable, 1936).

Monboddo
[James Burnet, Lord Monboddo], *Of the Origin and Progress of Language*, I (Edinburgh: A. Kincaid & W. Creech; London: T. Cadell, 1773).

Monod
Jacques Monod, *Chance and Necessity; An Essay on the Natural Philosophy of Modern Biology*, trans. Austryn Wainhouse (London: Collins, 1972).

Moorman, I
Mary Moorman, *William Wordsworth; A Biography; The Early Years, 1770-1803* (Oxford: The Clarendon Press, 1957).

Moorman, II
Mary Moorman, *William Wordsworth; A Biography; The Later Years, 1803-1850* (Oxford: The Clarendon Press, 1965).

Müller, *Elemente*
Adam Müller, *Die Elemente der Staatskunst . . .* , ed. Jakob Baxa (Jena: Verlag von Gustav Fischer, 1922), 2 vols.

Müller, *Schriften*
Adam Müller, *Kritische, ästhetische, und philosophische Schriften*, critical edition, ed. Walter Schroeder and Werner Siebert (Neuwied and Berlin: Hermann Luchterhand Verlag, 1967), 2 vols.

Murry, *Keats*
John Middleton Murry, *Keats*, fourth edition (New York: Minerva Press, 1968).

Murry, *Style*
John Middleton Murry, *The Problem of Style* (London: Oxford University Press, 1961).

Neumann
Erich Neumann, *The Origins and History of Consciousness*, trans. R.F.C. Hull (Princeton: Princeton University Press, 1969).

Nietzsche
Friedrich Nietzsche; Werke in drei Bänden, ed. Karl Schlechta (Munich: Carl Hanser Verlag, 1954-56), 3 vols.

Notebooks
The Notebooks of Samuel Taylor Coleridge, ed. Kathleen Coburn (London: Routledge & Kegan Paul, 1957-   ), 3 vols. to date.

Novalis
Novalis Schriften; Die Werke Friedrich von Hardenbergs, ed. Paul Kluckhohn and Richard Samuel, second edition, enlarged and corrected, supplemented from the manuscripts, in four volumes and a companion volume (Stuttgart: W. Kohlhammer Verlag, 1960-   ), 4 vols. to date.

O'Connell
Marvin R. O'Connell, *The Oxford Conspirators; A History of the Oxford Movement 1833-1845* (London and Toronto: The Macmillan Company [Collier-Macmillan Ltd.], 1969).

Oken
Lehrbuch der Naturphilosophie, by Dr. [Lorenz] Oken, Professor in Jena, member of several learned societies (Jena: bei Friedrich Frommann, 1809-11), 3 vols.

Ortega, *Crisis*
Jose Ortega y Gasset, *Man and Crisis*, trans. Mildred Adams (New York: W. W. Norton & Co., Inc., 1962).

Ortega, *Velazquez*
Jose Ortega y Gasset, *Velazquez, Goya and The Dehumanization of Art*, trans. Alexis Brown (New York: W. W. Norton & Company, Inc., 1972).

Painter
George D. Painter, *Marcel Proust; A Biography* (London: Chatto & Windus, 1959-65), 2 vols.

Paracelsus
Paracelsus; Samtliche Werke, ed. Karl Sudhoff et al. (Munich: O. W. Barth, 1922-   ), 22 vols. to date.

Perkins
David Perkins, *The Quest for Permanence; The Symbolism of Wordsworth, Shelley, and Keats* (Cambridge, Mass.: Harvard University Press, 1965).

Pfleiderer
Otto Pfleiderer, *Religionsphilosophie auf geschichtlicher Grundlage*, second, extensively enlarged edition (Berlin: Druck und Verlag von Georg Reimer, 1883-84), 2 vols.

Philosophical Lectures
The Philosophical Lectures of Samuel Taylor Coleridge; Hitherto Unpublished, ed. Kathleen Coburn (London: The Pilot Press Limited, 1949).

Platens Werke
August Graf von Platens sämtliche Werke in zwölf Bänden, ed. Max Koch and Erich Petzet (Leipzig: Max Hesses Verlag, 1910), 12 vols. in 4.

Poe

The Works of Edgar Allan Poe, ed. Edmund Clarence Stedman and George Edward Woodberry (New York: Charles Scribner's Sons, 1914), 10 vols.

Pope

The Twickenham Edition of the Poems of Alexander Pope, ed. John Butt et al. (London: Methuen & Co., Ltd.; New Haven: Yale University Press, 1939-1969), 11 vols. in 12.

Popper, *Conjectures*

Karl Popper, *Conjectures and Refutations: The Growth of Scientific Knowledge* (New York: Harper Torchbooks, 1968).

Popper, *Open Society*

Karl Popper, *The Open Society and Its Enemies*, fifth edition revised and enlarged (London: Routledge & Kegan Paul, 1974), 2 vols.

Prelude

William Wordsworth, *The Prelude; Or, Growth of a Poet's Mind*, ed. Ernest de Selincourt, second edition revised by Helen Darbishire (Oxford: The Clarendon Press, 1959). Unless otherwise indicated, citation of book and line numbers are to the 1805-1806 version.

Prose

The Prose Works of William Wordsworth, ed. W.J.B. Owen and Jane Worthington Smyser (Oxford: The Clarendon Press, 1974), 3 vols.

Quartets

T. S. Eliot, *Four Quartets* (New York: Harcourt, Brace & Company, 1943).

Reed, *Chronology*

Mark L. Reed, *Wordsworth; The Chronology of the Early Years; 1770-1799* (Cambridge, Mass.: Harvard University Press, 1967).

Reinhold

Karl Leonhard Reinhold, *Versuch einer neuen Theorie des menschlichen Vorstellungsvermögens* (Prague and Jena: C. Widtmann and I. M. Mauke, 1789).

Ricoeur

Paul Ricoeur, *Freud and Philosophy; An Essay on Interpretation*, trans. Denis Savage (New Haven: Yale University Press, 1970).

Rilke

Rainer Maria Rilke, *Sämtliche Werke*, ed. by the Rilke-Archive in association with Ruth Sieber-Rilke, supervised by Ernst Zinn (Frankfurt am Main: Insel-Verlag, 1955-67), 6 vols.

Robinson

Henry Crabb Robinson on Books and their Writers, ed. Edith J. Morley (New York: AMS Press, 1967), 3 vols.

Salvesen
Christopher Salvesen, *The Landscape of Memory; A Study of Wordsworth's Poetry* (Lincoln: University of Nebraska Press, 1965).

Santayana
Selected Critical Writings of George Santayana, ed. Norman Henfrey (Cambridge: Cambridge University Press, 1968), 2 vols.

Sartre, *Baudelaire*
Jean-Paul Sartre, *Baudelaire*, trans. Martin Turnell (New York: New Directions, 1950).

Sartre, *Critique*
Jean-Paul Sartre, *Critique de la raison dialectique* (Paris: Gallimard, 1960).

Sartre, *L'Être et le néant*
Jean-Paul Sartre, *L'Être et le néant; Essai d'ontologie phénoménologique* (Paris: Gallimard, 1943).

Schellings Werke
Friedrich Wilhelm Joseph von Schellings sämmtliche Werke, ed. K.F.A. Schelling (Stuttgart and Augsburg: J. G. Cotta'scher Verlag, 1856-61). The edition is in two *Abtheilungen*, the first consisting of volumes numbered 1-10, the second of volumes numbered 1-4. To avoid cumbersome identifications of *Abtheilungen*, references to the first *Abtheilung* are cited as volumes i-x, to the second as volumes xi-xiv.

Schillers Werke
Schillers sämtliche Werke, Secular Edition, ed. Eduard von der Hellen, in asociation with Richard Fester et al. (Stuttgart and Berlin: J. G. Cotta'sche Buchhandlung Nachfolger [1904-05]), 16 vols.

Schneider
Elisabeth Schneider, *Coleridge, Opium and* Kubla Khan (New York: Octagon Books, 1970).

Schopenhauer
Arthur Schopenhauer, *Sämtliche Werke*, ed. Arthur Hübscher, third edition (Wiesbaden: F. A. Brockhaus, 1972), 7 vols.

Shaffer
E. S. Shaffer, *"Kubla Khan" and The Fall of Jerusalem; The Mythological School in Biblical Criticism and Secular Literature 1770-1880* (Cambridge: Cambridge University Press, 1975).

Shaftesbury
Anthony, Earl of Shaftesbury, *Characteristics of Men, Manners, Opinions, Times*, ed. John M. Robertson (Indianapolis: The Bobbs-Merrill Company, Inc., 1964).

Sheats
Paul D. Sheats, *The Making of Wordsworth's Poetry, 1785-1798* (Cambridge, Mass.: Harvard University Press, 1973).

Shelley, *Letters*
The Letters of Percy Bysshe Shelley, ed. Frederick L. Jones (Oxford: The Clarendon Press, 1964), 2 vols.

Shelley, *Poems*
The Complete Poetical Works of Percy Bysshe Shelley, ed. Thomas Hutchinson (London: Oxford University Press, 1948).

Shelley, *Prose*
Shelley's Critical Prose, ed. Bruce R. McElderry, Jr. (Lincoln, Neb.: University of Nebraska Press, 1967).

Shenstone
William Shenstone, *Essays on Men and Manners* (London: Bradbury, Evans, & Co., 1868).

Shklar
Judith Shklar, *After Utopia; The Decline of Political Faith* (Princeton: Princeton University Press, 1969).

Shumaker
Wayne Shumaker, *Literature and the Irrational; A Study in Anthropological Backgrounds* (Englewood Cliffs, N.J.: Prentice-Hall, Inc., 1960).

Sidney
The Prose Works of Sir Philip Sidney, ed. Albert Feuillerat (Cambridge: Cambridge University Press, 1968-70), 4 vols.

Snyder
Alice D. Snyder, *The Critical Principle of the Reconciliation of Opposites as Employed by Coleridge* (Ann Arbor: The Graduate School of the University of Michigan, 1918).

Southey
New Letters of Robert Southey, ed. Kenneth Curry (New York and London: Columbia University Press, 1965), 2 vols.

Southey, *Poems*
The Poetical Works of Robert Southey, collected by himself (London: Longman, Orme, Brown, Green, & Longmans, 1838-49), 10 vols.

Sperry
Willard L. Sperry, *Wordsworth's Anti-Climax* (Cambridge, Mass.: Harvard University Press, 1935).

Spinoza
Spinoza Opera, commissioned by the Heidelberg Academy of Sciences,

ed. by Carl Gebhardt (Heidelberg: Carl Winters Universitaetsbuch-handlung, 1972), 4 vols.

Staiger
Emil Staiger, *Grundbegriffe der Poetik* (Zurich: Atlantis Verlag, 1963).

Starkie
Enid Starkie, *Petrus Borel the Lycanthrope; His Life and Times* (Norwalk, Conn.: New Directions, 1954).

Stephen
Leslie Stephen, *Hours in a Library* (London: Smith, Elder & Co., 1909), 3 vols.

Stevens
The Collected Poems of Wallace Stevens (New York: Alfred A. Knopf, 1964).

Table Talk
The Table Talk and Omniana of Samuel Taylor Coleridge, ed. T. Ashe (London: George Bell and Sons, 1888).

Taine
H[ippolyte] Taine, *Les Origines de la France contemporaine* (Paris: Librairie Hachette et Cie, 1875-1893), 6 vols.

Tetens
Johann Nicolas Tetens, *Philosophische Versuche über die menschliche Natur und ihre Entwickelung* (Leipzig: bey M. G. Weidmanns Erben und Reich, 1777), 2 vols.

Theory of Life
Hints Towards the Formation of a More Comprehensive Theory of Life, by S. T. Coleridge, ed. Seth B. Watson, M.D. (London: John Churchill, 1848).

Thomas
Dylan Thomas, *Collected Poems; 1934-1952* (London: J. M. Dent & Sons Ltd., 1959).

Todd
F. M. Todd, *Politics and the Poet; A Study of Wordsworth* (London: Methuen & Co., Ltd., 1957).

Trilling, *Imagination*
Lionel Trilling, *The Liberal Imagination; Essays on Literature and Society* (Garden City, N.Y.: Doubleday Anchor Books, 1954).

Trilling, *Self*
Lionel Trilling, *The Opposing Self; Nine Essays in Criticism* (New York: The Viking Press, 1959).

Wallace
  William Wallace, *Prolegomena to the Study of Hegel's Philosophy and Especially of His Logic*, second edition (Oxford: The Clarendon Press, 1931).

Warren
  Robert Penn Warren, "Pure and Impure Poetry," *The Kenyon Review*, 5 (1943).

Whitehead
  Alfred North Whitehead, *Science and the Modern World* (Cambridge: Cambridge University Press, 1926).

Wilbrand
  Johann Bernhard Wilbrand, *Das Gesetz des polaren Verhaltens in der Natur* (Giessen: bey C. G. Müller, 1819).

Williams
  The Autobiography of William Carlos Williams, second printing (New York: New Directions, 1967).

Winters
  Yvor Winters, *Forms of Discovery; Critical & Historical Essays on the Forms of the Short Poem in English* ([Denver]: Alan Swallow, 1967).

Woodring
  Carl Woodring, *Politics in English Romantic Poetry* (Cambridge, Mass.: Harvard University Press, 1970).

Wordsworth, *Poems*
  The Poetical Works of William Wordsworth, ed. Ernest de Selincourt and Helen Darbishire (Oxford: The Clarendon Press, 1940-49), 5 vols.

Yeats
  The Collected Poems of W. B. Yeats, Definitive Edition, With the Author's Final Revisions (New York: The Macmillan Company, 1956).

Zeltner
  Hermann Zeltner, *Schelling* (Stuttgart: Friedrich Frommanns Verlag, 1954).

ROMANTICISM
AND THE FORMS
OF RUIN

Fragmented Modalities and the
Criteria of Romanticism

◊♦◊

T HE phenomenology of the fragment is the phenomenology of human awareness. I look out my study window as I write this sentence and see a fragment made up of fragments: a mass of stone and concrete that is part of New York City: buildings in such a variety of size, shape, and architecture, mostly bad, juxtaposed in such randomness, and showing such heterogeneous effects of time, as to constitute a visual junk heap. I happen to take a book from my shelves, Lucien Goldmann's *Le Dieu caché*, and see the argument that Pascal's *Pensées*, a masterpiece even though fragmentary and incomplete, should not be reorganized toward its hypothethical completeness, because "the paradox and the fragment" are the "two forms of literary expression demanded by its own philosophy," and therefore the *Pensées* "are in truth a paradoxical masterpiece, achieved by its inachievement."

To varying extents all endeavor participates in this paradox. I take down another book, Peter Brown's *Augustine of Hippo*, and read of another realization of incompleteness, fragmentation, and ruin:

Augustine lived to see violence destroy his life's work in Africa. *"He who puts on wisdom, puts on grief; and a heart that understands cuts like rust in the bones."* "The man of God saw whole cities sacked, country villas razed, their owners killed or scattered as refugees, the churches deprived of their bishops and clergy, and the holy virgins and ascetics dispersed; some tortured to death, some killed outright, others, as prisoners, reduced to losing their integrity, in soul and body, to serve an evil and brutal enemy. The hymns of God and praises in the churches had come to a stop; in many places, the church-buildings were burnt to the ground."

Incompleteness, fragmentation, and ruin marked the inner life of Augustine no less than they did his cognizance of outer reality. Speaking of a certain treatise, Brown notes that "it was only a sketch. . . . This book is the first of Augustine's many 'left-overs'. . . his life will be littered with lines of thought that are not worked through to their conclusion, and with abandoned literary enterprises." What was true here is true for all writers. Even Shakespeare is not exempt from disintegrative vicissitudes. "I cannot say he is every where alike," writes Dryden, "He is many times flat, insipid; his Comick wit degenerating into clenches, his serious swelling into Bombast"; "I cannot deny that he has his failings." "It cannot be denied, further," says Bradley, "that in many of Shakespeare's plays, if not in all, there are inconsistencies and contradictions, and also that questions are suggested to the reader which it is impossible for him to answer with certainty."

But the diasparactions[1] of external configuration indicated by such judgments are as nothing compared to the diasparactive inner witness of Shakespeare's art. The sonnets tell a story of the breaking of hope and the sundering of relationship; the great comedies achieve longing visions of final wholeness only through a process that sets in motion individual tearings of society's fabric; and the tragedies, with their dramatic collisions of individual aspirations and their rendings of human life, are the very stuff of diasparactive realization—of incompleteness, fragmentation, and ruin. "CLEOPATRA. This mortal house I'll ruin,/ Do Caesar what he can." "GLOUCESTER. O, let me kiss that hand. LEAR. Let me wipe it first; it smells of mortality. GLOUCESTER. O ruined piece of nature; this great world/ Shall so wear out to naught." "POLONIUS. My honorable lord, I will most humbly take my leave of you. HAMLET. You cannot, sir, take from me anything that I will more willingly part withal—except my life, except my life, except my life." In Shakespeare's tragedies, indeed, it is as though the general surface of human existence, like a pristine field of ice, is constricted by forces that crumple it into human fragments thrusting against one another in agonized individuality, wracked grotesquely out of their plane. *Hamlet* is simply a vision of dismemberment—of the tearing apart of an existence and all its contiguities.

Other kinds of cultural activity and perception are no less dia-

---

[1] Cf. *An Intermediate Greek-English Lexicon, Founded upon the Seventh Edition of Liddell and Scott's Greek-English Lexicon* (Oxford: The Clarendon Press, 1961), pp. 194-95: "διασπαρᾰκτός . . . *torn to pieces*, Eur. From δια-σπᾰράσσω . . . *to rend in sunder* or *in pieces*, Aesch."

sparactive than those present to the literary imagination. "We have got the world divided into boxes," notes Ortega y Gasset: "each box is a science, and inside it we have locked the splinters of reality that we have been prising from the vast maternal quarry, Nature. And so, in little heaps assembled by chance or perhaps caprice, we hold the debris of life."

My taking of books from my shelves to find these illustrations is itself a piece of diasparactive awareness. The books are fragments of my personal library; yet my personal library is in its turn radically fragmentary and incomplete when compared to the New York Public Library; which again is radically fragmentary and incomplete when compared to the ideal library—which does not exist. Moreover, the individual books in these collections, considered each as an entity, are inevitably fragmentary and incomplete in their treatments of their subjects: "Whoever thinks a faultless piece to see,/ Thinks what ne'er was, nor is, nor e'er shall be," writes Pope. For instance, Brown's magisterial study of Augustine is prefaced by a barrage of apologies: "led me to concentrate on some aspects of Augustine's life more than on others," "The study of Augustine is endless," ". . . others are to hand to remedy my omissions," "I am aware of having omitted the work of some scholars," ". . . by-passing many controversies, to do justice to even one of which could have taken up an entire volume."

Incompleteness, fragmentation, and ruin—the diasparactive triad—are at the very center of life. The phenomenological analysis of existence reveals this with special clarity. Heidegger's twin conceptions of *Geworfenheit* (the sense of being hurled into reality, broken off) and *Verfallen* (the sense within life of its continuing ruin) are ineradicable criteria of existence. In truth, the largest contention of this book can be rendered by Heidegger's formulation that "in existence there is a permanent incompleteness (*ständige 'Unganzheit'*), which cannot be evaded." "In the midst of these evils," writes Augustine's ancient biographer Possidius, "he was comforted by the saying of a certain wise man: 'He is no great man who thinks it a great thing that sticks and stones should fall, and that men, who must die, should die.' " Plotinus's awareness—for he was the "certain wise man"—attests the same understanding as Heidegger's.

It can accordingly not be very surprising—in the light of experience itself no less than in that of both ancient and modern testimony—that diasparactive forms, which permeate the human situation, should manifest themselves in the lives and achievements of Coleridge and Wordsworth. What is perhaps surprising, however, is the extent of their sway. Indeed, the sense of both men's diasparaction has become increasingly insistent for me as a byproduct of editorial labors on Coleridge's *magnum opus*. Not only is that treatise radically incomplete but also, as I have elsewhere argued, it could not have been completed; and yet it exists and is, in title no less than in undoubted intent, the most important realization of the endeavors of Coleridge's life. Still, the only completeness it has is its incompleteness.[2] Like Pascal's great work, it is "un chef-d'oeuvre paradoxal, achevé de par son inachèvement."

The paradox extends to other aspects of Coleridge's effort. Of his three greatest poems, two of them are famously incomplete, and the third, "The Ancient Mariner," is, in its author's own testimony, unsatisfactory in its completion. But his life itself was no less torn apart. His marriage, his friendship with Wordsworth, his love for Sara Hutchinson, his relations with his children, his poetic career itself, after initial strivings for wholeness, subsided into the phenomenology of fragmentation. As he said, "I have beheld the whole of all, wherein/ My Heart had any interest in this Life,/ To be disrent and torn from off my Hopes."

Nor was Wordsworth's existence, despite surface indications to the contrary, really less torn and broken. His sense of the wholeness of life began early to be assaulted by massive diasparactions: by the death of his mother when he was seven; by the resulting separation of the children left "destitute, and as we might/ Trooping together"; by the death of his father less than six years later ("Ah!" exclaims Vigny, "what may one expect from a world to which one comes with the assurance of seeing one's father and mother die?"); and most agonizingly by the death of his brother John in 1805. "I feel that there is something cut out of my life which cannot be restored," he writes of that disaster. More and still more was cut out. The successive and unexpected deaths of his two dearest children shook his being to its foundations; his shattering "anti-climax" constituted a poetic death-in-life of some forty years; his most ambitious work remained even more a ruin than did Coleridge's; he unwittingly destroyed the existence of his beloved sister; the collapse of his friendship with Coleridge was no less stunning to him than to his friend. His whole cultural orientation was diasparactive: the pursuit of a visionary gleam that had fled; and

[2] As Coleridge's literary executor, Joseph Henry Green, reported after a preliminary survey: "the system, which it was the occupation of my revered friend's life to construct exists only in detached fragments, hints, & unfinished essays."

the deepest theme of his maturity could as a result be nothing other than despondency and its attempted correction.

The cultural iconology of Wordsworth and Coleridge is mirrored in that of Romanticism itself. Incompleteness, fragmentation, and ruin—*ständige Unganzheit*—not only receive a special emphasis in Romanticism but also in a certain perspective seem actually to define that phenomenon. "A new tone has come to suffuse Augustine's life," writes Brown:

> He is a man who has realized that he was doomed to remain incomplete in his present existence, that what he wished for most ardently would never be more than a hope, postponed to a final resolution of all tensions, far beyond this life. . . . If to be a "Romantic," means to be a man acutely aware of being caught in an existence that denies him the fullness for which he craves, to feel that he is defined by his tension towards something else, by his capacity for faith, for hope, for longing, to think of himself as a wanderer seeking a country that is always distant, but made ever-present to him by the quality of the love that "groans" for it, then Augustine has imperceptibly become a "Romantic."

The formulation is just. The sense of longing—which is an inner form of the perception of reality as diasparactive—saturates Romanticism. There are explicit formulas, and many of them, such as Friedrich Schlegel's "Sehnsucht nach dem Unendlichen"— longing for the infinite; such as Schleiermacher's "Gefühl einer unbefriedigten Sehnsucht"—feeling of an unsatisfied longing. There are symbols, and many of them, of that which is longed for, such as Novalis's "blaue Blume" or Goethe's "Land wo die Zitronen blühn."

The land where the lemon trees bloom is congruent with Brown's "country that is always distant" (and both to the "kingdom which has no end" so ardently sought by Augustine [*De civitate Dei* xxii. 30]). The longing for and quest of such a realm are the very stuff of Romanticism. Shelley's Alastor leaves his "alienated home/ To seek strange truths in undiscovered lands." The questing voyages of the fictional Childe Harold parallel the questing voyages of the actual Lord Byron. The Ancient Mariner, the Wandering Jew, Cain—the restless and unsatisfied wanderings of these mythic Romantic figures find counterparts in the actual journeyings of figures such as Chateaubriand, Lenau, Nerval. And Rimbaud and Wordsworth's Wanderer have at least homelessness in common.

The always distant country could be removed in time, as with the Romantic mania for the medieval (what Uhland calls "ein phantastischer Wahn des Mittelalters"), or removed in space, as with the Romantic preoccupation with the oriental (e.g., *The Giaour; A Fragment of a Turkish Tale*, or *West-östlicher Divan*, or *Les Orientales*, or *Lalla Rookh*, or *Ueber die Sprache und Weisheit der Indier*, or *Voyage en Orient*, to cite titles representing diverse embodiments of Romantic orientalism[3]—"It is in the Orient," proclaimed Friedrich Schlegel, "that we must seek the highest Romanticism"; "The East," confirmed Wackenroder, "is the home of everything wonderful"). Alternatively, the sought-for realm could be removed in space, in time, and in reality as well: a faery land forlorn, approached across perilous seas.[4]

In this latter manifestation especially, the apprehension of the distant country frequently partook of the nature of dream or reverie, two emphases, the one largely bequeathed by Leibniz and the other by Rousseau, that wove themselves into the very fabric of Romanticism.[5] To Shelley, the means of penetrating even partly to the "inmost sanctuary" of the "Mother of this unfathomable world" was by "incommunicable dream,/ And twilight phantasms, and deep noon-day thought." "Poetry a rationalized dream," suggests Coleridge in 1804. "Compared to pure dream, to the un-

---

[3] For the prevalence of the vogue, consider Byron's mocking lines in "Beppo": "Oh that I had the art of easy writing . . . / How quickly would I print (the world delighting)/ A Grecian, Syrian, or Assyrian tale;/ And sell you, mix'd with Western sentimentalism,/ Some samples of the finest Orientalism." (Elsewhere Byron notes that "I can't empty my head of the East," that his head was full of "*orientalities* [I can't call them *isms*].") Even the topographically entrenched Wordsworth was challenged by the rage for the oriental. "You have no oriental poem," wrote Barron Field to the great poet: "I wish you would write me one." Wordsworth replied the following day that "I should like to write a short Indian piece, if you would furnish me with a story." For comprehensive discussion of the larger aspects of the phenomenon, see Raymond Schwab's *La Renaissance orientale* (Paris: Payot, 1950), and E. S. Shaffer's chapter called "The Oriental Idyll" in her "*Kubla Khan" and the Fall of Jerusalem* (Cambridge: Cambridge University Press, 1975). Also see A. Leslie Willson's *A Mythical Image: The Ideal of India in German Romanticism* (Durham, N.C.: Duke University Press, 1964).

[4] "Heine, that saddest of all humorists," recalls Liszt, "listened with the eagerness of a fellow-countryman to the stories told him by Chopin of that mysterious country which also haunted his ethereal fancy, and the beautiful shores he too had explored."

[5] Cf., e.g., Rousseau: "Quelquefois mes rêveries finissent par la méditation, mais plus souvent mes méditations finissent par la rêverie, et durant ces égarements mon âme erre et plane dans l'univers sur les ailes de l'imagination dans des extases qui passent toute autre jouissance."

analyzed impression," says Baudelaire in *La Chambre double*, "definite art, positive art is a blasphemy." "I must devote some one or more Days exclusively to the Meditation on *Dreams*," muses Coleridge: "Days? Say rather Weeks!" "Dreams! always dreams!" exclaims Baudelaire in *L'Invitation au voyage*, "and the more the soul is ambitious and delicate, the more the dreams diverge from the possible. Every man carries within himself his dose of natural opium." Béguin's classic *L'Ame romantique et le rêve* reveals much about "les aspects nocturnes de la vie" in German speculation of the period; for our purposes here, however, it suffices merely to point out that, of Coleridge's two greatest poems, one was called "Kubla Khan, or, A Vision in a Dream," and the other was published in 1800 under the title "The Ancient Mariner. A Poet's Reverie." Such rubrics are typical for others besides their author. Lamb, for instance, denied himself any claim to Coleridgean or poetic richness of dream:

> For the credit of my imagination, I am almost ashamed to say how tame and prosaic my dreams are grown. They are never romantic. . . . The poverty of my dreams mortifies me. There is Coleridge, at his will can conjure up icy domes, and pleasure-houses for Kubla Khan, and Abyssinian maids, and songs of Abara . . . when I cannot muster a fiddle.

Yet even Lamb, his gentle self-deprecation notwithstanding, produced—in prose—the poignant longing of "Dream-Children; A Reverie."[6]

All such diasparactive *éloignement* testifies to the pervasiveness of Romantic longing and the incompleteness it implies. Always and everywhere there is longing, for Wordsworth's "light that never was, on sea or land,/ The consecration, and the Poet's dream"; or, in Tieck's words, for that rose-red key to open up our true home ("mit rosenrotem Schlüssel die Heimat aufschliessen"), where

[6] In a different vein, one more in keeping with the Gothic element in Romanticism, De Quincey, summoning both Romantic dream and Romantic orientalism to describe the effect of Romantic opium-addiction, summarizes "the unimaginable horror" of "my oriental dreams": "I was stared at, hooted at, grinned at, chattered at, by monkeys, by paroquets, by cockatoos. I ran into pagodas, and was fixed for centuries at the summit, or in secret rooms; I was the idol; I was the priest; I was worshipped; I was sacrificed. I fled from the wrath of Brama through all the forests of Asia; Vishnu hated me; Seeva lay in wait for me. . . . Thousands of years I lived and was buried in stone coffins, with mummies and sphinxes, in narrow chambers at the heart of eternal pyramids."

the intimations of childhood dwell, that glittering land where the most golden dreams swim in the blue-green sea, where forms of light play between fiery blossoms and extend to us hands to press against our heart

The corollary to such longing is the sense that life in the here-and-now is torn and broken. "The soul," said Wordsworth, striking the keynote of his greatest poetry, "Remembering how she felt, but what she felt/ Remembering not, retains an obscure sense/ Of possible sublimity." Again and again his longing flames forth: "How shall I seek the origin? Where find/ Faith in the marvellous things which then I felt?" "Oh! mystery of man," he writes,

> from what a depth
> Proceed thy honours. I am lost, but see
> In simple childhood something of the base
> On which thy greatness stands. . . .
> The days gone by
> Return upon me almost from the dawn
> Of life: the hiding-places of man's power
> Open; I would approach them, but they close.
> I see by glimpses now; when age comes on,
> May scarcely see at all

Again and again Wordsworth expresses in his greatest moments the sense of having been broken off and torn apart from true being: "I cannot paint/ What then I was. . . . That time is past,/ And all its aching joys are no more." And the diasparaction of actual life was only emphasized by longing glimpses of fulfillment:

> Those shadowy recollections,
> Which, be they what they may,
> Are yet the fountain light of all our day. . . .
> Which neither listlessness, nor mad endeavour . . .
> Can utterly abolish or destroy!
> Hence in a season of calm weather
> Though inland far we be,
> Our Souls have sight of that immortal sea
> Which brought us hither,
> Can in a moment travel thither,
> And see the Children sport upon the shore,
> And hear the mighty waters rolling evermore.

"Could I revive within me,/ Her symphony and song," writes

Coleridge in a similar ecstasy of longing for a reality from which he
has been torn away,

> I would build that dome in air . . .
> And all should cry, Beware! Beware!
> His flashing eyes, his floating hair!
> Weave a circle round him thrice,
> And close your eyes with holy dread,
> For he on honey-dew hath fed,
>   And drunk the milk of Paradise.

Rousseau, too, expresses the paradisal longing of Romanticism,
and its diasparactive form, in tones that, though in prose, are
hardly less impassioned:

> If all my dreams had turned into reality, I would still remain un-
> satisfied: I would have kept on dreaming, imagining, desiring.
> In myself I found an unexplainable void that nothing could have
> filled; a longing of the heart toward another kind of fulfillment of
> which I could not conceive but of which I nevertheless felt the
> attraction.

But the pervasive longing of the Romantics for an absent reality
was at the same time an index to a prevailing sense of incomplete-
ness, fragmentation, and ruin. "With us," said Schiller in 1795,

> the image of the race is scattered on an amplified scale among
> individuals—but in a fragmentary way . . . so that you have to go
> the rounds from individual to individual in order to gather the
> totality of the race. . . . We see not merely individual persons but
> whole classes of human beings developing only a part of their
> capacities, while the rest of them, like a stunted plant, show only
> a feeble vestige of their nature. . . .
> It was culture itself that inflicted this wound upon modern
> humanity. As soon as enlarged experience and more precise
> speculation made necessary a sharper division of the sciences on
> the one hand, and on the other, the more intricate machinery of
> states made necessary a more rigorous dissociation of ranks and
> occupations, the essential bond of human nature was torn apart.
> . . .
> This disorder, which art and learning began in the inner man,
> was rendered complete and universal by the new spirit of gov-
> ernment. . . . The simple organization of the first republics . . .
> now gave place to an ingenious piece of machinery, in which out

of the patching together of a vast number of lifeless parts a collective mechanical life results. State and church, law and customs, were now torn apart; enjoyment was separated from labor, means from ends, effort from reward. Eternally chained to only one single little fragment of the whole, man himself grew to be only a fragment.

The fragmentation and ruin that Schiller saw as the index of the social and economic reality of the time were identified by Burke in 1790 as the index of its central political reality as well:

All circumstances taken together, the French Revolution is the most astonishing that has hitherto happened in the world. The most wonderful things are brought about in many instances by means the most absurd and ridiculous, in the most ridiculous modes, and apparently by the most contemptible instruments. Everything seems out of nature in this strange chaos of levity and ferocity, and of all sorts of crimes jumbled together with all sorts of follies. . . .

The fresh ruins of France, which shock our feelings wherever we can turn our eyes, are not the devastations of civil war; they are the sad but instructive monuments of rash and ignorant counsel in time of profound peace. . . . The persons who have thus squandered away the precious treasure of their crimes . . . have met in their progress with little or rather with no opposition at all. . . . Their pioneers have gone before them and demolished and laid everything level at their feet. Not one drop of *their* blood have they shed in the cause of the country they have ruined.

And what Schiller and Burke spoke of from social and political perspectives, Hegel observed from a philosophical standpoint. The journey of *Geist* in his monumental and Romantically paradigmatic *Phänomenologie des Geistes* is in a fundamental sense a threading of a way through constantly recurring ruin:

. . . our epoch is a birth-time, and a period of transition. The spirit of man has broken with the old order of things. . . . The spirit of the time, growing slowly and quietly ripe for the new form it is to assume, disintegrates one fragment after another of the structure of its previous world.

The "life of mind," he says again, "only wins to its truth when it finds itself utterly torn asunder." In the *Phänomenologie*'s later argumentation, such an orientation eventuates in repeated invocations of the forms of ruin—as a single illustration may dramatize:

Since the pure ego sees itself outside self, and torn in sunder, everything that has continuity and universality, everything that bears the name of law, good, and right, is thereby torn to pieces at the same time, and goes to rack and ruin: all identity and concord break up, for what holds sway is the purest discord and disunion, what was absolutely essential is absolutely unessential, what has a being on its own account has its being outside itself: the pure ego itself is absolutely disintegrated.

That diasparactive hegemony to which Hegel's thought responded, and that Schiller and Burke described as obtaining in society at large, found correlates in the lives and efforts of the individual. "The further I go in my story," said Rousseau in his *Confessions*:

the less order and sequence I can put into it. The disturbances of my later life have not left events time to fall into shape in my head. They have been too numerous, too confused, too unpleasant to be capable of straightforward narration. The only strong impressions they have left me is that of the horrible mystery enveloping their cause, and of the deplorable state to which they have reduced me. Now the story can only proceed at haphazard, according as the ideas come back into my mind.

And if the story proceeded at haphazard, it ended as a fragment. For the *Confessions* is not completed; it simply breaks off at its author's fifty-third year.

With such varied testimonies to the prevalence of diasparactive forms in the cultural structures of the era, it can hardly be surprising that incompleteness, fragmentation, and ruin occupy both the theory and the actuality of Romanticism. Romanticism, as Friedrich Schlegel said in his *Athenäums-Fragment* 116, was an eternal "becoming" that had as its chief characteristic that it "nie vollendet sein kann"—can never be completed. Schubert's "Unfinished Symphony" participates in this characteristic no less certainly than does Keats's "Hyperion" (and even the "heavenly length" of Schubert's great C-Major Symphony implies a sense of incompleteness in its reachings and longings; in any event, as Hegel said, "the keynote of Romanticism is musical"). From another perspective, Schubert's death at thirty is existentially diasparactive no less than Keats's still more tearingly early death at twenty-five.

Early death is not merely early demise—it is a diasparaction that emphasizes the sense of incompleteness and fragmentation. Diasparaction that incorporated the sense of ruin was also pervasive, whether the ruin was conceived as work uncompleted or as edifice decayed, whether as psychic inner ruin or material outer ruin. The Gothic Church to which Wordsworth compared his lifework is no less a ruin than the heap of West Country stone called Tintern Abbey; the existence of his Margaret is as shattered as the ruined cottage that is its emblem: "In sickness she remained; and here she died;/ Last human tenant of these ruined walls!" Novalis, his own life soon to be shattered by consumption, hails in his early "Ans Kloster in Ruinen" a ruined medieval monastery: "Da liegst du nun und bist gefallen,/ Zerstöret von der mächtigern Zeit"—there liest thou now and art fallen, shattered by the mightier Time. "What mouldering Temples we seem to be!" exclaimed Coleridge (and T. S. Eliot observed that "The author of *Biographia Litteraria* was already a ruined man"). "My public and private hopes have been left a ruin," laments Hazlitt. "My soul wanders," confirms Byron, "I demand it back/ To meditate amongst decay, and stand/ A ruin amidst ruins." The "sentiment des ruines"—an attitude present in all eras but reaching a special pitch of intensity in Romanticism[7]—found in fragments and torn forms deeper meanings and presentiments than in completions. In Shelley's vision, the Romantic quest leads with "wandering step" to "The awful ruins of the days of old," where "among the ruined temples . . . poring on memorials/ Of the world's youth," there flashes "meaning" on the wanderer's mind. "There is a power/ And magic in the ruin'd battlement," said Byron, "For which the palace of the present hour/ Must yield its pomp and wait till ages are its dower." "A broken column," writes Mme de Staël, "a bas-relief half ruined, some stones linked in the indestructible workmanship of ancient architects, reminds you that there is an eternal power, a divine spark, in man."

[7] As in so many other instances, the intellectual contours of Romanticism were here prefigured by those of the Renaissance. Spenser's "The Ruines of Time" (and its predecessor, Du Bellay's "Les Antiquitez de Rome"—Henri Chamard, in his history of the *Pléiade* [II, 350], says that Du Bellay was the first among the moderns to express "le sentiment des ruines . . . et condensa ses émotions en quelques sonnets que traversa le frisson mystérieux du passé") prepared the ground for this sort of confession in *The Duchess of Malfi*: "I do love these ancient ruins: . . . all things have their end; Churches and cities, which have diseases like to men,/ Must have like death that we have" (v.iii.9-19). For further discussion of the historical continuity of the "sentiment des ruines" see Roland Mortier, *La Poétique des ruines en France* (Geneva: Librairie Droz, 1974). See also Laurence Goldstein, *Ruins and Empire: The Evolution of a Theme in Augustan and Romantic Literature* (Pittsburgh: University of Pittsburgh Press, 1977); Rose Macaulay, *Pleasure of Ruins* (London: Weidenfeld and Nicolson, 1953).

But the sense of eternal power and of a divine spark was inseparable from diasparactive limitation—from incompleteness, fragmentation, and ruin. "Tous les hommes," says Chateaubriand, "ont un secret attrait pour les ruines. Ce sentiment tient à la fragilité de notre nature, à une conformité secrète entre ces monuments détruits et la rapidité de notre existence." Shelley translates:

> I met a traveller from an antique land
> Who said: Two vast and trunkless legs of stone
> Stand in the desert . . . Near them, on the sand,
> Half sunk, a shattered visage lies . . .
> And on the pedestal these words appear:
> 'My name is Ozymandias, king of kings:
> Look on my works, ye Mighty, and despair!'
> Nothing beside remains. Round the decay
> Of that colossal wreck, boundless and bare
> The lone and level sands stretch far away.

There is a "sentiment des ruines" in our own backward glance at the Romantic era. To a striking degree a correlation seems to obtain between what posterity has judged to be the significant existences of that epoch and a diasparactive form in those existences. Lives are radically broken; early death not only afflicted Schubert and Keats but became almost a norm: by suicide, as with Chatterton, by misadventure, as with Shelley, by disease, as with Byron. Other lives are broken in other ways: by drugs, as with Coleridge or Baudelaire; by madness, as with John Clare or Lenau. In a scant half-decade no fewer than three among the small group who stood in relationship to Shelley—Fanny Godwin, Harriet Westbrook, and Dr. John Polidori—committed suicide, and of these Polidori, at twenty-six, was the oldest.[8] Lives are radically broken: Novalis, dead in 1801 in his twenty-ninth year; Hölderlin, insane in 1802 in his thirty-second year; Caroline von Günderode, a suicide in 1806 in her twenty-sixth year; Kleist, a suicide in 1811 in his thirty-fourth year; Platen, dead in 1835 in his thirty-ninth year (and gladly so: "Und wäre nicht das Leben kurz," he wrote, "das stets der Mensch von Menschen erbt,/ So gäb's Beklagenwerteres auf diesem weiten Runde Nichts!"—and were not the life short that

[8] For similar phenomena in France during the Romantic era, see, e.g., Charles Simond, *La Vie parisienne à travers le xix*^{e} *siècle. Paris de 1800 à 1900* (Paris: E. Plon, Nourrit et cie, 1900-01) II, 22-23, 49-51, 117-218. Compare Friedrich Schlegel's *Lucinde*: "For a human being who is a human being, there is no death other than his own self-induced death, his suicide." Still further, compare Novalis: "The authentic philosophical act is suicide; this is the real beginning of all philosophy."

man inherits from man, there would be nothing more lamentable on this wide earth). Of the five major figures in English Romanticism, it could easily be argued that the two whose lives and endeavors constitute the focus of this book are in diasparactive respects hardly more unusual, simply on the face of the matter, than the three who are not treated.[9] The days of our years are threescore and ten, but of Byron, Keats, and Shelley, only Byron saw his thirty-fifth birthday, and even Byron survived but a single one beyond that. And no one was more aware of ruin than Byron:

> We wither from our youth, we gasp away—
> Sick—sick; unfound the boon—unslaked the thirst,
> Though to the last, in verge of our decay,
> Some phantom lures . . .

Others died not so young, but died in little pieces. "Faculty after faculty, attachment after attachment," writes Hazlitt, "we are torn from ourselves piecemeal while living; year after year takes something from us; and death only consigns the last remnant of what we were to the grave." "Es schwinden, es fallen/ Die leidenden Menschen/ Blindlings von einer/ Stunde zur andern," sang Hölderlin—suffering humans grow less, they sink, blindly, from hour to hour. We think of Wordsworth. We think again of Nerval, who was one of Romanticism's suicides, but one who, like his English contemporary Beddoes, spent years of death-in-life beforehand. "La misère a rendu ma pensée invalide"; "Il voulait tout savoir mais il n'a rien connu." "Je suis sanglant, brisé, souffrant pour bien des jours!" The motif of the "disinherited one" from Ivanhoe became the profoundly serious rubric for his very existence:

> Je suis le Ténébreux,—le Veuf,—l'Inconsolé,
> Le prince d'Aquitaine à la Tour abolie

The "Tour abolie" of an inner life is here a counterpart to the Romantically external "sentiment des ruines."

The melancholy that accompanied Nerval's sense of ruin—"le Soleil noir de la Mélancolie"—was a darkened image of Romantic longing, and was scarcely less current in that era than more hopeful expressions of the soul's incompleteness. Thus Victor Hugo spoke of "un sentiment nouveau, inconnu des anciens et sin-

---

[9] I regard Blake as occupying a category all his own, at the center as it were of a triangle whose sides are Romanticism, Enlightenment, and pietistic traditions of inner light; although I do not thereby hesitate to cite him when appropriate in this volume.

gulièrement développé chez les modernes, un sentiment qui est plus que la gravité et moins que la tristesse: la mélancolie." "For classicists," wrote Charles Nodier in 1820, "the ideal was found in the perfection of our human nature. The ideal for romantic poets is found in our sorrows." Like longing, melancholy is a diasparactive form—witnesses a sense that things as they are provide no fulfillment, that they partake of incompleteness, fragmentation, and ruin:

> Le malheur n'en fait plus qu'une immense ruine,
> Où comme un grand débris le désespoir domine!

The lines are from Lamartine, and strike a recurring note in his poetry. "J'ai vécu; j'ai passé ce désert de la vie." He speaks of "mon esprit abattu," of having been "deceived by existence":

> —Combien de fois ainsi, trompé par l'existence,
> De mon sein pour jamais j'ai banni l'espérance

Like Wordsworth, he felt himself the inhabitant of a world torn and rent apart from its wholeness:

> Je ne veux pas d'un monde où tout change, où tout passe;
> Où, jusqu'au souvenir, tout s'use et tout s'efface;
> Où tout est fugitif, périssable, incertain;
> Où le jour du bonheur n'a pas de lendemain.

In those lines we see the defining structure of Romantic melancholy in its relationship to longing. Like longing, melancholy rejects the here-and-now as containing no fulfillment. Unlike longing, it is shorn of hope and therefore posits no otherness toward which to strive—no land where the lemon trees bloom, or to utilize Lamartine's own distinctive vision as elsewhere expressed, "Où l'oranger fleurit sous un ciel toujours pur."

Perhaps, however, melancholy's involvement with incompleteness, fragmentation, and ruin is as instructively shown by Lenau as by any other Romantic figure. "Anyone who has a feeling for history," he writes,

cannot help . . . feeling a deep sadness. Waste, omission, irretrievable omissions, and the failure of the fairest plans—these are what a lover of history finds everywhere in history and in nature. . . . It is striking that the most thoughtful men of our age—like Leo, Görres, Baader, Schelling, and others—stretch their arms toward the past, that their desires are somewhat backward-looking. Such geniuses have . . . a deep-seated awareness of the failure of the divine purposes in history. . . . They sense that the creating, shaping, weaving hand of nature . . . suddenly trembled as it was working on the . . . fabric of the past, that the thread fell out of its hand and the happiness of nations and ages was thus irretrievably lost. So they are driven by a powerful instinct to go back and seek the fallen thread and pin it again to the fabric. . . . The history of mankind is repeated in concentrated form as the history of the individual human being. I am aware of what I have omitted to do, wasted, done wrongly.

The diasparactive sense is here particularly strong, and is a constant in Lenau's outlook. For him poetry itself was a diasparaction: "The poetic organ which the poet possesses . . . belongs to another life in which it has its full unfolding, hence its disharmony with our present life."[10] In one of his finest poems, the breeze that blows over the ruined castle ("die Burgruine") speaks solely of passing away ("Vergänglichkeit!").

Lenau's feeling that mankind had somehow been broken off from the richest possibilities of the past was one expressed by Shelley as well. Surveying the ruins of Pompeii, the English poet noted that

This scene was what the Greeks beheld. (Pompeii you know was a Greek city.) They lived in harmony with nature, & the interstices of their incomparable columns, were portals as it were to admit the spirit of beauty which animates the glorious universe. . . . If such is Pompeii, what was Athens? . . . O, but for that series of wretched wars which terminated in the Roman conquest of the world, but for the Christian religion which put a finishing stroke to the antient system; but for those changes which conducted Athens to its ruin, to what an eminence might not humanity have arrived!

The thought that our present was a ruin of the past's possibilities was one to which Shelley recurred. On another occasion he restated the surmise in a still more insistent context of diasparaction:

I envy you the first reading of Theocritus.—Were not the Greeks

[10] Compare Wilhelm Schlegel: "In der Dichtkunst und den anderen Künsten habe ich nur noch den Widerschein der himmlischen Schönheit erblickt, ein schwaches Abbild der ehemaligen Vollkommenheit der Welt, ehe sie durch Verderbnis entstellt und ihre großartige Harmonie zerstöret wurde."—In poetry and the other arts I have caught sight only of the reflection of heavenly beauty, a faint image of the former perfection of the world, before it was disfigured by ruin and its sublime harmony shattered.

a glorious people? . . . If the army of Nicias had not been defeated under the walls of Syracuse, . . . Rome might have been all that its intellectual condition entitled it to be, a tributary not the conqueror of Greece; the Macedonian power would never have attained to the dictatorship of the civilized states of the world. . . . What then should we have been? As it is, all of us who are worth any thing spend our manhood in unlearning the follies, or expiating the mistakes of our youth; we are stuffed full of prejudices, & our natural passions are so managed that if we restrain them we grow intolerant & precise . . . & if we do not restrain them we all do sorts of mischief to ourselves & others. Our imagination & understanding are alike subjected to rules the most absurd.

In addition to such bleak presentiments, shared by figures as different as Shelley and Lenau, that man was historically broken off from his true heritage, melancholy could in the Romantic era sometimes be conceived under the explicit form of thwarted longing. "Denn jeder sucht ein All zu sein, und jeder ist im Grunde nichts," mourned Platen—for each seeks to be an all, and each is at bottom nothing. Byron felt himself no less an exile in the imperfect than did Baudelaire, but for him the paradisal longing was one of despair. "Of its own beauty is the mind diseased," he says, "—where,/ Where are the forms the sculptor's soul hath seized. . . . Where are the charms and virtues which we dare/ Conceive in boyhood and pursue as men/ The unreach'd Paradise of our despair."

In such despair, the era's melancholy sometimes dictated a more somber variant of the Romantic quest, one in which movement toward a paradise—even one unreached—gave way to a state of expiatory homelessness:

> a wanderer *must* I go . . .
> No human dwelling ever give me food
> Or sleep, or rest: but over waste and wild
> In search of nothing that this earth can give
> But expiation, will I wander on—
> A man by pain and thought compelled to live,
> Yet loathing life

The lines seem to be quintessential Byron, but are in fact Wordsworth, as too are these words from another locus:

> Day and night my toils redouble,
> Never nearer to the goal;

> Night and day, I feel the trouble
> Of the wanderer in my soul.

But Byron also (unlike Nerval) experienced the diasparaction of melancholy without that of suicide:

> I live
> But live to die: and, living, see no thing
> To make death hateful, save an innate clinging,
> A loathsome, and yet all invincible
> Instinct of life

As those lines from "Cain" suggest, what was true for real figures in the Romantic age was true for fictional ones as well—we hardly need Hazlitt's reminder with respect to Byron that "The Giaour, the Corsair, Childe Harold, are all the same person, and they are apparently all himself." Among such fictional figures, the three most symbolically representative for Romanticism as a whole might well be Goethe's Werther, Byron's Manfred, and Chateaubriand's René; all three, in different ways, are emblems of torn existence: one a suicide, one isolated and destroyed by his past, one a rejecter of life. "Notre coeur est un instrument incomplet," muses René—"Our heart is an incomplete instrument, a lyre where some strings are lacking, and where we are forced to convey the accents of joy under the tone consecrated to sighs."[11]

In another emphasis, the era is marked by a turning to diasparactive vehicles in writing. I have in mind not only the fragmentary poem (and whether fragmentary by intent or by accident makes little difference), such as "that spectacular literary ruin, *The Four Zoas*" (the phrase is Jean Hagstrum's), such as "Christabel" or "The Fall of Hyperion" or "The Triumph of Life," but also poems, such as "Don Juan" or "The Excursion," or such prose pieces as the vast unfinished autobiography of De Quincey, that were open forms and could be added to indefinitely (of "The Excursion" Hazlitt suggested that "this very original and powerful performance" was "like one of those stupendous but half-finished structures, which have been suffered to moulder into decay, because the cost and labour attending them exceeded their use or beauty"). Coleridge tried to convince Wordsworth not to dissipate himself in "little poems," but Wordsworth had a natural propensity for brief forms—"he cannot form a whole," judged Hazlitt. "The Title-page

---

[11] Compare Jean Paul: "Romanticism is an Aeolian harp through which the storm of reality strums melodies. . . . But melancholy trembles on the strings; indeed, at times a cry of pain tears through."

announces that this is only a Portion of a Poem," said Wordsworth himself of "The Excursion." Not only did the great poet not fret in the narrow confines of the sonnet form, but in fact he wrote more sonnets than Sidney, Spenser, Shakespeare, Donne, and Milton combined. Of course in a sense an individual sonnet is a completed venture; in contrast to Wordsworth's urgent commitment to "The Recluse," however, his repeated indulgences in sonnets testify to diasparactive uses of his energy. "In the course of the same afternoon," he writes in 1822, "I produced 3 sonnets, and soon after many others; and since that time, and from want of resolution to take up anything of length, I have filled up many a moment in writing sonnets, which might easily have been better employed."

Coleridge himself, his vision of the vast systematic philosophical whole notwithstanding, presents almost a thesaurus of diasparactive forms. Not only are there unfinished poems and partially written treatises, but there are promised yet unwritten letters, projected epics, planned yet unrealized philosophical and theological studies. (Lamb wrote jokingly in 1815 that "Coleridge is just dead. . . . Poor Col., but two days before he died he wrote to a bookseller proposing an epic poem on the 'Wanderings of Cain,' in twenty-four books. It is said he has left behind him more than forty thousand treatises in criticism and metaphysics, but few of them in a state of completion.") There are in particular what might be called rubble-heap works, such as *Biographia Literaria*, where a mosaic content of borrowed passages from various sources is complemented by meandering inattention to and indeed denial of conventional structure. The book is fittingly enough subtitled "Sketches of my Literary Life and Opinions," and contains internal subheadings such as "A Chapter of digression and anecdotes." As Pater noted, Coleridge's "very language is forced and broken"; and of the *Biographia*, the *Aids to Reflection*, and *The Friend*, the same critic further notes:

> perhaps, of all books that have been influential in modern times, they are furthest from artistic form—bundles of notes; the original matter inseparably mixed up with that borrowed from others; the whole, just that mere preparation for an artistic effect which the finished literary artist would be careful one day to destroy. Here, again, we have a trait profoundly characteristic of Coleridge.

I have just opened quite at random *The Friend*—a work heaped together in journalistic sections—and see that No. 26 for March 1, 1810, bears the entirely typical title of "Sketches and Fragments of the Life and Character of the Late Admiral Sir Alexander Ball." As Hazlitt unkindly but not inaccurately said of that work, "What is his *Friend* . . . but an enormous title-page; the longest and most tiresome prospectus that ever was written; an endless preface to an imaginary work."

In truth, it is my judgment, and I believe that of many and perhaps even most scholars actively engaged in Coleridge studies, that Coleridge's most pregnant, vital, and idiosyncratic work is to be found in his pure fragments: in the haphazard entries of his notebooks, and in the immediacies of marginal notations in books he was reading. Even his famous definition of imagination and fancy in the thirteenth chapter of the *Biographia Literaria* is in his own words like "the fragments of the winding steps of a ruined tower." "Exclusively of the abstract sciences," he once said, "the largest and worthiest portion of our knowledge consists of aphorisms: and the greatest and best of men is but an aphorism."

Yet even this apotheosis of the fragment is not unique. If Coleridge's most vital work, despite his attempts at conventional achievement, is in his jagged pieces—momentary epiphanies of a mind continuously in the process of thought—such is precisely the parallel truth for Novalis. His fragments are his glory. Indeed, the very treatise, *Die Christenheit oder Europa*, where he celebrates the oneness and wholeness of life in medieval times, is itself subtitled "A Fragment." So, too, with Friedrich Schlegel: if we look into the second and eighteenth volumes of the great modern edition of his works, we find in his disconnected and cryptic fragments the throbbing heart of the intellectual life of the time. "Many works of the ancients," he notes, "have become fragments. Many works of the moderns are so at their genesis."

The statement can be justified from differing perspectives and documented by varied examples. "I have turned for consolation to the past," says Hazlitt, "gathering up the fragments of my early recollections, and putting them into a form that might live." "Despite isolated moments of hope in some of his later fragments," writes a recent commentator, "Hölderlin is a poet who failed ultimately to create (or discover) those principles of integration by which things could be made whole."[12] Blake's three great prophetic poems—"The Four Zoas," "Milton," and "Jerusalem"—are simply studies in the fragmentation of the human psyche ("Constantly descending and fragmenting into Emanations and

[12] Richard Unger, *Hölderlin's Major Poetry* (Bloomington: Indiana University Press, 1975), p. 8.

Spectres," says for instance Helen McNeil, "the Zoas act according to the requirements of the present situation, not according to a concept of stable personality"). And Arnold, speaking of Goethe's criticisms of the "faults" that "impaired Byron's poetical work," notes the "straining after the unlimited, which made it impossible for Byron to produce poetic wholes such as the *Tempest* or *Lear*."

Moreover, fragmentariness, whether in Romantic consciousness or elsewhere, can be a feature even of supposed wholes—a phenomenon that Rilke signalized when he wrote to Lou Andréas-Salomé: "Yes, the two Elegies are there—but I can tell you when we meet how small and how sharply broken a fragment they form of what was then delivered into my power" ("the most glorious poetry that has ever been communicated to the world," observes Shelley, "is probably a feeble shadow of the original conception of the Poet"). Indeed, Tennyson's stately "In Memoriam," published as the nineteenth century reached its mid-point, was fragmentary in its very essence, although it was published as a supposed whole. One of the names Tennyson considered for the poem was "Fragments of an Elegy," and, as he explained, "The sections were written at many different places. . . . I did not write them with any view of weaving them into a whole . . . until I found I had written so many." Elsewhere he confessed that "the general way of its being written was so queer that if there were a blank space I would put in a poem." Conversely Shelley, complaining of Keats's "Endymion" that "the Author's intention" appeared to be "that no person should possibly get to the end of it," suggested that Keats would have done better "if he had printed about 50 pages of fragments from it" instead of the whole poem.

In addition to such fragmentariness within nominal wholes, Romanticism is especially fecund in explicit fragmentation and incompleteness. "The Bride such as it is is my first *entire* composition of any length," writes Byron in 1813, "for the G[iaou]r is but a string of passages—& C[hil]d Ha[rol]d is & I think always will be unconcluded." Earlier, he said that he had added to "The Giaour"—'but still in foolish fragments"; and in his journal he recorded his liking of "my Fragment. It is no wonder that I wrote one—my mind is a fragment." Again, Rousseau informs us in a statement prefixed to his *Contrat social* that

> this little treatise was originally part of a larger work begun in the past without considering my ability to finish it, and long since abandoned. Of the various segments that could have been taken from what I had written, this one is the longest, and seems to me

the least unworthy of being offered to the public. The rest no longer exists.

Rousseau was writing in the second half of the eighteenth century; by the second half of the nineteenth, Nietzsche, in hailing the "charm of imperfection" ("Reiz der Unvollkommenheit"), praised that poet

who, like so many men, achieves a higher attractiveness through his imperfections than through everything that comes to perfection under his hand—indeed, his advantage and fame stem rather from his ultimate incapacity than from his sufficient power. His work never quite expresses what he really would like to express and what he would *like to have seen*. It seems that he has had the foretaste of a vision and not the vision itself; but an immense desire for this vision has remained in his soul, and it is from this that he derives his equally immense eloquence of desire and craving. . . . It benefits his fame that he does not really achieve his goal.

Nietzsche's contemporary, Ruskin, was even more accepting of the inevitability of *Unvollkommenheit*:

. . . accurately speaking, no good work whatever can be perfect, and *the demand for perfection is always a sign of a misunderstanding of the ends of art*.

This for two reasons, both based on everlasting laws. The first, that no great man ever stops working till he has reached his point of failure; that is to say his mind is always far in advance of his powers of execution. . . . I believe there has only been one man who would not acknowledge this necessity, and strove always to reach perfection, Leonardo; the end of his vain effort being merely that he would take ten years to a picture, and leave it unfinished. . . .

The second reason is that imperfection is in some sort essential to all that we know of life. . . . Nothing that lives is, or can be, rigidly perfect; part of it is decaying, part nascent. The foxglove blossom—a third part bud, a third part past, a third part in full bloom—is a type of the life of this world. And in all things that live there are certain irregularities and deficiencies. . . . [T]o banish imperfection is to destroy expression, to check exertion, to paralyze vitality.

Ruskin here makes triumphant virtue out of iron necessity. But the reality addressed by him, no less than by Nietzsche, is that of dia-sparactive form.

By early in the twentieth century, Proust could look back and say, in *La Prisonnière*, that the "quality of being—albeit mar-vellously—incomplete" was "the peculiarity of all the great works of the nineteenth century." And still later, Kenneth Burke, in *The Philosophy of Literary Form*, commented on "the increasing propor-tion of *fragmentary* poems to be noted since the beginning of the nineteenth century."

To approach a single aspect of the matter more directly, one can simply open the Oxford edition of Shelley's poetical works (one could do the same with the new Penguin edition of Wordsworth's poems), and in the table of contents observe such titles as "Prince Athanase. A Fragment"; "Fragment: Home"; "Fragment of a Ghost Story"; "Fragment: To One Singing"; "A Fragment: To Music"; "Another Fragment to Music." Or, to limit attention merely to poems written in 1819, one notes "Fragment: To the People of England"; "Fragment: 'What men gain fairly' "; "Frag-ment: 'Follow to the deep wood's weeds' "; and then farther down in the work of the same year, a veritable barrage of additional fragments—seventeen by actual count.

But Shelley's fragmentariness is only one illustration of the in-tensified occurrence of diasparactive forms in the Romantic era. In this respect the Elgin Marbles—those supreme testimonies to sig-nificance within ruin—serve as a kind of objective correlative for the culture and history of the epoch. "On Monday last," writes Benjamin Haydon in 1817, "there were one thousand and two people visited the Elgin marbles! a greater number than ever vis-ited the British Museum since it was established. It is quite interest-ing to listen to the remarks of the people. . . . We overheard two common looking decent men say to each other, 'How broken they are, a'ant they?' 'Yes,' said the other, 'but how *like life*.' "

As an analogon of life itself, such brokenness marked all aspects of the period's reality. To cite an example from a special perspec-tive, Friedrich Schlegel observed that "Schelling's philosophy, which one could call criticized mysticism, ends, like the *Prometheus* of Aeschylus, with earthquake and ruin." To cite another from a modern perspective, a commentator has recently urged that "The later Byron is the castaway, but he is so because he is now the fragmented Byron. . . . In the dramas and long poems of the final period—in *Don Juan*, *The Island*, and even in *The Vision of Judgment*—he is the split man. . . . This problem is at its height in the final period . . . where the fragmentation of Byron's *oeuvre* is the clearest index of the fragmentation of his personality. . . . The fragmentation itself proceeds from the first trap of childhood misery and neurosis."[13] A second recent commentator notes that "The effort to find the structure of *Don Juan* is . . . the single greatest difficulty we have with the poem. *Don Juan* itself repudiates formality, in both senses, so that if we are ever to understand . . . the design of this work, we must I think begin by renouncing our ordinary thoughts about poetic structure. After all, as everyone knows, the poem stops—it does not end; nor is *Don Juan* seriously weakened by being a 'fragment.' "[14] Still another commentator says of yet another figure, Shelley, that "The burden of *Alastor* is despair of the human condition"; that "Beautiful and extreme as it is, *Alastor* remains a dead end, as any poem of a ruined quest must be, for it closes in a wasteland from which no salvation is possible"; that "The ruin and desolation that shadow the heart's affections in *Prometheus* haunt all of his later poetry"; that Shelley's last poem is a "poem of total despair."[15]

Other identifying features of the era are not only diasparactive in their structure but actually find in this fact a unifying denominator for their seeming heterogeneity. It would perhaps be generally agreed that two of the touchstones for the Romantic sensibility were the doctrine of organism and the doctrine of symbol. For instance, René Wellek, in a classic essay, has insisted on "three criteria" for Romanticism in general: "imagination for the view of poetry, nature for the view of the world, and symbol and myth for poetic style." As he develops the second and third criteria, he concludes that "All romantic poets conceived of nature as an organic whole, on the analogue of man rather than a concourse of atoms," and that "All the great romantic poets are mythopoeic, are symbolists."

But organism and symbolism address themselves to the same problem: they both are endeavors to adjudicate the relationship of parts to wholes.[16] They are, moreover, concerns in which, although the wholes are accorded theoretical honor, the experienced reality is that of parts.

[13] Bernard Blackstone, *Byron; A Survey* (London: Longman, 1975), pp. 177-83.

[14] Jerome J. McGann, Don Juan *in Context* (Chicago: University of Chicago Press, 1976), pp. 3-4.

[15] Bloom, pp. 285, 290, 323, 358.

[16] Cf. Hölderlin. "There is only one real quarrel in the world: which is more important, the whole or the individual part."

In truth, the very word symbol, in its Greek derivation, implies a putting together of something torn apart ("the juncture of two parts," is one of its root definitions [*Liddell and Scott*, p. 759]); and though the emphasis on putting together honors the idea of a whole, the inescapable fact is that the symbol as such is always jagged, is always a fragment incomplete in itself ("a sign or token by which one infers a thing" say Liddell and Scott of another variant of the root [*ibid.*]). The symbol is a diasparact. As Coleridge explains it,

> The Symbolical cannot perhaps be better defined in distinction from the Allegorical, than that it is always a part of that, of the whole of which it is representative.—"Here comes a sail,"—(that is a ship) is a symbolical expression. "Behold our lion!" when we speak of some gallant soldier is allegorical. Of most importance to our present subject is this point, that the latter (allegory) cannot be other than spoken consciously;—whereas in the former it is very possible that the general truth may be unconsciously in the writer's mind during the construction of the symbol.

The contention could hardly be more unequivocal. The symbol is parallel to the rhetorical figure of synecdoche: it is a part that indicates a whole, but only the part is present. Indeed, the whole ("the general truth") may not even be accessible to consciousness. The symbol, the diasparact, is the real; the whole the hypothetical.

It would be difficult to conceive of any theory of symbol for which this would not be true. In every symbol the mind proceeds from the contemplation of a fragment of reality to the apprehension but not the comprehension (to use a distinction favored by Coleridge and by Kant before him) of a larger entity, which in direct proportion to the grandeur of its putative wholeness eludes all conceiving. A passage in Wordsworth can establish the typology for this process:

> Never did a Child stand by the side of a running Stream, pondering within himself what power was the feeder of the perpetual current, from what never-wearied sources the body of water was supplied, but he must have been inevitably propelled to follow this question by another: 'towards what abyss is it in progress? what receptacle can contain the mighty influx?' and the spirit of the answer must have been, though the word might be Sea or Ocean, accompanied perhaps with an image gathered from a

Map, or from the real object in Nature—these might have been the *letter*, but the *spirit* of the answer must have been *as* inevitably, a receptacle without bounds or dimensions, nothing less than infinity.[17]

The logic of incompleteness is thus ultimately the logic of infinity. As Fritz Strich has argued in a well-known work (even if his theorizing perhaps depends too much on *a priori* polarities), the difference between Classic and Romantic awareness lies in their solutions to the problems of temporality and its dissipations. The Classic looks to the idea of perfection and completeness (*Vollendung*), the Romantic to infinity (*Unendlichkeit*). "Our destiny, our being's heart and home," said Wordsworth, "Is with infinitude, and only there." "The striving for the infinite," said Novalis, "is the ruling motive in a healthy, active soul." A chief characteristic of "romanticism," said Baudelaire, must be "aspiration toward the infinite." "The Romantic," said Jean Paul, "is the beautiful without boundary or the beautiful infinite." "All high poetry," urged Shelley still more inclusively, "is infinite." "The desire of Man being Infinite," wrote Blake, "the possession is Infinite & himself Infinite."

We see the same Romantic concern with infinity, and the attend-

[17] The passage is remarkable not only in its own right but as a paradigm of central interrelationships in the Romantic complex. The ocean as symbol of infinity is complemented by the stream as symbol of process, two concepts, and two images, under which much of Romanticism can be subsumed, and perhaps all of it implied. Compare Wordsworth's emphasis on the philosophical extensions of stream-reverie with Shelley's question: "O stream!/ Whose source is inaccessibly profound,/ Whither do thy mysterious waters tend?" For the ocean as icon of infinity, compare Hegel: "The ocean gives us the idea of the indefinite, the unlimited, and infinite; and in *feeling his own infinite* in that infinite, man is stimulated and emboldened to stretch beyond the limited." Compare Baudelaire: "Why is the spectacle of the sea so infinitely and eternally agreeable? Because the sea offers simultaneously the idea of immensity and of movement. . . . It suffices to suggest the idea of total infinity." Compare further Goethe: "Ah, how often at that time has the flight of a crane soaring above my head inspired me with the desire to be transported to the shores of the immeasurable ocean, there to quaff the pleasures of life from the foaming goblet of the infinite." Shortly further on, Goethe summons the same complex of factors, including now the stream of process: "I paused where we boys used to amuse ourselves making ducks and drakes upon the water. I remember so well how I sometimes watched the course of that stream, following it with strange feelings, and romantic ideas of the countries it was to pass through. . . . I knew that the water continued flowing on and on . . . and I lost myself completely in the contemplation of the infinite distance." It is only a step from here to "Mahomets-Gesang" or the last twenty-five lines of the third book of "The Excursion"—and later in the nineteenth century to "Le Bateau Ivre" or the ending of "Sohrab and Rustum."

ant paradox whereby the perception of parts and fragments implies the hypothetical wholeness of infinity, but the impossibility of grasping that entity simultaneously witnesses the actual dominance of diasparactive forms, in a Coleridgean statement that is hardly less pregnant than the one by Wordsworth:

I can contemplate nothing but parts, and parts are all *little*—!
—My mind feels as if it ached to behold and have something great—something *one and indivisible*—and it is only in the faith of this that rocks or waterfalls, mountains or caverns give me the sense of sublimity or majesty!—But in this faith *all things* counterfeit infinity!

Coleridge here speaks of "sublimity" as somehow co-ordinate with infinity and summons the natural phenomenology of rocks, waterfalls, and mountains as exemplars.[18] In doing so, he not only participates in that fascination with the sublime that increasingly agitated aesthetic theorists in the years leading to the crescendo of Romanticism but also indicates a common structure as obtaining between the sublime and the symbolic. "For all that meets the bodily sense," he writes in 1796, "I deem/ Symbolical, one mighty alphabet/ For infant minds." Yet in this universal democracy of symbolism, some things are more symbolic than others, and those things receive the special definition of the sublime. As a companion of Coleridge's reported in 1798:

When we were ascending the Brocken, and ever and anon stopping to take breath, as well as to survey the magnificent scene, a long discussion took place upon the sublime and beautiful. We had much of Burke, but more of Coleridge. Of beauty much, but more of sublimity, which was in accordance with the grandeur of surrounding objects. Many were the fruitless attempts made to define sublimity satisfactorily, when Coleridge, at length, pronounced it to consist in a suspension of the power of comparison.

The sublime, in other words, is the perception of very large fragments, such as mountains, with the accompanying awareness that this largeness implies still larger conceptions that can have no such objectivization and therefore cannot be compared. The sublime is, so to speak, an implied comparison in which only the dia-

[18] Cf. Wordsworth: "the rock & the Waterfall: these objects will be found to have exalted the mind to the highest state of sublimity . . . the absolute crown of the impression is infinity, which is a modification of unity."

sparactive object exists. This structure is made rigorously clear by Kant:

> Precisely because there is a striving in our imagination towards progress *ad infinitum*, while reason demands absolute totality, as a real idea, that same inability on the part of our faculty for the estimation of the magnitude of the world of sense to attain to this idea, is the awakening of a feeling of a supersensible faculty within us; and it is the use to which judgment naturally puts particular objects on behalf of this latter feeling, and not the object of sense, that is absolutely great, and every other contrasted employment small. Consequently it is the disposition of a soul evoked by a particular representation engaging the attention of the reflective judgment, and not the object, that is to be called sublime.

> The sublime is that, the mere capacity of thinking which evidences a faculty of mind transcending every standard of sense.

Both the sublime and the symbolic, accordingly, have in common a diasparactive structure: the object itself, which is present to the mind, implies a larger whole, which is not.[19] Indeed, it would be fitting to term the sublime a negative symbol, in that it turns the mind back to become aware of the unboundedness within itself, whereas the symbolic awareness seeks unboundedness within the implications of the object. Goethe's understanding of symbol bears direct witness to this truth. In some definitions, themselves fragments in a diasparactive heap, *Maximen und Reflexionen*—a work that emerged into being, to quote the commentary of the Hamburg edition, "on loose sheets, old scraps of paper and envelopes of letters, theater bills and schematic diagrams, notebooks and rough drafts of letters"[20]—he says that

> Symbol transfers the appearance into the idea, the idea into an image, in such a way that the idea remains always infinitely active and unattainable, and, even if expressed in all languages, remains in fact inexpressible.

---

[19] Cf. Kant: "the sublime is to be found in an object even devoid of form, so far as it immediately involves, or by its presence provokes, a representation of *limitlessness*, yet with a super-added thought of its totality."

[20] It is interesting to observe that the compositional method was utilized also by Rousseau, who "began writing the *Rêveries du promeneur solitaire* in the form of notes scrawled on odd slips of paper or playing cards" (Lester Crocker, *Jean-Jacques Rousseau* [New York: The Macmillan Company, 1968-73], II, 345).

That is the true symbolism where the particular represents the more universal, not as dream and shadow, but as living and momentary revelation of the *Unerforschlichen*.

The symbol is the "particular" (*das Besondere*) in space and momentary in time: a diasparact. The larger entity it expresses is "inexpressible," and is an aspect of the *Unerforschlichen* (the impenetrable).

So too with Kant. Although his conception of symbol is different in some ways, it agrees with Goethe's on the centrality of the diasparact. "Die symbolische ist . . . eine Art der intuitiven"—the symbolic is a mode of the intuitive. It contains "indirect representations of concepts." The symbolic transfers "our reflection upon an object of intuition to quite a new concept, and one with which perhaps no intuition can ever directly correspond. . . . All our knowledge of God is merely symbolic."

Here, although there is a disjunction between intuition and concept that differs from the emphasis of Coleridge, the definition agrees with Coleridge's in insisting that the symbolic is a diasparactive perception that expresses a larger awareness, with the larger awareness less comprehensible than the diasparact.

If for Kant, as for Goethe, the symbol is a jaggedness that implies a wholeness, this truth is honored still more thoroughly by Coleridge's requirement that symbol is actually a "part" of its more universal implication. He was undeviating in this insistence. "Symbols = 'the whole, yet of the whole a part,' " he writes in a notebook entry that isolates vividly the fragmentary nature of symbol. "By a symbol I mean, not a metaphor or allegory or any other figure of speech or form of fancy, but an actual and essential part of that, the whole of which it represents." Symbols are "consubstantial with the truths of which they are the *conductors*." And in a brilliantly stated passage he warns against the confounding of "SYMBOLS with ALLEGORIES," saying that a symbol is characterized

> above all by the translucence of the Eternal through and in the Temporal. It always partakes of the Reality which it renders intelligible; and while it enunciates the whole, abides itself as a living part in that Unity, of which it is the representative.

Although the symbol "enunciates the whole," it is only as "a living part"—a diasparact—that it exists; the whole relates to it by "translucence" of the larger concern in the living part; and ultimately—if we take "eternity" and "infinity" as synonyms for the incomprehensibly vast—the conception pours into that prospect of infinity suggested by Wordsworth's ocean. The symbol is characterized "above all" by the translucence of "the Eternal through and in the Temporal." "In the Symbol," agrees Carlyle, ". . . there is ever, more or less distinctly and directly, some embodiment and revelation of the Infinite; the Infinite is made to blend itself with the Finite."[21] This is the ultimate logic of the diasparact; this is also the ultimate logic of Romanticism as such. Racking his brains to describe the special quality of Delacroix' paintings, Baudelaire arrives at the formula: "C'est l'infini dans le fini"—it is the infinite in the finite. "Das Unendliche endlich dargestellt ist Schönheit," defined Schelling earlier—the infinite finitely represented is beauty. "Das Schöne," confirmed Wilhelm Schlegel, "ist eine symbolische Darstellung des Unendlichen"—the beautiful is a symbolic representation of the infinite. But in this relationship that which is finite does the representing. Although Carlyle could proclaim that "the Universe is but one vast Symbol of God," that "a Symbol is ever . . . some dimmer or clearer revelation of the Godlike," Goethe, in 1785, said: "Forgive me for so gladly remaining silent when talk arises about a divine being, for I recognize one only in and from particular things."[22]

Schelling's formula of "the infinite finitely represented" carried over into his specific conception of symbol. It was a central doctrine of his philosophy of art that "representation of the absolute with absolute indifference of the universal and particular *in the particular* is only symbolically possible." Utilizing Kant's division into "symbolic" and "schematic" (e.g. Kant: "the intuitive mode of representation is divisible into the schematic and the symbolic. Both are hypotyposes, i.e. presentations (*exhibitiones*), not mere marks"), Schelling proceeds to an "elucidation" of the symbolical:

That representation, in which the universal signifies the particular, or in which the particular is perceived through the universal, is schematism.

That representation, however, in which the particular signifies the universal, or in which the universal is perceived through the particular, is allegorical.

---

[21] Again: "in all true works of Art . . . (if thou know a work of Art from a Daub of Artifice) wilt thou discern Eternity looking through Time."

[22] Cf. Novalis: "Wir *suchen* überall das Unbedingte, und *finden* nur Dinge"—we seek everywhere the infinite, and find merely things.

The synthesis of these two, where the universal neither signifies the particular, nor the particular the universal, but where both are absolutely one, is the symbolic.

It may seem that Schelling, by his commitment to polarities resolving themselves into a synthesis, is here having it both ways. But his insistence that "representation of the absolute . . . *in the particular*" is only symbolically possible underscores the primacy of the diasparact. And his conception of the synthesis of universal and particular in the symbol does account for one practical difficulty in symbolic theories: that is, that no matter how many distinctions one makes between the symbolic and the allegorical (Creuzer says that symbol "seizes all our powers of soul. The symbol is a beam which falls upon our eyes directly from the dark ground of being and thought." Allegory, on the other hand, "entices us to search out and follow the way which thought hidden in image takes. The former is momentary totality; the latter a progression into a series of moments"), that whatever distinctions are made in theory,[23] in practical matters of interpretation, there tends to be only one mode: the allegorical. As Angus Fletcher, for instance, has said,

> The word "symbol" in particular has become a banner for confusion, since it lends itself to a falsely evaluative function whenever it is used to mean "good" ("symbolic") poetry as opposed to "bad" ("allegorical") poetry. . . . A critic may say of *The Castle* or *The Trial* . . . that they are "mythic," and then proceed to read them . . . as the purest sort of allegory.

Schelling's synthesis allows him a ready explanation of this phenomenon: "All symbolical things are easy to allegorize, because the symbolic meaning encloses the allegorical in itself."

None the less, the practical currency of allegory in such a fusion shows still again that the whole invoked by symbol is indeed impenetrable. Whether we maintain distinctions between symbol and allegory or collapse them into the single mode of allegory, what really present themselves are fragments; the larger wholes are al-

[23] In introducing Schelling in 1803 to a man named Martin Wagner, Goethe tells the former that "If you could make comprehensible to him the difference between allegorical and symbolic treatment, you would be his benefactor, for so much turns upon that axis." Goethe's own definition of allegory, in contradistinction to his definition of symbol cited above, is that "allegory transforms the appearance into the concept, the concept into an image, in such a way that the concept is forever delimited in the image and completely fixed and expressed there."

ways hypothetical extensions. "All beauty is allegory," writes
Friedrich Schlegel: "The highest thing can only be said allegori-
cally, just because it is inexpressible." "All art is allegorical," says
Tieck: "What can man represent, singly and consisting in itself,
broken off and eternally cut away from the rest of the world, which
is the way we see objects before us? Art does not do this: we join
together, we seek to fasten onto the particular a universal sense,
and thereby arises allegory. The word indicates nothing else than
true poetry, which seeks the high and noble and can find it only by
this path." Such too is the process of Romanticism itself. "The
world must be romanticized," proclaims Novalis: "When I give to
the commonplace a high sense, to the customary a secret authority,
to the known the dignity of the unknown, to the finite an infinite
appearance, then I romanticize." In these formulations, the sym-
bolic and the Romantic are conceived as virtually one and the same
diasparactive awareness.

So much—for the time being at any rate—for the Romantic sym-
bol and its testimony to fragmentation. The same factors inhere in
another and at least equally important criterion of Romantic cul-
tural consciousness. For the theory of organism was no less dear to
the Romantic sensibility than was the theory of symbol. Coleridge,
Wordsworth, Kant, and Schelling—simply to continue with
figures already brought forward—each devoted himself no less to
the conceptualizing of the former than to that of the latter. Indeed,
by something of a paradox, although an adequate history of the
doctrine of organism has yet to be written, the relative cultural
preoccupation from about 1740 to about 1840 was, I should think,
even greater for organism than for symbol. ("In the field of natural
history," writes Goethe excitedly to Herder in 1787, in his
Italienische Reise, "I have things for you that you don't expect. I be-
lieve I have pushed very near to the How of organism.") M. H. Ab-
rams, in his classic study, *The Mirror and the Lamp*, has adduced
important quotations from late eighteenth-century English theo-
rists that help document this contention, and Oskar Walzel goes so
far as to say that "the concept of organism is the key to the Roman-
tic view of the world."

The larger outlines of the doctrine's historical transmissions are
fairly well known. "The view of an organic nature," says Wellek,
"descends from neo-Platonism through Giordano Bruno, Böhme,
the Cambridge Platonists, and some passages in Shaftesbury." In
addition, and perhaps of more detailed importance for the de-
velopment of Romantic concern, the contributions of Leeuwen-

hoek (for the microscope gave a tremendous if as yet unassessed impetus to awareness of organism),[24] Leibniz, Buffon, Bonnet, and Kielmeyer should be in our minds. Of special interest in this line of conceiving was Turbervill Needham's description, at the mid-point of the eighteenth century, of "vegetative Force."[25]

The new awareness of organism generated by these and other investigators was correlated not only with a changed view of external nature but with evolving conceptions of society and the life of a people as well (for a brief but authoritative summary of this aspect of organic analogy see Paul Kluckhohn's *Das Ideengut der deutschen Romantik*). Still further, it became the basis for a widespread conviction that the form of a work of art was or should be analogous to the structure of an organism.

Such a view constituted a rejection of eighteenth-century formalities of rule and prescript; happily so, for it was one of the defining tasks of the Romantic sensibility to throw off these rigidities.[26] Boileau and his followers, in Keats's impassioned if not entirely accurate description, were considered to be

> closely wed
> To musty laws lines out with wretched rule
> And compass vile: so that ye taught a school
> Of dolts to smooth, inlay, and clip, and fit,
> Till, like the certain wands of Jacob's wit,
> Their verses tallied. Easy was the task:
> A thousand handicraftsmen wore the mask
> Of Poesy.

[24] For instance, when Henry Oldenburg, the secretary of the Royal Society of London, translated Leeuwenhoek's famous 18th letter of 9 October 1676, he expanded the Dutch investigator's name for protozoa, "animalcules," to read *"animalcula* or living Atoms" (*Philosophical Transactions*, xii [1677], 821). I suspect that Leibniz's prescription for his own monads, that they were alive, and that in fact death itself was only an indiscernible smallness of life, was actually a syncretism of certain insistences in the Hermetic tracts with the results of Leeuwenhoek's microscopic researches (Leibniz not only corresponded with Leeuwenhoek later in life and mentioned him in the *Théodicée* but also had been the emissary who bore back to Leeuwenhoek Oldenburg's acknowledgment of the 18th letter). In any event, for Leibniz, "la matiere" was "organique par tout" (*Leibniz*, v, 65).

[25] *Observations upon the Generation, Composition, and Decomposition of Animal and Vegetable Substances* (London, 1749), p. 39.

[26] Cf. Hazlitt: "Our poetical literature had, towards the close of the last century, degenerated into the most trite, insipid, and mechanical of all things, in the hands of the followers of Pope and the old French school of poetry. It wanted something to stir it up."

For Keats, the antidote to such mechanically external clipping and fitting was organic form: "If Poetry come not as naturally as the Leaves on a tree it had better not come at all."

Nor was Keats alone in his view. Wordsworth provides a similar rejection of rule and espousal of organism:

> A POET!—He hath put his heart to school,
> Nor dares to move unpropped upon the staff
> Which Art hath lodged within his hand—must laugh
> By precept only, and shed tears by rule.
> Thy Art be Nature; the live current quaff,
> And let the groveller sip his stagnant pool,
> In fear that else, when Critics grave and cool
> Have killed him, Scorn should write his epitaph.
> How does the Meadow-flower its bloom unfold?
> Because the lovely little flower is free
> Down to its root, and, in that freedom, bold;
> And so the grandeur of the Forest-tree
> Comes not by casting in a formal mould,
> But from its *own* divine vitality.

In short, the Romantic theory of art became virtually inseparable from the doctrine of organic form. "Remember," said Coleridge, "that there is a difference between form as proceeding, and shape as superinduced;—the latter is either the death or the imprisonment of the thing;—the former is its self-witnessing and self-effected sphere of agency."

But the preference for proceeding form over superinduced shape—for divine vitality as opposed to formal mould—came about not only as an effect of a shift in sensibility and a deepening of scientific enquiry, but as an outcome of philosophical argumentation as well. While we should beware of underestimating the continuity of the organic tradition, at least as far back as Leibniz and actually as far as classical antiquity, it was Kant who most authoritatively channeled this underground current into a great river that flowed into the historical ocean of Romanticism. Comparisons of nature to the handiwork of the artist had been familiar at virtually all periods in Western culture. In the seventeenth century, for instance, Henry Vaughan told John Aubrey that "all things are artificial, for Nature is the Art of God."[27] Kant, however, criticized the validity of the comparison, and insisted that

[27] Again, Richard Kroner notes that "there are countless places in Leibniz's writ-

We do not say half enough of nature and her capacity in organized products when we speak of this capacity as being the *analogue of art*. For what is here present to our minds is an artist—a rational being—working from without. But nature, on the contrary organizes itself. . . . We might perhaps come nearer to the description of this impenetrable property if we were to call it an analogue of life. . . . But strictly speaking, the organization of nature has nothing *analogous* to any causality known to us . . . *intrinsic natural* perfection, as possessed by things that are only possible as *ends of nature*, and that are therefore called organisms, is unthinkable on any analogy to any known physical, or natural, agency, not even excepting—since we ourselves are part of nature in the widest sense—the suggestion of any strictly apt analogy to human art.

In reversing the equation, Kant provided the paradigm for the Romantic attitude toward organism. Instead of comparing nature to, and thereby deriving it from, art, Romanticism simply restated the old comparison in the light of Kant's objection: the parallelism of nature and art was maintained, but now with art as subordinate to and imitative of nature. Poetry should come like "the Leaves on a tree," in Keats's phrase; or in Wordsworth's simile, should "unfold" like the bloom of "the Meadow-flower." "That which is beautiful," said Friedrich Schlegel, "reminds us of nature and therefore excites the feeling of the infinite fullness of life. Nature is organic, and the highest beauty is therefore eternally and always plantlike (*vegetabilisch*)."[28] "Organische Natur: ins Kleinste lebendig; Kunst: ins Kleinste empfunden"—such was one of Goethe's equations. "The great Artist," said Coleridge, "does what Nature would do, if only the disturbing Forces were abstracted.—" Not much more than a decade after Kant's statement, Schelling was saying that

---

ings where the universe is termed a work of art; indeed, the central concept of Leibnizian philosophy, that of pre-established harmony, is itself of aesthetic provenance" (*Von Kant bis Hegel*, II, 292 n. 2). For the Renaissance view by which the world was "God's poem," see, e.g., Alistair Fowler, *Triumphal Forms; Structural Patterns in Elizabethan Poetry* (Cambridge: Cambridge University Press, 1970), pp. 16 f. See further M. C. Nahm, "The Theological Background of the Artist as Creator," *Journal of the History of Ideas*, VII (1947).

[28] Cf. his even more rhapsodic statement from another place: "The more divine a man or a work of man is, the more it will be like the plant; this is of all forms of nature the most moral, and the most beautiful."

He lags far behind to whom art has not appeared as a closed, organic, and in all its parts necessary whole, as is the case with nature. If we feel ourselves incessantly urged to behold the inner essence of nature, and fathom that fruitful source that pours out of itself so many great appearances with eternal uniformity and adherence to law, how much more must it interest us to penetrate the organism of art, in which the highest unity and lawfulness produce themselves out of absolute freedom, and which allows us to know the wonder of our spirit far more immediately than nature does. If it interests us to pursue, as far as possible, the construction, the inner plan, the relations and intricacies of a plant or an organic being in general,[29] how much more would it have to entice us to perceive the same intricacies and relationships in the still more highly organized and intertwined plant that we call a work of art.

In such a manifesto, the Romantic preoccupation with freedom—"absolute freedom" as Schelling here says (and compare Wordsworth's asseveration that "the lovely little flower is free/ Down to its root, and, in that freedom, bold")—is not only emphasized but also constitutes a connecting link between organism and such essentially Romantic manifestations as the French Revolution. (For evidence of the interrelation of political revolution and Romantic awareness we are not restricted to Wordsworth's sojourn in France during the Revolution—and its reflection in "The Prelude"; nor to such forms as Beethoven's "Fidelio," as well as other of the era's operatic and symphonic works. On the contrary, we realize that the entire cultural complex of the time, including the enormous philosophical upsurge in Germany, was bound up with the same mystique of freedom as was the political upheaval.[30] "The French Revolution," said Friedrich Schlegel, was "an admirable allegory on the system of transcendental idealism." "The French Revolution," he said again, "Fichte's *Wissenschaftslehre*, and

[29] Cf. Rousseau: "Je n'ai ni dépense à faire ni peine à prendre pour errer nonchalamment d'herbe en herbe, de plante en plante, pour les examiner, pour comparer leurs divers caractères, pour marquer les rapports et leurs différences, enfin pour observer l'organisation végétale de manière à suivre la marche et le jeu de ces machines vivantes, à chercher quelquefois avec succès leurs lois générales, la raison et la fin de leurs structures diverses."

[30] See further Xavier Léon, *Fichte et son temps* (Paris: Librairie Armand Colin, 1954-59), I, 166 ff.; M. H. Abrams, *Natural Supernaturalism; Tradition and Revolution in Romantic Literature* (New York: W. W. Norton & Company, Inc., 1971), pp. 348 ff.; *CPT.*, pp. 149 ff.

Goethe's *Meister* are the greatest tendencies of the age.") The valuing of freedom, however, stems logically from the deficiency of the actual situation and is thus a variant of diasparactive perception. "The history of the world," said Hegel, "is nothing but the development of the idea of freedom." But that history and that development were and are partial, fragmentary, and incomplete.

Just a few years after Schelling's manifesto, Coleridge warned against "confounding mechanical regularity with organic form." His dichotomy was an almost verbatim appropriation of a fresh new formula by "a continental critic," Wilhelm Schlegel:

> The form is mechanic when on any given material we impress a predetermined form, not necessarily arising out of the properties of the material, as when to a mass of wet clay we give whatever shape we wish it to retain when hardened. The organic form, on the other hand, is innate; it shapes as it develops itself from within, and the fullness of its development is one and the same with the perfection of its outward form. Such is the life, such the form. Nature, the prime genial artist, inexhaustible in diverse powers, is equally inexhaustible in forms. Each exterior is the physiognomy of the being within, its true image reflected and thrown out from the concave mirror.

But the Coleridge/Schlegel formula merely focused an awareness that by that time was in the process of permeating all recesses of Romantic sensibility. "It is the same sap," said Victor Hugo, for instance, speaking from the Napoleonically delayed efflorescence of French Romanticism, "propagated in the sun, that produces all the trees of the forest, so diverse in presence, in fruits, in foliage. It is the same nature that fecundates and nourishes the most different geniuses. The true poet is a tree who can be battered by every gale and watered with every dew, who bears his works as his fruits." And by the second half of the century the situation had become such that Taine, in his *Philosophie de l'art*, could assert that "Cultural science must employ the same methods as botany. . . . As a matter of fact, cultural science is nothing other than a form of applied botany, concerned not with plants but with human achievements."

Indeed, to the Romantic sensibility organic form was the paradigm for philosophical no less than for artistic endeavor. "Philosophism," wrote Novalis, "is a higher analogue of organism. Organism is completed by philosophism and vice versa. Both symbolize one another." Here, as in other instances, Kant broke ground for Romanticism. As early as 1781, in a noteworthy formulation, he described the organic model for philosophical systematizing:

> In accordance with reason's legislative prescriptions, our diverse modes of knowledge must not be permitted to be a mere rhapsody, but must form a system. Only so can they further the essential ends of reason. . . . This idea is the concept provided by reason—the form of a whole—in so far as the concept determines *a priori* not only the scope of its manifold content, but also the positions which the parts occupy relatively to one another. The unity of the end to which they all stand in relation to one another, makes it possible for us to determine from our knowledge of the other parts whether any part be missing, and to prevent any arbitrary addition. . . . The whole is thus an organized unity (*articulatio*), and not an aggregate (*coacervatio*). It may grow from within (*per intussusceptionem*), but not by external addition (*per appositionem*). It is thus like an animal body, the growth of which is not by the addition of a new member, but the rendering of each member, without change of proportion, stronger and more effective for its purposes.

Now in a sense, and certainly at first glance, the doctrine of organic form seems to deny the diasparactive. As Walzel says, "the chief characteristic of the organic point of view was the wish to conceive an appearance as a whole." Schelling insisted that

> there is no true system that is not at the same time an organic whole. . . . If in every organic whole everything supports and underlies everything else, then this organization would have to exist as a whole in pre-existence to its parts; the whole could not arise from the parts, rather the parts would have to arise from the whole.

Such a view restates Kant's dictum that "the *first* prerequisite of a thing, considered as an end to nature [i.e. an organism],[31] is that its parts, both as to their existence and their form, are only possible by their relation to the whole." Kant also had said that the "principle, the statement of which serves to define what is meant by organisms, is as follows: *an organized natural product is one in which every part is reciprocally both end and means.*" The formula seems to

---

[31] "Organisms are . . . the only beings in nature that, considered in their separate existence and apart from any relation to other things, cannot be thought possible except as ends of nature."

contravene the diasparactive separation of part from whole, and it is normative for Romantic understanding.[32] Coleridge later indicated virtually an identical sense of parity between part and whole:

> The spirit of poetry, like all other living powers, must of necessity circumscribe itself by rules. . . . It must embody in order to reveal itself; but a living body is of necessity an organized one,—and what is organization but the connection of parts to a whole, so that each part is at once end and means.

And yet, upon closer examination, the doctrine of organic form is seen to be unsuccessful in its attempt to abridge the power of the diasparact—indeed, is seen to exist precisely as a kind of despairing response to that power. In the passages from Kant and Coleridge just cited, the equation subtly shifts the emphasis from an ascendancy of a monolithic whole to a wholeness of the parts. The tendency is even more marked in Goethe. For him it is "a higher maxim of organism" that

> every living thing is no singleness, but rather a manifold; even insofar as it appears to us as an individual, it is in fact an assembly of living, independent substances. . . . The more imperfect the plant is, the more these parts are alike or similar to one another, and the more they resemble the whole. The more perfect the plant becomes, the more dissimilar become the parts to one another. In the former case the whole is more or less like the parts, in the latter the whole is dissimilar to the parts. The more similar the parts are to one another, the less are they subordinate to one another. The subordination of the parts points to a more perfect plant.

In this view, the prior definition of "parts" is paradoxically necessary to the perfection of organism. If an organism is "no singleness, but rather a manifold," it is thereby true that perfect wholeness, which must be a singleness, tends to lie outside the fact—to become as it were a hypothetical construct. Thus for Goethe the

[32] Thus, for random example, Johann Wilhelm Ritter in 1797 defined an animal organism as "a system of forces acting upon one another, where the part is that which is for the whole, where the whole has its foundation in the parts, where the whole and the parts are reciprocally means and end." Much the same formulation is supplied by Schiller's friend Christian Gottfried Körner, in a letter of 6 December 1790: "und hierdurch unterscheidet sich eben ein *Aggregat* von Elementen, die einzeln als Produkte eines höheren geistigen Lebens ihren Wert haben, von einem *organisierten Ganzes*, wo Teil und Ganzes gegenseitig Mittel und Zweck sind, wie bei den organisierten Naturprodukten."

complete organism was a primal plant that existed only as an infer-ence, not as an object of experience. As the "relationships" of plants "gathered themselves under one conception," the idea "hovered before me in the sensible form of a supersensible *Urpflanze*."[33]

So despite the concern of organic metaphors with the idea of the whole, such concern is actually correspondent to symbol's stress on the larger meaning. In both cases, the total conception spills out into the incommensurable, and what is left as objectively real is the fragment. The very fact that organic growth is a process means that at any moment of its cognition that part must symbolically imply the whole. When the violet past prime is present to consciousness, the entire process of the violet's growth exists by implication. But it never exists in any other way: its wholeness is dispersed within a state of temporal *différance* (to adapt Derrida's special term); it is at any one time an inference proceeding from fragmentary cognition.

If for Goethe the ultimate organism must leave the realm of the sensible to seek its wholeness in a supersensible entity, for Cole-ridge too the organic ultimately implied the supersensible. In a passage that M. H. Abrams describes as having "haunted" him "since Dr I. A. Richards brought it to my attention when I was a student at Cambridge several decades ago," Coleridge communi-cates what Abrams calls his "informing vision" of nature:

> I seem to myself to behold in the quiet objects, on which I am gazing, more than an arbitrary illustration, more than a mere *simile*, the work of my own Fancy! I feel an awe, as if there were before my eyes the same Power, as that of the REASON—the same Power in a lower dignity, and therefore a symbol estab-lished in the truth of things. I feel it alike, whether I contemplate a single tree or flower, or meditate on vegetation throughout the world, as one of the great organs of the life of nature. Lo!—with the rising sun it commences its outward life and enters into open communion with all the elements. . . . At the same moment it strikes its roots and unfolds its leaves, absorbs and respires, steams forth its cooling vapour and finer fragrance. . . . Lo!—at the touch of light how it returns an air akin to light, and yet with the same pulse effectuates its own secret growth. . . . Lo!—how

---

[33] Cf. Kant: "For a given conditioned, reason demands on the side of the condi-tions absolute totality, and in so doing converts the category into a transcendental idea. For only by carrying the empirical synthesis as far as the unconditioned is it enabled to render it absolutely complete, and the unconditioned is never to be met with in experience, but only in the idea."

upholding the ceaseless plastic motion of the parts in the profoundest rest of the whole it becomes the visible organismus of the whole *silent* or *elementary* life of nature and, therefore, in incorporating the one extreme becomes the symbol of the other; the natural symbol of that higher life of reason, in which the whole series (known to us in our present state of being) is perfected. . . . We had seen each in its own cast, and we now recognize them all as co-existing in the unity of a higher form, the Crown and Completion of the Earthly, and the Mediator of a new and heavenly series.

In this vision, organism, no less than symbol, becomes a form of Romantic longing, and a witness to the diasparactive nature of Romantic structures.

Indeed, reflection leads us inescapably to the realization that such diasparactions are parallels of human perception itself, and that Romanticism is merely the intensification of certain attitudes inseparable from human experience. "Thou seest not all," writes Byron, "but piecemeal thou must break/ To separate contemplation the great whole."

If we accept Kant's analysis by which all possible experience occurs in inner and outer fields maintained respectively as time and space, then we see that the "separate contemplation" called organism is an analogy of the inner time sense, while that of symbolism parallels our perception of spatial reality. When, for example, I drive a motorcar along a road at night, what I actually perceive in my headlights is a white line and a sign indicating a curve to the right; what I infer from that is that the road is actually going to continue and will indeed turn to the right. But my perception as such is fragmentary—a piecemeal breaking; I act from faith in the symbolic implications of that fragment. If I enter a New York apartment, I glimpse perhaps two walls, some furniture, a door; I infer that two other walls exist, that other furnishings exist, that behind the door another room exists. In short, as Carlyle says, "It is in and through *Symbols* that man, consciously or unconsciously, lives, works, and has his being." By the same token, I am organically existent only at this moment; it is an inference and an act of faith that the organism will continue tomorrow.

Were my faith in such symbolic extensions and organic continuations to be in vain, life would be madness if it could be lived at all. We would all be like the boy in Stevenson's novel, sent up a broken staircase supposedly to a bedroom, to discover by a flash of lightning that an abyss looms before us.

Without faith, in other words, diasparactive awareness would be horror. "Nous ne voyons jamais qu'un seul côté des choses," says Victor Hugo, "L'autre plonge dans la nuit d'un mystère effrayant." It is no accident that Coleridge's most complete definition of symbol occurs immediately after this statement: "Faith is either to be buried in the dead letter, or its name and honors usurped by a counterfeit product of the mechanical understanding, which in the blindness of self-complacency confounds SYMBOLS with AL-LEGORIES." Nor is it fortuitous that Edwyn Bevan chooses as the title of his Gifford Lectures the rubric *Symbolism and Belief*. Faith is the necessary complement of the diasparactive perception of real-ity; it is, as the Bible says, "the evidence of things not seen, the substance of things hoped for"—a formulation that recognizes both the spatial and temporal perspectives. (Indeed, one of the progenitors of the Romantic sensibility, Friedrich Jacobi, based an entire philosophy on the necessary intertwinement of faith and the perception of reality.[34] As Coleridge said at one point, "This is not a fair Criticism on Jacobi. What was his Object? To prove, that FAITH, which the Philosophers of his Day, held in contempt, was sensuous Evidence. . . . No! But to prove that the sensuous Evi-dence itself was a species of Faith.")

If, despite reality's fragmentary presentation to our perception, we are enabled to function externally by means of faith, another principle allows us to maintain inner coherence despite the chaos of such fragmentation considered as pure objectivity. This second enabler is what Kant called "the highest principle in the whole sphere of human knowledge"—that of apperception. Pure apper-ception is the "transcendental unity of self-consciousness," the "abiding and unchanging 'I.' " It reveals itself to formal argument by the consideration that "it must be possible for the 'I think' to accompany all my representations. . . . All the manifold of intuition has, therefore, a necessary relation to the 'I think' in the same sub-ject in which the manifold is found."

It is the principle of apperception that provides the foundation for Husserl's entire phenomenology of noematic objectivity (and even Sartre, in attacking Husserl's postulate of a transcendent ego, admits, at the very outset of *La Transcendance de l'Ego: Esquisse d'une description phénoménologique*, that "it must be conceded to Kant that 'the I Think *must be able* to accompany all our representations' ").

[34] E.g.: "Das Element aller menschlichen Erkenntniß und Wirksamkeit ist Glaube." (*Jacobi's Werke*, IV-1, 223). We may conjecture that the source of Jacobi's contention was in large measure provided by certain arguments in Hume. See Sec-tions 5-10 in Book I of Hume's *Treatise*.

Moreover, it seems not unlikely that the first of Wellek's criteria for
Romanticism, that of imagination—a faculty that Kant in his own
analysis left shrouded in mystery—may well be simply the tran-
scendental unity of apperception considered as an activity. At any
rate it seems so if we accept Sartre's phenomenological under-
standing that the "imagination is not an empirical and superadded
power of consciousness; it is the whole of consciousness as it
realizes its freedom." "The imagination is not a state," agrees
Blake: "it is the Human Existence itself." Specifically, as Sartre in-
sists, "the imagination . . . is the necessary condition for the free-
dom of empirical man in the midst of the world." "Nothing is more
free," concurs Hume, "than the imagination of man." If the
Romantic preoccupation with freedom is a form of diasparactive
awareness, as we have argued above, the imagination by that view
would in its turn function as a response to diasparactive limita-
tion.[35] "Imagination," as Wordsworth observes, "almost always
transcends reality." Kant elucidates the structure of that truth:
"Though the imagination, no doubt, finds nothing beyond the
sensible world on which it can lay hold, still this thrusting aside of
the sensible barriers gives it a feeling of being unbounded; and that
removal is thus a presentation of the infinite. As such it can never
be anything more than a negative presentation—but still it expands
the soul."

In any event, it seems by the burden of the foregoing argumenta-
tion that diasparactive forms not only are intrinsic to human con-
sciousness but receive a special emphasis in Romantic attitudes. It
is with such emphasis in mind that this volume has been conceived
as a series of diasparactions; whatever else may be true of it, the
book accepts its own postulates. Its Coleridgean table of contents is
designedly jagged, and its various chapters, though intensely in-
tertwined in theme and concern, are at the same time deliberately
fragmentary and autonomous in formal conception. "A fragment,"
as Friedrich Schlegel said, "must like a small work of art be quite
separated from the surrounding world and complete in itself like a
hedgehog." The twin landing places, along with what at least on
the surface might seem the arbitrariness of the topics treated, are
designed to be impedances to a conventionally unitive reading—to
be reminders of the hedgehog status of its parts.

In its nominal focus on Coleridge and Wordsworth, further-

---

[35] Thus in his *Metaphysica* of 1739 Alexander Baumgarten defines "Lex imagina-
tionis" as "percepta idea partiali recurrit eius totalis"—the law of imagination is that
an idea perceived of a part of something recurs as the whole of it (§ 561). Likewise
for Coleridge "IMAGINATION" is the "completing power."

more, the book by its very doubling of figures under consideration renders obeisance to the principle of diasparaction. And it rejects the temptation to develop a symmetrical treatment of its two subjects. In particular, instead of comparing Wordsworth and Coleridge primarily as poets and secondarily as thinkers, it jaggedly distorts the equation: an underlying assumption of all the book's discussion is that Wordsworth's spirit realized itself most fully in poetry ("His genius," said Coleridge, "is most *apparent* in poetry"), and that Coleridge's realized itself most fully in the role of Christian philosopher ("If there be any two subjects which have in the very depth of my Nature interested me, it has been the Hebrew & Christian Theology, & the Theology of Plato").

Yet this asymmetry, like other Romantic jaggednesses, implies its paradoxical unity. That Wordsworth had thoughts, and that Coleridge was an at times distinguished poet, though true enough, are not the factors in the unity. Rather it coheres by another feature of Romantic consciousness, one that renders supererogatory any formal attempt at a symmetry of poetic and philosophical treatment; for to Romantic sensibilities poetry and philosophy tended to be the same activity. In the light of this understanding, an emphasis on poetry for Wordsworth and on philosophy for Coleridge is one and the same emphasis. "I regard Berkeley's system," said Herder, "like the systems of Spinoza, Fénelon, Leibniz, and Descartes, as being fiction—as being poetry. What system is anything else or should be regarded as anything else?"

Herder's words perhaps relate too much to the spirit of the *Aufklärung* to be taken as normative of the Romantic tone, however much his formal contention may coincide with Romantic awareness. But within high Romanticism itself, the unity of poetry and philosophy was repeatedly urged. "That which can be done as long as philosophy and poetry are separated," said Friedrich Schlegel, "is done and completed. Therefore the time has come to unite them both." And he hails Novalis: "Thou dost not hover on the border, but in thy spirit have poetry and philosophy inwardly intermingled." Novalis himself said that "Poetry is what is absolutely and genuinely real. That is the kernel of my philosophy. The more poetic, the more true." Again, he said that "poetry is the key, as it were, to philosophy—its goal and meaning."

Perhaps the union of philosophy and poetry seemed so feasible and desirable at least in part because Romantic philosophy no less than Romantic poetry was a fragmented form that embodied the era's longing for completeness and wholeness. We need think only of the systematic wholes striven for by the thinkers of the time—of Hegel's *Begriff* reaching toward its fulfillment in "absolute Idea," of Schelling's attempt to incorporate the absolute by abandoning "negative" or partial philosophy for "positive" or total philosophy. "Religion," maintained Coleridge, is "the ultimate aim of philosophy, in consequence of which philosophy itself becomes the supplement of the sciences, both as the convergence of all to the common end . . . and as supplying the copula, which modified in each in the comprehension of its parts to one whole, is in its principles common to all, as integral parts of one system."

It is not simple happenstance, therefore, that Coleridge on more than one occasion pondered, as did Schelling in Germany, the setting of his philosophy into the form of a vast poem. Nor is it anything less than a manifestation of the deep Romantic sensibility that he considered Wordsworth the greatest "philosophical" poet: "the only man who has effected a compleat and constant synthesis of Thought & Feeling and combined them with Poetic Forms."

Such a conception was essential to Coleridge's valuation of both intellectual modes. He reverenced Plato as "a Poetic Philosopher" and Shakespeare as "a Philosophic Poet." He always sought "that delightful harmony which ever will be found where philosophy is united with . . . poetry."

In these views he was at one with his compeers. Schelling, for a single instance, says in 1800 that "just as, in the childhood of knowledge, philosophy was born from and nourished by poetry, so, after its maturity, will it flow back as so many individual streams into the universal ocean of poetry." Again, Coleridge asks, in 1796, "Why so violent against *metaphysics* in poetry?"

Comparison of the dates indicates how much "in the air" was the aim to poeticize philosophy and to philosophize poetry. Here, as elsewhere in the structures favored by the Romantic consciousness, a diasparactive form is evident: an actual incompleteness striving toward a hypothetical unity. The unity in this instance was one that appealed on the deepest instinctive levels to the best sensibilities of the era. Thus when Keats says, in a poetic statement noteworthy for the plethora of uncomprehending commentary it has elicited, that "Beauty is truth, truth Beauty," the words are not a mere random coupling of abstractions, but a considered testimony to the prevailing desire for the union of poetry and philosophy. It is important to understand that the formula arose from the deepest intuitive layers of Keats's view of the world. "What the imagination seizes as Beauty must be truth," he writes; and elsewhere he speaks of a "regular stepping of the Imagination towards a Truth." "I never can feel certain of any truth," he writes again, "but from a clear perception of its Beauty." The meaning of such a persistent linkage is made explicit by Schelling's words of 1802: "O friend, after we have demonstrated the highest unity of beauty and truth, it then appears to me that we have also demonstrated the unity of philosophy and poetry; for what does philosophy strive after except precisely that eternal truth which is one and the same as beauty, and poetry after that unborn and immortal beauty, which is one and the same with truth?"

The reciprocity was one of Schelling's fundamental insistences. "Beauty and truth are in themselves or according to their idea one and the same." Again, "As the absolute is for philosophy the prototype of truth, so for art it is the prototype of beauty." Indeed, as early as 1796, in a fragment called by Rosenzweig "The Oldest Program for a System of German Idealism," Schelling expressed himself as follows:

> And lastly the idea that unites everything, the idea of beauty, taking the word in the high Platonic sense. I am now convinced that the highest act of reason, encompassing all ideas, is an aesthetic act, and that truth and goodness come together only in beauty—the philosopher must possess just as much aesthetic power as the poet.[36] The men without aesthetic sense are our philosophers of the letter. The philosophy of the spirit is an aesthetic philosophy.

Similar beliefs are to be found repeatedly among Schelling's contemporaries.[37] "The poetic philosopher, the philosophizing poet is a prophet," said Friedrich Schlegel. "The poetic philosopher," said Novalis, "is en état de Createur absolu." "Universality," wrote the former, "is reciprocal saturation of all forms and all materials. It attains harmony only through the union of poetry and philosophy." "The poem of the understanding is philosophy," said the latter—

[36] Cf. Keats: "axioms in philosophy are not axioms until they are proved upon our pulses."

[37] Indeed, an interesting aspect of this particular fragment, and one that dramatizes the extent to which such thoughts were "in the air" among the Romantics, is that its authorship is not certain. The passage is in Hegel's handwriting; Rosenzweig attributes it to Schelling; Fuhrmans includes it in his edition of Schelling's letters (Briefe und Dokumente, I, 69-71); Beissner, however, includes it in the Stuttgart edition of Hölderlin (IV, 1, 297-99). What can be said with certainty is that it represents the beliefs of all three men: Schelling, Hegel, and Hölderlin.

"Without philosophy man remains disunified in his most existential powers—there are two men—an understander—and a poet." "The transcendental poesy," he affirms, "is compounded of philosophy and poetry." "The distinction between poets and prose writers," says Shelley, "is a vulgar error. The distinction between philosophers and poets has been anticipated. Plato was essentially a poet. . . . Lord Bacon was a poet. . . . Shakespeare, Dante, and Milton (to confine ourselves to modern writers) are philosophers of the very loftiest power."

Accordingly, the paradox by which this volume emphasizes Wordsworth as poet and Coleridge as philosopher, and at the same time asserts the unity of its treatment, is identical with that for Romanticism as such. And if each of the chapters here protects its hedgehog status, it is also true, in Friedrich Schlegel's words, that "each thinking member of an organization does not feel its boundaries without its unity in relation to the whole." The mutual dependence of that which is separated and that which is bound together is recognized by Novalis too: "Alles Getrennte wird im Verbindenen—alles Verbundene im Trennenden wahrgenommen." Thus, though the book is a diasparactive study of diasparactive things, its form as a volume asserts its unity.

The fragmented character of the book's contents claims still another function. Their hedgehog nature isolates and thereby particularizes each topic of discussion, and such particularization is desirable as a complement to the conception of Romanticism as a universal sensibility or spirit of the age. Although every informed commentator—or at least every informed commentator capable of thought—must, it seems to me, reject the perverse nominalism of Lovejoy's unseeing denial of such a general entity as Romanticism, Leavis's insistence on particularity constitutes a worthier objection:

> "The romantic view of the world," a view common to Blake, Wordsworth, Shelley and others—yes, I have heard of it; but what interest can it have for the literary critic? For the critic, for the reader whose primary interest is in poetry, those three poets are so radically different, immediately and finally, from one another that the offer to assimilate them in a common philosophy can only suggest the irrelevance of the philosophic approach.

In light of the cultural data adduced above, Leavis's arbitrary elevation of a "primary interest . . . in poetry" at the expense of "the philosophic approach" is clearly unhistorical and leads to interpre-

tational distortion. But his sensitivity to idiosyncrasy and particu-
larity is exemplary. Such particular understanding is as necessary
to a more generalized conception as the lattter is to the former. It is
in the interests of particular understanding that hedgehog essays
seem especially appropriate. Their individuality stands in polar
tension to the more generalized arguments of the introductory
chapter. And in such a matrix—the polarity of the particular with
the general, of the separated with the bound together—the book
has no hesitation in extending its concern into questions about the
nature of poetry and about the existence of poetry's polar reciproc-
ity with philosophy.

The movement and purport of the book's various relationships
and tendencies, therefore, may perhaps not inappropriately be
compared to the weaving of a tapestry. The patterning of the fab-
ric's particolored strands forms an image of the diasparactive triad.
The warp of the weave is constituted by the strivings, achieve-
ments and ruins of Wordsworth and Coleridge, as seen against the
background of Romanticism as an epoch in the history of sensibil-
ity and thought. The woof insinuates a pervasive theme, that of the
interpenetration of poetry and philosophy.

The reciprocity of poetry and philosophy, in truth, is a theme
that exists in protean forms in all parts of the volume. The First
Landing Place, for instance, not only takes up philosophically the
question of poetry's content, but in a different perspective serves
as a transition between the chapters dealing primarily with
Wordsworth's and Coleridge's poetry and the chapters dealing
primarily with Coleridge's philosophy.

The Second Landing Place, like the first, debouches into theoret-
ical questions implied by the volume's preceding argumentation.
It, too, mingles the interests of poetry and philosophy. Even more
importantly, it constitutes the conclusion and keystone of the
book's enterprise; for it elucidates a major mode of artistic activity
as arising from the fragmented condition of our reality.

It thus brings into focus a problem that has been subliminal in all
the book's earlier discussion of diasparactive forms, that is, how
can a fragment be identified as a fragment unless there is also the
conception of a whole from which it is broken off? On the other
hand, if wholes exist, either in conception, or, as seems the case, in
actual experience, how can it be maintained that our perception of
reality is in fact fragmented?

In truth, notwithstanding the massive testimony of the Romantic
era to incompleteness, fragmentation, and ruin, that era was al-

most equally preoccupied with at least the idea of a whole. "The common end of all *narrative*," says Coleridge, "nay, of *all*, Poems is to convert *a series* into a *Whole*." Schelling, again, looked to an eventual system of knowledge that would be a complete whole: "If this system be once presented and known in its totality (*in seiner Totalität*), then the absolute harmony of the universe and the divinity of all beings in the thought of man will be established forever." "I feel in all things," wrote Novalis to Friedrich Schlegel in pantheistic rhapsody, "more and more the sublime components of a wonderful whole."[38]

The conception of a whole was also invoked in more limited contexts. As Coleridge wrote to his son, "Let a man be known first, as capable of doing, and as having done, some one objective Whole, having a Beginning, Middle, and End—a Whole, in which the Thinker and the Man of Learning appears as the Base of the Poet." The entity here prescribed is identical to that supplied by Ben Jonson under the heading *"What wee understand by Whole"*: "*Whole*, wee call that, and perfect, which hath a *beginning*, a *mid'dst*, and an *end*. So the place of any building may be whole, and intire, for that work; though too little for a palace."

But the unity invoked in such definitions, which is perhaps the most common conception of those wholes we encounter in daily experience, is a whole only by its own inner assertion of beginning, middle, and end; as it arises in our imagination or vision it is not absolutely a whole, but rather a fragment of a mental field—as Jonson himself indicates when he appends that "the place of any building may be whole, and intire, for that worke; though too little for a palace." Such a whole, in terms of a phenomenological accounting of the content of our consciousness, can never be anything more, precisely speaking, than a part or portion in a field of perception; it can never be more, even when as aesthetically symmetrical as a Greek vase, than *fragmentum formosum*, a shapely fragment. This kind of entity we may accordingly identify by the term *nominal whole*.

A second formulation of the idea of a whole is one that answers to the doctrine of organic form. Jonson, sounding quite like an organically oriented Romantic, concludes as follows respecting this notion of the whole: *"For the whole, as it consisteth of parts; so*

---

[38] Cf. Rousseau: "Je ne médite, je ne rêve jamais plus délicieusement que quand je m'oublie moi-même. Je sens des extases, des ravissements inexprimables à me fondre pour ainsi dire dans le système des êtres, à m'identifier avec la nature entière."

without all the parts it is not the whole; and to make it absolute, is required, not only the parts, but such parts as are true. For a part of the whole was true; which if you take away, you either change the whole, or it is not the whole." In this understanding, the whole exists as one pole of a linguistic dyad. Its existence depends syntactically on the conception of part, as that of part depends on the syntactic implication of whole. Each conception takes its being from and is defined by the complementarity of the other, and we may accordingly identify this second version of the whole as *contingent wholes*.

As Coleridge saw, all wholes of this second order, as a consequence of their polar involvement, are necessarily involved in ambiguity. Speaking of the two axioms underlying the idea of organic form, he says that "The first of the axioms is: In every true whole, the whole is prior to its parts; the second: The parts constituting the whole are necessarily prior to the whole so constituted. It is clear that both in the term Whole, and the term Parts, there must lurk a double meaning."

A third kind of whole is that indicated by Novalis's pantheistic effusion in which all things are felt to be parts of a wonderful whole. A classic illustration for this third order is provided by Lamartine's poem "L'Occident," where, in response to the question of where all things ultimately go, the answer given is that they go into that "vast ocean of being" that constitutes the "great whole":

> A toi, grand Tout, dont l'astre et la pâle étincelle,
> En qui la nuit, le jour, l 'esprit, vont aboutir!
> Flux et reflux divin de vie universelle,
> Vaste océan de l'Être où tout va s'engloutir!

Lamartine's "grand Tout" recalls "the great whole" of Byron referred to above (and may quite possibly have been suggested by Byron's phrase). But Wordsworth too invokes "the great whole": "the one Presence, and the Life/ of the great whole" (*Prelude*, 1805 version, III, 130-131). Yet again, Coleridge says that " 'Tis the sublime of man,/ Our noontide Majesty, to know ourselves/ Parts and proportions of one wondrous whole!" Taken together, the effect of such invocations is to reveal a deep-lying concern among the Romantics for the conceptions of wholeness and unity.

Another kind of example for this third order of whole is provided by Shelley's "Adonais":

The One remains, the many change and pass;
Heaven's light forever shines, Earth's shadows fly;
Life, like a dome of many-coloured glass,
Stains the white radiance of Eternity,
Until Death tramples it to fragments.

All such dispositions of reality, however, whether those of "The One" or those of "the great whole," are assumed rather than perceived or imaged, and we may accordingly term this third kind of entity *wholes of faith*. As Jonson says, speaking not of pantheistic assumption but of any whole too large for cognitive perception, "in a *Fable*, if the Action be too great, wee can never comprehend the whole together in our Imagination."

Wholes of faith are characterized by ambiguity of structure no less than are *contingent wholes*. For example, Schelling asserts a *whole of faith*: mankind, he said, "could not proceed into the infinite; mankind has a goal, where the striving after knowledge attains its long sought end, where the thousands of years old unrest of the human spirit comes to rest." Yet Schelling also said that "philosophy has till now not come to a true end." As Jaspers comments, "Schelling said both that there can be only one true system, and that no one has it. 'That philosophy is one, and can be only one, rests on the fact that reason is the same for all.' On the other hand, 'who can say: the true philosophy is here or over there?' "

If wholes recognized in our language and experience all suffer themselves to be categorized and modified under the headings of *nominal wholes, contingent wholes*, and *wholes of faith*, it seems clear that no invocation of a whole can countervail the truth that we live in a world of fragments. This truth was especially apparent in the transactions of Romanticism. Coleridge's *"expectations"* were that Wordsworth's "Poem on the growth of your own mind was as the ground-plat and the Roots, out of which the Recluse was to have sprung up as the Tree," and that they were together "to have formed one compleat Whole." But such expectations were crumbled by diasparactive vicissitude: "The Recluse" remained largely unwritten and wholly fragmentary; "The Prelude," after continual revision, remained unpublished in Wordsworth's lifetime. The same complex illustrates also a corollary truth: that the necessity to formulate or somehow to apprehend some true whole is an abiding need of the human spirit. This is the concern addressed in the Second Landing Place.

In a more general way, the paradox inherent in the relationship of part to whole extends to the structure of the book itself; it is both a series of fragments and a self-asserted whole. Its fragmentary dividings, along with its claim as a self-subsisting unity, parallel, as a matter of fact, the structure of Romanticism's most favored poetic form, the ode. For in no other vehicle available to the poet is the tension between fragmentation and wholeness so much the very essence of the form as it is with the ode. In an ode, the varied and deliberately uneven line lengths and stanzaic accumulations persistently urge the analogy of boulders hurled by a giant hand into a configuration that suggests the disorder of fragmentation simultaneously with the order of wholeness.

In truth, one way of viewing this book might be to see it as a prose embodiment of that displaced form of "the greater ode" that M. H. Abrams has termed the "greater Romantic lyric"—a possibility made more fitting by the Romantic dislike of any essential distinction between poetry and prose ("the popular division into prose and verse is inadmissible in accurate philosophy," said Shelley; "which of us," asks Baudelaire, "has not dreamed, in his days of ambition, of the miracle of a poetic prose, musical without rhythm and without rhyme"). Abrams's phrase emphasizes well enough the unevenness, the mass, and at the same time the unity claimed both by this volume and its poetic analogues; and it also engages the notion of that commerce between the subjective and the objective inherent both here and in the poems of which Abrams speaks.

A final observation. The opposed conceptions of organic form and diasparactive form are cast into a polar reciprocity by the volume's intent as a process of criticism. As was noted earlier, the idea of an organism, like that of a symbol, is in important respects fictional or at least heuristic; just as symbol, when subjected to practical interpretation, tends to become allegory, so does the organic whole, when inspected, resolve itself into a perception of parts. As Goethe says:

> In a living object its form as an entity first meets our eyes, then the parts of this form, their configuration and combination. Natural history occupies itself with the form in general and with the relation and combination of the parts, in so far as the object is first set before the eye; if the form is separated, we call this endeavor dissection or anatomization—it looks not merely to the configuration of the parts, but even to their inner structure, and justly calls the microscope to help. If in this way the organic

body has been more or less destroyed, so that its form is annulled and its parts can be regarded as matter, then sooner or later chemistry comes in and gives us new and beautiful conclusions about the final parts and their compound.

Such, *mutatis mutandis*, is the act of criticism. It is a diasparactive process: a tearing apart of a cultural configuration. Every critic in some sense murders to dissect; his armed vision, like Goethe's microscope, gains greater understanding at the cost of less naturalness. Every critic to some extent peeps and botanizes on the grave of richer emotion.

And yet without this rendering of an entity into its components, no criticism is possible. The organism, or the life, or the work of art, exists as a whole for itself alone or for naive intuition; when it becomes an object of analyzing consciousness, this condition is compromised by the assessment of its parts. "Unfortunately," notes Schiller, "the understanding must first destroy the objects of the inner sense before it can appropriate them. Like the chemist, the philosopher finds combination only through dissolution. . . . In order to seize the fleeting appearance he must bind . . . dissect . . . and preserve its living spirit in a sorry skeleton of words. Is it any wonder if natural feeling does not recognize itself in such a likeness, and if truth appears in the analyst's report as paradox?"

To the other reasons for the diasparactive emphasis of this book, accordingly, its intent as a process of critical inspection can be added. Taken as a whole, its most paradoxical ambition is to seem the first instance of a "genre" that Friedrich Schlegel described as not yet existing, one that "is fragmentary both in form and content, simultaneously completely subjective and individual, and completely objective." But perhaps the fullest and at the same time the most Platonically playful formula under which to indicate all the volume's intended aspects would be to say that it is a tearing up of and tearing about in torn up things. It is thereby both an examination of and an exemplar for the primacy of diasparactive forms.

CHAPTER ONE

The Symbiosis of Coleridge
and Wordsworth

◊ ♦ ◊

THE intellectual relationship of Coleridge and Wordsworth has scarcely any cultural counterpart. It is almost impossible to bring to mind any other two figures, so important each in his own right, but also so dependent the one upon the other during his richest intellectual years. The interchange between Goethe and Schiller occurred after each had established his own reputation and his own mode. That between Socrates and Plato was the relationship of master to pupil, while that between Plato and Aristotle, likewise a master-pupil situation, involved fundamental disagreements. The relationship of Beaumont and Fletcher was perhaps as close as that of Coleridge and Wordsworth, but in this instance neither figure achieved major stature in his own right.

But Coleridge and Wordsworth not only profoundly influenced one another; they did so in a way that challenges ordinary methods of assessment. As H. M. Margoliouth notes, in commenting on the Wordsworthian tone of the last ten lines of Coleridge's "The Dungeon,"

> There are so many "Wordsworthian" passages in Coleridge that one begins to wonder how much of "Wordsworth" is Coleridge. One cannot tell. The two blossomed together, each a fostering sun for the other. [1]

What Margoliouth says of the poetic interrelationship, another commentator has recently affirmed of the critical:

> It was the very differences between the two that brought them together, and in the years of their deepest intimacy, from 1797 to 1804, each man left an indelible imprint on the other. (*The Prel-*

[1] Margoliouth, pp. 94-95.

ude, after all, was Wordsworth's letter to Coleridge, and the *Biographia Literaria* was Coleridge's reply.) It is therefore impossible to isolate Wordsworth's theory of poetry from that of Coleridge, just as it is impossible to measure the exact amount of Wordsworth's intellectual debt to his friend.[2]

On the other hand, Norman Fruman's recent study of Coleridge's plagiarisms and weaknesses depicts the relationship as one of slavish dependence by Coleridge on his sturdier friend's stores of mind, heart, and poetry.[3]

Such a view, Coleridge's frequent disingenuousness and unreliability of testimony notwithstanding, is assuredly mistaken. Although most intellectual relationships mutually fecundate their participants at least to some extent, that of Wordsworth and Coleridge was nothing less than a symbiosis, a development of attitude so dialogical and intertwined that in some instances not even the participants themselves could discern their respective contributions. As Goethe said of a similar situation, "Friends such as Schiller and I, bound together over the years, with like interests, in daily contact and reciprocal exchange, existed in one another so thoroughly that there could be no question at all, in the case of individual thoughts, whether they belonged to one or to the other. We composed many couplets in common; often I had the thought and Schiller wrote the verse; often it was the other way around; and often Schiller wrote one verse and I the other. How can there then be any talk of mine and thine? One must really be mired deep in Philistinism to want to ascribe even the slightest importance to the resolving of our respective contributions."[4]

So, too, and even more comprehensively, for Coleridge and Wordsworth. As a recent investigator has said, Coleridge's poetry in 1798 "literally interbraids with Wordsworth's. Themes, motifs, and technical innovations pass from one mind to the other and back again, enriched and transformed at each passage."[5]

It is not impossible to find examples that provide a very clear glimpse of how symbiotic was the aetiology of an expressed viewpoint. As a single instance, Coleridge once called his friend and dedicated opponent of the slave trade, Thomas Clarkson, "the moral steam engine, or Giant with one idea."[6] This statement, made to Allsop during Coleridge's Highgate years and incorpo-

---

[2] Heffernan, p. 5.

[3] Fruman, pp. 265-333 *et passim.*

[4] *Gedenkausgabe,* xxiv, 300.

[5] Sheats, p. 163.

[6] *Table Talk,* p. 330.

rated into the *Table Talk* by Thomas Ashe, utilizes a metaphor developed jointly by Coleridge and Wordsworth in 1803:

> When we drew nearer [writes Dorothy Wordsworth] we saw, coming out of the side of the building, a large machine or lever, in appearance like a great forge-hammer, as we supposed for raising water out of the mines. It heaved upwards once in half a minute with a slow motion, and seemed to rest to take breath at the bottom, its motion being accompanied with a sound between a groan and *jike*. There would have been something in this object very striking in any place, as it was impossible not to invest the machine with some faculty of intellect; it seemed to have made the first step from brute matter to life and purpose, showing its progress by great power. William made a remark to this effect, and Coleridge observed that it was like a giant with one idea.[7]

The passage is particularly interesting because it shows that the attitude was developed mutually by Coleridge and Wordsworth—and indeed by Dorothy, too, who must never be left out of account as a factor in the symbiosis (she was, recalls Coleridge in 1833, "a Woman of Genius, as well as manifold acquirements; and but for the absorption of her whole Soul in her Brother's fame and writings would, perhaps, in a different style have been as great a Poet as Himself").[8] Before Coleridge expresses the actual formula, "a giant with one idea," conversation among the three friends has isolated the machine for observation, has noted the "sound between a groan and *jike*," has proceeded from this analogy to "invest the machine with some faculty of intellect," and has noted that it "seemed to have made the first step from brute matter to life and purpose, showing its progress by great power." Significantly, it was Wordsworth who "made a remark" to this last effect, thereby providing the stepping stone from which Coleridge then reached for the phrase, "a giant with one idea." The passage, in sum, though trivial in itself, demonstrates both the complete intertwinement of symbiotic development and the paradoxical integrity of the individual members in the process.

In the light of such process, therefore, one is inclined to credit Coleridge's testimony in a letter to Southey in July 1802 that "Wordsworth's Preface [to the 1800 edition of *Lyrical Ballads*] is half a child of my own Brain/ & so arose out of Conversations, so frequent, that with few exceptions we could scarcely either of us

[7] *Journals*, I, 207-208.   [8] *Collected Letters*, VI, 959.

perhaps positively say, which first started any particular Thought."[9] The possible objection that the 1800 Preface does not particularly sound like Coleridge, either in style or in idea may partly be answered by noting that it is a more remarkable theoretical document than we usually associate with Wordsworth, partly also by the fact that a symbiotic product incorporates the attitudes of both its authors and therefore does not necessarily seem entirely characteristic of either, but most of all by a third consideration: namely, that Coleridge had an almost chameleonlike ability to alter his own tone to conform to that of his friend. The phenomenon of his "plagiarisms," in fact, bears witness to this compulsion: instead of digesting an outer stimulus into his own mode of expression, Coleridge, to an almost unique extent, projects his psyche into the outer stimulus.

It seems clear, in short, that Coleridge's deep masochism not only asserted itself in repeated vices of procrastination, repeated indulgences in hypochondria, and repeated improprieties of "plagiarism," but also made him uncannily able to subordinate himself to the style of his friend.

For instance, in his beautiful poem written after hearing Wordsworth recite "The Prelude," Coleridge not only expresses his full understanding of Wordsworth's achievement and the agony of his own sense of comparative failure but does so in lines that almost perfectly imitate his friend's blank verse:

> Into my heart have I received that Lay
> More than historic, that prophetic Lay

---

[9] *Ibid.*, II, 830. For instance, in the famous passage in the 1800 Preface where Wordsworth broaches the opinion that "all good poetry is the spontaneous overflow of powerful feelings," the statement's complementary clause asserts that "Poems to which any value can be attached, were never produced on any variety of subjects but by a man who being possessed of more than usual organic sensibility had also thought long and deeply" (*Prose*, I, 126). This, *mutatis mutandis*, is precisely what is later said, not by Wordsworth, but by Coleridge, in the fifteenth chapter of the *Biographia Literaria*, when Shakespeare is being discussed: "What then shall we say? even this; that Shakespeare, no mere child of nature; no automaton of genius, no passive vehicle of inspiration . . . first studied patiently, meditated deeply, understood minutely, till knowledge, become habitual and intuitive, wedded itself to his habitual feelings, and at length gave birth to that stupendous power, by which he stands alone" (*Biographia*, II, 19-20). The emphasis here on a process by which "habitual feelings" wed themselves to "knowledge, become habitual and intuitive" also is prefigured in the passage from the 1800 Preface: "by the repetition and continuance of this act feelings . . . will be nourished, till at length . . . habits of mind will be produced" (*Prose*, I, 126).

> Wherein (high theme by thee first sung aright)
> Of the foundations and the building up
> Of a Human Spirit thou hast dared to tell
> What may be told; . . .
>   . . . and what within the mind
> By vital breathings secret as the soul
> Of vernal growth, oft quickens in the heart
> Thoughts all too deep for words!—
>   Theme hard as high!
> Of smiles spontaneous, and mysterious fears . . .
> And currents self-determined, as might seem,
> Or by some inner Power; of moments awful,
> Now in thy inner life, and now abroad,
> When power streamed from thee . . .[10]

The lines are pure Wordsworth, both in their cadences and in their great Wordsworthian abstractions: "heart," "Spirit," "vital breathings," "inner Power," "mysterious fears," "thoughts too deep," "Now in thy inner life, and now abroad." More remarkable even than the closeness of the imitation, however, is the fact that hardly anywhere else does Coleridge achieve this peculiar Miltonicity of style in which "The Prelude's" great moments are couched.

It is this ability of Coleridge to project himself into Wordsworth's style that makes the relationship of "The Mad Monk" to Wordsworth's "Intimations Ode" so difficult to determine. The opening stanza of Wordsworth's great ode seems to be modeled on the second stanza of Coleridge's "The Mad Monk." Wordsworth's poem begins:

> There was a time when meadow, grove, and stream,
> The earth, and every common sight,
>   To me did seem
>   Apparelled in celestial light,
> The glory and the freshness of a dream.
> It is not now as it hath been of yore;—
>   Turn wheresoe'er I may,
>   By night or day,
> The things which I have seen I now can see no more.[11]

The second stanza of "The Mad Monk" is notably similar, not only in sentiment but in cadence as well:

---

[10] Coleridge, *Poems*, I, 403-405.   [11] Wordsworth, *Poems*, IV, 279.

'There was a time when earth, and sea, and skies,
  The bright green vale, and forest's dark recess,
With all things, lay before mine eyes
    In steady loveliness:
But now I feel, on earth's uneasy scene,
  Such sorrows as will never cease;—
    I only ask for peace;
If I must live to know that such a time has been!'[12]

The unmistakable resemblance of the two passages accredits them as a key text in the symbiosis of Coleridge and Wordsworth. It is, however, not at all certain just what aspect of the symbiosis they illustrate. If "The Mad Monk" is a poem written and published by Coleridge in 1800, and the "Intimations Ode" is a poem begun on 27 March 1802 (accepting Dorothy's journal entry that "William wrote part of an ode" as referring to its opening stanzas) and finished, according to De Selincourt's deduction, in March 1804, then the similarity shows that Wordsworth was in this instance inspired by Coleridge's actual poetic work, and not merely by his intellectual presence and critical encouragement.[13]

That Coleridge did write "The Mad Monk," however, is not accepted beyond all question. E. H. Coleridge included it in the standard edition of Coleridge's *Poetical Works* because, under the title "The Voice from the Side of Etna; or, the Mad Monk," it appeared in the *Morning Post* for 13 October 1800 over the pseudonymous signature "CASSIANI, jun." Coleridge was at the time writing regularly for the *Morning Post*—or at least supposed to be writing regularly ("I am doing little worthy the relation," he says to Davy on 9 October 1800, "I write for Stuart in the Morning Post—& I am compelled by the God Pecunia").[14] Furthermore, the poem was reprinted in 1804 in Maria Robinson's collection called *The Wild Wreath*, and there it was, with a few other changes, entitled "The Mad Monk/ By S. T. Coleridge, Esq."

In 1960, however, S. M. Parrish, in a debate with David Erdman, argued that though Coleridge undoubtedly submitted the poem to the newspaper, and probably also to Maria Robinson, Wordsworth had in fact written it himself. Coleridge, under obligation to produce essays for which he had already been paid (he wrote to Stuart on 7 October 1800, and spoke of "the accidental constitution of my

---

[12] Coleridge, *Poems*, I, 348.
[13] *Journals*, I, 129; Wordsworth, *Poems*, IV, 465.
[14] *Collected Letters*, I, 631.

intellect—in which my taste in judging is far, far more perfect than my power to execute"), promised once more to supply the essays and then said, "I shall fill up these Blanks with a few Poems—."[15] As Parrish observes:

> Stuart cut the letter up to send it directly to his printer, and only one of the poems survives on it. It is a lyric, probably in its origins a Lucy poem, which Wordsworth had written in Germany and sent to Coleridge. Coleridge probably supplied the title, *Alcaeus to Sappho*, intended as a compliment to Mrs. Robinson, who was "Sappho" to *Morning Post* readers. The other poems in the letter can be identified conjecturally by looking through the *Morning Post* for the period following the letter's dispatch and arrival in London. *Alcaeus to Sappho* was not printed until November 24, but on October 13 appeared *The Mad Monk*, on October 14 Wordsworth's *Solitude of Binnorie, or the Seven Daughters of Lord Archibald Campbell* (published in *Poems*, 1807 as *The Seven Sisters*), and on October 21 Wordsworth's *Inscription for a Seat by the Road Side*.[16]

The strange but ineluctably established fact that Coleridge did submit other poems by Wordsworth to the *Morning Post* is much the strongest argument for suspicion about "The Mad Monk." The most important of these poems was "Lewti, or the Circassian Love-chaunt," which Coleridge extensively reworked from a juvenile poem of Wordsworth's composed in 1786 and called "Beauty and Moonlight." Southey had annotated his copy of "Lewti" with the remark, "A school poem of W. W. corrected by S. T. C.," but Lowes nevertheless imperiously maintained that the poem "is as unmistakably Coleridge's as it is unmistakably not Wordsworth's."[17] When "Beauty and Moonlight" was published by De Selincourt in the *Poetical Works of Wordsworth*, however, "Lewti's" dependence on it was pointed out by E.H.W. Meyerstein and quickly accepted by the scholarly community.[18]

Along with "Lewti," two other poems, entitled respectively "Inscription for a Seat by the Road Side" and "Alcaeus to Sappho" —both of them mentioned by Parrish in the passage quoted

[15] *Ibid.*, p. 629.

[16] Stephen M. Parrish and David Erdman, "Who Wrote *The Mad Monk*?; A Debate," *Bulletin of the New York Public Library*, 64 (1960), 218.

[17] Lowes, p. 516.

[18] "Wordsworth and Coleridge," *Times Literary Supplement*, 29 Nov. 1941, p. 596; 6 Dec. 1941, p. 611.

above—were revealed by De Selincourt's publication of Wordsworth's juvenilia to be the work of Wordsworth. Both had previously appeared as Coleridge's in E. H. Coleridge's edition of his poems (ɪ, 349, 353).

In 1950, Jane Worthington Smyser added four more examples of Coleridgean poems that were actually Wordsworth's:

> Since the publication of Wordsworth's juvenilia [she writes] I have found three more poems in the works of Coleridge which De Selincourt failed to note as also originally belonging to Wordsworth: "To Lesbia" (ɪ, 60), "The Death of the Starling" (ɪ, 61), and "Morienti Superstes" (ɪ, 62); besides these, a conjecture may be made as to the authorship of a fourth, "Moriens Superstiti" (ɪ, 61), for it is paired with a poem clearly belonging to Wordsworth.[19]

In the course of her essay, Mrs. Smyser notes that Coleridge was under great pressure to furnish material to the *Morning Post*; and so, as she drily says, "The poems which Coleridge sent were not only the 'emptying out of his Desk,' as he later described his newspaper contributions, but also the emptying out of Wordsworth's desk." She concludes with the observation that "on the whole the confusion in bibliography speaks well for the inextricable ties of a great collaboration; and on Wordsworth's part, at least, the confusion indicates his practical and ready support of a friend badgered by a contract."

So all this, although not explicitly summoned by him, underlies Parrish's argument. He further buttresses his case with the contention that on the basis of internal evidence as shown by concordance tabulations of the two poets' vocabularies, certain words in "The Mad Monk" are Wordsworthian but not Coleridgean.

To these considerations Erdman makes extended rebuttal, the chief point of which is that the poem is a Coleridgean parody of Wordsworth. Although the matter, in view of Coleridge's deviousness, is one where the utmost caution must be exercised, I agree on the whole with Erdman. Parrish's notice that "The Mad Monk" seems to echo Wordsworth's " 'Tis said, that some have died for love," published in the second edition of *Lyrical Ballads* and praised by Coleridge in the *Biographia Literaria*, actually suggests to me that this poem, together with "Strange Fits of Passion Have I Known," provide the basis for a reasonable judgment

---

[19] "Coleridge's Use of Wordsworth's Juvenilia," *PMLA*, 65 (1950), 419.

that "The Mad Monk" is, as Erdman maintains, a parodic imitation of Wordsworth's production. And to my ear, at least, there are internal considerations of tone and theme that bulwark this view. For instance, with reference to the comparative stanzas from "The Mad Monk" and the "Intimations Ode" quoted above, where the latter exhibits the wholly Wordsworthian sentiment that "It is not now as it hath been of yore," the former, in the statement that "I feel . . . Such sorrows as will never cease," seems to strike the idiosyncratic note of Coleridge's dejection—the note of "positive negation."

Resurveying the problem in 1962, Robert Woof suggested, against Parrish but not entirely for Erdman, that "Coleridge wrote 'The Mad Monk' with parody in mind perhaps, though not of Wordsworth. . . . The poem seems to be directed at Mrs. Radcliffe, but it recalls Mrs. Robinson too and even hints, perhaps, at Joseph Cottle."[20] Parrish, for his part, has recently reasserted his own view, but without decisive new evidence.[21]

In any event, the relationship of "The Mad Monk" to the very great "Intimations Ode" testifies to the deeply symbiotic ties between Coleridge and Wordsworth, whatever in this particular instance the dynamics of the symbiosis may be supposed to have been. That the diction of "The Mad Monk" is, by concordance test, more Wordsworthian than Coleridgean would seem, in the light of Coleridge's ability to project himself into his friend's mode, an inconclusive argument.

Indeed, Coleridge's ability—or, better, his need—to project himself into other men's modes is witnessed by his first published reference to Wordsworth. In "Lines, Written at Shurton Bars . . ." he writes, in 1795, as follows:

> Nor now with curious sight
> I mark the glow-worm, as I pass,
> Move with 'green radiance' through the grass,
> An emerald of light

and in a footnote he then says:

> The expression 'green radiance' is borrowed from Mr. Words-
> worth, a Poet whose versification is occasionally harsh and his
> diction too frequently obscure; but whom I deem unrivalled

[20] "Wordsworth's Poetry and Stuart's Newspapers: 1797-1803," *Studies in Bibliography*, 15 (1962), 174.
[21] *Art of the* Lyrical Ballads, pp. 189-213.

among the writers of the present day in manly sentiment, novel imagery, and vivid colouring.[22]

The phrase "green radiance" is patently a kind of symbiotic talisman that Coleridge clutches to himself—a claim that he stakes, so to speak, to participation in Wordsworth's poetic life—and it seems clear that its function prefigures that of the unacknowledged quotations, or "plagiarisms," that exist as mosaic fragments throughout his work. As he said of himself, with the penetrating insight that is no less astonishing than his neurotic convolution, the "first lesson, that innocent Childhood affords me, is—that it is an instinct of my Nature to pass out of myself, and to exist in the form of others."[23]

His relationship to Wordsworth, therefore, is as a feminine principle to its masculine counterpart. "Of all the men I ever knew," said Coleridge, "Wordsworth has the least femineity in his mind. He is *all* man."[24] But in his own stance with regard to this tower of masculinity, Coleridge expressed in 1805 the poignant and clinging wish "that my Spirit purged by Death of its Weaknesses, which are alas! my *identity* might flow into *thine*, & live and act in thee, & be Thou."[25]

So during the time of their closest friendship, Coleridge and Wordsworth, impelled by Coleridge's need to have his own identity flow into that of his friend, collaborated symbiotically. The prose fragment, "The Wanderings of Cain," testifies to Coleridge's initiative in the intertwinement. As he said, in a prefatory note composed in 1828, the piece was

> written in the year 1798, near Nether Stowey, in Somersetshire.
> . . . The work was to have been written in concert with another
> [Wordsworth], whose name is too venerable within the precincts
> of genius to be unnecessarily brought into connection with such
> a trifle. . . . The title and subject were suggested by myself, who
> likewise drew out the scheme and the contents for each of the
> three books or cantos, of which the work was to consist. . . . My
> partner undertook the first canto: I the second: and which ever

---

[22] Coleridge, *Poems*, i, 97 and note. For Coleridge's borrowing of "green radiance," and the composition of the footnote, see Robert Woof, "Wordsworth and Coleridge: Some Early Matters," *Bicentenary Wordsworth Studies in Memory of John Alban Finch*, ed. Jonathan Wordsworth (Ithaca, N.Y.: Cornell University Press, 1970), pp. 76-91.

[23] *Inquiring Spirit*, p. 68.   [24] *Ibid.*, p. 296.

[25] *Notebooks*, ii, 2712.

had *done first*, was to set about the third. Almost thirty years have passed by; yet at this moment I cannot without something more than a smile moot the question which of the two things was the more impracticable, for a mind so eminently original to compose another man's thoughts and fancies, or for a taste so austerely pure and simple to imitate the Death of Abel? Methinks I see his grand and noble countenance as at the moment when having despatched my own portion of the task . . . I hastened to him with my manuscript—that look of humourous despondency fixed on his almost blank sheet of paper, and then its silent mock-piteous admission of failure struggling with the sense of the exceeding ridiculousness of the whole scheme— which broke up in a laugh: and the Ancient Mariner was written instead.[26]

"The Ancient Mariner" too was to have been a collaboration. But again Wordsworth withdrew; not, however, without contributing important images and even lines to the poem. In 1836 Henry Crabb Robinson noted in his diary that Wordsworth gave him an

account of *The Ancient Mariner* written in Devonshire when Coleridge and Wordsworth were together and intended to be published in the *Monthly Magazine* to pay the expense of their journey. It was to have been a joint work. But Wordsworth left the execution to Coleridge after suggesting much of the plan. The idea of the crime was suggested by a book of travels by [Shelvocke] in which the superstition of sailors towards that bird [the albatross] is mentioned.[27]

Some seven years later, in the explanatory notes to his poems dictated to Isabella Fenwick in 1843, Wordsworth himself enlarged upon this information; he spoke of

one of the most remarkable facts in my own poetic history and that of Mr. Coleridge. In the spring of the year 1798, he, my Sister, and myself, started from Alfoxden, pretty late in the afternoon, with a view to visit Linton and the valley of Stones near it; and as our united funds were very small, we agreed to defray the expenses of the tour by writing a Poem, to be sent to the New Monthly Magazine set up by Phillips the bookseller, and edited by Dr. Aikin. Accordingly we set off and proceeded along the Quantock Hills . . . and in the course of this walk was planned

---

[26] Coleridge, *Poems*, i, 285-87.   [27] *Robinson*, ii, 481.

the Poem of The Ancient Mariner, founded on a dream, as Mr. Coleridge said, of his friend, Mr. Cruikshank. Much of the greatest part of the story was Mr. Coleridge's invention; but certain parts I myself suggested, for example, some crime was to be committed which should bring upon the Old Navigator, as Coleridge afterwards delighted to call him, the spectral persecution, as a consequence of that crime, and his own wanderings. I had been reading in Shelvock's Voyages a day or two before that while doubling Cape Horn they frequently saw Albatrosses in that latitude . . . some extending their wings 12 or 13 feet. "Suppose," said I, "you represent him as having killed one of these birds on entering the South Sea, and that the tutelary Spirits of those regions take upon them to avenge the crime." The incident was thought fit for the purpose and adopted accordingly. I also suggested the navigation of the ship by the dead men, but do not recollect that I had anything more to do with the scheme of the poem. . . . We began the composition together on that, to me, memorable evening. I furnished two or three lines at the beginning of the poem, in particular:

> 'And listened like a three years' child;
> The Mariner had his will.'

These trifling contributions, all but one (which Mr. C. has with unnecessary scrupulosity recorded) slipt out of his mind as they well might. As we endeavoured to proceed conjointly (I speak of the same evening) our respective manners proved so widely different that it would have been quite presumptuous in me to do anything but separate from an undertaking upon which I could only have been a clog. . . . The Ancient Mariner grew and grew till it became too important for our first object.[28]

A briefer statement to the same effect was made by Wordsworth in some autobiographical memoranda dictated to Mrs. Christopher Wordsworth in November 1847.[29]

In 1852 Sara Coleridge published a note by the Shakespearean

[28] Wordsworth, *Poems*, I, 360-61. The date was actually not spring of 1798, but 13 November 1797. See *Early Years*, p. 194.

[29] "Coleridge, my sister, and I, set off on a tour to Linton and other places in Devonshire; and in order to defray his part of the expense, Coleridge on the same afternoon commenced his poem of the Ancient Mariner; in which I was to have borne my part, and a few verses were written by me, and some assistance given in planning the poem; but our styles agreed so little, that I withdrew from the concern, and he finished it himself" (*Prose*, III, 374).

scholar Alexander Dyce, who recalled Wordsworth's telling him in conversation that

> "The Ancient Mariner" was founded on a strange dream, which a friend of Coleridge had, who fancied he saw a skeleton ship, with figures in it. . . . I had very little share in the composition of it, for I soon found that the style of Coleridge and myself would not assimilate. Besides the lines (in the fourth part),
>
> > 'And thou art long, and lank, and brown,
> > As is the ribbed sea-sand'—
>
> I wrote the stanza (in the first part),
>
> > 'He holds him with his glittering eye—
> > The Wedding-Guest stood still,
> > And listens like a three-years' child:
> > The Mariner hath his will'—
>
> and four or five lines more in different parts of the poem, which I could not now point out. The idea of *"shooting an albatross" was mine*. . . . I also suggested the reanimation of the dead bodies, to work the ship.[30]

If we accept all this as precisely true (Dyce's exact retention of a lengthy *viva voce* utterance—". . . the following statement, which I am quite sure, I give you correctly"—must surely be one of the most extraordinary memorial feats on record), we find in the "long, and lank, and brown" figure of the Mariner an avatar of the discharged soldier—"stiff, lank, and upright"—of "The Prelude's" fourth book, of the dead man in Esthwaite Lake in the fifth book, and even of the old Leech-gatherer. The Mariner, in short, is thereby a projection from the psycho-dramatic center of Wordsworth's fantasy more than from that of Coleridge. Indeed, David Beres has suggested that in the poem Coleridge's own most psychologically revealing fantasy is the Nightmare Life-in-Death, which is a guilty representation of the mother for whom he entertained an unconscious ambivalence of love and fierce hatred.[31] The relation of the Mariner to Life-in-Death would thus be a curious

[30] *The Poems of Samuel Taylor Coleridge*, ed. Derwent and Sara Coleridge (London: Edward Moxon, 1852), pp. 383-84.

[31] "A Dream, a Vision and a Poem: A Psycho-Analytic Study of the Origins of the Rime of the Ancient Mariner," *International Journal of Psycho-Analysis*, 32 (1951), 105-106.

extrapolation of the symbiosis of the masculine Wordsworth and the masochistic Coleridge as it existed outside the poem.

Whatever the validity of such speculation, however, "The Ancient Mariner" is Coleridge's, not Wordsworth's, poem (as Wordsworth said, "Much the greatest part of the story was Mr. Coleridge's invention"). Fruman's implications to the contrary are countered by L. C. Knights in a review of *Coleridge, The Damaged Archangel*:

> Marion Milner, in an essay, "Psychoanalysis and Art," says: "What is most important about this thing we call a work of art . . . is not the original primary unconscious wish or wishes that it symbolizes but the fact that a new thing has been created." "The Ancient Mariner" is "a new thing," an achieved work of art, and to "understand" it we need a knowledge neither of Coleridge's "sources" nor of his dreams, but only the capacity for imaginative response that we bring to any other poem.[32]

It is, in fact, important not to be misled by Coleridge's psychic masochism into overestimating, as Fruman does, his intellectual dependence on his friend. Alongside the need to have the sanctifying collaboration of another, Coleridge maintained the needs of the healthier aspects of his psyche. We see this very clearly in one of his statements of admiration for Wordsworth: "I speak with heartfelt sincerity & (I think) unblinded judgement, when I tell you, that I feel myself a *little man by his* side; & yet do not think myself the less man, than I formerly thought myself."[33] The structure of symbiosis presupposes a principle of opposition or polarity as the very condition of the urge toward submersion and oneness.

So we find Coleridge's distinct individuality no less actual than his dependence. "I am far from going all lengths with Wordsworth," he writes to Southey in 1802:

> He has written lately a number of Poems (32 in all) some of them of considerable Length/ (the longest 160 Lines) the greater number of these to my feelings very excellent Compositions/ but here & there a daring Humbleness of Language & Versification, and a strict adherence to matter of fact, even to prolixity, that startled me/ his alterations likewise in Ruth perplexed me/ and I

---

[32] "Coleridge: The Wound Without the Bow," *New York Review of Books*, 18 (4 May 1972), 26.

[33] *Collected Letters*, I, 325.

have thought & thought again/ & have not had my doubts solved
by Wordsworth/ On the contrary, I rather suspect that some
where or other there is a radical Difference in our theoretical
opinions respecting Poetry—/ this I shall endeavor to go to the
Bottom of.[34]

What we here see, of course, is the genesis of the superb Words-
worth criticism in the *Biographia Literaria*. Wordsworth's "strict
adherence to matter of fact" that startled Coleridge in 1802 is
criticized in the *Biographia* of 1817, in cool exactness, as "an appar-
ent minute adherence to *matter-of-fact* in characters and incidents; a
biographical attention to probability, and an *anxiety* of explanation
and retrospect."[35] But all Coleridge's lifelong and unswerving ad-
miration of his friend's genius receives its definitive critical form in
the *Biographia*'s public assessment that

> pre-eminently, I challenge for this poet the gift of IMAGINATION
> in the highest and strictest sense of the word. In the play of
> *Fancy*, Wordsworth, to my feelings, is not always graceful, and
> sometimes *recondite*. . . . But in imaginative power, he stands
> nearest of all modern writers to Shakespeare and Milton; and yet
> in a kind perfectly unborrowed and his own.[36]

In ranking Wordsworth just below Shakespeare and Milton in the
pantheon of English poets, Coleridge anticipates the independent
judgment of another great critic, Arnold, who discerned that "be-
sides Shakespeare and Milton . . . Wordsworth's name deserves to
stand, and will finally stand, above them all."[37]

From such impeccably accurate critical formulations we see that
Coleridge's masochism did not diminish his luminous intelligence
nor distort the rightness of his judgment. Nor did it really succeed

[34] *Ibid.*, II, 830; cf. II, 812. It is interesting to note on the other hand that
Wordsworth in the 1800 Preface says that he "believed that the poems of my Friend
would in a great measure have the same tendency as my own, and that, though
there would be found a difference, there would be found no discordance in the col-
ours of our style; as our opinions on the subject of poetry do almost entirely coin-
cide" (*Prose*, I, 120). Wordsworth's egotistical sublime, along with Coleridge's ea-
gerness to please his friend, may have been the grounds for this opinion, which is
certainly not consonant with later statements by the two men. See further Mark L.
Reed, "Wordsworth, Coleridge, and the 'Plan' of the *Lyrical Ballads*," *University of
Toronto Quarterly*, 34 (1965), 238-53.

[35] *Biographia*, II, 103. The statement about an "*anxiety* of explanation and retro-
spect" perfectly forecasts and sums up the fact and meaning of Wordsworth's
Fenwick notes of 1843.

[36] *Ibid.*, II, 124.   [37] Arnold, *Essays*, p. 132.

entirely in blending the two friends into one literary entity—the anonymity of *Lyrical Ballads* notwithstanding. The principle of polar opposition was continually apparent. For instance, a re-perusal of some of the passages adduced above reveals that "The Wanderings of Cain" ran aground on the ridiculousness of Wordsworth's mind "so eminently original" being expected "to compose another man's thoughts and fancies." When it came to the actual writing of "The Ancient Mariner," "our respective man-ners," as Wordsworth says in the Fenwick note, "proved . . . widely different." In the statement to Dyce, Wordsworth says that "the style of Coleridge and myself would not assimilate." Moreover, "Christabel" was not included in *Lyrical Ballads* because, as Coleridge wrote to Humphry Davy in October 1800, "the poem was in direct opposition to the very purpose for which the Lyrical Ballads were published—viz—an experiment to see how far those passions, which alone give any value to extraordinary Incidents, were capable of interesting, in & for themselves, in the incidents of common Life."[38]

Such a statement, of course, seems somewhat at variance with Coleridge's later recollection, in the *Biographia*, of the purpose of *Lyrical Ballads*:

> it was agreed, that my endeavours should be directed to persons and characters supernatural, or at least romantic; yet so as to transfer from our inward nature a human interest and a semblance of truth sufficient to procure for these shadows of imagination that willing suspension of disbelief for the moment, which constitutes poetic faith. Mr. Wordsworth, on the other hand, was to propose to himself as his object, to give the charm of novelty to things of every day, and to excite a feeling analo-gous to the supernatural, by awakening the mind's attention from the lethargy of custom, and directing it to the loveliness and the wonders of the world before us.[39]

Whichever—if either—of the two versions of purpose is correct (certainly the one in the *Biographia* more nearly corresponds to the actual content of *Lyrical Ballads*), both testify to a distinct principle of polarity and opposition in the relationship.

The opposition becomes quite explicit on the well-known issue of poetic diction. In the 1800 Preface to *Lyrical Ballads*, Wordsworth had declared for "the real language of men," "the very language of

---

[38] *Collected Letters*, I, 631.   [39] *Biographia*, II, 6.

men," had chosen "subjects from common life, and endeavoured to bring my language near to the real language of men"; and had bluntly rejected "poetic diction."[40] In 1817, in *Biographia Literaria*, Coleridge replied with extended criticism of what he regarded as Wordsworth's false dichotomy. He urged, among other points, that "it is not possible to imitate truly a dull and garrulous discourser, without repeating the effects of dullness and garrulity."[41] All this, of course, though one of Coleridge's most acute displays of critical and theoretical prowess, is familiar to interested scholars and need not be summarized here. But Parrish, in a skillful article, has maintained that what lay beneath the controversy above poetic diction was "a disagreement about dramatic method":[42]

> the crucial difference lay in Wordsworth's adoption of the dramatic method in his ballads, and Coleridge's rejection of it. To put it in the simplest way, the passion that Wordsworth expressed in poetry was likely to be that of his characters, the passion that Coleridge looked for was mainly that of the poet. For Wordsworth, the passion could appear only if the poet maintained strict dramatic propriety; for Coleridge, the passion was obscured unless the poet spoke in his own voice.[43]

In Parrish's analysis of the course of this opposition, a longstanding and ultimately wide-ranging divergence is revealed: "It should be apparent," he says, "how wide a gulf has opened . . . between the partners in *Lyrical Ballads*." Especially important for our purposes, because it demonstrates both the intertwinement and the polarity of the symbiosis, is Parrish's utilization of the history of Coleridge's "The Three Graves" in its relationship to Wordsworth's "The Thorn," and of "The Thorn" to "The Ancient Mariner."

Coleridge's "The Three Graves," it was discovered by De Selincourt, was in its first two parts actually written by Wordsworth. It is unclear whether the poem, which was to have had six parts, was Coleridge's reworking of a subject that Wordsworth had thrown aside (as with "Lewti") or whether it represented an effort at collaboration (as with "The Wanderings of Cain"). Either possibility is

---

[40] *Prose*, I, 118, 130, 150, 130.   [41] *Biographia*, II, 36.

[42] The third of the defects Coleridge alleged in 1817 against Wordsworth's poetic practice was "an undue predilection for the *dramatic* form in certain poems" (*ibid.*, II, 109).

[43] Stephen Maxfield Parrish, "The Wordsworth-Coleridge Controversy," *PMLA*, 73 (1958), 371.

congruent with the structure of the symbiosis. Of the six parts, Wordsworth wrote two, Coleridge wrote and published two more in *The Friend* (1809), and the last two remained unwritten. Wordsworth's portion exhibits significant similarities to his poem, "The Thorn" (it contains both a thorn tree and an old narrator).[44] As Parrish says:

> In later years, these two poems [i.e. "The Three Graves" and "The Thorn"] have occasionally been compared, to Wordsworth's disadvantage. Swinburne was among the first to indicate a preference. . . . But Wordsworth's own opinion was quite different. Coleridge, he told Barron Field, was unable to project himself dramatically into his characters: having "always too much personal and domestic discontent," he could not "afford to suffer/ With those whom he saw suffer." "I gave him the subject of his Three Graves," Wordsworth continued, "but he made it too shocking and painful, and not sufficiently sweetened by any healing views. Not being able to dwell on or sanctify natural woes, he took to the supernatural, and hence his Antient Mariner and Christabel."
>
> Wordsworth's remark clearly implies that "The Ancient Mariner"—the partners' third attempt at collaboration—embodied Coleridge's solution to the problems presented by their first attempt—"The Three Graves." It should by now be equally clear that "The Thorn," in turn, embodied Wordsworth's solution to the same problems.[45]

The joint authorship of "The Three Graves" therefore underwent metamorphosis into Wordsworth's "The Thorn" and Coleridge's "Ancient Mariner" (with its own symbiotic evidences), and then grew into still wider oppositions. The symbiosis, as such an example shows, paradoxically emphasized as well as submerged the individual differences of the two writers.

Indeed, a recurring pattern in the poetic practice of Wordsworth and Coleridge was for one partner's poem to elicit a kind of com-

[44] These similarities had been remarked much earlier than Parrish's article (and before De Selincourt's discovery that part of "The Three Graves" was actually Wordsworth's) during the course of a commentator's perceptive discussion of the two poems, with the conclusion that "These features point not merely to a general Wordsworthian 'influence,' but to specific suggestions from Wordsworth in planning the poem [i.e. The Three Graves'], or to the adaptation of processes and details from *The Thorn*." (W. Strunk, Jr., "Some Related Poems of Wordsworth and Coleridge," *Modern Language Notes*, 29 [1914], 203.)

[45] "The Wordsworth-Coleridge Controversy," p. 369.

petitive poem from the other. "Wordsworth's most wonderful as well as admirable Poem, Peter Bell,"[46] is generally regarded as an answer to "The Ancient Mariner." The supernatural fantasies of Coleridge's poem are countered by Wordsworth's adherence to a strict naturalism. "The Poem of Peter Bell," says Wordsworth in his 1819 dedicatory epistle, ". . . was composed under a belief that the Imagination not only does not require for its exercise the intervention of supernatural agency, but that . . . the faculty may be called forth . . . by incidents within the compass of poetic probability, in the humblest departments of daily life."[47] So, to confine ourselves to merely one example, where Coleridge has the memorable image of the "frightful fiend," "Peter Bell" projects a correspondent but determinedly unsupernatural image. Coleridge says:

> Like one, that on a lonesome road
> Doth walk in fear and dread,
> And having once turned round walks on,
> And turns no more his head;
> Because he knows, a frightful fiend
> Doth close behind him tread.[48]

And Wordsworth counters:

> When Peter spied the moving thing,
> It only doubled his distress;
> 'Where there is not a bush or tree,
> The very leaves they follow me—
> So huge hath been my wickedness!'[49]

A more complicated kind of interaction existed between Wordsworth's "The Rainbow," his "Intimations Ode," and Coleridge's "Dejection: An Ode" on the one hand, and Coleridge's "Dejection" and Wordsworth's "Resolution and Independence" on the other. Briefly stated, the matter is this: Coleridge's "Dejection" was probably an answer to the philosophy of joy from nature expressed by "The Rainbow" and the "Intimations Ode";[50] "Resolution and Independence" was probably a correction of the despondency of the first version of "Dejection"; and the revised version of "Dejection" that was published on Wordsworth's wedding

---

[46] *Notebooks*, II, 2583.
[48] Coleridge, *Poems*, I, 203.
[47] Wordsworth, *Poems*, II, 331.
[49] Wordsworth, *Poems*, II, 365.
[50] See Fred Manning Smith, "The Relation of Coleridge's *Ode on Dejection* to Wordsworth's *Ode on Intimations of Immortality*," *PMLA*, 50 (1935), 224-34.

day became a kind of wedding gift and affectionate acquiescence in the philosophy of joy once more.

The dates of these pieces show how closely intertwined the psychic processes of competition were. Wordsworth wrote "The Rainbow" on Friday, 26 March 1802. He began the "Intimations Ode" the next morning (and in 1815 he emphasized the continuity of the two poems by using the last three lines of the first poem, now known as "My Heart Leaps Up," as the epigraph to the "Intimations Ode"). Nine days later, on 4 April 1802, Coleridge, after hearing Dorothy repeat certain of Wordsworth's verses at tea at Greta Hall, poured out in a letter to Sara Hutchinson some lengthy verses indicating his own unhappiness:

> A Grief without a pang, void, dark, & drear,
> A stifling, drowsy, unimpassion'd Grief
> That finds no natural Outlet, no Relief
>
> . . . . . .
> My genial Spirits fail—[51]

It was, of course, the first draft of "Dejection: An Ode," and it was prompted by the juxtaposition of Wordsworth's happy plans for forthcoming marriage against Coleridge's own ruined marriage and his hopeless love for Sara Hutchinson, by Wordsworth's continuing productivity in great poetry as against his own drying up of the poetical faculty, and by his own psychosomatic misery.[52]

In the April 4 draft of "Dejection," the connection with the "Intimations Ode" is strikingly apparent. Even if we compare the two poems using the easily accessible *textus receptus* of "Dejection" printed in 1817, we note the following linkages. Wordsworth says:

> There was a time when meadow, grove, and stream,
>
> . . . . . .
> To me did seem
> Apparelled in celestial light,
>
> . . . . . .
> It is not now as it hath been of yore;—[53]

Coleridge says:

[51] *Collected Letters*, II, 790-91. "My genial Spirits fail" is a counter to "Tintern Abbey": "Nor . . . should I the more/ Suffer my genial spirits to decay" (lines 111-13).

[52] Cf. Ernest de Selincourt, "Coleridge's *Dejection: An Ode*," *Essays and Studies by Members of the English Association*, ed. Helen Darbishire, 22 (London, 1937), 14-15.

[53] Wordsworth, *Poems*, IV, 279.

There was a time when, though my path was rough,

. . . . . .

. . . hope grew round me, like the twining vine,

. . . . . .

But now afflictions bow me down to earth:[54]

Wordsworth says that "The earth" did seem "Apparelled in celestial light/ The glory and the freshness of a dream" (ll. 2-5); Coleridge counters with the statement that "Ah! from the soul itself must issue forth/ A light, a glory, a fair luminous cloud/ Enveloping the earth" (ll. 53-55). Wordsworth says (l. 41): "The fulness of your bliss, I feel—I feel it all"; Coleridge counters (l. 38), "I see, not feel how beautiful they are." Wordsworth says (ll. 22-23): "To me alone there came a thought of grief:/ A timely utterance gave that thought relief"; Coleridge counters: "A stifled, drowsy, unimpassion'd grief,/ Which finds no natural outlet, no relief" (ll. 22-23). Wordsworth: "Doth the same tale repeat" (l. 55); Coleridge: "It tells another tale" (l. 117). Wordsworth: "the freshness of a dream" (l. 5); Coleridge: "Reality's dark dream" (l. 85).

In Coleridge's version of 4 April 1802, moreover, still more parallelisms and contrasts occur. Where Wordsworth writes "The things which I have seen I now can see no more" (l. 9), Coleridge's first draft contains the line, "They are not to me the Things, which once they were." Wordsworth's "My head hath its coronal" (l. 40) is almost pathetically echoed in Coleridge's "I too will crown me with a Coronal."[55]

The status of the poem as an answer to Wordsworth was further emphasized in a version communicated to William Sotheby on 19 July 1802. Where in the first version "Sara" had been apostrophized, the person addressed now became "Wordsworth":

> It were a vain Endeavor,
> Though I should gaze for ever
> On that green Light, that lingers in the West.
> I may not hope from outward Forms to win
> The Passion & the Life, whose Fountains are within.
>
> O Wordsworth! we receive but what we give,
> And in our Life alone does Nature live:[56]

It is perhaps not without significance that in this moment of pro-

---

[54] Coleridge, *Poems*, I, 366.   [55] *Collected Letters*, II, 797; 793.
[56] *Ibid.*, p. 817.

found response to, and disagreement with, his friend, Coleridge uses the phrase "green light"; for in 1795 the phrase "green radiance" had been the talisman that signaled the beginning of the symbiosis.

Wordsworth first heard the "Dejection Ode" read on 21 April 1802. It was a fortissimo note in an entire symphony of his friend's unhappiness, which is revealed to us not only in Coleridge's letters and notebooks, but also in Dorothy's journals and William's and Dorothy's letters. As a commentator says:

> it is clear that Coleridge's performance drove Wordsworth to deep thought on the mysteries of life. In the days which followed the reading of the *Ode* Wordsworth meditated the possibility of peace in the grave, and the manner in which afflictions, real or imagined, should be borne by men. . . . A disturbing letter from Coleridge kept Wordsworth awake the night of 29 April and caused his head to ache the next day. Another letter came from Coleridge on 2 May, and that night Wordsworth began to write *Resolution and Independence*—originally called *The Leech Gatherer*. Wordsworth worked at the poem for a week, put it aside for nearly two months, and finished it on 4 July. . . . We see at once that it is an answer to Coleridge's *Dejection Ode*. It begins, as the *Ode* does, with mention of a storm.[57]

Other pointed reactions to Coleridge's "Dejection" can be seen in "Resolution and Independence" in the lines:

> As high as we have mounted in delight
> In our dejection do we sink as low;[58]

and

> We Poets in our youth begin in gladness;
> But thereof come in the end despondency and madness.
>
> (ll. 48-49)

Though Burns and Chatterton are invoked in the poetic context of this last statement, in the context of Wordsworth's life at the time Coleridge looms uppermost. And Coleridge again seems to be the object of these lines:

> But how can He expect that others should

---

[57] George W. Meyer, "*Resolution and Independence:* Wordsworth's Answer to Coleridge's *Dejection: An Ode,*" *Tulane Studies in English*, 2 (1950), 64-66.

[58] Lines 24-25; Wordsworth, *Poems*, II, 236.

> Build for him, sow for him, and at his call
> Love him, who for himself will take no heed at all?
>
> (ll. 40-42)

Rebuked by the parable of the resolution and independence he so conspicuously lacked, and reclaimed somewhat from his dejection by the very poem of that name—for his "shaping Spirit of Imagination" returned to him in its composition—Coleridge accordingly, in the version of "Dejection" published in the *Morning Post* on Wordsworth's wedding day, 4 October 1802, hails Wordsworth, now under the sobriquet "Edmund," and subscribes once more to the philosophy of joy:

> Thou need'st not ask of me
> What this strong music in the soul may be?
> What, and wherein it doth exist,
> This light, this glory, this fair luminous mist,
> This beautiful and beauty-making pow'r?
> Joy, virtuous EDMUND! joy that ne'er was given,
> Save to the pure, and in their purest hour,
> Joy EDMUND! is the spirit and the pow'r
> Which wedding Nature to us gives in dow'r.[59]

Although these are the most familiar examples of the dialogical interchange between the poetic productions of Wordsworth and Coleridge, they do not exhaust the symbiotic aspects of the two poets' practice. For instance, a commentator has taken note of a

> theme which, with remarkable consistency, runs through the major efforts of both poets during the 1790's. This . . . theme is as follows: a man commits a crime; the crime sets in motion the machinery of justice and punishment; it also calls down a curse upon his head; the criminal suffers severe pangs of remorse; and finally, through remorse, he finds regeneration and salvation.
>
> This is the story that both Wordsworth and Coleridge, during their early years, tell over and over again. It is to be found in Wordsworth's *Guilt and Sorrow*, *The Borderers*, and *Peter Bell*, and in Coleridge's *Osorio*, *The Wanderings of Cain*, and *The Rhyme of the Ancient Mariner*—as well as in a half dozen lesser pieces.[60]

To pursue more fully a still further instance, Coleridge's frag-

[59] Coleridge, *Poems*, II, 1078.
[60] Charles J. Smith, "Wordsworth and Coleridge: The Growth of a Theme," *Studies in Philology*, 54 (1957), 53-54.

ment "The Dungeon" is not only written in a Wordsworthian style and shares the emphases of Wordsworth's "The Convict" (both poems appeared in the first edition of *Lyrical Ballads*) but it is also thematically related to the last part of Wordsworth's "The Old Cumberland Beggar." Both sets of lines develop the theme of life in nature *versus* life in an institution, and both eloquently choose the former.

It seems likely that the two ventures were written not as statement and answer but as independent voicings of a mutual attitude developed in conversation; for the passages exhibit thematic, but not verbal, similarities. Coleridge's lines present the imagination with the thought of a man incarcerated in a dungeon:

> And this place our forefathers made for man!
> This is the process of our love and wisdom,
> To each poor brother who offends against us—
> Most innocent, perhaps—and what if guilty?
> Is this the only cure? Merciful God![61]

Wordsworth's poem conceives the situation of an old and derelict man being incarcerated in a public institution for the poor:

> But deem not this Man useless—Statesmen! ye
> Who are so restless in your wisdom, ye
> Who have a broom still ready in your hands
> To rid the world of nuisances; ye proud,
> Heart-swoln, while in your pride ye contemplate
> Your talents, power, or wisdom, deem him not
> A burthen of the earth!
>
>   . . . . . .
>
> May never HOUSE, misnamed of INDUSTRY,
> Make him a captive![62]

Both poems thus confront the conception of a man isolated from society, and both attack the conventional wisdom that justifies the isolation. Both then assert the view that even social misfits would be better if allowed their freedom in the healing environment of nature. Coleridge's lines say:

> With other ministrations thou, O Nature!
> Healest thy wandering and distemper'd child:
> Thou pourest on him thy soft influences,
> Thy sunny hues, fair forms, and breathing sweets,

[61] Coleridge, *Poems*, i, 185.   [62] Wordsworth, *Poems*, iv, 236, 239.

Thy melodies of woods, and winds, and waters,
Till he relent and can no more endure
To be a jarring and a dissonant thing. . . .

(ll. 20-26)

Wordsworth's lines affirm the same conviction:

Let him be free of mountain solitudes;
And have around him, whether heard or not,
The pleasant melody of woodland birds. . . .
And let him, *where* and *when* he will, sit down
Beneath the trees, or on a grassy bank
Of highway side, and with the little birds
Share his chance-gathered meal; and, finally,
As in the eye of Nature he has lived,
So in the eye of Nature let him die!

(ll. 183-197)

If I am correct in thinking that the thematic similarities of the two sets of lines indicate a common basis in the friends' conversation rather than a consciously competitive statement and response, then the chronological details of their respective compositions would not be of decisive significance. Coleridge's poem was published in the first edition of *Lyrical Ballads*; Wordsworth's, not until the second. In date of composition also the Coleridge lines appear to have a slight priority. "The Old Cumberland Beggar" was probably written between 25 January and 5 March 1798;[63] "The Dungeon," which was designed for the fifth act of Coleridge's play *Osorio*, was probably composed before 6 September 1797.[64]

The two poems attest their authors' symbiosis in still other ways. For the prison in Coleridge's poem, like the poorhouse in Wordsworth's, seems to be a version, more or less unconscious, of Coleridge's experience at Christ's Hospital; while the salute to nature in both poems seems to represent Wordsworth's contrasted enthusiasm for his own early environment ("For I, bred up in Nature's lap, was even/ As a spoil'd Child . . .").[65] The comparison of their differing early histories seems to have occupied an important place in the conversation of the two friends. In "Dejection," where the juxtaposition of his situation with that of Wordsworth is so evident a factor, Coleridge remembers in the first draft that

---

[63] Reed, *Chronology*, p. 342. [64] *Early Years*, p. 192.
[65] *Prelude*, p. 90 (III, 358-59).

> At eve, sky-gazing in 'ecstatic fit'
> (Alas! for cloister'd in a city School
> The Sky was all, I knew, of Beautiful)
> At the barr'd window often did I sit,
> And oft upon the leaded School-roof lay[66]

The "barr'd window," along with the absence of nature, makes the recollection of this "city School" not very much different from the situation in "The Dungeon."

The lines in "Dejection" are prefigured by lines in "Frost at Midnight":

> For I was reared
> In the great city, pent 'mid cloisters dim,
> And saw nought lovely but the sky and stars.[67]

That the matter was much discussed by the two friends can be inferred from Wordsworth's invoking precisely the same fact in the second book of "The Prelude":

> Thou, my Friend! wert rear'd
> In the great City, 'mid far other scenes;[68]

Interestingly enough, to this version of the situation in the thetic statement of "The Dungeon," Wordsworth then adds the contrasted nature-salutation of its antithetic vision:

> But we, by different roads, at length have gained
> The self-same bourne. . . .
>   . . . For thou hast sought
> The truth in solitude, and Thou art one,
> The most intense of Nature's worshipper,
> In many things my Brother, chiefly here
> In this my deep devotion.
>   (ll. 468-69, 475-79)

Likewise, Coleridge, in "Frost at Midnight," provides the same antithetic salutation. Where he himself had been "pent 'mid cloisters dim,"

> . . . *thou*, my babe! shalt wander like a breeze
> By lakes and sandy shores, beneath the crags

---

[66] *Collected Letters*, II, 791.

[67] Coleridge, *Poems*, I, 242. Cf. "This Lime-tree Bower my Prison," both in the implications of its title and in lines 28-32 (*ibid.*, I, 179).

[68] *Prelude*, p. 68 (II, 466-67).

> Of ancient mountain, and beneath the clouds,
> Which image in their bulk both lakes and shores . . .
>
> (ll. 54-57)

Still again, in the sixth book of "The Prelude" Wordsworth returns to the theme of Coleridge imprisoned in Christ's Hospital, and there too he appends the antithetic vision of nature's ministering beauty:

> Of Rivers, Fields,
> And Groves, I speak to Thee, my Friend; to Thee,
> Who, yet a liveried School-Boy, in the depths
> Of the huge City, on the leaded Roof
> Of that wide Edifice, thy Home and School,
> Wast used to lie and gaze upon the clouds
> Moving in Heaven; or haply, tired of this,
> To shut thine eyes, and by internal light
> See trees, and meadows, and thy native Stream
> Far distant, thus beheld from year to year
> Of thy long exile. . . .
>
> . . . . . .
>
> I have thought
> Of Thee, thy learning, gorgeous eloquence,
>
> . . . . . .
>
> The self-created sustenance of a mind
> Debarr'd from Nature's living images,
> Compell'd to be a life unto itself . . . [69]

In these lines, the schoolboy, like the man in "The Dungeon," exists "in the depths"; the schoolboy, like the man in "The Dungeon," is "Debarr'd from Nature's living images."[70]

Thus the contrast, repeatedly summoned by both poets, between institutional captivity and freedom in nature testifies to an intermingling of their primary orientations. To achieve such a remarkable feat, there must have been extended and repeated conversation; for as Fruman well says, "We must never cease to remind ourselves that the documentary record of the relations be-

[69] *Prelude*, pp. 188-90 (vi, 264-314).

[70] As a further example, it is interesting to recall that Wordsworth's Ruth, who went mad and was "in a prison housed," fled thence and "Among the fields she breathed again" (Wordsworth, *Poems*, ii, 233). Coleridge dejectedly said that he "would rather have written Ruth . . . than a million . . . poems" such as "Christabel" (*Collected Letters*, i, 632).

tween Wordsworth and Coleridge represents but a minuscule pro-
portion of what passed between them."[71]

With such a fact in mind, we can look beyond "The Old Cumber-
land Beggar" and find a Wordsworthian counterpart to still
another theme enunciated in "The Dungeon." In Coleridge's
poem, the thought of humanity blunted by unfavorable conditions
of environment receives expression in passionate lines:

> Each pore and natural outlet shrivell'd up
> By Ignorance and parching Poverty,
> His energies roll back upon his heart,
> And stagnate and corrupt; till chang'd to poison,
> They break out on him . . .
> So he lies
> Circled with evil, till his very soul
> Unmoulds its essence, hopelessly deform'd
> By sights of ever more deformity![72]

The same idea—of the human soul deformed by inhuman condi-
tions around it—is expressed by Wordsworth, in lines of compara-
ble power, in the twelfth book of the 1805 "Prelude." The context
of the two passages is not at all the same, but their larger concern
is identical:

> True is it, where oppression worse than death
> Salutes the Being at his birth, where grace
> Of culture hath been utterly unknown,
> And labour in excess and poverty
> From day to day pre-occupy the ground
> Of the affections, and to Nature's self
> Oppose a deeper nature, there indeed,
> Love cannot be;[73]

In the certainty that much more was discussed between the two
friends than is explicitly recorded, one is tempted to extend recog-
nition of the symbiosis still further. An ideal understanding of the
mutual interaction would have to go beyond verifiable dates and
documentary backing, would be to some extent what Friedrich
Schlegel called "a divinatory criticism."[74] Such a criticism, how-
ever, would not be made up of irresponsible guesses; it would
rather entail something of the same process by which an as-

---

[71] Fruman, p. 310.
[72] Coleridge, *Poems*, I, 185.
[73] *Prelude*, p. 466 (XII, 194-201).
[74] *Friedrich Schlegel*, II, 183.

tronomer deduces the presence of a hidden astral body by interpreting variations in the behavior of a celestial object already known.

By this conception of the gravitational pulls of the two friends on one another, certain things become clear. It seems likely, as many have noted, that Coleridge's preoccupation with nature in some of his finest poetry of 1797 and 1798 ("This Lime-Tree Bower," "Frost at Midnight," "Fears in Solitude") bears witness to Wordsworth's insistent proselytizing. To please his friend, Coleridge did for a while become, if not the "most intense of Nature's worshippers," at least, as the 1850 version changes the expression to read, "the most assiduous of her ministers." Thus, in "This Lime-Tree Bower," he voices a Wordsworthian trust in nature:

> Henceforth I shall know
> That Nature ne'er deserts the wise and pure;
> No plot so narrow, be but Nature there . . .
>
> (ll. 59-61)

Thus, in "Frost at Midnight," a Wordsworthian benediction scarcely less memorable (and earlier) than that expressed in the great lines at the end of "Tintern Abbey":

> Therefore all seasons shall be sweet to thee,
> Whether the summer clothe the general earth
> With greenness, or the redbreast sit and sing
> Betwixt the tufts of snow on the bare branch
> Of mossy apple-tree, while the nigh thatch
> Smokes in the sun-thaw;
>
> (ll. 65-70)

Thus, in "Fears in Solitude," a Wordsworthian emotional pantheism:

> Here he might lie on fern or withered heath,
> While from the singing lark (that sings unseen
> The minstrelsy that solitude loves best),
> And from the sun, and from the breezy air,
> Sweet influences trembled o'er his frame;
> And he, with many feelings, many thoughts,
> Made up a meditative joy, and found
> Religious meanings in the forms of Nature!
>
> (ll. 17-24)

On the other hand, Wordsworth's preoccupation with books

seems to reflect Coleridge's emphasis. The entire fifth book of "The Prelude," I suspect, exists as a testimony not to Wordsworth's but to Coleridge's reverence for books. "I am, & ever have been," says Coleridge, "a great reader—& have read almost every thing—a library-cormorant—I am *deep* in all out of the way books."[75] Such was always the Coleridgean reality; Dorothy's testimony in 1810, to cite a single additional example, confirms Coleridge's statement of 1796: "Coleridge is still at Keswick where, as at Grasmere, he has done nothing but read."[76] Thus Wordsworth's "Expostulation and Reply," and "The Tables Turned," seem, by their form as dialogue and by their discussion of the relative claims of books and nature, to be an extrapolation of conversations that must have occurred between the two friends. The argument to "quit your books," to "Close up those barren leaves," to "Come forth into the light of things,/ Let Nature be your Teacher" witnesses, one can hardly doubt, the Wordsworthian egotistical sublime attempting to reject his friend's influence.[77]

But the friend's influence, Wordsworth's struggle against it notwithstanding, was formidable. In the fifth book of "The Prelude" it almost succeeded in pulling Wordsworth out of orbit. Certainly that book's topic represents a curious counterstroke to the paeans to nature that have occupied so much of the preceding portion of Wordsworth's great poem. As he says:

> Hitherto,
> In progress through this Verse, my mind hath look'd
> Upon the speaking face of earth and heaven
> As her prime Teacher,[78]

but now, although reluctant to interrupt his celebration of nature, Wordsworth salutes the world of books:

> Mighty indeed, supreme must be the power
> Of living Nature, which could thus so long
> Detain me from the best of other thoughts.
>
> (ll. 166-68)

So the fifth section is determinedly entitled "Books," and Wordsworth concludes it with the dutiful statement that

---

[75] *Collected Letters*, I, 260.   [76] *Middle Years*, I, 412.

[77] Wordsworth, *Poems*, IV, 57. Although it is widely accepted that Hazlitt's visit in the late spring of 1798 prompted the two poems, their truer background must surely be the immensely deeper and more lasting dialogue with Coleridge.

[78] *Prelude*, p. 136 (v, 10-13).

> Thus far a scanty record is deduced
> Of what I owed to Books in early life;
> Their later influence yet remains untold;
>
> (ll. 630-32)

But the actual testimony of the fifth section of "The Prelude," despite these obeisances, is that the subject of books is ultimately alien to Wordsworth; he talks about almost anything rather than books: about the boy of Winander, about the dead man in Esthwaite Lake, about childhood, about visionary power, about raptures forever flown, about his mother's death. And in this very section he says that "This Verse is dedicate to Nature's self,/ And things that teach as Nature teaches."[79]

The gravitational pull of Coleridge is apparent in still other ways, and it accounts, I believe, for what seems to be a major contradiction in Wordsworth's expressed attitudes on a deeply important topic, that of the relation of the mind to the external world. That topic, indeed, was to be the central theme of Wordsworth's greatest work, "The Recluse" (and may well have been supplied by Coleridge).[80] As Wordsworth writes in the "Prospectus" to "The Recluse," he wished to proclaim

> How exquisitely the individual Mind
> . . . to the external World
> Is fitted:—and how exquisitely, too—
> Theme this but little heard of among men—
> The external World is fitted to the Mind;[81]

But in this fitting, Wordsworth's own instinctive understanding of the matter was that the mind passively fills itself from the greater reality of nature:

> The eye—it cannot choose but see;
> We cannot bid the ear be still;

[79] *Ibid.*, p. 149; lines 230-31. The nominal topic of Book Five is a continuation of matters broached in Book Three, where Wordsworth discusses his Cambridge education. It is significant, I think, that there he says that the "lovely forms" found in nature "left less space within my mind," that "other passions" than books had been his, "making me less prompt, perhaps/ To in-door study than was wise or well" (*Prelude*, p. 90 [III, 366-74]).

[80] Cf. *Friend*, I, 463; *Collected Letters*, IV, 574; *Table Talk*, 21 July 1832. In my book, *Coleridge and the Pantheist Tradition*, I attempt to demonstrate at length that the adjudication of the claims of mind as opposed to external reality was the consuming topic of Coleridge's philosophical activity.

[81] Wordsworth, *Poems*, v, 5.

> Our bodies feel, where'er they be,
> Against or with our will.

> Nor less I deem that there are Powers
> Which of themselves our minds impress;
> That we can feed this mind of ours
> In a wise passiveness.[82]

It seems almost unarguably to be the case, as a commentator has recently pointed out, that Wordsworth projected his infant relationship with his mother into his conception of nature.[83] We thereby understand his "wise passiveness" as a psychoanalytical corollary to his rapture about nature: in such rapture he is forever the infant at the breast.[84] The statements of this passive relationship, some of them very great poetic moments, are repeated and insistent:

> A Child, I held unconscious intercourse
> With the eternal Beauty, drinking in
> A pure organic pleasure from the lines
> Of curling mist, or from the level plain
> Of waters colour'd by the steady clouds.[85]

Again:

> From Nature and her overflowing soul
> I had receiv'd so much that all my thoughts
> Were steep'd in feelings; I was only then
> Contented when with bliss ineffable
> I felt the sentiment of Being spread
> O'er all that moves, and all that seemeth still,[86]

And again:

---

[82] *Ibid.*, IV, 56.

[83] Richard J. Onorato, *The Character of the Poet; Wordsworth in "The Prelude"* (Princeton, N.J.: Princeton University Press, 1971), e.g. p. 64: "In our account of Wordsworth he is seen as fixated to a trauma, obsessed by a vital relationship with Nature which has come to stand unconsciously for the lost mother."

[84] Immediately after saying that he was "left alone" (by his mother's death), and that "the props" of his affections "were remov'd," Wordsworth says that "yet the building stood," that "All that I beheld/ Was dear to me, and from this cause it came,/ That now to Nature's finer influxes/ My mind lay open" (*Prelude*, p. 58 [II, 292-99]).

[85] *Prelude*, p. 34 (I, 589-93).

[86] *Ibid.*, pp. 64-66 (II, 416-21).

> Thus deeply drinking-in the soul of things,
> We shall be wise perforce;[87]

And again:

> How bountiful is Nature! he shall find
> Who seeks not; and to him, who hath not asked,
> Large measures shall be dealt.[88]

And again:

> Far and wide the clouds were touched,
> And in their silent faces could be read
> Unutterable love. Sound needed none,
> Nor any voice of joy; his spirit drank
> The spectacle: sensation, soul, and form,
> All melted into him; they swallowed up
> His animal being; in them did he live,
> And by them did he live; they were his life.[89]

And again:

> I was as wakeful, even, as waters are
> To the sky's motion; in a kindred sense
> Of passion was obedient as a lute
> That waits upon the touches of the wind.[90]

And still again:

> One impulse from a vernal wood
> May teach you more of man,
> Of moral evil and of good,
> Than all the sages can.[91]

To such a fundamental and pervasive acceptance of the passive relationship of mind to the activity of nature, Coleridge opposed himself absolutely; and he did so not merely from his own differing data of personal experience (we recall that his intellectual characteristics, as described by Wordsworth, were "The self-created sustenance of a mind/ Debarr'd from Nature's living images,/ Compell'd to be a life unto itself") but from his philosophical understanding as well:

---

[87] "The Excursion," IV, 1265-66; Wordsworth, *Poems*, V, 149.
[88] *Ibid.*, lines 466-68; p. 123.   [89] *Ibid.*, I, 203-10; p. 15.
[90] *Prelude*, p. 78 (III, 135-38).
[91] 'The Tables Turned"; Wordsworth, *Poems*, IV, 57.

I may not hope from outward Forms to win
The Passion & the Life, whose Fountains are within.

O Wordsworth! we receive but what we give,
And in our Life alone does Nature live:[92]

Thus Coleridge in 1802. Again, in 1807, the "moments awful,/ Now in thy inner life, and now abroad" celebrated by Wordsworth were actually, in Coleridge's view, moments

When power streamed from thee, and thy soul received
The light reflected, as a light bestowed—[93]

It was "not from any external impulses, not from any agencies that can be sought for" that human life and meaning derived; for to Coleridge "man comes from within, and all that is truly human must proceed from within."[94] "That which we find in ourselves is . . . the substance and the life of all our knowledge. Without this latent presence of the 'I am', all modes of existence in the external world would flit before us as colored shadows."[95] To his philosophical collaborator, J. H. Green, he said in 1829:

We behold our own light reflected from the object as light bestowed *by* it.[96]

Again, in 1832, near the end of his life:

The pith of my system is to make the senses out of the mind—not the mind out of the senses, as Locke did.[97]

Undoubtedly Coleridge explained to Wordsworth the moral and philosophical reasons for this attitude; undoubtedly, too, he explained the pantheistic implications of "wise passiveness" (Wordsworth's increasingly orthodox Christianity and the theistic tendency of his revisions for the 1850 "Prelude" both reflect—of this I have no doubt at all—the impact of Coleridge's philosophical and theological conversation).[98] Such explanation, it seems likely, accounts for the fact that Wordsworth, in direct contradiction to his own powerful instinct for "wise passiveness," incorporates into "The Prelude" the principle of the mind's pre-eminence. In doing so, he sounds not like himself but like his friend:

[92] *Collected Letters*, II, 817.
[93] Coleridge, *Poems*, I, 404, 405.
[94] *Philosophical Lectures*, p. 226.
[95] Coleridge, *Complete Works*, I, 465.
[96] *Collected Letters*, VI, 813.
[97] *Table Talk*, 25 July 1832.
[98] For comprehensive discussion of both issues see *CPT*.

> Not prostrate, overborne, as if the mind
> Itself were nothing, a mean pensioner
> On outward forms . . .[99]

And in one of the most important passages in the poem, he entirely adopts the argument of "Dejection":

> Oh! mystery of Man, from what a depth
> Proceed thy honours! I am lost, but see
> In simple childhood something of the base
> On which thy greatness stands, but this I feel,
> That from thyself it is that thou must give,
> Else never canst receive.[100]

The 1850 revision of the last two lines makes them even more Coleridgean:

> That from thyself it comes, that thou must give,
> Else never canst receive.[101]

Coleridge's gravitational influence is no less discernible in Wordsworth's distinction of fancy and imagination. The friends must often have discussed these faculties, and in the note to "The Thorn" in 1800, Wordsworth speaks of "imagination, by which word I mean the faculty which produces impressive effects out of simple elements" and of "fancy, the power by which pleasure and surprize are excited by sudden varieties of situation and by accumulated imagery."[102] Coleridge's own first recorded definition occurs in September 1802, although, in the *Biographia*, he asserts his "belief that I had been the first of my countrymen, who had pointed out the diverse meaning of which the two terms were capable."[103] In his distinction of 1802, Coleridge, in a letter to Sotheby, speaks somewhat offhandedly of "Fancy, or the aggregating Faculty of the mind—not *Imagination*, or the *modifying*, and *co-adunating* Faculty."[104] The discrimination was one of lasting importance to both poets. Wordsworth, in the 1815 edition of his poems, re-arranged them under various headings, two of which

[99] *Prelude*, p. 216 (vi, 666-68). In Book Two, we can almost see a tug-of-war between Coleridge's influence and Wordsworth's instinctive attitude, for Wordsworth there concedes somewhat equivocally that "An auxiliar light/ Came from my mind which on the setting sun/ Bestow'd new splendor" (*Prelude*, p. 64 [ii, 387-89]).

[100] *Ibid.*, p. 448 (xi, 329-34).   [101] *Ibid.*, p. 449 (xii, 276-77).

[102] *Literary Criticism of William Wordsworth*, ed. Paul M. Zall (Lincoln, Neb.: University of Nebraska Press, 1966), p. 12.

[103] *Biographia*, i, 63.   [104] *Collected Letters*, ii, 865-66.

were "poems of the fancy" and "poems of the imagination";[105] and in the prefatory material to that edition he discussed at length the theoretical signification of the two terms. Coleridge, noting his "frequent conversation" with Wordsworth on this subject, said in the *Biographia* that one of his own chief purposes was "to investigate the seminal principle" of the distinction.[106]

But Wordsworth's formulation of the two functions has always seemed somewhat obscure. (I remember, for instance, Frederick A. Pottle once telling his seminar that he had never fully been able to see the point of what Wordsworth said in the 1815 Preface.) That obscurity, I suggest, results from the fact that Wordsworth, once privy to Coleridge's conversation but never to Coleridge's reading, and by 1815 estranged from his friend and hence no longer able to call on him for theoretical clarification, actually did not himself fully understand the philosophical ramifications of the distinction.[107] This, at any rate, is what Coleridge politely suggests. Wordsworth had said in the 1815 Preface that

> To the mode in which Fancy has already been characterised as the power of evoking and combining, or, as my friend Mr. Coleridge has styled it, "the aggregative and associative power," my objection is only that the definition is too general. To aggregate and to associate, to evoke and to combine, belong as well to the Imagination as to the Fancy. . . .[108]

But Coleridge, in the *Biographia*, retorted:

> I shall now proceed to the nature and genesis of the imagination; but I must first take leave to notice, that after a more accurate perusal of Mr. Wordsworth's remarks on the imagination, in his preface to the new edition of his poems, I find that my conclusions are not so consentient with his as, I confess, I had taken for granted. . . . [Wordsworth says that] "To aggregate and to associate, to evoke and to combine, belong as well to the imagination as to the fancy." I reply, that if, by the power of evoking and combining, Mr. Wordsworth means the same as, and no more than, I meant by the aggregative and associative, I continue to

---

[105] See James Scoggins, *Imagination and Fancy; Complementary Modes in the Poetry of Wordsworth* (Lincoln, Neb.: University of Nebraska Press, 1966), pp. 71-138.

[106] *Biographia*, I, 64.

[107] See in general Clarence D. Thorpe, "The Imagination: Coleridge *versus* Wordsworth," *Philological Quarterly*, 18 (1939), 1-18.

[108] *Prose*, III, 36.

deny, that it belongs at all to the imagination; and I am disposed to conjecture, that he has mistaken the co-presence of fancy with imagination for the operation of the latter singly. [109]

What Coleridge means here is clarified by referring to the main source of his own theory of imagination. I have elsewhere attempted to demonstrate that his formula of 1802, with its conception of imagination as a *"modifying, and co-adunating* Faculty,"* rests largely upon conceptions propounded by the eighteenth-century German psychologist Tetens. [110] Coleridge's secondary imagination, or *"modifying,* and *co-adunating* Faculty,"* is Tetens's *Dichtkraft,* that is, poetic and joining power. Coleridge adopts the differentiation of *Dichtkraft* from *Phantasie* because Tetens demonstrates that *Dichtkraft* cannot be accounted for by Hartley's association psychology. The whole point, in other words, of the distinction was that fancy is conceded to "aggregate and to associate" on Hartleyan lines, but imagination witnesses the principle that "we receive but what we give." This crucial difference Wordsworth clearly does not understand, hence his version seems somewhat pointless.

That it was Coleridge's mediating of Tetens that actually gave Wordsworth his imagination-fancy dichotomy can be indicated by an example. Wordsworth says in the 1815 Preface that

Fancy does not require that the materials which she makes use of should be susceptible of change in their constitution. . . . Directly the reverse of these, are the desires and demands of the Imagination. She recoils from every thing but the plastic, the pliant, and the indefinite. She leaves it to Fancy to describe Queen Mab as coming,

> "In shape no bigger than an agate-stone
> On the fore-finger of an alderman."[111]

But it is not made plain why fancy should be clear and precise, while imagination should be indefinite. Presumably the specification came from Coleridge, for in a note of 1803 he says: "Mix up Truth & Imagination, so that the Imag. may spread its own indefi-

---

[109] *Biographia,* I, 193-94.

[110] McFarland, "The Origin and Significance of Coleridge's Theory of Secondary Imagination," *New Perspectives on Coleridge and Wordsworth,* ed. Geoffrey H. Hartman (New York and London: Columbia University Press, 1972), pp. 195-246.

[111] *Prose,* III, 36.

niteness over that which really happened."[112] Yet Coleridge also fails to explain.

If we turn to Tetens, however, the matter is resolved. Fancy is clear, says Tetens, because it is a faculty that directly receives images from the outside. Linnaeus, whom Tetens nominates as an example of a man with a fanciful mind, takes in "a countless multitude of clear representations of sensation from bodily objects . . . ; receives them in their clarity and reproduces them."[113] But imagination or *Dichtkraft* must, in its function of "endowing or modifying" (I use Wordsworth's phrase), expend some of its power; the resultant image thereby becomes less distinct, or as Tetens says, "dimmer" (*dunkler*). *Dichtkraft*'s

> new forms are perhaps only shadow work in comparison to the images which are received in new sensations from outside. But this is not surprising. While the fancy produces two distinct images and maintains them in the present, each one then has its own associated ideas, which are different, and resist being modified. . . . The blending is therefore weakened, and the whole dimmer. A portion of the representing power must be used up to suppress these distinct side ideas; and it therefore cannot be applied to the blended images to maintain them in their previous vividness.[114]

Still another place where Wordsworth almost certainly writes with dependence on Coleridge's philosophical knowledge can be found in "The Excursion." In the fourth book Wordsworth rejects philosophical solipsism; he speaks of

> Philosophers, who, though the human soul
> Be of a thousand faculties composed,
> And twice ten thousand interests, do yet prize
> This soul, and the transcendent universe,
> No more than as a mirror that reflects
> To proud Self-love her own intelligence;
> That one, poor, finite object, in the abyss
> Of infinite Being, twinkling restlessly![115]

The reference could scarcely be to anyone other than Fichte and Schelling, who derived all reality from the ego positing both itself and the non-ego. If so, the information must have come from Cole-

---

[112] *Notebooks*, I, 1541.
[114] *Ibid.*, p. 124.
[113] Tetens, I, 81.
[115] Wordsworth, *Poems*, v, 140.

ridge, for Wordsworth did not read German philosophy, and indeed, in W. W. Robson's words, "meditative as he was, his mind was radically unphilosophical."[116] Coleridge, however, not only lengthily preoccupied himself with Fichte and Schelling but also mocked the Fichtian ego-philosophy in some doggerel lines in the *Biographia*. Fichte's theory, says Coleridge by way of preliminary, "degenerated into a crude egoismus, a boastful and hyperstoic hostility to NATURE"; and in a footnote he produces "the following burlesque on the Fichtean Egoismus":

> Here on this market-cross aloud I cry:
> I, I, I! I itself I!
> The form and the substance, the what and the why,
> The when and the where, and the low and the high,
> The inside and outside, the earth and the sky,
> I, you, and he, and he, you and I,
> All souls and all bodies are I itself I![117]

From such and similar examples, it becomes plain that Coleridge's reliance on Wordsworth, though masochistic and psychically clinging, was not accompanied by reliance in the realm of thought. In that realm, indeed, the reliance was reversed. It is significant that Wordsworth never lost his enormous respect for his friend's mental powers, despite his growing disgust at Coleridge's weaknesses, despondency, and self-indulgence. If Coleridge was overwhelmed by Wordsworth, Wordsworth, in another way, was no less impressed by Coleridge. "Coleridge was over at Grasmere a few days ago," writes Wordsworth in April 1801—long after any initial enthusiasm should have been worn away by Coleridge's shortcomings—"he was both in better health and in better spirits than I have seen him for some time. He is a great man, and if God grant him life will do great things."[118] In 1838 he says in passing that "It will hardly be disputed" that Coleridge "was a man of first-rate genius and attainments."[119] Even in his period of almost complete disillusionment in the relationship, Wordsworth never doubted his friend's quality of mind. In 1812, many months after the estrangement, he spoke to Crabb Robinson of "Coleridge's mind, the powers of which he declared to be greater than those of any man he ever knew. From such a man, under favourable influ-

---

[116] *Critical Essays* (London: Routledge & Kegan Paul, 1966), p. 139.
[117] *Biographia*, I, 101-102.   [118] *Early Years*, p. 324.
[119] *Prose*, III, 310.

ences, everything might be looked for."[120] In May 1809, at the most intense moment of his exasperation with Coleridge, Wordsworth wrote Poole of his

> deliberate opinion, formed upon proofs which have been strengthening for years, that he neither will nor can execute any thing of important benefit either to himself his family or mankind. Neither his talents nor his genius mighty as they are nor his vast information will avail him anything; they are all frustrated by a derangement in his intellectual and moral constitution—In fact he has no voluntary power of mind whatsoever, nor is he capable of acting under any *constraint* of duty or moral obligation.[121]

But even here, where his denunciation of Coleridge is so forthright, the estimate of Coleridge's mind could hardly be more admiring. Such passages, indeed, of themselves show that the relationship with Coleridge could never have been the one-way dependency that Fruman's lamentably tendentious arguments depict it as being. Quite the contrary, Wordsworth relied deeply upon his friend's "vast information" and discerning judgment. He thought of Coleridge and himself as "Twins almost in genius and in mind," and Coleridge had lent "a living help/ To regulate my Soul."[122] As Parrish points out:

> We can only guess how large a part Coleridge may have played, in the early years, in turning his partner away from the dramatic monologue and toward the "philosophic" mode. But there is no need to guess at the impression left by *Biographia Literaria*. For the 1820 edition of his collected poems Wordsworth revised the passages that Coleridge had singled out for criticism. The revisions had a consistent aim—to elevate the language, making it accord more closely with Coleridge's notion of poetic diction.[123]

Coleridge helped his friend in still other ways. It was not only Coleridge who borrowed poetic lines from Wordsworth; Wordsworth too borrowed from Coleridge. The first stanza of Wordsworth's "We Are Seven" was written by Coleridge, as Wordsworth told Crabb Robinson in 1836 and Isabella Fenwick in

[120] *Robinson*, I, 76. [121] *Middle Years*, I, 352.
[122] *Prelude*, pp. 188, 418 (VI, 263, X, 907-908). It is significant of the oppositions inherent in the symbiosis, however, that the first of these statements was removed by Wordsworth in the 1850 version.
[123] "The Wordsworth-Coleridge Controversy," p. 373.

1843.[124] There may have been other instances,[125] but this one is firmly documented, and it demonstrates that the relationship, even in poetic composition, was truly symbiotic, not merely one of Coleridge's dependency. Furthermore, as George Watson pointed out in 1966, "Coleridge was already a poet of original accomplishment before he knew Wordsworth; and . . . he is rather more likely than Wordsworth to have evolved the blank-verse monody which he came to call the conversation poem and which, in Wordsworth's more industrious hand, became 'Tintern Abbey' and, in a vastly extended form, the Prelude of 1805."[126] As another commentator further observes:

> After all, in 1795 when Coleridge had written "The Aeolian Harp" Wordsworth was still working on such poems as "Guilt and Sorrow," an imitation of Juvenal (Satire VII), and translations from Catullus. "This Lime-Tree Bower," "Frost at Midnight" and "The Nightingale" all preceded "Tintern Abbey."[127]

But perhaps the best example of Coleridge's counterinfluence on Wordsworth, and also the last one to be adduced here, relates to Wordsworth's projected work, "The Recluse." This vast poem was to be the supreme achievement of his life, and he placed the highest kind of value on its completion. He mentions his hopes to Tobin in March 1798:

> I have written 1300 lines of a poem in which I contrive to convey most of the knowledge of which I am possessed. My object is to give pictures of Nature, Man, and Society. Indeed I know not any thing which will not come within the scope of my plan.[128]

To De Quincey in March 1804, he said that "The Prelude" was not to be

> published these many years, and never during my lifetime, till I have finished a larger and more important work to which it is tributary. Of this larger work I have written one Book and several scattered fragments: it is a moral and Philosophical Poem, the subject whatever I find most interesting, in Nature Man So-

[124] Robinson, ii, 481; Wordsworth, Poems, i, 361-62.

[125] For instance, in a letter to Poole in 1809, Coleridge says that of the installments of Wordsworth's The Convention of Cintra that had appeared in The Courier, "The two last Columns of the second, excepting the concluding Paragraph, were written all but a few sentences by me" (Collected Letters, iii, 174).

[126] Coleridge the Poet (London: Routledge & Kegan Paul, 1966), p. 64.

[127] Heath, pp. 169-70.   [128] Early Years, p. 212.

ciety, most adapted to Poetic Illustration. To this work I mean to devote the Prime of my life and the chief force of my mind.[129]

It was a plan that had matured under the admiration and encouragement of Coleridge, who had always thought of his friend as "the first & greatest philosophical Poet."[130] As Coleridge wrote to Wordsworth on 12 October 1799:

> I long to see what you have been doing. O let it be the tail-piece of 'The Recluse!' for of nothing but 'The Recluse' can I hear patiently. That it is to be addressed to me makes me more desirous that it should not be a poem of itself. To be addressed, as a beloved man, by a thinker, at the close of such a poem as 'The Recluse' . . . is the only event, I believe, capable of inciting in me an hour's vanity.[131]

But Wordsworth, despite his daily and dutiful labor (he was not afflicted, as was Coleridge, by the disease of procrastination), was never able to finish "The Recluse." As Helen Darbishire has said, "all that was accomplished of the great philosophical poem, apart from Book I and the magnificent Prospectus, was a Prelude to the main theme, and an Excursion from it."[132]

The cause of his failure, it seems clear, was too great a dependency upon Coleridge's "vast information," critical discernment, and philosophical understanding. Wordsworth's letters to Coleridge convey the greatest urgency in his sense of this dependence:

> I am very anxious to have your notes for the Recluse. I cannot say how much importance I attach to this, if it should please God that I survive you, I should reproach myself for ever in writing the work if I had neglected to procure this help.[133]

A letter of about three weeks later, 29 March 1804, is almost frantic:

> Your last letter but one informing us of your late attack was the severest shock to me, I think, I have ever received. . . . I will not speak of other thoughts that passed through me; but I cannot help saying that I would gladly have given 3 fourths of my possessions for your letter on The Recluse at that time. I cannot say what a load it would be to me, should I survive you and you die without this memorial left behind. Do for heaven's sake, put this out of the reach of accident immediately.[134]

---

[129] *Ibid.*, p. 454.
[130] *Collected Letters*, II, 1034.
[131] *Ibid.*, I, 538; see also I, 527.
[132] Darbishire, p. 90.
[133] *Early Years*, p. 452.
[134] *Ibid.*, p. 464.

Coleridge, however, departed to Malta, sliding ever deeper into opium. His departure was tantamount to the doom of Wordsworth's poem. Dorothy notes in December 1805 that Wordsworth "is very anxious to get forward with The Recluse, and is reading for the nourishment of his mind, preparatory to beginning; but I do not think he will be able to do much more till we have heard of Coleridge."[135] Wordsworth himself writes in August 1806 that "Within this last month I have returned to the Recluse, and have written 700 additional lines. Should Coleridge return, so that I might have some conversation with him upon the subject, I should go on swimmingly." But what Wordsworth had actually written was part of "The Excursion."[136]

When Coleridge returned to England, he was on the brink of psychic ruin. As a consequence, the estrangement of 1810 was preceded by four years of deteriorating friendship. So it was not until 1815 that he sketched to Wordsworth the plan that he had not written in 1804:

> in the very Pride of confident Hope I looked forward to the Recluse, as the *first* and *only* true Phil. Poem in existence. Of course, I expected the Colors, Music, imaginative Life, and Passion of *Poetry*; but the matter and arrangement of *Philosophy*. . . . I supposed you first to have meditated the faculties of Man in the abstract, in their correspondence with his Sphere of action, and . . . to have laid a solid and immoveable foundation for the Edifice by removing the sandy Sophisms of Locke, and the Mechanic Dogmatists, and demonstrating that the Senses were living growths and developments of the Mind & Spirit in a much juster as well as higher sense, than the mind can be said to be formed by the Senses. . . . to have affirmed a Fall in some sense, as a fact, the possibility of which cannot be understood from the nature of the Will, but the reality of which is attested by Experience & Conscience . . . and not disguising the sore evils, under which the whole Creation groans, to point out however a manifest Scheme of Redemption from this Slavery, of Reconciliation from this Enmity with Nature . . . and to conclude by a grand didactic swell on the necessary identity of a true Philosophy with true Religion. . . .

Such or something like this was the Plan, I had supposed that you were engaged on—.[137]

[135] *Ibid.*, p. 664.
[137] *Collected Letters*, IV, 574-75.
[136] *Middle Years*, I, 64, and n. 1.

From such a statement it is apparent that "The Recluse," if it could have been produced by Wordsworth at all, would have required a joint effort recalling the happy togetherness of the late 1790s; for Wordsworth did not have the philosophical capabilities to incorporate Coleridge's deeply felt opinions into a poem. As Sheats has said with regard to that part of Wordsworth's work that culminated in "Tintern Abbey": "One cannot doubt Coleridge's immense contribution to these achievements. A brilliant and profoundly generous man, he offered a philosophic and poetic comradeship. . . . Coleridge furthermore was probably the only man in England who recognized the achievement of the Racedown poems and could articulate its philosophical and historical significance."[138] To lose such support was to experience a crippling blow.

"The Recluse" in its failure is thus parallel to the fate of Coleridge's own *magnum opus*. Indeed, in a statement made near the end of his life, Coleridge suggests as much. It is a fact, remarkable only if one does not know of the younger man's need to project himself into his friend's identity, that Wordsworth's great philosophical poem was really to have been a version of the *magnum opus*:

I cannot help regretting that Wordsworth did not first publish his thirteen books on the growth of an individual mind—superior, as I used to think, upon the whole, to the "Excursion." You may judge how I felt about them by my own poem upon the occasion. Then the plan laid out, and, I believe, partly suggested by me, was, that Wordsworth should assume the station of a man in mental repose, one whose principles were made up, and so prepared to deliver upon authority a system of philosophy. He was to treat man as man . . . in contact with external nature, and informing the senses from the mind, and not compounding a mind out of the senses; then he was to describe the pastoral and other states of society, assuming something of the Juvenalian spirit as he approached the high civilization of cities and towns, and opening a melancholy picture of the present state of degeneracy and vice; thence he was to infer . . . a redemptive process in operation, showing how this idea reconciled all the anomalies, and promised future glory and restoration. Something of this sort, was I think, agreed on. It is, in substance, what I have been all my life doing in my system of philosophy.[139]

[138] Sheats, p. 163.
[139] *Table Talk*, 21 July 1832. Coleridge, in another variation of his symbiotic im-

So the most ambitious symbiotic venture of them all—it illustrates Borges's dictum that "any collaboration is mysterious"[140]— ended in diasparactive ruin for both Wordsworth and Coleridge. Indeed, the symbiosis by its very nature involved forces of fragmentation as unmistakably as it did those of unity. "A dialogue," said Friedrich Schlegel, in words that eminently pertain to the dialogical interchange between Coleridge and Wordsworth, "is a chain or garland of fragments."[141] The relationship of the two men involved distortions as well as fecundations of their abilities. If Wordsworth allowed himself to be pushed into the uncongenial role of philosophical poet in order to satisfy Coleridge's propensities for abstract thought, Coleridge for his part allowed Wordsworth's poetic genius, along with his friend's sparseness of encouragement, to occultate his own poetic self-confidence. As a commentator concludes, "Coleridge slowly and reluctantly began to recognize that Wordsworth, being as he was a glutton of praise with little to spare for another, had been greatly instrumental in suspending the 'shaping spirit of Imagination' in the friend to whom he owed so much."[142]

Thus Coleridge writes to Thelwall, on 17 December 1800: "As to Poetry, I have altogether abandoned it, being convinced that I never had the essentials of poetic Genius, & that I mistook a strong desire for original power."[143] A letter to Godwin on 25 March 1801 makes it clear that self-comparison to Wordsworth precipitated this opinion:

The Poet is dead in me—my imagination . . . lies, like a Cold Snuff on the circular Rim of a Brass Candlestick. . . . If I die, and the Booksellers will give you any thing for my Life, be sure to say—'Wordsworth descended on him, like the Γνῶθι σεαυτόν from Heaven; by shewing to him what true Poetry was, he made him know, that he himself was no Poet.'[144]

Still again, on 29 July 1802 he writes to Southey: "As to myself, all

---

pulse, planned also to write a vast poem called "The Brook," which, in containing "impassioned reflections on men, nature, and society" (*Biographia*, I, 129), was to have been clearly an alternate version of his friend's "Recluse." In yet another convolution of the symbiosis, Wordsworth's "The River Duddon" was in turn a version of Coleridge's "The Brook" (see Wordsworth, *Poems*, III, 503-504).

[140] Borges, p. 96.   [141] *Friedrich Schlegel*, II, 176.

[142] A. M. Buchan, "The Influence of Wordsworth on Coleridge (1795-1800)," *University of Toronto Quarterly*, 32 (1963), 365.

[143] *Collected Letters*, I, 656.   [144] *Ibid.*, II, 714.

my poetic Genius, if ever I really possessed any *Genius*, & it was not rather a mere general *aptitude* of Talent, & quickness in Imitation/ is gone."[145] To be sure, this last statement was written after Coleridge had begun the "Dejection Ode"; but that poem, as well as the lines "To William Wordsworth" of 1807, which seem to contradict his gloomy self-assessment, are both directly informed by Wordsworth's proximity. Besides these two poems, there is almost nothing further on in time that can be called poetic achievement.

So for Coleridge the symbiosis was a mixture of stimulation and defeat. His self-confidence was assuredly not helped by Wordsworth's critical ineptitude and lack of generosity, which contrast starkly with his own superb appreciations of Wordsworthian accomplishment. Not only did Wordsworth manage to keep "Christabel" from being published in *Lyrical Ballads*,[146] he even considered dropping "The Ancient Mariner" from the second edition:

> From what I can gather [he writes Cottle] it seems that The Ancyent Mariner has upon the whole been an injury to the volume, I mean that the old words and strangeness of it have deterred readers from going on. If the volume should come to a second Edition I would put in its place some little things which would be more likely to suit the common taste.[147]

But even this astonishing statement cannot match the critical inaneness (to say nothing of the personal insensitivity) of the apologetic "Note to the Ancient Mariner" that Wordsworth inserted in the 1800 edition of *Lyrical Ballads*:

> The Poem of my Friend has indeed great defects; first, that the principal person has no distinct character, either in his profession of Mariner, or as a human being who . . . might be sup-

[145] *Ibid.*, p. 831.

[146] On the seriousness of this action as a blow to Coleridge's self-confidence, cf. Parrish: "What the dropping of 'Christabel' meant to Coleridge came out only very slowly as the months and years rolled by. . . . [Wordsworth's] rejection of it, together with Coleridge's inability to finish it, must have helped to give Coleridge the keenest sense of frustration and defeat he had yet experienced. Some of this feeling Coleridge betrayed in a notebook entry of 30 October (no. 834): 'He knew not what to do—something, he felt, must be done—he rose, drew his writing-desk suddenly before him—sate down, took the pen—& found that he knew not what to do' " (*Art of the* Lyrical Ballads, p. 200).

[147] *Early Years*, p. 264. Wordsworth's eager insistence in later years on his own share in the composition of "The Ancient Mariner" (see notes 27-30 above) seems, in the light of this ungenerous intent, a rather glaring example of *mauvaise foi*.

posed himself to partake of something supernatural: secondly, that he does not act, but is continually acted upon.[148]

Lamb's retort was properly biting, and we treasure its discernment:

> For me, I was never so affected with any human Tale. After first reading it, I was totally possessed with it for many days. . . . I totally differ from your idea that the Marinere should have had a character and profession. . . . The Ancient Marinere undergoes such Trials, as overwhelm and bury all individuality or memory of what he was, like the state of man in a Bad dream. . . . Your other observation is I think as well a little unfounded. . . . You will excuse my remarks, because I am hurt and vexed that you should think it necessary, with a prose apology, to open the eyes of dead men that cannot see.[149]

At least in part, therefore, because his friend could not see his poetical achievement, Coleridge withdrew into metaphysics: "He is a great, a true Poet—I am only a kind of a Metaphysician."[150] This acquiescence of 1800 gave way in 1818 to a more bitter and less self-deprecating remembrance of the Wordsworths' "cold praise and effective discouragement of every attempt of mine to roll onward in a distinct current of my own."[151] But the whirligig of time brought in his revenges. After the estrangement of 1810, Wordsworth himself published no more important poetry; and indeed, all his really important statements were completed or in

---

[148] *Lyrical Ballads; The Text of the 1798 Edition with the Additional 1800 Poems and Prefaces,* ed. R. L. Brett and A. R. Jones (London: Methuen and Co., Ltd., 1965), pp. 276-77.

[149] Lamb, *Letters,* I, 240.   [150] *Collected Letters,* I, 658.

[151] *Ibid.,* I, 631 n. Cf. IV, 669, 688. With regard to distinct currents of his own, it should be noted that some themes Coleridge held in common with Wordsworth were apparently, their similarity notwithstanding, not the products of the symbiosis. For example, nothing seems more exclusively characteristic of Wordsworth than the dislike of cities, so memorably expressed in Book Seven of "The Prelude" but also elsewhere; "Love," he says in Book Twelve, does not "easily thrive/ In cities, where the human heart is sick" (p. 466; lines 201-202). Yet in March 1795, presumably before meeting Wordsworth, Coleridge speaks of "proof, that Man was not made to live in Great Cities!" (*Collected Letters,* I, 154). Again, speaking of the "theme" that Wordsworth and Coleridge shared, Smith notes that "The next two years, 1796 and 1797, find both Wordsworth and Coleridge giving this theme fuller treatment in their simultaneous attempts at verse tragedy, *The Borderers* and *Osorio.* Interestingly enough, there is no indication that either knew of the other's work, each having taken up this theme independently" ("Wordsworth and Coleridge: The Growth of a Theme," p. 55).

progress by the time Coleridge left for Malta in 1804. Heath even suggests that Wordsworth's marriage in 1802, by altering the structure of the relationship existing among Wordsworth, Coleridge, and Dorothy, sealed Wordsworth's poetic decline; it was the first step in the process by which he "gained a public and lost an audience."[152]

So if Wordsworth, one of the supremely great poets in the entire history of literature, overshadowed the formidable poetical abilities of Coleridge, the latter, for his part, possessed powers of insight and understanding no less indubitably unique than his friend's poetic gifts. With his vast information and his gorgeous eloquence, Coleridge was one of the most comprehensive philosophical intelligences and the subtlest critic England has produced. The history of Wordsworth's career shows that the "friend so prompt in sympathy" was quite as important to him as he was to the friend. Although he had "seen little of him for the last twenty years," Wordsworth wrote on the occasion of Coleridge's death that "his mind has been habitually present with me."[153] And in a final moment of explanation and retrospect, he realized that Coleridge was "the most *wonderful* man" he had ever known.[154]

[152] Heath, p. 174.   [153] *Later Years*, II, 710.
[154] Grosart, III, 469.

CHAPTER TWO

Coleridge's Anxiety

◊♦◊

Mᴜᴄʜ of Coleridge's existence was a death in life. His deep commitment to the Christian religion was sustained, on the one hand, by the need to feel that there must be something better than the torment in which he so mysteriously found himself and, on the other, by the sense of his inability to cope with his manifold failings:

> I profess a deep conviction [he wrote] that Man was and is a *fallen* Creature, not by accidents of bodily constitution, or any other cause, which *human* Wisdom in a course of ages might be supposed capable of removing; but diseased in his *Will*.[1]

Certainly this view, central to Christian faith, corresponded exactly to the facts of life as he himself experienced them.[2] His intellect, noted Southey in 1815, was "as clear and as powerful as ever was vouchsafed to man," but "he labours under a disease of the volition."[3] Earlier, in May 1809, Wordsworth, in a moment of intense exasperation, had informed Thomas Poole of his "deliberate opinion" about Coleridge, that

> Neither his talents nor his genius mighty as they are nor his vast information will avail him anything; they are all frustrated by a derangement in his intellectual and moral constitution—In fact he has no voluntary power of mind whatsoever, nor is he capable of acting under any *constraint* of duty or moral obligation.[4]

To these statements by outside observers, one could add re-

---

[1] *Aids to Reflection* (London: Taylor and Hessey, 1825), p. 136.

[2] "My Faith is simply this—that there is an original corruption in our nature, from which & from the consequences of which, we may be redeemed by Christ . . . and this I believe—not because I *understand* it; but because I *feel*, that it is not only suitable to, but needful for, my nature" (*Collected Letters*, ɪɪ, 807. To George Coleridge, 1 July 1802).

[3] *Southey*, ɪɪ, 117-18.　　　　　　　　　[4] *Middle Years*, ɪ, 352.

peated self-awarenesses by Coleridge himself. To cite a single instance, which by its almost trivial context may seem to show his "disease of the volition" in all its mysteriousness, a note of January 1804 says:

> All this evening, indeed all this day . . . I ought to have [been] reading & filling the Margins of Malthus—I had begun & found it pleasant/ why did I neglect it? . . . —surely this is well worth a serious Analysis, that understanding I may attempt to heal/ for it is a deep & wide disease in my moral Nature. . . . Love of Liberty, Pleasure of Spontaneity . . . these all express, not explain, the Fact.[5]

If the unexplainable fact of a diseased volition was the most mysterious and destructive of the ills under which Coleridge labored, it was, as we all know, by no means the only one. His dependence of almost forty years upon the specious consolations of opium (or "laudanum," which, as he says at one point, "I had taken in enormous doses for 32 years")[6] filled him even more with self-loathing than did his inability to discharge his duty, indeed, was at times charged with responsibility for that defect:

> What crime is there scarcely which has not been included in or followed from the one guilt of taking opium? Not to speak of ingratitude to my maker for the wasted Talents; of ingratitude to so many friends who have loved me . . . of barbarous neglect of my family. . . . I have in this one dirty business of Laudanum an hundred times deceived, tricked, nay, actually & consciously LIED—[7]

Everywhere he found a bewildering sense of his own inadequacy. "There *is* a something, an essential something wanting in me."[8] Again, he writes of "A sense of weakness—a haunting sense, that I was an herbaceous Plant, as large as a large Tree . . . but with *pith within* the Trunk, not heart of Wood/—that I had *power* not *strength*—an involuntary Imposter. . . . This . . . is as fair a statement of my habitual Haunting, as I could give before the Tribunal of Heaven."[9]

Beset as it was by such inner hauntings, Coleridge's life, in many

---

[5] *Notebooks*, I, 1832.
[6] *Collected Letters*, VI, 910 (to William Worship, May 1832).
[7] *Ibid.*, III, 490.   [8] *Ibid.*, II, 1102 (to Davy, Mar. 1804).
[9] *Ibid.*, p. 959 (to Southey, Aug. 1803).

of its most important outward manifestations, became a shambles. He failed to take his degree at Cambridge; he married the wrong woman;[10] he was unable to capture the lasting respect of the women he did love; he managed, at great cost to his own self-esteem and their patience, continually to be supported by admirers; he became estranged from his dearest friend; he was humiliated by the abject failure of his first born, which seemed a repetition of his own disasters;[11] he reneged on his aspirations as a poet and did not adequately realize those as a philosopher. Furthermore, he did not bear his troubles with the stoic dignity of Wordsworth; rather he lived a life of desperation made unquiet by interminable self-justifications and hypochondriac fancies, by a querulous inability to accept criticisms or anything less than uncritical affection. He plagiarized; he procrastinated; he spent a dismaying amount of effort, as Dorothy Wordsworth said, "in deceiving himself, and seeking to deceive others."[12] In sum, he was, as Humphry House has said, "not a glamorous or systematic Romantic sinner who, like Byron or Baudelaire, seized on the idea of evil as a stimulus: he was a genuine sinner, who did what he believed to be wrong against his conscience and his better judgement; he was an important sinner, whose sins were meanness, hypocrisy, self-deceit . . . a tortured, tearful, weak, self-humiliating sinner."[13] In such massive contexts of woe, it is difficult to imagine a more apposite epitaph than the one Coleridge himself supplied:

> Beneath this sod
> A poet lies, or that which once seem'd he.
> O, lift one thought in prayer for S. T. C.;
> That he who many a year with toil of breath
> Found death in life, may here find life in death![14]

The sense of the cumulatively battering effect of Coleridge's voyage through this world can be experienced in the simple record of his physical presence as seen by others. An aura of exuberant vitality surrounded him in young manhood. "You had a great loss in not seeing Coleridge," writes Dorothy Wordsworth in 1797:

[10] As Dorothy Wordsworth observed of Coleridge's wife, "she has several great merits. . . . She would have made a very good wife to many another man, but for Coleridge!! Her radical fault is want of sensibility and what can such a woman be to Coleridge?" Later: "Mrs. Coleridge is a most extraordinary character—she is the lightest weakest silliest woman!" (*Early Years*, pp. 330-31, 363).

[11] See especially *Collected Letters*, v, 232-33.

[12] *Middle Years*, i, 399.   [13] House, pp. 18-19.

[14] Coleridge, *Poems*, i, 491-92.

He is a wonderful man. His conversation teems with soul, mind, and spirit. Then he is so benevolent, so good tempered and cheerful, and, like William, interests himself so much about every little trifle. At first I thought him very plain, that is, for about three minutes: he is pale and thin, has a wide mouth, thick lips, and not very good teeth, longish loose-growing half-curling rough black hair. But if you hear him speak for five minutes you think no more of them. [15]

But by 1806, upon Coleridge's return from Malta, Dorothy witnessed quite a different sight:

never did I feel such a shock as at first sight of him. We all felt exactly in the same way—as if he were different from what we expected to see; . . . I know not what to hope for, or what to expect; . . . his misery has made him so weak, and he has been so dismally irresolute in all things since his return to England, that I have more of fear than hope. He is utterly changed. [16]

By 1810 things were even worse. The man who had been described in the 1805 "Prelude" as "The most intense of Nature's worshippers" was now almost wholly withdrawn and cast scarcely a glance on the outer world:

He lies in bed [wrote Dorothy], always till after 12 o'clock, sometimes much later; and never walks out—Even the finest spring day does not tempt him to seek the fresh air; and this beautiful valley seems a blank to him. He never leaves his own parlour except at dinner and tea, and sometimes supper, and then he always seems impatient to get back to his solitude—he goes the moment his food is swallowed. Sometimes he does not speak a word, and when he does talk it is always very much and upon subjects as far aloof from himself or his friends as possible. [17]

After 1816, to be sure, when Coleridge came under the devoted care of the physician James Gillman, his life became more stable and, at least in comparison with the horrors of the preceding fifteen years, more happy. But the impression he conveyed was of a man swamped by existence:

he was now getting old, towards sixty perhaps [writes Carlyle of the Coleridge of the Highgate years]; and gave you the idea of a life that had been full of sufferings; a life heavy-laden, half-

[15] *Early Years*, pp. 188-89. [16] *Middle Years*, I, 86.
[17] *Ibid.*, p. 399.

vanquished, still swimming painfully in seas of manifold physical and other bewilderment. Brow and head were round, and of massive weight, but the face was flabby and irresolute. The deep eyes, of a light hazel, were as full of sorrow as of inspiration; confused pain looked mildly from them, as in a kind of mild astonishment. . . . A heavy-laden, high-aspiring and surely much-suffering man.[18]

This outer testimony to stress and bewilderment is paralleled by extensive inner witness by Coleridge himself. In his "Dejection: An Ode," he writes in 1802 of a deep-lying malaise that he called

> A Grief without a pang, void, dark, & drear,
> A stifling, drowsy, unimpassion'd grief,
> That finds no natural Outlet, no Relief . . .[19]

In 1804, he writes in this way:

> Sleep a pandemonium of all the shames & miseries of the past Life from early childhood all huddled together, & bronzed with one stormy Light of Terror & Self-torture[20]

All this went on for many years. For instance, to Josiah Wade, in June 1814, Coleridge asks his correspondent to

> conceive whatever is most wretched, helpless, and hopeless, and you will form as tolerable a notion of my state, as it is possible for a good man to have.[21]

In short, Coleridge's "Terror & Self-torture," his "Grief without a pang, void, dark, & drear," his sense of being "wretched, helpless, and hopeless," all are testimony to a consuming misery that continued with little abatement for most of his life. Like Cowper, he felt himself a psychic castaway, overwhelmed and drowning in an ocean of inner torment.

This torment, it seems clear, was deeper than the opium-addiction, deeper than the hypochondria, deeper than the plagiarisms, deeper than the inability to work. It was in fact the universal substructure upon which they reared their individual ruins. Indeed, it is probably true that the repeated recourses to opium, the repeated indulgences in hypochondria, the repeated indecorums of plagiarism, and the repeated vices of procrastination were neurotic attempts to cope with this deeper malaise rather than unmixed evi-

---

[18] *Carlyle*, xi, 54.
[20] *Notebooks*, ii, 2091.

[19] *Collected Letters*, ii, 790.
[21] *Collected Letters*, iii, 511.

dence of the malaise itself. Certainly they all have in common the characteristic neurotic form of compulsive repetition.[22]

The opium addiction, for instance, though sometimes referred to by Coleridge as though it were the underlying cause of his unhappiness—he speaks at one point of "the poison that has been the curse of my existence, my shame and my *negro-slave* inward humiliation and debasement"[23]—is at other times identified as merely a symptom:

> I have never loved Evil for its own sake; no! nor ever sought pleasure for its own sake, but only as the means of escaping from pains that coiled round my mental powers.[24]

The pains that coiled around his mental powers were the indeterminate convulsions of his drowning psyche, or, as he calls it, "infantine nervousness":

> most men [he notes in December, 1806] affected by belief of *reality* attached to the wild-weed spectres of infantine nervousness—but I affected by them simply, & of themselves—/ but for the last years I own & mourn a more deleterious Action of *Fear*—fear of horrors in *Sleep*, driving me to dreadful remedies & stimuli . . . to purchase daily a wretched Reprieve from the torments of each night's Daemons.[25]

At one point "intolerable Despair" is termed the underlying cause of the addiction:

> O me! now racked with pain, now fallen abroad & suffocated with a sense of intolerable Despair/ & no other Refuge than Poisons that degrade the Being.[26]

As with the opium addiction, so with the bodily illness. One can scarcely doubt that Coleridge did suffer much physical pain and discomfort; but one can also not doubt that a very substantial portion of it was psychic, not organic, in origin. He spent an extraordinary amount of time worrying about his intestinal functions, and in his letters and notebooks the repeated reports on the state of his bowels can be wearisome to read. Some of his experiences were both fearsome and revolting. Thus on ship to Malta in 1804, he writes of

---

[22] See *Freud*, xviii, 18-23.
[23] *Collected Letters*, vi, 892 (to Green, 23 Mar. 1832).
[24] *Notebooks*, ii, 2368.   [25] *Ibid.*, 2944.
[26] *Ibid.*, 2860.

the dull quasi finger-pressure on the Liver, the endless Flatulence, the frightful constipation when the dead Filth *impales* the lower Gut—to weep & sweat & moan & scream for the parturience of an excrement with such pangs & such convulsions as a woman with an Infant.[27]

For the last three decades of his life he believed that his troubles were caused by an obstruction of the bowels and was confident that an autopsy would prove him correct.[28] At one point he speaks of a "not unfrequent tragico-whimsical fancy" in which he is present at his post-mortem dissection, "infusing . . . this and that thought into the Mind of the Anatomist. . . . Be so good as to give a cut just *there*, right across the umbilicar region—there lurks the fellow that for so many years tormented me on my first waking!"[29] But when the autopsy was actually performed, no obstruction was revealed. As Sara Coleridge wrote to her brother Hartley after Coleridge's death:

He had made a solemn injunction on Mr Gillman that his body should be opened—which was accordingly done. . . . There was more than a pint of water in the chest, & the heart & liver were enlarged. But nothing was observed which could be ascribed to laudanum, & the internal pain & uneasiness which he has suffered from all his life, & which my mother remembers him complaining of before he ever had recourse to opium, is supposed to have been some sympathetic nervous affection.[30]

Coleridge appears to have suspected that at least some aspects of his discomfort were psychic in origin (he admits at one point to being "horribly hypochondriacal")[31] and at times his report is openly psychosomatic. Thus he speaks of

frightful Dreams with screaming—*breezes* of Terror blowing from the Stomach up thro' the Brain/ always when I am awakened, I find myself stifled with wind/ & the wind the manifest cause of the Dream/ frequent paralytic Feelings—sometimes approaches to Convulsion fit.[32]

---

[27] *Ibid.*, 2091.
[28] See, for instance, his complaint of June 13, 1809: "Sleep or even a supine Posture does not fail to remind me that something is organically amiss in some one or other of the Contents of the Abdomen" (*Collected Letters*, III, 212).
[29] *Ibid.*, VI, 769 (to Sotheby, 9 Nov. 1828).
[30] *Ibid.*, p. 992.   [31] *Ibid.*, II, 710 (to Poole, 24 Mar. 1801).
[32] *Ibid.*, p. 976.

And that the organic pain, psychosomatic pain, and imaginary pain all were enormously amplified by an extreme psychic stress seems still more clear from the fact that he felt them most when alone, and had innumerable turns for the better when in company.[33] Doubtless the fear of being alone was an important element in his fame as a conversationalist, for to talk to another was to ward off the psychic agony that erupted when he was by himself.[34] At any rate, numerous observers noted an almost obsessive quality in his discourse: "he lays down his pen to make sure of an auditor," said Hazlitt, "and mortagages the admiration of posterity for the stare of an idler."[35] Once the auditor was gone, terror could engulf Coleridge. As he writes in 1803, in "The Pains of Sleep,"

> . . . yesternight I pray'd aloud
> In Anguish & in Agony,
> Awaking from the fiendish Crowd
> Of Shapes & Thoughts that tortur'd me!
>
> . . . . . .
>
> For all was Horror, Guilt & Woe . . .
> Life-stifling Fear, Soul-stifling Shame![36]

The life-stifling fear, and its hypochondriac manifestations, were very hard on his friends. As Dorothy Wordsworth notes in her Grasmere Journal in 1801: "[William] went to meet Mary, and they brought 4 letters—2 from Coleridge. . . . Coleridge's were melancholy letters, he had been very ill in his bowels. We were made very unhappy." Again: "A heart-rending letter from Coleridge— we were sad as we could be. Wm. wrote to him." And again: "two very affecting letters from Coleridge. . . . I was stopped in my writing, and made ill by the letters."[37]

Although Wordsworth pronounced Dorothy's intense concern

---

[33] Cf. Wordsworth to Thomas Poole in July 1801: "He is apparently quite well one day, and the next the fit comes on him again with as much violence as ever" (*Early Years*, pp. 338-39). As Mary Lamb noted in November 1810, during a virtual nadir of Coleridge's deterioration: "We have had many pleasant hours with Coleridge,—if I had not known how ill he is I should have had no idea of it, for he has been very chearful" (Lamb, *Letters*, II, 106).

[34] "The stimulus of Conversation suspends the terror that haunts my mind; but when I am alone, the horrors . . . almost overwhelm me—" (*Collected Letters*, IV, 630).

[35] *Hazlitt*, XI, 30. Cf. Wordsworth: "He talks as a bird sings, as if he could not help it" (*Middle Years*, II, 664).

[36] *Collected Letters*, II, 983.

[37] *Journals*, I, 92-93, 103, 107 (21 Dec. 1801; 29 Jan. and 6 Feb. 1802).

about Coleridge's health to be "nervous blubbering,"[38] he himself could become scarcely less upset. For instance, on 29 March 1804, as was noted in the previous chapter, he writes to Coleridge that a letter informing them "of your late attack was the severest shock to me, I think, I have ever received."[39]

Coleridge once spoke of "the accumulating embarrassments of procrastination."[40] Hypochondria, too, accumulates its embarrassments, for when one arouses the sympathy and fears of his friends as often as Coleridge did, the only thing he can decently do is to die. When time goes on, and the heart-rending complaints are followed, not by death but simply by more complaints, the attitudes of the friends begin to harden. We can see this in a sad but also almost ludicrously indignant letter written by Dorothy to Catherine Clarkson in 1811:

> How absurd, how uncalculating of the feelings and opinions of others, to talk to your Father and Sister of dying in a fortnight, when his dress and everything proved that his thoughts were of other matters. Such talks will never more alarm me. Poor William went off to London [i.e. in February 1808] . . . in consequence of [Coleridge] having solemnly assured Mrs. Coleridge that he *could* not live three months; and, when William arrived, he . . . saw no appearance of disease which could not have been cured, or at least prevented by himself.[41]

From these and other examples, it seems probable that a massive *anxiety*, rather than any more specific ailment, was the true source of Coleridge's varied miseries. Indeed, he himself suspected as much. "My 44th Birth-day," he exclaims in 1815:

> and in *all* but the Brain I am an *old* man! Such ravages do anxiety & mismanagement make.[42]

Elsewhere, he identifies anxiety, or, as he calls it, "dread," as the common denominator of his woes:

> It is a most instructive part of my Life [he writes in 1805] . . . that I have been always preyed on by some Dread, and perhaps all my faulty actions have been the consequence of some Dread or other on my mind/ . . . So in my childhood & Boyhood the horror of being detected with a sorehead . . . then a short-lived Fit of

---

[38] *Ibid.*, p. 79 (10 Nov. 1801).
[40] *Biographia*, I, 31.
[42] *Collected Letters*, IV, 609.

[39] *Early Years*, p. 464.
[41] *Middle Years*, I, 495.

Fears from sex . . . then came Rob. Southey's alienation/ my marriage—constant dread in my mind respecting Mrs Coleridge's Temper . . . and finally stimulants in the fear & prevention of violent Bowel-attacks from mental agitation/ then almost epileptic night-horrors in my sleep/ . . . all this interwoven with its minor consequences, that fill up the interspaces—the cherry juice running in between the cherries in a cherry pie/ procrastination in dread of this—& something else in consequence of that procrast. &c/ [43]

The multiplication of symptoms testifies to the depth and intensity of the anxiety, which runs like cherry juice through their interspaces. For as Freud has pointed out, in his treatise *Hemmung, Symptom, und Angst,*

symptoms are only formed in order to avoid anxiety: they bind the psychical energy which would otherwise be discharged as anxiety.[44]

It follows that "anxiety," as Freud says, is "the fundamental phenomenon and main problem of neurosis."[45] Symptom formation is

synonymous with substitute-formation. . . . The defensive process is analogous to the flight by means of which the ego removes itself from a danger that threatens it from outside.[46]

If we seek the origin of an anxiety so pervasive, so shattering and so neurotically persistent as Coleridge's, we look, in this post-Freudian age, almost as a matter of course to his childhood. Even before more precise investigation, one might suspect that his position as the youngest of ten children, nine of whom were brothers, was psychologically precarious. The likelihood of fragmentation of attention and relation on the part of the parents, and of damaging aggressiveness from the jealously competing brothers, would inevitably be very high in such a situation.

More specifically, the enormous extent of Coleridge's anxiety points compellingly to two sources in his childhood: an extension of what Freud calls a primal anxiety, arising from his relationship

---

[43] *Notebooks,* ii, 2398.   [44] *Freud,* xx, 144.

[45] *Ibid.* Again: "the generating of anxiety sets symptom formation going and is, indeed, a necessary prerequisite of it." Cf. Fenichel: "the problem of anxiety is the essence of any psychology of neurotic conflicts" (p. 132). See further *Freud,* xvi, 393, 404, 411.

[46] *Freud,* xx, 145. "Symptom-formation . . . does in fact put an end to the danger-situation."

with his mother, and what in that same terminology is called a castration anxiety,[47] which in this instance would be connected with his older brothers.

The subject of motherhood was one that for Coleridge seemed to be charged with a special burden of morbid emotion. To cite an example, some lines in "The Three Graves" run as follows:

> Beneath the foulest Mother's curse
> No child could ever thrive:
> A Mother is a Mother still;
> The holiest thing alive.[48]

As an equally revealing example, one might consider a letter Coleridge wrote to his son Derwent in 1807, after having decided to separate from his wife. The letter rather terrifyingly impresses upon the child the need for respect for the mother:

> she gave *you* nourishment out of her own Breasts . . . and she brought you into the world with shocking pains. . . . So it must needs be a horribly wicked Thing ever to forget, or wilfully to vex, a Father or a Mother: especially, a Mother.[49]

Despite the piety of such admonitions, Coleridge's relations to his own mother, as the psychoanalyst David Beres first and most authoritatively noted, were characterized by a peculiar coldness. For instance, in his remarkable series of autobiographical letters to Thomas Poole in 1797, all he finds to say about her was that "My Mother was an admirable Economist, and managed exclusively."[50] Perhaps a more unmistakably significant datum, however, is his virtual disregard of the fact of her death. He had always been reluctant to return to the family home;[51] indeed, in 1802, although near

[47] See *Freud*, xxii, 86-87.

[48] *Friend*, ii, 90. Cf. Coleridge to Mary Robinson in 1802: "Your dear Mother is more present to my eyes, than the paper on which I am writing—which indeed swims before my sight—for I can not think of your Mother without Tears." "What, dear Miss Robinson! ought *you* to feel for yourself—& for the memory of a Mother—of all names the most awful, the most venerable, next to that of God!" (*Collected Letters*, ii, 904-905).

[49] *Collected Letters*, iii, 1-2.

[50] *Ibid.*, i, 310 (to Poole, Mar. 1797). For this and other of my materials with respect to Coleridge's view of his mother I am indebted to Beres's pioneering article (cited below, note 60).

[51] For example, he writes to Southey on 12 Feb. 1800 that "In May I am under a kind of engagement to go with Sara to Ottery—My family wish me to fix there, but *that* I must decline, in the names of public Liberty & individual Free-agency. Elder Brothers, not senior in Intellect, & not sympathizing in main opinions, are subjects

enough to Devonshire, he declined to make a visit that would have entailed very little trouble.[52] And early in November 1809, he wrote to Southey that

> my poor Mother is near her end, and dying in great torture, death eating her piecemeal . . . & she wishes to see me before her death—But tho' my Brother knows I am penniless, not an offer of a Bank note to en[able] me to set off. In truth, I know not what to do—for [there] is not a shilling in our whole House—[53]

Even allowing for the differences of individual temperaments, for the differences in family traditions, for the differences in custom in various locales and eras, and allowing also for the realness of Coleridge's poverty, this declaration sounds strange.

No less curious is the fact that Coleridge does not mention his mother's death in any form of writing, even though Dorothy Wordsworth, to whom his mother can have meant nothing, writes on 18 November 1809, that "Mrs. Fricker and Coleridge's Mother are both dead."[54] Coleridge's wife also takes note of the event, saying that Coleridge was "greatly distressed," but that she and his "Grasmere friends" had opposed his going because of the "effect such a scene would have upon his mind & health."[55] That Coleridge was greatly distressed shows what is psychoanalytically predictable, that is, the existence of love for his mother; that he did not, however, go to Ottery St. Mary either for her sickness or for her death, nor again mention the matter with his customary loquacity or even at all, shows how strong was the inhibition under which he labored. Freud defines inhibitions as "the expression of a *restriction of an ego-function*"; "they are restrictions of the functions of the ego which have been either imposed as a measure of precaution or brought about as a result of an impoverishment of en-

---

of occasional Visits, not temptations to a Co-township" (*Collected Letters*, I, 570). More bluntly, to Poole, he writes on 7 Sept. 1801 of "My family—I have wholly neglected them—I do not love them—their ways are not my ways, nor their thoughts my thoughts" (II, 756).

[52] He writes to Southey on 31 Dec. 1801 that "I have not yet made up my mind whether or no I shall move Devonward. My Relations wish to see me, & I wish to avoid the uneasy feelings I shall have, if I remain so near them without gratifying the wish" (*Collected Letters*, II, 778-79). Nevertheless he informs his wife, little more than a fortnight later, that "I shall not go to [Otter]y; but shall return to London" (II, 779).

[53] *Collected Letters*, III, 261.   [54] *Middle Years*, I, 373.

[55] E. Betham (ed.), *A House of Letters* (London, 1905), p. 116.

ergy."[56] The concept of inhibition as "precaution" would here seem to relate directly to Coleridge's anxiety about his brothers. That as "impoverishment of energy" could arise from the love-hate ambivalence toward his mother.[57] In any case, his lack of action in the face of being "greatly distressed" and in view of a conception of a mother as "the holiest thing alive" seems most unusual. A comparison of his conduct with that of Dr. Johnson in the same relationship comes naturally to mind.

Such a remarkable distancing could have been achieved, I suggest, only as the result of traumatic experience. Although Coleridge at one point says that as a child "I was my mother's darling,"[58] the recollection refers directly to his mildly preferential treatment with regard to his brother Francis. Any further claim must surely be either fantasy or what psychoanalysts call a "screen memory,"[59] for had he in any deep sense been his mother's darling, his self-confidence, as in our post-Freudian sophistications we all now know, would have been far greater than it was. If we judge by the results, his mother's affection must have alternated with periods of neglect or coldness, which developed an extreme anxiety in the child. According to psychoanalytic theory, moreover, it developed rage and an equally great guilt in response to the rage. As Beres suggested in 1951, the Nightmare Life-in-Death of the intensely psychodramatic "Ancient Mariner" seems to be a representation of the mother, deformed by the mixture of rage and guilt projected onto her:[60]

> Her skin was as white as leprosy,
> The Night-mare LIFE-IN-DEATH was she,
> Who thicks man's blood with cold.[61]

[56] *Freud*, xx, 89, 90.

[57] *Ibid.*, x, 241.

[58] *Collected Letters*, I, 347 (to Poole, Oct. 1797).

[59] See *Freud*, III, 301-22; vi, 43-52.

[60] David Beres, "A Dream, A Vision and a Poem: A Psycho-Analytic Study of the Origins of the Rime of the Ancient Mariner," *International Journal of Psycho-Analysis*, 32 (1951), 97-116. See also Fenichel: "In a symbolic way, [the] pursuit of rest and of protection at the mother's breast is expressed in the frequent yearning for the boundless ocean" (p. 370). In this symbolism the Mariner's quest on the ocean/ breast, harassed by the shipmate/brothers, is a kind of counterpart to the situation in "Kubla Khan," where the pleasure dome/breast is lost, though it leaves behind the memory of "the milk of paradise." As Freud says, "If an infant could speak, he would no doubt pronounce the act of sucking at his mother's breast by far the most important in his life" (xvi, 314).

[61] Coleridge, *Poems*, I, 194.

Such a threatening figure reappears in the dreams that Coleridge, so helpfully for future attempts to understand his psychic life, recorded in his notebooks:

Friday Night, Nov. 28, 1800, or rather Saturday Morning—a most frightful Dream of a Woman whose features were blended with darkness catching hold of my right eye & attempting to pull it out—I caught hold of her arm fast—a horrid feel—[62]

In 1802 this baleful apparition is followed by another "Spectre-Woman," as the Nightmare Life-in-Death is called:

I was followed up & down by a frightful pale woman who, I thought, wanted to kiss me, & had the property of giving a shameful Disease by breathing in the face/
& again I dreamt that a figure of a woman of a gigantic Height, dim & indefinite & smokelike appeared—& that I was forced to run up toward it—& then it changed to a stool—& then appeared again in another place—& again I went up in great fright.[63]

We need not suppose that Coleridge's mother was in fact either a monster, or even, by her own lights and situation, particularly a bad mother. She was, however, very probably somewhat neurotic, for the existence of a neurotic son implies neurotic parents. Her neurosis seems to have expressed itself in a certain coldness of disposition; James Dykes Campbell stresses that "she was comparatively an uneducated woman, and unemotional," while Gillman says that she was "a very good woman . . . over careful in many things, very ambitious for the advancement of her sons in life, but wanting perhaps that flow of heart which her husband possessed so largely."[64] No great crime, surely, but her diminished store of warmth, further dissipated by the natural demands of caring for nine other children, could have seemed to her infant son to be total abandonment, and the anxiety thus generated would be very great indeed.

For as Freud has emphasized, the prototypal pattern of anxiety is the birth trauma of separation from the mother;[65] in the infant, accordingly, absence or neglect by the mother is the specific source of normal anxiety and, if pronounced enough, can become the source of neurotic anxiety:

[62] *Notebooks,* I, 848. [63] *Ibid.,* 1250.
[64] Campbell, *Samuel Taylor Coleridge* . . . (London, 1894), p. 3; James Gillman, *Life of Coleridge* (London, 1838), p. 7. Cited in Beres, 102.
[65] *Freud,* xx, 84, 133. Cf. xvi, 396-97.

Only a few of the manifestations of anxiety in children are comprehensible to us, and we must confine our attention to them. They occur, for instance, when a child is alone, or in the dark, or when it finds itself with an unknown person instead of one to whom it is used—such as its mother. These three instances can be reduced to a single condition—namely, that of missing someone who is loved and longed for. But here, I think, we have the key to an understanding of anxiety. . . . The child's mnemic image of the person longed for is no doubt intensely cathected [i.e. invested with emotion], probably in a hallucinatory way at first. But this has no effect; and now it seems as though the longing turns into anxiety.[66]

The mother, as is indicated in Freud's description of the genesis of anxiety, must have been identified in Coleridge's unconscious mind as no less a benign than a vengeful figure: the two states expressing respectively the infant's love for the mother and the rage-guilt complex occasioned by her absence. Although the Ancient Mariner is harrowed by the Nightmare Life-in-Death, he is also, as the gloss informs us, "By grace of the holy Mother . . . refreshed with rain." Coleridge's love of his mother was such as any infant might feel; it was the rage and guilt that were abnormally intense. As he wrote in 1794, "Alas! my poor Mother! What an intolerable weight of guilt is suspended over my head by a hair on one hand—and if I endure to live—the look ever downward—insult—pity—and hell.—"[67]

The anxiety produced in the infant Coleridge by his mother's coldness and inattentiveness was probably not only a source of his lifelong neurotic malaise but also a factor in his failure to develop a strong sense of his own being. He says as an adult that "I know, I feel, that I am weak—apt to faint away inwardly, self-deserted & bereft of the confidence in my own powers."[68] The poignant statement is co-ordinate with Freud's formula that "anxiety is seen to be a product of the infant's mental helplessness."[69]

Coleridge, however, was probably bereft of the confidence in his own powers by still another psychologically damaging situation. His mother apparently was not the only cause of his woe; the Nightmare Life-in-Death had a companion with whom she cast

[66] *Ibid.*, xx, 136-37.
[67] *Collected Letters*, i, 63 (to G. L. Tuckett, 6 Feb. 1794).
[68] *Ibid.*, ii, 1054 (to Sir George Beaumont, 1 Feb. 1804).
[69] *Freud*, xx, 138.

dice for the Mariner's soul. To understand the possibility of this doubling effect, we again have recourse to Freud. "Anxiety arises," he says, "by a kind of fermentation, from a libidinal cathexis [emotional attachment] whose processes have been disturbed."[70] Such disturbance can be provided not only by situations that separate the infant psychologically from its mother but also by threats from a male. After pointing out that anxiety is an expression of the helplessness of the infant, "as though in its still very undeveloped state it did not know how better to cope with its . . . longing," Freud concludes that

anxiety appears as a reaction to the felt loss of the object; and we are at once reminded of the fact that castration anxiety, too, is a fear of being separated from a highly valued object, and that the earliest anxiety of all—the "primal anxiety" of birth—is brought about on the occasion of a separation from the mother.[71]

To continue with psychoanalytic theory, therefore, it seems that Coleridge developed an extreme anxiety from his relation to his brothers, and that this, as another form of the infantile sense of object loss, operated in conjunction with the more basic anxiety connected with his mother.[72] On his very deathbed, as Henry Crabb Robinson noted in his diary, Coleridge expressed "his sense of the unkindness with which he had been treated by his brothers."[73] Nor had he ever felt himself "their Brother in any sense that gives to that title aught that is good or dear."[74] "The shipmates," says the gloss to Coleridge's great poem, "would fain throw the whole guilt on the ancient Mariner."[75] It is surely not without psychological significance that he declined to visit his mother during her last days on the curious stipulation that a brother had not provided him money to do so.

Of Coleridge's numerous brothers, Francis seems to have been

---

[70] *Ibid.*, p. 123. [71] *Ibid.*, p. 137.

[72] In a neurotic, the replacement of one phase of anxiety by another need not take place. As Freud puts it, "each period of the individual's life has its appropriate determinant of anxiety. . . . Nevertheless, all these . . . determinants of anxiety can persist side by side and cause the ego to react to them with anxiety at a period later than the appropriate one; or, again, several of them can come into operation at the same time" (xx, 142). Cf. xxii, 88.

[73] *Robinson*, i, 446.

[74] *Collected Letters*, ii, 757 (to Poole, 7 Sept. 1801). Again: "I have three Brothers/ that is to say, Relations by Gore . . . but alas! we have neither Tastes or Feelings in common" (*Collected Letters*, i, 528. To Poole, 16 Sept. 1799).

[75] Coleridge, *Poems*, i, 191 (gloss of 1815-16).

the most harmful to his development. He recalls to Poole that "Frank hated me" and that "Frank had a violent love of beating me." The relationship was not exclusively violent. Whenever Frank's love of "beating me" was "superseded by any humour or circumstance, he was always fond of me—& used to regard me with a strange mixture of admiration & contempt."[76] Such ambivalent behavior might well induce psychological damage, with the affection binding the younger brother, as it were, to the hammer blows of hatred. And he records an almost classically Oedipal memory of a double assault by Francis, together with the guilt it aroused:

> I had asked my mother one evening to cut my cheese *entire*, so that I might toast it: this was no easy matter, it being a *crumbly* cheese—My mother however did it—/ I went into the garden for some thing or other, and in the mean time my Brother Frank *minced* my cheese. . . . I returned, saw the exploit, and in an agony of passion flew at Frank—he pretended to have been seriously hurt by my blow, flung himself on the ground, and there lay with outstretched limbs—I hung over him moaning & in great fright—he leaped up, & with a horse-laugh gave me a severe blow in the face—I seized a knife, and was running at him, when my Mother came in & took me by the arm—/ I expected a flogging—& struggling from her I ran away, to a hill at the bottom of which the Otter flows—about one mile from Ottery.[77]

In such a nightmare of mincing, knife play, seeming death, guilt, and retribution, we are made directly aware of how psychologically harrowing Coleridge's childhood situation in fact was.[78] "I

[76] *Collected Letters*, I, 347-48 (to Poole, Oct. 1797).

[77] *Ibid.*, pp. 352-53.

[78] Douglas Angus points out that a fraternally Oedipal situation is also the burden of *Osorio*: "If one doubts the highly autobiographical nature of Coleridge's writing during this period, he should read this play carefully. It is concerned with the rivalry of Osorio with an older brother, Albert, for the love of a woman named Maria. . . . It is, in short, his old rivalry with Francis that reappears in the play. Osorio plots to murder his brother so that he can have Maria, but instead he murders another character, Ferdinand. This murder is completely irrational from beginning to end. It is without motivation" ("The Theme of Love and Guilt in Coleridge's Three Major Poems," *Journal of English and Germanic Philology*, 59 [1960], 658). The connection of this play with the cheese-mincing episode seems still more clear in another commentator's description: "Once again a crime has been committed: the attempted murder of a man by his younger brother, Osorio. The attempt fails, although Osorio thinks it has succeeded, and the intended victim returns in disguise to punish Osorio" (Charles J. Smith, "Wordsworth and Coleridge: The Growth of a

was hardly used from infancy to Boyhood," he writes to Sir George Beaumont in 1804, "& from Boyhood to Youth most, MOST cruelly."[79] As in the episode with Francis he tried to solve the problem by removing himself, so, in a certain sense, did the double anxiety always remove him from himself, evacuate, as it were, his inner feeling of self. He felt "self-deserted and bereft," that he was "a crumbling wall, undermined at the foundation," that there was "*pith within* the Trunk, not heart of Wood."[80] The anxiety made him feel worthless and isolated. "From my Youth upward," he wrote near the end of his life, "the most unpleasant if not the most worthless Object of direct Thought has ever been my individual Self." He speaks elsewhere of his "sense of my own small Worth & of others' superiority."[81] "Mine is a sensibility gangrened with inward corruption," he writes self-loathingly in February 1794.[82] "I feel, with an intensity unfathomable by words, my utter nothingness, impotence, & worthlessness, in and for myself—."[83] Still again: "My past life seems to me like a dream, a feverish dream! all one gloomy huddle of strange actions, and dim-discovered motives! Friendships lost by indolence, and happiness murdered by mismanaged sensibility!"[84] In a notebook entry of August 1805, the sense of isolation is poignantly connected with the fact that "by poor Frank's dislike of me when a little Child I was even from Infancy forced to be by myself."[85]

As a counter to his sense of being "self-deserted and bereft," Coleridge developed a clinging reliance on his friends. "I cannot be happy," he writes in a continuation of the note just quoted, "but while awakening, enjoying, and giving *sympathy* to one or a few eminently loved Beings"; otherwise, he says, "I *feel* my Hollowness." "To be beloved is all I need," he says at the conclusion of his recountal of night-horrors in "The Pains of Sleep," "and whom I love, I love indeed."

Theme," *Studies in Philology*, 54 [1957], 56-57). Doubtless Francis's early death, by intensifying Coleridge's sense of guilt, made the fraternal relationship even more neurotically damaging. In this respect, of course, it is significant that the title of *Osorio* was eventually changed to *Remorse*.

[79] *Collected Letters*, II, 1053.

[80] *Ibid.*, 1054 (1 Feb. 1804); 929, 959 (to Southey, 1803).

[81] *Ibid.*, VI, 984 (to Eliza Nixon, 7 June 1834); *Notebooks*, II, 2998.

[82] *Collected Letters*, I, 62 (to G. L. Tuckett, 6 Feb. 1794).

[83] *Ibid.*, III, 498 (to J. Cottle, 27 May 1814).

[84] *Ibid.*, I, 184 (to Wade, 10 Feb. 1796).

[85] *Notebooks*, II, 2647.

In his reliance on his friends, Coleridge seems often to have sought not merely a single but a double dependency, that is, he seems to have attempted to replace the threatening brother and cold mother with an accepting brother and warm mother. His early enthusiasm for Southey is marked by such an emphasis: "Remember me to your Mother—to our Mother—am I not affiliated? I will write her when I arrive at Cambridge."[86] He was equally enthusiastic for his bachelor friend Thomas Poole and Poole's mother. ("My filial love to your dear Mother|& believe me, my best dear friend!| ever, ever most affectionately your's"; "In this hurly burly of unlucky Things, I cannot describe to you how pure & deep Joy I have experienced from thinking of your dear Mother!")[87] The friendship with Wordsworth seems to have been enhanced by Dorothy's motherlike concern that came with it. "Wordsworth & his exquisite Sister are with me," he writes in July 1797: "She is a woman indeed!"[88] Even his strange willingness to be led by Southey into a disastrous marriage perhaps derives from the unconscious expectation that Sarah Fricker would form with Southey a combination of mother and brother. Certainly Southey's agency seems crucial in the venture.

After the estrangement from Wordsworth, Coleridge managed to find still other combinations. The most lasting was the one with the Gillmans. Here the longed for mother was transformed into something like a daughter or younger sister, and the accepting older brother into a less potentially threatening son and younger brother; and Coleridge often and fervently recorded his gratitude to both James and Anne Gillman. They were people "to whom under Heaven I owe my Life and more than words can express!"[89] In short as De Quincey says,

> in one respect at least he was eminently favoured by Providence: beyond all men who ever perhaps have lived, he found means to engage a constant succession of most faithful friends; and he levied the services of sisters, brothers, daughters, sons, from the hands of strangers. . . . Fast as one friend dropped off, another,

[86] *Collected Letters*, i, 99 (to Southey, 1 Sept. 1794).

[87] *Ibid.*, p. 381 (27 Jan. 1798); p. 480 (6 April 1799); and cf. i, 529 (16 Sept.) and, still more emphatically, ii, 758 (19 Sept. 1801): "She was the only Being whom I ever *felt* in the relation of Mother."

[88] *Collected Letters*, i, 330 (to Cottle).

[89] *Ibid.*, vi, 580 (to Cattermole, 25 May 1826); and cf. v, 164; vi, 607-608, 804.

and another, succeeded: perpetual relays were laid along his path in life, of judicious and zealous supporters.[90]

Thus Coleridge sought to ameliorate both orders of anxiety by having himself adopted, as it were, by the various mother-brother combinations; for in the relation to his own family he always felt himself, as he angrily wrote his brother George, to be "a deserted Orphan."[91] In all of these relationships he assumed something of the situation of a child, for the neurotic nature of his needs froze him into certain infantile attitudes, as though (and Freud has emphasized the point) in the psychic arena where the problem originated, there must it forever be ministered to.[92] Ensconced benignly on the top floor of the hard-working Gillman's house in Highgate, Coleridge seems to us, by his obliviousness to many aspects of adult responsibility, to be something like a pink, friendly infant of enormous mental powers. Indeed, a constant feature of his rejection of adulthood was his lifelong refusal to work sensibly for money; and one of the necessary signs of love that he awaited seems to have been that, like a child, he be given money by someone. He was perpetually poor as a boy (he speaks of his "want of money all the first two or three and 20 years of my Life"),[93] and his infrequent monetary gifts were presumably invested with great emotional significance against the penurious background of Ottery St. Mary and Christ's Hospital. "I am remarkably fond of Beans &

[90] *De Quincey*, II, 210-11.

[91] *Collected Letters*, III, 103 (11 May 1808). Cf. p. 31: "releasing my conscience wholly from all connection with a family, to whom I am indebted only for misery."

[92] For example, "It seems quite normal that at four years of age a girl should weep painfully if her doll is broken; or at six, if her governess reproves her; or at sixteen, if she is slighted by her young man; or at twenty-five, perhaps, if a child of her own dies. Each of these determinants of pain has its own time and each passes away when that time is over. . . . We should think it strange if this same girl, after she had grown to be a wife and mother, were to cry over some worthless trinket that had been damaged. Yet that is how the neurotic behaves. . . . [He] behaves as though the old danger-situations still existed, and keeps hold of all the earlier determinants of anxiety" (xx, 147). Again, after pointing out that "a great many people remain infantile in their behaviour in regard to danger and do not overcome determinants of anxiety which have grown out of date," and that it is "precisely such people whom we call neurotics," Freud speaks of "the element of persistence in these reactions" and notes that "the affect of anxiety alone" seems to enjoy the "advantage over all other affects of evoking reactions which are distinguished from the rest . . . and which, through their inexpediency, run counter to the movement of life" (p. 148). Cf. xvi, 365.

[93] *Notebooks*, II, 2647.

Bacon—and this fondness I attribute to my father's having given me a penny for having eat a large quantity of beans, one Saturday."[94] We hark back again to the unusual explanation that he could not visit his dying mother because the brother would not give him money; and he reacted almost hysterically to Poole's reasonable refusal to lend him fifty pounds that Wordsworth had begged in his behalf.[95] The gifts from the Wedgwoods, De Quincey, and Byron, or the Wordsworths' dividing of their money with him on the Scottish tour, in this respect all assume symbolic significance.[96]

The attempt to find a forgiving brother was particularly important to his unconscious need to reinstate his sense of self. "My anxieties eat me up," he laments to Poole, "I want consolation, my friend! my Brother!" "Dear Friend—and Brother of my Soul—," he writes to Gillman in October 1822, "God only knows! how truly and in the depth you are loved & prized by your affectionate/ Friend S. T. Coleridge."[97] The ardor that marks these declarations recurs repeatedly throughout his career; although when directed to an older friend such statements frequently take on overtones of masochism. Poole, for instance, who had himself been hailed as "the man in whom *first* and in whom alone, I had felt an *anchor*," somewhat jealously but also accurately accused Coleridge of "prostration" with regard to Wordsworth.[98] How much anxiety was suspended in such relationships can be gauged from a dream Coleridge records about his friend, Thomas Middleton, who had been the object of his hero worship both at Christ's Hospital and at Cambridge:

> Wonderful blending of Ideas in Dreams. . . . Middleton, who was my superior, my friend and Patron at School, my friend for the first year at College, who never quarrelled with me, but was quietly alienated, was there and received me kindly . . . he went

[94] *Collected Letters*, I, 347 (to Poole, Oct. 1797).

[95] *Early Years*, pp. 338-40; *Collected Letters*, II, 756, 1124; III, 210.

[96] In this same line, it is interesting to note that Coleridge's almost passionate friendship with Thomas Allsop entailed Allsop's "sending Coleridge a present of £100 in admiration of his genius" (*Robinson*, I, 315).

[97] *Collected Letters*, I, 257 (15 Nov. 1796); v, 255.

[98] *Ibid.*, I, 491 (6 May 1799); 584 (31 Mar. 1800). As late as 1815 Coleridge, in writing to Wordsworth, termed him "an absent friend, to whom for the more substantial Third of a Life we have been habituated to look up . . . our Love, tho' increased by many and different influences, yet begun and throve and knit it's Joints in the perception of his Superiority" (IV, 571).

away—& I lay down at the bottom of the Desk. . . . Then Middleton returned & reproved me severely for taking Liberties on the slightest encouragement, & sitting thus by *his Fire!* Till that moment it had been the bottom of a Desk, & no *Fire!* but now there was a little obscure Fire-place . . . & I awoke—[99]

Middleton was only one of a number of older men who filled the role of accepting brother for Coleridge. His rather priggish brother, George, was also cast into that role:

My Brother George is a man of reflective mind & elegant Genius. He possesses Learning in a greater degree than any of the Family, excepting myself. His manners are grave, & hued over with a tender sadness. In his moral character he approaches every way nearer to Perfection than any man I ever yet knew—indeed, he is worth the whole family in a Lump.[100]

This was written in 1797. Earlier, in May 1794, he had written to George himself and closed with these ardent words: "God bless you—my Brother—my Father!"[101] Inevitably, however, there came an estrangement, the nature of which is implicit in this statement of October 1794: "I have heard from my Brothers—from him particularly, who has been Friend, Brother, Father—'Twas all remonstrance, and Anguish, & suggestions, that I am deranged!!—"[102]

The role occupied and relinquished successively by George Coleridge, by Middleton, by Southey and by Poole was filled longer and more deeply by Wordsworth. Indeed, in the relation to Wordsworth we not only glimpse the depth of Coleridge's need to reclaim his evacuated sense of self by dependence on another but see also the dim outlines of his compulsion to plagiarize. As he wrote in a note of 1806, "absorption and transfiguration of Consciousness" were what he groaned for. In a note of 1805 he utters the clinging wish with reference to Wordsworth "that my Spirit purged by Death of its Weaknesses, which are alas! my *identity* might flow into *thine,* & live and act in thee, & be Thou."[103] In this poignant statement, Coleridge's masochistic submersion of his own self in his friend's strength becomes strikingly apparent.

[99] *Notebooks,* ii, 2539.
[100] *Collected Letters,* i, 311.
[101] *Ibid.,* p. 80.
[102] *Ibid.,* p. 118. The immediate cause of the estrangement was George's informing Coleridge, in 1807, that because of the latter's impending separation from Sarah Coleridge, he would not "receive" him (see *Collected Letters,* iii, 102-105).
[103] *Notebooks,* ii, 2860, 2712.

The tendency to self-denigration is hardly less evident in a de-pressed statement of September 1807: "W[ordsworth] is greater, better, manlier, more dear, by nature, to Woman, than I—I—miserable I!"[104] Masochism, however, is not an unalloyed mis-ery to the masochist, and Coleridge accordingly can say that "My instincts are so far dog-like/ I love beings superior to me better than my Equals." Again: "at times I derive a comfort even from my in-firmities, my sins of omission & commission, in the joy of the deep feeling of the opposite Virtues in the two or three whom I love in my Heart of Hearts."[105]

Of those two or three, Wordsworth was first. "Wordsworth is a very great man," writes Coleridge to Southey in July 1797, "—the only man, to whom *at all times* & in *all modes of excellence* I feel my-self inferior." In March 1798, he speaks to Cottle of "The Giant Wordsworth—God love him!—even when I speak in the terms of admiration due to his intellect, I fear lest tho[se] terms should keep out of sight the amiableness of his manners."[106] The relationship, even with all its indications of neurotic dependency on the part of the younger man, was one of the deepest realities of Coleridge's entire life. As late as 1822, a dozen years after the painful but no doubt inevitable breach between the two friends (in 1807 Coleridge had already spoken of being prevented from *"entire* Love" of the Wordsworths),[107] he wrote to Allsop that "in the course of my past Life I count four griping and grasping Sorrows, each of which seemed to have my very heart in it's hands, compressing or wring-ing," and one of these was the estrangement from Wordsworth, "when all the Superstructure raised by my idolatrous Fancy during an enthusiastic & self-sacrificing Friendship of 15 years . . . burst like a Bubble—but the Grief did not vanish with it, nor the Love which was the Stuff & Vitality of the Grief."[108]

It was, I believe, this need to allay the castration anxiety in his own ego by identification with the strength of an accepting brother that provided much of the basis for Coleridge's compulsion to plagiarize. Indeed, his need to merge himself with other men's modes is witnessed by his very first published reference to Wordsworth. In "Lines written at Shurton Bars . . . ," he writes, in 1795, as follows:

---

[104] *Ibid.,* 3148.   [105] *Ibid.,* 2726.

[106] *Collected Letters,* I, 334, 391. In June 1797, Coleridge had written to Estlin that "Wordsworth is a great man" (I, 327).

[107] *Notebooks,* II, 3146.   [108] *Collected Letters,* V, 249-50.

> Nor now with curious sight
> I mark the glow-worm, as I pass,
> Move with 'green radiance' through the grass,

and in a footnote he says:

> The expression 'green radiance' is borrowed from Mr. Words-
> worth . . . whom I deem unrivalled among the writers of the
> present day.[109]

The phrase "green radiance"—as was noted in the previous
chapter—is unmistakably a kind of fetish, an entity that Coleridge
clasps to himself. Of similar psychic import was his later publica-
tion of some of Wordsworth's juvenilia in *The Morning Post*, or the
reworking of a youthful Wordsworthian poem into his own poem
"Lewti."[110] The function of these Wordsworthian borrowings
prefigures that of the unacknowledged quotations, or "plagia-
risms," that exist as mosaic fragments throughout his work. All
testify not to intellectual poverty but to the need to relieve his
over-powering anxiety: to rejoin the brothers, as it were, and at the
same time to reclaim the "essential something" that he always felt
to be wanting in himself.[111]

---

[109] Coleridge, *Poems*, I, 97 and n. See above, Chapter One, note 22.

[110] See above, pp. 62-63.

[111] Cf. De Quincey: "Had, then Coleridge any need to borrow from Schelling?
Did he borrow *in forma pauperis*? Not at all: there lay the wonder. He spun daily, and
at all hours, for mere amusement of his own activities, and from the loom of his
own magical brain, theories more gorgeous by far, and supported by a pomp and
luxury of images such as neither Schelling—no, nor any German that ever
breathed, not John Paul—could have emulated in his dreams. With the riches of El
Dorado lying about him, he would condescend to filch a handful of gold from any
man whose purse he fancied . . . applying . . . to intellectual wealth, that maniacal
propensity which is sometimes well known to attack enormous proprietors and mil-
lionaires for acts of petty larceny" (*De Quincey*, II, 146-47).
If we accept De Quincey's shrewd surmise that Coleridge's compulsive plagia-
risms were in fact a variant form of kleptomania, then, in this context, psycho-
analytical theory connects to both his mother and his brothers his haunted feeling
that he was missing an "essential something." In view of the importance of the mat-
ter for our ultimate understanding of Coleridge's struggle, we must force ourselves
to confront precise significances—no matter how strongly they are resisted by the
psychoanalytically uninformed. Accordingly, we must entertain the possibility,
with regard to Coleridge's damaged relationship with his mother, that the "essen-
tial something" represents what he memorably terms the once imbibed but now lost
"milk of paradise." Cf. Fenichel: "If it is true that the cleptomaniac is striving for a
lost sexual satisfaction which has been protection, forgiveness, and regulator of
self-esteem simultaneously, the property stolen must of necessity symbolically rep-

Coleridge's plagiarisms are not the only testimony to the compulsion to reclaim his identity by merging himself with the brothers. We see it also in his lifelong fondness for joining marginalia to the books he read, a form of composition that, in terms of the number and of the variety of books so adorned, and of the worth of the notations themselves, has no real counterpart in either English or continental literature. The compulsion appears in still another of its protean manifestations in his *Aids to Reflection*. There, late in life, he seems to attempt to give up his indulgence in outright plagiarism, but substitutes instead a technique by which his own thoughts blossom around the work of another man, Archbishop Leighton. As he says in 1824,

> a little volume will soon appear under the title *Aids to Reflection*, which was at first intended only for a Selection of Passages from Leighton's Works but in the course of printing has become an original work almost.[112]

Again, he found that he increasingly preferred to compose only when dictating to an amanuensis, especially a benign brother-figure such as Gillman or Joseph Henry Green.[113]

All such phenomena are symptomatic of Coleridge's attempt to restore the self that had been evacuated by his anxieties. As he said of himself, the "first lesson, that innocent Childhood affords me, is—that it is an instinct of my Nature to pass out of myself, and to exist in the form of others." "My nature," he says again, "requires another Nature for its support, & reposes only in another from the necessary Indigence of its Being." Still again, he intended to write a biography of Lessing "because it would give me an opportunity

---

resent milk." (Fenichel, p. 370.) With regard to his damaged relationship with his brothers, we should be aware of the theoretical insistence, no matter what our reluctance to accept it may be, that "In the cleptomanic strivings of patients who are not very deeply disturbed, the significance of 'penis' will be the foreground" (*ibid.*). In this context of the formal theory of impulse neurosis, Coleridge's drug addiction would be related as an attempt "to satisfy the archaic oral longing which is sexual longing, a need for security, and a need for the maintenance of self-esteem simultaneously. Thus the origin and nature of the addiction are not determined by the chemical effect of the drug but by the psychological structure of the patient" (*ibid.*, p. 376). See Molly Lefebure, Samuel Taylor Coleridge (Gollancz, 1974).

[112] *Collected Letters*, v, 336.

[113] Referring in 1825 to his "friendly Amanuensis," he says that "the slowness, with which I get on with the pen in my own hand, contrasts most strangely with the rapidity with which I dictate" (*Collected Letters*, v, 423).

of conveying under a better name, than my own ever will be, opinions, which I deem of the highes[t] importance."[114]

If much of what Coleridge did in his literary career attests the pervasive demands of his anxiety, much that he did not do testifies as well. His procrastination and inability to work seem to be complications arising from his traumatically threatening anxiety situations.[115] "I deeply regret," he writes in 1797, "that my anxieties and my slothfulness, acting in a combined ratio, prevented me from finishing my 'Progress of Liberty. . . .' "[116] They prevented him from finishing, or even doing, many other things. "I became a proverb to the University for Idleness," he writes of his later Cambridge days, "—the time, which I should have bestowed on the academic studies, I employed in dreaming out wild Schemes."[117] The inhibition of his ability to work continued throughout his career. "He will tell me," writes Dorothy Wordsworth in 1810, "that he has been writing, that he *has* written half a Friend; when I *know* that he has not written a single line."[118]

The unfinished state of the legendary *magnum opus* is the most notorious monument to his procrastination, but it is not psychologically the most revealing; it is rather in Coleridge's minor procrasti-

---

[114] *Inquiring Spirit*, p. 68; *Notebooks*, I, 1679; *Collected Letters*, I, 519 (to Wedgwood, 21 May 1799).

[115] For instance, he says at one point that "an indefinite indescribable Terror . . . drove me. . . . The worst was, that in *exact proportion* to the *importance* and *urgency* of any Duty was it, as of a fatal necessity, sure to be neglected" (*Collected Letters*, III, 489 [to J. J. Morgan, 14 May 1814]). Cf. Freud's statement, with regard to "symptom-formation in obsessional neurosis," that symptoms "which once stood for a restriction of the ego come later on to represent satisfactions as well," and that the "result of this process . . . is an extremely restricted ego which is reduced to seeking satisfaction in the symptoms. The displacement of the distribution of forces in favour of satisfaction may have the dreaded final outcome of paralysing the will of the ego" (xx, 118). Thus Coleridge in 1808: "I have been for years almost a paralytic in mind" (*Collected Letters*, III, 131). Cf. Southey's surmise (p. 104 above) that Coleridge was laboring under "a disease of the volition," and Hazlitt: "He was a man without a will" (*Robinson*, I, 11). At one point Coleridge wished for "a few hundred Pounds, but 200£, half to send to Mrs Coleridge, & half to place myself in a private madhouse . . . —O God! how willingly would I place myself under Dr Fox in his Establishment—for my Case is a species of madness, only that it is a derangement, an utter impotence of the *Volition*, & not of the intellectual Faculties—You bid me rouse myself—go, bid a man paralytic in both arms rub them briskly together, & that will cure him. Alas! (he would reply) that I cannot move my arms is my Complaint & my misery—" (*Collected Letters*, III, 477). See further *Freud*, x, 241.

[116] *Collected Letters*, I, 329 (to Cottle, June 1797).

[117] *Ibid*., p. 67 (to George Coleridge, Feb. 1794).

[118] *Middle Years*, I, 399.

nations, his inability, for instance, not only to answer letters but even to open them in the first place, that the roots of the inhibition in anxiety become most apparent. "As to letters," recallls De Quincey, "unless the address were in some female hand that commanded his affectionate esteem, he tossed them all into one general *dead-letter bureau*, and rarely, I believe, opened them at all."[119] Coleridge muses on this deficiency in 1803:

> received a Letter which I knew would contain interesting matter—not quite certain whether it would be affectionate or reproachful, mournful or happy—this I have kept in my pocket sometimes half a day, sometimes a whole day—have opened it at length, just looked at the end . . . —then let it lie on my Desk, or put it up once more in my pocket—& have walked about my garden or Study an hour or more, wasting the activity & flutter of feeling excited by the letter in planning compositions, or have sate & read a book of Kant/ & last of all read my Letter, my spirits tamed—[120]

The trivial nature of his anxiety's object here testifies to the authentic structure of the anxiety itself, for as Freud insists, anxiety "has a quality of *indefiniteness and lack of object*. In precise speech we use the word 'fear' rather than 'anxiety' if it has found an object."[121]

Freud's distinction between anxiety (*Angst*) and fear (*Furcht*), with the former being characterized by the lack of a definite object, is parallel to, although independent of, Heidegger's phenomenological distinction of the same two states. To Heidegger "the object of anxiety is completely indefinite." *Furcht*, to Heidegger, is fear of a definite danger; *Angst*, fear of nothing at all. In Heidegger's conception, *Angst* comes about simply from the fact of our being thrown into the world ("das Wovor der Angst ist das geworfene In-der-Welt-sein"); it arises from the sense of "naked existence cast into psychic homelessness."[122] And the conception corre-

---

[119] *De Quincey*, ɪɪ, 149. Cf. Coleridge's own anguished confession, in 1808, that on occasion he "left every letter received lie unopened for weeks together, all the while thoroughly ashamed of the weakness and yet without power to get rid of it" (*Collected Letters*, ɪɪɪ, 148). At another time he speaks of his "accursed Letterophobia" (ɪᴠ, 584). In 1807 he writes Josiah Wedgwood that he has "sunk under such a strange cowardice of Pain, that I have not unfrequently kept Letters from persons dear to me for weeks together unopened" (ɪɪɪ, 19).

[120] *Notebooks*, ɪ, 1517.

[121] *Freud*, xx, 165. Cf. xvɪ, 395.

[122] Heidegger, *Sein und Zeit*, pp. 186, 185, 186-87, 191, 343.

sponds closely to Freud's description of anxiety's origin as the birth trauma of separation from the mother.

It is useful to cross this bridge between the psychoanalytical and the existential conceptions of anxiety, and to view Coleridge's drowning struggles from the existential shore. It is possible to do so because both conceptions of anxiety, despite their difference in focus, are attempts to analyze a psychic phenomenon that arises in experience; neither conception is merely the verbal construct of psychologist or philosopher. As Sartre says in his own discussion of *angoisse*:

> Kierkegaard, in describing anxiety in the face of what one lacks, characterizes it as anxiety in the face of freedom. But Heidegger, whom we know to have been greatly influenced by Kierkegaard, considers anxiety instead as the apprehension of nothingness. These two descriptions of anxiety do not appear to us contradictory; on the contrary the one implies the other.[123]

The various descriptions of *Angst*, therefore, whether by Freud, by Heidegger, or by Kierkegaard, are complementary rather than mutually exclusive, and all provide perspectives on the sea of anxiety in which Coleridge was engulfed.

A second reason for crossing over to the standpoint of existential anxiety is that the Freudian analysis of the condition tends to make Coleridge seem, as it were, a special case, a patient. Existential analysis of anxiety, on the other hand, emphasizes its human unavoidability. As Kierkegaard says, "if a man were a beast or an angel, he would not be able to be in the state of anxiety. Since he is a synthesis he can be in such a state, and the greater the anxiety, the greater the man."[124] To transfer such a contention to a Freudian matrix, one could point out that it was precisely Coleridge's unusual mental receptivity that made him so vulnerable to the unfavorable childhood influences that surrounded him. His neurosis is, as it were, the index of his intellectual power.

Kierkegaard further relates to Coleridge's situation by connecting anxiety with that original sin so often avowed by the English poet. "I believe most stedfastly [writes Coleridge] in original Sin; that from our mothers' wombs our understandings are darkened; and even where our understandings are in the Light, that our organization is depraved, & our volitions imperfect; and we some-

[123] Sartre, *L'Être et le néant*, p. 66.
[124] Kierkegaard, p. 139. With the translator's "dread" rendered by me throughout as "anxiety."

times see the good without *wishing* to attain it, and oftener *wish* it
without the energy that wills & performs."[125] Such a conviction is
entirely consonant with the emphasis of Kierkegaard, whose pri-
mary definition of anxiety is "the presupposition of original sin."
"The consequence of original sin," Kierkegaard says again,
". . . is anxiety."[126] But original sin is the affliction of the race, not
merely the problem of the individual, and for both Coleridge and
Kierkegaard the conception socializes the woes of existence.

In these terms, Coleridge's anxiety, or dread, not only brings
him into the communal fold but actually becomes a special mark of
spirit; for as Kierkegaard insists, "the less spirit, the less anxi-
ety."[127] To accept this is to reverse the tendency of a long tradition,
current no less in our own day than in an earlier one, that ap-
proaches Coleridge with an attitude of moralistic finger-pointing
and pious head-shaking. This tradition, I think, is mistaken. As
Dr. Johnson says of Savage:

> For his Life, or for his Writings, none who candidly consider his
> Fortune, will think an Apology either necessary or difficult . . .
> nor will a wise Man easily presume to say, 'Had I been in
> *Savage*'s Condition, I should have lived, or written, better than
> *Savage*.'[128]

So too for Coleridge. But I should go still further, and urge the
validity of Kierkegaard's formula: "the greater the anxiety, the
greater the man."[129] Despite Coleridge's own frequent laments for
his weakness, in a larger reference I do not find that term properly
descriptive. Certainly the conception is a relative one. If we see
legs buckle under a burden, we might ascribe the effect to weak-
ness; but if the legs belong to Atlas, the ascription makes little
sense. Coleridge, I have always felt, is in a special way a hero of
existence: though life bore him down, he fought from his knees.[130]
He did not take refuge in suicide, which was the solution of Kleist,
of Chatterton, of Nerval; he did not become mentally unbalanced,
as did Hölderlin, Cowper, Ruskin; he did not become misan-
thropic, as did Swift, or Schopenhauer, of whom Nietzsche said
that "he raged for the sake of raging."[131]

---

[125] *Collected Letters*, I, 396 (to George Coleridge, Mar. 1798).

[126] Kierkegaard, pp. 41, 47.   [127] *Ibid.*, p. 38.

[128] *Life of Savage*, ed. Clarence Tracy (Oxford: The Clarendon Press, 1971), pp.
139-40.

[129] Kierkegaard, p. 139.   [130] Cf. Seneca, *De Providentia*, II, 6-7.

[131] *Nietzsche*, II, 848.

On the contrary, he preserved his life, his reason, and his humanity. Querulous and often feline he could be, but he was not twisted or distortedly bitter. As Leslie Stephen noticed, "at his worst Coleridge was both loved and eminently lovable. . . . He was always full of kindly feelings, never soured into cynicism."[132] Wordsworth, even after his estrangement from Coleridge, spoke, as Henry Crabb Robinson records, of his "goodness of heart."[133] And after Coleridge's death, Lamb, who knew the worst about his friend, said that "his great and dear spirit haunts me."[134]

Coleridge's spirit manifested itself in other ways as well. He warred constantly against the neurotic symptoms that, in binding his anxiety, deprived his life of happiness. Thus De Quincey, no ordinary observer of the drug habit, notes that "Coleridge did make prodigious efforts to deliver himself from this thraldom."[135] So, too, he struggled against the crippling inhibition of his ability to work. During the very months of the deterioration that Dorothy Wordsworth noted so vividly, he managed, despite his diseased volition, a certain productivity. Thus the Wordsworths record on 12 September 1809 that "Coleridge has been very busy lately"; on 18 November that "Coleridge goes on with his work briskly"; on 28 December that "Coleridge has been very well of late, and very busy."[136] But in a letter to Lady Beaumont, in February 1810, Dorothy revealed the internal struggle with diseased volition that such activity entailed:

> By the great quantity of labour that he has performed since the commencement of the Friend [she writes] you will judge that he has upon the whole been very industrious; and you will hardly believe me when I tell you that there have been weeks and weeks when he has not composed a line. The fact is that he either does a great deal or nothing at all; and that he composes with a rapidity truly astonishing, if one did not reflect upon the large stores of thought which he has laid up, and the quantity of knowledge which he is continually gaining from books—add to this his habit of expressing his ideas in conversation in elegant language. He has written a whole Friend more than once in two days.[137]

It is in the way Coleridge met his death, however, that the element of heroism in his life becomes most apparent. For death, of all

---

[132] Stephen, III, 329.
[134] Lamb, Works, I, 351.
[136] Middle Years, I, 371, 375, 380.
[133] Robinson, I, 80.
[135] De Quincey, II, 211.
[137] Ibid., pp. 390-91.

human possibilities, is the one most fraught with anxiety. As Shakespeare's Richard II says, "The worst is death, and death will have his day." For Heidegger, it is death that awakens man to his own authenticity, but this opening up of existence is achieved only through anxiety: "Das Sein zum Tode," he says, "ist wesenhaft Angst"—being toward death is in its nature anxiety. As the nothingness that is the final object of all anxiety, as the anxiety in which existence confronts the possible impossibility of itself ("In ihr befindet sich das Dasein *vor* dem Nichts des möglichen Unmöglichkeit seiner Existenz"),[138] death is the most genuine terror. It should, one thinks, have paralyzed Coleridge, had he been truly weak. But throughout his life he not only said that he did not fear death,[139] he actually proved as much when the moment of agony arrived. "My father," recalls his daughter,

> since he first felt his end approaching had expressed a desire that he might be as little disturbed as possible . . . he then said that he wished to evince in the manner of his death the depth & sincerity of his faith in Christ . . . he then fell asleep—from sleep into a state of coma, Torpor, as I understood it, and ceased to breathe at half past six in the morning of Friday. . . . In the middle of the day on Thursday, he had repeated to Mr Green his formula of the Trinity. His utterance was difficult—but his mind in perfect vigour & clearness—he remarked that his intellect was quite unclouded & he said "I could even be witty."[140]

As his nephew, Henry Nelson Coleridge, remarked: "He shrank from mere uneasiness like a child, and bore the preparatory agonies of his death-attack like a martyr."[141] It was as though the Nightmare Life-in-Death had indeed pre-empted the claims of death itself.

If Coleridge's ruined existence thus contains elements of heroism, so too does his fragmentary work function culturally with no less power than work of more conventionally praised structure. Both effects are possible because "every life," as Ortega y Gasset has insisted, "is, more or less, a ruin among whose debris we have

[138] Heidegger, *Sein und Zeit*, p. 266.

[139] E.g. in 1801: "though I wish to live, yet the Thought of Death is never for a moment accompanied by Gloom, much less terror, in my feelings or imagination" (*Collected Letters*, II, 719).

[140] *Ibid.*, VI, 991-92.

[141] "H. N. Coleridge's Preface," *Table Talk*, p. 13.

to discover what the person ought to have been."[142] Accordingly, when Dr. Leavis judges that "Coleridge's prestige is very understandable, but his currency as an academic classic is something of a scandal," and that "he was very much more brilliantly gifted than Arnold, but nothing of his deserves the classical status of Arnold's best work,"[143] what seems to be called in question is not so much Coleridge's achievement as the relevance of this conception of the academic classic.

There are actually only incomplete human lives and the gestures that occur within them. Where does the evidence arise, except in such an arena, that could make a "prestige very understandable," or that could justify the conviction that Coleridge was "very much more brilliantly gifted than Arnold"? Coleridge's ruin, in both life and work, is, I suggest, the true human fact; the academic classic and the conventional achievement the illusion. Such ruin is testimony to what Karl Jaspers, the greatest philosopher of our century—or at least the one nearest my heart—has elucidated as "die Zerrissenheit des Seins": the tatteredness of being. Coleridge's prestige could hardly *be* understandable to us if he stood outside the mainstream of human reality; it *is* understandable, on the contrary, because his tragic existence is an icon for the larger nature of our situation.

For tragedy and human existence are synonymous. Human life is not only nasty, brutish, and short; it is also uncertain in its hopes, vulnerable in its affections, and unsatisfactory in its achievements.[144] The proudest of the world's empires was evacuated of its subjects in response to a simple invitation: "Come unto me all ye

---

[142] "In Search of Goethe from Within," *The Dehumanization of Art and Other Essays on Art, Culture and Literature*, trans. Helene Weyl *et al.* (Princeton, N.J.: Princeton University Press, 1968), pp. 143-44.

[143] "Coleridge in Criticism," *Scrutiny*, 9 (1940), 69.

[144] Compare, for instance, Byron: "we are all heirs to misfortune and disappointments—but *poets* especially seem to be a marked race—who has not heard of the blindness of *Milton*—the wretched life, and still more unhappy death of *Otway*—the long sufferings & unrequited services of *Cowley* and of *Butler*—the struggles against poverty & malice which occupied the life of *Dryden*—the constitutional infirmities which embittered the existence of *Pope*—the lamentable idiocy & madness of *Swift*—the almost unparalleled miseries and unhappy end of *Savage*—the frenzy of *Collins*—the indigence of *Goldsmith*—the morbid melancholy and sullen discontent of *Johnson*—the hypochondrianism of *Gray* and of *Beattie*—the tragical catastrophe of *Chatterton*—the disappointed hopes and premature death of *Burns*—and the sickness, despondency, and madness of *Cowper*?" (Byron, *Letters*, VI, 85).

that labour and are heavy laden, and I will give you rest." From the Biblical Preacher's "vanity of vanities" to the universal "foundering" Jaspers describes, our annals sound warnings of the shipwreck that awaits everyone.[145]

Of those who foundered, and left a record of their foundering,[146] Coleridge occupies an honored role in our cultural memory. His life was tormented by anxiety and his work torn by imperfection. But neurotic anxiety, as Freud contends, is an intensification of the anxiety that all men feel; while to Kierkegaard, anxiety is the mark of the human spirit itself. And the imperfection so evident in Coleridge's work is, from the perspective of the larger truths of existence, nothing less than the final shape of every man's effort.

[145] Jaspers, *Philosophie*, III, 222-36 *et passim*; Jaspers, *Wahrheit*, pp. 299, 956.

[146] As he wrote to Josiah Wade in 1814: "After my death, I earnestly entreat, that a full and unqualified narration of my wretchedness, and of its guilty cause, may be made public" (*Collected Letters*, III, 511).

CHAPTER THREE

The Significant Group: Wordsworth's Fears in Solitude

◇◆◇

In 1818 Keats, in distinguishing the sort of "poetical Character" to which he belonged, contrasted it to "the wordsworthian or egotistical sublime; which is a thing per se and stands alone."[1] The statement seems to define in an important way a certain irreducible attitude in Wordsworth's life and art. Benjamin Haydon, for instance, said that though Wordsworth was a "great Being," he could use his intense feelings only "as referring to himself."[2] Coleridge, indeed, observed as early as 1799 that "Wordsworth appears to me to have hurtfully segregated & isolated his Being/ Doubtless, his delights are more deep and sublime;/ but he has likewise more hours, that prey on his flesh & blood."[3] Elsewhere Coleridge suggested that Wordsworth was "a man of whom it might have been said,—'It is good for him to be alone.' "[4]

The egotism first noted by Coleridge was insisted on more forcefully by Hazlitt than by anyone else. "An intense intellectual egotism swallows up every thing," he observed of Wordsworth's "Excursion." He contrasted "Mr. Wordsworth's arbitrary egotism and pampered self-sufficiency" with Byron's nihilism. Wordsworth's poetry, said Hazlitt, "is not external, but internal; it does not depend upon tradition, or story, or old song; he furnishes it from his own mind, and is his own subject." "He sees nothing but himself and the universe," said Hazlitt again. "The power of his mind preys upon itself. It is as if there were nothing but himself and the universe. He lives in the busy solitude of his own heart; in the deep silence of thought."[5] To Hazlitt, such a characteristic was inseparable from Wordsworth's idiosyncratic greatness as a poet:

---

[1] Keats, *Letters*, I, 387. [2] *Haydon*, I, 451.
[3] *Collected Letters*, I, 491. [4] *Inquiring Spirit*, p. 296.
[5] *Hazlitt*, IV, 113; XIX, 36; V, 156; V, 163; IV, 113.

He is the greatest, that is, the most original poet of the present day, only because he is the greatest egotist. . . . He sits in the centre of his own being, and 'there enjoys bright day.' He does not waste a thought on others.[6]

On the other hand, and by what seems, thus, a radical paradox, Wordsworth presents himself, both in his own life and in his poetic stance, as a deeply social being. "No poet is more emphatically the poet of community," said Bradley. "A great part of his verse . . . is dedicated to the affections of home and neighborhood and country, and to that soul of joy and love which links together all Nature's children."[7] Where Coleridge abandoned his own wife and children (he reproaches himself—justifiably—for "barbarous neglect of my family," for "*unnatural cruelty to my poor children*"),[8] Wordsworth was an exemplary and deeply devoted husband and father. To have separated from his wife would have been as literally unthinkable for him as it was literally inevitable for Coleridge. Again, Coleridge, to whom Wordsworth appeared "to have hurtfully segregated and isolated his Being," conceived in his own greatest poem a nightmare experience of precisely such isolation of being: "Alone, alone, all, all alone,/ Alone on a wide wide sea!/ And never a saint took pity on/ My soul in agony." Segregated and isolated being is in fact the most memorable emphasis of "The Ancient Mariner";

> O Wedding-Guest! this soul hath been
> Alone on a wide wide sea:
> So lonely 'twas, that God himself
> Scarce seeméd there to be.[9]

Wordsworth, conversely, entitled the eighth book of *his* greatest poem "Love of Nature Leading to Love of Mankind," and describes how "man" was

> Ennobled outwardly before mine eyes,
> And thus my heart at first was introduc'd
> To an unconscious love and reverence
> Of human Nature; hence the human form
> To me was like an index of delight,
> Of grace and honour, power and worthiness.[10]

---

[6] *Ibid.*, VIII, 44.
[8] *Collected Letters*, III, 490, 511.
[10] *Prelude*, p. 286 (VIII, 411-16).

[7] Bradley, pp. 143-44.
[9] Coleridge, *Poems*, I, 196, 208.

In another of his greatest poetic moments he speaks memorably of "The still, sad music of humanity," and hails "that best portion of a good man's life,/ His little, nameless, unremembered, acts/ Of kindness and of love."[11]

And yet the "egotistical sublime" was certainly there—in ways, in truth, that had less of the sublime than of the egotistical. "I am sorry," writes Keats, "that Wordsworth has left a bad impression wherever he visited in Town—by his egotism, Vanity and bigotry—yet he is a great Poet if not a Philosopher."[12] Such egotism, vanity, and bigotry are apparent in many aspects of the great poet's life. They appear in especially naked form in Henry Crabb Robinson's account of a dinner attended by Wordsworth and Coleridge in 1817:

> Coleridge spoke of painting in that style of mysticism which is now his habit of feeling. Wordsworth met this by dry, unfeeling contradiction. The manner of Coleridge towards Wordsworth was most respectful, but Wordsworth towards Coleridge was cold and scornful. Coleridge maintained that painting was not an art which could operate on the vulgar, and Wordsworth declared this opinion to be degrading to the art. Coleridge illustrated his assertions by reference to Raphael's Madonnas. Wordsworth could not think that a field for high intellect lay within such a subject as a mother and child, and when Coleridge talked of the divinity of those works, Wordsworth asked whether he thought he should have discerned those beauties if he had [not] known that Raphael was the artist; and when Coleridge said that was an unkind question, Wordsworth made no apology.[13]

Another example of egotism and vanity is provided by Wordsworth's harsh and contemptuous defense of his own achievement:

> By this time, I trust that the judicious Reader, who has now first become acquainted with these poems, is persuaded that a very senseless outcry has been raised against them and their Author. . . . I am not wholly unacquainted with the spirit in which my most active and persevering Adversaries have maintained their hostility; nor with the impudent falsehoods and base artifices to which they have had recourse. . . . But the ignorance of those who have chosen to stand forth as my enemies . . . has unfortu-

[11] Wordsworth, *Poems*, II, 261, 260.   [12] Keats, *Letters*, I, 237.
[13] *Robinson*, I, 214-15.

nately been still more gross than their disingenuousness, and their incompetence more flagrant than their malice. . . . By what fatality the orb of my genius . . . acts upon these men like the moon upon a certain description of patients, it would be irksome to inquire; nor would it consist with the respect which I owe myself to take further notice of opponents whom I internally despise.[14]

In simple fact, contempt and cold disdain were never far from Wordsworth's attitudes toward the world at large, or even toward his friends if he felt himself threatened. As Hazlitt said, "Wordsworth would not forgive a single censure mingled with however great a mass of eulogy"; he was "satisfied with nothing short of indiscriminate eulogy."[15] In this respect, Coleridge's profound criticisms in the *Biographia Literaria*, which did so much to establish Wordsworth's reputation as a great poet, none the less apparently contained enough reservations for Wordsworth characteristically to indicate, in Robinson's words, that "Coleridge's book has given him no pleasure. . . . With the criticism on the poetry too he is not satisfied. The praise is extravagant and the censure inconsiderate."[16]

Again, when Lamb reported that his highly affirmative review of "The Excursion" had been verbally tampered with by an editor, Wordsworth did not so much share his vexation as he simply retreated—or ascended rather—into the egotistical sublime: "As to the Excursion I have ceased to have any interest about it, since I read Lamb's Letter, let this benighted age continue to love its own darkness and to cherish it. I shall continue to write with I trust the light of Heaven upon me."[17]

Another generous recognition of the achievement of "The Excursion," that of Hazlitt, ran afoul Wordsworth's egotistical sublime in quite another way. Mrs. Moorman summarizes the matter:

> During this visit to London Wordsworth made a dangerous enemy. Discourteously and most unwisely, he had let it be known that he did not wish to meet Hazlitt at the houses of their common friends. This was because he was now convinced that Hazlitt's behaviour twelve years before in Keswick had been inexcusably bad. But Hazlitt was an ill man to cross. Not only now in the *Examiner*, but again and again in the ensuing years, in his critical and political writings, he took his revenge on Words-

[14] *Prose*, III, 62n.
[16] *Ibid.*, p. 213.

[15] *Robinson*, I, 213, 179.
[17] *Middle Years*, II, 187.

worth. Haydon, writing to Wordsworth in April 1817, told him candidly what Hazlitt's feelings had been and how Wordsworth could have placated them. 'Had you condescended', he said, 'to visit him when he praised your Excursion just before you came to town his vanity would have been soothed and his virulence softened—he was conscious from what an emergency you had helped to rescue him—he was conscious of his conduct while in your neighbourhood—and then your taking no notice of his praise, added to his acid feelings.' Wordsworth would have lost no dignity and lowered no moral standards had he been more gracious, but he chose to maintain his resentment, and so to make a formidable enemy of the greatest critic of the age.[18]

Mrs. Moorman, whose sympathies for Wordsworth of course run very deep, here speaks with what is for her some heat. But Wordsworth's rigidity and gaucherie in personal relationships—for these were aspects of the egotistical sublime—were always able to arouse indignation even among those most favorably disposed toward him. However badly Hazlitt may have behaved, Keats had certainly not done so; and yet Keats too was the victim of Wordsworth's egotistical clumsiness. Haydon, one of Wordsworth's most devoted admirers, reports an instance with undisguised indignation:

As you alluded to Keats opinion of Wordsworth. If he (Keats) Complained he had a right—because Wordsworth did not behave to Keats when I introduced Keats to him as he ought—

I have a letter of Keats wherein he expresses the most glorious respect & love of Wordsworth. . . . When Wordsworth came to Town, I brought Keats to him. . . . Keats expressed to me . . . the greatest, the purest, the most unalloyed pleasure at the prospect. Wordsworth received him kindly, & after a few minutes,

---

[18] Moorman, II, 280-81. But cf. Haydon: "The misfortune is with him you can never get a genuine principle or an honest thought from Hazlitt. His passions & petty revenges so influence his thoughts and his opinions are entirely guided by them. In early life having offended Wordsworth, when he heard Wordsworth was coming to town, he wrote a fine puffing criticism on the Excursion, in hopes of preparing the way for a reconciliation. Wordsworth's utter contempt for his character induced him to take no notice whatever of this piece of petty finesse. Hazlitt now became amazed, & stung at Wordsworth's neglect, thundered forth those attacks on the whole Lake School, which, on the commonest appearance of any attention on their part, he would have defended their apostasy, & lauded by some paradox their talents" (Haydon, II, 494-95). It seems to me, however, that Haydon seriously underestimates Hazlitt's critical integrity.

Wordsworth asked him what he had been lately doing, *I* said he has just finished an exquisite ode to Pan—and as he had not a copy I begged Keats to repeat it—which he did in his usual half chant, (most touching) walking up & down the room—when he had done I felt really, as if I had heard a young Apollo— Wordsworth drily said

"a Very pretty piece of Paganism—

This was unfeeling, & unworthy of his high Genius to a young Worshipper like Keats—& Keats felt it *deeply* . . . he was wounded—and though he dined with Wordsworth after at my table—he never forgave him.[19]

Wordsworth's egotism here seems still more blatant when we consider that he himself was inordinately sensitive to precisely such charges of paganism and pantheistic sentiment. Thus in 1815 he reacts angrily to a lady's criticisms:

I have alluded to the Ladys errors of opinion—she talks of my being a worshipper of Nature—a passionate expression uttered incautiously in the Poem upon the Wye has led her to this mistake, she reading in cold-heartedness and substituting the letter for the spirit. . . . She condemns me for not distinguishing between nature as the work of God and God himself. But where does she find this doctrine inculcated? Where does she gather that the Author of the Excursion looks upon nature and God as the same?[20]

In such a context, Wordsworth's comment to Keats constitutes a painful example of how he could use his feelings only "as referring to himself."

But it was Coleridge, of course, who suffered most bitterly from Wordsworth's egotistical ineptitude in personal relationships. To those astonishing comments of Wordsworth on "The Ancient Mariner" noted in our first chapter (see above, page 101) a single, and no less astonishing, further example may be added. Writing to Coleridge in 1815 about Coleridge's poem "To Wordsworth," which is surely one of the most satisfying tributes ever offered by one poet to the achievement of another, Wordsworth said:

Let me beg out of kindness to me that you would relinquish the intention of publishing the Poem addressed to me after hearing

---

[19] *Keats Circle,* ɪɪ, 143-44. [20] *Middle Years,* ɪɪ, 188.

mine to you. The commendation would be injurious to us both, and my work when it appears, would labour under a great disadvantage in consequence of such a precursorship of Praise.[21]

As Hazlitt said, "His egotism is in some respects a madness; for he scorns even the admiration of himself, thinking it a presumption in any one to suppose that he has taste or sense enough to understand him."[22]

It seems desirable at this point, as the evidences of Wordsworth's egotism accumulate, to interpose a caveat. If, in the present discussion, Wordsworth's gaucherie seems to contrast most unfavorably with Coleridge's sympathy and subtlety in personal relationships, no such invidious assessment is intended. The unfavorable contrast is rather an inevitable appearance arising from the special perspective of the investigation. In the process of critically inspecting the life of any figure, we are always led to see more than we really want to see: the critic's microscope reveals and magnifies blemishes as well as structural subtleties. There are many proverbs answering to this universal and unavoidable sense of the less attractive concomitants of biographical intimacy—those about familiarity breeding contempt, about prophets being without honor in their own country, about no man being a hero to his valet. Conversely, proximate figures not in the foreground always seem by contrast less blemished. When, for instance, it is Coleridge's life that is under close inspection, Wordsworth then seems a tower of integrity, wisdom, and stability—as appears to a notorious extreme in one widely noticed study of Coleridge.

The present volume expressly disclaims invidious intent with respect to either figure, and it regards the negative appearances of both Wordsworth and Coleridge as simply predictable byproducts of our intense scrutiny. Neither man, in intellectual or in human terms, needs an apology. Quite the contrary, Coleridge was, as Wordsworth saw, a *"wonderful* man"; and Wordsworth in simple truth was, as Coleridge saw, "a very great man." Indeed, my own considered opinion is that scarcely any cultural figure short of Shakespeare himself gives evidence of more depth of human feeling than does Wordsworth.[23]

[21] *Ibid.*, p. 238.

[22] *Hazlitt*, v, 163.

[23] Cf. Haydon: "Wordsworth's great power is an intense perception of human feelings regarding the mystery of things by analyzing his own, Shakespeare's an intense power of laying open the heart & mind of man by analyzing the feeling of

Moreover, even the less praiseworthy aspects of the personalities and actions of both men (if Coleridge was guilty of "plagiarism," Wordsworth was guilty of "usury")[24] are not, in all instances and perspectives, necessarily to their human detriment. Wordsworth's bluntness in personal relationship, which frequently appeared as egotistical gaucherie, could at other times be manly truthfulness; Coleridge's sympathy and tact, conversely, could sometimes be duplicity. For illustration we may consider an occasion in which each man confronted an older brother. Coleridge wrote to Poole in September 1801 and unequivocally declared his hostility and lack of affection toward his brothers:

> My family—I have wholly neglected them—I do not love them—their ways are not my ways, nor their thoughts my thoughts—I have no recollections of childhood connected with them, none but painful thoughts in my after years—at present, I think of them habitually as commonplace rich men, bigots from ignorance, and ignorant from bigotry.[25]

Writing to his brother James, however, scarcely more than a year later, Coleridge replaces such cold home truths with fulsome protestations:

> I long very much—indeed, my whole inside *yearns*—to see you all—& your dear little ones.—My best duty to my Mother—my Love to Mrs James, love to the big Children, & kisses to the little ones—love to George, Mrs George, to Edward & his Wife. May Heaven bless you all!
>
> I am, dear Brother, your's with unfeigned Affection, & a deep Esteem
>
> S. T. Coleridge[26]

We see quite clearly that normally acceptable social tact has here degenerated into a cringing display of bad faith.

Wordsworth, on the other hand, writes to his own older brother Richard, on July 3, 1802, in terms of blunt rebuke that seem, par-

---

others acting on themselves." "In moral grandeur of Soul and extension of scope, he [Wordsworth] is equal to Milton" (*Haydon*, II, 171, 148).

[24] See, e.g., Wallace W. Douglas "Wordsworth as Business Man," *PMLA*, 63 (1948), 625-41. Cf. Wordsworth: "I suppose in a court of justice this note would have no other effect but that of exposing me to a prosecution for usury . . ." (*Early Years*, p. 183).

[25] *Collected Letters*, II, 756.

[26] *Ibid.*, p. 898.

ticularly in contrast to the passages from Coleridge, to radiate manly integrity and healthy directness:

> My dear Brother,
>
> I have this evening received two Letters from you, one of the 26th, the other the 29th June.
>
> Before I say any thing in answer to what relates to business in them, I feel it proper to inform you that I must disapprove of the tone which pervades your second Letter. Many parts of it are totally deficient in that respect with which Man ought to deal with Man, and Brother with Brother. You seem to speak to me as if you were speaking to a Child: this is very unbecoming on your part: and it is not fit that I should hear it without informing you, that it is your duty to guard against any thing of the kind in the future. I hope this is the last time I shall have occasion to speak on this subject.[27]

Having recalled to mind such nuances and variations, however, it is still necessary for an observer to insist upon the very large and idiosyncratic role of the egotistical sublime in Wordsworth's life. "I was taught to feel, perhaps too much,/ The self-sufficing power of solitude," admits Wordsworth himself.[28] "Mr. Wordsworth," confirms Hazlitt, "is 'himself alone,' a recluse philosopher, or a reluctant spectator of the scenes of many-coloured life; moralising on them, not describing, not entering into them."[29] Coleridge indicated the same judgment of Wordsworth as isolated spectator rather than as member of community:

> it seems to me that [Wordsworth] ought never to have abandoned the contemplative position, which is peculiarly—perhaps I might say exclusively—fitted for him. His proper title is *Spectator ab extra*.[30]

Some six months later he repeats the judgment, this time pairing Wordsworth and Goethe:

> Although Wordsworth and Goethe are not much alike, to be sure, upon the whole; yet they both have this peculiarity of utter non-sympathy with the subjects of their poetry. They are always, both of them spectators *ab extra*,—feeling *for*, but never *with*, their characters.[31]

---

[27] *Early Years*, p. 371.
[28] *Prelude*, p. 46 (II, 77-78).
[29] *Hazlitt*, v, 131.
[30] *Table Talk*, pp. 171-72 (July 21, 1832).
[31] *Ibid.*, p. 193 (Feb. 16, 1833).

More recently a commentator has spoken of the long tradition, from Hazlitt on, by which "critics have tended to deny that Wordsworth possessed much sympathetic receptivity to the life around him. If it existed at all, it was certainly selective in accordance with his own intense preoccupations, directed only to some things, and specifically to nonhuman identities."[32] Another modern commentator goes so far as to contend that "Wordsworth is not a great lover of man but almost a great despiser of him."[33]

But such conclusions, it seems to me, though in some sense unavoidable, leave too much unaccounted for in Wordsworth's life and work, just as do interpretations that gloss over his egotism. A more desirable, even if more difficult, alternative is to maintain our awareness of his egotism and our awareness of his sense of community as well, and attempt to elucidate the psychic and intellectual paradox by which both were central in his attitudes.

I shall further argue that not only did both exist simultaneously, but also that each was in certain ways the condition for the emphasis on the other. The failure to recognize the interdependence of these characteristics has repeatedly led observers into open contradiction with themselves. Keats, for instance, who first applied the phrase "egotistical sublime" to Wordsworth, and who was painfully aware of the extent of Wordsworth's self-preoccupation, judges, in startling paradox, that "Wordsworth is deeper than Milton" because Milton "did not think into the human heart, as Wordsworth has done."[34] Hazlitt again, who insisted even more than did Keats upon Wordsworth's self-isolation and egotism, can upon one of the same occasions complain that Wordsworth possesses too wide a range of human sympathies:

> However we may sympathise with Mr. Wordsworth in his attachment to groves and fields, we cannot extend the same admiration to their inhabitants, or to the manners of country life in general. We go along with him, while he is the subject of his own narrative, but we take leave of him when he makes pedlars and ploughmen his heroes and the interpreters of his sentiments. It is, we think, getting into low company, and company, besides, that we do not like. We take Mr. Wordsworth himself for a great poet, a fine moralist, and a deep philosopher; but if he insists on introducing us to a friend of his, a parish clerk, or the barber of

[32] Perkins, pp. 51-52.   [33] Ferry, p. 52.
[34] Keats, *Letters*, I, 281, 282.

the village, who is as wise as himself, we must be excused if we draw back with some little want of cordial faith.[35]

If Hazlitt and Keats did not quite see the interdependence of Wordsworth's egotism and his communal commitment, Coleridge was more aware of their paradoxical intertwinement; to him Wordsworth's "Self-involution" was maintained by "living wholly among *Devotees*." As he says in 1803:

> I owe it to Truth & Justice as well as to myself to say, that the concern, which I have felt in this instance, and one or two other more *crying* instances, of Self-involution in Wordsworth, has been almost wholly a Feeling of friendly Regret, & disinterested Apprehension—I saw him more & more benetted in hypochondriacal Fancies, living wholly among *Devotees*—having every the minutest Thing, almost his very Eating & Drinking, done for him by his Sister, or Wife—& I trembled, lest a Film should rise, and thicken on his moral Eye.[36]

What Coleridge saw was the irreducible Wordsworthian truth: the most egotistical, subjective, and withdrawn of poets was in curious fact almost never alone (of his ménage of Dorothy, Mary Hutchinson Wordsworth, and Sara Hutchinson, Crabb Robinson is reported to have said that "he never saw a man so happy in *three wives* as Mr. Wordsworth is").[37] "Wordsworth's needs," confirms Parrish,

> evolved rather strangely from his egotism, which, sublime or not, was a central principle of his nature. Though solitary and self-isolated, he was rarely self-sufficient; both his literary taste and his self-confidence were nourished by drawing compulsively upon the energies and talents of other people, notably his sister and Coleridge. As this process continued, what had begun as a normal dependence on the literary advice of friends became an immoderate need for praise.[38]

By this view, the egotism assumes meaning as a kind of defense or "reaction formation," serving the same function as did his dependence on friends and family. That function was a fending off of the sense of being isolated, lost, and helpless. The egotistical sublime is the visible tip of an iceberg the larger but hidden portion of

[35] *Hazlitt*, IV, 121.
[37] Lamb, *Letters*, II, 199.
[36] *Collected Letters*, II, 101,3.
[38] *Art of the* Lyrical Ballads, pp. 46-47.

which is the fear of being alone. With this as a fundamental conten-
tion, I shall attempt to elucidate both Wordsworth's well-known
stoicism and his equally well-known political conservatism as as-
pects of the special tension that maintained at once his sense of iso-
lated being and his need for human relationship.

To state the matter in small, it seems that Wordsworth's egotisti-
cal sublime was in its origins and development not a misanthropic
withdrawal, but, quite the contrary, an intensification of his sense
of human relationship; it came about as an attempt to maximize
such relationship, and in fact served that purpose in his develop-
ment. Secondly, this process of intensification, which at first led to
an unusually strong sense of the goodness of human life as such,
gradually gave way, under the twin impacts of personal loss and
political disillusionment, to what others have found to be rigidity
of attitude and a rather notorious political conservatism. In short,
Wordsworth's feeling for humanity was always strong—startlingly
so, in fact; but it came more and more to be concentrated in the
idea not of people in general but in that of a *significant group* of
people. This concentration, which in one way was a deepening of
human commitment, involved by its very existence a lessening of
concern with what, from our twentieth-century perspectives, may
be called the liberal myth of the *a priori* value of mankind in
general.

Now Onorato's recent psychoanalytical study of "The Prelude,"
referred to in our first chapter, has demonstrated quite conclu-
sively that Wordsworth's enormous and idiosyncratic sensitivity to
and valuation of natural objects arose as a projection of his rela-
tionship with his mother; and it fixated itself as a denial of the loss
of that relationship when she died:

> I was left alone
> Seeking the visible world, nor knowing why.
> The props of my affections were removed,
> And yet the building stood, as if sustained
> By its own spirit!

Previous to such a removing of the props of his affections, the cen-
tral reality in Wordsworth's life was his mother and the love that
she furnished. With an insight that seems the more remarkable in
that it antedates Freud by a century, Wordsworth—in "best conjec-
ture" seeking to "trace/ Our Being's earthly progress"—says that
"blest" is

> the Babe,
> Nursed in his Mother's arms, who sinks to sleep,
> Rocked on his Mother's breast; who with his soul
> Drinks in the feelings of his Mother's eye!

What we see here is undoubtedly not only the origin of Wordsworth's special preoccupation with the wonder of childhood but the origin of his sense of "wise passiveness" as well.

No less remarkably, he continues with an explicit recognition of how "the discipline of love" develops "the filial bond/ Of Nature." The infant finds that "in one dear Presence"—that of the mother—there exists

> A virtue which irradiates and exalts
> Objects through widest intercourse of sense.
> No outcast he, bewildered and depressed:
> Along his infant veins are interfused
> The gravitation and the filial bond
> Of nature that connect him with the world.
> Is there a flower, to which he points with hand
> Too weak to gather it, already love
> Drawn from love's purest earthly fount for him
> Hath beautified that flower

And all this originates from the situation of human relationship, from that time

> In which, a Babe, by intercourse of touch
> I held mute dialogues with my Mother's heart[39]

These awarenesses, supplied by Wordsworth himself in the course of a rigorous self-examination, seem to be an unassailably correct assessment of the situation. Not only do they accord with a Freudian interpretation of the structure of Wordsworth's nature worship, but they also have impressed themselves upon commentators not viewing from the Freudian perspective. Mrs. Moorman, for a single instance, speaks of "the exalted importance" that Wordsworth attached to "the relation of the infant to its mother"; and she says that

> Soon he learnt to transfer to Nature the affection, the faith, the 'religious love' which he had felt for his mother. Wordsworth's

[39] *Prelude*, 1850 version, p. 59 (II, 277-81), p. 57 (II, 234-37), p. 57 (II, 238-48), p. 59 (II, 267-68).

maternal conception of Nature echoes throughout his poetry—
she was

> The anchor of my purest thoughts, the nurse,
> The guide, the guardian of my heart, and soul
> Of all my moral being . . .
> Surely I was led by her.

The awe and fear of Nature in him were never hideous or terri-
ble, but rather a source of strength and love. Doubtless this had
its analogy in his desire for his mother's approval—his con-
sciousness sometimes of her disapproval.[40]

In this understanding, the Wordsworthian formula, "Love of
Nature Leading to Love of Man," can be understood as a divagated
version of a more usual procedure: primary love of one human
being leading to the capacity for love in general. As Coleridge ob-
served, in pre-Freudian insight no less remarkable than that of
Wordsworth (and the matter was doubtless a symbiotic topic of
their conversation), the "first dawnings" of a baby's "humanity"
will break forth in

> the Eye that connects the Mother's face with the warmth of the
> mother's bosom, the support of the mother's Arms. A thousand
> tender kisses excite a finer life in its lips & there first language is
> imitated from the mother's smiles. Ere yet a conscious self exists
> the love begins & the first love is love to another. The Babe ac-
> knowledges a self in the Mother's form, years before it can rec-
> ognize a self in its own.[41]

But this emotional sense of what Coleridge often called "alterity"
was for Wordsworth displaced, or detoured, rather, into the forms
of nature and the objects within it. As he says, he "first . . . look'd/
At Man through objects that were great and fair,/ First communed
with him by their help."[42] In the process an almost incredibly in-
tense object-cathexis—to adopt Freudian terminology—was devel-
oped. "Mr. Wordsworth's characteristic is one, and may be ex-
pressed in one word," said Hazlitt in summary, "—a power of
raising the smallest things in nature into sublimity by the force of

[40] Moorman, I, 3.   [41] MS. of the *Opus Maximum*.
[42] *Prelude*, p. 289 (VIII, 315-17). Again: "But he had felt the power/ Of Nature, and
already was prepared,/ By his intense conceptions, to receive/ Deeply the lesson of
love which he,/ Whom Nature . . . has taught/ To feel intensely, cannot but receive"
(Wordsworth, *Poems*, V, 14).

sentiment. He attaches the deepest and loftiest feelings to the meanest and most superficial objects."[43] Elsewhere Hazlitt recalls his first meeting with Wordsworth and, significantly for our purposes, stresses at the outset the unusual sense of the poet's fixation upon external objects:

> I think I see him now. . . . There was a severe, worn pressure of thought about his temples, a fire in his eye (as if he saw something in objects more than the outward appearance).[44]

In short, "deep feelings had impressed/ So vividly great objects that they lay/ Upon his mind like substances."[45]

From the fact of Wordsworth's divagation of human emotion into natural objects, we can account for the ambivalence that generated his intense concern for others simultaneously with his egotistical sublime. The same path that led to the maintenance of his departed mother's love led in theory to the extension of that love to mankind in general:

> For I have learned
> To look on nature, not as in the hour
> Of thoughtless youth; but hearing oftentimes
> The still, sad music of humanity[46]

The claims of reality, however, will inevitably assert themselves: natural objects are not people, and to direct oneself almost obsessively toward such objects is to move toward an antisocial isolation. There are moments when both factors in this necessary ambivalence are revealed simultaneously:

> Yet could I only cleave to solitude
> In lonesome places; if a throng was near
> That way I lean'd by nature; for my heart
> Was social, and lov'd idleness and joy.[47]

As Lionel Trilling maintains, "the great Hillel" had a "Wordsworthian personality" and was in the habit of saying " 'if I am not for myself, who, then is for me? And if I am for myself, what then am I?' "; and this parallels what Trilling identifies as "the Wordsworthian moral essence." That essence is "the interplay between individualism and the sense of community, between an awareness

---

[43] *Hazlitt*, ix, 243.
[45] Wordsworth, *Poems*, v, 12-13.
[47] *Prelude*, p. 84 (iii, 233-36).

[44] *Ibid.*, xvii, 118.
[46] *Ibid.*, ii, 261.

of self that must be saved and developed, and an awareness that the self is yet fulfilled only in community."[48]

Such a statement, while closer to my own understanding than the opinion that Wordsworth was "not a great lover of man but almost a great despiser of him," still does not indicate the special psychological mechanism that generated the paradox. That agency can be conceptualized as a funneling in the emotional current, one by virtue of which feeling was at once intensified and narrowed as Wordsworth proceeded toward pure communion with nature. The sense of narrowing at the end of the funnel made him retreat from isolation and solitude (for narrowing implies eventual extinction); the sense of dispersal and attenuation of feeling at the opening of the funnel made him draw back from too general an involvement with masses of people. Impelled toward but at the same time retreating from both isolation and community, Wordsworth came to be as it were suspended in an emotional force-field between them. The components of the field were on the one hand the fears in and of solitude that accompanied the "Love of Nature," and on the other, accompanying the "Love of Man," the rewards of the significant group: richness of feeling without loss of community. But the investment in the significant group was by its very fact a turning away from undifferentiated social concern. "I am not fond of making myself hastily beloved and admired," he says in revealing rebuke to Coleridge, "you take more delight in it than a wise man ought. I am naturally slow to love and to cease loving."[49]

Both the fears in solitude and the sense of the significant group can be illustrated from many places in Wordsworth's utterance. Indeed, as Bréhier said of Plotinus, all of Wordsworth seems to exist in each unit of his work. Both elements are present in "The Prelude," in "The Excursion," in the "Intimations Ode," in "Tintern Abbey," in "Michael"—even in a poem such as "Peter Bell" (of this last it was Robinson's gloomy view that "Wordsworth has set himself back ten years by the publication of this unfortunate work").[50] But sometimes briefer and less complex statements reveal the structure of an attitude more unequivocally than do more ambitious works. In this context we may take two minor poems, "Lines Left upon a Seat in a Yew-Tree" and "We Are Seven," as emblematic of the depth of Wordsworth's anxieties at the smaller and larger ends of the funnel.

[48] Trilling, Self, p. 127.   [49] Middle Years, I, 245.
[50] Robinson, I, 230.

"Lines Left upon a Seat in a Yew-Tree" is a recollection sug-
gested by a "lonely Yew-tree" that "stands/ Far from all human
dwelling." The poet is led to remember the man who "piled these
stones and with the mossy sod/ First covered, and here taught this
aged Tree/ With its dark arms to form a circling bower." This man,
it turns out, was a representative of the egotistical sublime: "He
was one who owned/ No common soul." Going forth into the
world, he found himself neglected:

> wherefore he at once
> With indignation turned himself away,
> And with the food of pride sustained his soul
> In solitude.[51]

It seems clear enough that the proud and indignant retreat into
solitude is parallel to a strong impulse in Wordsworth himself.
What the man in the poem is prepared to find in the great world—
"the taint/ Of dissolute tongues, and jealousy, and hate,/ And
scorn"—is precisely what Wordsworth finds there as expressed in
"Tintern Abbey": "evil tongues/ Rash judgments . . . the sneers of
selfish men,/ . . . greetings where no kindness is."[52] The man's
withdrawal from the "world" parallels Wordsworth's own later
withdrawal into the relative isolation of the Lake District—a resi-
dency that never ceased to puzzle such urban devotees as Hazlitt
and the Lambs ("I am very sorry for Mr. De Quincey," writes Mary
Lamb to Dorothy Wordsworth in 1817, "—what a blunder the poor
man made when he took up his dwelling among the moun-
tains").[53]

It is noteworthy, however, that in the poem such withdrawal is
censured; indeed, the lines become a kind of warning against the
dangers of solitude. The solitary

> many an hour
> A morbid pleasure nourished, tracing here
> An emblem of his own unfruitful life.

He is termed a "lost Man," and "In this deep vale/ He died,—this
seat his only monument." A final stanza turns the poem into a
homily:

> Stranger! henceforth be warned; and know that pride,
> Howe'er disguised in its own majesty,

[51] Wordsworth, Poems, I, 92-93.   [52] Ibid., II, 262.
[53] Lamb, Letters, II, 217.

Is littleness; that he who feels contempt
For any living thing, hath faculties
Which he has never used; . . .
          The man whose eye
Is ever on himself doth look on one,
The least of Nature's works. . . .
          O be wiser, Thou!
Instructed that true knowledge leads to love;[54]

The sentiments of the final stanza seem strikingly Coleridgean. For instance, the exhortation not to feel "contempt/ For any living thing" and the apotheosis of "love" insistently parallel the moral of "The Ancient Mariner": "He prayeth best, who loveth best/ All things both great and small." There is even the possibility that the last stanza could be either wholly or in part the actual work of Coleridge, and in any event, the poem presents itself unmistakably as still another datum in the symbiotic activity of the two men.[55]

But Coleridgean though its sentiments are, they are also Wordsworthian; if not in the concern for "any living thing," at least in the warning about the egotistical sublime ("pride,/ Howe'er disguised") and in the statement about the fundamental necessity of love. Inasmuch as the Wordsworthian emphasis on nature was in its origin a projection of love, love by that fact always takes precedence, in the Wordsworthian hierarchy of values, over all other considerations:

          From love, for here
Do we begin and end, all grandeur comes,
All truth and beauty, from pervading love,
That gone, we are as dust.[56]

The implications of love are by definition opposed to the implications of the isolated self. As Wordsworth says in "Laodamia":

          Love was given,
Encouraged, sanctioned, chiefly for that end;
For this the passion to excess was driven—
That self might be annulled:[57]

The intensification of love that resulted from Wordsworth's original progress toward pure communion with nature always had as

[54] Wordsworth, *Poems*, I, 93-94.
[55] Cf., e.g., Jonathan Wordsworth, pp. 199-201.
[56] *Prelude*, p. 488 (XIII, 149-52).   [57] Wordsworth, *Poems*, II, 271.

ultimate possibility, if pursued far enough, the loss of all love in a pure egotism and selfishness: we recall that the whole point of the yew-tree poem is that "The man whose eye/ Is ever on himself doth look on one,/ The least of Nature's works." He who

> Affronts the eye of Solitude, shall learn
> That her mild nature can be terrible;
> That neither she nor Silence lack the power
> To avenge their own insulted majesty.[58]

This chasm, it seems, loomed before Wordsworth as an absolute limit on the possibilities of the egotistical sublime; and his awareness of it as lying along his path in life generated a special anxiety.

Repeatedly he warns himself against plunging into the abyss of total isolation. The characterization of Vaudracour provides such a warning: "Into a deep wood/ He fled, to shun the haunts of human kind"; but there, "Cut off from all intelligence with man," his life became waste and madness:

> in those solitary shades
> His days he wasted,—an imbecile mind.[59]

Another warning appears in "Elegiac Stanzas":

> Farewell, farewell the heart that lives alone,
> Housed in a dream, at distance from the Kind!
> Such happiness, wherever it be known,
> Is to be pitied, for 'tis surely blind:[60]

In "A Poet's Epitaph," again, Wordsworth speaks with contempt of "A Moralist" who "has neither eyes nor ears;/ Himself his world, and his own God."[61] He convulsively rejects the ego-philosophy of Fichte and Schelling:

> Philosophers, who, though the human soul
> Be of a thousand faculties composed,
> And twice ten thousand interests, do yet prize
> This soul, and the transcendent universe,
> No more than as a mirror that reflects
> To proud Self-love her own intelligence;
> That one, poor, finite object, in the abyss
> Of infinite Being, twinkling restlessly![62]

[58] Ibid., v, 142.
[60] Wordsworth, Poems, iv, 260.
[62] Ibid., v, 140.

[59] Prelude, p. 364 (ix, 302-308).
[61] Ibid., p. 66.

Yet again, in the "Preface to 'The Borderers' " he sketches a remarkable variant of the egotistical sublime, a kind of prototype of the Byronic hero ("Let us suppose a young man. . . . His master passions are pride and the love of distinction"; he has "shaken off the obligations of religion & morality in a dark and tempestuous age").[63] The young man and his unruly impulses seem to be a rejected version of the sense of Wordsworth's own possibility; like Wordsworth "He goes into the world and is betrayed into a great crime" (if we accept that Wordsworth on at least an unconscious level considered his relationship with Annette Vallon as such). Like Wordsworth, the young man withdraws from the world ("he quits the world in disgust, with strong misanthropic feelings"), but, significantly, the withdrawal is judged to involve a vicious loss of humanity:

> assisted by disgust and misanthropic feeling, the character we are now contemplating will have a strong tendency to vice. His energies are most impressively manifested in works of devastation. . . . He presses truth and falshood into the same service. He looks at society through an optical glass of peculiar tint.[64]

Here, as with the man in the yew-tree poem, we seem to see a homily preached by Wordsworth against his own tendency to withdraw into egotism.

Conversely, he was continually preoccupied with the problem of loneliness and isolation. Despite the truth that he was, in fact, almost never alone, his tendency toward the egotistical sublime made the possibility of eventual solitude an especially intense fear; and it is in this fear that we see the substratum of his concern with derelicts and lonely people, especially with the lonely aged—the "sole survivor" such as Simon Lee.

There is a kind of inexorable logic to it all. If, for Wordsworth, the earliest part of life was the state of fullest being ("trailing clouds of glory do we come/ . . . Heaven lies about us in our infancy!"), and the process of growth was accompanied by a loss of being ("Shades of the prison-house begin to close/ Upon the growing Boy"),[65] it follows that the worst of all possible states must be age, where the process of diminution reaches its nadir. It is in age, moreover, that one is most likely to be cast into solitude. For instance, in "Tintern Abbey," the poet's attention sweeps from the

[63] *Prose*, I, 76, 78.   [64] *Ibid.*, p. 77.
[65] Wordsworth, *Poems*, IV, 281.

"aching joys" and "dizzy raptures" of boyhood to a future when "solitude, or fear, or pain, or grief" might be one's portion.[66] Again, the Old Cumberland Beggar "travels on, a solitary Man;/ His age has no companion." Against this fearful isolation, Wordsworth summons up the thought that "man is dear to man," that "we have all of us one human heart," and imagines the villagers supplying at least enough charity and human companionship to alleviate the absoluteness of the beggar's lot:

> Then let him pass, a blessing on his head!
> And while in that vast solitude to which
> The tide of things has borne him, he appears
> To breathe and live but for himself alone,
>   . . . while life is his,
> Still let him prompt the unlettered villagers
> To tender offices and pensive thoughts.[67]

As such examples suggest, Wordsworth's fear of isolated age involved strategies for coping with that fear. In "Tintern Abbey," the possible future of "solitude, or fear, or pain, or grief" will be countered by "healing thoughts" of "these my exhortations"—that is, by the hope that in this moment of "present pleasure" there will be "life and food/ For future years."[68] In "The Old Cumberland Beggar," benign nature and the villagers' solicitude will make the beggar's isolation less terrifying.

One of the most revealing of the poems about isolated old age is "Resolution and Independence." Here the situation is one in which nature fails in its function as nurse, guide, and guardian. The poem projects at its outset an archetypally Wordsworthian view of glorious nature:

> But now the sun is rising calm and bright;
> The birds are singing in the distant woods;
> Over his own sweet voice the Stock-dove broods;
> The Jay makes answer as the Magpie chatters; . . .
>
> All things that love the sun are out of doors;
> The sky rejoices in the morning's birth;
> The grass is bright with rain-drops;—on the moors
> The hare is running races in her mirth;

But unlike many other Wordsworthian celebrations, this one wit-

[66] *Ibid.*, II, 263.   [67] *Ibid.*, IV, 239.
[68] *Ibid.*, II, 261.

nesses a disjunction; nature is glad, but the observer is not. The ways of men seem "vain and melancholy," and "fears and fancies thick upon me came;/ Dim sadness—and blind thoughts, I knew not, nor could name." It eventually becomes clear that the cause of the "dim sadness" is the thought of solitude, focused as usual upon the thought of life advancing toward age:

> But there may come another day to me—
> Solitude, pain of heart, distress, and poverty.

He thinks of Coleridge's dejection, of Chatterton's suicide, of Burns, and the thoughts do nothing to alleviate his anxiety about the future:

> We Poets in our youth begin in gladness;
> But thereof come in the end despondency and madness.

Into this despondent prospect comes the Old Leech-Gatherer, an actualization of the fact of solitary and isolated old age. Indeed, he is still more isolated, if possible, than the Old Cumberland Beggar, in that not even the sustaining society of the village is available to him; he is the ultimate in age and isolation: "The oldest man he seemed that ever wore grey hairs." He appears to be:

> not all alive nor dead,
> Nor all asleep—in his extreme old age:
> His body was bent double, feet and head
> Coming together in life's pilgrimage;
> As if some dire constraint of pain, or rage
> Of sickness felt by him in times long past,
> A more than human weight upon his frame had cast.

And then, and we can scarcely be insensitive to the accents of profound relief with which the fact is discovered, the old man reveals himself as having lost neither his humanity nor his sanity; and the observer's anxiety is almost explosively dispelled:

> I could have laughed myself to scorn to find
> In that decrepit Man so firm a mind.

It is apparent from such a release of tension, as well as from other emphasis, that the Old Leech-Gatherer focuses the deepest of Wordsworth's fears in solitude:

> . . . the lonely place,
> The old Man's shape, and speech—all troubled me;

In my mind's eye I seemed to see him pace
About the weary moors continually,
Wandering about alone and silently.

He therefore represents for Wordsworth a kind of existential boundary-situation (to use the terminology of Jaspers). He is "like a man from some far region sent,/ To give me human strength, by apt admonishment."[69] But only as a figure representing what for Wordsworth was the possibility of existence in extremis is the Old Leech-Gatherer so important. It is his role as an embodiment of Wordsworth's own anxieties that makes him a central rather than a peripheral figure. For Wordsworth, not death but solitude was the ultimate dread.

In the "so firm a mind" possessed by the old man, we see a choice example of the stoicism that was so special a feature of Wordsworth's outlook and of much of his poetry. In the Latin literature of Stoicism, with which we know Wordsworth to have been well acquainted, to live as a Stoic is to live in accordance with nature.[70] In Wordsworth's version, however, stoic endurance is necessary only when nature has failed. It is as though there are two lines of defense against the final horror of absolute solitude: the outer wall is nature; the keep of the castle is stoic endurance. This is precisely the situation in "Resolution and Independence": the poet feels himself failed by nature, but then reassures himself by the emblem of the stoically uncomplaining Leech-Gatherer, whose spirit survives the worst that age and isolation can do.

Again, Wordsworth's testament to nature in "Tintern Abbey" reveals nature as functioning in the same way as stoic fortitude: it erects a defense against the assaults of existence:

Oh! yet a little while
May I behold in thee what I was once,
My dear, dear Sister! and this prayer I make,
Knowing that Nature never did betray
The heart that loved her; 'tis her privilege,

[69] Ibid., ii, 235, 236, 236, 237, 240, 240, 239.

[70] See, e.g., Jane Worthington, Wordsworth's Reading of Roman Prose (New Haven: Yale University Press, 1946). For perhaps the most comprehensive modern study of Stoicism see Max Pohlenz, Die Stoa; Geschichte einer geistigen Bewegung, second edition (Göttingen: Vandenhoeck & Ruprecht, 1959). 2 vols. For the Stoic formula whereby the highest good is to live in accordance with nature, see, e.g., Cicero: "summum bonum . . . est convenienter congruenterque naturae vivere" (De Finibus iii.9).

Through all the years of this our life, to lead
From joy to joy: for she can so inform
The mind that is within us, so impress
With quietness and beauty, and so feed
With lofty thoughts, that neither evil tongues,
Rash judgments, nor the sneers of selfish men,
Nor greetings where no kindness is, nor all
The dreary intercourse of daily life,
Shall e'er prevail against us, or disturb
Our cheerful faith, that all which we behold
Is full of blessings.[71]

It can be instructive to analyze the statement that "Nature never did betray/ The heart that loved her." One remarks the feminine personification; also the attribution of human agency. Most of all, however, the note of protestation is the striking feature of the passage. It is not necessary to state that one will not be betrayed unless fear of betrayal does in fact exist. Such fear is more clearly revealed in other statements; to cite an example, Wordsworth says in "The Excursion" that "A piteous lot it were to flee from Man—/ Yet not rejoice in Nature."[72]

Indeed, Wordsworth's philosophy of joy almost always seems to be at least in part a product of the mechanism of denial. He himself admitted having "two natures in me, joy the one/ The other melancholy, and withal/ A happy man."[73] Yet the stipulation, "withal a happy man," seeks to deny the melancholy even as it is granted half his being. The pattern is recurrent in Wordsworth. For example, perhaps the strongest embodiment of the philosophy of joy is in the "sing, ye Birds, sing, sing a joyous song!/ And let the young Lambs bound/ As to the tabor's sound!" of the "Intimations Ode"; but this is a conclusion reached not as an apex of ascending gladness, but as a response to the dismal sense that "there hath past away a glory from the earth." The exclamation, "O joy!" is engendered not by the sense of life's fullness, but by the diminished thought "that in our embers/ Is something that doth live."[74]

Again and again we see that Wordsworth's "cheerful faith that

[71] Wordsworth, *Poems*, II, 262-63.   [72] *Ibid.*, v, 127.

[73] *Prelude*, p. 416 (x, 869-71). As a graphic instance, in one context Wordsworth denies unhappiness with the assurance: "No outcast he, bewilder'd and depress'd" (*Prelude*, p. 56 [II, 261]); yet in another context he admits to sadness in precisely the same combination of adjectives: "Depressed, bewildered thus . . ." (*Prelude*, 1850 version, p. 419 [XI, 321]).

[74] Wordsworth, *Poems*, IV, 284, 283.

all which we behold/ Is full of blessings" is an attempt to assert mastery over fears to the contrary. Though "The thought of our past years in me doth breed/ Perpetual benediction," other Wordsworthian testimony allows us glimpses of unease beneath this serene façade—as when he speaks of the occurrence in childhood of "terrors, pains, and early miseries,/ Regrets, vexations, lassitudes interfused/ Within my mind."[75] Elsewhere he records that his mother had said

> that the only one of her five children about whose future life she was anxious, was William; and he, she said, would be remarkable either for good or for evil. The cause of this was, that I was of a stiff, moody, and violent temper; so much so that I remember once going into the attics of my grandfather's house at Penrith, upon some indignity having been put upon me, with an intention of destroying myself with one of the foils which I knew was kept there.[76]

There is assuredly nothing in *that* memory to "breed/ Perpetual benediction." And if such malaise existed while his mother was alive, we can only speculate on how vastly it was increased by her untimely death. The projection of emotion into nature, corresponding with the period of latency in the child's development, damped the overt expression of shock at his mother's death. But it burst forth with, as it were, a double power upon the death of his brother John in 1805; for we can scarcely doubt that this second disaster was shattering not only in its own right but as a confirmation and reawakening of the losses of his father, and especially of his mother, in his childhood. Moreover, the death of his brother in a storm at sea was particularly traumatic for Wordsworth in that it was a betrayal by Nature of the heart that loved her:

> Not for a moment could I now behold
> A smiling sea, and be what I have been:
> The feeling of my loss will ne'er be old[77]

---

[75] *Prelude*, 1850 version, p. 23 (I, 345-47). Compare a statement later in the same poem, where he speaks of being "inwardly oppressed/ With sorrow, disappointment, vexing thoughts,/ Confusion of the judgment, zeal decayed,/ And, lastly, utter loss of hope itself/ And things to hope for" (p. 431 [XII, 3-7]). Again, in a prose tract on education he says, significantly, that "We have made no mention of fear, shame, sorrow, nor of ungovernable and vexing thoughts; because, although these have been and have done mighty service, they are overlooked in that stage of life when Youth is passing into Manhood,—overlooked, or forgotten" (*Prose*, II, 17).

[76] *Prose*, III, 372.   [77] Wordsworth, *Poems*, IV, 260.

The betrayal by Nature cast Wordsworth back upon his final de-
fense: stoicism. The egotistical sublime was not merely an attitude
emanating from his early substitution of nature for his mother, but
also and specifically from that self-sufficiency in solitude combined
with stoic imperturbability:

> O blest seclusion! when the mind admits
> The law of duty; and can therefore move
>
> Through each vicissitude of loss and gain,
> Linked in entire complacence with her choice[78]

The ideas of "joy" and "cheer" and "happiness" more and more
accreted to the idea of stoic endurance; it was not enough simply to
bear, but to bear proudly and even gladly. "I am myself," he told
Robinson in May 1812, "one of the happiest of men, and no man
who does not partake of that happiness, who lives a life of constant
bustle, and whose felicity depends on the opinions of others, can
possibly comprehend the best of my poems."[79] This was enun-
ciated just before the deaths of two of his children; none the less,
four years later he presented to Robinson much the same picture of
outward happiness:

> it was a serious gratification to behold so great and so good a
> man as Wordsworth in the bosom of his family enjoying those
> comforts which are apparent to the eye. He has two sons and a
> daughter surviving. They appear to be amiable children, if not of
> superior intellectual endowments. And adding to these external
> blessings the *mind* of the man, he may justly be considered as
> one of the most enviable of mankind.[80]

Thus stoic conceptions were his armor. The "Character of the
Happy Warrior"—and the rubric itself is indicative of this concep-
tion of stoic cheer—sets forth as a Wordsworthian model the figure

> Whom neither shape of danger can dismay,
> Nor thought of tender happiness betray;
> Who, not content that former worth stand fast,
> Looks forward, persevering to the last . . . [81]

Again, in "Elegiac Stanzas," a poem responding—as does the
"Character of the Happy Warrior"—to the loss of his brother John,

---

[78] *Ibid.*, v, 142.
[80] *Ibid.*, p. 188.

[79] *Robinson*, I, 73.
[81] Wordsworth, *Poems*, IV, 88.

his reaction to the sense that "A power is gone, which nothing can restore" is stoic cheerfulness:

> But welcome fortitude, and patient cheer,
> And frequent sights of what is to be borne![82]

The denial always inherent in the philosophy of joy thus became strengthened by the repeated demands for fortitude that life made on Wordsworth. It might be rewarding to examine an instance in some detail. The loss of his two dearest children in a half-year's space constituted a crushing blow, especially to a man whose emotions ran as deep as did their father's. Yet Wordsworth remarks on their death in tones that, if taken without our contextual knowledge of his grief, sound so serene as almost to be uncaring:

> You probably know how much I have suffered in this way myself; having lost within the short space of half a year two delightful creatures a girl and a boy of the several ages of four and six and a half. This was four years ago—but they are perpetually present to my eyes—I do not mourn for them; yet I am sometimes weak enough to wish that I had them again. They are laid side by side in Grasmere Churchyard.[83]

At what cost this particular manifestation of the egotistical sublime was maintained, however, can be gauged from other statements of almost unbearable poignance—if indeed this one itself is not so. Without summoning those heart-rending passages in "The Excursion" where the Solitary's despondency is connected to the deaths of his daughter and son, we may simply note the testimony of Dorothy. "It would have pitied the hardest heart to witness what he has gone through," she writes of her brother's reaction to his son's death. "It has been a cruel stroke for William—he loved Thomas with such a peculiar tenderness." "My Brother is grown very thin," she writes again, "and at times I think he looks ten years older since the death of Thomas." On occasion an overt grief filters through even Wordsworth's own stoic calm:

> The Boy whom we have lost was the pride and darling of the House—as sweet and faultless a child as ever breathed. . . . We shall quit this House for Rydale Mount; we have too many distressful Memorials here. . . . I hope we shall be something less sad when we get away from the heavyness of this Dwelling in

[82] *Ibid.*, p. 260.   [83] *Middle Years*, ii, 361.

which we have been so pitiably smitten by the hand of provi-
dence.[84]

But excruciatingly as he felt his son's death, so, and if possible
even more deeply, did he feel his daughter Catharine's:

> Surprised by joy—impatient as the Wind
> I turned to share the transport—Oh! with whom
> But Thee, deep buried in the silent tomb,
> That spot which no vicissitude can find?
> Love, faithful love, recalled thee to my mind—
> But how could I forget thee? Through what power,
> Even for the least division of an hour,
> Have I been so beguiled as to be blind
> To my most grievous loss!—That thought's return
> Was the worst pang that sorrow ever bore,
> Save one, one only, when I stood forlorn,
> Knowing my heart's best treasure was no more;
> That neither present time, nor years unborn
> Could to my sight that heavenly face restore.[85]

The public fortitude of "I do not mourn for them; yet I am some-
times weak enough to wish that I had them again" was a stoicism
that covered an ocean of grief at "Knowing my heart's best treasure
was no more."

The attitude of defense—the armored attitude of the happy
warrior—was one that Wordsworth maintained against the as-
saults of life for more than seventy years. So constant a posture of
defense had as concomitant the rigidity that is so notable a feature
of his later period. Almost everything Wordsworth espoused be-
came rigid. For instance, his Christianity, which had developed in
part under Coleridge's warnings against Spinozistic pantheism
("this inferred dependency of the human soul on accidents of
Birth-place & Abode together with the vague misty, rather than
mystic, Confusion of God with the World & the accompanying
Nature-worship, of which the asserted dependence forms a part, is
the Trait in Wordsworth's poetic Works that I most dislike, as un-
healthful, & denounce as contagious. . . . It conjures up to *my* fancy
a sort of *Janus*-head of Spinoza and Dr Watts"),[86] became so rigid
that Coleridge himself commented adversely on its orthodoxy.[87]

Again, Wordsworth's pattern of first supporting, then repudiat-

[84] *Ibid.*, pp. 64, 62, 76, 75.
[86] *Collected Letters*, v, 95.
[85] Wordsworth, *Poems*, iii, 16.
[87] *Robinson*, i, 288.

ing, the revolutionary tendencies of the age was one he shared with many intellectuals; but with him the reaction was peculiarly rigid. "Most intensely did I rejoice at the Counter Revolution," admits Crabb Robinson: "I had also rejoiced when a boy at the Revolution, and I am ashamed of neither sentiment." Yet in the very entry in which this statement occurs, Robinson says of Wordsworth's hardening conservatism that "I am sorry that Wordsworth cannot change with the times. . . . Wise men and great men when carried away by strong feelings run with fools. Of the integrity of Wordsworth I have no doubt, as of his genius I have an unbounded admiration; but I doubt the discretion and wisdom of his latest political writings."[88]

It was as though Wordsworth's psychic muscles were constantly tensed. The initial life-giving radiance—the sense that "Heaven lies about us in our infancy"—was left further and further behind as the years went by. Though the growing boy beheld "the light, and whence it flows," the "Youth" daily traveled "farther from the east"; at length "the Man" perceived it "die away,/ And fade into the light of common day."[89] The course of existence therefore offered the prospect not of an accession but a deprivation of being: "I see by glimpses now; when age comes on/ May scarcely see at all";[90] "Life's autumn past, I stand on winter's verge;/ And daily lose what I desire to keep."[91] In this respect Wordsworth's life of eighty years, in itself an anomaly among ruptured Romantic existences, was a cruel irony, a long day's dying to augment his pain. What he always wanted was to experience unchangingly the joy he had felt as a child—"Stability without regret or fear;/ That hath been, is, and shall be evermore."[92] Thus the Solitary, commenting on the happiness of a "cottage boy," says "Far happiest . . . / If, such as now he is, he might remain."[93]

But into the longing for eternal and blessèd childhood obtruded the iron claims of ravaging time:

> . . . a thought arose
> Of life continuous, Being unimpaired;
> That hath been, is, and where it was and is
> There shall endure,—existence unexposed
> To the blind walk of mortal accident;
> From diminution safe and weakening age;

[88] Ibid., pp. 183, 183-84.
[90] Prelude, p. 448 (xi, 337-38).
[92] Ibid., p. 86.

[89] Wordsworth, Poems, iv, 281.
[91] Wordsworth, Poems, v, 128.
[93] Ibid., p. 81.

> While man grows old, and dwindles, and decays;
> And countless generations of mankind
> Depart; and leave no vestige where they trod.[94]

We recognize the lines as not merely the poetic precursor of Keats's "Ode to a Nightingale," but also as an index for the peculiarly tragic sense of Wordsworth's life. The cheerfulness of the egotistical sublime was an attempt to maintain the thought of "life continuous, Being unimpaired." The cost of such continual straining against the true situation of "mortal accident," "diminution," and "weakening age" was the Wordsworthian rigidity: the psychic muscles were always tensed. A trifling comment from the last decade of Wordsworth's life reveals, perhaps better than larger evidence, Wordsworth's own haunted sense of this fact:

> Nothing however said or done to me for some time has in relation to myself given me so much pleasure as a casual word of Anna's that the expression of my face was ever varying. I had begun to fear that it had lately been much otherwise.[95]

Both Wordsworth's rigidity and his stoic defenses were raised to ideational formulation in his conception of "duty." The word, indeed, received an honorific charge in his vocabulary that only "love" and "joy" and "nature" can match. Even Kant's apotheosis of *Pflicht*[96] at the expense of *Neigung* is no more insistent than was Wordsworth's rejection of "wayward inclination" for what he apostrophizes as the "Stern Daughter of the Voice of God."[97]

The honorific charge seems to derive from two related defensive services that duty performed in Wordsworth's lifelong struggle against loss of being. First of all, duty was a principle by which an existence kept itself from being broken up and dissipated in protean change. It maintained the commitments of childhood in the circumstances of age, and thus bulwarked the aspiration to "life continuous, Being unimpaired." Without it, one would be, to use a phrase from the "Ode to Duty," the "sport of every random gust." For Wordsworth change meant loss, time was horror ("Mutability is Nature's bane");[98] he longed for "a repose that ever is the same."[99] Underlying any possibility of a life of joy and love there

---

[94] *Ibid.*, p. 133. [95] *Later Years*, III, 1133.
[96] Cf. Friedrich Schlegel: "Duty is Kant's 'One and All.' Out of the duty of thankfulness he maintains that one must defend and treasure the old; and only out of duty has he himself become a great man" (*Friedrich Schlegel*, II, 166).
[97] Wordsworth, *Poems*, IV, 83. [98] *Ibid.*, V, 89.
[99] *Ibid.*, IV, 85.

accordingly was the necessity of keeping the past green; and duty
helped to achieve this:

> Serene will be our days and bright,
> And happy will our nature be,
> When love is an unerring light,
> And joy its own security.
> And they a blissful course may hold
> Even now, who, not unwisely bold,
> Live in the spirit of this creed;
> Yet seek thy firm support, according to their need.[100]

The "firm support" of duty thus was a major ally in the war
against fears in solitude. As such, its call became in its largest de-
scription an obligation toward the significant group; as we see, to
cite only one instance, in Wordsworth's dismay about Coleridge:

> He *ought* to come to see after Hartley. . . . But because he ought
> to come, I fear he will not; and how is H. to be sent to College?
> These perplexities no doubt glance across his mind like
> dreams—but nothing ever will rouze the Father to his duty *as
> Duty*.[101]

As we can infer from that passage and others like it, Coleridge's
failure to recognize the sacredness of duty was, at least from
Wordsworth's perspective, perhaps the single most important fac-
tor in the eventual estrangement of the two men.

The second function of duty was a complement to the first. If
duty helped maintain the bonds of the significant group, it also
rescued an individual from chaotic solitude—from the "being to
myself a guide" that characterized the egotistical sublime. As
Wordsworth says in the "Ode to Duty":

> I, loving freedom, and untried; . . .
> Yet being to myself a guide,
> Too blindly have reposed my trust: . . .
> But thee I now would serve more strictly, if I may.

The isolated self is free, but this freedom divorced from relation-
ship and its responsibilities paradoxically becomes a burden: "Me
this unchartered freedom tires;/ I feel the weight of chance-
desires."[102]

Duty therefore both redeems one from the emptiness of self and

---

[100] *Ibid.*, p. 84. [101] *Middle Years*, II, 124.
[102] *Poems*, IV, 85.

asserts the bond with the significant group.[103] In such functions
we can understand the enormous importance Wordsworth at-
tached to the idea, at the same time that we realize how rigid is the
tendency of a life dominated by so demanding an allegiance. Both
the importance and the rigid tendency can perhaps be illustrated
by a single idiosyncratic example. Dorothy, in mourning the death
of Thomas, ascribes as one of his finest qualities the attachment to
"duty" as opposed to "wayward inclination." She is speaking of a
child six years old! That Wordsworth's sister expressed such an
almost grotesque sentiment about his son shows how magical, al-
most, was the conception of duty in the psychic economy of his
own significant group. Dorothy writes:

> The ways of Providence are inscrutable. That child was taken
> from us who never disturbed our minds with one wayward
> inclination—Right forward did he tread the path of duty—and
> we looked at him with the fondest hopes, that in after years he
> would be our pride and comfort as he was then a source of ten-
> der delight.[104]

Such a statement indicates very precisely the nature of duty in
Wordsworth's vision. A child who treads "the path of duty" will,
unlike Michael's Luke, be able to resist change and dissipation of
being, will in "after years" support the significant group and be a
"pride and comfort" to those of its members assaulted by diminu-
tion and weakening age.

If the Wordsworthian rigidity is apparent in the conception of
duty, it also is a factor, as we have suggested above, in the almost
feudal quality of his political conservatism. But the more *outré* as-
pects of that conservatism (he threatened to leave the country if the
Reform Bill of 1832 were enacted!)[105] were the result not solely of
rigidity but of rigidity compounded with withdrawal of emotional
affect. The affect withdrawn from the conception of society at large
was bestowed on the significant group, whose features we now
can clearly discern. For the significant group might most simply be
defined as that society the loss of any member of which attacks the

---

[103] Thus when John Wordsworth, a charter member of the significant group,
died, Wordsworth characteristically says that "his whole life was dignified by pru-
dence and firmness and self-denial—as far as my knowledge goes never did a man
live who had less to repent of than he. He was steady to his duty in all situations. I
praise him in a manner that would have shocked him, but I fall far, far, below the
truth" (*Early Years*, p. 565).

[104] *Middle Years*, II, 77-78.   [105] *Robinson*, I, 405.

participant's sense of his own being. Furthermore, the significant group is composed exactly of those people, the loving of whom and then the loss of whom tested Wordsworth's stoic fortitude throughout his life. His mother, we remember, died in his early childhood; his father, in his early adolescence; his brother, in the poet's early manhood; his son and daughter together, in his early middle age. His best friend dropped off; his beloved sister became insane; his favorite remaining daughter died before him in his extreme old age. To all these hammer blows Wordsworth reacted with cheerful stoicism; but surely his was a being under assault, an existence exposed to "the blind walk of mortal accident." Central to the whole situation was the extreme depth of Wordsworth's capacity for emotional attachment. Only by loving so deeply could he lose so deeply.[106] "We weep much to-day, and that relieves us," he said after his brother's death:

> As to fortitude, I hope I shall show that, and that all of us will

[106] Even through the protective armor of Wordsworth's stoicism we can, by accumulating his brief remarks to various correspondents after his brother's death, perhaps see—as in time-lapse photography—this depth of feeling. Their amassed weight is overwhelming: ". . . a great affliction . . . the set is now broken . . ."; "I can say nothing higher of my ever dear Brother than that he was worthy of his Sister who is now weeping beside me . . ."; "We have done all that could be done to console each other by weeping together"; ". . . oh my dear Friends! what have we not endured!"; "We know what we have lost, and what we have to endure; our anguish is allayed, but pain and sadness have taken place of it; with fits of sorrow which we endeavour to suppress but cannot"; ". . . let me again mention my beloved Brother"; "I shall never forget him, never lose sight of him"; "This affliction weighs so heavy on the hearts of all in this house, that we have neither strength nor spirits for any thing. Our Brother was the pride and delight of our hearts . . ."; "The distress of mind under which we are at present labouring is not to be measured by any living person but one, and that is poor Coleridge, who is now far from us, at Malta. Our Brother was so modest and shy a man, that not a tenth part of his worth, above all, his Taste, Genius, and intellectual merits was known to anybody but ourselves and Coleridge . . ."; ". . . he was innocent as he was brave . . ."; "I never wrote a line without a thought of its giving him pleasure . . ."; "We have lost so much hope and gladsome thought . . ."; "He loved every thing which we did, and every thing about us here incessantly reminds us of him and our irreparable loss. But I will not distress you, for you can give us no relief"; "He did not know how I loved and honored him, and how often he was in my thoughts"; ". . . to encourage you to write to us. I have now and then in my distress, turning here and turning there, a thought of this kind, and then I said to myself what can he write, or what can any body write to us" (Early Years, pp. 540, 541, 543, 544, 546, 547, 553, 562, 565, 566, 571, 572). What is especially clear in this accumulation is Wordsworth's constant referral of the dead brother to Dorothy and to Coleridge—the other charter members of the significant group—and to the idea of the group itself.

show it, in a proper time, in keeping down many a silent pang hereafter. [107]

It is in this regard that "We Are Seven"—a poem that shows marks of Coleridge's compositional symbiosis no less than does our other example of the yew-tree poem—can be seen as paradigmatic for the structure of the significant group. "We Are Seven" is a poem about diasparaction denied: about the breaking of the significant group and the refusal to accept that breaking:

> "Sisters and brothers, little Maid,
> How many may you be?"
> "How many? Seven in all," she said,
> And wondering looked at me.
>
> "And where are they? I pray you tell."
> She answered, "Seven are we;
> And two of us at Conway dwell,
> And two are gone to sea.
>
> "Two in the church-yard lie,
> My sister and my brother;
> And, in the church-yard cottage, I
> Dwell near them with my mother."

The primary speaker in the poem, who ironically combines worldly wisdom with the denudation of being that for Wordsworth accompanied adulthood, repeatedly attempts to insist on the fragmentation of the significant group; but the child, combining in counter-irony inexperience of reality and more intense feeling for human relationship, has the last word:

> "How many are you, then," said I,
> "If they two are in heaven?"
> Quick was the little Maid's reply,
> "O Master! we are seven."
>
> "But they are dead; those two are dead!
> Their spirits are in heaven!"
> 'Twas throwing words away; for still
> The little Maid would have her will,
> And said, "Nay, we are seven!" [108]

In the light of the foregoing discussion, it is evident that this

[107] *Early Years*, p. 542.   [108] Wordsworth, *Poems*, I, 236-37, 238.

poem, its deliberate simplicity notwithstanding, goes to the very heart of what Wordsworth valued and what he feared. Naive though its surface statement is, its deeper attitudes intertwine in a special complexity. The little girl is at once one who refuses to accept reality and one who serves a higher reality: she is that "best Philosopher" of the "Intimations Ode"; she is that "Eye among the blind"—and here as there the one who is blind is the informed adult who is the speaker. She is a specification of the way in which the child is "Mighty Prophet! Seer blest!/ On whom those truths do rest,/ Which we are toiling all our lives to find." She serves, still again, as parallel in figure and function to Dorothy in "Tintern Abbey":

> . . . thou my dearest Friend,
> My dear, dear Friend; . . . in thy voice I catch
> The language of my former heart, and read
> My former pleasures in the shooting lights
> Of thy wild eyes. Oh! yet a little while
> May I behold in thee what I was once,
> My dear, dear Sister![109]

The little girl of "We Are Seven" represents for Wordsworth the "language of my former heart"; he beholds in her "what I was once."

The child's denial of reality ironically echoes that tendency toward denial that guaranteed Wordsworth's own stoic cheerfulness, and that in a sense dictated his entire poetic effort—that thought of "life continuous, Being unimpaired," "existence unexposed/ To the blind walk of mortal accident;/ From diminution safe and weakening age." Still further, the "seven" who constitute the child's significant group contain among them both the living and the dead, and this, in Wordsworth's most mature conception, was indispensable to the idea of meaningful community:

> There is
> One great society alone on earth:
> The noble Living and the noble Dead.[110]

He expounds more fully upon this fundamental of the significant group in his prose writing, where he refers to the great society as a "spiritual community":

---

[109] *Ibid.*, II, 262.
[110] *Prelude*, 1850 version, p. 423 (XI, 393-95).

There is a spiritual community binding together the living and the dead; the good, the brave, and the wise, of all ages. We would not be rejected from this community; and therefore do we hope. We look forward with erect mind, thinking and feeling: it is an obligation of duty: take away the sense of it, and the moral being would die within us.[111]

Here again we see "duty" functioning to bind together the significant group.

The child's significant group, lastly, is constituted by her family circle. Family relationships were for Wordsworth those most cherished, and those that, when torn apart by death, generated the most pain. "My loss is great, and irreparable," he writes of the death of his brother—and might well have written of any of the losses he sustained within his family group.[112] On this occasion, indeed, he was so agonized as to pose the question whether "however inferior we may be to the great Cause and ruler of things, we have *more of love* in our Nature than he has?"[113]—an attitude that, at least in this instance, is not far from Blake's gnostic essential that "the Creator of this World is a very Cruel Being."[114] As De Quincey charged in 1816, with pique but not wholly without point, Wordsworth "is incapable of friendship out of his own family, and . . . is very secular in his feelings."[115]

The family, in brief, was for Wordsworth both the archetype of the ideal society and the center of all he held holy:[116] "the household of man" is his revealing phrase from the revised preface to *Lyrical Ballads*.[117] In his remarkable letter to Fox, which constitutes an enchiridion for his social beliefs, he draws an implied distinction between human life that has meaning and human life that does not (the great society is not simply the living and the dead, but the *noble* living and the *noble* dead). Life that does have meaning is possible only through "domestic affections":

[111] *Prose*, I, 339.

[112] *Early Years*, p. 548; and see above, note 106.

[113] *Ibid.*, p. 556.

[114] *Blake*, p. 555.

[115] *Robinson*, I, 196.

[116] Compare his statement to Robinson: "He repeated emphatically what he had said before to me, that he did not expect or desire from posterity any other fame than that which would be given him for the way in which his poems exhibit man in his essentially human character and relations—as child, parent, husband, the qualities which are common to all men as opposed to those which distinguish one man from another" (*Robinson*, II, 535).

[117] *Prose*, I, 141.

The domestic affections will always be strong amongst men who live in a country not crowded with population, if these men are placed above poverty. But if they are proprietors of small estates, which have descended to them from their ancestors, the power which these affections will acquire amongst these men is inconceivable by those who have only had an opportunity of observing hired labourers, farmers, and the manufacturing Poor. Their little tract of land serves as a kind of permanent rallying point for their domestic feelings, as a tablet upon which they are written which makes them objects of memory in a thousand instances when they would otherwise be forgotten. It is a fountain fitted to the nature of social man from which supplies of affection, as pure as his heart was intended for, are daily drawn.[118]

If the human life that is most meaningful requires placement in a natural setting—proprietorship of "small estates" that have descended from "ancestors"—the insistence not only accords with values that others have emphasized but reflects the structure of Wordsworth's psychic investment as well. For if his preoccupation with nature be ultimately a projection of human situation, so it seems fitting that nature then be reintegrated into human needs and concerns. And if the "small estates" are a sheltering of exposed existence by the protective cloak of nature, so does their descent from their owners' ancestors sanctify the child's wisdom of denial in "We Are Seven." The inheritance of the "small estate" is precisely a major agency in "binding together the living and the dead." One may remark parenthetically that Wordsworth's stress on his kind of property ownership stands at the antipodes from that most corrupt practice of modern capitalism: New York speculators buying unseen land to subdivide in the Rocky Mountains. Against such desecration he might have sided with Proudhon and declared property to be theft; for the implication of Wordsworth's attitude is that property not *lived into* by its owner is immoral.[119] The property should be both an extension of and bul-

---

[118] *Early Years*, pp. 314-15.

[119] E.g.: "Among the holders of fixed property (whether labourers in the field, or artisans;) among those who are fortunate enough to have an interest in the soil of their Country; these human sentiments of civil life are strengthened by additional dependencies.—I am aware how much universal habits of rapacious speculation . . . —how much the spread of manufactories . . . have done to impair these indigenous and salutary affections. I am conscious of the sad deterioration . . . but sufficient vitality is left in the Stock of ancient virtue to furnish hope . . . were it not for the base artifices of Malignants, who, pretending to invigorate the tree, pour scalding water and corrosive compounds among its roots" (*Prose*, III, 187).

wark for the unique personality that inhabits it (Wordsworth, had he known them, would almost surely have found himself in agreement with the social theories of his contemporary, Adam Müller, whereby possessions are justified by being regarded as extensions of the limbs of the body).[120] Finally, the lived-into property, by its descent from ancestors, is above all the locus of family relationships.

This complex of Wordsworthian emphases is perhaps nowhere better illustrated than in what Coleridge termed "the divine Poem called Michael."[121] The work contains some of the most limpid verse Wordsworth ever composed, and constitutes possibly the finest realization of his prosodic theories of simplicity and naturalness of diction. Furthermore, its charge of emotion is so strong that the pathos achieved is almost sublime—matched only, one thinks, if at all, by the pathos of "The Ruined Cottage."[122]

"Michael" is, in short, a great and quintessentially Wordsworthian achievement,[123] and thereby added significance is lent to the fact that in it the three aspects of the complex just elucidated are classically presented: the family as archetypal society; the small estate as extension of its owner's personality; and *lived-into* land as the arena of communal interaction.

Michael's land is the projection of his own heart, and his heart is in turn the land:

> Those fields, those hills—what could they less? had laid
> Strong hold on his affections, were to him

---

[120] Müller's argument runs thus: "If the relation of man to his physical possessions were completely and absolutely different from the other relations of man to persons . . . there would be, outside the realm of persons, in which a living law reigns, a special realm of things, subjugated to a merely mechanical law of understanding. . . . It would be an easy task to trace all real-relations back to personal-relations, to show that all property has worth not for the man in himself but for the man in civil society and for the sake of this society . . . that accordingly the whole of civil society is interested in the use of the most insignificant possession of the individual; that things possessed are therefore nothing other than necessary accessories—I might say extended limbs (*erweiterte Gliedmaßen*) of the human body—with the consequence that what we call 'person' is a little world of things possessed (*Sachen*)" (Müller, *Elemente*, I, 155-56).

[121] *Collected Letters*, II, 707. Cf. *Notebooks*, I, 1782.

[122] The latter effort was praised by Coleridge as "the finest poem in our Language" (*Collected Letters*, IV, 564).

[123] Cf. Arnold: "If I had to pick out poems of a kind most perfectly to show Wordsworth's unique power, I should rather choose poems such as *Michael, The Fountain, The Highland Reaper*" (Arnold, *Essays*, pp. 159-60).

> A pleasurable feeling of blind love,
> The pleasure which there is in life itself.

This land is not inhabited in selfish isolation, however; it is the natural setting for the small but complete society of Michael's love:

> His days had not been passed in singleness.
> His Helpmate was a comely matron, old—
> Though younger than himself full twenty years.
> She was a woman of a stirring life,
> Whose heart was in her house:

The conception of the land as binding together the "great society" of living and dead, and simultaneously the sense of this society as personally connected—as familial in its history—is unequivocally set forth:

> I have been toiling more than seventy years,
> And in the open sunshine of God's love
> Have we all lived; yet if these fields of ours
> Should pass into a stranger's hand, I think
> That I could not lie quiet in my grave.

The significant group is completed by the son, Luke, who by his status as child symbolizes the blessedness of the situation and the hope of its continuation:

> The Shepherd, if he loved himself, must needs
> Have loved his Helpmate; but to Michael's heart
> This son of his old age was yet more dear—
> Less from instinctive tenderness, the same
> Fond spirit that blindly works in the blood of all—
> Than that a child, more than all other gifts
> That earth can offer to declining man,
> Brings hope with it, and forward-looking thoughts

But then the group is broken; Michael's heart and life are broken; the relationship to the land itself is broken. The monument to this massive onset of diasparaction is the sheepfold, eternally fragmentary and incomplete: "The length of full seven years, from time to time,/ He at the building of this Sheepfold wrought,/ And left the work unfinished when he died." And this monument focuses the pathos of the poem:

> Among the rocks
> He went, and still looked up to sun and cloud,

> And listened to the wind; and, as before,
> Performed all kinds of labour for his sheep,
> And for the land, his small inheritance.
> And to that hollow dell from time to time
> Did he repair, to build the Fold of which
> His flock had need. 'Tis not forgotten yet
> The pity which was then in every heart
> For the old Man—and 'tis believed by all
> That many and many a day he thither went,
> And never lifted up a single stone.

Luke's defection not only breaks the significant group but also indicates the kind of human assembly that to Wordsworth was the enemy of significance: the society of the city:

> . . . Luke began
> To slacken in his duty; and, at length,
> He in the dissolute city gave himself
> To evil courses: ignominy and shame
> Fell on him, so that he was driven at last
> To seek a hiding-place beyond the seas.[124]

To Wordsworth, the transitory, anonymous, and chaotic life of the city stood in horrible antithesis to all he held dear in society. The significant group that redeemed man from the abyss of egotism was maintained by fewness in number, spatial placement in lived-into property, and continuity in time. London, on the contrary, was a "monstrous ant-hill on the plain/ Of a too busy world!" The variety of types and multiplication of numbers that to many have been fascinations in city life were to Wordsworth a deprivation of all meaning:

> How oft, amid those overflowing streets,
> Have I gone forward with the crowd, and said
> Unto myself, "The face of every one
> That passes by me is a mystery!"

This effect, whereby multiplication of people breaks down human meaning, is symbolized by the blind beggar—a derelict figure whose blankness as a city-dweller presents a strong contrast to the Old Leech-Gatherer's humanity in the country:

> Amid the moving pageant, I was smitten
> Abruptly, with the view (a sight not rare)

[124] Wordsworth, *Poems*, ii, 83, 83, 87-88, 85, 94, 93-94, 93.

Of a blind Beggar, who, with upright face,
Stood, propped against a wall, upon his chest
Wearing a written paper, to explain
His story, whence he came, and who he was.
Caught by the spectacle my mind turned round
As with the might of waters; an apt type
This label seemed of the utmost we can know,
Both of ourselves and of the universe

The groupings of the city thus diminished rather than enhanced the sense of the unique personality, and thereby paradoxically suppressed the very variety of relationship that for Wordsworth was necessary to redeem the egotistical sublime. Bartholomew Fair, which in Ben Jonson's art had been a place for affectionate if therapeutic sporting with human weakness and folly, became in Wordsworth's vision little less than pandemonium itself:

What a shock
For eyes and ears! what anarchy and din,
Barbarian and infernal,—a phantasma,
Monstrous in colour, motion, shape, sight, sound!

It was a collection of "All out-o'-the-way, far-fetched, perverted things,/ All freaks of nature." But most of all, it negated, rather than preserved, the very spatiality and uniqueness of the individual necessary to a significant group:

Oh, blank confusion! true epitome
Of what the mighty City is herself,
To thousands upon thousands of her sons,
Living amid the same perpetual whirl
Of trivial objects, melted and reduced
To one identity[125]

Wordsworth thus recoiled from what we have termed the liberal mythology of the meaningfulness of life in and of itself. If egotistical isolation was to be feared, so too was the immersion—the drowning rather—of the individual in the experience of the multitude. Only concrete and continuing relationships, constantly defined and renewed by love, gave value to existence.

Thus in his largest commitments—to begin to proceed to more modern instances—Wordsworth stood at the opposite extreme

---

[125] *Prelude*, 1850 version, p. 229 (vii, 149-50); p. 255 (vii, 626-29); p. 257 (vii, 639-46); p. 259 (vii, 685-88); p. 261 (vii, 714-15); (vii, 722-27).

from Dickens's Mrs. Jellyby, who worried about Africa while her household and children were neglected. Mrs. Jellyby's eyes "had a curious habit of seeming to look a long way off," as if "they could see nothing nearer than Africa!"; and she held a discussion "of which the subject seemed to be—if I understood it—the Brotherhood of Humanity; and gave utterance to some beautiful sentiments." But her daughter bursts out:

> "I wish Africa was dead!" she said, on a sudden. I was going to remonstrate.
> "I do!" she said. "Don't talk to me, Miss Summerson. I hate and detest it. It's a beast!"[126]

The point of Dicken's satire is not restricted to Mrs. Jellyby. If Wordsworth's conservatism was to some extent dictated by a withdrawal of emotion from mankind at large and a redirection toward the significant group, the "radical chic" of our own day often simply reverses that process. I am mindful of a paradigmatic cocktail party conversation a few years ago, in which, after expressions of agonized concern for Biafra, my interlocutress briskly dismissed the suicide of a man we both knew with an attitude equivalent to sweeping him into the trash bin. What was true in this instance has been, in my rather dishearteningly extensive experience, almost a norm for the relationship of humanitarian protestation to actual practice. One recalls Burke's trenchant attack on Rousseau, who exhausted "the stores of his powerful rhetoric in the expression of universal benevolence, whilst his heart was incapable of harboring one spark of common parental affection." In Burke's observation, "Benevolence to the whole species, and want of feeling for every individual with whom the professors come in contact," were the hallmarks of Rousseau's philosophy.[127] The spiritual descendants of Rousseau are with us yet and evermore.

As with Burke, Wordsworth's reaction against the French Revolution came about not as a rejection of humane ideals, but as a judgment that those ideals had been betrayed; and ultimately as the conclusion that they could not practically be realized. In a sense he always remained a republican; the structure of the significant group incorporated an honoring of liberty, equality, and fraternity. It was not in any way dependent upon a privilege of birth or wealth, and its feudal nature is qualified by that idiosyncrasy:

[126] *Bleak House*, Chapter IV; "Telescopic Philanthropy."
[127] *Burke's Writings*, p. 387.

> It was my fortune scarcely to have seen,
> Through the whole tenor of my school-day time,
> The face of one, who, whether boy or man,
> Was vested with attention or respect
> Through claims of wealth or blood

Membership in a significant group was on the contrary open to all, for such a group was maintained by a valuing of human life that radiated out from primary relationships:

> . . . my affections first were led
> From kindred, friends, and playmates, to partake
> Love for the human creature's absolute self

His "heart" was through such relationships, and through nature,

> early introduced
> To an unconscious love and reverence
> Of human nature.[128]

With such idealism, he, like ardent spirits throughout Europe, greeted the Revolution as a great step forward for humanity:

> Bliss was it in that dawn to be alive,
> But to be young was very Heaven!
> . . . the whole Earth
> The beauty wore of promise[129]

From the wreck of the overthrown Bastille

> A golden palace rose, or seemed to rise
> . . . The potent shock
> I felt: the transformation I perceived,
> As marvellously seized as in that moment
> When, from the blind mist issuing, I beheld
> Glory—beyond all glory ever seen[130]

He soon became "a patriot, and my heart was all/ Given to the

---

[128] *Prelude*, 1850 version, p. 327 (ix, 218-22); p. 273 (viii, 121-23); p. 287 (viii, 277-79).

[129] *Ibid.*, p. 407 (xi, 108-18). Cf. Hegel, who with reference to the French Revolution speaks of "a glorious dawn [*ein herrlicher Sonnenaufgang*]. All thinking things shared in the jubilation of this epoch. Emotions of a lofty character stirred men's minds at that time; a spiritual enthusiasm thrilled through the world, as if the reconciliation between the divine and the secular were now first accomplished" (*Hegel's Werke*, ix, 535-36).

[130] Wordsworth, *Poems*, v, 101.

people, and my love was theirs"; "in the People was my trust."
The ideals of the Revolution seemed such a logical extension of
"love and reverence/ Of human nature" that to stand against its
tide seemed to argue a personal malignancy of spirit. All the weight
of humanity seemed on the side of the great stirring—the "Domes-
tic severings, female fortitude/ At dearest separation, patriot love/
And self-devotion, and terrestrial hope" that accompanied the
early days of the Revolution were like

> arguments from Heaven, that 'twas a cause
> Good, and which no one could stand up against,
> Who was not lost, abandon'd, selfish, proud,
> Mean, miserable, wilfully deprav'd,
> Hater perverse of equity and truth

Such a hater Wordsworth neither was nor ever wanted to be.

His mind, as did that of other noble-spirited young men of the
time, could move quickly from obvious wrong to exalted visions of
apocalyptic amelioration:

> And when we chanced
> One day to meet a hunger-bitten Girl,
> Who crept along fitting her languid self
> Unto a Heifer's motion
>   . . . at the sight my Friend
> In agitation said, ' 'Tis against *that*
> Which we are fighting,' I with him believed
> Devoutly that a spirit was abroad
> Which could not be withstood, that poverty
> At least like this, would in a little time
> Be found no more . . .
> All institutes for ever blotted out
> That legalized exclusion, empty pomp
> Abolish'd, sensual state and cruel power,
> Whether by edict of the one or few,
> And finally, as sum and crown of all,
> Should see the People having a strong hand
> In making their own Laws, whence better days
> To all mankind.[131]

In this view of futurity, all society would participate in the struc-
ture of a significant group:

[131] *Prelude*, 1850 version, pp. 321 (ix, 123-24), 401 (xi, 11); 1805 version, pp. 328-30
(ix, 276-92); pp. 340-42 (ix, 509-32).

> . . . prophetic harps
> In every grove were ringing, 'War shall cease;
> Did ye not hear that conquest is abjured?
> Bring garlands, bring forth choicest flowers, to deck
> The tree of Liberty. . . .
> Henceforth, whate'er is wanting to yourselves
> In others ye shall promptly find;—and all,
> Enriched by mutual and reflected wealth,
> Shall with one heart honour their common kind.'[132]

Disillusionment, when it came, was harsh. The very residence in France that so exhilarated Wordsworth made him more vividly aware of the rapid degeneration of Revolutionary ideals than was, for instance, "English Blake." His first realizations that "Lamentable crimes,/ . . . the work/ Of massacre" had been committed were hopefully dismissed. Such occurrences were "Ephemeral monsters, to be seen but once!"; and "inflamed with hope,/ To Paris I returned." But as terror continued, and the Moloch-figure of Robespierre rose over the scene, the exhilaration vanished:

> O Friend!
> It was a lamentable time for man. . . .
> A woeful time for them whose hopes did still
> Outlast the shock; most woeful for those few,
> They had the deepest feeling of the grief
> Who still were flattered, and had trust in man. . . .
> Most melancholy at that time, O Friend!
> Were my day-thoughts, my dreams were miserable; . . .
> I scarcely had one night of quiet sleep
> Such ghastly visions had I of despair
> And tyranny, and implements of death,
> And long orations which in dreams I pleaded
> Before unjust Tribunals,—[133]

Robespierre—"a Caligula with the cap of Liberty on his head," in Coleridge's image[134]—was followed by Napoleon and the Revolutionary mockery of the empire: "to close/ And rivet up the gains of France, a Pope/ Is summon'd in, to crown an Emperor—/ This last opprobrium, when we see the dog/ Returning to his vomit." From being the nourisher of human hopes France became a defiler of those hopes:

[132] Wordsworth, *Poems*, v, 101.
[133] *Prelude*, p. 368 (x, 29-39); pp. 386-88 (xi, 355-78).
[134] *Lectures 1795*, p. 35.

And now, become Oppressors in their turn
Frenchmen had changed a war of self-defense
For one of conquest, losing sight of all
Which they had struggled for[135]

The cumulative effect of these progressive disillusionments led
Wordsworth to what he memorably terms a "loss of confidence in
social man."[136] He had glimpsed and been repelled by what Taine
retrospectively described as the social bestiality of the French Revo-
lution: "from the peasant, the laborer, the bourgeois, pacified and
tamed by an old civilization, we see suddenly spring forth the bar-
barian, and still worse, the primitive animal, the grinning, bloody,
wanton baboon, who chuckles while he plays, and gambols over
the ruin (dégâts) he has accomplished."[137] Wordsworth had ini-
tially approached, "like other Youth, the Shield/ Of human nature
from the golden side";[138] but the Terror forced him to conclude
that "the weak functions of one busy day" could not reclaim, extir-

[135] Prelude, p. 420 (x, 933-36); p. 412 (x, 792-95).

[136] Wordsworth, Poems, v, 117.

[137] Taine, ii, 70. Taine's view finds its polar opposite in that of Michelet, who saw
the Revolution as the most glorious event of world history: "I define the
Revolution,—The advent of the Law, the resurrection of Right, and the reaction of
Justice." The Revolution was "the tardy reaction of Justice against the government
of favor and the religion of grace." "What is the old regime, the king, the priest, in
the old monarchy?" he asks, and his answer is: "tyranny in the name of grace."
"What is the Revolution?" he then asks, and his answer is: "The reaction of equity,
the tardy coming of eternal justice" (Michelet, i, 17, 29, 87-88). The Revolution was
the "day of Judgment"; it overthrew "The unjust transmission of good, perpetuated in
the rights of the nobility; the unjust transmission of evil, by original sin" (Michelet, i,
32, 10). The Revolution "began by loving everything"; the Terror, explained
Michelet, was almost as nothing compared to the injustices perpetrated by the long
history of established Christianity: "Let the revolutionary reign of Terror beware of
comparing herself with the Inquisition. Let her never boast of having, in her two or
three years, paid back to the old system what it did to us for six hundred years! The
Inquisition would have good cause to laugh! What are the sixteen thousand men
guillotined of the one, to the millions of men butchered, hanged, broken on the
wheel,—to that pyramid of burning stakes, to those masses of burnt flesh, which
the other piled up to heaven" (i, 11, 34). Michelet, like Shelley, was especially out-
raged by the thought of "tyrants" ('Though a sworn enemy to barbarous fictions
about everlasting punishment, I found myself praying to God to construct a hell for
tyrants" [Michelet, i, 82]); and if we feel justified in looking to Sir Timothy Shelley
for the origin of his son's preoccupation with tyranny, we might also find it signifi-
cant that Michelet was still living with his own father at the age of forty-eight. At
any rate, the French historian reacted with fury to "Two paternal powers: ecclesias-
tical paternity, characterized by the Inquisition; monarchical paternity, by the Red
Book and the Bastille" (i, 72).

[138] Prelude, p. 404 (x, 663-64).

pate, and perform "What all the slowly-moving years of time,/ With their united forces, have left undone."[139] His vision of building "social upon personal Liberty" gave way to ever more unrewarding examination of doctrine:

> Thus I fared,
> Dragging all passions, notions, shapes of faith,
> Like culprits to the bar, suspiciously
> Calling the mind to establish in plain day
> Her titles and her honours, now believing,
> Now disbelieving, endlessly perplex'd
> With impulse, motive, right and wrong, the ground
> Of moral obligation, what the rule
> And what the sanction, till, demanding *proof*,
> And seeking it in everything, I lost
> All feelings of conviction, and, in fine,
> Sick, wearied out with contrarieties
> Yielded up moral questions in despair

From this retreat into confusion and disillusionment, he was saved by the significant group—by his sister, "Companion never lost through many a league," who "Maintained for me a saving intercourse/ With my true self"; and by Coleridge, "Thou, most precious Friend!" who "didst lend a living help/ To regulate my Soul."

It was those two, Coleridge and Dorothy, who vitalized for Wordsworth the conception of the significant group. The entity as a whole contained also his brother John, his wife Mary, and his sister-in-law Sara; Coleridge and Dorothy, however, were the defining members. "But Thou art with us," writes Wordsworth of Coleridge,

> with us in the past,
> The present, with us in the times to come.
> There is no grief, no sorrow, no despair,
> No languor, no dejection, no dismay,
> No absence scarcely can be there, for those
> Who love as we do.

The emotional triplicity—that is, the changing of simple adhesion into the special structure of group—was completed by Dorothy. Wordsworth felt himself, and Coleridge as well, to be "blest" with a joy

[139] Wordsworth, *Poems*, v, 117.

Above all joys, that seem'd another morn
Risen on mid noon, the presence, Friend, I mean
Of that sole Sister, she who hath been long
Thy Treasure also, thy true friend and mine,
Now, after separation desolate
Restor'd to me—[140]

Wordsworth withdrew into the significant group after having been both pulled away and pushed away from the vision of social panacea initially offered by the French Revolution. The pushing away was effected by the Terror and its bloodshed; the pulling away, by his personal and idiosyncratic involvement in the egotistical sublime—the need to restore "intercourse/ With my true self." It was henceforth no longer the case that "in the People was my trust"; rather, his idealism was displaced into the conviction that only the few can raise themselves to meaningful life: "Endeavour thus to live . . . / . . . and a stedfast seat/ Shall then be yours among the happy few/ Who dwell on earth, yet breathe empyreal air,/ Sons of the morning."[141] The displacement in effect aligned him morally and politically with Plato, who, to the continuing dismay of Karl Popper and his followers, equated the many with a "great beast," and was convinced that "Philosophy, then, the love of wisdom, is impossible for the multitude."[142]

In this altered vision, Wordsworth's love of humanity (even as early as "An Evening Walk" he had expressed "Entire affection for all human kind")[143] became increasingly qualified by recognitions of disabling defects in social man:

[140] Prelude, pp. 416-18 (x, 891-901); 418-20 (x, 914-16); 418 (906-908); 188 (vi, 251-56); 184-86 (vi, 210-17). For the structure of the significant group, compare John Beer: "If the power of the heart was as strong as he [Wordsworth] and Coleridge believed, the various cross-links of affection and love (William-Mary, William-Dorothy, Coleridge-Sara, John-Sara, and so on) could all support and draw sustenance from that central nexus, so that the members of the group with their various gifts (Wordsworth and the three women as a rooted and creative household; Coleridge as visiting intelligence; John giving the world its due for the time being by serving at sea and then returning in the future to help support his relatives) would form a strong and fruitful community, an organism linked both to the ideal and the real. The interlinked initials, W. W., D. W., M. W., S. H., J. W., S.T.C., which they carved on a rock-face by Thirlmere (—significantly, on a rock by a spring) evidently formed a visual charm expressive of this shared faith." (Wordsworth and the Human Heart [London and Basingstoke: The Macmillan Press Ltd., 1978], pp. 165-66).

[141] Wordsworth, Poems, v, 116.
[142] Republic 493C, 494A.
[143] Wordsworth, Poems, I, 11.

Neither vice nor guilt,
Debasement undergone by body or mind,
Nor all the misery forced upon my sight,
Misery not lightly passed, but sometimes scanned
Most feelingly, could overthrow my trust
In what we *may* become.[144]

Thus he came in effect to share the sentiment of Keats: "I admire Human Nature but I do not like *Men*."[145]

As years went by, both Wordsworth's tendency to rigidification and his withdrawal of emotional affect from the idea of society at large left their marks. The husks of these later attitudes are well described by Mrs. Moorman:

His extreme horror of Lord Grey's Reform Bill has to be understood in the light of his own depressive temperament which always tended to expect the worst consequences from all measures which he could not approve. He had given way entirely to his uncontrollable dread of 'the mob' which had been increasing in him ever since the days of Robespierre.[146]

His fear of and contempt for the undifferentiated mass—"the mob" (an abhorrence he shared with Shakespeare no less than with Plato)—were complemented, however, by the more positive aspect of his ever-deepening commitment to the significant group.

---

[144] *Prelude*, 1850 version, p. 309 (viii, 645-50).

[145] Keats, *Letters*, i, 415.

[146] Moorman, ii, 466. Cf. Wordsworth in 1817: "Faction runs high—The Friends of liberty and good order are alarmed at the corruption of opinion among the lower classes, and the Reformers and Revolutionists are irritated and provoked that their plans have for the present been defeated. For my own part I am full of fears, not for the present; the immediate danger will, I think be got over, but there is a malady in our social constitution which it will require the utmost skill to manage, and which if it is not met with firmness and knowledge will end in the dissolution of the body Politic. When I have the pleasure of seeing you, I will explain my views at length, and state to you the grounds of my apprehensions" (*Middle Years*, ii, 377). Wordsworth was scarcely starting at shadows, for England's stability and continuity become apparent only in historical hindsight; actually, from about 1812 on into the 1830s England teetered on the brink of the French example. Thus Shelley in 1819: "Many thanks for your attention in sending the papers which contain the terrible and important news of Manchester. These are, as it were, the distant thunders of the terrible storm which is approaching. The tyrants here, as in the French Revolution, have first shed blood" (Shelley, *Letters*, ii, 119). Again: "These, my dear Hunt, are awful times . . . whatever revolutions are to occur, though oppression should change names & names cease to be oppressions, our party will be that of liberty & of the oppre[ss]ed" (p. 148).

For the "mob" was merely people too crowded and deracinated to participate in meaningful relationship. In this context, we are justified in saying that Wordsworth's ideals never changed; only his cognizance of their possibilities changed. As a commentator sees:

Wordsworth's sympathy with the French Revolution was . . . never an independent or a primary matter. It was the corollary of a prior loyalty, his faith in the sort of persons whom he later made his chosen heroes. . . . At this point Legouis, and all who have followed his lead, have misread the poet. William Wordsworth was from first to last a stubborn north-country Englishman, anxious above all else, in political matters, to perpetuate the society in which he had grown up as a boy and youth.

His one desire was to insure to the world men like Michael. He was a revolutionist as long as the Revolution promised to yield him such men. When the Revolution failed him here, degenerating into a new tyranny, he lost all interest in it. He turned to Toryism because political thinking of that type seemed to him at the time more likely than any other to guarantee him his freeman.[147]

There is a third factor that demands consideration. Pushed into commitment to the significant group by disillusionment with universal social solutions, and pulled into it by his tendency to the egotistical sublime, Wordsworth held ever-tighter to it in response to the dwindling of those who constituted its being. The loss of each uniquely valuable relationship hammered him, as it were, further into himself, and caused him to question the whole purpose and meaning of mankind. "Alas! what is human life!"[148] he exclaimed after his brother's death; and such a shaking of assumption and value could hardly help restore his loss of confidence in social man.

Rigid and reactionary though Wordsworth's political attitudes eventually became, however, they should not be dismissed as nothing more than idiosyncrasy. The name of Burke alone should remind us that Wordsworth's cherishing of the significant group was not solely the expression of his special cognizance of meaning in human life, but also participated in broader historical currents. It would, indeed, be an interesting and illuminating task to explore in detail the historical analogies to Wordsworth's conservatism. Al-

[147] Sperry, p. 75.　　　　　　　　[148] *Early Years*, p. 541.

though, as we have been at pains to elucidate, his attitudes arose primarily from tensions in his own psychological development and needs, they none the less conformed in important respects to those of contemporary conservative thinkers.

Romanticism, in fact, though in a sense inaugurated by the French Revolution (which was, in Shelley's words to Byron, "the master theme of the epoch in which we live"),[149] distributed the energy thus stirred up in a polar form. Although figures such as Blake, and Shelley himself, espoused what may loosely be termed the Jacobin tradition ("The system of society as it exists at present," said Shelley, "must be overthrown from the foundations with all its superstructure of maxims & of forms"),[150] figures such as Wordsworth and Coleridge opposed it.[151] "No man," claimed Coleridge in retrospect,

> was more enthusiastic than I was for France and the Revolution: it had all my wishes, none of my expectations. Before 1793, I clearly saw and often enough stated in public, the horrid delusion, the vile mockery of the whole affair. When some one said in my brother James's presence that I was a Jacobin, he very well observed—"No! Samuel is no Jacobin; he is a hot-headed Moravian!" Indeed, I was in the extreme opposite pole.[152]

In this polar opposition, Burke, as Cobban and others have shown, was the intellectual leader. But Burke was not the only philosopher of conservatism, and Wordsworth's opinions exhibit affinities to the thought of such continental writers as Justus Möser—"der herrliche Justus Möser," in Goethe's words[153]—and Adam Müller

---

[149] Shelley, *Letters*, I, 504. [150] *Ibid.*, II, 191.

[151] For European Romanticism as a whole, those who took the Jacobin side of the future, and those who took the conservative side of the past were fairly evenly divided. The pattern exhibited by Wordsworth and Coleridge, of first welcoming, and then rejecting the Revolution occurred repeatedly among figures on the continent as well. For instance, a commentator speaks as follows of Joseph Görres: "Görres started his remarkable career as a Jacobin and as an enthusiastic follower of French ideals." "The breach with France resulting from his disillusionment became final when in 1800 he went to Paris as a deputy of the Rhineland . . . 'I have seen the actors undressed behind the scenes,' Görres wrote from Paris." "With the 18th Brumaire the Revolution had in his opinion ceased to be a movement which set the pace for the world and had degenerated into an immoral dictatorship. Görres became anti-French not because he lost his belief in republican principles but because he lost his confidence in the French Republicans" (Aris, pp. 321, 329).

[152] *Table Talk*, pp. 172-73 (July 23, 1832).

[153] *Gedenkausgabe*, x, 651. Goethe also refers to Möser as "this incomparable man" and provides an excellent summary of a major contention in Möser's line of

(the latter's *Die Elemente der Staatskunst* [1809] is of special relevance to Romantic conservatism in general).[154] Later contributions, such as Taine's massive *Les Origines de la France contemporaine* and the writings of Maurice Barrès, extend the historical perspective of anti-revolutionary conservatism. In fact, Barrès, both by his insistence on the continuity between the living and the dead, and by his stress on human relationship to the soil, seems in certain ways an unintentional epigone of Wordsworth. In Wordsworth's own era, moreover, other conservative thinkers such as Bonald, Joseph de Maistre, and Friedrich Schlegel were active and are pertinent to his position.

Among these and other theorists, however, and without discounting the special importance of Wordsworth's similarity to both Müller and Möser, one might say that the conservative analogies for the great poet's stance are most satisfyingly embodied by Burke.[155] Hazlitt identifies the "clue" to all Burke's "reasoning on politics" in these words:

---

thought: "Where one as a rule reproached the German *Reich* with splintering, anarchy, and powerlessness, from the standpoint of Möser it was precisely the crowd of small states that seemed highly desirable for the spreading of culture in the particular, according to the needs that proceed from the situation and condition of the different provinces" (x, 703). Had this essential of Möser's conservatism been heeded, it is obvious that German militarism, from Bismarck through Hitler, could never have gained a significant foothold. "Möser opposed the rationalism of the Enlightenment," notes a commentator: "He most strongly rejected the *philosophes'* tendency to want to make life and society uniform." "He consistently stressed the individual, the historical, the unique, and the manifold in his refutation of the uniformity of rationalism. The individual unit of most concern to him . . . was the small state." "That value which Möser missed the most on the local scene and in all of Germany was honor. . . . Honor comprised the rights and obligations of the property-owner, or shareholder" (William F. Sheldon, *The Intellectual Development of Justus Möser: The Growth of a German Patriot* [Osnabruck: Kommissionsverlag H. Th. Wenner, 1970], pp. 103, 106, 114-15). For Möser's emphasis on political honor, cf. Wordsworth: "Sir Philip Sidney, of whom it has been said, that he first taught this country *the majesty of honest dealing*" (*Prose*, I, 257). Again: "How base! how puny! how inefficient for all good purposes are the tools and implements of policy. . . . Justice must . . . be enthroned above might, and the moral law take place of the edicts of selfish passion" (*Prose*, I, 292).

[154] See Reinhold Aris, *Die Staatslehre Adam Müllers in ihrem Verhältnis zur deutschen Romantik* (Tübingen: J.C.B. Mohr [Paul Siebeck], 1929).

[155] But the essentials of conservative thought, which involve the idea of organic form, the importance of the family as a model for the state, and a deferring to the historical reality of the feudal past, tend to appear again and again in thinkers widely separated in place and circumstance; and we should heed the opinion of a commentator: "It does in fact seem that many of the principles and opinions which

He saw in the construction of society other principles at work, and other capacities of fulfilling the desires, and perfecting the nature of man, besides those of securing the equal enjoyment of the means of animal life. . . . He thought that the wants and happiness of men were not to be provided for, as we provide for those of a herd of cattle, merely by attending to their physical necessities. He thought more nobly of his fellows. He knew that man had affections and passions and powers of imagination, as well as hunger and thirst and the sense of heat and cold. He took his idea of political society from the pattern of private life, wishing, as he himself expresses it, to incorporate the domestic charities with the orders of the state, and to blend them together. He strove to establish an analogy between the compact that binds together the community at large and that which binds together the several families that compose it. He knew that the rules that form the basis of private morality are not founded in reason . . . but in the nature of man, and his capacity of being affected by certain things from habit, from imagination, and sentiment, as well as from reason. [156]

The congruence of these essentials of Burke's political philosophy with Wordsworth's object-oriented, family-vitalized social vision is apparent. Equally so is that between Wordsworth's commitment to the significant group and Burke's ordering of the priorities of human concern. To Burke, in Hazlitt's words,

---

the later Wordsworth held and which are so similar to Burke's were arrived at more as a consequence of his own experience than as the result of his study of the politician's writings. He drew conclusions from the course of the French Revolution almost identical with those which Burke had prophetically drawn; his attitude to nature and his life among the statesmen of the Lake District led him to opinions about the role of tradition, permanence and gradualism in national life which were again almost identical with Burke's. It seems as though it were only when he realized the large area of agreement which had been unconsciously established between them that he turned to Burke's writings for confirmation" (Todd, p. 170).

[156] *Hazlitt*, VII, 306. Among numerous other common emphases, Burke and Wordsworth shared this proleptic rejection of the Marxist referral of all cultural meanings to the economic infrastructure. Thus in *The Convention of Cintra* Wordsworth says: "Not by bread alone is the life of Man sustained; not by raiment alone is he warmed;—but by the genial and vernal inmate of the breast, which at once pushes forth and cherishes; by self-support and self-sufficing endeavours; by anticipations, apprehensions, and active remembrances; by elasticity under insult, and firm resistance to injury; by joy, and by love; by pride which his imagination gathers in from afar; by patience . . . ; by admiration; by gratitude" (*Prose*, I, 326).

the reason why a man ought to be attached to his wife and children is not, surely, that they are better than others, (for in this case every one else ought to be of the same opinion) but because he must be chiefly interested in those things which are nearest to him, and with which he is best acquainted, since his understanding cannot reach equally to every thing; because he must be most attached to those objects which he has known the longest, and which by their situation have actually affected him the most . . . ; that is, because he is by his nature the creature of habit and feeling, and because it is reasonable that he should act in conformity to his nature.[157]

Such, in Hazlitt's description, were Burke's basic tenets. Strikingly apposite to those of Wordsworth, they assume special importance as the considered conclusions of a political mind of the first magnitude. As Hazlitt says (his tribute is the more remarkable in that he regarded Burke as "an enemy" of his own radically democratic principles), Burke's "stock of ideas did not consist of a few meagre facts, meagrely stated, of half a dozen common-places tortured in a thousand different ways; but his mine of wealth was a profound understanding, inexhaustible as the human heart, and various as the sources of nature. He therefore enriched every subject to which he applied himself, and new subjects were only the occasions of calling forth fresh powers of mind which had not been before exerted. It would therefore be in vain to look for the proof of his powers in any one of his speeches or writings: they all contain some additional proof of power."[158]

In addition to the correspondences obtaining between the basic priorities of Burke and Wordsworth, Wordsworth's turning from support to repudiation of the French Revolution duplicated in his private experience the pattern that Burke, on the larger stage of national political life, exhibited in turning from espousal of the American Revolution to rejection of the French; and perhaps the

[157] Hazlitt, vii, 306. With the emphasis on the family shared by Burke and Wordsworth, compare Adam Müller: "it must become clear that the state is nothing other than the expanded family, and that the first fundamental test of all constitutions and laws is the investigation: whether and how far they harmonize with family relationships, and whether the two relations that constitute the inner unity of every family, that of old and young on one side, and of male and female on the other, uniformly permeate the whole legal structure" (Müller, Elemente, i, 89).

[158] Hazlitt, vii, 301. Compare Matthew Arnold's judgment that "Burke is so great because, almost alone in England, he brings thought to bear upon politics, he saturates politics with thought."

best political commentary to the metamorphosis of Wordsworth's attitude to French Republican dogma is supplied by the *Reflections on the Revolution in France*.[159]

In such contexts of similar conviction and fellow-feeling, it was entirely fitting that the 1850 version of "The Prelude" should incorporate a direct salutation to Burke:

> Genius of Burke! forgive the pen seduced
> By specious wonders. . . .
> I see him,—old, but vigorous in age,—
> Stand like an oak. . . .
> While he forewarns, denounces, launches forth,
> Against all systems built on abstract rights,
> Keen ridicule; the majesty proclaims
> Of Institutes and Laws, hallowed by time;
> Declares the vital power of social ties
> Endeared by Custom; and with high disdain,
> Exploding upstart Theory, insists
> Upon the allegiance to which men are born—[160]

To be sure, there are differences between Burke and Wordsworth; Wordsworth was a relative novice in politics, whereas Burke was one of the great govenmental practitioners and theorists ("He knew more of the political machine than a recluse philosopher," said Hazlitt, "and he speculated more profoundly on its principles and general results than a mere politician").[161] But the differences are less urgent than the deep-lying similarities. Indeed, two similarities not previously adduced are that, for both men, the reaction to the French Revolution was the result of proximity in both space and time to its specific features; and, secondly that neither endorsed those more aggressive strains of conservative thought that, departing from Maistre's glorification of warfare and Stirner's celebration of pure egotism, led through Nietzsche and Sorel to fascism and the Nazi cataclysm.

---

[159] Cf. the judgment of a modern historian sympathetic both to the Jacobins and to Robespierre: "In the previous November, Burke had brought out his celebrated *Reflections on the Revolution in France*, which became and has remained the gospel of counter-revolution. Forcefully arguing that decrees do not suffice to give a sense of freedom and civic virtue, he introduced into history and politics the concept of evolution. His thought was profound. . . . Better than any of his contemporaries, he perceived the most essential and enduring aspect of the Revolution in France" (Lefebvre, I, 189).

[160] *Prelude*, 1850 version, p. 251 (VII, 512-30).

[161] *Hazlitt*, VII, 227.

The latter fact is especially important. It is necessary to understand that men such as Burke and Wordsworth were not only wholly humane but also were not opposed to progress in human affairs[162]—most certainly not to the alleviation of human suffering.[163] But they both rejected the equating of change as such with progress.[164] It was precisely the point of their opposition that to them wholesale innovation did not constitute progress.[165] "Thoughtless people," as Ortega y Gasset has said, "imagine that human progress consists in a quantitative increase of things and ideas. Not at all: true progress is the growing intensity with which

[162] Wordsworth accepted the reality of progress, but saw it in a more problematic light than did such enthusiasts as Priestley or Condorcet: "The progress of the Species neither is nor can be like that of a Roman road in a right line. It may be more justly compared to that of a River, which both in its smaller reaches and larger turnings, is frequently forced back towards its fountains, by objects which cannot otherwise be eluded or overcome; yet with an accompanying impulse that will ensure its advancement hereafter, it is either gaining strength every hour, or conquering in secret some difficulty, by a labour that contributes as effectually to further it in its course, as when it moves forward uninterrupted in a line, direct as that of the Roman road with which we began the comparison" (*Prose*, ɪɪ, 11).

[163] Wordsworth saw and sympathized with the difficulties of his fellow men—how could he not? For an instance almost at random, he observed in 1835 that "Despair is no friend to prudence, the springs of industry will relax, if chearfulness be destroyed by anxiety; without hope men become reckless, & have a sullen pride in adding to the heap of their own wretchedness. Again, every one, who has looked round him, must have observed how distress creeps upon multitudes without misconduct of their own. . . . Let it not be forgotten also that there are thousands with whom vicious habits of expense are not the cause why they do not store up their gains" (*Prose*, ɪɪɪ, 264). Again, "By having put an end to the Slave Trade and Slavery, the British people are exalted in the scale of humanity" (*Prose*, ɪɪɪ, 247). Yet again, Wordsworth pronounced "a harsh judgment" on Carlyle's *French Revolution*: "It is not only his style that he condemns, but his *inhumanity*. He says there is a want of due sympathy with mankind" (*Robinson*, ɪɪ, 566). For the evolution of Wordsworth's social concern and awareness of human suffering as expressed in his poetry, see the discussion in Jacobus, pp. 133-83.

[164] In our own day, change and progress have become so merged in popular conception that it is necessary to remind ourselves that they are two things, not one thing, and that change itself can be a sinister rather than a benign phenomenon. Thus F. R. Leavis: "That there *has* been swift and radical change, and that more is upon us, no one will question, and there is a general recognition, helpless enough, of a deep and frightening human disorder (the consequence, or concomitant, of change) that menaces civilization itself" (*Sword*, p. 36).

[165] E.g.: "Reform is a word under which in this particular, as in so many others injurious fallacies lie hid; it implies that the change demanded, is a restoration of something that formerly existed, & it presumes further, that the change must be an improvement" (*Prose*, ɪɪɪ, 270).

we perceive the very few cardinal mysteries that pulsate in the shadow of history."[166]

Wordsworth could have subscribed to such a statement. Innovative change took men away from rather than nearer to true being:[167] "Mutability is Nature's bane." The only beneficial change takes place on the analogy of the gradual unfoldings of organic growth ("By nature's gradual processes be taught").[168] Accordingly, the attempt to engineer social attitudes would always threaten the conditions of those relationships in which alone the individual can flourish. As Coleridge says,

> I have no faith in act of parliament reform. All the great—the permanently great—things that have been achieved in the world, have been so achieved by individuals, working from the instinct of genius or of goodness. The rage now-a-days is all the other way: the individual is supposed capable of nothing; there must be organization, classification, machinery . . . as for . . . breaking up the cottage home education, I think it one of the most miserable mistakes which the well-intentioned people of the day have yet made[169]

To conservative thinkers such as Burke, Wordsworth, and in this instance, Coleridge, manipulated egalitarianism and social leveling attacked the *spacing* necessary to human meaning. The word "spacing" needs construal, for it refers to three separate but interlinked requirements for full humanity. First of all, it refers to the relation of an individual to his environment: he must pertain to the physical space around him, and there must be a certain amount of it—as with Michael's farm. Secondly, it refers to a viewing of the present

---

[166] Ortega, *Velazquez*, p. 14.

[167] How reluctantly Wordsworth accepted change, while still understanding that some change must occur, is illustrated by Carl Woodring: "As late as 1838 he could make a slight variation in a line borrowed from Spenser, 'All change is perilous and all chance unsound,' in order to permit some change where Spenser had allowed none: 'Perilous is sweeping change, all chance unsound.' Nor is he quite ready to declare all change 'sweeping change' " (Woodring, p. 146). In a related emphasis, characteristic lines in "The Excursion" speak of "the spirit" being "oppressed by sense/ Of instability, revolt, decay,/ And change, and emptiness, these freaks of Nature" (Wordsworth, *Poems*, v, 79). Compare Burke: "By this unprincipled facility of changing the state as often, and as much, and in as many ways as there are floating fancies or fashions, the whole chain and continuity of the commonwealth would be broken. No one generation could link with the other. Men would become little better than the flies of summer" (Burke, *Reflections*, p. 108).

[168] Wordsworth, *Poems*, v, 117. [169] *Table Talk*, p. 173 (July 24, 1832).

as a continuation of the past—what Ruskin so eloquently expatiates on as "the lamp of memory." As Karl Mannheim wrote in 1933, "a man for whom nothing exists beyond his immediate situation is not fully human."[170] Finally, there must be enough space between a man and other men so that the individual is not lost in the group. One should live, in Wordsworth's phrase, in an area "not crowded with population," so that people are not "melted and reduced to one identity." The vision of such spatiality of relationships, with the concomitant enhancement of meaningful individuality, is glimpsed by Burke in a famous passage:

> The age of chivalry is gone. That of sophisters, economists, and calculators has succeeded, and the glory of Europe is extinguished forever. Never, never more shall we behold that generous loyalty to rank and sex, that proud submission, that dignified obedience, that subordination of the heart which kept alive, even in servitude itself, the spirit of an exalted freedom.[171]

Burke's sense of loss, his seeing of the ideal in the past rather than in the future, is a hallmark of the conservative attitude toward life. Although the word "conservative" was first used in its political sense by Chateaubriand, the attitude, if not the name, applies to Shakespeare as well as to Wordsworth, and there, too, ideality inheres in the past. A collage of passages from a modern commentator serves the point:

> Shakespeare was no revolutionary—indeed, if one had to label his political "position," it would be as that of a natural conservative whom the stress of events, internal and external, had driven

---

[170] *Mannheim*, p. xvi.

[171] Burke, *Reflections*, p. 86. Though related to the feudalism of such continental theorists as Müller, Burke's invocation of chivalry is, as a commentator emphasizes, different: "When Burke praised the age of chivalry he was using a historic flourish to strengthen his position, but he would have been horrified at the idea that someone would use his arguments to revive feudalism. He had, as Lord Morley remarks, 'no puny sentimentalism, and none of . . . mere literary or romantic conservatism. . . . He lived in the real world, and not in a false dream of some past world that had never been.' Müller's conservatism, strongly though it was influenced by Burke, had more in common with De Maistre's mysticism and Chateaubriand's poetic visions" (Aris, p. 309). With Burke's nostalgia for the feudal past compare Carlyle's: "The Feudal Baron had a Man's Soul in him; to which anarchy, mutiny, and the other fruits of temporary mercenaries, were intolerable. . . . He felt it precious, and at last it became habitual, and his fruitful enlarged existence included it as a necessity, to have men round him who in heart loved him. . . . It was beautiful; it was human!" (*Carlyle*, x, 274).

to the edge of anarchism. . . . To construct an idealized Middle Ages is no Romantic or Victorian invention; the Middle Ages, indeed, seem to have become "romantic" almost as soon as they came to an end. . . . Modern research has undoubtedly shown how deeply medieval, in all spheres of life, the Elizabethans still were; but if we think that *they* saw themselves as such, we shall see them wrong. *They* thought they were very different from the men of the Middle Ages: thought it and regretted it. . . . [T]here is no doubt . . . the young man of the Sonnets, embodied for Shakespeare this dream of a beautiful past. . . . Not only the past, but more precisely the past of medieval chivalry, the past which Drayton lamented. . . . Lost innocence, lost simplicity, lost certainty, all symbolized in a lost and regretted past: these themes, strong both in the Sonnets and in the age when they were written, are equally strong in the plays which Shakespeare wrote round the turn of the century. A great deal of *Hamlet* is a lament for these losses.[172]

Shakespeare's orientation in this description stood in contrast to the progressive futurism of Sir Francis Bacon, and it would be both feasible and interesting to institute an extended comparison of Shakespeare and Wordsworth, on the one hand, with Bacon and Shelley on the other.

But rather than attempt such a delicate and complicated task, or even that of examining in detail Wordsworth's social philosophy in the general historical context of conservative thought—which must be left for another occasion, and preferably for another commentator—it seems more urgent to conclude this chapter with a briefer kind of examination. Inasmuch as Wordsworth's conservatism represents an attitude almost wholly alien to the intellectual fashion of our day, it seems desirable to try to penetrate to the "deep structure," as it were, of the grounds on which his transference of emotional affect away from innovative social amelioration to a cherishing of the significant group can be said—for this is what I do maintain—to entail neither a diminution of the sense of reality nor a loss of humane feeling.

It might seem necessary at first glance to defend this kind of displacement against the implication of proto-fascism. Such a defense is not required, however, if only for a cynical reason. Even if for the sake of argument—it is assuredly not the case—the cumulative course of conservative thought be accepted as leading directly

[172] Cruttwell, pp. 30, 32-37.

to the horrors of Nazism, it would still in dismal truth have been in no way more destructive of human life and meaning than has been the historical progress to the Finland Station and beyond. The communist societies have been no less murderous and repressive than were the Nazis—a fact that the noble indignation of Solzhenitsyn has been drumming into the reluctant conscience of our time.

Without dwelling on cynical parallels, however, we can unequivocally say that Wordsworth's conservatism had no connection with what became fascism and Nazism simply because it rejected the conception of coercive power. Wordsworth felt that

> tyrannic power is weak,
> Hath neither gratitude, nor faith, nor love,
> Nor the support of good or evil men
> To trust in; that the godhead which is ours
> Can never utterly be charmed or stilled;
> That nothing hath a natural right to last
> But equity and reason; that all else
> Meets foes irreconcilable, and at best
> Lives but by variety of disease.[173]

Long before Lord Acton's famous aphorism, he recognized that power corrupts:

> There is a maxim laid down in my Tract on the Convention of Cintra, which ought never to be lost sight of. It is expressed I believe nearly in the following words. "There is, in fact, an unconquerable tendency in all power save that of knowledge acting by and through knowledge, to *injure the mind* of him by whom that power is exercised."[174]

Confidently leaving aside all questions of virulent historical typology, therefore, we may briefly turn to the presuppositions underlying Wordsworth's commitment to the significant group. As Mannheim notes, "If only one penetrates deeply enough, one will

---

[173] *Prelude*, 1850 version, pp. 377-39 (x, 200-208). Again: "a Tyrant's domain of knowledge is narrow, but melancholy as narrow; inasmuch as—from all that is lovely, dignified, or exhilarating in the prospect of human nature—he is inexorably cut off; and therefore he is inwardly helpless and forlorn" (*Prose*, i, 298). "Despotism, in a general sense, is but another word for weakness" (*Prose*, i, 312). "It is immutably ordained that power, taken and exercised in contempt of right, never can bring forth good" (*Prose*, i, 330).

[174] *Middle Years*, ii, 388.

find that certain philosophical assumptions lie at the basis of all political thought, and similarly, in any kind of philosophy a certain pattern of action and a definite approach to the world is implied."

Mannheim himself has attempted to illuminate conservative attitudes in contrast to what we have here loosely called the Jacobin, and what he calls the "progressive," tradition. He distinguishes two forms of conservatism, one instinctive or "natural," and the other intellectually elaborated. In the first instance, conservatism subsists as what Max Weber termed "traditionalism," and is "bound up with magical elements in consciousness; conversely, among primitive peoples, respect for traditional ways of life is strongly linked with the fear of magical evils attendant on change." "Traditionalism is a general psychological attitude which expresses itself in different individuals as a tendency to cling to the past and a fear of innovation. But this elementary psychological tendency may attain a special function in relation to the social process."[175] Such a psychological tendency, as we have seen, characterizes Wordsworth very strongly.

Yet Mannheim's analysis does not in this first instance seem very enlightening. It requires supplementation; and without discounting it, we may add to it the following considerations. Conservative thought may stem from three disparate sources, each sufficient in itself but all intermingling easily. We may term them the source of reason, the source of inertia, and the source of human structure. Conservatism stemming from reason is simply the recognition that a previous or present state of affairs, whatever its inequities or inadequacies, is still better than a hypothetical state of affairs yet unknown, especially if the latter must be brought about by the trauma of revolution. As Coleridge said, "A system of fundamental Reform will scarcely be effected by massacres mechanized into Revolution."[176] The American Revolution was more an orderly transfer of power from one elite to another than a true revolution ("England has had fifty years' experience," observed Hegel, "that *free* America is more profitable to her than it was in a state of *dependence*").[177] But a true revolution—a turning of the world upside down—produces the profoundest dislocations, destructions, and crimes; and one may feel that not only have there never been exceptions to this consequence, but even that in theory there cannot

[175] *Mannheim*, pp. 142, 153, 157.
[176] *Lectures 1795*, p. 48.
[177] *Hegel's Werke*, ix, 107.

be.[178] France took generations to recover from the ruins of the Revolution—if indeed France has ever recovered. There is less freedom today in Russia than there was under the czars, and literally millions of lives have been sacrificed to obtain the dubious fullness—dullness rather—of Russian life under the Communist regime. Although there are more material goods in Russia now, such an outcome would have followed under the czars as well, since it developed simply from the improved technologies that became available all over the world with the passage of years. Furthermore, the only conditions that might justify the disruptions of revolution—those of absolute tyranny—are the very conditions under which revolutions cannot gain their necessary momentum; for as Coleridge saw, "Revolutions are sudden to the unthinking only."[179]

From the point of view of rational conservatism, the watchword of social change must always be evolution, never revolution. As Burke realized, the French government before the Revolution was "full of abuses":

These abuses accumulated in a length of time, as they must accumulate in every monarchy not under the constant inspection of a popular representative. I am no stranger to the faults and defects of the subverted government of France. . . . But . . . is it, then, true that the French government was such as to be incapable or undeserving of reform, so that it was of absolute necessity that the whole fabric should be at once pulled down and the area cleared for the erection of a theoretic, experimental edifice in its place? All France was of a different opinion in the beginning of the year 1789.[180]

In truth, a revolution in a nation seems much like a "nervous breakdown" in a person—an apocalyptic change that in part is allowed to happen and in part is willed, under the illusion that such radical change will lift seemingly unbearable burdens. But quotid-

[178] Compare Taine on the inevitable result of "overthrowing an established government by force," which is that "every interregnum is a return to barbarism" (Taine, III, 68). See also Taine, III, 263-64, 266, 302-304; IV, iii-iv. Compare further Conrad in *Under Western Eyes*: "in a real revolution the best characters do not come to the front. A violent revolution falls into the hands of narrow-minded fanatics and of tyrannical hypocrites at first. Afterwards comes the turn of all the pretentious intellectual failures of the time. . . . Hopes grotesquely betrayed, ideals caricatured—that is the definition of revolutionary success."

[179] *Lectures 1795*, p. 36.

[180] Burke, *Reflections*, p. 145.

ian reality exacts its harsh demands: life must go on, with all its inadequacies and frustrations, but now amid the ruins of self-destruction. As Simone Weil points out, with wisdom no less than wit, it is not religion, but revolution, that is the true opiate of the masses.

The second source of conservatism, inertia (and what would physics and physical reality itself be without inertia?), derives its philosophical validity from the superiority or at least the ontological priority of something that does exist to something that does not exist. What a mind like Voltaire's could not understand about a mind like Leibniz's was not simply that existence itself is flawed—or rather, metaphysically considered, that existence constitutes precisely *the* flaw in the fabric of being[181]—but also that this is the best of possible worlds because it exists and the others do not. The simple wonder of existence is a perennial source of the wish to cleave to given reality and reject its dissipation by change. As any child knows, a flawed marble is better than no marble at all, as it is better than a cinder given in exchange. As Burke said, "it is with infinite caution that any man ought to venture upon pulling down

---

[181] To the many philosophical formulations of this conception, we may add two from twentieth-century science. The biochemist Jacques Monod says that both the development and the disintegration of life are functions of the same abnormalities or "perturbations": "modern biology recognizes . . . that all the properties of living beings are based on *a fundamental mechanism of molecular invariance.* For modern theory *evolution is not a property of living beings*, since it stems from the very *imperfections* of the conserving mechanism which indeed constitutes their unique privilege. It must, then, be said that the same source of fortuitous perturbations, of 'noise,' which in a nonliving . . . system would gradually lead to the disintegration of all structure, is the progenitor of evolution in the biosphere" (Monod, p. 113). Again, Freud says that "the phenomena of organic development must be attributed to external disturbing and diverting influences." He speaks of the "deceptive appearance" of instincts as "forces tending towards change and progress, whilst in fact they are merely seeking to reach an ancient goal. . . . It would be in contradiction to the conservative nature of the instincts if the goal of life were a state of things which had never yet been attained. On the contrary, it must be an *old* state of things. . . . If we are to take it as a truth that knows no exception that everything living dies for *internal* reasons—becomes inorganic once again—then we shall be compelled to say that '*the aim of all life is death*' and, looking backwards, that '*inanimate things existed before living ones*' " (*Freud*, xviii, 38). From another standpoint, Leibniz says that "all reality purely positive or absolute is a perfection, and . . . all imperfection comes from limitations, that is to say from the privative; for to limit is to refuse progress, or the further beyond. Now God is the cause of all perfections, and consequently of all realities, considered as purely positive. But limitations, or privations, result from the original imperfection of creatures that bound their receptivity" (*Leibniz*, vi, 383). See further *Leibniz*, vi, 108-10, 115, 120-22, 341.

an edifice which has answered to any tolerable degree for ages the common purposes of society, or on building it up again without having models and patterns of approved utility before his eyes." But with the revolutionaries

> it is a sufficient motive to destroy an old scheme of things because it is an old one. As to the new, they are in no sort of fear with regard to the duration of a building run up in haste, because duration is no object to those who think little or nothing has been done before their time, and who place all their hopes in discovery. They conceive, very systematically, that all things which give perpetuity are mischievous, and therefore they are at inexpiable war with all establishments. They think that government may vary like modes of dress, and with as little ill effect; that there needs no principle of attachment, except a sense of present convenience, to any constitution of the state. They always speak as if they were of opinion that there is a singular species of compact between them and the magistrates which binds the magistrate, but which has nothing reciprocal in it.

Burke's own conviction, on the other hand, was that "People will not look forward to posterity, who never look backward to their ancestors." This opinion lies at the root of the third source of conservatism, which is the desire to accumulate the best aspects of human life by saving the past in the present. Such a desire is based upon the perception that not all human possibilities are of equal value, and it is expressed by Wordsworth's vision of the "one great society" composed of "the noble living and the noble dead." It is, again, Burke's "partnership" between "those who are living, those who are dead, and those who are to be born" that constitutes "the great primeval contract of eternal society, linking the lower with the higher natures."[182] It is a reflection in the social sphere of the structure of human personality, whereby the conscience of a man is not his ego, but his superego—that is, the introjection into his life of another identity standing prior to his own in time, a prior identity that he ignores or dishonors only at peril to his humanity. So Freud, in speaking of present and future forms of society, notes "the important claims made by the super-ego, which represents tradition and the ideals of the past and will for a time resist the incentives of a new economic situation."[183] In this context, it is in-

[182] Burke, *Reflections*, pp. 70, 99-100, 38, 110.

[183] *Freud*, XXII, 178. Again: "A child's super-ego is in fact constructed on the model not of its parents but of its parents' super-ego; the contents which fill it are

triguing to speculate about possible links between the Jacobin mania of our own recent past and the "psychopathy"—the absence of superego—that has been described as endemic in our contemporary social behavior.[184] On the other hand, in some polities, such as that of China over several millennia, where the superego is especially strong, the outcome can be not only ancestor worship but virtual stasis in the society. The true conservative ideal, however, is not stasis, but what Coleridge defined as the polarity of permanence and progression or, to use his own words, the "harmonious balance of the two great correspondent, at once supporting and counterpoising, interests of the state, its permanence, and its progression."[185] Progression by revolution, however, fractures the polarity and endangers the element of permanence so essential to the conservative sense of meaning in life.

With these substitutions, supplementations, and elucidations in mind, we may proceed to Mannheim's second criterion for conservative attitudes. "Conservative thought," he says, "emerged as an independent current when it was forced into conscious opposition to bourgeois-revolutionary thought, to *the natural-law mode of thought*." Natural-law thought, which encompasses the assumptions of present-day liberalism, is analyzed by Mannheim in terms both of its contents and of its methodological features, some of the former of which are the doctrines of "social contract," "popular sovereignty," and "the inalienable Rights of Man." Among the latter are "rationalism as a method of solving problems," "a claim of *universal validity* for every individual," "a claim to universal

---

the same and it becomes the vehicle of tradition and of all the time-resisting judgements of value which have propagated themselves in this manner from generation to generation. You may easily guess what important assistance taking the super-ego into account will give us in our understanding of the social behaviour of mankind. . . . It seems likely that what are known as materialistic views of history sin in under-estimating this factor. . . . Mankind never lives entirely in the present. The past, the tradition of the race and of the people, lives on in ideologies of the super-ego, and yields only slowly to the influences of the present and to new changes; and so long as it operate through the super-ego it plays a powerful part in human life, independently of economic conditions" (*Freud*, XXII, 67). In referring pointedly to economic factors, Freud is of course rejecting the Marxist hypothesis.

[184] See Alan Harrington, *Psychopaths* . . . (New York: Simon and Schuster, 1973). Cf. Christopher Lasch's recent recognition of "the organized assault on the superego, which has liberated pleasure only to transform it into another form of pain," and which "reflects the devaluation of authority in modern society" (*Haven in a Heartless World; The Family Besieged* [New York: Basic Books, Inc., 1979], p. 183).

[185] *Church and State*, p. 29.

applicability of all laws to all historical and social units," and "static thinking (right reason conceived as a self-sufficient, autonomous sphere unaffected by history)."

Wordsworth, who praised Burke's denunciation of "all systems built on abstract rights," was opposed, and became ever more so, to natural-law thought. His own views, at least by extension, accorded with the conservative repudiation both of the contents and of the methodology of that thought. Mannheim identifies six aspects of such repudiation:

(i) The conservatives replaced Reason with concepts such as History, Life, the Nation.

(ii) To the deductive bent of the natural-law school, the conservative opposes the *irrationality of reality*.

(iii) In answer to the liberal claim of universal validity for all, the conservative poses the problem of *individuality* in radical fashion.

(iv) The concept of the social *organism* is developed by the conservatives to counter the liberal-bourgeois belief in the universal applicability of all political and social innovations.

(v) Against the construction of collective units from isolated individuals and factors, the conservative opposes a kind of thought which starts from a concept of a whole which is not the mere sum of its parts.

(vi) One of the most important logical weapons against the natural-law style of thought is the *dynamic conception of Reason*. At first, the conservative merely opposed the rigidity of the static theory of Reason with the movement of 'Life' and history. Later, however, he discovered a much more radical method of disposing of the eternal norms of the Enlightenment. Instead of regarding the world as eternally changing in contrast to a static Reason, he conceived of Reason and of its norms themselves as changing and moving.[186]

All of these emphases, some directly and some with qualification, apply to Wordsworth's position, and, where they have not already received documentation in the cumulative course of this chapter, could be interestingly illustrated from Wordsworth's utterance. To take a single, previously unmentioned example, Wordsworth amply confirms Mannheim's second criterion, the *"irrationality of reality."* To the great poet reality should not be ap-

---

[186] *Mannheim*, pp. 174, 175, 175-76.

proached rationalistically, but was and should remain emotional and even mystical. Thus in "Tintern Abbey" he invokes

> that blessed mood
> In which the burthen of the mystery,
> In which the heavy and the weary weight
> Of all this unintelligible world,
> Is lightened . . .
> And even the motion of our human blood
> Almost suspended, we are laid asleep
> In body, and become a living soul:
> While with an eye made quiet by the power
> Of harmony, and the deep power of joy,
> We see into the life of things.[187]

Any attempt to change this apprehension into the forms of analytic reason is unequivocally rejected by Wordsworth:

> Our meddling intellect
> Mis-shapes the beauteous forms of things:—
> We murder to dissect.
>
> Enough of Science and of Art;
> Close up those barren leaves;
> Come forth, and bring with you a heart
> That watches and receives.[188]

The anti-rationalistic bias appears repeatedly and in varying forms in his writing. In "A Poet's Epitaph" he speaks with scorn of physical science:

> Physician art thou?—one, all eyes,
> Philosopher!—a fingering slave,
> One that would peep and botanize
> Upon his mother's grave?[189]

Elsewhere he asks, "who shall parcel out/ His intellect by geometric rules/ Split like a province into round and square?"[190] In "The Excursion," for our last illustration, he says,

---

[187] Wordsworth, *Poems*, II, 260.

[188] *Ibid.*, IV, 57. Compare with Wordsworth's "murder to dissect" Blake's "murder by analyzing" (*Blake*, p. 249).

[189] Wordsworth, *Poems*, IV, 66.

[190] *Prelude*, 1850 version, p. 55 (II, 203-205).

> go, demand
> Of mighty Nature, if 'twas ever meant
> That we should pry far off yet be unraised;
> That we should pore, and dwindle as we pore,
> Viewing all objects unremittingly
> In disconnexion dead and spiritless;
> And still dividing, and dividing still,
> Break down all grandeur, still unsatisfied
> With the perverse attempt, while littleness
> May yet become more little; waging thus
> An impious warfare with the very life
> Of our own souls![191]

Intriguing though such confirmations of Mannheim's analysis are, however, they do not establish so profoundly the parallelism between Wordsworth's poetic sensibility and his conservatism as do the implications of "a further radical difference between progressive and conservative patterns of experience." The difference lies in "the way of experiencing time," and is formulated by Mannheim as follows:

> the progressive experiences the present as the beginning of the future, while the conservative regards it simply as the latest point reached by the past. . . . Primarily, the conservative experiences the past as being one with the present.[192]

Such a schematism pertains directly to Wordsworth, and indeed could supply a rubric for the subsumption of his entire vital effort. His whole poetic endeavor might be described as the maintaining of the past in the present. There is, for instance, possibly no more exalted passage anywhere in the Wordsworthian corpus than this one in which he describes the need to have the past in his present consciousness:

> The days gone by
> Return upon me almost from the dawn
> Of life: the hiding-places of man's power
> Open; I would approach them, but they close.
> I see by glimpses now; when age comes on,
> May scarcely see at all; and I would give,
> While yet we may, as far as words can give,

[191] Wordsworth, *Poems*, v, 139. [192] *Mannheim*, pp. 169-70.

> Substance and life to what I feel, enshrining,
> Such is my hope, the spirit of the Past
> For future restoration.[193]

As a commentator has recognized, "the deepest current of feeling in his nature" was "the continuous presence of his own past."[194]

Still another of the conservative characteristics identified by Mannheim might be seen as deriving from such superimposition of the past upon the present. By the doubling effect, the sense of the present becomes intensified, with a consequent treasuring of the concrete and the immediate:

> One of the most essential characteristics of this conservative way of life and thought seems to be the way in which it clings to the immediate, the actual, the *concrete*.

> Non-romantic conservatism always starts with the particular case at hand, and never broadens its horizon beyond its own particular surroundings. It is concerned with immediate action, with changing concrete details, and therefore does not really trouble itself with the *structure* of the world in which it lives. On the other hand, all progressive activity feeds on its *consciousness of the possible*.[195]

How relevant such strictures are for Wordsworth may be gauged from a typical figure such as the Old Leech-Gatherer, who is immediate, actual, and concrete—a particular case at hand. The structure of his world is not questioned; only his response to that structure is at issue (a "progressive" might well denounce the social conditions that reduced the old man to gathering leeches). It is in such immediacy and concreteness that Wordsworth elsewhere can say:

> I remember well
> That in life's every-day appearances
> I seemed about this time to gain clear sight
> Of a new world.[196]

Indeed, inasmuch as the poet is almost generically defined by adherence to "the immediate, the actual, the *concrete*," then con-

---

[193] *Prelude*, 1850 version, pp. 449-51 (xII, 277-86).
[194] Salvesen, p. 45.   [195] *Mannheim*, pp. 160-61.
[196] *Prelude*, 1850 version, pp. 475-77 (xIII, 367-70).

servatism would in this perspective as well be a stance benign to Wordsworth as a great poet ("Language and science are abbreviations of reality," observes Cassirer; but "art is an intensification of reality. Language and science depend upon one and the same process of abstraction; art may be described as a continuous process of concretion").[197]

It is instructive to contrast the correlation obtaining between Wordsworth's conservatism and his poetic sensibility with that between Shelley's progressivism and his own kind of poetry. "Ideologically," as Harold Bloom has said, "Shelley is of the permanent Left, in politics and religion. . . . He is nothing short of an extremist."[198] Politically visionary and future-directed, he is a fine example of someone almost wholly opposed to conservatism. The drives and awarenesses that made his politics progressive, however, seem to have rendered his general intellectual mode so possibility-oriented that in much of his poetry he virtually deserted "the immediate, the actual, the *concrete*." His poems are, in Hazlitt's assessment, "filmy, enigmatical, discontinuous, unsubstantial." "Spurning the world of realities, he rushed into the world of nonentities and contingencies, like air into a *vacuum*." "We have everywhere a profusion of dazzling hues, of glancing splendours, of floating shadows, but the objects on which they fall are bare, indistinct, and wild." Shelley's stanzas "abound in horrible imaginings like records of a ghastly dream;—life, death, genius, beauty, victory, earth, air, ocean, the trophies of the past, the shadows of the world to come, are huddled together in a strange and hurried dance of words, and all that appears clear is the passion and paroxysm of thought of the poet's spirit."[199]

Now the preoccupations with the respective structures of their social feeling in both Shelley and Wordsworth rest upon a valuing of human life in its generality, as do all genuine progressivisms and conservatisms of attitude. Between the two social orientations, however, there exists a fundamental difference in how life's value is conceived. That difference, I suggest, can be formulated as follows: humane liberal or progressive attitudes tend to assume life to be theoretically valuable in its substance, and humane conservative attitudes conceive it as theoretically valuable in its function.

The ultimate differences surface in attitudes toward capital punishment. Where the liberal's valuing of life's substance tends to-

[197] *Essay on Man*, p. 143.   [198] Bloom, p. 284.
[199] Hazlitt, xvi, 274, 268, 272, 273.

ward *a priori* rejection of the death penalty, the conservative's treasuring of function tends to rate the protection of the functioning individual or society itself higher than the protection of the malfunctioning individual. One thinks of Plato's penalties in *The Laws*, or of Wordsworth's "Sonnets upon the Punishment of Death": "But O, restrain compassion, if its course,/ As oft befals, prevent or turn aside/ . . . acts whose higher source/ Is sympathy with the unforewarned, who died/ Blameless"; "Lawgivers, beware,/ Lest, capital pains remitting till ye spare/ The murderer, ye . . . / . . . debase the general mind."[200]

In other words, at the root of the democratic and egalitarian impulse there is a sense that every life is actually valuable in its fact (Blake's "Every Harlot was once a Virgin: every Criminal an Infant Love"),[201] and at the root of the conservative impulse the sense that every life is potentially valuable in its realization. But in this latter case the value must be earned, developed, conferred, or in some other way attained in the course of living. Accordingly, although both liberal and conservative would agree that "No man is an island, entire of itself," only the liberal would conclude that "any man's death diminishes me."

Donne's beautiful conceit was pre-Malthusian and pre-Darwinian, and, at least in our own day, it could as cogently be argued that any man's birth diminishes me, inasmuch as the conditions for realizing one's full individuality are lessened by each additional competitor for life's rewards. Indeed, seen against nature's unwillingness to concur in humane formulas, the ascription of value to a human life—either to others or to the liver of that life—solely by virtue of its existence, can in countless instances seem a sentimentality, and in many a cruel lie. In the claim to significance and amelioration for all, the actual and concrete miseries of individual deficiency are almost obscenely passed over. As Ortega y Gasset has pointed out, the "cosmic injustices" are not affected by visionary zeal about the state of mankind as such:

> Among the inexorable questions of human existence is that of social justice. It is one, undoubtedly; but also undoubtedly, it is *only* one. There are many other questions, a great many of them. . . . But suppose that some despairing men resolve that there is no question other than this, or that this at least is the decisive one . . . [nevertheless they] cannot do much about solving prob-

[200] Wordsworth, *Poems*, IV, 135, 136.
[201] *Blake*, p. 210.

lems which are even more important: those of organic life, the biological problems, the problem of sorrow and death, or the terrible cosmic injustices of bodily and psychic inequalities among human beings.[202]

In the light of the pulverizing reality of "cosmic injustices," the ameliorative fixations of a Trotsky, or of a Shelley, can seem peculiarly blind, as can every variety of natural-law thought. If the "truths" asserted as "self-evident" in the Declaration of Independence were in actuality so, their manifesto would not be necessary. Indeed, if espoused without qualification, the ameliorative vision can seem hardly sane, as was the judgment of Dostoevsky with regard to the Russian Jacobins who were Trotsky's prototypes, or of Arnold with regard to Shelley's entire personal and intellectual existence: "The man Shelley, in very truth, is not entirely sane, and Shelley's poetry is not entirely sane either."[203]

In addition to the disquieting ineffectuality, the utter impotence, rather, of progressivist dreams of amelioration in the face of life's most shattering woes (with the concomitant indication that one's investment in such dreams should be cautious, precise, and carefully meditated), there is a perhaps even more compelling consideration. The ascription of value to life's substance depends on the testimony of nature, which, if we agree with Dostoevsky's Shatov that "socialism is by its very essence bound to be atheism," must for the progressive constitute ultimate reality. Yet what nature reveals to us, to quote the words of Schopenhauer, is that "the life or death of the individual is of absolutely no consequence."

The grim vision of this great and comprehensive intellect ("a truly self-dependent mind, a man and knight with a gaze of bronze," is Nietzsche's tribute)[204] should be considered more fully:

> We know, of course, of no higher gamble than that of life and death. We watch every decision concerning them; for in our view all in all is at stake. On the other hand, nature, which never lies . . . speaks quite differently on this theme. . . . Her statement is that the life or death of the individual is of absolutely no consequence. She expresses this by abandoning the life of every animal . . . to the most insignificant accidents without coming to the rescue. . . . Now, since nature abandons without reserve her

---

[202] Ortega, *Crisis*, pp. 145-46. [203] Arnold, *Essays*, p. 251.
[204] *Nietzsche*, II, 844.

organisms constructed with such inexpressible skill, not only to the predatory instinct of the stronger, but also to the blindest chance, the whim of every fool, and the mischievousness of the child, she expresses that the annihilation of these individuals is a matter of indifference to her, does her no harm, is of no significance at all. . . . With man she does not act otherwise than she does with the animals; hence her declaration extends to him also; the life or death of the individual is a matter of indifference to her. Consequently, it should be, in a certain sense, a matter of indifference to us; for in fact, we ourselves are nature.[205]

Those bedrock truths of existence glimpsed by Ortega and by Schopenhauer underlie the conception of the significant group. From a natural standpoint, or in itself, life is neutral with regard to meaning; it is not natural reality, but human need, that claims importance for mankind. Only from a human standpoint can life be said to be valuable. But value, if it justifies its name, must be a concrete bestowal, not an abstract fiction. Those who assert benign concern for all humankind are necessarily indulging in cant— loneliness, bereavement, personal betrayal, incurable disease, crippling ugliness, malformed personality, and human aggressiveness all remain in their full reality, untouched by such easy sentiments. As Blake so pointedly says,

> He who would do good to another, must do it in
> Minute Particulars
> General Good is the plea of the scoundrel,
> hypocrite & flatterer[206]

What in our own day is called the "liberal" mentality is of necessity, because of the necessary limitations of the capacity for human relationship, involved in hypocrisy. Despite its beneficent posture, it is characteristically quite selective in its objects of human sympathy. Take, for instance, Darwin, a "born" progressivist (he was the scion of two major "liberal" households, the Wedgwoods and the Darwins), and esteemed as a good man by family and friends—as no doubt he was, to the extent, that is, that men can be good. "Notwithstanding provocations which might have excused any outbreak," wrote Huxley, he "kept himself clear of all envy, hatred, and malice, nor dealt otherwise than fairly and justly with the unfairness and injustice which was showered upon him."[207]

---

[205] Schopenhauer, III, 541-42.   [206] *Blake*, p. 203.
[207] Darwin, *Life*, I, 533.

Well and good. And yet Darwin, so irenic to those around him, could produce the following awesomely blood-thirsty sentiment at the outbreak of the American Civil War:

I have not seen or heard of a soul who is not with the North. Some few, and I am one of them, even wish to God, though at the loss of millions of lives, that the North would proclaim a crusade against slavery. In the long-run, a million horrid deaths would be amply repaid in the cause of humanity. What wonderful times we live in![208]

This is fairly throwing out the baby with the bath. Saul slaying his thousands and David his ten thousands seem like innocent play in comparison. Indeed, if we agree with Augustine that moral good and evil refer to the will of man, not solely to his deeds, then Darwin here takes a place of pride with Genghis Khan slaying his millions and Stalin his ten millions. After all, Stalin's "liquidations" also were undertaken in the "long-run" cause of "humanity" (I may add that Lincoln, too, was not entirely free of such blood-thirstiness; and as I understand the Christian *kerygma*, would have much to answer for at the Day of Judgment).

Few if any, in actual fact, can or do maintain concern for very many of their fellow humans. Almost anyone who has had burdens to bear can attest the truth of Platen's melancholy lines:

Es liegt an eines Menschen Schmerz, an eines Menschen
     Wunde nichts,
Es kehrt an das, was Kranke quält, sich ewig der
     Gesunde nichts[209]

—a human's pain, a human's wound matters nothing; the healthy never pay attention to what torments the sick. "I am," wrote the stricken John Clare, "yet what I am, none cares or knows,/ My friends forsake me like a memory lost."[210] As Keats lay dying, his companion, Joseph Severn, recorded the reluctance of others to share in the ordeal: "here I am by our poor dying friend—my spirits—my intelects and my health are breaking down—I can get no one to change me—no one will relieve me—they all run away—."[211]

Severn, however, remained in true and significant relationship to Keats, and that action is of another order of value than the prot-

[208] *Ibid.*, ii, 166.
[210] *Clare*, p. 195.

[209] *Platens Werke*, iii, 127.
[211] Keats, *Letters*, ii, 375-76.

estations of radical chic, or the pronouncements of Hollywood actors under the name of social concern. Claims to universal benevolence must unfortunately be met with skepticism. By their very nature such attitudes involve suppressions of awareness—as when, in our own day, the same humanitarian feeling that wishes to protect and conserve criminal life is unconcerned by the exposure and dissipation of foetal life.

Such a contradiction shows two things about the structure of social benevolence: first, that no ameliorative formula, no matter how well-intentioned its assertions, can in fact account for all the variations of real situation; secondly, that although benevolent formulas exist in everyone's mind—be he progressive or conservative—such general formulas are always adjusted in actual experience by the individual's interests and by group fashion. Everyone, as it were, keeps two sets of books, and it is in what he actually intends and does, not in what he says, that meaning and morality inhere.

Blake can serve as a case in point. Neither his humanity nor his integrity can be questioned; and his attitudes were radically progressive. The largeness of his concern is indicated by his favorite words, "every thing that lives is Holy." Again:

> We live as One Man; for contracting our infinite senses
> We behold multitude; or expanding: we behold as one,
> As One Man all the Universal Family . . .

Yet with another voice and in another perspective—opening his second set of books, as it were—Blake can say:

> I profess not Generosity to a Foe
> My Generosity is to my Friends . . .
> The Generous to Enemies promote their Ends
> And become the Enemy & Betrayer of his Friends

And he asserts that "the Worship of God, is honouring his gifts/ In other men: & loving the greatest men best."[212]

So the fact, as opposed to the pretense, is that for everyone some people are valued more than others. "Those whom I know already," confessed Keats in 1819, "and who have grown as it were a part of myself I could not do without: but for the rest of Mankind, they are as much a dream to me as Miltons Hierarchies."[213] It is the understanding that in the relativities and limitations of human intercourse some existences always seem more important and more

[212] *Blake*, pp. 44, 178, 493, 248.   [213] Keats, *Letters*, II, 146.

worthy than others that legitimizes the commitment to the significant group. The noblest natures of our history have insisted on this truth, which no amount of visionary egalitarianism can obviate. To Milton, some were master spirits, but others were not: "Many a man lives a burden to the earth."[214] "What a pity," said Keats to Haydon, "there is not a *human dust hole*."[215] "A Last Judgment is Necessary," said Blake, "because Fools flourish."[216] "The good die first," wrote Wordsworth, "and they whose hearts are dry as summer dust/ Burn to the socket."[217]

In light of these facts, the commitment to the significant group simply observes the structure of reality. On the other hand, commitments to the amelioration of every human existence, however cant-ridden they necessarily are in their individual utterance, can in their cumulative voice set in motion economic, social, and political changes the outcome of which no man can foresee, and the desirability of which can accordingly never be assured. The one assured, unarguable, and constant truth in human goodness resides precisely in those "little, nameless, unremembered, acts/ Of kindness and of love" that to Wordsworth were at the center of moral life. As a Marxian apologist recalls of Wittgenstein, perplexedly: "Wittgenstein told me firmly that political work was the worst possible thing for me to do; it would do me great harm. 'What you should do is to be kind to others. Nothing else. Just be kind to others.' "[218]

The great philosopher and the great poet were in this instance of one mind. For the larger issues of human welfare, flail as we may, remain in the grip of history; they will be determined, for better or for worse, by economic, scientific, and socio-political tides and accidents the forecasting and control of which no man can legitimately claim. Only a bigotry of the present can say that the twentieth century, with its hideous devastations, is a better time to live—or as the case may be, to die—than was the eighteenth, its own miseries notwithstanding. It has not been shown, nor can it

---

[214] Milton, *Prose*, p. 207.   [215] *Haydon*, II, 107.

[216] *Blake*, p. 551. Again: "there will always be as many Hypocrites born as Honest Men" (p. 554). "Jesus does not treat [?all ?alike] because he makes a Wide Distinction between the Sheep & the Goats consequently he is Not Charitable" (p. 673).

[217] Wordsworth, *Poems*, v, 25. Again, his "theme" in "The Prelude" is "No other than the very heart of man/ As found among the best of those who live" (*Prelude*, p. 468 [XII, 240-42]).

[218] Fania Pascal, "Wittgenstein; A Personal Memoir," *Encounter*, 41 (August 1973), p. 27.

be shown, that the England of present-day ameliorative socialism is a better realm than the England of Wordsworth's youth. Indeed, whether life becomes better or worse is a meaningless judgment unless defined as an answer to the question "for whom?" And this "for whom" is always and unchangingly not a statistical assembly, but an undividual awareness.[219]

The insurmountable defect in progressivisms of attitude is that no amount of visionary confidence, or paradisal hope of societal transformation, can compensate for the inherent unpredictability of the future. No theory or plan can guarantee or even take into account all the factors and contingencies involved in radical changes encouraged or imposed. Lavoisier was an ornament to the human species, and he welcomed the French Revolution with a heart full of hope. But his gaze was fixed on the ideal rather than on the real, and the real exacted its payment: he died at the hands of Revolutionary executioners. Condorcet sang paeans to progress, but he for his part was deprived of existence by the very machinery he hailed: he perished in a revolutionary dungeon.

Freud saw reality more clearly and was less burdened by sentimentality. "The writings of Marx," he says, "have taken the place of the Bible and the Koran as a source of revelation, though they would seem to be no more free from contradictions and obscurities than those older sacred books." He continues:

> although practical Marxism has mercilessly cleared away all idealistic systems and illusions, it has itself developed illusions which are no less questionable and unprovable than the earlier ones.

[219] "Is it possible," asks Rilke, "that the whole history of the world has been misunderstood? Is it possible that the past is false, because one has always spoken of its masses just as though one were telling of a coming together of many human beings, instead of speaking of the individual around whom they stood because he was a stranger and was dying? Yes, it is possible." "Is it possible that one says 'women,' 'children,' 'boys,' not guessing (despite all one's culture, not guessing) that these words have long since had no plural, but only countless singulars? Yes, it is possible" (Rilke, VI, 727-28). Cf. Leavis: "It sometimes seems to me that the central [cliché], to reclaim which would be to 'place' standard enlightenment for the cock-a-hoop folly it is, callously lethal in its witless inhumanity, is 'social.' 'The individual condition,' we are told, 'is tragic,' but—'there is social hope.' I commented on that characteristic proposition. . . . Where, I asked, is the postulated hope located—where *could* it be located unless in individuals? I half thought I might get from someone the reply that when people had identified themselves . . . with the 'social hope' they would cease to brood on the inevitability of personal death, and of 'tragic' things such as bereavement" (Leavis, *Sword*, pp. 163-64).

In order to effect the paradisal future envisaged by radical Marxism it would, Freud points out, be impossible to proceed "without compulsion" in education, "without the prohibition of thought and without the employment of force." He concludes with biting irony:

> I should admit that the conditions of this experiment would have deterred me and those like me from undertaking it; but we are not the only people concerned. There are men of action, unshakable in their convictions, inaccessible to doubt, without feeling for the sufferings of others if they stand in the way of their intentions. We have to thank men of this kind for the fact that the tremendous experiment of producing a new order of this kind is now actually being carried out in Russia.[220]

So much for the Jacobin mania of our own era. In its systematic form as Marxism, it has been identified by Octavio Paz as an "intellectual vice" and, still more inclusively, as "the superstition of the 20th century."[221] All its elements were present in the time of Wordsworth and were rejected by him. To Wordsworth, paradisal progress could only be an illusion, for an unsurpassable intensity and fullness of experience had already taken place in his early life. As Arnold said of him,

> He grew old in an age he condemn'd.
> He look'd on the rushing decay
> Of the times which had shelter'd his youth;
> Felt the dissolving throes
> Of a social order he loved;
> Outlived his brethren, his peers,
> And, like the Theban seer,
> Died in his enemies' day.[222]

There is accordingly little or no contradiction in the fact that though his politics were conservative and even reactionary, Wordsworth's feelings were those of an exquisite humanity. "A line of Wordsworth's," in Lamb's judgment, "is a lever to lift the immortal spirit!"[223] Few have lamented more than Wordsworth

---

[220] *Freud*, xxii, 180-81.
[221] *New York Times*, Thursday, May 3, 1979, p. A2.
[222] Arnold, *Poems*, p. 229.
[223] Lamb, *Letters*, ii, 426.

> The differences, the outside marks by which
> Society has parted man from man,
> Neglectful of the universal heart[224]

Few have recognized with more agony the discrepancy between what human life should be and what it too often is:

Oh! it makes the heart groan, that with such a beautiful world as this to live in, and such a soul as that of man's is by nature and gift of God, we should go about on such errands as we do, destroying and laying waste; and ninety-nine of us in a hundred never easy in any road that travels towards peace and quietness![225]

No words could express a more exalted sense of the possibilities of human life. Yet Wordsworth's realization of those possibilities was broken and torn away from earlier visions of general societal apocalypse. Amid the ruins of his earlier confidence in social man, there was formed, because of his idiosyncratic development toward the egotistical sublime, and because of the extraordinary power of his feelings, a passionate and unchanging commitment to that significant group that assuaged his fears in solitude.

[224] *Prelude,* p. 466 (xii, 217-19).   [225] *Early Years,* p. 543.

Problems of Style in the Poetry of
Wordsworth and Coleridge

◊♦◊

WHEN we see cultural figures lacquered, dusted, shined, and resting in those handsome display cases called the canon, little is apparent to us but achievement and wholeness. But when we view the process of their life and thought as those figures themselves did, with the sheets of blank paper before them, and with their prospects on the future everywhere bardered and problematic.[1] It is from this second perspective, when nacled with indecision, doubt, and anxiety, then all becomes hin- we see their efforts as tentative and their achievement as only a partial fulfillment of what they hoped, that their humanity comes to the fore. More paradoxically, it is only when we see their attainment as filtered through the *aporiae* of their effort, that both the value and the price of that attainment are revealed.

The *aporiae* wrestled with by Wordsworth and Coleridge are more than ordinarily instructive for our understanding of what the two men were, what they wanted, and what they achieved. The word indicates precisely the relationships I propose to address in this chapter, because as a technical term (it is I think less frequently

---

[1] Compare, for instance, Byron's private reflection: "To-morrow is my birthday—that is to say, at twelve o' the clock, midnight, i.e. in twelve minutes, I shall have completed thirty and three years of age!!!—and I go to bed with a heaviness of heart at having lived so long, and to so little purpose"; "I don't regret them [the years] so much for what I have done, as for what I *might* have done. Through life's road, so dim and dirty,/ I have dragged to three-and-thirty./ What have these years left to me?/ Nothing—except thirty-three" (Byron, *Letters*, VIII, 31-32). Alongside this we may set Coleridge's lament: "O why have I shunned & fled like a cowed Dog from the Thought that yesterday was my Birth Day, & that I was 32—So help me Heaven! as I looked back, & till I looked back I had imagined I was only 31—so completely has a whole year passed, with scarcely the fruits of a *month*.—O Sorrow & Shame! I am not worthy to live—Two & thirty years.—& this last year above all others!—I have done nothing!" (*Notebooks*, II, 2237).

encountered in literary than in philosophical studies) *aporiae* refers
not only to problems, but to problems necessarily dealt with—its
etymology concerns the blocking of a passage, with the concomit-
ant suggestion of the desirability of proceeding up the passageway
despite the hindrance.

If we begin by mentally surveying the poetic *oeuvre* of Words-
worth and of Coleridge and at the same time summon to mind the
poetic achievement of the precursor who loomed largest in their
respective endeavors—I speak of course of Milton—we note im-
mediately that the ratio of the poetically meretricious to the po-
etically first rate alters drastically in the two Romantic poets. Put
quite simply, it seems that the gestation of the first class work in
Coleridge and in Wordsworth involved an enormously greater
amount of unsuccessful or even bad poetry than it did in Milton. I
suspect that if we substituted Donne for Milton the statement
would still hold true, and probably would hold true even if we
substituted Dryden. For whatever Dryden's deficiencies as seen
from Romantic or Victorian perspectives, his verse at least resides
on a more or less level plane of craftsmanship. But Wordsworth
notoriously wrote too much; his poetic anticlimax is a palpable real-
ity whose explanation has exercised the ingenuity of many and
able commentators. Those who, like Bernard Groom, attempt to
solve the problem by denying that there was in fact an anticlimax
simply gain no credence.[2] I happen to own Wordsworth's volume
of 1835 called *Yarrow Revisited*, and in its more than three hundred
and twenty pages of verse there are hardly as many *lines* of what
might, even by the most liberal standards, be called poetry. The
entire volume, when perused as an entity, is a sombre spectacle of
poetic desiccation.

Moreover, the decline set in long before 1835. H. W. Garrod felt
that the entire last forty years of Wordsworth's life constituted, as
he said, "the most dismal anti-climax of which the history of litera-
ture holds record."[3] Such an opinion would place the beginning of
Wordsworth's poetic decline in 1810, some quarter of a century be-
fore the *Yarrow Revisited* volume appeared. Even the date of 1810 is
perhaps later than the facts warrant. Matthew Arnold speaks of
Wordsworth's "golden prime," that decade between "1798 and

[2] See Bernard Groom, *The Unity of Wordsworth's Poetry* (London: Macmillan,
1966). I must however concur with Garrod about "that decline in Wordsworth's po-
etical powers which no obtuseness can miss and no ingenuity satisfactorily explain"
(Garrod, p. 136).

[3] Quoted in Sperry, p. 29.

1808" when "almost all his really first-rate work was produced."[4] W. L. Sperry, whose book on the anticlimax is still one of the better general studies of Wordsworth as well, lowers the onset of the decline by yet another two years: "Wordsworth," he says, "could not be relied upon, after about 1806, to write poetry which bore upon its face the credentials of its greatness, and, failing inspiration, he manufactured verses."[5] As noted in a previous chapter, the date could be lowered to 1804,[6] or even 1802.[7] Whatever the year at which it began to predominate, moreover, the quantity of meretricious verse in Wordsworth's poetry as a whole is striking. "In his seven volumes," summarizes Arnold, "the pieces of high merit are mingled with a mass of pieces very inferior to them. . . . Work altogether inferior, work quite uninspired, flat and dull, is produced by him with evident unconsciousness of its defects, and he presents it to us with the same faith and seriousness as his best work."[8]

Nor was the early decline of Wordsworth's poetic abilities compensated for by an equally early efflorescence of those powers. On the contrary, as Sperry notes, "Wordsworth was late in his authentic arrival. . . . The authentic poet . . . did not begin to write until he was nearly thirty."[9] Three of Coleridge's stronger poems, "This Lime-Tree Bower," "Frost at Midnight," and "The Nightingale," all preceded "Tintern Abbey."

Yet if Coleridge came to poetic fruition earlier than Wordsworth, the ratio of chaff to wheat in his own poetic production is even more dismaying. Side by side with Arnold's conception of a "golden prime" for Wordsworth limited to a "single decade," we may place E. K. Chambers's even more diminutive accounting of Coleridge's achievement, that he left nothing of value behind but "a handful of golden poems."[10]

Now it is probable that very few of my readers would wish to contest, at least as far as poetry is concerned, the negative contentions I have just set forward. They are comfortably established in the traditional criticism of both poets, and their truth is constantly renewed for anyone who engages in comprehensive study of either Coleridge or Wordsworth. At the same time, however, that most of us concede the startling ratio of the meretricious to the first

[4] Arnold, *Essays*, p. 136.   [5] Sperry, p. 29.
[6] See above, Chapter One, pp. 102-103.
[7] See above, Chapter One, note 152.
[8] Arnold, *Essays*, p. 135.   [9] Sperry, p. 36.
[10] Chambers, p. 331.

rate in both poets, we also usually prefer to let the matter rest at that point. One tends to prefer, in the words of the song, to accentuate the positive and eliminate the negative. Furthermore, the problem of an adverse ratio of the unsuccessful to the successful in the two poets would seem to be readily resolved by the principle of selectivity; it would appear that we could easily put together a kind of Crocean "what is living and what is dead" anthology for both men. As early as 1819, a writer for the *Eclectic Review* suggested as much:

> Mr. Wordsworth has one chance of being read by posterity. . . . If Wordsworth's best pieces could be collected into one volume, some of his early lyrics, a few of his odes, his noble sonnets, all his landscape sketches and the best part of the Excursion, while his idiots and waggoners were collected into a bonfire on the top of Skiddaw, the "Sybilline leaves" would form a most precious addition to our literature.[11]

Solution by anthology, indeed, is precisely Arnold's own prescription in the matter. He felt that "Wordsworth needs to be relieved of a great deal of the poetical baggage which now encumbers him." He sought "to clear away obstructions" from around "Wordsworth's best work," "to disengage the poems which show his power, and to present them to the English-speaking public and to the world."[12]

Yet I maintain, even against so high an authority as that of Arnold, that selectivity does not in fact solve the problem. On the contrary, in the context of an author's life-effort, to select is to obscure, to anthologize is to distort. Anthologies are for cursory readers, not for those who really need to understand.

For that apex we call achievement is not suspended in air; it always rests upon a base of lower and less perfect effort. It is scarcely accidental that scholarship founds its standard editions not upon the principle of selectivity, but upon that of fullness: the six exhaustive volumes of Wordsworth's poems published for the Clarendon Press by Ernest de Selincourt and Helen Darbishire are now in part being superseded by the Cornell Wordsworth, which in still greater fullness presents not only the texts of Wordsworth's major poems but intermediate versions and rough drafts as well. We need to know it all, the tentative and failed and incomplete no less than the rounded and achieved; the negative no less than the

---

[11] Quoted in Sperry, p. 15.   [12] Arnold, *Essays*, pp. 140, 160-61.

positive. The silhouette does not become more clearly defined by eliminating the negative or outside field; it simply disappears altogether.

More formally, in a principle that modern philosophers have found useful, Karl Popper has argued that the truth content of a scientific theory should be measured not, as the Vienna positivists would have it, by its verifiability, but by its falsifiability; that is to say, the more possible falsifiers a theory has, the greater its empirical content. On the other hand, if a theory is unfalsifiable, it is nugatory and devoid of substance.[13]

If we extrapolate Popper's principle for the purposes of criticism, it applies to our present task in roughly this way: the theory is the proposition that Wordsworth and Coleridge are both major poets; the empirical content of this theory will be revealed precisely to the degree that we understand the ways in which they are both partial, incomplete, and unsatisfactory in their poetic production. After all, the twenty-second chapter of the *Biographia Literaria* urges the same truth by calling itself "The characteristic defects of Wordsworth's poetry . . ."; and in general Coleridge's prime critical maxim, which he called "this *golden rule* of mine," was that "*until you understand a writer's ignorance, presume yourself ignorant of his understanding*."[14]

In our attempt to understand the characteristic defects of both Coleridge and Wordsworth, or, if one wishes, their poetic ignorance, we may divide the hindered paths by which their achievement took shape into three interrelated groupings. The first group of these *aporiae* is constituted by the two men's mutual influence, with its accompanying distraction of poetic ambition into philosophical ambition; the second involves the struggles of each man to find his own appropriate poetic voice; and a third stems from the disrupted and disruptive nature of Romanticism itself.

This chapter will be addressed mainly to the second group of *aporiae*, that is, to those hindrances against which each man had to struggle in order to find his own poetic voice. In order to make my contentions clear, however, it will be necessary to enter to some extent, or at least to take glancing account of, the other two groups of *aporiae*. As to the first of these, the hindrances arising from the mutual interaction of the two men, and in particular the way in which this interaction pertained to their philosophical commit-

---

[13] "One can sum up all this by saying *the criterion of the scientific status of a theory is its falsifiability, or refutability, or testability*" (Popper, *Conjectures*, p. 37).

[14] *Biographia*, I, 160.

ments, a considerable amount of the materials for such an aware-
ness has already been supplied in the preceding chapters of this
book. Accordingly, the pertinent truth of that interrelationship
may now be stated in summary form: to a very large extent Cole-
ridge and Wordsworth created one another as great poets; but to
an equally large extent they also extinguished one another as great
poets.

In the beginning, indeed, it was almost as though Coleridge
simply decreed poetic greatness for Wordsworth, somewhat as
Kubla Khan decreed the pleasure dome. Thus on May 13, 1796,
Coleridge mentions Wordsworth for the first time, as "a very dear
friend of mine, who is in my opinion the best poet of the age."[15] As
more than one bewildered critic has wondered, how on earth could
Coleridge, on the basis of anything his new friend had done up to
that time, have known that Wordsworth was the best poet of the
age? That Wordsworth was in fact soon to reveal himself as the
best poet of the age makes the mystery still more intriguing. But
certainly one large part of Wordsworth's emergence in the role of
great poet was Coleridge's unstinting praise, encouragement, and
discerning criticism. For a single instance from a rather humorous
perspective, when Lamb ventured to omit effusive praise of some
portions of the *Lyrical Ballads*, Wordsworth wrote him a customar-
ily egotistical rebuke, which was followed by a second castigation
from Coleridge. As Lamb wryly described the second episode,

> Coleridge, who had not written to me some months before,
> starts up from his bed of sickness to reprove me for my hardy
> presumption: four long pages, equally sweaty and more tedious,
> came from him; assuring me that, when the works of a man of
> true genius such as W. undoubtedly was, do not please me at
> first sight, I should suspect the fault to lie 'in me and not in
> them,' etc. etc. etc. etc. etc. What am I to do with such people?
> I certainly shall write them a very merry Letter.[16]

Both language and idea in Wordsworth frequently, and in fact in
many more ways than anyone has ever documented, reflect Cole-
ridge's influence. For example, in "Tintern Abbey," the "pres-
ence" that disturbs Wordsworth with the joy of elevated thoughts
bears unmistakable resemblance to a Coleridgean emphasis in an
earlier poem. Wordsworth's "presence" involves

[15] *Collected Letters*, I, 215.
[16] Lamb, *Letters*, I, 247.

> a sense sublime
> Of something far more deeply interfused. . . .
> A motion and a spirit, that impels
> All thinking things, all objects of all thought,
> And rolls through all things.[17]

At the end of his predecessor poem, "Religious Musings," however, Coleridge, in speaking of "creative Deity," hails

> . . . ye of plastic power, that interfused
> Roll through the grosser and material mass
> In organizing surge! Holies of God![18]

The use in both passages of the unusual word "interfused," along with the similarity of Wordsworth's "motion and a spirit, that . . . rolls through all things" to Coleridge's "Holies of God" that "Roll through the grosser and material mass," seems to document the importance of Coleridgean pattern in Wordsworth's poetic process, for the Wordsworthian passage at issue is one of the most central in all his poetry.

Many more comparative passages could be brought forward, but Wordsworth's dependence upon Coleridge is most strikingly revealed, as suggested earlier, in the plan and eventual failure of "The Recluse." Wordsworth was as serious about the aspiration of his poem as a man could well be. As noted earlier, he intended it to convey "most of the knowledge of which I am possessed," and he meant "to devote the prime of my life and the chief force of my mind" to its completion. Remarkably, however, he could do virtually nothing at all on this vast project without Coleridge's help, and, as he strikingly confessed to his friend, "I cannot help saying that I would gladly have given 3 fourths of my possessions for your letter on The Recluse."[19]

Thus when Coleridge became estranged from Wordsworth, the non-existence of "The Recluse" was assured. But not only that; the shipwreck of Wordsworth as a poet was assured as well. Wordsworth was not a poet of major significance before he came under Coleridge's influence; he was never a poet of major significance after their break. Indeed, it is interesting to note that most of the dates for the beginning of Wordsworth's decline listed earlier in this chapter also refer to crises in Wordsworth's relation to Coleridge. Garrod's date of 1810 is the year in which Coleridge and

[17] Wordsworth, *Poems*, II, 262.   [18] Coleridge, *Poems*, I, 124.
[19] *Early Years*, p. 464.

Wordsworth broke off their friendship. Sperry's date of 1806 is the year in which clear evidences of strain in that friendship begin to be apparent. My own date of 1804 is the year in which Coleridge left for his sojourn in Malta. Heath's date of 1802 is the year in which Wordsworth's marriage involved a dislodgement of Coleridge from his position as prime counselor and helper.

Yet the case is hardly less extreme with the counter-influence of Wordsworth upon Coleridge. As we have noted, not only did Coleridge rework some of Wordsworth's juvenilia and publish the poems as his own, but "The Ancient Mariner" itself could hardly have been written without Wordsworth's help, for Wordsworth supplied the albatross, its killing by the mariner, and the navigation of the ship by the dead men, as well as actually composing a number of lines in the poem as we have it. Still again, some of Coleridge's most successful poetry of the late 1790s incorporates Wordsworthian emphases, and indeed the very tone of Wordsworth's poetic voice. In this respect, an example deserves to be repeated from earlier argumentation; in Coleridge's "Fears in Solitude" we actually seem to hear Wordsworth, not only in theme but in language as well:

> Here he might lie on fern or withered heath,
> While from the singing lark (that sings unseen
> The minstrelsy that solitude loves best),
> And from the sun, and from the breezy air,
> Sweet influences trembled o'er his frame;
> And he, with many feelings, many thoughts,
> Made up a meditative joy, and found
> Religious meanings in the forms of Nature!
>
> (ll. 17-24)

Above all, perhaps, Wordsworth's presence, in the early raptures of their friendship, encouraged Coleridge, whose nature, as he himself said, needed "another nature for its support," to the remarkable year of poetic productivity in 1797 to 1798 that scholars have agreed to call the *annus mirabilis*.

Yet "the Giant Wordsworth," though he made possible the *annus mirabilis*, by that same strength was able to turn off Coleridge's poetic fountain with scarcely a trickle left. We shall not here rehearse, but merely summarize, the melancholy story, for it has been recounted in a previous chapter.[20] Wordsworth managed to

[20] See above, Chapter One, pp. 100-102.

block "Christabel" from inclusion in *Lyrical Ballads* and probably ensured its forever remaining unfinished; he considered dropping "The Ancient Mariner" from the second edition; he did in fact insert an apologetic note in that edition in which he talked of the "great defects" of the poem. Coleridge's tenuous self-confidence could hardly withstand such vicissitudes; and he soon found that "The poet is dead in me," that Wordsworth had "descended on him, like the Γνῶθι σεαυτόν from Heaven; by shewing to him what true Poetry was, he made him know, that he himself was no Poet." Years later, Coleridge in a more hostile manner spoke of the adverse effects of Wordsworth's "cold praise and effective discouragement."

I have been at some pains to emphasize the ambivalent truth that Wordsworth and Coleridge largely created and also largely extinguished one another as great poets because such a double effect also characterizes the related *aporia* that consists of displacements of poetic energy into philosophical ambitions. The philosophical commitments made by both poets were not simply a block to their poetic achievements; they were also essential to the very conception of what those achievements were to have been. In this respect, T. S. Eliot's complaint, that Coleridge's poetry was hurt by the "stupefaction of his powers in transcendental metaphysics"[21] somewhat misconceives the dynamics of the situation, as does F. R. Leavis's enmity to approaching any aspect of Romanticism in other than exclusively literary terms. On the contrary, and as urged in the introduction to this volume, Coleridge, like his fellow-Romantics in Germany, thought of poetry and philosophy as interchangeable activities. Though in moments of dejection he could attribute the "loss" of his poetic genius "to my long & exceedingly severe Metaphysical Investigations,"[22] and say that he had been forced to give up poetry for *"downright metaphysics,"*[23] what he actually laments is not metaphysics as such, but metaphysics exclusively—that is, downright metaphysics to the exclusion of poetry. It was the upsetting of the balance that he deplored, for he believed unequivocally that "No man was ever yet a

---

[21] Eliot, *Use of Poetry*, p. 67.

[22] *Collected Letters*, II, 831. Earlier, he said that he had been "compelled" to "seek resources in austerest reasonings" and had thereby "denaturalized my mind" (725). Again, he says that he "found no comfort except in the driest speculations" (875).

[23] *Ibid.*, p. 814.

great poet without being at the same time a profound philosopher."[24]

He also was "convinced that a true System of Philosophy . . . is *best* taught in Poetry."[25] So in accordance with this view he early projected philosophical poems on the four elements, and another one on Spinoza.[26] His three most famous poems, to be sure, do not seem overtly—though they may well be so symbolically—especially philosophical, but we must remember that these three poems were all more casual in their inception than we are accustomed to realize, and that Coleridge's own esteem for them evolved during the passage of time and the praise of outside observers. Coleridge thought of "The Ancient Mariner" as merely a ballad at first, never was entirely satisfied with its conclusion, and by adding the gloss nearly two decades later attempted to give it more weight. "Kubla Khan" he apparently had so little confidence in that he did not publish it for nearly twenty years after it was written, and then anxiously attempted to deflect judgment by saying that it was incomplete—though it seems in fact about as fully terminated as any poem in the language. "Christabel," which was conceived under Wordsworth's benign influence, became hateful to Coleridge when Wordsworth withdrew his approval. As Coleridge dejectedly said, he would rather have written Wordsworth's "Ruth" than "a million" poems such as "Christabel."[27]

So Coleridge's three most famous poems were somethat provisional and even anomalous in their relationship to his total enterprise. On the other hand, the conversation poems, which more and more intrigue modern commentators, reveal themselves, in the light of the elucidation of their common underlying structure by Gérard and others, as profoundly philosophical in movement and concern, especially in their characteristic drawing together of subject and object.[28] Coleridge's later poetry, such as "Human Life; On the Denial of Immortality," is often philosophical where it is not merely occasional. The same holds true for his early

[24] *Biographia*, ii, 19.

[25] *Collected Letters*, iv, 687.

[26] *Notebooks*, i, 174, 556, 1561.

[27] See above Chapter One, note 70.

[28] See Albert S. Gérard, "The Discordant Harp: The Structure of Coleridge's Conversation Poems," *English Romantic Poetry; Ethos, Structure, and Symbol in Coleridge, Wordsworth, Shelley, and Keats* (Berkeley & Los Angeles: University of California Press, 1968), pp. 20-39.

poetry—a large part of it is either occasional or experimental, but when he draws himself up for a serious effort, we almost unfailingly encounter his peculiar mixture of theological and philosophical commitment. A ready example is provided by the long poem, "Religious Musings," where Hartley, Priestley, and the "sublime system of Berkeley" are invoked.

For a more detailed instance, in "The Destiny of Nations" we find such relentlessly philosophical lines as these:

> But Properties are God: the naked mass . . .
> Acts only by its inactivity.
> Here we pause humbly. Others boldlier think
> That as one body seems the aggregate
> Of atoms numberless, each organized;
> So by a strange and dim similitude
> Infinite myriads of self-conscious minds
> Are one all-conscious Spirit, which informs
> With absolute ubiquity of thought . . .
> All his involvéd Monads[29]

Such a Leibnizian embroiderment is an interesting datum in Coleridge's struggle with the attractions of pantheism, but as verse it seems rather clearly undigested into the language and movement of an effective poetic statement. As Coleridge himself realized, "I cannot write without a *body* of *thought*"; hence, as he said, "my *Poetry* is crowded and sweats beneath a heavy burthen of Ideas and Imagery."[30] Another burden of ideas, in the still earlier poem "The Eolian Harp," seems to work better in purely poetic terms:

> And what if all of animated nature
> Be but organic Harps diversely fram'd,
> That tremble into thought, as o'er them sweeps
> Plastic and vast, one intellectual breeze,
> At once the Soul of each, and God of all?[31]

But here, too, it is apparent that Coleridge's ideal view of himself as a poet entailed a profound intermingling of poetic activity with philosophical concern, and that such an intertwinement posed special problems in his poetic development.

The two poems from which I have just quoted were written prior to his deep friendship with Wordsworth. That "The Ancient Mari-

---

[29] Coleridge, *Poems*, i, 133.
[30] *Collected Letters*, i, 137.
[31] Coleridge, *Poems*, i, 102.

ner," "Kubla Khan," and "Christabel" do not carry so heavy an ostensible burden of ideational commitment—and that thereby, if one wishes, they were able to become better poems—is perhaps due not only to their quasi-provisional nature but also to the fact that Coleridge had by then unconsciously shifted the weight of his poetico-philosophical aspiration onto Wordsworth. At any rate, by 1800 he was able to announce that "I abandon Poetry altogether—I leave the higher & deeper Kinds to Wordsworth."[32] The higher and deeper kinds, as we have seen, necessarily mingled philosophy with poetry, and Coleridge's bequest was to doom much of Wordsworth's later poetic possibility. For not only was Wordsworth's mind "radically unphilosophical," it was not even theoretical. "I never cared a straw about the theory," he said of his own "Preface" to *Lyrical Ballads*, "& the Preface was written at the request of Coleridge out of sheer good nature."[33] The real truth about Wordsworth's mental activity is the one enunciated for his own work by William Carlos Williams: "The poet thinks with his poem, in that lies his thought, and that in itself is the profundity."[34]

Yet Coleridge was even more insistent about Wordsworth's role as philosophical poet than he was about Wordsworth's role as poetic theorist. Wordsworth was, said Coleridge, nothing less than "the first & greatest philosophical poet." Coleridge "looked forward," as he said, "to the Recluse, as the *first* and *only* true Phil. Poem in existence . . . not doubting . . . that the Totality of a System was not only capable of being harmonized with, but even calculated to aid, the unity . . . of a *Poem*."[35] The outcome of such massive proselytizing was inevitable. Wordsworth, always enormously under Coleridge's intellectual influence, took up, not his own, but Coleridge's intellectual cross, and struggled with faltering feet beneath it. As Sperry notes, Wordsworth was "strangely wanting in the power of abstract thought and curiously dependent upon others to supply him with the stuff of his speculations. . . . His systems were borrowed clothes and betray a foreign quality wherever they appear in his work."[36]

So much for the hindrances, as well as the strengths, that Wordsworth and Coleridge generated for one another. Such am-

---

[32] *Collected Letters*, I, 623.

[33] *Prose*, I, 167. As Coleridge said, "The Preface contains our joint opinions on Poetry" (*Collected Letters*, I, 627).

[34] *Williams*, pp. 390-91.   [35] *Collected Letters*, IV, 574.

[36] Sperry, p. 43.

bivalent effects exist of course on their own terms, but they also relate to the second group of *aporiae* for the achievement of both poets, which center upon the difficulties of finding authentic voices in which to utter their poetry, and to the third, which involves the disrupted nature of Romanticism itself.

Without at this point undertaking an exhaustive discussion of the latter phenomenon—which after all is the main theme of this book as a whole—we shall still probably all concede that the struggle of the two poets to find appropriate voices was greatly complicated by their role as establishers of the new Romantic sensibility. For their appropriate voices had to be authentic in terms of their poetic individualities, and yet had at the same time to embody the as yet indistinct character of the cultural shift. Moreover, that cultural shift, in expanding the boundaries of what had hitherto been considered proper technique and proper subject matter, tended to disorient the poet. "The range of poetic feeling," said Wordsworth, "is far wider than is ordinarily supposed, and the furnishing new proofs of this fact is the only *incontestible* demonstration of genuine poetic genius."[37] "Art has nothing to do with restrictions, gags or manacles," wrote Victor Hugo: "It bids you go, and leaves you free to wander in the great garden of poetry where there are no forbidden fruit."[38] Romantic poetry, in Friedrich Schlegel's epochal prescription, "embraces everything . . . from the greatest system of art . . . down to the sigh, the kiss"; "it tries to and should mix and fuse poetry and prose, inspiration and criticism, the poetry of art and the poetry of nature."[39] To Shelley, a "poem is the image of life expressed in its eternal truth"; and "all the great historians, Herodotus, Plutarch, Livy, were poets."[40] To Wordsworth, "a large portion of the language of every good poem can in no respect differ from that of good Prose," and as for subject matter, "The objects of the Poet's thoughts are every where."[41] According to Coleridge, poetry "brings the whole soul of man into activity";[42] and in Hazlitt's description, the basic premise of the

---

[37] *Middle Years*, II, 178.

[38] Hugo, *Poésies*, I, 577. Again, he urges "the freedom of art against the despotism of systems, of codes, and of rules" (Hugo, *Théatre*, I, 444). Compare Blake's rejection of "the modern bondage of Rhyming": "I therefore have produced a variety in every line, both of cadences & number of syllables. . . . [T]he terrific numbers are reserved for the terrific parts—the mild & gentle, for the mild & gentle parts, and the prosaic, for inferior parts . . ." He follows this with a quintessentially Romantic manifesto: "Poetry Fetter'd, Fetters the Human Race!" (*Blake*, p. 144).

[39] *Friedrich Schlegel*, II, 182.   [40] Shelley, *Prose*, p. 10.

[41] *Prose*, I, 135, 141.   [42] *Biographia*, II, 12.

Romantic poet was "that all things are by nature equally fit subjects for poetry."[43]

Such largeness of aspiration and expansion of range were willy-nilly accompanied by an uncertainty of taste and a blurring of poetic focus. Before the advent of Romanticism, the reigning traditions of poetic theory, from antiquity onward, tended to limit poetic language and poetic subject matters. In the words of a noted guardian of ancient learning, George Chapman,

> worthiest poets
> Shun common and plebeian forms of speech;
> Every illiberal and affected phrase
> To clothe their matter; and together tie
> Matter and form, with art and decency[44]

All this changed with Romanticism. Kierkegaard mounted a "protest against the view that romanticism can be comprehended in one concept, for romanticism implies overflowing all boundaries";[45] and his conception was exactly commensurate with Wordsworth's pronouncement that "poetry is the spontaneous overflow of powerful feelings."[46] But such overflow could also have the effect of an inundation of form and sense. In Romanticism, said Hulme trenchantly, "the concepts that are right and proper in their own sphere are spread over, and so mess up, falsify and blur the clear outlines of human experience. It is like pouring a pot of treacle over the dinner table."[47]

Of course the neo-classic period, as Pope deliciously demonstrated, had its own forms of bathos. But in the new Romantic era it was this abrogation of traditional boundaries for subject matters, forms of treatment, and choice of diction that led poets to perilous brinks. Thus Southey in his "Botany-Bay Eclogues" attempts a pastoral substitution of penal Australia for the Sicily and Arcadia of Theocritus and Virgil:

[43] *Hazlitt*, v, 163.

[44] *The Revenge of Bussy D'Ambois*.

[45] Kierkegaard, *Journals*, p. 25. Cf. Shelley: "I love all waste and solitary places; where we taste / The pleasure of believing what we see / Is boundless, as we wish our souls to be" (Shelley, *Poems*, p. 190). Cf. Blake: "The bounded is loathed by its possessor" (*Blake*, p. 2). From an opposed perspective, compare Francis Jeffrey's complaint that Keats's "ornamental images" were "poured out without measure and restraint, and with no apparent design but to unburden the breast of the author, and give vent to the overflowing vein of his fancy" (*Keats; The Critical Heritage*, ed. G. M. Matthews [London: Routledge & Kegan Paul, 1971], p. 203).

[46] *Prose*, I, 127.   [47] Hulme, *Speculations*, p. 118.

> Welcome, ye wild plains
> Unbroken by the plough, undelved by hand
> Of patient rustic; where for lowing herds,
> And for the music of the bleating flocks,
> Alone is heard the kangaroo's sad note
> Deepening in the distance[48]

If the kangaroo is dangerous game for a poet, it teeters hardly less vertiginously on the rim of the ludicrous than does the pig elsewhere hailed by the eventual poet laureate:

> Jacob! I do not like to see thy nose
> Turn'd up in scornful curve at yonder Pig.
> It would be well, my friend, if we, like him,
> Were perfect in our kind! . . . And why despise
> The sow-born grunter?[49]

The sow-born grunter, in Southey's menagerie, carries no more poetic risks than does the goose that he still elsewhere celebrates:

> If thou didst feed on western plains of yore;
> Or waddle wide with flat and flabby feet
> Over some Cambrian mountain's plashy moor;[50]

Poetic risks of this kind were not assumed by Southey alone. We find Coleridge extending human sympathy to an equally risible animal in his notorious "To a Young Ass," while Wordsworth, not to be outdone, sentimentalized another jackass in "Peter Bell." Again, in a different but still chance-taking emphasis, Wordsworth hails an incongruous inanimate object: "Spade!" he apostrophizes, and then proceeds to the thought that whoever "inherit[s] Thee," "That man will have a trophy, humble Spade!/ A trophy nobler than a conqueror's sword."[51] As Hazlitt maliciously but acutely commented about these kinds of risks, the Romantic poets—"these sweeping reformers and dictators in the republic of letters"— founded "the new school on a principle of sheer humanity, on pure nature void of art. . . . They were surrounded, in company with the Muses, by a mixed rabble of idle apprentices and Botany Bay convicts, female vagrants, gipsies . . . of ideot boys and mad mothers."[52]

Not merely in lesser works did the broadened range claimed by

[48] Southey, *Poems*, II, 73.
[50] *Ibid.*, II, 96.
[52] *Hazlitt*, v, 162-63.

[49] *Ibid.*, III, 65.
[51] Wordsworth, *Poems*, IV, 75-76.

the Romantic sensibility lead poets to faultily conceived or even ludicrous statement. In the very greatest poems of the Romantic masters there occur uncertainty of diction and banality of reference. Like Keats's melancholy, these characteristically Romantic forms of ruin dwell not in some limbo, but at the shrine of the temple itself. Although Arnold was aware that in Wordsworth there is "a mass of inferior work . . . imbedding the first-rate work and clogging it, obstructing our approach to it, chilling, not unfrequently, the high-wrought mood with which we leave it,"[53] he seems less clearly aware that such diasparactive reality not only afflicts Wordsworth's patently unsuccessful poetry but marbles his finest achievement as well. Indeed, this is a second reason why the attempt to solve the problem of Wordsworth's meretricious productivity by an anthology cannot succeed; the first-rate work is not only conditioned by the meretricious work, but in truth is inextricably intermixed with it.

As one pregnant example, we may consider the "Intimations Ode," which almost without question is one of Wordsworth's greatest poems. It is an inspired statement; but it is also one that in places is almost embarrassing.[54] The "six years' Darling of a pigmy size!" of stanza VII, despite the claims of apologists, was when it was written and will always remain a false note, one both cloying and jarring in the combined sentimentality and grotesquerie of its

[53] Arnold, *Essays*, p. 136.

[54] Among the criticisms of Wordsworth's "Intimations Ode," we may note Arnold's restive comment that it is "not wholly free from something declamatory" (Arnold, *Essays*, p. 159). Again, Bradley notes of Wordsworth that "where his metrical form is irregular his ear is uncertain. The Immortality Ode, like *King Lear*, is its author's greatest product, but not his best piece of work" (Bradley, p. 117). Still again, Trilling comments that "the Ode is not wholly perspicuous. . . . The difficulty does not lie in the diction, which is simple, or even in the syntax, which is sometimes obscure, but rather in certain contradictory statements which the poem makes, and in the ambiguity of some of its crucial words" (Trilling, *Imagination*, p. 130). Compare the denunciation of Yvor Winters, which, though characteristically exaggerated, encloses—again characteristically—a kernel of perception: "*Ode: Intimations of Immortality* is loosely associational in method. . . . Wordsworth gives us bad oratory about his own clumsy emotions and a landscape that he has never really perceived" (Winters, pp. 171-72). Leavis, again, speaks of "empty grandiosity" and "general factitiousness," of "falsity" and "rhythmic vulgarity" (Leavis, *Revaluation*, pp. 184-85). More specific is Coleridge's comment on the lines, "Thou, over whom thy immortality/ Broods like the day, a master o'er the slave," where he says that "without examining the propriety of making a 'master *brood* o'er a slave,' or the *day* brood *at all*; we will merely ask, what does all this mean?" (*Biographia*, II, 111). One might append that the very metaphor of master and slave is incongruous in the sublimity of the stanza's diction, cadence, and statement.

reference. A few lines further down in the same stanza we wince at another false note:

> The little Actor cons another part;
> Filling from time to time his 'humorous stage'
> With all the Persons, down to palsied Age,
> That Life brings with her in her equipage;

But the succeeding stanza, unencumbered by the ghost of Shake-speare and uncontaminated by labored rhyme, rises to majestic heights:

> Thou, whose exterior semblance doth belie
>   Thy Soul's immensity;
> Thou best Philosopher, who yet dost keep
> Thy heritage, thou Eye among the blind

The co-presence of the meretricious and the sublime is even more proximate in one of the loftiest passages in the poem—one of the most elevated, one thinks, that any poet has ever achieved:

> Hence in a season of calm weather
>   Though inland far we be,
> Our Souls have sight of that immortal sea
>   Which brought us hither,
>   Can in a moment travel thither,
> And see the Children sport upon the shore,
> And hear the mighty waters rolling evermore.[55]

The onomatopoeic grandeur of the cadence and the thalassic depths of primal experience engaged by the reference authenticate the lines as one of the touchstones of world poetry. Yet in their very midst occurs the impoverished rhyme of "hither" and "thither."

But surely, we think, such flaws are Wordsworth's alone, are unique to him; surely they cannot be found in Coleridge at his best. "Of all our writers of the briefer narrative poetry," judged Leigh Hunt, "Coleridge is the finest since Chaucer; and assuredly he is the sweetest of all our poets." "Of pure poetry, strictly so called, that is to say, consisting of nothing but its essential self, without conventional and perishing helps, he was the greatest master of his time."[56] Notwithstanding such praise, however, Coleridge, like Wordsworth, even at his best presents a flawed texture, skirts, even in his greatest moments, the banal and the misconceived.

---

[55] Wordsworth, *Poems*, IV, 282, 284.
[56] Hunt, pp. 163, 162.

Take for example "Kubla Khan." The last four lines of that poem are perfection, are, in their incantatory splendor, possibly the most wonderful he ever achieved:

> Weave a circle round him thrice,
> And close your eyes with holy dread,
> For he on honey-dew hath fed,
> And drunk the milk of Paradise.

For such poetry we may utilize the judgment of Dr. Johnson on Gray: had Coleridge written often thus, it had been vain to blame, and useless to praise him. In the very same stanza, however, there appear lines that are much less felicitous in their language and reference:

> It was an Abyssinian maid,
> And on her dulcimer she played,
> Singing of Mount Abora.

The near-doggerel rhyme of "maid" and "played" can hardly support the weight of the two exotic references, "Abyssinian" and "dulcimer." The language that follows dips to outright banality:

> Could I revive within me
> Her symphony and song,
> To such a deep delight 'twould win me,
> That with music loud and long,
> I would build that dome in air,[57]

"Symphony" followed by "song"—a redundancy not redeemed by the alliteration—seems to exist merely to fill the line. "Deep" delight is banal. The contraction "'twould" is execrable—even though the Romantics, in the continuing process of disentangling themselves from eighteenth-century forms, lapsed not infrequently into such usages. But that falseness is as nothing before the appalling cliché, "loud and long." The linkage is inert even in colloquial prose; but in a poem, to say nothing of this great poem, its presence is startling testimony to the effect of diasparactive pressure on the Romantic sensibility.

The matter is at once so central and so conventionally unrecognized as to require further illustration. We bring to mind a palpably great work by a third Romantic master: the "Ode to a Nightingale" of Keats, a poem worthy to stand with any in the English language. It too, like the "Intimations Ode" and "Kubla Khan," is visited by a

---

[57] Coleridge, *Poems*, I, 298.

form of ruin.[58] Where Coleridge, despite his reluctance to think of "Kubla Khan" as completed, somehow found the poetic tact to terminate his statement with its most soaring lines—and what single word could be more elevated and more final than "Paradise"?—Keats overflowed his own poem's most wonderful lines, which were also a possible point of termination, and produced a disastrous final stanza. The close of Keat's penultimate stanza matches the close of "Kubla Khan" in imaginative expansion and melody:

> The voice I hear this passing night was heard
> In ancient days by emperor and clown:
> Perhaps the self-same song that found a path
> Through the sad heart of Ruth, when, sick for home,
> She stood in tears amid the alien corn;
> The same that oft-times hath
> Charm'd magic casements, opening on the foam
> Of perilous seas, in faery lands forlorn.

A more absolute climax would be hard to conceive—it opens onto that prospect of infinity so cherished by Romanticism; and yet Keats, seemingly hypnotized by the word "forlorn," extends himself into a last stanza that carries with it ruinous consequences:

> Forlorn! the very word is like a bell
> To toll me back from thee to my sole self!
> Adieu! the fancy cannot cheat so well
> As she is fam'd to do, deceiving elf.
> Adieu! adieu! thy plaintive anthem fades . . .
> Was it a vision, or a waking dream?
> Fled is that music:—Do I wake or sleep?[59]

Keats, in the very month in which this poem was composed—May 1819—suppressed an inappropriate opening stanza that he had composed for the "Ode on Melancholy." Why then did he not do so here? What set the word "forlorn" tolling in his head; what led him to this diasparactive anadiplosis? The postposed adjectival emphasis of the word's first appearance points us to the answer. Consciously or more probably unconsciously, Keats was, one surmises, rapt by Shakespeare's great postposed "forlorn" in *King Lear*: "And wast thou fain, poor father,/ To hovel thee with swine

[58] Winters says fiercely that "The *Ode to a Nightingale* is a mediocre poem with a very few good lines and some of the worst lines of the century" (Winters, p. 179).
[59] Keats, *Poems*, pp. 259, 260.

and rogues forlorn,/ In short and musty straw?"[60] We know how important *King Lear* was to Keats; we know that "passages of Shakespeare" shared with "Sun Moon & Stars" the proud category of "Things real" in his spiritual hierarchy. "I sat down yesterday to read King Lear once again," he writes on one occasion: "once again the thing appeared to demand" a Keatsian response.[61] In that instance the response was "the prologue of a Sonnet"; in the instance we are considering it seems to have been the final stanza of his greatest poem. The duplication of the word "forlorn" in that stanza parallels the duplication of Shakespeare's usage by that of his ephebe; and it is the urging ghost of Shakespeare again that produces the "Adieu" of the stanza's third line and its second and third utterances in the fifth line. "Adieu! adieu!" is a singularly mannered expression to find in a nineteenth-century English poem; one surmises that it is there, however, not as a febrile affectation from French, but as a duplication of the ghost's three adieus in *Hamlet*: "Adieu, adieu, adieu! Remember me" (i.v.91). Structurally, it is clear what Keats was trying to do: bring the poem full circle back to its starting point. But in this attempt to serve its structure, he compromises his poem's texture.

The ghostly presence of Shakespeare, here no less than in its haunting of Wordsworth's "Intimations Ode," distorts and clogs the poem's natural movement. Indeed, the questions posed by the last stanza, "Do I wake or sleep?" and "Was it a vision, or a waking dream?" should not, by Keats's own theories of poetry, have been asked at all. They represent a precise instance of that "irritable reaching after fact & reason," that incapability of "being in uncertainties, Mysteries, doubts," which violates the desideratum of "*Negative Capability*."[62] Just how ruinously inappropriate the stanza is can perhaps be sensed in another way simply by reflecting upon the full banality of the intrusive personification, "deceiving elf," which, though not so grotesque as Wordsworth's "six years' Darling of a pigmy size!" is even more false.

To some extent, therefore, even the greatest Romantic poetry (with occasional exceptions such as "To Autumn"—though even there line seventeen is not quite right) may be seen as exhibiting uncertainty of tone, diction, and focus. This characteristic was in part an inevitable accompaniment to the overflowing of traditional limits by Romanticism's new and fervid aspiration. As Hazlitt saw, "this school of poetry had its origin in the French revolution, or

[60] Act iv, Scene vii, lines 37-40. [61] Keats, *Letters*, i, 243, 214.
[62] *Ibid.*, p. 193.

rather in those sentiments and opinions which produced that revo-
lution. . . . From the impulse it thus received, it rose at once from
the most servile imitation and tamest common-place, to the utmost
pitch of singularity and paradox." He continues:

> The change in the belles-lettres was as complete, and to many
> persons as startling, as the change in politics, with which it went
> hand in hand. There was a mighty ferment in the heads of
> statesmen and poets, kings and people. According to the prevail-
> ing notions, all was to be natural and new. Nothing that was es-
> tablished was to be tolerated. All the common-place figures of
> poetry . . . were instantly discarded . . . rhyme was looked upon
> as a relic of the feudal system, and regular metre was abolished
> along with regular government. Authority and fashion, elegance
> or arrangement, were hooted out of countenance, as pedantry
> and prejudice. Every one did that which was good in his own
> eyes. The object was to reduce all things to an absolute level; and
> a singularly affected and outrageous simplicity prevailed in dress
> and manners, in style and sentiment. A striking effect produced
> where it was least expected, something new and original, no
> matter whether good, bad, or indifferent, whether mean or lofty,
> extravagant, or childish, was all that was aimed at. . . . The licen-
> tiousness grew extreme. . . . The world was to be turned topsy-
> turvy; and poetry, by the good will of our Adam-wits, was to
> share its fate and begin *de novo*. It was a time of promise, a re-
> newal of the world and of letters; and the Deucalions who were
> to perform this feat of regeneration, were the present poet-
> laureat and the two authors of the Lyrical Ballads. The Germans,
> who made heroes of robbers, and honest women of cast-off mis-
> tresses, had already exhausted the extravagant and marvellous
> in sentiment and situation; our native writers adopted a wonder-
> ful simplicity of style and matter. The paradox they set out with
> was, that all things are by nature equally fit subjects for poetry.[63]

Although Hazlitt's description may itself exhibit some extrava-
gance, its kernel is sound: Romanticism represented, or at least
tried to represent, radical change. And radical change, whether
cultural or political, though it liberates, also dissipates the energies
of its participants. One may indeed take it as axiomatic that from a
cultural standpoint evolution is easier than revolution. Mozart, for
instance, was able to harvest a highly sophisticated musical idiom
that had been brought to supple perfection by his contemporaries

[63] *Hazlitt*, v, 161-62.

and immediate predecessors; Beethoven, on the other hand, had first to disentangle himself from the mode in which Mozart composed, and then forge his own giant forms as he progressed. But even the Promethean powers of the revolutionary Beethoven were taxed by the demand for a new cultural expression: his lifework encompasses hardly more than one hundred and thirty compositions, while the legatee of evolutionary process, Mozart, unencumbered by the draining demands of new forms and styles, produced scarcely less than *six* hundred and thirty.

The same principle of culturally encumbered genius holds true for Wordsworth and Coleridge as for Beethoven. Indeed, Wordsworth's "Prelude" is a work that can properly be termed Beethovenian, not only in its grandeur but also in the tentativeness with which it searches for themes and prospects after it is actually under way. Our admiration for the poem is by now so well established that we rarely pause to think what an enormously encumbered and hard won work of art it is. It emerged with all the difficulty of one of Michelangelo's slaves from the stone that bound it. I have elsewhere called "The Prelude" the "only great poem that does not have a text, for its *substantia* hovers in *Aufhebung* somewhere between the facing page editions of the 1805 and 1850 versions."[64] Actually, "The Prelude" could as well be printed in, as it were, a septuagint edition as one on facing pages, for it existed successively in two books, five books, thirteen books, and fourteen books, along with whatever tentative versions lay in between.[65] The testimony of all this revision is simply and on its face that of an immense struggle with form and statement. In addition there are still further paradoxes that indicate an encumberment in the emergence of "The Prelude." The greatest poem of the nineteenth century, after being worked on approximately fifty years, was not even published by its author, nor was it even called "The Prelude" by him. It was in fact not even designed as a prelude, but rather as a postlude or appendix[66]—or in Coleridge's term, a "tail-piece."

[64] "Recent Studies in the Nineteenth Century," *Studies in English Literature*, 16 (1976), 712.

[65] It is instructive to note that Jonathan Wordsworth delivered an address at the Eighth Annual Wordsworth Summer Conference at Grasmere on July 31, 1978, that was entitled "Seventeen Versions of the Prelude." All this is a long way from Havens's statement of about four decades earlier that "By '*The Prelude*' is generally understood *The Prelude* of 1850. It has always been so; presumably it always will be so" (Raymond Dexter Havens, *The Mind of a Poet* [Baltimore: The Johns Hopkins Press, 1941], I, xiii).

[66] Compare Dorothy on February 13, 1804: "William . . . is chearfully engaged in

Furthermore, the poem is entangled with three other works, all of which are even more encumbered than it is. I shall not dwell on this here, other than to present the preliminary suggestion that "The Prelude" relates exactly to the "Recluse" as Coleridge's *Biographia Literaria* does to his *magnum opus*, that also "The Prelude" is the *Biographia* as the "Recluse" is to the *magnum opus*, and that the proportion is strictly mathematical in its possible substitutions. But another kind of encumbrance for Wordsworth's poem pre-empts my concern in this chapter, that imposed by his predecessor figure, or, to use Harold Bloom's term, his "strong precursor," Milton. Indeed, I should like license to invoke another mathematical metaphor: that of a triangle in which the apex is "Paradise Lost" and the two angles of the base are "The Prelude" and Coleridge's "Kubla Khan." For whatever else both "The Prelude" and "Kubla Khan" may be, they are both celebrations of paradises that have been lost, and Milton's work is undeniably the parent of them both. As Elisabeth Schneider has argued, it is not, as Lowes had supposed, to travel books that Coleridge's poem owes its origin, but to Milton, who, as she says, "hovers over Coleridge's poem."[67] Moreover, despite "Kubla Khan's" relative brevity, especially as compared with "The Prelude," we may feel justified in regarding our triangle as isosceles in shape; for E. S. Shaffer has recently argued that "Kubla Khan" is in fact a collapsed epic, the residue or precipitate of the great epic poem on the Fall of Jerusalem that Coleridge had planned to write.[68]

Still, a collapsed or condensed epic is not exactly a true epic, for length is a necessary criterion of the epic form. In the respective epic ventures of the two Romantic poets at least, it would seem, therefore, that Milton might have been more beneficial to Wordsworth's struggle with form than to Coleridge's, or at any rate less harmful. This same truth obtains, I believe, in Milton's influence on the respective poetic languages employed by Wordsworth and by Coleridge.

To state the matter in brief, Milton provided Wordsworth, not with his most authentic style of utterance, but at least with *an* au-

---

composition, and goes on with great rapidity. He is writing the Poem on his early life which is to be an appendix to the Recluse" (*Early Years*, 440).

[67] Schneider, p. 264. Interestingly enough, I. A. Richards pointed out the poem's Miltonic antecedence in 1924, some three years before Lowes's *Road to Xanadu* appeared. See Richards, *Principles of Literary Criticism* (New York: Harcourt, Brace and Company; London: Routledge & Kegan Paul Ltd., 1950), pp. 30-31.

[68] See Shaffer, e.g., p. 95.

thentic utterance, while Coleridge, following the same pattern, became involved in deleterious aspirations toward the sublime. An example of this last effect can be seen in Coleridge's "Religious Musings":

> There is one Mind, one omnipresent Mind,
> Omnific. His most holy name is Love.
> Truth of subliming import! with the which
> Who feeds and saturates his constant soul,
> He from his small particular orbit flies
> With blest outstarting!

Again, from the same poem:

> Contemplant Spirits! . . .
> I haply journeying my immortal course
> Shall sometime join your mystic choir! Till then
> I discipline my young and novice thought
> In ministeries of heart-stirring song,
> And aye on Meditation's heaven-ward wing
> Soaring aloft I breathe the empyreal air
> Of Love, omnific, omnipresent Love[69]

The passages are so shrill in diction and so earnest in tone as to verge on the bathetic, and the word "omnific," lifted bodily out of Milton, somehow here sounds like a particularly heavy-handed coinage.

But the aspiration toward the sublime was only one of the problems with which Coleridge wrestled. Two other aspects of his early struggles with poetic style are almost equally bound up with the failure of his verse—or at the least to the keeping of it simply verse rather than poetry. The first was too large a commitment to occasional poems, especially humorously occasional poems, and the second was a tendency to experiment with poetic language. Of this latter characteristic, Wordsworth himself said that Coleridge devoted "inconceivable" time and labor to new experiments in meter, and was "an epicure in sound."[70] Even his three greatest poems are notably experimental from metrical and stanzaic standpoints—we need think only of the protosprung rhythm of "Christabel," of the experiments in ballad stanzas in "The Ancient Mariner," and of Schneider's surmise that "it is difficult not to suppose that the effect of free or imperfect rhyming in *Kubla Khan* was in

---

[69] Coleridge, *Poems*, i, 113, 124.   [70] Schneider, p. 270.

part a deliberate reflection of *Lycidas*, for in later years Coleridge described this very feature of *Lycidas* in words that fit his own poem quite as well."[71]

When one is not borne along by the currents of a great poem, however, the experimental tendency can be baneful. Thus there are Coleridgean imitations of "Ossian" that may have historical interest, but as poetry are unspeakable:

> Through the high-sounding halls of Cathlóma
> In the steps of my beauty I strayed;
> The warriors beheld Ninathóma
> And they bléssed the white-bosom'd Maid![72]

The same could be said for a poem in imitation of Akenside,[73] and again for "Lines in the Manner of Spenser," where Coleridge expresses the wish that from the pinions of the dove of peace "One quill withouten pain ypluck'd might be," for to his lady he fain some soothing song would write,

> Lest she resent my rude discourtesy,
> Who vow'd to meet her ere the morning light,
> But broke my plighted word—ah! false and recreant wight![74]

This is of course apprentice work, but even in his poetic maturity Coleridge devoted an unusual amount of time to the metrically and linguistically experimental. Thus there are poetic exemplifications of the Homeric hexameter, of the Ovidian elegiac metre, of the Catullian hendecasyllables; and there are imitations of Stolberg's hexameters, and an experimental paraphrase of Psalm 46 in sprung rhythm.[75] Still again, Coleridge sent some experimental hexameters to William and Dorothy in Goslar, which begin, charmingly enough, as follows:

> William, my teacher, my friend! dear William and dear
>   Dorothea!
> Smooth out the folds of my letter, and place it on desk or on
>   table;
> Place it on table or desk; and your right hands loosely
>   half-closing,
> Gently sustain them in air, and extending the digit didactic,
> Rest it a moment on each of the forks of the five-forkéd left hand,

[71] *Ibid.*, p. 272.
[72] Coleridge, *Poems*, i, 39.
[73] *Ibid.*, p. 69.
[74] *Ibid.*, p. 95.
[75] *Ibid.*, pp. 307, 308, 307, 327-29, 326.

Twice on the breadth of the thumb, and once on the tip of each
    finger;
Read with a nod of the head in a humouring recitativo;
And, as I live, you will see my hexameters hopping before you.
This is a galloping measure; a hop, and a trot, and a gallop!

He continues in the same vein:

All my hexameters fly, like stags pursued by the stag-hounds,
Breathless and panting, and ready to drop, yet flying still
    onwards

And in due course he becomes somewhat more serious:

William, my head and my heart! dear Poet that feelest and
    thinkest!
Dorothy, eager of soul, my most affectionate sister!
Many a mile, O! many a wearisome mile are ye distant.[76]

In this instance, of course, Coleridge's metrical experimentations
share the scene with his urge toward the occasional and the
humorous. Throughout his *oeuvre* there is an abundance of the lat-
ter, from a youthful poem called "The Nose" ("A Nose, a mighty
Nose I sing"),[77] to his verse of 1800 to Mr. Pye:

Your Poem must *eternal* be,
    Eternal! it can't fail,
For 'tis *incomprehensible*,
    And without head or tail![78]

Some "Lines to Thomas Poole," both occasional and humorous,
are interesting in their biographical re-creation of joking evenings
in the two men's friendship, but are poetically null:

Such Verse as Bowles, heart honour'd Poet sang,
That wakes the Tear, yet steals away the Pang,
Then, or with Berkeley, or with Hobbes romance it,
Dissecting Truth with metaphysic lancet.
Or, drawn from up those dark unfathom'd wells,
In wiser folly chink the Cap and Bells.
How many tales we told! what jokes we made,
Conundrum, Crambo, Rebus, or Charade;

[76] *Ibid.*, p. 304.   [77] *Ibid.*, p. 8.
[78] *Ibid.*, II, 959.

Aenigmas that had driven the Theban mad,
And Puns, these best when exquisitely bad;[79]

There are many occasional verses even more trifling, such as
"Lines to a Friend in Answer to a Melancholy Letter."[80] But we
need not dwell further on either the experimental or the occasional
in Coleridge's *oeuvre*, for the point seems clear: namely, that a sub-
stantial amount of the verse he produced was not undertaken in
any real poetic seriousness or designed to participate in any high
poetic moment.[81]

What he *was* serious about were the poems that entailed the as-
piration to the sublime. There he sought to pile up tonal masses in
the manner of Milton—to do in poetry what Handel could do in
music—but what he actually achieved was shrill turgidity:

> And lo! the Great, the Rich, the Mighty Men,
> The Kings and the Chief Captains of the World,
> With all that fixed on high like stars of Heaven
> Shot baleful influence, shall be cast to earth,
> Vile and down-trodden, as the untimely fruit
> Shook from the fig-tree by a sudden storm.
> Even now the storm begins: each gentle name,
> Faith and meek Piety, with fearful joy
> Tremble far-off—for lo! the Giant Frenzy
> Uprooting empires with his whirlwind arm
> Mocketh high Heaven; burst hideous from the cell
> Where the old Hag, unconquerable, huge,
> Creation's eyeless drudge, black Ruin, sits
> Nursing the impatient earthquake.[82]

If we seek the reason for Coleridge's repeated attempts, however
unsuccessful, to achieve the sublime, we should ascribe only part
of it to his reverence for Milton, or to the interest in the sublime
that he, as a theorist, shared with other theorists of the age.[83] The

---

[79] *Ibid.*, p. 977.   [80] *Ibid.*, I, 90.

[81] As additional examples compare such trifles as "Written in an Album" (Cole-
ridge, *Poems*, II, 972), "To a Lady Who Requested Me to Write a Poem Upon Noth-
ing" (p. 973), "Sentimental" (p. 973), "My Godmother's Beard" (p. 976), "The
Silver Thimble" (I, 104-106). There seems a patently disproportionate amount of
such foolery in Coleridge's poetic effort.

[82] Coleridge, *Poems*, I, 121.

[83] For general background see, e.g., Samuel H. Monk, *The Sublime; A Study of
Critical Theories in XVIII-Century England* (Ann Arbor: University of Michigan Press,
1960); Walter John Hipple, Jr., *The Beautiful, The Sublime, and The Picturesque in*

largest part of the reason, one can hardly doubt, was neither rever-
ence for Milton nor interest in the sublime as such, but the urge to
find a proper voice for his conception of the necessary mingling of
poetry and philosophy—which for Coleridge meant religious phi-
losophy. For such philosophical poetry, Milton provided the true
poetic voice. For instance, in praising Wordsworth, Coleridge said
that he had "more of the genius of a great philosophical poet than
any man I ever knew, or, as I believe, has existed in England since
Milton."[84] By the same token, the unserious character of Cole-
ridge's experimental and occasional verse is generated precisely by
the absence of the poetico-philosophical intent. But even in the
experimental verse and the occasional verse we can glimpse the
depth of his commitment to the mixing of poetry and philosophy.
Simply to restrict ourselves to passages already quoted, the
hexameters sent to Dorothy and William contain in their playful-
ness the entirely serious specification that Wordsworth is a "Poet
that feelest *and* thinkest"; and in the near-doggerel lines to Poole,
the salutation of Bowles's verse is followed by the couplet:

> Then, or with Berkeley, or with Hobbes romance it,
> Dissecting Truth with metaphysic lancet.

That, almost certainly, is the key to Coleridge's continuing
involvement in what Shaftesbury termed the "false sublime."[85]
When a theologico-philosophical intent is present, the sublime en-
sues as the chosen voice for its realization. Thus "The Destiny of
Nations" begins this way:

> Auspicious Reverence! Hush all meaner song,
> Ere we the deep preluding strain have poured
> To the Great Father, only Rightful King,
> Eternal Father! King Omnipotent!
> To the Will Absolute, the One, the Good!
> The I AM, the Word, the Life, the Living God!

If we enquire as to why Coleridge's sublime was almost always
false, we might ascribe the cause, or part of it, to the inherent dif-

---

Eighteenth-Century British Aesthetic Theory (Carbondale: Southern Illinois University
Press, 1957); Thomas Weiskel, *The Romantic Sublime: Studies in the Structure and Psy-
chology of Transcendence* (Baltimore: The Johns Hopkins University Press, 1976); Al-
bert O. Wlecke, *Wordsworth and the Sublime* (Berkeley: University of California Press,
1973).

[84] *Table Talk*, p. 171 (July 21, 1832).

[85] Shaftesbury, p. 160.

ficulties of melding poetry and philosophy. But whatever the cause, the effect is one of misplaced pitch; Coleridge's voice is so shrill and agitated as to verge on hysteria:

> I mark'd Ambition in his war-array!
>   I heard the mailéd Monarch's troublous cry—
> 'Ah! wherefore does the Northern Conqueress stay!
> Groans not her chariot on its onward way?'
>   Fly, mailéd Monarch, fly!
>   Stunn'd by Death's twice mortal mace,
>   No more on Murder's lurid face
> The insatiate Hag shall gloat with drunken eye!

The lines are from "Ode to the Departing Year." The same sense of shrill frenzy, of hubbub really, attends characteristic lines from "Religious Musings":

>   Whence that cry?
> The mighty army of foul Spirits shrieked
> Disherited of earth! For she hath fallen
> On whose black front was written Mystery;
> She that reeled heavily, whose wine was blood;
> She that worked whoredom with the Daemon Power,
> And from the dark embrace all evil things
> Brought forth and nurtured: mitred Atheism!
> And patient Folly who on bended knee
> Gives back the steel that stabbed him; and pale Fear
> Haunted by ghastlier shapings than surround
> Moon-blasted Madness when he yells at midnight!
> Return pure Faith! return meek Piety!

As we see from that passage, the sense of hysteria in Coleridge's sublime is continually reinforced by the repeated appearance of words such as "shrieked," "yells," "moaned," and "groaned"; as, to take another instance, in these Miltonic lines from "The Destiny of Nations":

>   Wherefore not vain,
> Nor yet without permitted power impressed,
> I deem those legends terrible, with which
> The polar ancient thrills his uncouth throng:
> Whether of pitying Spirits that make their moan
> O'er slaughter'd infants, or that Giant Bird
> Vuokho, of whose rushing wings the noise

Is Tempest, when the unutterable Shape
Speeds from the mother of Death, and utters once
That shriek, which never murderer heard, and lived.[86]

Perhaps a few disconnected lines and passages, drawn more or less at random from the same poem, will illustrate still better the pervasiveness of Coleridge's frenetic pitch: "The Maid gazed wildly at the living wretch"; "Yet amid his pangs,/ With interruptions long from ghastly throes,/ His voice had faltered out this simple tale"; "They saw the neighbouring hamlets flame, they heard/ Uproar and shrieks! and terror-struck drove one"; "The weeping wife/ Ill hushed her children's moans; and still they moaned,/ Till Fright and Cold and Hunger drank their life"; "From his obscure haunt/ Shrieked Fear, of Cruelty the ghastly Dam"; "The infuriate spirits of the murdered make/ Fierce merriment, and vengeance ask of Heaven"; "Shriek'd Ambition's giant throng, . . . And such commotion made they, and uproar,/ As when the mad Tornado bellows through/ The guilty islands of the western main."[87]

One does not wish to labor the point: Coleridge's diction here is kinetic enough for great poetry, but not weighty enough, and its continuing shrillness perhaps reflects certain psychological aspects of his emotional personality as it responded to stress.[88] Inter-

---

[86] Coleridge, *Poems*, I, 131, 162, 121, 134.

[87] *Ibid.*, pp. 138-46.

[88] In terms of the historical background of predecessor styles, however, as distinguished from the psychological dynamics of Coleridge's inner life, we may see the hysterical sublime as an overlaying of the Miltonic model by the bardic style of Gray. Thus, from Gray's "The Triumphs of Owen": "There the press, and there the din;/ Talymalfra's rocky shore/ Echoing to the battle's roar/ Where his glowing eyeballs turn,/ Thousand Banners round him burn./ . . . There Confusion, Terror's child,/ Conflict fierce, and Ruin wild,/ Agony, that pants for breath." How close this kind of hubbub comes to Coleridge's usage may be gauged still better by comparing a few lines from "The Bard" itself: "On dreary Arvon's shore they lie,/ Smear'd with gore, and ghastly pale:/ Far, far aloof th' affrighted ravens fail;/ The famish'd Eagle screams . . ."; "When Severn shall re-eccho with affright/ The shrieks of death, thro' Berkley's roofs that ring./ Shrieks of an agonizing King!"; "She-Wolf of France, with unrelenting fangs,/ That tear'st the bowels of thy mangled Mate." Similarities to other varieties of Coleridgean formulation may be found in "The Progress of Poesy" ("Nor second He, that rode sublime/ Upon the seraph-wings of Extasy,/ The secrets of th' Abyss to spy") and "The Descent of Odin," but it seems clear enough even from these few examples that the youthful Coleridge, in his quest for the sublime, was much under the influence of the bardic style. As Dr. Johnson severely said of Gray's odes, for which that style was developed: "These odes are marked by glittering accumulations of ungraceful ornaments; they strike, rather than please; the images are magnified by affectation; the language is laboured into harshness. The

estingly, however, the elocutionary uproar of his false sublime, which seems to be caused by the anxiety of trying to combine theology, philosophy, and poetry, is almost entirely absent from the conversation poems, and it would seem that the very idea of conversation, with its lowering of the voice in a mutual give and take, may have effected the change. Certainly his prowess as a conversationalist, as we observed when discussing the nature of Coleridge's anxiety, appears to have developed as a palliative for the psychological terrors that beset him. In any event, "The Nightingale," which is the only poem directly identified by Coleridge as a conversation poem, opens with a quietness that is in stark contrast to the frenetic notes of the hysterical sublime:

> No cloud, no relique of the sunken day
> Distinguishes the West, no long thin slip
> Of sullen light, no obscure trembling hues.
> Come, we will rest on this old mossy bridge!
> You see the glimmer of the stream beneath,
> But hear no murmuring: it flows silently,
> O'er its bed of verdure. All is still.

In the matrix of stillness, Coleridge is able to cope with the anxiety generated by the figure of Milton. In the twelfth line of the poem, he quotes Milton directly in calling the nightingale "Most musical, most melancholy" bird, and he then discharges the anxiety invoked by his poetic father into a footnote, where he says that he comments as he does in order "to rescue himself from the charge of having alluded with levity to a line in Milton; a charge than which none could be more painful to him, except perhaps that of having ridiculed his Bible." Immediately after this obeisance, however, Coleridge is actually able to take issue with Milton, and he does so with remarkable calm. In a passage that rebukes the "fame is the spur" confession in "Lycidas," Coleridge chooses instead a form of sporting with Amaryllis in the shade—or rather with Wordsworth in the shade. Thus he censures the

> Poet who hath been building up the rhyme
> When he had better far have stretched his limbs

---

mind of the writer seems to work with unnatural violence." Hazlitt was possibly even more apposite in his *Lectures on the English Poets*, where he characterized the style of the odes as "a kind of methodical borrowed phrenzy" (*Hazlitt*, v, 118). The phrase could serve as an almost perfect description of Coleridge's hysterical sublime as well.

Beside a brook in mossy forest-dell,
By sun or moon-light, to the influxes
Of shapes and sounds and shifting elements
Surrendering his whole spirit, of his song
And of his fame forgetful! so his fame
Should share in Nature's immortality

The same modulation of pitch and lowering of tone, with the same lessening of shrillness and poetic anxiety, characterizes the conversation poem that is possibly Coleridge's most perfect poetic production, and in the opinion of some critics his greatest one as well. For "Frost at Midnight" opens with perhaps an even more absolute sense of calm than does "The Nightingale":

The Frost performs its secret ministry,
Unhelped by any wind. The owlet's cry
Came loud—and hark, again! loud as before.
The inmates of my cottage, all at rest,
Have left me to that solitude, which suits
Abstruser musings: save that at my side
My cradled infant slumbers peacefully.
'Tis calm indeed! So calm, that it disturbs
And vexes meditation with its strange
And extreme silentness.[89]

The passage is in complete antithesis to the hubbub of the hysterical sublime. The sole sound, the owl's cry, simply accentuates the pervading calm and stillness, which is inaugurated by the secret ministry of frost on a windless night. The inmates of the cottage are all at rest, the poet is in solitude, the infant slumbers peacefully. The two uses of the word "calm" lead naturally into the invocation of "extreme silentness."

One should observe of these two poems, finally, that their lovely calmness of diction and tone perhaps results not only from their conversational form but also from the fact that their philosophical content arises from within them rather than being confronted as an edifice of thought already existing on the outside.

So much for some of the varied characteristics of Coleridge's poetic endeavor. If a large part of his problems as a poet arose from the difficulty of steering a path between the Scylla of occasional and experimental verse and the Charybdis of philosophic poetry rendered in the language of the Miltonic sublime, the situation of

[89] Coleridge, *Poems*, I, 264, 265, 240.

his fellow-struggler, Wordsworth, was quite different. Where Milton aroused anxiety in Coleridge, Wordsworth was able to utilize the predecessor poet as a support for his own authentic voice. A particularly intriguing witness to this truth is provided by Coleridge's lines to Wordsworth after hearing "The Prelude" recited over a period of weeks. For here we see the style of the Miltonic sublime utilized as common property; not, however, in Coleridge's own voice, but in an almost perfect imitation of that of Wordsworth himself:

> Friend of the Wise! and Teacher of the Good!
> Into my heart have I received that Lay
> More than historic, that prophetic Lay
> Wherein (high theme by thee first sung aright)
> Of the foundations and the building up
> Of a Human Spirit thou hast dared to tell
> What may be told, . . .
>   Theme hard as high!
> Of smiles spontaneous, and mysterious fears . . .
>   of moments awful,
> Now in thy inner life, and now abroad[90]

The imitation is virtually perfect, not only of Wordsworth, but also of Wordsworth's use of the highly enjambed cadences and drawn-out rhythms of the so-called Miltonic paragraph.

In "The Prelude," in particular, Wordsworth relies on and incorporates Milton's way of speaking. Thus, in the first book of the 1850 version, in line 7 Wordsworth lifts the phrase "vast city" from *Areopagitica*; in line 15, the statement that "The earth is all before me" echoes Milton's "The world was all before them" of "Paradise Lost" (XII, 646); lines 102-103 hail the sun "that sheds/ mild influence," which takes up Milton's "the Pleiades . . . shedding sweet influence" (VII, 374-75); in lines 140-41, Wordsworth's "dove" that "sits brooding" echoes Milton's divine spirit in "Paradise Lost" that "Dove-like sat'st brooding"; in line 175 Wordsworth's "dire enchantments" echoes Milton's "enchantments drear" of "Il Penseroso," and so on.[91]

---

[90] *Ibid.*, pp. 403-404 (ll. 1-7, 12-13, 15-16).

[91] See J. C. Maxwell's notes to his edition of "The Prelude" (Harmondsworth: Penguin Books, 1971), pp. 539-65. The starting point for any general consideration of the important topic of Milton's presence among the Romantics is Joseph Wittreich, *The Romantics on Milton; Formal Essays and Critical Asides* (Cleveland and London: The Press of Case Western Reserve University, 1970).

These examples could be multiplied indefinitely; and all of them show that not only Milton's cadences but his actual statements were deeply interwoven into the fabric of Wordsworth's poetic discourse. That they could be so interwoven suggests, however, a certain malleability in Wordsworth's style, and in fact the first of the characteristic defects of Wordsworth that Coleridge identifies in the *Biographia Literaria* is "the INCONSTANCY of the *style*."[92] Indeed, leaving aside the desiccated verse of his later utterance, one may find in Wordsworth perhaps as many as half a dozen styles, including the ballad doggerel of poems like "The Idiot Boy" and "Peter Bell," the venturesome rhymed style, featuring the alternation of short and long lines to achieve a rough-hewn effect, that he employs in the "Intimations Ode," and at least two blank verse styles, both of them lofty, but otherwise quite different. The one that we have been talking about, the one that is so compatible with the poetic voice of Milton and that Wordsworth uses in much of "The Prelude," is stately and beautifully cadenced, with frequent enjambment and liberal use of inversions.

The other style does not occur very often. It is, however, in my judgment Wordsworth's deepest form of utterance, his own true and authentic style, compared to which all the others, even the Miltonic, are provisional. It was to the perfection of this style, I believe, that his whole unconscious being tended. For want of a better name, I shall call it the limpid style; it is a blank verse of almost crystalline purity and directness, characterized by virtually no inversions, few tropes, and almost no ornament or specialness of diction. Like Coleridge's conversational style, it is quiet. Were it not for its cadence, which flows as naturally and as unremittingly as a mountain stream, this limpid style could almost be a form of prose. If we need an example for its illustration, we may look to perhaps the most distinctively Wordsworthian of all Wordsworth's achievements, "Michael":

> Upon the forest-side in Grasmere Vale
> There dwelt a Shepherd, Michael was his name;
> An old man, stout of heart, and strong of limb.
> His bodily frame had been from youth to age
> Of an unusual strength: his mind was keen,
> Intense, and frugal, apt for all affairs,
> And in his shepherd's calling he was prompt
> And watchful more than ordinary men.

[92] *Biographia*, II, 97.

In such a style, the dominant characteristics are simplicity and directness. Subject precedes verb, and verb precedes object. The tone neither rises nor falls, but is the same at any point, even and inevitable:

> I have been toiling more than seventy years,
> And in the open sunshine of God's love
> Have we all lived; yet if these fields of ours
> Should pass into a stranger's hand, I think
> That I could not lie quiet in my grave.

Though it does not rise or fall, the limpid style is keyed to a pitch of quiet but intense emotion:

> but to Michael's heart
> This son of his old age was yet more dear—
> Less from instinctive tenderness, the same
> Fond spirit that blindly works in the blood of all—
> Than that a child, more than all other gifts
> That earth can offer to declining man,
> Brings hope with it, and forward-looking thoughts,[93]

It is the existence of this limpid style, one can hardly doubt, that caused Arnold to say that "Wordsworth's poetry, when he is at his best, is inevitable, as inevitable as Nature herself. It might seem that Nature not only gave him the matter for his poem but wrote his poem for him. He has no style." It is the existence of the limpid style, again, that caused Arnold to say that "if we are to seize [Wordsworth's] true and most characteristic form of expression," we would find it in a line like this in "Michael": "And never lifted up a single stone." In that line, observes Arnold, there is "nothing subtle," there is "no heightening," yet it is "expression of the highest and most truly expressive kind."[94]

It is the limpid style, furthermore, that supplies us with clues to the profoundest directions and goals of Wordsworth's poetic strivings. First of all, it reveals why he was so concerned to free himself from poetic diction, and it reveals also why Coleridge, despite his superior critical skills, never really addressed the point of Wordsworth's stand on poetic diction.[95] Coleridge himself, both in his

[93] Wordsworth, *Poems*, II, 81-82 (ll. 40-47); 87-88 (ll. 228-32); 85 (ll. 142-48).

[94] Arnold, *Essays*, pp. 155, 157-58.

[95] Another commentator comes independently to the same conclusion: "Coleridge in tearing the theory to pieces in the *Biographia Literaria* was demolishing what was his own invention rather than Wordsworth's, and removing from Words-

metrical experiments and in the examples of the sublime that we have noted, typically moved toward a heightened diction and a complex syntax. He aimed in general at an intricate artifact. He strove to erect a verbal structure adequate to support and to display the monumental mass of theological philosophy that he intended it to convey. Wordsworth, on the contrary, was in a sense always trying to diminish, not augment, the artifact. He sought a direct expression of an inner truth that was felt with a literally prophetic conviction and certainty, and it was necessary that the poem not come between that truth and its proclamation. Wordsworth needed, not to hypostasize his poetry by an ornate style, but rather so to purify the style that the poem disappeared and only the distilled truth remained. Thus Coleridge, significantly, realizes that the speaker in "The Prelude" is not primarily a poet, but "Friend of the wise, and teacher of the Good," that "The Prelude" is not so much an artifact as a "prophetic Lay."

If the limpid style, or, to utilize Arnold's metaphor, the style of nature, were to be achieved, it must be purged of the accreted artificialities that Wordsworth called poetic diction. Poetic diction, in fact, though Coleridge elaborately skirts the issue, was merely the conglomerate poetic style offered to every poet in every age by his immediate predecessors, what Pound in 1934 called in terms of his own background "the common verse of Britain from 1890 to 1910," "a horrible agglomerate compost, not minted, most of it not even baked, all legato, a doughy mess of third-hand Keats, Wordsworth, heaven knows what, fourth-hand Elizabethan sonority blunted, half-melted, lumpy."[96] It was from the late eighteenth-century version of this eternally renewed poetic pabulum that Wordsworth first took nourishment, and then asceticized himself.[97] Or, to vary the metaphor, he began to block off the muddy rills of outworn formulation so that his own stream could flow both

---

worth's genius an incrustation which was largely deposited by himself" (Murry, *Keats*, p. 271).

[96] Kenner, p. 80.

[97] As Eliot realizes, "Every revolution in poetry is apt to be, and sometimes to announce itself to be, a return to common speech. That is the revolution which Wordsworth announced in his prefaces, and he was right; but the same revolution had been carried out a century before by Oldham, Waller, Denham and Dryden; and the same revolution was due again something over a century later. The followers of a revolution develop the new poetic idiom . . . they polish or perfect it; meanwhile the spoken language goes on changing, and the poetic idiom goes out of date" (*On Poets*, p. 23).

deep and clear. His early poem, "An Evening Walk," as Legouis long ago pointed out, is virtually an anthology of those stock eighteenth-century usages called poetic diction:

> In thoughtless gaiety I coursed the plain,
> And hope itself was all I knew of pain;

Or

> There, bending o'er the stream, the listless swain
> Lingers behind his disappearing wain.[98]

No authentic voice could emerge from such an agglomerate compost; the very fact, however, that Wordsworth had to purge his own practice of this style gives point to his animadversions against poetic diction. For a single instance, even in a poem of such maturity and finish as "Resolution and Independence," we suddenly encounter a doughy mess of undigested poetic diction in the phrase "sable orbs," and this in a poem where direct speech such as "A gentle answer did the old Man make" prevails. Indeed, the phrase "sable orbs" contaminates two whole lines:

> Ere he replied, a flash of mild surprise
> Broke from the sable orbs of his yet-vivid eyes[99]

In order to achieve the purities of the limpid style, such language had to be purged.

The existence of the limpid style, and the inferences to be drawn from it, serve to answer, finally, two of the questions posed by or at least implied in this chapter: first, why was Milton not so baneful for Wordsworth as he was for Coleridge; and secondly, why did Coleridge so unswervingly cast Wordsworth in the role of philosophical poet? The solution to both problems is contained in a single word of a Wordsworthian grandeur and simplicity. That word is "truth." Wordsworth's task was simply to record a truth he already knew. "The days gone by," he says in one of his ultimate statements,

> Return upon me almost from the dawn
> Of life: the hiding-places of man's power
> Open; I would approach them, but they close

---

[98] Wordsworth, *Poems*, I, 7, 11 (ll. 21-22, 70-71).

[99] *Ibid.*, II, 238 (ll. 90-91). Such eighteenth-century contamination recurs, interestingly enough, so late as the 1850 version of "The Prelude," where line 315 of Book XIII says that Wordsworth "ranged at will the pastoral downs."

> I see by glimpses now; when age comes on,
> May scarcely see at all; and I would give,
> While yet we may, as far as words can give,
> Substance and life to what I feel[100]

Coleridge, on the other hand, was faced with a far more daunting prospect—not simply to record the truth, but to ascertain it and to examine it by philosophical argument in contexts of philosophical learning. For Coleridge, accordingly, Milton's style and its philosophical weight suggested a task of Herculean proportions, while for Wordsworth it was simply another, and eventually discardable, vehicle for an abiding knowledge lodged in his own feeling and experience.

The same certainty that Wordsworth possessed the truth caused Coleridge to fasten upon him as the great philosophical poet. For however formally unphilosophical and untheoretical Wordsworth may have been, truth, which his whole being radiated the confidence of possessing, is what all philosophers have always sought. Therefore Wordsworth, like his six years' child, was, despite his innocence of formal learning, a best philosopher and an eye among the blind.

So the poetic problems encountered by Coleridge and Wordsworth, though frequently similar, varied in difficulty as the needs and goals of the two men varied. It seems proper to conclude this chapter, which has dealt with problems and negativities, with an example of poetic vindication for both figures that restores also our sense of the goodness of their mutual dependency. At the end of "Frost at Midnight," Coleridge, writing in his recently achieved quiet style, achieves also a new poetic form, one fittingly enough borrowed from the benediction in a church service. The lines, addressed to his infant son, are among the most exquisite he ever wrote:

> Therefore all seasons shall be sweet to thee,
> Whether the summer clothe the general earth
> With greenness, or the redbreast sit and sing
> Betwixt the tufts of snow on the bare branch
> Of mossy apple-tree, while the nigh thatch
> Smokes in the sun-thaw; whether the eave-drops fall
> Heard only in the trances of the blast,
> Or if the secret ministry of frost

[100] *Prelude*, 1850 version, pp. 449-51 (XII, 275-84).

> Shall hang them up in silent icicles,
> Quietly shining to the quiet Moon. [101]

With the words "secret," "silent," "quietly," and "quiet," the style of the benediction triumphantly banishes the hysterical sublime that had plagued its author. And both its style and its form were bequeathed by him, this time with benign effect, to his friend. For "Tintern Abbey," like "Frost at Midnight," concludes with a benediction. Where Coleridge had blessed and prophesied for his son, Wordsworth blesses and prophesies for his sister; and like Coleridge, Wordsworth signals the occasion with the summarizing word "therefore":

> Therefore let the moon
> Shine on thee in thy solitary walk;
> And let the misty mountain-winds be free
> To blow against thee; and, in after years . . .
> If solitude, or fear, or pain, or grief,
> Should be thy portion, with what healing thoughts
> Of tender joy wilt thou remember me . . .
> Nor wilt thou then forget,
> That after many wanderings, many years
> Of absence, these steep woods and lofty cliffs,
> And this green pastoral landscape, were to me
> More dear, both for themselves and for thy sake! [102]

The diction, syntax, and cadence of the lines, so serene, pure, and inevitable, make us realize that they constitute a prime example of Wordsworth's limpid style. And both the benediction here and that in Coleridge's predecessor poem are examples of the most authentic voices of their authors as well as some of the truest poetry in our language.

[101] Coleridge, *Poems*, I, 242 (ll. 65-74).
[102] Wordsworth, *Poems*, II, 263 (ll. 134-59).

Poetry and the Poem: The Structure of Poetic Content

◊♦◊

I<small>F MUCH</small> of the intellectual effort expended in the lives of both Coleridge and Wordsworth—expended and continually summoned up again despite the formidable obstacles surveyed in the preceding chapter—if much of this effort went toward the ideal of writing great poetry, the question presents itself: why is poetry worthy of such dedication, and why, furthermore, is it so persistently intertwined with the different even if related realm of philosophy? Arnold provides a kind of answer: "Poetry is nothing less than the most perfect speech of man, that in which he comes nearest to being able to utter the truth. It is no small thing, therefore, to succeed eminently in poetry."[1]

But Arnold's statement, one to which most of us no doubt would willingly subscribe, actually signalizes the high respect in which the world holds poetic achievement more than it answers the questions just raised. For we require to know the nature of "truth," or at least of that "truth" that poetry utters or approximately utters. Once we realize the importance of such truth, and the uniqueness of poetry's apprehension of it, we shall have a cognitive basis for a better understanding both of what poetry is and of why it merits the large role it assumes in the lives and activities of men such as Wordsworth and Coleridge.

Our approach to such an understanding will in this chapter proceed through a gateway formed by two terms, "poetry" and "poem," which are used freely by everyone when speaking of poetic concerns.

Now the use of the two words "poetry" and "poem" in ordinary discourse uncovers a paradox. On the one hand, we customarily invoke them both as referring interchangeably to the same artistic activity; and on the other we sense in them, the more so upon re-

[1] Arnold, *Essays*, p. 128.

flection, a certain difference in semantic overtone—a difference that at first seems slight but eventually reveals itself as crucial. The word "poetry" suggests something unbounded, a current only adventitiously caught in words (as in "The poetry of earth is never dead"), while "poem" suggests something closed and delimited, a verbal artifact.

"Poetry," in the former signification, represents a conception that might fittingly be called Platonic (although the adjective is intended not at all in Ransom's sense). In Plato's approval of a poetry that is at once a mania and a philosophical glimpse of ultimate reality, we see a tendency to supplant the notion of "poem" as artifact with that of "poetry" as current of feeling:

> There is a third form of possession or madness, of which the muses are the source. This seizes a tender, virgin soul and stimulates it to rapt passionate expression, especially in lyric poetry. . . . But if any man come to the gates of poetry without the madness of the Muses, persuaded that skill alone will make him a good poet, then shall he and his works of sanity with him be brought to nought by the poetry of madness.[2]

The same sense of enraptured flow, by which poetry is precisely not delimited artifact but a momentary participation in an unlimited current of feeling, is emphasized by Plato in another place:

> as the worshipping Corybantes are not in their senses when they dance, so the lyric poets are not in their senses when they make these lovely lyric poems. No, when once they launch into harmony and rhythm, they are seized with the Bacchic transport— as the bacchants, when possessed, draw milk and honey from the rivers, but not when in their senses. So the spirit of the lyric poet works, according to their own report. For the poets tell us, don't they, that the melodies they bring us are gathered from the rills that run with honey, out of glens and gardens of the Muses, and they bring them as the bees do honey, flying like the bees. And what they say is true, for a poet is a light and winged thing, and holy, and never able to compose until he has become inspired, and is beside himself, and reason is no longer in him.[3]

Poetry, in this understanding, boasts an extraordinarily distinguished lineage of practitioners and guardians. It is, to cite a single instance, what Shelley pays homage to in his *Defence*:

[2] *Phaedrus* 245A. [3] *Ion* 534A-B.

Poetry, in a general sense, may be defined to be "the expression of the imagination": and poetry is connate with the origin of man. Man is an instrument over which a series of external and internal impressions are driven, like the alternations of an ever-changing wind over an Aeolian lyre, which moves it by their motion to ever-changing melody. . . . In the infancy of society every author is necessarily a poet, because language itself is poetry; and to be a poet is to apprehend the true and the beautiful. . . . A poet participates in the eternal, the infinite, and the one.[4]

But in such formulations the conception of "poem" is devalued; the hardness of outline that we associate with artifact is blurred and veiled.

The conception of poetic act as "poem"—that is, as artifact—is, however, nearly as ancient and quite as distinguished in its partisans, as is that of poetic act as "poetry." It is implied in Aristotle's insistence that poetry, whether tragic or of other kind, should involve the idea of "a whole," with "a beginning, middle and end."[5] All those aspects of the poet's utterance that we associate with the notion of craftsmanship, as opposed to that of a divine current of inspiration, tend toward the same understanding. Thus Du Bellay argues that it is not enough to allege that poets are simply born: whoever wants poetic immortality must remain long in his chamber, must "sweat and tremble repeatedly," must endure "hunger, thirst, and long vigils"; for it is on these wings that "the writings of men mount up to the sky."[6] Again, Ben Jonson praises Shakespeare for his "well torned, and true-filed lines", and says that he "Who casts to write a liuing line, must sweat,/ . . . and strike the second heat/ Vpon the *Muses* anuile."[7] It is in this tradition that Pope can complain that "Ev'n copious Dryden wanted, or forgot,/ The last and greatest Art, the Art to blot."[8] It is in this tradition, too, that T. S. Eliot speaks of "the intolerable wrestle/ With words and meanings."[9] And in his *Discoveries* Jonson, asking *"how differs a Poeme from what wee call Poesy,"* concludes that *"A Poeme* . . . is the worke of the Poet; the end, and fruit of his labour, and studye."[10] All such attitudes tend toward an emphasis on the poem as artifact, as consciously formed verbal structure. This is the "art" that in the Renaissance and the seventeenth century was so

[4] Shelley, *Prose*, pp. 4, 6, 7.
[6] Du Bellay, pp. 105-106.
[8] *Pope*, IV, 219.
[10] *Jonson*, VIII, 636.

[5] *Poetics* 1450^{b}25-30; 1459^{a}15-20.
[7] *Jonson*, VIII, 392.
[9] *Quartets*, p. 13.

frequently differentiated from "nature," or the unconscious product of inspiration.[11]

The divergence in conception between unconsciously or carelessly voiced "Platonic" poetry and carefully wrought "Aristotelian" poem is further indicated by the simultaneous currency, in both antiquity and the Renaissance, of the dual conception of the poet as reflected in the Greek *poietes*, on the one hand, and the Latin *vates* on the other. *"What is a Poet?"* asks Jonson. *"A Poet* is that which by the *Greeks* is called . . . ὁ ποιητής, a Maker, or a fainer: . . . From the word ποιεῖν, which signifies to make or fayne."[12] Sidney, however, notes that "Among the *Romanes* a Poet was called *Vates*, which is as much as a diviner, foreseer, or Prophet."[13] *Poietes*, in other words, refers to the maker of "Aristotelian" poems; *vates* to the communicant of "Platonic" poetry.

To view the matter from another perspective, we see evidence of the difference between "poetry" and "poem" in Poe's well-known insistence that "a long poem does not exist." It is, indeed, the recognition of this difference, together with an unwillingness to accept it, that underlies Poe's whole contention:

> a poem deserves its title only inasmuch as it excites, by elevating the soul. The value of the poem is in the ratio of this elevating excitement. . . . That degree of excitement which would entitle a poem to be so called at all, cannot be sustained throughout a composition of any great length. . . . *"Paradise Lost"* . . . in fact, is to be regarded as poetical, only when, losing sight of that vital requisite in all works of Art, Unity, we view it merely as a series of minor poems. . . . After a passage of what we feel to be true poetry, there follows, inevitably, a passage of platitude which no critical pre-judgment can force us to admire.[14]

But obviously, long poems *do* exist. Long poems, that is, as verbal artifacts. What might not exist are long, seamless flows of "poetry." In short, Poe expects "poem" to mean "poetry"—the Platonic current. His phrase "elevating the soul" indicates this bias, as does the still more significant phrase "true poetry."

Coleridge, on the other hand, observes and reports the same facts as Poe does but interprets them in a different awareness. For

---

[11] See, e.g., Edward Tayler, *Nature and Art in Renaissance England* (New York: Columbia University Press, 1964). The differentiation of nature and art was inherited from classical antiquity, e.g., Horace, *Ars poetica*, lines 408-409.

[12] *Jonson*, VIII, 635.   [13] *Sidney*, III, 6.

[14] *Poe*, VI, 3-4.

Coleridge, the conception of "poem" is not dictated absolutely by the conception of "poetry." Like Poe, he observes that poetry and poem are not always identical; unlike Poe, he accepts rather than suppresses the resulting postulation of two entities:

> whatever *specific* import we attach to the word, poetry, there will, be found involved in it, as a necessary consequence, that a poem of any length neither can be, or ought to be, all poetry. Yet if an harmonious whole is to be produced, the remaining parts must be preserved *in keeping* with the poetry; and this can be no otherwise effected than by such a studied selection and artificial arrangement, as will partake of *one*, though not a *peculiar* property of poetry.[15]

Actually, the dual existence of "poetry" and "poem" is an omnipresent reality in poetic practice, and our recognition of it can shed light on certain aesthetic problems. For instance, it is a common practice for a poet, even a major one, to neglect "poetry" in order to serve the structure of "poem." Take, for a single example, Wordsworth's fine sonnet, the first part of which runs as follows:

> The world is too much with us; late and soon,
> Getting and spending, we lay waste our powers:
> Little we see in Nature that is ours;
> We have given our hearts away, a sordid boon![16]

Here the phrase "late and soon" adds little or nothing to the poetic statement. The poetry would mean the same if it simply ran, "The world is too much with us:/ Getting and spending we lay waste our powers." The redundant "late and soon" is there because of the demands of the "poem," that is, it satisfies the requirements of the metrical pattern adopted in the sonnet. Likewise, the dubious phrase "a sordid boon," which though not redundant is clumsily archaic, and which is justified mainly as the rhyme to "soon," serves the need of the "poem" more than that of the "poetry."

On the other hand, one frequently encounters instances where diminished concern with the "poem" occurs alongside heightened concern for the "poetry." An example is "Kubla Khan." Here the "poem" is a broken form, but the "poetry" is dipped from the high Platonic stream. Indeed, as Elisabeth Schneider has pointed out, the concluding lines are drawn directly from the *Ion*:[17]

[15] *Biographia*, II, 11.   [16] Wordsworth, *Poems*, III, 18.
[17] Schneider, pp. 245-46.

Weave a circle round him thrice,
And close your eyes with holy dread,
For he on honey-dew hath fed,
And drunk the milk of Paradise.[18]

This intensification of "poetry," however, is set against a denigration of "poem": at this very moment the poetic whole is simply denied, for the "poem" ends, uncompleted. So Coleridge seems in this instance to elevate the conception of *vates* at the expense of that of *poietes*.

To be sure, poetry as the artifact of a *poietes* and poetry as the vision of a *vates* were not, and are not, emphases that ought necessarily to exclude one another; indeed, the interchangeability of the words "poem" and "poetry" in ordinary use, as well as repeated statements of poets and theorists, demonstrates that the optimum situation would be one in which the two terms coincide. Shelley, to cite an instance, fuses emotional "Platonic" flow and perdurable "Aristotelian" artifact in his ideal of a "great poem":

A great poem is a fountain for ever overflowing with the waters of wisdom and delight; and after one person and age has exhausted all its divine effluence which their peculiar relations enable them to share, another and yet another succeeds, and new relations are ever developed, the source of an unforeseen and an unconceived delight.[19]

In actual practice, however, the two conceptions coincide less often than one might expect. A whole class of poetic phenomena, grouped by Addison under the rubric "false wit"—that is, Herbert's "Easter Wings" or, as Addison says, "Poems cast into the Figures of *Eggs, Axes* or *Altars*"[20]—testifies to the tendency of some poets to lay disproportionate stress on the conception of "poem." Although few actually claim that the poem as it appears on the page is the "real" poem (Wellek's essay, "The Mode of Existence of a Literary Work of Art," provides the classic argument against such a fallacy), the analogical thrust of "poem" as the product of a maker seems to extend toward a certain preoccupation with the literally visual object. Cummings's eccentricities about capitalization and José García Villa's comma poems both attest this preoccupation. One of the best poets to whom such matters have been impor-

---

[18] Coleridge, *Poems*, I, 298.　　　　　　[19] Shelley, *Prose*, p. 26.
[20] *Spectator*, 62.

tant is Stefan George, who designed his own typefaces and subscribed to a mystique of the poem's appearance on the page.

George's poetry, even aside from such a mystique, exhibits a strong sense of the artifact, a sense that is accentuated by a characteristically static subject matter, as is perhaps conveyed by the simple title of one of his best poems: "Der Teppich" ("The Tapestry"). A briefer poem may be adduced in full to particularize the contention:

> Komm in den totgesagten park und schau:
> Der schimmer ferner lächelnder gestade,
> Der reinen wolken unverhofftes blau
> Erhellt die weiher und die bunten pfade.

> Dort nimm das tiefe gelb, das weiche grau
> Von birken und von buchs, der wind ist lau,
> Die späten rosen welkten noch nicht ganz,
> Erlese küsse sie und flicht den kranz,

> Vergiss auch diese letzten astern nicht,
> Den purpur um die ranken wilder reben
> Und auch was übrig blieb von grünem leben
> Verwinde leicht im herbstlichen gesicht.[21]

> Come to the park they say is dead, and view
> The shimmer of the smiling shores beyond,
> The stainless clouds with unexpected blue
> Diffuse a light on motley path and pond.

> The tender grey, the burning yellow seize
> Of birch and boxwood, mellow is the breeze.
> Not wholly do the tardy roses wane,
> So kiss and gather them and wreathe the chain,

> The purple on the twists of wilding vine,
> The last of asters you shall not forget,
> And what of living verdure lingers yet,
> Around the autumn vision lightly twine.

Here both Platonic frenzy and Platonic current are absent; the lapidary precision of diction, meter, and pattern is complemented by near neutrality of emotion. The poetry is muted; the poem is strong—almost palpably "there," a fine example of *poesis* as *pictura*.

[21] *George*, IV, 12.

Indeed, the similarity of this emotionally neutralized poem to Robert Penn Warren's prime example of "pure" poetry (in his essay, "Pure and Impure Poetry") suggests that possibly his example is not one of "pure poetry" so much as one of "pure poem," and that its limitations are less the lack of the strengthening alloy of impurity than simply a lack of poetry. Warren takes as his example Tennyson's lines,

> Now sleeps the crimson petal, now the white;
> Nor waves the cypress in the palace walk;
> Nor winks the gold fin in the porphyry font:
> The firefly wakens: waken thou with me.[22]

The stillness of the emotional current, alongside the heightened sense of artifice, seems to indicate that the lines are pure poem; as is also the tendency in such traditions as *haiku*.

Many poems diminish poetry in quite another way. I have in mind particularly certain aspects of the poetic practice of Dryden, Pope, and their contemporaries, where the epigrammatic compression, tightly reined couplets, and extraordinary attention to "numbers" emphasize the idea of poem, while the poetry is evacuated, as it were, to such a degree that Arnold called these writers "not classics of our poetry" but "classics of our prose."[23] Think, for instance, of Dryden's "Religio Laici," which begins,

> Dim as the borrow'd beams of moon and stars
> To lonely, weary, wand'ring travelers
> Is Reason to the soul

and ends, nearly nine hundred lines later, with the statement

> And this unpolish'd, rugged verse, I chose
> As fittest for discourse, and nearest prose;
> For while from sacred truth I do not swerve,
> Tom Sternhold's, or Tom Sha—ll's rhymes will serve.[24]

Yet despite Arnold's dictum, and despite Dryden's own admission of the interchangeability of verse and prose in this instance, "Religio Laici" is, one thinks, clearly a poem. It is prosaic but not prose. For a poem, though we often use the term to indicate the full coincidence of artifice and poetry, can contain a minimum of poetry and maintain itself simply by artifice. That is to say, a poem in one sense is simply anything that first of all looks like other

[22] Warren, p. 230. [23] Arnold, *Essays*, pp. 41-42.
[24] *Dryden*, p. 168.

poems, and secondly is claimed to be a poem by its author or someone else. As Coleridge says:

> If a man chooses to call every composition a poem, which is rhyme, or measure, or both, I must leave his opinion uncontroverted. The distinction is at least competent to characterize the writer's intention. . . . But if the definition sought for be that of a *legitimate* poem, I answer, it must be one, the parts of which mutually support and explain each other; all in their proportion harmonizing with, and supporting the purpose and known influences of metrical arrangement.[25]

By the first part of Coleridge's standard, "Religio Laici" is indubitably a poem, and by the second (which does seem to beg the question somewhat), it is, if not quite so indubitably, still a respectable candidate for the title. For Coleridge, significantly, does not in this definition insist that a poem must be characterized by poetry.

Much the same claim could be made for Pope's "Essay on Man." We find it a more significant poem than "Religio Laici," probably because its technical proficiency is greater, its argument more subtle, and its leaven of poetry somewhat more evident (e.g. "die of a rose in aromatic pain"). But, like Dryden's poem, it is an artifice for prosaic, not poetic awareness. "This I might have done in prose," writes Pope in a foreword prefixed to all editions from 1734 on, "but I chose verse, and even rhyme, for two reasons. The one will appear obvious; that principles, maxims, or precepts so written, both strike the reader more strongly at first, and are more easily retained by him afterwards: The other may seem odd, but is true, I found I could express them more *shortly* this way than in prose itself."[26]

It should be observed that such prosaic poems are not "bad" poems. If "poem" and "poetry" were in our common understanding actually synonymous, then the absence of poetry would make it necessary to say that "Religio Laici" either was no poem at all or was at best a bad poem. But few of us think of the work in that way; and almost no one, I believe, would seriously maintain that "An Essay on Man" is bad as an expression of verbal art. "The question, whether Pope was a poet," writes Hazlitt, "has hardly yet been settled, and is hardly worth settling; for if he was not a great poet, he must have been a great prose-writer, that is, he was a great writer of some sort."[27]

[25] *Biographia*, II, 10.   [26] *Pope*, III, 7-8.
[27] *Hazlitt*, v, 69.

In short, whatever the genre of "An Essay on Man," its quality is not "bad." Even Arnold concedes such efforts the status of "classic." His own "Rugby Chapel," on the other hand, provides an example of what we call the "bad" poem: its verbal artifice is strained, its measure uncertain, and its diction false.[28] Arnold's emotion about his father rings counterfeit (perhaps because he himself was unaware of its ambivalence), and its shrillness is especially evident in the use of archaic second-personal forms. In the following lines from "Rugby Chapel" the badness verges on the ludicrous; the tongue-twisting "Sternly repressest the bad!" and "reviv'st, Succorest!" represent a bathos that Pope would have treasured:

> Still thou upraisest with zeal
> The humble good from the ground,
> Sternly repressest the bad!
> Still, like a trumpet, doth rouse
> Those who with half-open eyes
> Tread the border-land dim
> 'Twixt vice and virtue; reviv'st,
> Succorest!—this was thy work
> This was thy life upon earth.[29]

Yet even "Rugby Chapel" is a poem, though an inadequate one. It is not a strong poem with a minimum of poetry, as is "An Essay on Man," but a weak poem with an abundance of false poetry. It is not, however, any more than Pope's work, a piece of prose.

Still, one must concede that the distinction between poetry and prose is in fact an important aesthetic problem. Further, it is a problem that reveals the existence of a fundamental difference between poetry and the poem. Poetry, if sufficiently weak, can fade into prose (even though the actual line of demarcation, like that between the state of sleep and the state of being awake, is in the event elusive). The poem, on the other hand, never fades by badness into prose.[30] As we see in the instance of "Rugby Chapel," it

[28] Though capable of true poetic achievement on some occasions, Arnold was peculiarly prone to create "bad poems." See, for instance, Leavis's devastating critique of the sonnet to Shakespeare in his *Education and the University* (London: Chatto & Windus, 1965), pp. 73-76.

[29] Arnold, *Poems*, pp. 287-88.

[30] Shelley seems to recognize this distinction, at least by implication, when he says that the "parts of a composition may be poetical, without the composition as a whole being a poem" (Shelley, *Prose*, p. 10).

simply becomes increasingly a bad poem. The writings of Robert W. Service and Edgar Guest are bad poems, not prose. Doggerel of the "Roses are red/ Violets are blue" type constitutes a poem. Nonsense verse such as "Jabberwocky" is a poem. The result of party games where each of several guests supplies a line in a predetermined meter and rhyme scheme is a poem. Even a poem composed to be a deliberate fraud will still be a poem. For pattern and figure in language are of themselves sufficient to maintain the conception of "poem."

The boundary between the poetic and the prosaic becomes difficult to define only when we speak of "poetry" versus prose rather than of "poem" versus prose. Most of us conclude intuitively that certain impassioned prose is really poetry; and that certain attempts at poetry never leave the realm of prose, particularly those attempts that are not protected by the artifice of "poem." We recall T. S. Eliot's observation that "a great deal of bad prose has been written under the name of free verse."[31] The fact, however, that fine things have been written in free verse, as well as the fact that certain prose seems to qualify as poetry, indicates that verse form alone is not crucial. Coleridge notes that "The writings of PLATO, and Bishop TAYLOR, and the 'Theoria Sacra' of BURNET, furnish undeniable proofs that poetry of the highest kind may exist without metre";[32] and Shelley says that

> The distinction between poets and prose writers is a vulgar error. . . . Plato was essentially a poet—the truth and splendour of his imagery, and the melody of his language, is the most intense that it is possible to conceive.[33]

If the distinction between verse and prose is not necessary to the conception of "poetry," neither is the conception of beginning, middle, and end—that is, of completed form. The most obvious examples are supplied by Shakespearean tragedy, where parts of the language are in verse that is not poetic, where other parts are not in verse at all, and where the incidence of "poetry" does not occur in the context of "poem." One doubts whether greater poetry can exist than that which incorporates the paradisal exhilaration of Lear:

> No, no, no, no! Come, let's away to prison;
> We two alone will sing like birds i' th' cage.

[31] Eliot, On Poetry, p. 31.   [32] Biographia, II, 11.
[33] Shelley, Prose, p. 9.

When thou dost ask me blessing, I'll kneel down
And ask of thee forgiveness. So we'll live,
And pray, and sing, and tell old tales, and laugh
At gilded butterflies, and hear poor rogues
Talk of court news; and we'll talk with them too
Who loses and who wins; who's in, who's out;
And take upon's the mystery of things
As if we were God's spies; and we'll wear out,
In a wall'd prison, packs and sects of great ones,
That ebb and flow by th' moon.

(V.iii.8-19)

There is no question here of free verse; the language is at once pat-
terned and figured. And yet the speech is not a poem, that is, it is
not something complete in itself as an artifact. It could not be taken
out of its dramatic context and retain its full power. Nor is it part of
a poem, for although the play as a whole is doubtless a literary ar-
tifact, it is (despite the efforts of some Shakespearean critics to
maintain the contrary) not a poem—not even a greatly extended
poem. It is a play. The completed form in which Lear's speech re-
sides is an existential configuration: a symbolic representation of
human interaction. The "poetry" relates to the currents of this in-
teraction, not to the artifice of "poem" as such.

We can see this distinction still more plainly by comparing two
other Shakespearean passages, similar in statement but different in
context. The first is his sonnet 66:

Tir'd with all these, for restful death I cry:
As, to behold desert a beggar born,
And needy nothing trimm'd in jollity,
And purest faith unhappily forsworn,
And gilded honour shamefully misplac'd,
And maiden virtue rudely strumpeted,
And right perfection wrongfully disgrac'd,
And strength by limping sway disabled,
And art made tongue-tied by authority,
And folly, doctor-like, controlling skill,
And simple truth miscall'd simplicity,
And captive good attending captain ill:
    Tir'd with all these, from these would I be gone,
    Save that, to die, I leave my love alone.

The second is a portion of Hamlet's "To be or not to be" speech:

For in that sleep of death what dreams may come,
When we have shuffl'd off this mortal coil,
Must give us pause. There's the respect
That makes calamity of so long life.
For who would bear the whips and scorns of time,
The oppressor's wrong, the proud man's contumely,
The pangs of dispriz'd love, the law's delay,
The insolence of office, and the spurns
That patient merit of the unworthy takes,
When he himself might his quietus make
With a bare bodkin?

(III.i.66-76)

The passages are strikingly similar: each is in verse, each expresses a sense of gloom about existence, each lists a catalogue of generally experienced woes, each asserts that life is not worth living "except for." Both passages are what we call poetry. Yet the first passage is also a poem; the second one is not. The first needs no context other than that supplied by the reader's own past. The second calls not only upon the general experience of the reader, but also upon a knowledge of Hamlet's situation.

The import of these examples and others like them becomes increasingly clear. Although we often use "poetry" and "poem" to mean the same thing ("verse" is perhaps the most neutral name for this congruence), at other times we use the words as though they refer to matters that can exist separately from one another. At still other times we use them as coinciding, but only in the sense that the former is "in" the latter. In this usage, we seem to think of the poem as a kind of receptacle for the poetry. Such variations indicate, I believe, that in the living use of language there is constantly recognized and maintained an undefined, but indispensable, distinction between the ideal identity and possible separability of poetic form and poetic content.

"Poetry," I suggest, often means that which corresponds to our intuitive sense of the content of a poetic act; and "poem," that which corresponds to our perception of its form.

I have been at pains to point out the unavoidability and constant recurrence of our sense of the difference between "poetry" and "poem," for to speak of significant distinctions between "content" and "form" requires the strongest kind of empirical foundation. The best established traditions of modern critical and aesthetic thought run counter to such dichotomies. We can see this in the change, which occurred some decades ago, in the teaching of poetry in our schools. Before the advent of the New Criticism, it was customary to teach the beauty of poetry, and especially to isolate individual passages as representative of that beauty. The procedure perhaps expressed itself with greatest prestige in Arnold's conception of "touchstones": fragments of poetry taken to represent absolute poetry. The poem as such tended to be neglected, beyond classifying it as a sonnet, or as written in Spenserian stanzas. But after the rise of New Criticism (which was more a pedagogic than a theoretically novel revolution), the emphasis changed from the beauty of fragmentary "poetry" to the perception of the unity of the "poem." The poem was read as a whole, without a content separable from that whole; individual lines were read not as "poetic" but as coherent with the whole. In this perspective, the critical judgment changed from evaluation of "beauty" to judgment of coherence: a poem was declared to be "successful" or not depending mainly on whether it was a perceptible whole into which all images and statements fitted. The most influential single figure in this pedagogic revolution, Cleanth Brooks, accordingly asserted as "articles of faith" the contentions that *"in a successful work, form and content cannot be separated,"* and that *"form is meaning."*[34]

To be sure, some modern theorists have clung to distinctions of form and content.[35] Yvor Winters boldly announces, for instance, an "absolutist" theory of literature, in which the poem is "good in so far as it makes a defensible rational statement about a given human experience."[36] Both Richards's useful differentiation of "vehicle" and "tenor" and Ransom's discrimination of "structure" and "texture" seem to be covert dichotomies of form and content. Yet by and large modern critics and theorists usually reject any essential distinction between form and content.[37] As Wellek's and Austin Warren's formidable and pedagogically influential *Theory of Literature* puts it:

[34] "The Formalist Critics," *Kenyon Review*, 13 (1951), 72.

[35] For a survey of modern attitudes toward the idea of form, and incidentally of content, see Wellek's "Concept of Form and Structure in Twentieth-Century Criticism," *Concepts of Criticism* (New Haven: Yale University Press, 1963), pp. 54-68.

[36] *In Defense of Reason*, third edition (Denver: Alan Swallow, n.d.), p. 11.

[37] But it is interesting to note, in view of our equation of "poetry" with Platonic current of feeling, that Susanne Langer, in her discussion of "feeling" and "form," equates the former with music, which is above all a current, e.g.: "The tonal structures we call 'music' bear a close logical similarity to the forms of human feelings. . . . Music is a tonal analogue of emotive life" (Langer, p. 27).

"Content" and "form" are terms used in too widely different senses for them to be, merely juxtaposed, helpful; indeed, even after careful definition, they too simply dichotomize the work of art.[38]

Even now, when New Criticism as a movement has passed into history, the most sophisticated theoretical attitudes continue to reject any attempt to define a significantly separable content in poetic form. As Samuel R. Levin, for instance, has recently said:

> In my view it is those linguistic properties in a poem which induce the responses of unity, novelty, compression, etc. that go to make up poetic form. Comprehended in this view of poetic form are of course also the conventions—rhyme, meter, etc.— since they also conduce to the responses in question. When seen in this way, we can understand why form is so fundamental to poetry. On this view it is the content of a poem, what can be paraphrased of it, that is superficial; all the rest is form.[39]

Such an attitude reflects the important and still growing effect of a movement somewhat similar to New Criticism but theoretically more satisfying: that is, the linguistically oriented formalist tradition stemming from the allied schools of Russian Formalism and Prague Structuralism.

The leading idea of these schools was to see a poem in its relation to language as such. Most language is either not expressed at all (remaining potential expression or, in Saussure's term, *langue*) or, if expressed, is forgotten after it has served its purpose of communication. A poem, however, tends to be special—to be an artifact, an autonomous linguistic structure—and hence not to be used up in the act of communication. The way it prevents itself from being used up is by certain kinds of linguistic emphasis that both assert its difference from ordinary language and indicate its unity as an artifact. Such emphasis is supplied by rhyme, meter, assonance, consonance, unexpected words and combinations of words: in short, by all those features we usually find in a poem.

Thus Paul Valéry, writing from the standpoint of the poet rather than that of the linguist, sees the poem as radically different from ordinary language:

[38] (New York: Harcourt, Brace and Company, 1949), p. 18.
[39] "The Analysis of Compression in Poetry," *Foundations of Language; International Journal of Language and Philosophy*, 7 (1971), 40 n.

the language I use to express my design, my desire, my command, my opinion; this language, when it has served its purpose, evaporates almost as it is heard. I have given it forth to perish, to be radically transformed into something else in your mind; and I shall know that I was *understood* by the remarkable fact that my speech no longer exists: it has been completely replaced by its *meaning*. . . .

The poem, on the other hand, does not die for having lived: it is expressly designed to be born again from its ashes and to become endlessly what it has just been. Poetry can be recognized by this property, that it tends to get itself reproduced in its own form: it stimulates us to reconstruct it identically.[40]

This same distinction, though nowhere so pointedly expressed, has repeatedly been urged by the formalist theoreticians. As Havránek said, nonpoetic language is characterized by "automatization":

By *automatization* we . . . mean such a use of the devices of the language . . . that the expression itself does not attract any attention; the communication occurs, and is received, as conventional in linguistic form and is to be "understood" by virtue of the linguistic system.

Poetic language, conversely, is made special by a process called "foregrounding," which Havránek defines as follows:

By *foregrounding*, on the other hand, we mean the use of the devices of the language in such a way that this use itself attracts attention and is perceived as uncommon, as deprived of automatization, as deautomatized, such as a live poetic metaphor (as opposed to a lexicalized one, which is automatized).[41]

Foregrounding is thus the central means by which language becomes poetic. Jan Mukarovský pointed out that

Poetic language cannot be called a brand of the standard. . . . The function of poetic language consists in the maximum of foregrounding of the utterance. Foregrounding is the opposite of automatization, that is, the deautomatization of an act; the more an act is automatized, the less it is consciously executed; the more it

---

[40] "Poetry and Abstract Thought," *The Art of Poetry*, trans. Denise Folliott (New York: Pantheon Books, 1958), pp. 71-72.

[41] *A Prague School Reader on Esthetics, Literary Structure, and Style*, trans. Paul L. Garvin (Washington, 1964), pp. 9-10.

is foregrounded, the more completely conscious does it become.
. . . In poetic language foregrounding achieves maximum inten-
sity to the extent . . . of being used for its own sake; it is not used
in the services of communication, but in order to place in the
foreground the act of expression.[42]

It is noteworthy that the kind of poetic language of which
Mukarovský speaks does not lead to "Platonic" poetry; rather, his
emphasis on the fact that the more language is foregrounded "the
more completely conscious does it become" identifies "Aristote-
lian" poem as the goal of that language.

The distinctions urged by these exponents of Prague Struc-
turalism confirm earlier insights of Russian Formalism. In 1917 Vic-
tor Shklovsky used the term "defamiliarization" to indicate what
the Structuralists called "foregrounding":

Habitualization devours works, clothes, furniture, one's wife,
and the fear of war. . . . And art exists that one may recover the
sensation of life; it exists to make one feel things, to make the
stone *stony*. . . . The technique of art is to make objects "unfamil-
iar," to make forms difficult. . . .

In studying poetic speech in its phonetic and lexical structure
as well as in its characteristic distribution of words and in the
characteristic thought structures compounded from the words,
we find everywhere the artistic trademark—that is, we find ma-
terial obviously created to remove the automatism of perception;
the author's purpose is to create the vision which results from
that deautomatized perception. . . . The language of poetry is,
then, a difficult, roughened, impeded language.[43]

It is obvious, even from such brief quotations from their writ-
ings, that the formalist theoreticians and their sympathizers, by
stressing the specialness of the poem as against the unspecialness
of ordinary language (we use the word "prosaic" simply to mean
the commonplace and unmemorable), have afforded a compelling
insight into the nature of poetic language and of the linguistic work
of art. Many kinds of problems are resolved by this insight. For a
single instance, the theoretical problem of how some poems can be

---

[42] "Standard Language and Poetic Language," *Essays on the Language of Literature*,
ed. Seymour Chatman and Samuel R. Levin (Boston: Houghton Mifflin Co., 1967),
pp. 241-43.

[43] *Russian Formalist Criticism: Four Essays*, trans. Lee T. Lemon and Marion J. Reis
(Lincoln, Neb.: University of Nebraska Press, 1965), pp. 12, 21-22.

written in meter and rhyme, but others in meter only (the paradox of Milton saying that rhyme is "no necessary adjunct or true ornament of poem or good verse," even though our most naive intuition identifies rhyme as the first requirement of a poem), immediately disappears. For rhyme and meter, whatever their tactical differences, are here revealed as being merely variations of the same thing: that is, as forms of foregrounding that by their nature as repetition indicate both the specialness and the unity of the linguistic statement (and it is interesting to reflect that from a compositional standpoint, the construction of meter and that of rhyme demand from the poet much the same kind of labor).

Despite the cogency of formalist analysis, however, I disagree with an important implication of that tradition: I deny that poetic "content" inheres in the linguistic code. It does not seem to me that a poetic act can be described as merely an activation of language, no matter how sophisticated that activation might be. Nor do I accept Brooks's similar contention that *"form is meaning."* Although Boris Eichenbaum writes that "poetic form . . . is not contrasted with anything outside itself—with a 'content' which has been laboriously set inside this 'form'—but is understood as the genuine content of poetic speech,"[44] and although Mukarovský says that "in a work of poetry . . . there is no fixed border, nor, in a certain sense, any essential difference, between the language and the subject matter,"[45] I do not believe that such views account for the whole truth of poetic act. I maintain that there is indeed an "essential difference" between the language and subject matter in the poetic act, that there is indeed content "set inside this 'form.' " The essential difference is the difference between poem and poetry; the content inside the form is the poetry within the poem.

In short, I hold that the formalist position accounts for poetic language, but not for the full poetic act. Or, stated another way, it is my contention that though linguistic manipulation can generate a poem, it cannot generate poetry as such.

In order to make this contention more clear, and to try to describe what a complete poetic act really *is*, I propose to conceive of the "isness" under the Greek word ὀυσία, which is a term of

[44] *Ibid.*, p. 127. So too Croce, although from a different standpoint: 'The aesthetic fact . . . is form, and nothing but form"; "Poetical material permeates the souls of all: the expression alone, that is to say, the form, makes the poet. . . . When we take 'content' as equal to 'concept' it is most true, not only that art does not consist of content, but also that *it has no content*" (Croce, pp. 16, 25).

[45] "Standard Language and Poetic Language," p. 245.

time-honored philosophical provenance.[46] The *ousia*, or "isness," can then be conceived under three Latin terms, each of which is a synonym for the Greek word; specifically, I propose considering the poem (that is, the form) as poetic *substantia*, and the poetry (or poetic content) under the twin terms of *ens* and *essentia*. By doing so, I hope to muffle any debilitating overtones that might reside in the words "form" and "content," where through long carelessness one tends to think of form as something like a stanza pattern and of content as some kind of hortatory message. By using synonyms rather than widely different words, I hope to indicate the sense of the indispensability of "form" and "content" in the full poetic act. And by using three terms instead of "form" and "content" I hope to be able to talk of certain complexities not rewardingly designated by the single word "content."

By *substantia* I mean not only stanza form, not only meter and rhyme, not only the semantic references of the words in the poem, not only the sense of beginning and end, but also the statement of the poem. For instance, in Edwin Arlington Robinson's "Mr. Flood's Party,"[47] the *substantia* would consist not only of the seven stanzas of eight lines each, and of the rhyme pattern *a b c b*, but of the story of the old man who gives himself a lonely drunken party; not only of whatever visual sense is implied by the invocation of "harvest moon," but of whatever literary complex of associations is summoned up by the image of "Roland's ghost winding a silent horn." In brief, *substantia* includes not only the words and their patterns but also their meanings. Under this term I would place almost everything that formalist theory has to say about poetry.

The *ens* is a characteristic scarcely accounted for by formalist theory. The *ens* is the interanimation of the sense of self in the poetic statement with the perspective of the outer world; it is the fusion of mind and nature. Alternate phrasings might be the sense of "I am" interpenetrating the sense of "it is"; or the subject revealing itself in the object, the object in the subject.[48] Keats speaks of "the

[46] I have in mind Kant's dictum that "to coin new words" is a "desperate expedient," and that we ought rather to "look around in a dead and learned language" to find appropriate terms (*Gesammelte Schriften*, III, 245).

[47] E. A. Robinson, pp. 573-75.

[48] One of the ways in which *ens* can reveal itself in *substantia* is through onomatopoetic metrical cadence. Compare Emil Staiger's observation: "The more purely lyrical a poem is, the more it renounces the neutral repetition of its beat, not in the direction of prose, but rather in favor of a rhythm transforming itself in harmony with the mood. That is merely the metrical expression of the fact that in lyric poetry an 'I' and an object scarcely face one another" (Staiger, p. 28). Examples

camelion Poet," who "has no Identity—he is continually in for—
and filling some other Body."[49] "A Poet's *Heart & Intellect*," says
Coleridge, "should be *combined, intimately* combined & *unified*, with
the great appearances in Nature."[50] "To end this eternal conflict
between our Self and the World," says Hölderlin, "to re-establish
the peace above all peace, which passeth all understanding, to
unite ourselves with Nature, into one infinite entity, that is the aim
of all our aspirations."[51]

The *ens* is the same for all art, although the manner of its realiza-
tion may vary almost infinitely. Where the poetic *substantia* is re-
markably different from the sculptural *substantia*, the poetic *ens* and
the sculptural *ens* are alike. (It is in its *ens* that the poetic act most
strongly connects itself with other art forms; indeed, part of the *ens*
in Blake's poetry consists in the illuminated engravings that ac-
company many of the poems.) As a theorist has said:

> The task of art is to *ingest* whatever can be learned objectively
> about the world of the non-I and then to *give out* an image which
> will accord not only with non-human truths . . . but also with the
> forms of universal human feelings.[52]

Ens is embodied in such a statement as "Eternal smiles his emp-
tiness betray,/ As shallow streams run dimpling all the way," or in
that where an observer says of wild swans that "Their hearts have
not grown old." Any interfusion of an aspect of the nonhuman
world with a human emotion or awareness is poetic *ens*. In Tenny-
son's exquisite "Break, Break, Break," the correlation of the break-
ing surf with the observer's sense of broken life provides a fine
example of *ens*. In "Mr. Flood's Party" we see *ens* in these words:

> Then, as a mother lays her sleeping child
> Down tenderly, fearing it may awake,
> He set the jug down slowly at his feet
> With trembling care, knowing that most things break:[53]

Leavis's famous attack on Shelley, that his most serious fault is a
"weak grasp upon the actual," is a judgment of that poet's defi-
ciency in poetic *ens* ("Poetry," concurs Hazlitt, "creates a world of

---

might be such lines as "And hear the mighty waters rolling evermore," or "The
murmurous haunt of flies on summer eves."

[49] Keats, *Letters*, I, 387.
[50] *Collected Letters*, II, 864.
[51] Hölderlin, II, 236.
[52] Shumaker, p. 275.
[53] *E. A. Robinson*, p. 574.

its own; but it creates it out of existing materials. Mr. Shelley is the maker of his own poetry—out of nothing").[54] When Coleridge says that "a great Poet" must have "the *ear* of a wild Arab listening in the silent Desart, the eye of a North American Indian tracing the footsteps of an Enemy upon the Leaves that strew the Forest—; the *Touch* of a Blind Man feeling the face of a darling Child,"[55] he is dramatizing the importance of *ens* in the poetic commitment. When Wordsworth observes that "there is not a single image from Nature in the whole body" of Dryden's work,[56] the reproach refers to Dryden's lack of *ens* (which, indeed, is part of the reason for Arnold's feeling—he says so in his essay on Gray[57]—that Dryden is not a poet). What Robert Langbaum has described as a characteristic of Romantic poetry is in fact a characteristic of poetry as such:

> The romantic lyric or poetry of experience . . . is both subjective and objective. The poet talks about himself by talking about an object; and he talks about an object by talking about himself.[58]

Indeed, as Coleridge says very simply, "in every work of art there is a reconcilement of the external with the internal."[59]

Accordingly, the poetic temperament often reveals itself, even outside the artifacts created by the poet, in an unusual sensitivity to the appearances and shadings of the natural world, in sight, smell, and sound. "Wordsworth," recalls Hazlitt of his first meeting with the young poet, "looking out of the low, latticed window, said, 'How beautifully the sun sets on that yellow bank!' I thought within myself, 'With what eyes these poets see nature!' and ever after, when I saw the sun-set stream upon the objects facing, conceived I had made a discovery, or thanked Mr. Wordsworth for having made one for me."[60] As for Wordsworth, so for Keats. "Keats was in his glory in the fields!" testifies Haydon: "The humming of the bee, the sight of a flower, the glitter of the sun, seemed to make his nature tremble! his eyes glistened! his cheek flushed! his mouth positively quivered & clentched!"[61]

Much of the flocking of imagery and metaphor to poetry, whereby one might note "How like a winter hath my absence been/ From thee," clusters in the area of poetic *ens*. When Byron says that "I live not in myself, but I become/ Portion of that around me; and

[54] Leavis, *Revaluation*, p. 206; *Hazlitt*, xvi, 265.
[55] *Collected Letters*, ii, 810.
[56] *Early Years*, p. 641.
[57] Arnold, *Essays*, pp. 95-96.
[58] Langbaum, p. 53.
[59] *Biographia*, ii, 258.
[60] *Hazlitt*, xvii, 118.
[61] *Haydon*, ii, 316.

to me/ High mountains are a feeling,'' the statement both describes and embodies poetic *ens*. [62] And as is apparent from such examples, the ways in which the intermixing of subject and object can occur in *ens* are exceedingly varied. But even Stefan George's poem about the "totgesagten Park" (the park they say is dead), which was cited above as an example of an almost muted "poetry," is replete with the correlation of perceived outer reality with inner attitude. For as Coleridge says, in a passage we may take as summarizing the whole truth of this aspect of poetry as "content":

> As soon as the human mind is intelligibly addressed by an outward image exclusively of articulate speech, so soon does art commence. . . . Art itself might be defined as of a middle quality between a thought and a thing, or . . . the union and reconciliation of that which is nature with that which is exclusively human. It is the figured language of thought. [63]

I have spoken somewhat briefly of a feature of "content" that actually could be shown to ramify into subtle examples, and I have done so in order to be able to devote slightly longer discussion to a more elusive aspect: that for which I adopt the term *essentia*. Poetic *essentia* is not dependent upon a linguistic code; it is not generated by foregrounded arrangement of language and its reference. It is, rather, an awareness that is "existential" or "metaphysical." It is represented by rather than derived from language. "Words are but under-agents" in this "language of the heavens."

Only by living and feeling, not by arrangement or inspection of mundane language as such, does poetic *essentia* occur. It expresses nothing less than the nature of human existence itself, wherein we find ourselves with "such large discourse,/ Looking before and after." For we live always in a "now" looking to a past and future "then." Our lives are split. We have a double nature: an existence "now," which is palpable and concrete, and an existence in the past and future, which though spectral is none the less truly our own existence. The paradox is what Jaspers recognizes by his two terms for existence: *Dasein* and *Existenz*. But the paradox, one stresses, is not the property of philosophers; it is the most inescapable fact of human life. It is a fact about which there can be no argument whatever, however strange it may seem when compared to the way in which a stone or a cow exists.

Poetic *essentia* is generated by the simultaneous awareness of our

---

[62] Byron, *Poems*, II, 261.   [63] *Biographia*, II, 254-55.

existence in these two forms. When we stand in a "now" and look at a "then," we generate *essentia* by making the sense of "now" more vivid (and thereby treasuring its nowness), and simultaneously becoming more aware of its difference from "then." Or conversely, we may devalue "now" and treasure "then." In Lear's speech, the gloom of "now" as defeat is impregnated with the joy of "then"; "now" is the prospect of "away to prison," but the tone implies "away to paradise."

In Lear's speech the relation of now to then is that of a present to a future; it is prophetic and accords with the conception whereby a poet serves as *vates*. Blake, whose "heart," as he so hauntingly says, was "full of futurity,"[64] strained in his own poetry toward a prophetic vision of a Jerusalem where fragmentations would be made whole and burdens lifted. In any such prophetic vision, however, the elements of the future are recombined from the past: Lear and Cordelia's paradise, where they will tell "old tales," is a restoration of earlier realizations as well as a new life.

Essentia, in short, is the feeling of the whole of our existence in its cloven reality. And to be fully aware of the cloven nature of existence is in a sense to restore its wholeness. Every act of true poetry succeeds in some way in rendering, in Wordsworth's beautiful phrase, "The life where hope and memory are as one."[65]

The perspective along which split existence is seen and symbolically healed, however, is more frequently that from a present turned to a past than from a present turned to a future. "I look into past times," says Wordsworth in an orientation that is the opposite and polar complement of Blake's, "as prophets look/ Into futurity."[66] *Essentia* is most typically the sense of a treasured "now" lost in "then," or the prospect of such loss. It is a sweet sadness. The sweetness comes from the intensified sense of being, and the sadness from the intensified sense of being's loss into the nonbeing of "then." As Shenstone said, in a scarcely expected *aperçu*, "The words 'no more' have a singular pathos," reminding us at once "of past pleasure" and of its loss.[67] "Deep as first love, and wild with all regret;/ O Death in Life, the days that are no more!"

Essentia, in its disposition of awareness between "now" and "then," is accordingly fleeting and intangible—is in the nature of an *evanescence*. Indeed, the most immediate awareness of "now" is that which not only vanishes into "then," but is in itself fragile. It

[64] Blake, *Letters*, p. 67.
[66] *Ibid.*, ii, 480.
[65] Wordsworth, *Poems*, v, 87.
[67] Shenstone, p. 191.

is noteworthy that Rilke's prescription, in *The Notebooks of Malte Laurids Brigge*, for how a poet is formed, insists not only on saturation in *ens* but also on saturation in the evanescences that characterize the "nows" of *essentia*:

> In order to write a single verse, one must see many cities, and men, and things. . . . One must be able to return in thought . . . to unexpected encounters, and to partings . . . to days of childhood . . . and to mornings by the sea. . . . There must be memories of many nights of love. . . . And still it is not yet enough to have memories. . . . Only when they have turned to blood within us . . . no longer to be distinguished from ourselves—only then can it happen that . . . the first word of a poem arises and goes forth from them.[68]

Poe, in cataloguing "the simple elements which induce in the Poet himself the true poetical effect," comes to a similar conclusion:

> He recognizes the ambrosia which nourishes his soul . . . in the volutes of the flower . . . in the waving of the grain-fields . . . in the blue distance of mountains—in the grouping of clouds . . . in the sighing of the night-wind . . . in the scent of the violet.[69]

The linkage between intensified nowness and evanescence is further underscored in Coleridge's statement that "poetry is the blossom and the fragrancy" of human thoughts and emotions.[70]

Because the intensified sense of being alive involves awareness of the most fleeting elements in our experience, the "then" that characterizes *essentia* is sometimes poetically implied in a "now" even without being summoned. We recognize this in such lines as

> Passions of rain, or moods in falling snow;
> Grievings in loneliness, or unsubdued
> Elations when the forest blooms; gusty
> Emotions on wet roads on autumn nights.[71]

Here, amid an abundance of *ens*, *essentia* is present though "then"

---

[68] Rilke, VI, 724-25.

[69] Poe, VI, 34. Cf. Yeats: "The poet must not seek for what is still and fixed . . . but be content to find his pleasure in all that is forever passing away that it may come again, in the beauty of women, in the fragile flowers of spring, in momentary heroic passion, in whatever is most fleeting" (*Essays and Introductions* [New York: Collier Books, 1968], p. 287).

[70] *Biographia*, II, 19.   [71] *Stevens*, p. 67.

is not stated. In other instances, the evanescence of a treasured "now" is emphasized by "then":

> And as I was green and carefree, famous among the barns
> About the happy yard and singing as the farm was home,
>
> . . . . . .
>
> All the sun long it was running, it was lovely, the hay
> Fields high as the house, the tunes from the chimneys, it was air
> And playing, lovely and watery
> And fire green as grass.[72]

There, as in these following lines, the evanescences of a treasured "now" are made more fragile by loss into a past "then":

> Oh, many a time have I, a five years' child,
> In a small mill-race severed from his stream,
> Made one long bathing of a summer's day;
> Basked in the sun, and plunged and basked again
> Alternate, all a summer's day, or scoured
> The sandy fields, leaping through flowery groves
> Of yellow ragwort.[73]

But perhaps no more revealing example of poetic *essentia* could be adduced than Keat's lines, uttered from the "now" of a visit to the Elgin marbles:

> Such dim-conceivèd glories of the brain
> Bring round the heart an undescribable feud;
> So do these wonders a most dizzy pain,
> That mingles Grecian grandeur with the rude
> Wasting of old Time—with a billowy main,
> A sun—a shadow of a magnitude.[74]

The "then" of Grecian antiquity is rendered as glimpses of a "now"—a "billowy main,/ A sun, a shadow of a magnitude"—but the nature of this "now" as glimpse confirms the countertruth of "then." The "heart," or full emotional awareness, experiences the recognition of existence's split into "now" and "then" as an "undescribable feud" or "dizzy pain." "Now" is intensified by the image of sun, but the specification "a" sun, rather than "the" sun, holds the sun in the real "now" and identifies the second sun as

---

[72] Thomas, p. 159.

[73] *Prelude*, 1850 version, p. 19 (I, 288-94).

[74] Keats, *Poems*, p. 478.

lost in "then." The last phrase, "a shadow of a magnitude," attenuates evanescence to the remotest point that can be indicated by words.

The moment when we most truly feel ourselves alive, and in the same awareness most feel ourselves passing into time—that is poetic *essentia*. That is the lyric instant. It is hardly an exaggeration to say that lyric awareness is always an awareness, however expressed, of "the rude/ Wasting of old Time"; or that the ultimate poetic theme is the elegiac theme. Great poems are monuments to our lost selves. "A Poet," says Shelley, in recognition of this unceasing loss of human experience in time's flow, "is a nightingale, who sits in darkness and sings to cheer its own solitude with sweet sounds."[75]

It is the sense of the "now" passing into the "then" that creates the feeling of "current" in Platonic poetry.[76] It is the existential, as opposed to the linguistic, awareness of this movement that accounts for the sense in such poetry that the essence lies outside the words in which it is caught ("True poesy," writes John Clare, "is not in words").[77] And it is the evanescence of *essentia* that accounts for that tradition's insistence that poetry comes from an inspired moment of vision rather than from consciously premeditated design. In this view, moreover, the poetic act reveals itself as diasparactive in both structure and function. The poem, or *substantia*, is a fragment of language—a configuration of words torn out of the vast mine of linguistic possibility. The poetry, in its aspect as *essentia*, is a paradoxical attempt to apprehend life's wholeness at the very moment of its fragmentation and dispersal by time.

Sometimes *essentia* occurs even where life is not treasured. Hardy's "The Darkling Thrush" and Donne's "A Nocturnal upon St. Lucy's Day" come to mind as examples. But the frosty desolation of the first poem, and the emphasis of the second upon "absence, darkness, death; things which are not," generate the positives by which alone their negatives have poetic force. Both poems are

[75] Shelley, *Prose*, p. 11. For another realization of the same sadness, compare a modern commentator: " 'Unsecure, here upon the mountain of the heart,' thus has Rilke, from within this existential experience himself, attempted to indicate the entire no-way-outness (*Ausweglosigkeit*) of mankind" (Bollnow, p. 15).

[76] Compare Plato: " . . . when a poet takes his seat on the Muses's tripod . . . he is like a fountain that gives free course to the rush of its waters" (*Laws*, 719C).

[77] *English Romantic Writers*, ed. David Perkins (New York: Harcourt, Brace & World, Inc., 1967), p. 1107.

realizations of loss; but loss does not exist by itself. Its "intentional structure" (to borrow a concept from Husserl) assures the presence of those correlatives of life and joy displaced by the overt stratagems in each case. The "lovers" and their "next Spring" in Donne's poem, and the "joy illimited" and "blessed Hope" of the bird's song in Hardy's, thereby become hints for an entire unexpressed treasuring of life.

Sometimes, to take another kind of example, the "now" of the poetic observer is desolate, but that of the poetic subject is treasured, so that the subject's "now" becomes the observer's "then," and vice versa. An illustration might be Gray's "Ode on a Distant Prospect of Eton College."

Essentia must be present in all poetry that merits the name, though it need not mark every line of that poetry. The lyric and the poetically essential are one and the same; but the lyric instant, or awareness of *essentia*, is the evanescent and life-giving breath, not the bricks and mortar, of poetry. As Emil Staiger says, "The lyric is the last attainable ground of everything poetic."[78] An individual poem, as contrasted to poetry, may generate much, little, or no *essentia*. Dryden, strong in *substantia* but weak in *ens*, writes page upon page with hardly a suggestion of *essentia* (although there are occasional exceptions, such as "To the Memory of Mr. Oldham"). As Young said, Dryden "was a stranger to the Pathos, and by numbers, expression, sentiment, and every other dramatic cheat, strove to make amends for it; as if a Saint could make amends for the want of conscience. . . . The noble nature of tragedy disclaims an equivalent; like virtue, it demands the heart; and *Dryden* had none to give."[79]

The lyric instant, however, thought related to tragic awareness, is slightly but significantly different from that awareness. The tragic realization is the vision of the conflicts of human aspiration at the brink of nonbeing; yet the tragic "then" is a future "then," usually symbolized by death. But the lyric instant does not involve a social perspective; it is rather art's most distinctive tribute to our individual selfhood. It looks upon the world from our own inner selves, not from the standpoints of interacting characters. The lyric instant occurs when, gazing directly from our own being into the double awareness of life as "now" and "then," we understand both what we treasure and what we lose. "What is Poetry?"

[78] Staiger, p. 207.   [79] *Conjectures*, pp. 82-83.

mused Byron, and the answer at which he arrived was this: "The feeling of a Former world and Future."[80]

The lyric "then" is less typically a future than a past, less a death than a loss in time (death as such is treated in lyric as the form of loss rather than as the tragic terminus). Keats's "Ode on Melancholy," where sadness is found to live not with darkness but with the sense of life ("She dwells with Beauty—Beauty that must die,/ And Joy, whose hand is ever at his lips/ Bidding adieu"), represents exactly the defining simultaneity of treasuring and loss suspended in *essentia*.

In "Mr. Flood's Party," which we have rather casually adduced to provide examples of *substantia* and *ens*, poetic *essentia* accordingly reveals itself in such lines as

> Alone, as if enduring to the end
> A valiant armor of scarred hopes outworn

and in general is revealed by the sense of the isolation of the old man and of his separation from his youthful existence:

> There was not much that was ahead of him,
> And there was nothing in the town below—
> Where strangers would have shut the many doors
> That many friends had opened long ago.[81]

In these lines we feel the essence of poetry.

Poetic *essentia* can often be found in the same group of words that embody *ens*; but the two aspects of "content" are not at all the same. The line, "Their hearts have not grown old," quoted from Yeats's "The Wild Swans at Coole" to illustrate *ens*, also illustrates *essentia*. The correlation of human emotion (hearts) with an object of nature (the swans) reveals *ens*; the simultaneous emphasis on the "now" of the observer and the "then" of his former self that is conveyed by the idea of growing old reveals *essentia*. For the line, in saying that "Their hearts have not grown old," simultaneously conveys the meaning "My heart *has* grown old."

"The Wild Swans at Coole," indeed, illustrates very well the way in which poetic *essentia* is generated. The first stanza establishes the almost palpable presence of "now":

> The trees are in their autumn beauty,
> The woodland paths are dry.
> Under the October twilight the water

[80] Byron, *Letters*, VIII, 37.   [81] *E. A. Robinson*, pp. 574, 575.

> Mirrors a still sky;
> Upon the brimming water among the stones
> Are nine-and-fifty swans.

The counting of the swans, which is further foregrounded by the archaic form "nine-and-fifty," provides transition to another form of counting—that in which the "then" is opposed to the "now":

> The nineteenth autumn has come upon me
> Since I first made my count;

And the two succeeding stanzas develop the poignance arising from the gap between "now" and "then":

> I have looked upon those brilliant creatures,
> And now my heart is sore.
> All's changed since I, hearing at twilight,
> The first time on this shore,
> The bell-beat of their wings above my head,
> Trod with a lighter tread.
>
> Unwearied still, lover by lover,
> They paddle in the cold
> Companionable streams or climb the air;
> Their hearts have not grown old;
> Passion or conquest, wander where they will,
> Attend upon them still.[82]

Essentia not only arises from the movement of poetic argument but inheres naturally in certain images. Among these we may think of twilight, which fuses the "now" of day with the "then" of night; of autumn, which fuses the "now" of summer's warmth with the "then" of winter's coldness; of flowers, which underscore the beauty of "now" while, by their fragility, they intensify the sense of loss into "then." For instance, the first stanza of "The Wild Swans at Coole" quoted immediately above suggests, by its images of "autumn beauty" and "October twilight," the lyric concatenation of "now" and "then."

Such images are the very stuff of poetic *essentia*, and are used again and again by poets. Consider Hopkins:

> Márgarét are you gríeving
> Over Goldengrove unleaving?
> Leáves, like the things of man, you

[82] *Yeats*, p. 129.

With your fresh thoughts care for, can you?
Áh! ás the heart grows older
It will come to such sights colder
By and by, nor spare a sigh
Though worlds of wanwood leafmeal lie;
And yet you will weep and know why.
Now no matter, child, the name;
Sórrows spríngs áre the same.
Nor mouth had, no nor mind, expressed
What heart heard of, ghost guessed:
It ís the blight man was born for,
It is Margaret you mourn for.[83]

The correlation of human sadness with the falling leaves of autumn is a classic example of *ens*. The contrast of the observer's "now" with the child's "now," however, emphasizes an unspoken contrast between his "now" and the "then" of his own childhood and also emphasizes that Margaret's "now" will become the "then" of the observer's "now": the sense of loss in falling leaves is that of the loss of self in time: "It is Margaret you mourn for." This is poetic *essentia*. In *essentia* "Sórrows Spríngs áre the same": the loss of "now" in "then." The concern in this poem with the knowledge that "the heart grows older" is the same *essentia* revealed in Yeats's poem by the line, "Their hearts have not grown old."

Hopkins's use of the *essentia* inherent in autumn might be compared with Rilke's variation, incorporated into even greater poetry:

Herr: es ist Zeit. Der Sommer war sehr gross.
Leg deinen Schatten auf die Sonnenuhren,
Und auf den Fluren lass die Winde los.

Befiehl den letzten Früchten voll zu sein;
Gib ihnen noch zwei südlichere Tage,
Dränge sie zu Vollendung hin und jage
Die letzte Süsse in den schweren Wein.

Wer jetzt kein Haus hat, baut sich keines mehr.
Wer jetzt allein ist, wird es lange bleiben,
Wird wachen, lesen, lange Briefe schreiben
Und wird in den Alleen hin und her
Unruhig wandern, wenn die Blätter treiben.[84]

---

[83] *Hopkins*, pp. 88-89. [84] Rilke, i, 398.

Lord: it is time. Most great the summer was.
Lay your shadow down upon the sundials now,
And across the meadows set the winds loose.

Make the last fruits mellow on the vine;
Spare them but two further southern days,
Speed them to fullness, and press
The last sweetness through the heavy wine.

Whoever does not have a house will build one now no more.
Whoever dwells alone now will long remain alone,
Will wakefully write long letters, read,
And restless to and fro
Will wander in the avenues, when the leaves are blown.

Here, in addition to a Keatsian opulence of *ens*, the lines "reek" (to misappropriate Donald Davie's term)[85] of *essentia*. The "now" of summer is held in autumnal suspension with the "then" of winter by such phrases as "den letzten Früchten," "zu Vollendung," "die letzte Süsse." The restlessness—an inspired combination of sadness and expectation—of the line "Wird wachen, lesen, lange Briefe schreiben" makes the sense of "Unruhig wandern" more poignant; for to write long letters is to attempt to reclaim life from "then" into "now," an attempt the more elegiac in the context of "allein" and blowing leaves.

The images of autumn and twilight coalesce with the metaphor, "In me thou see'st the glowing of such fire,/ That on the ashes of his youth doth lie," and together they generate the *essentia* of Shakespeare's sonnet 73:

That time of year thou mayst in me behold
When yellow leaves, or none, or few, do hang
Upon those boughs which shake against the cold,
Bare ruin'd choirs, where late the sweet birds sang;
In me thou see'st the twilight of such day
As after sunset fadeth in the west;
Which by and by black night doth take away,
Death's second self, that seals up all in rest:
In me thou see'st the glowing of such fire,
That on the ashes of his youth doth lie,
As on the death-bed whereon it must expire

---

[85] Davie, pp. 161-65.

Consum'd with that which it was nourish'd by.
This thou perceiv'st, which makes thy love more strong,
To love that well which thou must leave ere long.

The best of Shakespeare's sonnets, indeed, seem almost Platonic paradigmata for *ousia*'s interfusing of *substantia*, *ens*, and *essentia*. Despite Ransom's unseeing attack on these poems, despite animadversions by Winters, despite disparaging remarks by Auden, I agree with Keats that Shakespeare here "has left nothing to say about nothing or any thing,"[86] with Wordsworth that in no other place in Shakespeare is there found "in an equal compass a greater number of exquisite feelings felicitously expressed,"[87] and with Coleridge, who stated that no other sonnets were "so rich in metre, so full of thought and *exquisitest* diction" as the later sonnets. Of the cycle as a whole, Coleridge judged that "These sonnets . . . are characterised by boundless fertility and laboured condensation of thought, with perfection of sweetness in rhythm and metre."[88]

Above all, they reek of poetic *essentia*. "Now" is again and again embodied and cherished in the motif of love and the beauty of the beloved, caught in metaphors of light, flowering, and summertime; "then" is indicated again and again in time's corrosion of those metaphors:

When I do count the clock that tells the time,
And see the brave day sunk in hideous night;
When I behold the violet past prime,
And sable curls all silver'd o'er with white;
When lofty trees I see barren of leaves,
Which erst from heat did canopy the herd,
And summer's green all girded up in sheaves
Borne on the bier with white and bristly beard,
Then of thy beauty do I question make,
That thou among the wastes of time must go.

The murmuring lines that open the cycle like a breeze from the past, and never fail to stir my heart, annunciate the theme: the conflict of beauty and loss essential to the deepest poetry:

From fairest creatures we desire increase
That thereby beauty's rose might never die

[86] Keats, *Letters*, i, 189.   [87] *Prose*, iii, 69.
[88] *Table Talk*, pp. 222-23 (May 14, 1833).

The opposing tensions that generate *essentia* are perhaps nowhere else so powerfully realized as in the first two quatrains of sonnet 65:

> Since brass, nor stone, nor earth, nor boundless sea,
> But sad mortality o'ersways their power,
> How with this rage shall beauty hold a plea,
> Whose action is no stronger than a flower?
> Oh how shall summer's honey breath hold out
> Against the wrackful siege of batt'ring days,
> When rocks impregnable are not so stout,
> Nor gates of steel so strong, but Time decays?

Here the images of permanence in the first line—which pounds like the waves of the sea—are juxtaposed against equally powerful images of destruction by time, all made more memorable by extraordinary richness of *ens* and intricacy of *substantia* (as, for instance, in the consonantal *s*, *t* variations that permeate the diction, reaching an apex in the eighth line).

In Shakespeare's sonnets, finally, is achieved the truest relationship between "content" as poetry and "form" as poem. For that relationship is not merely the interpenetration of *substantia* by *ens* and *essentia*. It is also a radically paradoxical melding of disparate resistances to time. Poetic *essentia* is an evanescence—a "honey breath" assaulted by "the wrackful siege of batt'ring days." *Dum loquimur, fugerit invida aetas: carpe diem*. Poetic *substantia*, in absolute contrast, is that which abides. *Exegi monumentum perennius aere*. As Blackmur points out:

> Poetry names and arranges, and thus arrests and transfixes its subject in a form which has a life of its own forever separate but springing from the life which confronts it. Poetry is life at the remove of form and meaning; not life lived but life framed and identified. [89]

And Valéry, as noted above, emphasizes that "the poem . . . does not die for having lived: it is expressly designed to be born again from its ashes and to become endlessly what it has just been." So the paradox is this: poetry, the evanescent mingling of the sense of life's value within its loss, is itself free from such loss within the unchanging artifice of poem—"Ah happy, happy boughs! that cannot shed/ Your leaves, nor ever bid the Spring adieu." Of the

---

[89] Blackmur, p. 339.

many expressions of this ultimate paradox none is more satisfying than those supplied by Shakespeare's sonnets. The wonderful sonnet 107 concludes:

> And thou in this shalt find thy monument,
> When tyrants' crests and tombs of brass are spent.

Sonnet 60, which begins with the *ens* and *essentia* of "Like as the waves make towards the pebbled shore,/ So do our minutes hasten to their end," concludes with the couplet:

> And yet to times in hope my verse shall stand,
> Praising thy worth, despite his cruel hand.

The exquisite sonnet 18 provides an almost flawless example of the ideal balance of *substantia, ens,* and *essentia,* as well as an illustration of the fully realized relationship of poetry to poem:

> Shall I compare thee to a summer's day?
> Thou art more lovely and more temperate:
> Rough winds do shake the darling buds of May,
> And summer's lease hath all too short a date:
> Sometimes too hot the eye of heaven shines,
> And often is his gold complexion dimm'd;
> And every fair from fair sometimes declines,
> By chance, or nature's changing course, untrimm'd;
> But thy eternal summer shall not fade
> Nor lose possession of that fair thou ow'st
> Nor shall Death brag thou wand'rest in his shade
> When in eternal lines to time thou grow'st:
> > So long as men can breathe or eyes can see,
> > So long lives this, and this gives life to thee.

The sonnet does not exhibit quite so much richness of word and sound as does sonnet 30 ("When to the sessions of sweet silent thought"), but it exemplifies as well the complete poetic act—the coming together of evanescent "poetry" and immutable "poem"—as any in the whole inspired cycle.

CHAPTER FIVE

A Complex Dialogue: Coleridge's Doctrine

of Polarity and Its European

Contexts

◊♦◊

In all subjects of deep and lasting Interest," wrote Coleridge in 1820, "you will detect a struggle between two opposites, two polar Forces, both of which are alike necessary to our human Well-being, & necessary each to the continued existence of the other."[1] What he here enunciated was an ineradicable characteristic and compelling urgency of his thought. As a commentator has emphasized:

> Coleridge's conception of genre is based upon the method of the reconciliation of opposites, which embodies the characteristic method of his thought. . . . The reconciliation of opposites, indeed, is the Archimedes lever of Coleridge's criticism. His procedure and his terminology are dialectical or "polar." Reality is always organic unity or wholeness, but this reality can only be discursively revealed as two, in the form of polar opposites reconciled, or of centripetal and centrifugal forces in equilibrium.[2]

More recently, Owen Barfield, in his study entitled *What Coleridge Thought*, has seen the doctrine of polarity as the Archimedes lever not merely of Coleridge's criticism but of the entirety of his mental activity: "polarity," summarizes Barfield, "is at the root of what Coleridge thought"; "the apprehension of polarity is itself *the basic act of imagination*."[3]

Explicit testimony from Coleridge himself amply supports such assessments of polarity's importance in his intellectual commitment. We may isolate a single comprehensive statement:

---

[1] *Collected Letters*, v, 35. [2] Fogle, p. 4.
[3] Barfield, pp. 145, 36.

EVERY POWER IN NATURE AND IN SPIRIT *must evolve an opposite, as the sole means and condition of its manifestation:* AND ALL OPPOSITION IS A TENDENCY TO RE-UNION. This is the universal Law of Polarity or essential Dualism, first promulgated by Heraclitus, 2000 years afterwards re-published, and made the foundation both of Logic, of Physics, and of Metaphysics by Giordano Bruno.[4]

Coleridge's description of the provenance of the doctrine of polarity is historically admissible (if we except possibly even earlier formulations by ancient thinkers of the Orient). His awareness of Heraclitus's priority and Bruno's reassertion both indicates the lodgment of the doctrine in transmissions and indebtednesses going back to the origins of Western philosophy, and somewhat paradoxically suggests a continual rebirth in differing epochs as dictated by evolving needs and disparate intellectual situations.

Heraclitus promulgated the doctrine fully albeit cryptically. In their reduction of his thought to fourteen rubrics, Kirk and Raven devote no fewer than four to his involvement in the doctrine of polarity; and among the Heraclitean fragments brought forward to illustrate the first of them ("Different types of example of the essential unity of opposites"), they cite such statements as

Sea is the most pure and the most polluted water; for fishes it is drinkable and salutary, but for men it is undrinkable and deleterious

Again:

The path up and down is one and the same.

And yet again:

Disease makes health pleasant and good, hunger satiety, weariness rest.[5]

Diels's great collection can supply us additional examples of Heraclitus's conception of polarity. For instance:

That which is in opposition is in concert, and from things that differ comes the most beautiful harmony.

Again:

They do not understand how that which differs with itself is in

[4] *Friend*, I, 94n.   [5] Kirk and Raven, pp. 189-95.

agreement: harmony consists of opposing tensions, like that of the bow and the lyre.

And once more:

And what is in us is the same thing: living and dead, awake and sleeping, as well as old and young; for the latter having changed becomes the former, and this again having changed becomes the latter.[6]

How central was the principle of reconciled opposition to Heraclitus's dark understanding may be further emphasized by a collage of quotations from Burnet's classic study of early Greek philosophy:

A glance at the fragments will show that the thought of Herakleitos was dominated by the opposition of sleeping and waking, life and death, and that this seemed to him the key to the traditional Milesian problem of the opposites, hot and cold, wet and dry. . . . We see further that there is a regular alternation of the two processes; sleep alternates with waking, and life with death. . . . Such, so far as we can make it out, is the general view of Herakleitos, and now we may ask for his secret, the one thing to know which is wisdom. It is that, as the apparent strife of opposites in this world is really due to the opposite tension which holds the world together, so in pure fire, which is the eternal wisdom, all these oppositions disappear in their common ground.[7]

Guthrie—to add a more modern authority—interprets the harmony of opposites as one part of a threefold rationale for the Heraclitean "Logos." "Harmony is always the product of opposites, therefore the basic fact in the natural world is strife." Heraclitus's doctrine, observes Guthrie furthermore, was in fact a special realization of a more general intellectual preoccupation of his time:

The Heraclitean doctrine of the simultaneity of opposites and its paradoxical consequences is the result of intense concentration on a mental phenomenon common in the early Greek world, to which the name 'polarity' has been given. Thus for example H. Fränkel writes of 'a thought-form which after Homer, in the

6 Diels-Kranz, I, 152 (B8); 162 (B51); 170-71 (B88).
7 Burnet, pp. 47, 49.

archaic period of Greece, was the dominant one, namely the polar mode of thought: qualities cannot be conceived otherwise than together with their contraries.'[8]

As Coleridge was correct about Heraclitus's priority in focusing the polar doctrine of the harmony of opposites, so was he also correct about Bruno's re-establishment of that doctrine. "Harmony," writes Bruno, "is not effectuated except where there is contrariety. The spherical does not repose on the spherical, because they touch each other at a point; but the concave rests on the convex." The "coincidenza de contrarii," as Bruno calls it, is an arcane knowledge that may fairly be thought to provide, as Coleridge says it does, "the foundation both of Logic, of Physics, and of Metaphysics":

> if the matter is considered physically, mathematically, and morally, one sees that that philosopher who has arrived at the theory of the 'coincidence of contraries' has not found out a small thing, and that that magician who knows how to look for it where it exists is not an imbecile practitioner.

To this statement Bruno's narrator, Sophia, responds with nothing less than a paean to the importance of contraries:

> the beginning, the middle, and the end, the birth, the growth, and the perfection of all that we see, come from contraries, through contraries, into contraries, to contraries. And where there is contrariety, there is number, there is order, there are degrees, there is succession, there is vicissitude.[9]

In his great treatise *De la causa, principio e uno,* again, Bruno concludes that "contraries coincide in unity"; and that

> he who wants to know the greatest secrets of nature should regard and contemplate the minima and maxima of contraries and opposites. It is a profound magic to know how to draw out the contrary after having found the point of union.[10]

The contemplation of the minima and maxima of contraries and opposites, and the finding of their point of union, were for Coleridge not a mere intellectual fancy, but—entirely in the spirit of both Bruno and Heraclitus—a philosophical commitment dictated by the nature of reality. Thus, under the title "extremes meet," he

[8] Guthrie, I, 435, 446.   [9] Bruno, p. 573.
[10] *Ibid.,* pp. 335, 340.

frequently noted empirical evidences of polarity. For instance, on shipboard to Malta in 1804 he writes:

> Extremes meet. The Captains of a fastest-sailing Vessel & the obstinately Laggardmost of a Convoy, equally vexed, and restless.—[11]

In December 1803, he collected a number of examples of the coincidence of contraries:

> I have repeatedly said, that I could have made a Volume, if only I had noted down, as they occurred to my Recollection or Observations, the instances of the Proverb, Extremes Meet!—This Night, Sunday, Dec. 11, 1803, ½ past 11, I have determined to devote the last 9 pages of my Pocket[book] to the collection of the same.

He then produces the heading, in large capitals, "EXTREMES MEET." Immediately underneath he supplies, from Milton, a motto for the enterprise:

> The parching Air
> Burns frore, and Cold performs the Effect of Fire.
> Par. Lost, Book 2.594.

There follow ten instances, differing widely, of how extremes meet:

> Insects by their smallness, the Mammoth by its hugeness, terrible.

> Sameness in a Waterfall, in the foam Islands of a fiercely boiling Pool at the bottom of the Waterfall, from infinite Change.

> The excess of Humanity & Disinterestedness in polite Society, not to give Pain, e.g. not to talk of your own Diseases or misfortunes, & to introduce nothing but what will give pleasure, destroys all Humanity & Disinterestedness by making it intolerable thro' Desuetude, to listen to the Complaints of our Equals or of any where the Listening does not gratify or excite some vicious Pride, & sense of Superiority.

---

[11] *Notebooks*, ii, 2066. It should be emphasized that such notations were for Coleridge illustrations of a truth of fundamental importance, not idle observations. Thus he says that "extremes meet" is his "favorite proverb" (*Friend*, i, 529). Even more importantly: "Extremes meet—a proverb, by the bye, to collect and explain all the instances and exemplifications of which would constitute and exhaust all philosophy" (*Friend*, i, 110).

A perfectly unheard of Subject, & a crambe bis cocta, chosen by a man of Genius—difficult to say, which would excite in the higher degree the sense of Novelty. E.g. the Orestes of Sotheby.

Dark with excess of Light.

Self-absorption & Worldly-mindedness N.B. The latter a most philosophical word

The dim Intellect *sees* an absolute Oneness, the perfectly clear Intellect *knowingly perceives* it. Distinction & Plurality lie in the Betwixt.

9. The naked Savage, & the Gymnosophist.

10. Nothing & intensest absolutest Being.

11. Despotism and ochlocracy. [12]

The examples are Heraclitean enough in their obscurity as well as in their reliance on common observation. Two, however, differ somewhat from this characterization. The fourth from the last, about dim intellect seeing oneness, and clear intellect knowingly perceiving it, and the penultimate example, about the coincidence of "Nothing & intensest absolutest Being," are metaphysically abstract rather than gnomically empirical observations.

Indeed, they are virtually Hegelian in their abstraction. The statement that "Nothing & intensest absolutest Being" coincide is in fact almost identical with the first triad of Hegel's larger *Logik:* "*Das reine Seyn und das reine Nichts ist also dasselbe. Was die Wahrheit ist, ist weder das Seyn, noch das Nichts, sondern daß das Seyn in Nichts, und das Nichts in Seyn,—nicht übergeht,—sondern übergegangen ist*"—pure being and pure nothing are therefore the same; truth is neither being nor nothing, but the fact that being— not passes over—but has passed over into nothing, and nothing into being. [13]

The close similarity of these formulations, however, can be misleading if taken as an indication of a generalized congruence in the mental styles of Coleridge and Hegel. To step into that "maelstrom of thought" (the description is Geoffrey Hartman's) that consti-

---

[12] *Notebooks*, I, 1725.

[13] *Hegel's Werke*, III, 78-79. Again: "Das Seyn, das unbestimmte Unmittelbare ist in der That nichts, und nicht mehr noch weniger als Nichts"—being, the indeterminate immediacy, is in fact nothing, and neither more nor less than nothing (III, 78).

tutes Hegelian philosophy is to be swept into a dialectic of opposites pouring forth in the most stringent abstraction and fullness of philosophical formulation. The "primary concepts or starting-points of logic" are for Hegel "being and nothing, and as that which contains the two previous determinations as moments, becoming." In his first great treatise, *Die Phänomenologie des Geistes*, he intended to

> set out an example of the true method of philosophical science as applied to . . . consciousness. We have here modes of consciousness each of which in realizing itself abolishes itself, has its own negation as its result, and thus passes over into a higher mode. The one and only thing *for securing scientific progress* . . . is knowledge of the logical precept that negation is just as much affirmation as negation, or that what is self-contradictory resolves itself not into nullity, into abstract nothingness, but essentially only into the negation of its *particular* content, that such negation is not an all-embracing negation, but is *the negation of a definite somewhat* that abolishes itself, and thus is a definite negation; and that thus the result contains in essence that from which it results—which is indeed a tautology, for otherwise it would be something immediate and not a result. Since what results, the negation, is a *definite* negation, it has a *content*. It is a new concept, but a higher, richer concept than that which preceded; for it has been enriched by the negation or opposite of that preceding concept, and thus contains it, but contains also more than it, and is the unity of it and its opposite.

In general, for Hegel "it is in this dialectic . . . and in the comprehension of the unity of opposites, or of the positive in the negative, that *speculative knowledge consists*."[14]

Hegel differed from Coleridge, and from his own contemporaries and immediate predecessors, in the dynamic or progressive emphasis of his logic—the restless movement from thesis to antithesis to synthesis, and the continual reinstitution of the process (or, if we heed Kojève's observation that "The expressions 'Thesis,' 'Antithesis,' 'Synthesis' almost never appear" in Hegel's writing, we may substitute "the 'dialectical' expressions he commonly uses," that is, " 'Immediacy,' 'Mediation,' 'Overcoming,' [and their derivatives]").[15] Such logical movement was certainly implied, and frequently stated, in other theories of contrariety, as,

[14] *Ibid.*, pp. 23, 41, 44. [15] Kojève, pp. 208-209 n. 14.

for instance, in Blake's formula: "Without Contraries is no progression";[16] or again, in Oken's statement that "The revelation of polarity is movement."[17] It is also inherent in Coleridge's conception that "Distinction & Plurality" lie between "the dim Intellect" that sees an absolute oneness, and "the perfectly clear Intellect" that knowingly perceives it—an ideation not unlike the Hegelian progression from "notion" (*Begriff*) to "absolute knowledge" (*absolute Wissenschaft*); but the insistence and expansion of statement that accompany such formulations weave the distinctive fabric of Hegelian discourse. Coleridge's commitment to dialectical movement, though implied, is more tentative than that of Hegel.

Another difference between Hegel and Coleridge lies in the characteristic hiddenness of the latter's process of thought—what I have elsewhere referred to as the fact that Coleridge "customarily presents us with completed opinions based on unexpressed arguments rather than with the process of argument itself."[18] Hegel, on the other hand, explicates his arguments in relentlessly abstract accumulation; this powerful idiosyncrasy, indeed, is largely what guarantees him inclusion among the half-dozen or so greatest philosophers of our cultural history. We may compare Coleridge's Heraclitean terseness in "Nothing & intensest absolutest Being" with Hegel's pile-driving specification of the thought process involved in such a formula. Discussing the concept of "contradiction," toward the conclusion that "positive and negative are the same," the German philosopher writes:

> If we consider the two independent determinations of reflection for themselves, we see that the positive is positedness as reflected into self-equality; positedness which is not relation to an other, and thus persistence in so far as positedness is transcended and excluded. But hereby the positive converts itself into the relation of a not-being—into a positedness.—It is thus contradiction: it is the positing of self-identity, and, by excluding the negative, it makes itself into the negative of something, that is, into that other which it excludes from itself. This, as excluded, is posited as free from the excluding term, and consequently as introreflected and itself excluding. Thus exclusive reflection is the positing of the positive as excluding the other in such a manner that this positing is immediately the positing of its other, which excludes it.[19]

[16] *Blake*, p. 34.
[18] *CPT*, p. 236.
[17] Oken, I, 23.
[19] *Hegel's Werke*, IV, 58.

Although the principle of the reconciliation of opposites received its most varied and systematic exposition in Hegel's dialectical construction of the world, it was a principle that also pervaded Romantic thought in general. Under the name of "Polarität," and, conceived on the analogy of the positive and negative poles of magnetism, it dominated that whole spectrum of German scientific speculation called *Naturphilosophie*. As Hegel said, in his *Encyclopaedia Logic*:

> Positive and negative are supposed to express an absolute difference. The two, however, are at bottom the same: the name of either might be transferred to the other. Thus, for example, debts and assets are not two particular self-subsisting species of property. What is negative to the debtor, is positive to the creditor. A way to the east is also a way to the west. Positive and negative are therefore intrinsically conditioned by one another, and exist only in relation to each other. The north pole of the magnet cannot be without the south pole, and vice versa. If we cut a magnet in two, we do not have a north pole in one piece, and a south pole in the other. . . . The other is seen to stand over against *its* other. Thus, for example, inorganic nature is not to be considered merely something else than organic nature, but the necessary antithesis of it. . . . Nature in like manner is not without mind, nor mind without nature. . . . In modern physical science the opposition, first observed to exist in magnetism as polarity, has come to be regarded as a universal law pervading the whole of nature.[20]

Hegel's phrasing here indicates that "polarity" is the cultural property of an age and intellectual community rather than his own distinctive formulation. Indeed, the actual word "Polarität" is not very Hegelian in its occurrence, but is associated more usually with Goethe and with Schelling.[21] Furthermore, despite Hegel's own ambitious scientific schematizings, *Naturphilosophie* as such is customarily thought of as the peculiar domain of Schelling and his followers (though Hegel too used the name);[22] and in their treatises

---

[20] *Ibid.*, vi, 240-41.

[21] Cf. Zeltner, p. 123: "The two fundamental premises of Schelling's explanation of nature are *Polarität* and *Steigerung*, and here he is especially close to Goethe."

[22] Hegel in fact sharply rejected *Naturphilosophie* as presented by the school of Schelling, even though in his lectures he indulged in such speculation at length (see, e.g., Volumes 6-8 of the great edition-in-progress of his *Gesammelte Werke*). For instance, he writes to a correspondent in 1814 as follows: "You know that I have

the doctrine of polarity assumes a kind of absolute centrality. As Schopenhauer said, looking backward from an unsurpassed command of all the intricacies of German Romantic thought, a chief characteristic of the "Naturphilosophen der Schellingischen Schule" was their emphasis on the fact that

> *polarity*, that is, the splitting of a force into two qualitatively different and opposite activities striving for reunion . . . is a basic type of almost all the phenomena of nature, from the magnet and crystal up to man.[23]

To bring forward a striking example, Oken, one of the most ardent of the "Naturphilosophen der Schellingischen Schule," enunciated the sweeping dictum: "Keine Welt ohne polare Kraft"— there would be no world without polar force. "There is therefore no simple force in the world," said Oken further: "each is an appearance of itself, a position of + −, or a *polarity*." Yet again: "The cosmic entelechy is itself polarity, is the primal polarity (*Urpolarität*). Polarity breaks out in the moment where the world creation stirs itself. . . . Every individual thing is a doubleness."[24]

Oken was writing in 1809, in a three-volume work dedicated to "his friends Schelling and Steffens from Oken." He was proceeding confidently along a broad thoroughfare laid down more than a decade before by the first of the three friends. For Schelling, earlier than Hegel, and in no way less fully or insistently, had in the late 1790s projected a comprehensive philosophy of polar oppositions and their reconciliations. His imagination fired by the practical experiments of Franklin, Galvani, Volta, and other pioneer investigators of electrical phenomena,[25] Schelling turned to electricity and its laws as the model for an entire metaphysic of existence. "God as dyad is electricism," said his disciple Oken in witness to the radical fascination of electrical discovery. "Galvanism is the

---

had too much to do not merely with ancient literature, but even with mathematics, more recently with the higher analysis, differential calculus, physics, natural history, chemistry, to let myself be taken in by the humbug of *Naturphilosophie*, philosophizing without knowledge of facts and by mere force of imagination, and treating mere fancies, even imbecile fancies, as ideas" (*Briefe*, II, 31).

[23] Schopenhauer, II, 171.

[24] Oken, I, 22-3.

[25] A single instance may help to illustrate the excitement generated by these investigators. Johann Wilhelm Ritter's *Beweis, dass ein beständiger Galvanismus den Lebensprocess in dem Thierreich begleite*, which was published in Weimar in 1798, was dedicated to "the great men F. A. v. Humboldt and A. Volta." For Volta and Galvani see further Haym, pp. 578-79.

principle of life," said Oken again: "There is no other life force than galvanic polarity."[26]

Permeating as it does almost all the work of Schelling's most vital period, the theory of electrical polarity receives especially full discussion in a treatise of 1798 called *Von der Weltseele; eine Hypothese der höheren Physic zur Erklärung des allgemeinen Organismus,* which was an extension and documentation of emphases sketched in the programmatic *Ideen zu einer Philosophie der Natur* of the preceding year. For instance, in the first-named work, following a discussion of "the universal dualism of nature," Schelling says that electricity "is no form of combustion, which even Lavoisier had supposed; electrical activity belongs to a higher sphere of nature's operations than does combustion." He then sets forth "as the first fundamental of the doctrine of electricity, that no electricity without the Other exists—is there—or can exist," and that this empirical fact allows us to "deduce the concept of positive and negative forces. Neither positive nor negative principles are something in themselves or *absolutely real*. That they are called positive or negative is proof that they exist only in a definite *reciprocal relation*."[27]

When Schelling later in the same treatise proceeds to "define more exactly the concept of polarity," he observes that

> it is certain *a priori* that in the whole of nature there are divided—truly opposed—principles at work; these opposed principles united in one body impart to it polarity; through the phenomena of polarity we become acquainted with, so to speak, only the *narrower* and *more defined* sphere within which the universal dualism operates. (II, 476)

The conception of a universal dualism in nature, based on the phenomena of magnetic polarity, is central to Schelling's thought. To take another instance, in his *Erster Entwurf eines Systems der Naturphilosophie* of 1799, he speaks of "Franklin's idea" that "the differentiation of the world is probably not merely mathematical, but is founded on a *universally operative physical cause*. This physical cause can be nothing else than magnetism."[28] The universe, says Schelling, is "one self-maintaining system" that "has formed all things from one pulsating point" (III, 125). Although we "must think of the continuing of the universe as organic," and "the continuing of a system is nothing other than a reciprocity of expansion

---

[26] Oken, I, 112; II, 10.　　　　[27] *Schellings Werke*, II, 430, 432.
[28] *Ibid.*, III, 122 n. 1.

and contraction—an eternal metamorphosis" (III, 126 n.2); nevertheless, says Schelling, there is "no doubt that the organism first contracts and then expands itself through the same mechanism by which two electricities attract and then repel one another" (III, 167 n.3). It is *"one and the same universal dualism that extends from magnetic polarity through electrical phenomena, loses itself in chemical heterogeneities, and finally reappears in organic nature."* He continues: "If magnetism has brought about the first opposition in nature, there was thereby simultaneously planted the seed of an infinite evolution, the seed of that infinite splitting into ever new products in the universe" (III, 258). And Schelling concludes that there *"is therefore* ONE *cause, which has brought about the original opposition in nature; this cause we can denote by the* (unknown) *cause of the primal magnetism"* (III, 260).

Hegel, too, devoted close attention to the phenomena of magnetic polarity, and in his own *Naturphilosophie*, as expressed in the second part of his *Enzyklopädie*, he produces a discussion based on the understanding that

> the magnet represents in a simple, naive fashion the nature of the notion (*Begriff*), namely in its developed form as conclusion (*Schluss*). The poles are the materially existing ends of a real line (of a rod, or also in a body extended in all dimensions): as poles they possess, however, not a mechanically material reality, but an ideal one; they are absolutely inseparable. The *point of indifference*, in which they have their substance, is the unity in which they are as determinations of the notion; so that they have meaning and existence in this unity alone, and *polarity* is the relation solely of such moments.

In an expanded version of this discussion in the revised *Enzyklopädie* (the elements of the first passage were in the Heidelberg edition), Hegel further observes that

> If the magnet is cut in two, then each piece is again a whole magnet; the North pole arises again immediately in the broken piece. Each is the positing and excluding of the other from itself; the *termini* of the conclusion (*Schluss*) can exist not for themselves, but only in combination.[29]

Hegel's appeal to magnetic polarity, however, is on the whole less resonant than that of Schelling and his *naturphilosophische*

[29] *Hegel's Werke*, VII, i, 246, 249.

Anhänger—metaphysically more cautious, one might say. As Haering has stressed, "people have probably been all too hasty in allowing themselves to be carried along, through the outer similarity of the Schellingian concept of 'Polarität' and the Hegelian concept of 'Negativität,' opposition, dialectical unity etc. to a simple identification of the two standpoints—primarily for the reason that Hegel himself adduces the Schellingian examples, and especially magnetic polarity, as illustration for his own meaning. But when two do the same thing, then it is not the same thing."[30]

Doubtless some of the difference in Hegel's tone and emphasis from that of Schelling—and Haering provides extended discussion of such difference—was attendant upon his psychological position as "latecomer" (I use Harold Bloom's redaction of Nietzsche's term) with respect to Schelling's formulations. As Rudolf Haym notes, one of the most remarkable facts about Schelling was his extraordinary quickness in seeing the metaphysical possibilities of the discoveries made in late eighteenth-century physics and chemistry:[31] he was pre-eminently an early formulator ("Schelling," wrote Novalis in about 1798, "is the *philosopher of modern chemistry*").[32] None the less, I should urge, even if paradoxically, that chronological gradations are only schematically, not substantively, important for the understanding of the doctrines of polarity and the harmony of opposites.

Far more important than chronological awareness is the realization that the various enunciations of such doctrines in this period, like Romanticism itself, constitute a kind of cultural flood, one in which divisions into before or after have little relevance, and where creeks and branches of individual discovery or originality, though arising at different points along the banks, all flow inevitably to a common mingling in the larger current of the age. Indeed, the very

---

[30] Haering, I, 690. Pursuing this contention, Haering provides lengthy discussion of the ways in which the two men were in fact not doing "the same thing." But briefer illustration may suffice here. We may take a passage from each man as comparative example. First Hegel, then Schelling. "Das Seyn," says the former, "ist zuerst gegen Anderes überhaupt bestimmt"—being is in the first place determined as opposed to other in general (*Hegel's Werke*, III, 74). "Das Universum," says the latter, is "Ein selbständiges System" that has "alle von Einem pulsirenden Punkt aus sich gebildet"—the universe is one self-maintaining system that has formed all things out of itself from one pulsating point (*Schellings Werke*, III, 125). The characteristic abstractness of Hegel, and on the other hand the metaphorical dynamism of Schelling—what has been called his "dithyrambic" quality—are here fairly apparent.

[31] Haym, p. 578.   [32] *Novalis*, III, 266.

idea of "an age" or "a time" tends to repudiate the importance of smaller temporalities and priorities within the larger entity. For instance, Coleridge's "extremes meet" notation in which he sees the coincidence of "Nothing & intensest absolutest Being" precedes by about a decade the first triad of Hegel's *Logik*; on the other hand, since both Coleridge and Hegel had long been thinking about such topics, and continued to think about them much later, the special formulations should be seen as more or less arbitrary emergences from the deeper currents of the time. Although Schelling began serious publication earlier than did Hegel (the latter's *Phänomenologie des Geistes* did not appear until 1807, whereas Schelling's *System des transzcendentalen Idealismus* not only appeared as early as 1800 but also marked the close of Schelling's most dynamic phase), it would be difficult to say that either of the erstwhile friends and youthful roommates carried on the *process of thought* in chronological befores and afters.

In this respect, to attach honorific significance to Schelling's prior publication is like saying that upstream is somehow better than downstream. After all, as Richard Kroner emphasizes, Hegel's *Enzyklopädie* is

> the richest and most complete presentation that German idealism found; it is the form of that system that idealism was everywhere striving toward in its development, that Schelling in 1802 termed the "first task to be solved in the future," and of which he had prophetically said that if the system be "once presented and perceived in its entirety, the absolute harmony of the universe and the divinity of all natures in the thoughts of man will be established forever."[33]

In that perspective, surely, Hegel's "latecomer" status is a virtue rather than a defect; he becomes, as it were, the sea into which Schelling's river flows. And such, *mutatis mutandis*, is the ambivalent truth about the chronological befores and afters of Coleridge and of others in the Romantic community of thought.

Of more significance than chronological fixations is the apprehending of—to vary the metaphor—the *texture* of the Romantic involvement in polarity: the closeness of weave in the common emphasis no less than the differing threads in the historical transmission and the idiosyncratic patternings of individual commitment. Chronology in and of itself brings us little light. Goethe, for

---

[33] Kroner, II, 502-503.

instance, was as profoundly involved with polarity as were Schelling and Hegel, and became so earlier than either; but he was also involved contemporaneously with them, and continued in deep commitment perhaps even later than Schelling. Thus in 1810, in his *Farbenlehre*, he hails the doctrine of polar oppositions; he had, however, as a commentator emphasizes, been devoting "intensive work" to that treatise since 1790, and had begun thinking about the theory of color as early as 1777.[34]

Moreover, Goethe's tone is one that welcomes the agreement of other minds rather than insisting on his own priority (or indebtedness). As he says in the *Farbenlehre*:

> True observers of nature, however they otherwise consider themselves as differing, will nonetheless agree with one another that everything that appears, everything that is to meet us as a phenomenon, must indicate and in some way represent itself as either an original separation that is capable of being made one, or an original unity, which can attain to a division into two. To divide into two that which is united into one, to make into one that which is sundered into two, is the life of nature; this is the eternal systole and diastole, the eternal syncresis and diacresis, the breathing in and out of the world in which we live, move, and have our being.[35]

One of the "true observers of nature" who agreed with Goethe was Schelling, who, quite in accord with the emphasis of Goethe's passage, wrote that

> Where appearances are, there are already opposed forces. The theory of nature therefore supposes as immediate principle a universal heterogeneity of matter, and, in order to be able to conceive this, a universal homogeneity. Neither the principle of absolute heterogeneity nor that of absolute homogeneity is the true one; the truth lies in the union of both.[36]

Even where Goethe speaks of his own particular contribution, he connects his invocation of polarity with the laws of reality itself:

> It would be most highly to be desired, however, that the language by which the particularities of a certain sphere of investigation are designated be taken from the sphere itself; the

[34] Rike Wankmüller, in *Goethes Werke*, Hamburg Edition, XIII (Hamburg: Christian Wegner Verlag, 1955), 605.

[35] *Gedenkausgabe*, XVI, 199.   [36] *Schellings Werke*, II, 390.

simplest appearance treated as a basic formula and the manifold deduced and developed from that.

The necessity and propriety of such a language of signs, where the basic sign expresses the appearance itself, has been quite well sensed in the extending of the formula of polarity, borrowed from the magnet, to electricity and further matters. The plus and minus that can be posited in this situation have found a proper application in many other phenomena; indeed, the musical artist, probably without troubling himself about those other subjects, has been prompted by nature to express the main difference of musical tones by major and minor.

Thus we have for a long time wished to introduce the term polarity into the theory of colors; with what right and in what sense, let the present work reveal.[37]

The conception of polarity, as such quotations suggest, was never far from Goethe's mind; in truth, it was for him, possibly even more than for Romanticism in general, one of the most central of all propositions that made possible a world. The "two great drive wheels of all nature," he wrote in 1828, are "the concept of polarity and that of evolution (Steigerung), the former belonging to matter insofar as we think it material, the latter, on the contrary, belonging to it insofar as we think it spiritual; the former is in a state of ever-continuing attraction and repulsion, the latter in one of ever-striving ascent."[38] On one occasion, Goethe compiles— somewhat in the manner of Coleridge's "extremes meet" notations—a random list of examples of the "duality of the appearance as contrast":

> Ourselves and objects
> Light and dark
> Body and soul
> Two souls
> Mind and matter
> God and the world
> Thought and extension
> Ideal and real
> Sensuousness and reason
> Imagination and understanding
> Being and longing
> Two halves of a body

[37] Gedenkausgabe, XVI, 205. [38] Ibid., p. 925.

> Right and left
> Breathing
>   Physical experience:
> Magnet[39]

In Goethe's constant musings on the principle of polarity, however, personal reverie was not the sole preoccupation. On the contrary, he, like others in the Romantic era, participated in that frequent and varied interchange, that intense interweaving of thought, that raised certain matters, and polarity was importantly one of them, beyond the conception of source and influence to the status of being "in the air." For a single instance, on a visit to Tübingen in September 1797, he casually records a meeting with Karl Friedrich Kielmeyer, professor of chemistry and medicine, and an important authority on organic and dynamic topics:[40]

> Early this morning with Professor Kielmeyer, who visited me, various things about anatomy and physiology of organic natures. His program will be printed very soon for the purpose of his lectures. He harangued me with various thoughts as to how he is inclined to join the laws of organic nature to general physical laws—for example, to polarity, to the reciprocal modification and correlation of extremes, to the extendable force of expansible fluids.[41]

Such peripheral influence, as it were, may well to some extent have set up its own little harmonic eddy of opposites between Goethe and his interlocutor; that it could have "influenced" Goethe in the sense of placing hitherto unknown principles in his head, however, is surely not the case. For example, some five years earlier than this interview he writes to a correspondent as follows:

> Since our excellent Kant says in plain words that there can be no material without attraction and repulsion (that is, without polarity), I am much reassured to be able, under this authority, to proceed with my view of the world according to my own earliest convictions, in which I have never lost confidence.[42]

The statement to which Goethe refers had appeared in the

---

[39] *Ibid.*, pp. 863-64.

[40] See Kielmeyer, *Ueber die Verhältniße der organischen Kräfte unter einander in der Reihe der verschiedenen Organisationen, die Geseze und Folgen dieser Verhältniße* (Tübingen: Osiander, 1793).

[41] *Gedenkausgabe*, xii, 151.   [42] *Ibid.*, xix, 732.

course of a discussion of the dynamic in Kant's *Metaphysische An-fangsgründe der Naturwissenschaft*, which was published in 1786. In that treatise Kant had argued that the conception of matter depended entirely upon that of a tension of attracting and repelling forces.[43] His argument was of great importance to thinkers of the Romantic era.[44] Hegel refers to it repeatedly; for instance, in the *Wissenschaft der Logik*:

> Kant, as is well known, has *constructed matter from repulsive and attractive force*, or, at least, he has erected (as he calls it) the metaphysical elements of this construction.

But, objects Hegel in an extended discussion designed to validate his own thought against that of his predecessor, "at bottom Kant's method is *analytical* and not constructive."[45] As another example, taken almost at random, Carl August Eschenmayer, in a treatise of 1797 that attempts to apply Fichte's *Wissenschaftslehre* to natural science, and which was carefully studied by Novalis, explicitly summons the Kantian conception that "the dynamic teaches us that the existence of matter can be conceived only under the assumption of the concurrence of two elemental forces";[46] "in the metaphysics of nature the concept of matter in general is analyzed and deduced from two opposed forces, namely those of repulsion and attraction."[47]

Goethe himself refers on still another occasion in 1792 to Kant's analysis as a major presentation of the doctrine of polarity:

> I had not allowed it to escape me, in Kant's *Naturwissenschaft*, that attractive and repelling force belongs to the nature of matter, and neither can be separated from the other in the concept of matter; hence there became clear to me the primal polarity of all natures, a polarity that interpenetrates and animates the infinite manifoldness of all appearances.[48]

[43] *Gesammelte Schriften*, IV, 511.

[44] For Coleridge's enthusiasm for the *Metaphysische Anfangsgründe der Naturwis-senschaft*, see, e.g., *Biographia*, I, 99. Cf. Barfield: "This relatively brief treatise is more thickly annotated than any other volume I have come across, and the marginalia make it obvious that it was ardently studied and pondered by Coleridge" (Barfield, p. 248). See further W. Schrickx, "Coleridge Marginalia in Kant's *Metaphysische Anfangsgründe der Naturwissenschaft*," *Studia Germanica I* (Ghent, 1959), 161-87.

[45] *Hegel's Werke*, III, 201, 202.

[46] As copied by Novalis, in *Novalis*, II, 381.

[47] C. A. Eschenmayer, *Säze aus der Natur-Metaphysik auf chemische und medicinische Gegenstände angewandt* (Tübingen: J. F. Heerbrandt, 1797), p. 88.

[48] *Gedenkausgabe*, XII, 373.

Such statements by Goethe, occurring throughout a continuous course of thirty-six years, and with direct assurance that they pertain to his "earliest convictions," demonstrate an enormously personal involvement in the doctrine of polarity.[49] They also demonstrate, however, paradox though it may be, participation in what can accurately be described as the spirit of the age. The same double structure, I suggest, marks the involvement of Coleridge as well.

It seems desirable and even rather necessary to dwell upon this double character of Coleridge's own preoccupation with polarity and the reconciliation of opposites; for Barfield, in his otherwise useful and important study, largely neglects to present either the fact or the significance of the communal dimension of Coleridge's thought. Eschewing "the comparative approach," Barfield takes as "a fair description of what I myself should actually be trying to do" a statement from J. A. Appleyard's *Coleridge's Philosophy of Literature*:

> What is wanting in the sizable bibliography of literature on Coleridge is a full-scale study of the development of his philosophy which will consider him on his own terms and not as a representative of something else, whether it be German idealism, English Platonism, pantheistic mysticism, semantic analysis, or depth psychology. The idea or organizing insight ought to be internal to his thought, so as to see what that thought is and not merely what it is like or unlike.[50]

Despite the seeming reasonableness of such an approach, however, I find myself in disagreement with it, and indeed, I think it leads to misunderstandings as to the real nature of Coleridge's mentation. Strictly speaking, neither Coleridge nor any other philosopher can be said "on his own terms" to have thought anything at all. Not only the philosophical language he uses but the formulation of the very problems he confronts are given him by his intellectual culture. If there were no culture, there would be no thought. Dull and speechless tribes have no tradition of philosophy, and, having no tradition, they have no philosophers. One can only speculate how many mute, inglorious Miltons, alike of poetry, of science, and of philosophy, have been born, grown to adulthood in vain, and then vanished for want of a nurturing tradition. Texts are possible only in contexts.

[49] For additional discussion and illustration of Goethe's commitment to polarity see, e.g., Danckert, pp. 371-400.

[50] Barfield, p. 4; and Appleyard, p. ix.

In other words I should argue, in direct contravention of Appleyard's call, that it is precisely in the understanding of "something else" that philosophical meaning inheres; that to understand what a philosopheme is "like or unlike" is the very process of understanding "what that thought is." Cassirer insists that the chief contribution of Socrates was the transforming of philosophy from "an intellectual monologue" into a "dialogue":

> Truth is by nature the offspring of dialectic thought. It cannot be gained, therefore, except through a constant coöperation of the subjects in mutual interrogation and reply. It is not therefore like an empirical object; it must be understood as the outgrowth of a social act.[51]

Coleridge's thought, like that of other philosophers, is "the outgrowth of a social act." Only if it is heard as a voice in a complex dialogue with his forebears and contemporaries can its meaning be ascertained. There are no Robinson Crusoes of the intellect.

Indeed, in a cultural ambiance dominated by the vision of the reconciliation of polar oppositions, the largest of those oppositions suspended in the cultural act is exactly the one indicated above for Goethe: the polarity of the individual talent and the tradition in which it functions.

The approach sponsored by Appleyard and Barfield can accordingly never be more than an heuristic device, a Vaihingerian *as if* plea. Its attractiveness is that it greatly simplifies the task of the interpreter, and to some extent that of the reader as well. But to simplify in this way can also be to distort. Barfield's special virtue as a commentator is the tenacity with which he confronts passage after passage that has heretofore been ignored or dismissed as Coleridgean vaporing. But this very virtue of, so to speak, New Critical concentration on the passages at hand is also his main defect; for by taking everything at face value, without the safeguards of that "complex and allusive web of comparative philosophy" that he rejects,[52] Barfield does violence to two aspects of our understanding of Coleridge. First of all, he provides a system of Coleridge's thought that is really what Coleridge worked through and dismissed rather than what he finally endorsed. Secondly, to treat Coleridge's profound interest in polarity without reference to the cultural situation on the continent is to destroy the historical ecology of his thought.

---

[51] *Essay on Man*, p. 5.   [52] Barfield, p. 4.

With regard to the first of these limitations, we may take a re-
vealing instance. Barfield lays great stress on a clear understanding
of the two chapters at the end of the first volume of the *Biographia
Literaria*: "this is the place [he writes of Chapter Twelve] where,
more than anywhere else, the dynamic philosophy is brought to-
gether in epitome. It is impossible to master the chapter without
becoming substantially seised of what Coleridge thought. But that
is difficult and is likely to be attempted by comparatively few. If it
were otherwise, there would be the less need for such a book as
this."[53] But what Barfield's simplified approach does not allow him
to take into account is, first, that Chapter Twelve is mostly the
thought of Schelling and, secondly, that Coleridge, in direct rejec-
tion of the importance placed on it by Barfield, at the end of his life
dismissed "the metaphysical disquisition at the end of the first
volume of the 'Biographia Literaria' " as "unformed and imma-
ture."[54]

With regard to the other idiosyncrasy in Barfield's approach, that
is, the lack of referential placement in an intellectual tradition and
the attendant violence done to the historical ecology of Coleridge's
mental activity, a single citation may suffice for illustration. Led on
by a penchant for Rudolf Steiner, Barfield follows Steiner into the
realm of Goethe's morphological speculations:

> Goethe's *Metamorphosenlehre* [writes Barfield] . . . was published
> in 1790. Not only is its method based on precisely what Cole-
> ridge demands, namely penetration from *natura naturata* into
> *natura naturans*, but its "archetypal plant" (*Urpflanze*) is the very
> embodiment of the idea of polarity as the basis of life. In some of
> the other writings Goethe's epistemology (so far as he develops
> it philosophically) is thoroughly Coleridgean.[55]

Barfield is here standing at a threshold opening onto vast move-
ments of European thought; but all he can say, constricted as he is
by a method that refers everything to Coleridge "on his own
terms," is that the Goethean endorsement of polarity is "thor-
oughly Coleridgean." It is precisely this kind of Anglocentric dis-
tortion of perspective that has fueled the wrath of learned anti-
Coleridgeans from Ferrier to Wellek.

In truth, the first of the examples opens out into larger Romantic
ideational currents no less than does the second. For the twelfth

[53] *Ibid.*, p. 63.   [54] *Table Talk*, p. 293 (June 28, 1834).
[55] Barfield, p. 242.

chapter of the *Biographia Literaria* is concerned with the logical po-
larity of ego and external as represented by the formal terms "sub-
ject" and "object." The opposition was of recurring urgency in
Coleridge's thought, as is witnessed by Carlyle's wickedly hilari-
ous recollection of his characteristic discourse: "He had knowledge
about many things and topics, much curious reading; but generally
all topics led him, after a pass or two, into the high seas of
theosophic philosophy, the hazy infinitude of Kantean transcen-
dentalism, with its 'sum-m-mjects' and 'om-m-mjects.' "[56] "All
knowledge rests on the coincidence of an object with a subject,"
confirms Coleridge himself in the twelfth chapter of the *Biographia
Literaria*.[57]

But in so saying Coleridge translates exactly the opening state-
ment of Schelling's *System des transzcendentalen Idealismus*: "Alles
Wissen beruht auf der Uebereinstimmung eines Objektiven mit
einem Subjektiven."[58] Coleridge subsequently—and for a consid-
erable space in his larger argument he is following Schelling so
closely as to be simply translating, or "plagiarizing," his German
contemporary—produces ten theses having to do with the polarity
of subject and object. "It must be remembered," he says, "that all
these Theses refer solely to one of the two Polar Sciences, namely,
to that which commences with, and rigidly confines itself within,
the subjective, leaving the objective (as far as it is exclusively objec-
tive) to natural philosophy, which is its opposite pole." Still follow-
ing, although not exactly translating, Schelling, he then says that
"the true system of natural philosophy places the sole reality of
things in an ABSOLUTE, which is at once causa sui et effectus, . . . in
the absolute identity of subject and object, which it calls nature,
and which in its highest power is nothing else than self-conscious
will or intelligence."[59]

If Coleridge in these instances goes beyond the bounds of pro-
priety in his unacknowledged use of Schelling, he at least demon-
strates the critical acumen for which he is famous. For there is no
fuller or more explicit statement of the doctrine of universal polar-
ity in terms of subject and object than that provided by the opening
pages of Schelling's treatise. "We can call the content of everything

---

[56] *Carlyle*, xi, 56. Again: "I still recollect his 'object' and 'subject,' terms of con-
tinual recurrence in the Kantean province; and how he sang and snuffled them into
'om-m-mject' and 'sum-m-mject,' with a kind of solemn shake or quaver, as he
rolled along" (p. 55).

[57] *Biographia*, i, 174. [58] *Schellings Werke*, iii, 339.

[59] *Biographia*, i, 185, 187.

in our knowledge that is merely *objective, nature*," says Schelling there: "the content of everything subjective on the other hand is called the *ego*, or the *intelligence*. Both concepts are opposed to one another. Intelligence is originally thought as the merely representing, nature as the merely representable, the former as the conscious, the latter as being without consciousness. There is however in each knowledge a reciprocal coincidence of both." "If all *knowledge* has as it were two poles, which reciprocally presuppose and demand one another," continues Schelling, "then they must seek themselves in all sciences; there must accordingly be two fundamental sciences, and it must be impossible to go out from the one pole without being driven onto the other." Since "both opposed entities are necessarily reciprocal," says Schelling further, then "to make the objective pole the first, and to deduce the subjective from it" is "the task of *Naturphilosophie*." If there is a *"Transzcendental-Philosophie*, then there is left for it only the opposed direction—to go out from the subjective, as from the first and *absolute*, and to have the *objective* arise out of it." The "whole system of philosophy," concludes Schelling, is accordingly "completed by two fundamental sciences, which, opposed to one another in principle and in direction, reciprocally seek and supplement one another."[60] In this sweeping formulation, surely, we encounter an apex of the doctrine of polarity.

Despite these emphatic polar schematisms, however, it would be a serious historical error to think that Schelling had any special property rights, terminological or substantive, to the examination and manipulation of the logic of subject and object.[61] To cite merely one counter-claim, Ernst Bloch argues that the "seminal idea" (*Kerngedanke*) of all Hegel's thought is "dialectic subject-object mediation."[62] As Goethe, who knew both Schelling and Schelling's philosophy so very well and sympathetically, remarked, "where object and subject touch one another, there is life; if Hegel in his identity-philosophy puts himself in the middle between *Objekt* and *Subjekt* and maintains this place, then we want to render him praise."[63]

Neither Schelling nor Hegel, moreover, was the originator of the German commitment to subject/object philosophizing. Rather, as

---

[60] *Schellings Werke*, III, 339, 340, 342.

[61] For instance, compare Novalis: "Objective and subjective necessary signs,/ which is fundamentally one/ are therefore the only way whereby something thought allows itself to be communicated" (*Novalis*, II, 109).

[62] Bloch, p. 31.　　　　　　　　　　　[63] *Gedenkausgabe*, XXIII, 492.

in so many instances, it was to Kant, or possibly more precisely to Reinhold's presentation of Kant, that the Romantic preoccupation with subject/object logic owed its rise.[64] Thus in the same place where Goethe commends Hegel's position on the issue of *Subjekt* and *Objekt*, he also surveys the development of the topic from its beginning, with the observation that "Kant was the first who laid an orderly groundwork. On this foundation construction has proceeded in various directions."[65]

A single example should suffice to justify Goethe's contention as to Kant's direct priority. Schelling's initial proposition, quoted above, that "all knowledge (*Wissen*) rests on the agreement of an object (*Objektiven*) with a subject (*Subjektiven*)" is clearly a mere restatement of Kant's observation, in the course of distinguishing opinion (*Meinen*), belief (*Glauben*), and knowledge (*Wissen*), that "when the holding of a thing as true is sufficient both subjectively and objectively (*sowohl subjectiv als objectiv*), it is knowledge (*Wissen*)."[66]

Goethe himself participated in subject/object conceivings, even if less insistently for such logical oppositions than for polarities in the natural sciences he so much loved. "Everything that is in the subject," he said, "is in the object—and still something more. Everything that is in the object, is in the subject—and still something more. We are in a double manner lost and made safe: By conceding the object its more and renouncing our subjective more; by exalting the subject with its more and not recognizing the other more." His "general confession of belief" was that

a) In nature there is everything that is in the subject;
y) and something above it.
b) In the subject there is everything that is in nature;
z) and something above it.[67]

Of greater pertinence for judging the dissemination of subject/object preoccupation in Romantic thought, however, is a treatise of 1804 by the political theorist, Adam Müller, called *Die Lehre vom*

[64] See Reinhold, e.g., pp. 201 ff., 250-52, 256-57, 296-303. Cf. Kroner, I, 316-22, and Erdmann, p. 476. See further Alfred Klemmt, *Karl Leonhard Reinholds Elementarphilosophie; eine Studie über den Ursprung des spekulativen deutschen Idealismus* (Hamburg: Verlag von Felix Meiner, 1958), e.g., pp. 58-91.

[65] *Gedenkausgabe*, XXIII, 492.

[66] *Gesammelte Schriften*, III, 533.

[67] Both statements quoted in Danckert, p. 231, in the course of a chapter entitled "Subjekt-Objekt" (pp. 222-32).

Gegensatze—that is, Theory of Opposition. The book presents such typically polar section headings as "Object and Subject," "Positive and Negative," "Nature and Art," "Man and Wife," and "Youth and Age"; and among these oppositions that of subject and object receives explicit formulation:

> *Objekt* is that which stands in opposition to the *Subjekt*, and vice versa. Therefore a subject that might be opposed to no object is absolutely nothing; for of such a subject it would merely be affirmed that the *Gegenstand* [object] (*das Objekt, das Entgegenstehende*) does not stand opposite it—in short, that it is not a subject, which is a contradiction. . . . What would here be maintained of object and subject is valid for all possible applications of this formula, for all possible objects and subjects; and therefore something is only there (real) insofar as something is there standing against it (anti-real or ideal); force is there and functions only insofar as a counterforce stands against it, works against it; an activity, only insofar as opposite activity (passivity) stands against it; the I is only something insofar as the not-I (*Gegenich*) is there.[68]

If we pause at this juncture to take stock, we realize that the Romantic doctrine of polarity has up to now been revealed in three different, yet intertwined forms: firstly, as the preceding discussion illustrates, in the logical opposition of subject and object derived from Kant's analysis of representability; secondly, as the physical opposition of attractive and repelling forces derived from Kant's discussion of the metaphysical fundamentals of the dynamic; and thirdly, as an analogy of the phenomenon of magnetic polarity, made popular by eighteenth-century empirical investigations of electrical laws.

Coleridge's awareness and commitment, perhaps predictably, extended to all three of these major forms. For instance, in addition to his subject/object preoccupation of the twelfth chapter of the *Biographia* and elsewhere, he speaks of polarity in the form of attractive and repelling forces:

> If we pass to the construction of matter, we find it as the product, or *tertium aliud*, of antagonist powers of repulsion and attraction.[69]

Coleridge says again, invoking the same distinction,

---

[68] Müller, *Schriften*, II, 219-20.   [69] *Theory of Life*, p. 55.

That nothing real does or can exist corresponding to either pole *exclusively*, is involved in the very definition of a THING as the synthesis of opposing energies (p. 69).

It was the third form of polarity, however, the one analogized from electrical phenomena, that especially stimulated Coleridge's imagination, as, by its connection with new horizons of scientific possibility, it did also for that of Schelling and his school. "A new light," Coleridge recognizes,

> was struck by the discovery of electricity, and, in every sense of the word, both playful and serious, both for good and for evil, it may be affirmed to have electrified the whole frame of natural philosophy (p. 31).

Defining life as the "tendency to individuate," Coleridge says that

> this tendency to individuate cannot be conceived without the opposite tendency to connect, even as the centrifugal power supposes the centripetal, or as the two opposite poles constitute each other, and are the constituent acts of one and the same power in the magnet (pp. 49-50).

As with Schelling and Hegel, Coleridge's commitment to total system in philosophy led him necessarily to account for—or to attempt to account for—the relationship of nature to mind, of the inanimate to the animate. Accordingly, his own version of *Naturphilosophie*, although one of the three necessary realms addressed by the putative *magnum opus* (as was also true for the parallel but quite independent organization of Hegel's *Enzyklopädie*) finds its fullest sketch in the actually written but posthumously published treatise from which we have just been quoting, the *Hints Towards the Formation of a More Comprehensive Theory of Life*. In that essay, the principle of polarity, as was the case for the Schellingian school, became the key to the understanding of natural reality. "What is the most general law," queries Coleridge, for the tendency to individuation:

> I answer—*polarity*, or the essential dualism of Nature, arising out of its productive unity, and still tending to reaffirm it, either as equilibrium, indifference, or identity (p. 50).

His sense of systolic and diastolic flux is similar both to that of Goethe and to that of Schelling and his followers:

Thus, in the identity of the two counter-powers, Life *sub*sists; in their strife it *con*sists: and in their reconciliation it at once dies and is born again into a new form, either falling back into the life of the whole, or starting anew in the process of individuation (pp. 51-52).

Again:

the whole *actual* life of Nature originates in the existence, and consists in the perpetual reconciliation, and as perpetual re-surgency of the primary contradiction, of which universal polarity is the result and the exponent (p. 70).

He links *Polarität* and *Steigerung* as emphatically as do any of his continental compeers:

my opinions will be best explained by a rapid exemplification in the processes of Nature, from the first rudiments of individualized life in the lowest classes of its two great poles, the vegetable and animal creation, to its crown and consummation in the human body; thus illustrating at once the unceasing *polarity of life, as the form of its process, and its tendency to progressive individuation as the law of its direction* (p. 67).

As such quotations indicate, Coleridge was working in the spirit of his time no less wholeheartedly than were his German contemporaries. Indeed, if the Romantic era was in some fundamental sense inaugurated and characterized by the French Revolution and its reverberations, then it could also be complementarily defined as an allegiance to new theories of dynamic process, and in particular to those associated with the phenomena of electrical polarity; and it is entirely typical of Coleridge's unusual cultural sensitivity that he was able to see this twin truth with an accuracy usually afforded only by a much later historical perspective. "Henceforward," he writes of the emergence of electrical conceptions onto the intellectual scene,

the new path, thus brilliantly opened, became the common road to all departments of knowledge: and, to this moment, it has been pursued with an eagerness and almost epidemic enthusiasm which, scarcely less than its political revolutions, characterise the spirit of the age (p. 32).

A revealing illustration of the "eagerness and almost epidemic enthusiam" with which electrical polarity was pursued is supplied by a treatise published at Giessen in 1819 by a minor investigator named Johann Bernhard Wilbrand. Called—I cite the title at length in order to indicate the comprehensiveness of the treatment—*Das Gesetz des polaren Verhaltens in der Natur; dargestellt in den magnetischen, electrischen und chemischen Naturerscheinungen; in dem Verhalten der unorganischen Natur zur organischen Schöpfung; in den Erscheinungen des Pflanzen- und Thierlebens; in dem Verhalten unsers Weltkörpers zu dem umgebenden Planetensystem*, it plods with Teutonic thoroughness through almost every conceivable variation of polar relationship.[70] Part of the volume's interest lies in its fullness; a still larger part, at least in terms of the contextual interrelationships addressed by this chapter, lies in the fact that it is not, as one might suspect, an offshoot of Schellingian *Naturphilosophie*; nor again of Hegelian systematizing; nor still again of Goethe's morphological speculations. Indeed, Schelling, Hegel, and Goethe are not even mentioned; the book instead is a contribution to "the founding of a scientific physiology," and is dedicated to "physicists, physiologists, and scientific physicians." Its reference is to scientific writers all over Europe—Galvani, Volta, Alexander von Humboldt, and a host of other actual scientists.

Although the treatise acknowledges no debt to the figures with whom we have been most concerned, it takes up, in explicit fullness, most of the emphases—excepting those exclusively philosophical—that we have encountered. For instance, after an introduction tracing the "development of the concept of polarity," it begins, predictably enough, with a first chapter entitled "Polar Relation in the Phenomena of Magnetism." The second chapter is called "Polar Relation in the Phenomena of Electricity." The third is "Polar Relation in the Phenomena of the Chemical Process," while the succeeding chapter, "Reciprocal Relation of Magnetic, Electrical and Chemical Phenomena," is divided into three sections: "Comparison of Magnetic Polarity with Electrical Polarity"; "Comparison of Electrical Polarity with the Chemical"; and "Comparison of Magnetism with the Chemical Process."[71] By the eighth

[70] Wilbrand defines "the characteristics of the concept of polarity" by three related criteria: "(1) an opposition between two, which reciprocally presuppose one another, and where the one has a real meaning only in opposition to the other; (2) inner unity of this opposition in a third, which (3) as a unity of a peculiar kind owes its existence to the opposition and would not exist without the opposition" (Wilbrand, p. 12).

[71] With reference to the emphasis of these three divisions of Wilbrand's fourth chapter, compare Coleridge: "we revert again to potentiated length in the power of magnetism; to surface in the power of electricity; and to the synthesis of both, or

chapter, "Polar Relation in the Functions of Animal Life in General," we encounter subheadings such as "Nourishment, Respiration, Circulation"; and by the tenth we are presented with the polar relation of seasonal changes. In short, this is a work that in its preoccupation with electrical science as a model for universal polarity truly incorporates "the spirit of the age" and amply justifies Coleridge's words about "eagerness and epidemic enthusiasm."

As a defining component of the spirit of the age, polarity was naturally enough conceived in varying forms and in differing contexts. If we revert to our earlier metaphor of a textured fabric, we may see the Romantic tapestry not only as one in which polarity's strands weave themselves into symmetrically repeated figures, but also as one in which certain patterns appear but once; as one in which not only the three primary colorations, so to speak, of subject/object logic, attraction/repulsion dynamic, and—most important of all—magnetic analogy are evident but also in which secondary shadings and blendings occur. Thus, to take an example of a special patterning, the "demonic," a conception that was among Goethe's most personal intellectual emphases, rested on a unique version of the principle of polarity. "He thought," runs the passage in *Dichtung und Wahrheit*, "to discover something in nature, both as animate and inanimate, as souled and unsouled, that manifested itself only in contradictions and accordingly could be comprehended under no concept, still less under a word. It was not divine, for it seemed irrational; not human, for it had no understanding; not devilish, for it was beneficent. . . . This being (*Wesen*), that seemed to step in between all the rest, to part them, to combine them, I called demonic (*dämonisch*), after the example of the ancients."[72]

No less idiosyncratic than Goethe's conception of the demonic was Coleridge's conception of the state as depending on a polarity of permanence and progression. "The two antagonist powers or opposite interests of the state, under which all other state interests are comprised," he writes in *On the Constitution of the Church and State*, "are those of PERMANENCE and of PROGRESSION." To this declaration he appends a footnote in which with characteristic subtlety

---

potentiated depth, in constructive, that is, chemical affinity"; ". . . in the present state of science, the magnetic, electric, and chemical powers are the last and highest of inorganic nature" (*Theory of Life*, pp. 56, 59). Coleridge's treatise was almost certainly composed a few years before the appearance of Wilbrand's.

[72] *Gedenkausgabe*, x, 839-40.

he attempts to discriminate different forms of a general theory of oppositions:

> Permit me to draw your attention to the essential difference between *opposite* and *contrary*. Opposite powers are always of the same kind, and tend to union, either by equipoise or by a common product. Thus the + and − poles of the magnet, thus positive and negative electricity are opposites. Sweet and sour are opposites; sweet and bitter are contraries. . . . Even so in the present instance, the interest of permanence is opposed to that of progressiveness; but so far from being contrary interests, they, like the magnetic forces, suppose and require each other. Even the most mobile of creatures, the serpent, makes a *rest* of its own body, and drawing up its voluminous train from behind on this fulcrum, propels itself onward. On the other hand, it is a proverb in all languages, that (relatively to man at least) what would stand still must retrograde.

The doctrine of polarity runs all through Coleridge's political awareness. Indeed, not even Marx himself conceived political realities in a more insistently dialectic opposition than did Coleridge:

> We have thus divided the subjects of the state into two orders, the agricultural or possessors of land; and the merchant, manufacturer, the distributive, and the professional bodies, under the common name of citizens.

That polar archetype, the magnet, is repeatedly invoked as metaphorical underpinning of Coleridge's most fundamental political conceptions:

> In order to correct views respecting the constitution, in the more enlarged sense of the term, viz. the constitution of the *Nation*, we must, in addition to a grounded knowledge of the *State*, have the right idea of the *National Church*. These are the two poles of same magnet; the magnet itself, which is constituted by them, is the CONSTITUTION of the nation. [73]

As with individual patterns of realization, so with subsidiary

---

[73] *Church and State*, pp. 24, 26, 31. Elsewhere he speaks eloquently of "the contest between the two great moving Principles of social Humanity—religious adherence to the Past and the Ancient, the Desire & the admiration of Permanence, on the one hand; and the Passion for increase of Knowlege, for Truth as the offspring of Reason, in short, the mighty Instincts of *Progression* and *Free-agency*, on the other" (*Collected Letters*, v, 35).

strands in the historical provenance of Romantic concern with po-
larity. To the three major derivations noted above, one may add
two important but somewhat less culturally dispersed ones. The
first reflects the single influence of Spinoza. That philosopher had
observed that to define any object of thought, the conception of
negativity must be invoked—that is to say, to recognize that any-
thing is something, it must simultaneously be recognized that it is
not something else—and he expressed this insight in the formula
determinatio negatio est.[74] To Hegel, this was an insight of the most
profound importance. " 'Determinateness is negation posited af-
firmatively,' is the meaning of Spinoza's *omnis determinatio est
negatio*," he said: "this proposition is of infinite importance."[75]
"Determination is negation is the absolute principle of Spinoza's
philosophy," he said again.[76] It was also, in truth, the absolute
principle of his own insight; for the realization that being (*Sein*) and
nothing (*Nichts*) are one and the same is authenticated precisely by
the conception of *determinatio negatio est*, and this both Hegel and
his followers well understood. As Schopenhauer later remarked,
with the sarcasm that was inevitable whenever he referred to
Hegel, the vagueness and ambiguity of Spinoza

> did not prevent the Neo-Spinozists of our own day from taking
> all that he said as gospel. Of these the Hegelians, of whom there
> are actually still a few, are particularly amusing by their tradi-
> tional reverence for his proposition *omnis determinatio est negatio*.
> At this, in accordance with the charlatan spirit of the school, they
> put on a face as if it were able to shake the world to its founda-
> tions.[77]

Whether or not it shook the world, the formula did manage to ex-
press in a single concept a necessary polarity as the condition of
existence.

The second of these subsidiary historical strands in the transmis-
sion of the doctrine of polarity descended from thinkers of the
Renaissance, especially from a nucleus that included Bruno (and
Schelling's title of 1802, *Bruno*, perhaps serves as a single adequate
reminder of the Nolan philosopher's importance for Romanticism),
Nicholas of Cusa, Paracelsus, and Boehme.[78] As a commentator
has said of their differing versions of polarity,

[74] *Spinoza*, IV, 240.   [75] *Hegel's Werke*, III, 117.
[76] *Ibid.*, IV, 194.   [77] Schopenhauer, III, 96.
[78] A third major strand of pre-Romantic polar thought does not weave itself into
the center of Romantic concern, but its transformation for modern possibilities is so

the doctrine of the *coincidentia oppositorum* is as little a passing insight for Nicholas of Cusa as is the unity of microcosmos and macrocosmos, despite all tension, for Paracelsus, or the unity of light and dark, good and bad, etc. for Boehme; rather their thought's whole nature and being is thoroughly interpenetrated

---

very important—indeed, it vies with Newton's third law (see below, note 88) in its indispensability for the future of mankind—that it demands at least the notice of a footnote. The whole theory of modern computer science depends upon Leibniz's mathematical theory of binary oppositions (that all numbers can be represented by only two ciphers, 1 and 0) which he first propounded in 1679; and this mathematical theory was cherished by him as a development from and illustration of the Christian theological essential that God created the world out of nothing (for ancient background to the *creatio ex nihilo* as a philosophical and theological contention, see Gerhard May, *Schöpfung aus dem Nichts; Die Entstehung der Lehre von der Creatio ex Nihilo* [Berlin, New York: Walter de Gruyter, 1978]). Thus Leibniz entitled a paper of May 1696, in which he mathematically demonstrated the binary system, "Mira Numerorum omnium expressio per 1 et 0, repraesentans rerum originem ex Deo et Nihilo seu Mysterium creationis," and to a German redaction of the same paper, he prefixed "Unum necessarium, 1, 0, Nichts außer Eins" (in 1459, Nicholas of Cusa had said in his *De principio* that "Hoc unum necessarium vocatur Deus, ut dicebatur ISRAELI: '*Audi, Israel, Deus tuus unum est . . .*' "). Shortly afterward Leibniz became aware of the congruence between his binary system and the polar thought of the *I Ching*, and he welcomed this ancient confirmation: "But my principal goal has been . . . to furnish you with a new confirmation of the Christian religion with regard to the sublime article of creation by a fundamental that in my opinion will be of great importance with the philosophers of China. . . . To say simply that all numbers are formed by the combinations of unity with nothing, and that nothing suffices to diversify them, this seems as believable as to say that God has made all things out of nothing, without availing himself of any primal matter, and that there are only two prime principles, God and nothing! God for perfections, and nothing for imperfections or vacuities of essence." Later, Leibniz wrote to another correspondent that "by a marvelous encounter, it turns out that my mode of binary arithmetic, new to us in Europe, has been known from FOHY, who lived there more than four thousand years ago, and who is considered the founder of sciences and of the empire of China" (Hans J. Zacher, *Die Hauptschriften zur Dyadik von G. W. Leibniz; Ein Beitrag zur Geschichte des binären Zahlensystems* [Frankfurt am Main: Vittorio Klostermann, 1973], pp. 225, 229, 49, 247, 289). For extended discussion of the doctrine of polarity in Chinese thought one should of course consult Needham's majestic work, e.g.: 'The scientific or proto-scientific ideas of the Chinese involved two fundamental principles or forces in the universe, the Yin and the Yang, negative and positive projections of man's own sexual experience; and five 'elements' of which all process and all substance was composed." "As we have seen, the two fundamental forces are not mentioned in any of the surviving fragments of Tsou Yen, though his school was called the Yin-Yang Chia. . . . There can be very little doubt that the philosophical use of the terms began about the beginning of the -4th century. . . . Etymologically the characters are certainly connected with darkness and light respectively. The character Yin . . . involves graphs for hill (-shadows) and clouds; the character Yang has slanting sunrays or a flag fluttering in the sunshine. . . . Those who have

and supported by the doctrine of contrariety, which is for them the root and the basic experience out of which all individual things arise.[79]

One example of how subtly and variously the emphases of these thinkers pervaded Romanticism may be supplied by noting a passage in Coleridge in which Paracelsus's microcosm/macrocosm polarity blooms once again. Near the end of his *Theory of Life*, Coleridge comments that

> Man possesses the most perfect osseous structure, the least and most insignificant covering. The whole force of organic power has attained an inward and centripetal direction. He has the whole world in counterpoint to him, but he contains an entire world within himself. Now, for the first time at the apex of the living pyramid, it is Man and Nature, but Man himself is a syllepsis, a compendium of Nature—the Microcosm![80]

Despite the presumed lodgment of this discussion in the matrix of contemporary nineteenth-century biological argumentation, and especially in the *Naturphilosophie* of the speculative scientists of the Schellingian school, the passage is actually simply a restatement of the fundamentals of Paracelsus's position. Paracelsus—who considered himself "not an apostle or anything like an apostle, but a philosopher in the German manner" (*ein philosophus nach der teutschen art*)[81]—says, for instance, that

> The Great World, the macrocosm, is closed in itself in such a way that nothing can leave it, but that everything that is of it and

---

studied the first appearance of the words as philosophical terms find the *locus classicus* in the fifth chapter of the fifth appendix of the *I Ching* (the Hsi Tzhu; the 'Great Appendix'), where the statement is made 'One Yin and One Yang; that is the Tao.' (*I Yin i Yang chih wei Tao*). The general sense must be that there are only these two fundamental forces or operations in the universe, now one dominating, now the other, in a wave-like succession. This appendix would date (at the earliest) from the late Warring States period (early -3rd century)." (Joseph Needham, *Science and Civilisation in China*, II [Cambridge: Cambridge University Press, 1975 (1956)], 279, 273-74).

[79] Theodor Haering, "Cusanus-Paracelsus-Böhme. Ein Beitrag zur geistigen Ahnenforschung unsrer Tage," *Zeitschrift für deutsche Kulturphilosophie*, ed. Hermann Glockner and Karl Larenz, II (1935), 19.

[80] *Theory of Life*, p. 85. For Coleridge's knowledge of Paracelsus see, e.g., *Collected Letters*, IV, 973-74; *Notebooks*, III, 3616, 3616n., 3660. For discussion see Kathleen Coburn, *Experience into Thought; Perspectives in the Coleridge Notebooks*, the Alexander Lectures (Toronto: University of Toronto Press, 1979), pp. 35-39.

[81] *Paracelsus*, II, 1, 76.

within it remains complete and undivided. Such is the Great World. Next to it subsists the Little World, that is to say, man. He is enclosed in a skin, to the end that his blood, his flesh, and everything he is as a man may not be mixed with that Great World. . . . For one would destroy the other. Therefore man has a skin; it delimits the shape of the human body, and through it he can distinguish the two worlds from each other—the Great World and the Little World, the world and man—and can keep separate that which must not mingle.[82]

For Paracelsus the opposition of macrocosm and microcosm is polar, that is to say, each member is necessary to a unity that exists only by their opposition: "The mysteries of the Great and the Little World are distinguished only by the form in which they manifest themselves; for they are only *one* thing, *one* being."[83] Likewise, Coleridge's opposition of "Man and Nature," in which "Man himself is a syllepsis, a compendium of Nature—the Microcosm," is virtually identical to Paracelsus's insistence that "No brain can fully encompass the structure of man's body and the extent of his virtues; he can be understood only as an image of the macrocosm. . . . For what is outside is also inside, and what is not outside man is not inside. The outer and the inner are *one* thing, *one* constellation."[84]

Although all the Renaissance figures mentioned above—and others as well—were known in the Romantic era, not all were equally familiar to each philosophical or literary expositor of polarity; and consequently, when isolating strands of influence, we should be aware of interstices of stitching. For instance, Goethe, despite his consuming preoccupation with polarity, does not seem to have known Nicholas of Cusa and the *coincidentia oppositorum* of that thinker;[85] he paid special attention, on the other hand, to Telesio's doctrine of contraries.[86] Again, Barron Field, Wordsworth's friend and commentator, in discoursing of "the real peculiarity of Mr Wordsworth's poetical theory," cites "the philosophical dogma of Thomas Campanella, an Italian writer of the early part of the seventeenth century," and quotes Campanella as maintaining that

Contrariety is necessary for the decay and reproduction of Na-

[82] *Ibid.*, I, 9, 178. [83] *Ibid.*, I, 8, 280.
[84] *Ibid.*, I, 8, 180.
[85] See Ernst Hoffman, "Nikolaus von Cues und die deutsche Philosophie," *Neue Heidelberger Jahrbücher*, new series (1940), pp. 35-76, especially p. 52 n. 27.
[86] *Gedenkausgabe*, XVI, 397-98.

ture; but all things strive against their contraries, which they could not do, if they did not perceive what is their contrary.[87]

It may be said in general, however, that such minor figures as Campanella and Telesio, and even major figures such as Nicholas of Cusa and Paracelsus, were less important in the provenance of the Romantic doctrine of polarity than was Jacob Boehme (who was himself, like Bruno, obligated both to Cusanus and to Paracelsus). Speaking of Boehme's "influence on romanticism and occultist currents," Berdyaev has said that "Boehme is the fountainhead of the dynamism of German philosophy, one might even say of the dynamism of the entire thought of the nineteenth century. He was the first to conceive cosmic life as an impassioned battle, as a movement, as a process, as an eternal genesis."[88] Indeed, it is to Boehme that Blake seems to have looked more or less exclusively for his own awareness of the principle of contrariety; and Coleridge, too, through the same English translations that were available to Blake, was fully cognizant of Boehme's thought.[89] In that thought, the principle of contrariety receives repeated emphasis, as, for instance:

[87] Field, p. 120.
[88] Berdyaev, p. xxxiii. One of the most intriguing aspects of Boehme's possible influence is the question of whether or not Newton derived from him the third law of motion, which is undoubtedly the most important of all conceptions of polarity. Newton's third law states that "To every action there is always opposed an equal reaction or the mutual actions of two bodies on each other are always equal and directed to contrary parts" (*Isaac Newton's Philosophiae Naturalis Principia Mathematica* . . . ed. Alexandre Koyré and I. Bernard Cohen [Cambridge, Mass.: Harvard University Press, 1972], I, 55)—and this of course provides the basis, among other realities, for all future exploration of outer space. In 1742, several years after Newton's death, William Law wrote in a letter to a friend that "When Sir Isaac Newton died, there was found among his papers large abstracts out of Behmen's works written in his own hand," and in another statement Law said flatly that "the illustrious Sir Isaac ploughed with Behmen's heifer." In the absence of confirming documentation, however, the matter has remained problematic. For the conclusion that Boehme did not influence Newton, see, e.g., Stephen Hobhouse, "Isaac Newton and Jacob Boehme," *Philosophia; philosophorum nostri temporis vox universa*, ed. Dr. Arthur Liebert, II (1937), 25-54. For the conclusion, on the other hand, that Boehme did influence Newton, see, e.g., Karl Popp, *Jakob Böhme und Isaac Newton* (Leipzig: Hirzel, 1935).
[89] The English translations were published as *The Works of Jacob Behmen, the Teutonic Theosopher . . . with Figures, illustrating his principles*, left by the Reverend William Law, M.A. (London, 1764-81). Coleridge annotated a set of these important and rather rare volumes, now in the British Museum, and the marginalia, which occupy approximately 150 pages, were apparently composed over a number of

Nothing without contrariety can become manifest to itself; for it it has nothing to resist it, it goes continually of itself outwards, and returns not again into itself.

Again, from the same treatise:

were there no contrariety in life, there would be no sensibility, nor will, nor efficacy therein, also neither understanding nor science. For a thing that has only one will has no divisibility. If it finds not a contrary will, which gives occasion to its exercising motion, it stands still.[90]

The similarity between the contention of this passage, and Blake's "without contraries there is no progression," is obvious.[91]

Just as the Renaissance traditions of contrariety and coinciding opposites, especially as vitalized by Boehme, became only slightly less important a stimulus to Romantic theories of polarity than those supplied by electrical experimenters or by Kant, so too were there in use illustrative images only scarcely less important than that supplied by the magnet. Chief among them was probably that of the division of human sexuality into male and female, and both Schelling and Hegel found in this phenomenon illustration for their respective conceptions of polarity and dialectic.[92] As Wilbrand observed,

---

years—1808 to 1827 might be a reasonable supposition. See further *CPT*, "Excursus Note XIX: Coleridge and Boehme," pp. 325-32.

[90] Boehme, IV, 167, 168 (*Von göttlicher Beschaulichkeit*).

[91] Behind Boehme, however, lies Paracelsus, who also realizes that progression depends on polarity, e.g.: "But the seed of a single man does not yet make a complete man. God wills to make a man out of two, and not out of one; he wills man composed of two and not of one alone. For if man were born of the seed of one individual, he would not change in nature" (*Paracelsus*, I, 1, 262-63). As a commentator observes: "I believe Blake to have been influenced not only by the enormous figures of Paracelsus and Boehme whose thought was so important that whole literatures grew up around it and generations of men and women in Europe were affected by it: but by some of their humbler followers also" (Hirst, p. 303).

[92] See, e.g., Haering, I, 677 ff. But the illustration was so inevitable that it occurred everywhere—for instance, one of the section headings in the second chapter of the second book of Müller's *Die Lehre vom Gegensatze* is "Mann und Weib." Again, D. H. Lawrence, who, though not a scholar of the Romantic movement, was so entirely the unconscious heir of Romanticism as to be virtually a twentieth-century avatar of that sensibility, repeatedly invokes polarity in his discussions of sexuality, e.g., "What is sex, really? We can never say, satisfactorily. But we know so much: we know that it is a dynamic polarity between human beings, and a circuit of force *always* flowing. . . . There can be no vivid relation between two adult individuals which does not consist in a dynamic polarized flow of vitalistic force or magnetism

there exists between the two sexes, as far as reciprocal need is concerned, the same relation that obtains between magnetic or electrical polarity. Just as a magnetic polarity, as merely northern, or merely southern, is actually unthinkable, but rather the two reciprocally presuppose each other, so is it certainly true that a merely male or merely female sex is not only contrary to appearance in the whole of nature, but also unthinkable, because the female is female only in contrast to the male, and vice versa.[93]

Wilbrand further argues that woman cannot be considered an inferior or incomplete man, because such an hypothesis violates the structure of polarity: that "just as a polar relation cannot fail to be recognized between male and female," by the same token "it cannot be doubted that in each sex human nature is given perfect in itself."

Among the variations of the sexual metaphor, two, that of the androgyne, and that of elective affinity, deserve special note. The former was part of the heritage of antiquity, and a *locus classicus* is of course the myth of Aristophanes in Plato's *Symposium*.[94] But among the Renaissance progenitors of Romantic polarity, androgyny was a specific and recurrent feature of the thought of Paracelsus. Thus he speaks of "the *rebis*—the bisexual creature—that makes gold out of silver and out of other metals";[95] and his commentator, Yolande Jacobi, glosses the term as follows:

---

or electricity, call it what you will, between these two people"; "But what is this experience? Untellable. Only, we know something. We know that in the act of coition the *blood* of the individual man, acutely surcharged with intense vital electricity . . . rises to a culmination, in a tremendous magnetic urge towards the magnetic blood of the female. The whole of the living blood in the two individuals forms a field of intense, polarized magnetic attraction. So, the two poles must be brought into contact." (*Fantasia of the Unconscious* [London: Martin Secker, 1923], pp. 95, 196).

[93] Wilbrand, pp. 269-70.

[94] *Symposium* 189D-193D, especially 189D-E. In later aspects of ancient thought, the androgynous conception became essential to the cosmological speculations of Gnosticism, e.g.: "So there is a bisexual power and conception. . . . Being one is found to be two, a male-and-female being having the female within it"; "But after this they called themselves gnostics, alleging that they alone 'knew the deep things.' . . . These men, according to their own doctrine, reverence beyond all others Man and the Son of Man. Now this Man is bisexual and is called by them Adamas" (*Gnosis; A Selection of Gnostic Texts*, ed. Werner Foerster, trans. R. McL. Wilson [Oxford: The Clarendon Press, 1972-74], I, 260, 263).

[95] *Paracelsus*, I, 3, 141.

REBIS. The hermaphrodite, or bisexual being; in its unity, that is to say, by combining the two antitheses, the male and the female principle, it represents, in accordance with an old alchemistic idea, the highest and most desirable degree of the process of transmutation—totality.[96]

Such a polar variation was carried into Romanticism by the occultist currents so ably elucidated by scholars like Viatte; and probably its most recurrent appearance is in the work of Franz von Baader, Boehme's most devoted Romantic disciple.

To limit ourselves to perhaps the single most intriguing illustration of its currency, however, we must turn our attention to a curious late-Romantic French cult called *Évadanistes*. The doctrine of *Évadisme* derived its name from an amalgam of Adam and Eve, and as a commentator says,

It was an androgynous religion composed of male and female elements, and, to compensate for the humble part she had hitherto played in the religions of the world, her name, Eve, came first. The leader—or prophet—of this new religion was a man called Ganneau who styled himself *Le Mapah*—a name made from the first syllable of *maman* and the first syllable of *papa*.

In one of the *Mapah*'s "platras," or printed proclamations of religious androgyny, it is said that

Mary is no longer the Mother. She is the wife. Jesus Christ is no longer the son. He is the husband.

"Finally," continues the commentator,

the *Mapah* greets them both together as the great symbol, the personification of unity in duality, under one name *Androgyn-Évadam*.

'Humanity is now constituted for the great betrothal.
The hour of human virility has come.
The era of *Évadah* is at hand.
Hosannah!'[97]

The sexual, and even the androgynous, illustration of polarity was not entirely absent from the thought of Coleridge and of

[96] *Paracelsus; Selected Writings*, ed. Yolande Jacobi, trans. Norbert Guterman (New York: Pantheon Books, 1951), p. 331.
[97] Starkie, pp. 50-54.

Wordsworth, though it was not a large factor. Thus the *Mapah's* "great betrothal" is to some extent analogous to the polar union of Wordsworth's "great consummation" of nature and the mind of man, for which the "spousal verse" of *The Recluse* would chant the celebration.[98] And *Christabel's* Geraldine is sexually ambivalent (we recall Coleridge's indignation at Hazlitt's bruiting it about that Geraldine was in fact a man).[99] On more than one occasion, moreover, Coleridge observed that the feminine was an important element in the finest masculine natures. "The truth is," he said at one point, "a great mind must be androgynous."[100]

But more widespread than the metaphor of androgyny was that of elective affinity. The interest in this latter conception stemmed from a work of 1775 by the Swedish chemist, Torbern Bergman, entitled *De attractionibus electivis*, which, Germanized, became the title of Goethe's novel of human relationships published in 1809 as *Die Wahlverwandschaften*. As the author of the latter work told Riemer, "the moral symbols in the natural sciences (for example that of elective affinity discovered and used by the great Bergmann [*sic*]) are more spiritual, and allow themselves to be combined with poetry, indeed with society, above all others."[101]

Goethe was by no means the only Romantic figure to be intrigued by the scientific affinities of acids and alkalis. Hegel devoted philosophical consideration to elective affinity (*Wahlverwandtschaft*) in both the *Enzyklopädie*[102] and the *Wissenschaft der Logik*. In the latter, after arguing that musical harmonies are forms of elective affinity, he proceeds to a lengthy discussion of chemical affinities, based on the recent investigations of Berthollet, Johann Wilhelm Ritter, and Berzelius. Significantly for our interests in this chapter, he entertains the possibility not only that "every chemical effect is ultimately an electrical phenomenon but also that what appears to be the effect of so-called elective affinity is really brought about only by an electrical polarity which is stronger in

---

[98] Wordsworth, *Poems*, v, 4-5 (ll. 57-68).

[99] *Collected Letters*, IV, 918.

[100] *Table Talk*, p. 183 (Sept. 1, 1832). For additional discussion of the androgyne in Romantic conceiving see, e.g., Mircea Eliade, *The Two and the One*, trans. J. M. Cohen (Chicago: The University of Chicago Press, 1979), especially the section called "Mephistopheles and the Androgyne or The Mystery of the Whole" (pp. 78-124).

[101] *Gedenkausgabe*, xxII, 565. Bergman's work was translated into English in 1785, under the title *A Dissertation on Elective Attractions*, and the translator, Dr. Thomas Beddoes, was later to become a friend of Coleridge.

[102] *Hegel's Werke*, vII, i, 405-410.

some bodies than in others."[103] Wilbrand, working independently of Hegel, is more positive: "the doctrine of chemical affinity, and elective affinity (*chemischen Verwandtschaft, und Wahlverwandtschaft*) rests solely and singly on a polar relationship between the substances."[104]

How widely disseminated was the interest in this version of polarity is indicated by the unforgettable scene in *Madame Bovary* where Rodolphe conducts a seduction of Emma while both are listening from within the town hall to the speech of an official outside. In high Romantic fashion, Rodolphe discourses to Emma of "dreams, presentiments, magnetism"; and then he proceeds to "the affinities":

> From magnetism, Rodolphe little by little by little came to the affinities, and, while the president was citing Cincinnatus at his plow, Diocletian planting his cabbages, and the emperors of China inaugurating the year by the sowing of seed, the young man was explaining to the young woman that these irresistible attractions drew their cause from some previous existence.[105]

The "magnétisme" invoked by Rodolphe's sexual design encompassed not only the electrical phenomenon with which the era was so fascinated but also the all but equal fascination with Mesmerism, or "animal magnetism." The importance of this latter vogue for the late eighteenth and nineteenth centuries can hardly be overestimated;[106] and animal magnetism, like the affinities, seemed to be still another of the reasons for thinking, in the speculative intoxication of early Romanticism, that nature and spirit were but polar aspects of a common unity. Indeed, as a recent commentator has said,

> Of the many systems for bringing the world into focus, mesmerism had most in common with the vitalistic theories that had multiplied since the time of Paracelsus. Indeed, Mesmer's opponents spotted his scientific ancestry almost immediately. They showed that, far from revealing any new discoveries or ideas, his system descended directly from those of Paracelsus, J. B. van Helmont, Robert Fludd, and William Maxwell, who presented

---

[103] *Ibid.*, III, 430-31, 443.   [104] Wilbrand, p. 56.

[105] Flaubert, *Madame Bovary*, Part Two, Chapter VIII.

[106] See, e.g., Fred Kaplan, *Dickens and Mesmerism; The Hidden Springs of Fiction* (Princeton: Princeton University Press, 1975), especially "The Mesmeric Mania," pp. 3-33.

health as a state of harmony between the individual microcosm and the celestial macrocosm, involving fluids, human magnets, and occult influences of all sorts.[107]

Furthermore, as the same commentator notes, Mesmer himself explicitly utilized the conception of magnetic polarity in his own practice:

> Mesmer and his followers put on fascinating performances: they sat with the patient's knees enclosed between their own and ran their fingers all over the patient's body, seeking the poles of the small magnets that composed the great magnet of the body as a whole (p. 4).

Wilbrand, for his part, though unwilling as a scientist to speak too confidently about the inner truth of Mesmerism—and awake also to the possibilities that Mesmerism presented to the charlatan—observes that

> rapport occurs only between the magnetiser and the magnetised person, and it is established with a third person only when he enters into contact with the magnetiser, which points, as it were, to a linear relation similar to that which obtains in genuine magnetic phenomena. Likewise, the inner blending of the magnetised person with the magnetiser is similar to the inner blending of the two polar directions of a real magnet.[108]

Another major invocation of polarity and the coincidence of opposites in the Romantic period, but this one having to do with literary rather than with scientific issues was constituted by the adoption of the reconciliation of opposites as a guiding principle of art. Although both Schelling and Hegel adopted polarity as a principle of their aesthetic theories, it is perhaps true that no single German thinker applied polarity as unequivocally to literary definition as did Victor Hugo. In his *Préface de Cromwell* of 1827, a document that lies at the very heart of the French Romantic sensibility, Hugo incorporated the spirit of the age into a manifesto that proclaimed that "true poetry, complete poetry, is in the harmony of opposites."[109]

The necessity for the "harmonie des contraires" arises in Hugo's view, out of the fragmented nature of our reality and experience, as witnessed and influenced by Christianity:

---

[107] Darnton, p. 14.
[109] Hugo, *Théâtre*, I, 425.

[108] Wilbrand, pp. 276-77.

We come to see how . . . Christianity profoundly separates the breath from the matter. It puts an abysm between the soul and the body, an abysm between man and God (p. 414).

Because our experience is one of separation and sundering, the role of art, following Christianity, is to rejoin the original elements:

> Christianity leads poetry to truth. Like it, the modern muse will see things in a higher and larger glance. She will perceive that everything in creation is not humanly *beautiful*, that the ugly exists by the side of the beautiful, the deformed near the gracious, the grotesque on the reverse of the sublime, the evil with the good, the shadow with the light (p. 416).

Again:

> She will begin to create like nature, to mingle in her creations without however confounding them, the shadow with the light, the grotesque with the sublime . . . the body with the soul, the animal nature with the spirit; for the point of departure of religion is always the point of departure of poetry. Everything hangs together (p. 416).

We live as the heirs of Christianity, says Hugo, and Christianity assumes that man is double, composed of two beings, one mortal and one immortal: "From the day that Christianity has said to man: 'Thou art double, thou art composed of two beings . . .'; from this day drama has been created" (p. 425).

Drama is therefore the necessary form of modern art: "the poetry born of Christianity, the poetry of our time, is therefore drama; the character of the drama is the real; the real results from the natural combination of two types, the sublime and the grotesque" (p. 425). Having erected this arch of theory, Hugo—in true Romantic fashion—finds Shakespeare the keystone and completion. Shakespeare, he says, united the genius of Homer and the sublime with that of Dante and the grotesque:

> We have here arrived at the poetic summit of modern times. Shakespeare is drama, and drama incorporates in the same breath the grotesque and the sublime, the terrible and the ridiculous, tragedy and comedy (p. 422).

The "harmonie des contraires" that for Hugo is so perfectly exemplified by Shakespeare is the same motif that Coleridge—the greatest Shakespearean critic of the day[110]—describes as constituting the poetic imagination itself:

> The poet, described in *ideal* perfection, brings the whole soul of man into activity, with the subordination of its faculties to each other, according to their relative worth and dignity. He diffuses a tone and spirit of unity, that blends, and (as it were) *fuses*, each into each, by that synthetic and magical power, to which we have exclusively appropriated the name of imagination. This power . . . reveals itself in the balance or reconciliation of opposite or discordant qualities: of sameness, with difference; of the general, with the concrete; the idea, with the image; the individual, with the representative; the sense of novelty and freshness, with old and familiar objects; a more than usual state of emotion, with more than usual order; judgement ever awake and steady self-possession, with enthusiasm and feeling profound or vehement; and while it blends and harmonizes the natural and the artificial, still subordinates art to nature; the manner to the matter; and our admiration of the poet to our sympathy with the poetry.[111]

[110] The doctrine of reconciled oppositions figures no less prominently in Coleridge's conceptions of drama and of Shakespeare than it does in those of Hugo. Shakespeare is characterized by "signal adherence to the great law of nature that opposites tend to attract and temper each other." The one great principle of dramatic illusion is "that ever-varying balance, or balancing, of images, notions, or feelings . . . conceived as in opposition to each other" (Samuel Taylor Coleridge, *Shakespearean Criticism*, ed. T. M. Raysor [London: Dent; New York: Dutton, 1960], I, 199, 181).

[111] *Biographia*, II, 12. The literary application of the doctrine of reconciled contraries was prefigured in the Renaissance as fully as were philosophical or scientific versions. For a single instance, Tasso, in his *Discorsi del poema eroico* of 1594, says that "the world that contains in its womb so many diverse things is one . . . and one the bond that links its many parts and ties them together in discordant concord, and nothing is missing; . . . just so, I judge the great poet (who is called divine for no other reason than that as he resembles the supreme Artificer in his workings he comes to participate in his divinity) can form a poem in which, as in a little world, one may read here of armies assembling, here of battles on land or sea . . . there discord, wanderings, adventures, enchantments. . . . Yet the poem that contains so great a variety of matters none the less should be one . . . and all these things should be so combined that each concerns the other . . . that removing any one part or changing its place would destroy the whole. And if that is true, the art of composing a poem resembles the plan of the universe, which is composed of contraries" (Torquato Tasso, *Discourses on the Heroic Poem*, trans. Mariella Cavalchini and Irene Samuel [Oxford: The Clarendon Press, 1973], p. 78).

The comprehensiveness of this justly famous passage in its deployment of the principle of polarity cannot readily be matched by any single *locus* in either French or German literature. But it was written entirely in the spirit of the time, and other poets than Coleridge and Hugo saw the "reconciliation of opposite or discordant qualities" and the "harmonie des contraires" as the first task of successful poetry. Hölderlin, to restrict ourselves to a single illustration, reveals, in some turbulent notes connected with *Empedokles*, how constantly the principle of polarity was working in his conception of what he was doing as a poet:

> . . . thus it is necessary that the poetic spirit in its concord and harmonic progress also provide itself an infinite point of view. . . a unity, where in harmonic progress and alternation everything may go forward and backward, and by its thoroughly characteristic relation to this unity may win not merely objective connection, for the onlooker, but also felt and tangible connection and identity in the alternation of the opposites, and it is its final task, to have a thread, a memory in the harmonic alternation, by which the spirit may remain present to itself, never in a single moment, and again in a single moment, but continuing in one moment as in another, and in differing moods.

Further down in this same seamless outpouring, which is entitled *Über die Verfahrungsweise des poetischen Geistes*, Hölderlin strikes off a veritable *glissando* of invocations of opposites and their reconciliation:

> . . . in der unendlichen Einheit, welche einmal Scheidepunct des Einigen als Einigen, dann aber auch Vereinigungspunct des Einigen als Entgegengesezten, endlich auch beedes zugleich ist, so daß in ihr das Harmonischentgegengesezte weder als Einiges entgegengesezt, noch als Entgegengeseztes vereinigt, sondern als beedes in Einem als einig entgegengesezetes unzertrennlich gefühlt, und als gefühltes erfunden wird. Dieser Sinn ist eigentlich poetischer Karakter.[112]

The "Harmonischentgegengesezte," the "harmonie des contraires," the "reconciliation of opposite or discordant qualities," summoned as criteria of poetry and the poetic imagination, serve to conclude this conspectus, where much has been necessarily shortened or omitted, of the major appearances of the doctrine of

[112] Hölderlin, IV, 251.

polarity in the Romantic era (we have not even alluded, for one of numerous instances, to Byron's commitment to polarity—"the great double Mysteries! the *two Principles*" [Cain, Act II, line 609]; nor have we done more than barely mention polarity's role in Wordsworth—"So meet extremes in this mysterious world,/ And opposites melt into each other" [*The Borderers*, lines 1529-30]). There has throughout been no attempt to observe nominal distinctions between doctrines of contrariety and those of polarity or other supposedly significant differentiations of formulation, none of which to my mind has a real basis in the ontology of the problem.

Rather than developing this contention, however (which one would like to think self-evident), I shall devote the remaining space, before venturing briefly to assess the deeper significance of polar commitments in the Romantic era, to elucidating three minor but not unimportant historical points about the ramification of the nineteenth-century's protean concern with contraries and oppositions.

First of all, it is necessary to realize that the polar commitment sometimes appeared in disguised or inexplicit forms. "The *naturphilosophisch*-romantic doctrine that life is an oscillation between two poles," says Ricarda Huch in an insight that isolates the point, "is to be applied literally to the vacillating wanderlust and longing of the Romantics between the geographical poles."[113] One thinks here not only of the actual voyagings of Romantic authors such as Byron, Nerval, or Lenau but even more directly of Coleridge's Mariner, journeying specifically to and from the polar region, with contrarieties of sun and moon, the dead and the living, as *basso ostinato* of his progress.

Secondly, it is necessary to realize that the concern with a dialectic of oppositions did not suddenly disappear with the demise, whenever that may supposedly have been, of Romanticism proper. For instance, J. J. Bachofen, who despite his sobriquet of "Mythologe der Romantiker" actually wrote in the middle decades of the nineteenth century, based both his mythological exegeses and his anthropological conjectures squarely upon the conception of dialectical oppositions and their synthesis. To cite a single example from his essay on mortuary symbolism:

We shall now attempt to elucidate the original idea underlying the connection between eggs and circus games. . . . Material life

[113] Huch, p. 383.

moves between two poles. Its realm is not that of being but that of becoming and passing away, the eternal alternation of two colors, the white of life and the black of death. Only through the equal mixture of the two is the survival of the material world assured. . . . Indeed, the positive power cannot for one moment exist without the negative power. Death, then, is not the opposite but the helper of life, just as the negative pole of magnetism is not the adversary of the positive pole but its necessary complement, without which the positive pole would vanish immediately, and life give way to nothingness.[114]

Bachofen, though active in the middle of the century, might still be considered a Romantic. Other invocations of the doctrine of contraries, however, by figures clearly beyond any usual description as Romantics, exist in profusion. For instance, a recent commentator compares Ruskin with Hegel: "there can be no doubt that Ruskin was a dialectical thinker." "If one major theme has been the unity of Ruskin's thought, another has been its progression by opposites. . . . In practice Ruskin tended to use contrasting terms which acted as separate but parallel categories, each category containing polarities of an idea within it. . . . If Ruskin's terminology is thought of as a series of polarities . . . the apparent contradictions in what he says about art become comprehensible. . . . His critical theories depend upon a series of dynamic opposites."[115] Again, Browning not only adopted a thesis-antithesis-synthesis structure for *The Ring and the Book* but also, in the view of a modern commentator, devotes one part of his poetic endeavor to arguing that "men fail when they do not admit the dual thrusts of their natures and recognize only one pole of the dialectic tension," and another part to depicting "man held in tension by a polarity of opposing thrusts."[116]

But the doctrine of oppositions persists with hardly less vigor in this century than it did in the nineteenth. Major figures like Yeats and minor ones like Eli Siegel provide familiar examples, and even Edwin Arlington Robinson on one occasion espoused a "system of 'opposites,' " which consisted in "creating a fictitious life in direct

[114] *Bachofen*, pp. 33-34.

[115] Robert Hewison, *John Ruskin; The Argument of the Eye* (Princeton: Princeton University Press, 1976), pp. 208, 202-203.

[116] Clyde de L. Ryals, *Browning's Later Poetry; 1871-1889* (Ithaca and London: Cornell University Press, 1975), pp. 115, 64.

opposition to a real life which I know."[117] Again, Freud's biographer points out that

Running all through his work there is what Heinz Hartmann has called "a very characteristic kind of dialectical thinking that tends to base theories on the interaction of two opposite powers." This was of course most pronounced in his basic classifications: love-hunger; ego-sexuality; auto-erotism–hetero-erotism; Eros-Thanatos; life-death, and so on. I remember how alien this seemed to me, having been brought up in a biological school that thought of instincts in the plural. But the same fondness for pairs is to be found again and again: love-hate, exhibitionism-scopophilism, etc. It is as if Freud had difficulty in contemplating any topic unless he could divide it into two opposites, and never more than two. That there was a fundamental conflict between two opposing forces in the mind was for him a basic fact.[118]

More recently a critic of Shakespeare, J. W. Lever, has argued that modern scholarship has "grasped a latent dualism, an acceptance of multiple oppositions and polarities, at the roots of Shakespeare's response to thought and experience," and that Shakespeare is characterized by "an artistic philosophy and a philosophical art, mutually interacting, alike sustained by the willing acceptance of contraries."[119]

Lever's contention, which is put forth in apparent oblivion of all that Shakespeare represented to the Romantic sensibility,[120] illustrates the third of our concluding remarks about the historical ramification of concerns with polarity: that is, it illustrates the phe-

[117] James G. Hepburn, "E. A. Robinson's System of Opposites," *PMLA*, 80 (1965), 266-74.

[118] G. Ernest Jones, *The Life and Work of Sigmund Freud* (New York: Basic Books, 1953-57), II, 422.

[119] J. W. Lever, "Shakespeare and the Ideas of his Time," *Shakespeare Survey 29*, ed. Kenneth Muir (Cambridge: Cambridge University Press, 1976), pp. 89, 91. For perhaps the best of modern studies that conceives Shakespeare's art in terms of polarity or "complementarity," see Norman Rabkin, *Shakespeare and the Common Understanding* (New York: The Free Press, 1967), e.g., p. 12: "Shakespeare tends to structure his imitations in terms of a pair of polar opposites"; "The technique of presenting a pair of opposed ideals or groups of ideals and putting a double valuation on each is the basis of Shakespeare's comedy as well as his tragedy."

[120] For a single reminder, cf. Hazlitt: "Shakespeare's imagination . . . unites the most opposite extremes. . . . From the remoteness of his combinations, and the celerity with which they are effected, they coalesce the more indissolubly together."

nomenon of recurrence. The historical dimension becomes—such is the peculiar intermixture of cultural transmission in the group experience and logical inevitability for an individual's own process of thought—the serpent with its tail in its mouth. As a single instance, we may take the figure of Heraclitus with whom Coleridge conceives the polar tradition to have begun, and who has otherwise seemed only tangential to the historical appearances of polar awareness.

Now Marx, as we probably all know, adopted, with certain qualifications, the polar logic of Hegelian dialectic:

> My dialectic method is not only different from the Hegelian, but is its direct opposite. To Hegel, the life-process of the human brain, i.e., the process of thinking . . . is the demiurgos of the real world, and the real world is only the external, phenomenal form of "the Idea." With me, on the contrary, the ideal is nothing else than the material world reflected by the human mind, and translated into forms of thought.
>
> The mystifying side of Hegelian dialectic I criticized nearly thirty years ago. . . . [Since then] I have openly avowed myself the pupil of that mighty thinker. . . . The mystification which dialectic suffers in Hegel's hands by no means prevents him from being the first to present its general form of working in a comprehensive and conscious manner. With him it is standing on its head. It must be turned right side up again.[121]

Thus Marx. From him, the principles of dialectical materialism were transmitted to Lenin. Lenin, however, subsequently came across Heraclitus and rediscovered him as an exemplar of dialectical materialism: "A very good account of the elements of dialectical materialism," he wrote of one of Heraclitus's fragments.[122] Such circular confirmation seems peculiarly appropriate in its relationship to the theory of opposites, for the serpent with its tail in its mouth—or uroboros—has itself been elucidated at length as the Jungian archetype for the primal unity that precedes all separation and polar opposition.[123]

In truth, Heraclitus, though rarely at the cultural surface in the polar tradition, is everywhere just beneath that surface. "The only thinker to whom he is close," writes Berdyaev of Boehme, "is

[121] Marx, xxiii, 27.

[122] Quoted in Guthrie, i, 403 n. 1.

[123] See Neumann, e.g., pp. 10-12, 15-17. The uroboros symbolizes the "time of the beginning, before the coming of the opposites" (p. 12).

Heraclitus."[124] Coleridge, again, called a sketch of part of his own system *"Heraclitus redivivus,"* and in that same sketch summoned insistently the doctrine of polarity, e.g.:

> But observe that Poles imply a null punct or point which being both is neither, and neither only because it is the Identity of Both. The Life of Nature consists in the tendency of the Poles to re-unite, and to find themselves in the re-union[125]

Yet again, Hegel—to adduce a final illustration before the conclusion of this chapter—says, in his first observation to the first triad of the larger *Logik*, that "Heraclitus was profound enough to emphasize . . . the higher total concept of Becoming, saying: 'Being is not more than Nothing is,' or 'All things flow,' which means, everything is Becoming."[126]

So we arrive now at the necessity of attempting to formulate the deeper cultural significance of the efflorescence of the doctrine of polarity in the Romantic era. In part one must agree with Alice D. Snyder's assessment, in her pioneering study of the principle of the reconciliation of opposites in Coleridge:

> A theoretical insistence upon inclusiveness, in all spheres, and a temperament that found in abstract metaphysical entities, in mere words, real emotional values of almost enervating ultimateness, made it natural that Coleridge should pin his faith to the principle of the Reconciliation of Opposites. . . . The principle . . . serves primarily to define that which is positively inclusive, and absolute; at the same time it gives room for all the negations, oppositions and double meanings that must arise in any fundamental dealing with words and metaphysical concepts.[127]

Yet this understanding is merely the reverse side, so to speak, of a truth whose obverse is more deeply etched and culturally more revealing. As Whitehead has noted, "In the earlier times the deep thinkers were the clear thinkers—Descartes, Spinoza, Locke, Leibniz. They knew exactly what they meant and said it. In the nineteenth century, some of the deeper thinkers among theologians and philosophers were muddled thinkers. Their assent was claimed by incompatible doctrines; and their efforts at reconciliation produced inevitable confusion."[128] The Romantic commitment to reconciled oppositions is, in largest description, an at-

---

[124] Berdyaev, p. xxxvii.
[126] *Hegel's Werke*, III, 80.
[128] Whitehead, p. 115.

[125] *Collected Letters*, IV, 775, 771.
[127] Snyder, p. 17.

tempt to cope with the increasing incompatibility of the data that
impinged on cultural consciousness. In all its varied patterns and
emphases, such a commitment serves one overriding preoccupa-
tion: that of conceiving sundered entities as a reunited whole. Thus
Coleridge speaks of "the *polarizing* property of all finite mind, for
which Unity is manifested only by correspondent opposites.[129] In
such a formulation the real witness is not to reconciliation but to
fragmentation.

For incompleteness, fragmentation, and ruin—the diasparactive
triad—constitute the deepest underlying truth of Romanticism's
experience of reality. The normative awareness of the century as a
whole was what Hegel termed "das unglückliche Bewußtsein," the
unhappy consciousness. And the unhappy consciousness was a
consciousness of irreconcilable conflict[130]—was "the consciousness
of self as a divided nature, a doubled and merely contradictory be-
ing."[131] As a modern commentator has urged, "even a cursory
examination of the writings of the major Romantic poets reveals
that the traditional view is seriously oversimplified and mislead-
ing. . . . What seems at first glance triumphant affirmation, is re-
vealed on closer observation as a desperate struggle for affirmation
against increasingly powerful obstacles."[132]

Thus doctrines of contraries and oppositions flourished because
contraries and oppositions were ever more the stuff of cultural and
psychological awareness. Although the image of the magnet pro-
vided a paradigm for conceiving plurality within a larger unity, the
more frequent form of real experience was that of fragmentation.
The "harmonie des contraires" was necessary to Hugo precisely
because there is "un abîme entre l'âme et le corps, un abîme entre
l'homme et Dieu." And Novalis understood that "polarity is an
imperfection—there shall one day be no polarity. It enters a system

---

[129] *Friend*, ı, 515n.

[130] Cf. Shklar: "The aesthetic revolt of romanticism was . . . only part of a more
general dissatisfaction with the entire age. If we look deeper, beyond even the con-
scious expressions of romantic thought, we discover a specific consciousness . . .
described by Hegel as the 'unhappy consciousness.' This is the 'alienated soul' that
has lost all faith in the beliefs of the past, having been disillusioned by skepticism,
but is unable to find a new home for its spiritual longings in the present or future.
Hopelessly tossed back and forth between memory and yearning, it can neither ac-
cept the present nor face the new world. . . . It was not only that 'God is dead,' but
that culture had perished. . . . The sense of lostness in the 'real' world that marks
the unhappy consciousness, and that lies at the root of the romantic revival, is also
what gives the movement its continuity" (pp. 15-16).

[131] *Hegel's Werke*, ıı, 158.   [132] Bostetter, p. 5.

before it is perfect. . . . With polarity there arises a separation of that which is necessarily united."[133]

The conception of reconciled opposites is in this perspective nothing less than an attempt to overcome the ruptured awareness of existence; to the extent that it dominates modes of thought, to that same extent will the desire for unity, and the concomitant reality of incompleteness and fragmentation, be necessarily apparent.

Coleridge's own polar schematisms are, typically for him, but also generically for a wider definition of Romantic activity, almost invariably inconclusive or fragmentary. For a single instance, we may note the opening of a letter that contains some of his scientific speculations:

> In my literary Life you will find a sketch of the *subjective* Pole of the Dynamic Philosophy; the rudiments of *Self*-construction, barely enough to let a thinking mind see *what it is like* . . . while the inclosed Scrawl contains a very, *very* rude and fragmentary delineation of the *Objective* Pole, or the Science of the Construction of *Nature*.[134]

To the degree, however, that diasparactive awareness is a major criterion of Romantic consciousness, Coleridge's incompleteness as a practicing polar schematist becomes a badge of honor; and by the same paradox, Hegel's triumphant filterings of world and mind through the net of dialectical polarity into completed system are exercises in the mechanism of denial no less than they are completed wholes. Indeed, it was exactly because reality was not to be so easily tamed by *a priori* networks of logic that German idealism was historically discredited and gave way to positivism. For as Sir Francis Bacon, an honored figure in Coleridge's intellectual background, early and accurately realized, "The human understanding is of its own nature prone to suppose the existence of more order and regularity in the world than it finds. And though there be many things in nature which are singular and unmatched, yet it devises for them parallels and conjugates and relatives which do not exist."[135]

From this standpoint, the fact that Coleridge's own use of polarity is both less systematic and less complete than that of Hegel or

---

[133] *Novalis*, III, 342.   [134] *Collected Letters*, IV, 767.

[135] *Bacon*, I, 165. Several sections later (No. LIV) Bacon notes disparagingly that Gilbert also, after he had employed himself most laboriously in the study and observation of the magnet, proceeded at once to construct an entire system in accordance with his favorite subject.

Schelling perhaps testifies as much to the larger hegemony of diasparactive awareness in his life and work as it does to a less responsible reporting of reality. In any case, Nietzsche—for whom, too, Heraclitus was honored as an "incredible man" ("Unter Menschen war Heraklit als Mensch unglaublich")[136]—subjected the polar logic so lauded by his German predecessors to a sardonically skeptical scrutiny. Although he refers to the *"Gegensatz-Charakter"* of existence and says that the "fundamental belief of metaphysicians is *belief in the antitheses of values (Gegensätze der Werte),"* (III, 595; II, 568), he actually had little respect either for metaphysicians or for their fundamental beliefs. Speaking of the subject/object relationship, he says: "There are no oppositions: only from the oppositions of logic do we have the concept of polarity *(Begriff des Gegensatzes)*—and it is falsely carried from there over into the observation of things" (III, 541). The doctrine of polarity was for Nietzsche based on an "error of reason" (I, 447). It "may be doubted whether polarities *(Gegensätze)* exist at all" (II, 568). "General, imprecise observation sees everywhere in nature polarities (as, for instance, 'warm and cold') where there are no polarities *(Gegensätze)*, but only variations of degree *(Gradverschiedenheiten)"* (I, 907).

The recognition of "variations of degree" was a hallmark of Coleridge's nuanced observation of the particularities of nature and experience; and although such attention to degree was undoubtedly one of the reasons for his eminence as a literary critic, it worked against the completion of a system based on polar reconciliations. His intellectual activity, as House has noted, was "grounded in a minute analysis of the phenomena of sense. He is far more alert and sensitive to the modes in which sense-experience conditions the life of the mind than most technical philosophers. . . . His quivering alertness to every stimulus of sense was . . . the ground of his strengths and weaknesses."[137] The principle of reconciled opposites held out hope for unifying this mass of discrete data. But the diasparactive form of Coleridge's thought and experience was too pervasive. We are left finally not with a Coleridgean system, but with repeated testimonies to a mighty split in his allegiance and concern: reason and understanding, imagination and fancy, the head and the heart, 'I am' and 'it is,' subject and object—these and other characteristic dichotomies testify to the ineradicable presence of diasparactive process in Cole-

---

[136] *Nietzsche,* III, 269.   [137] House, p. 14.

ridge's deepest awareness. The principle of polarity that aligns these sunderings was treasured, by him and by his Romantic contemporaries, as a path to an ultimate wholeness. But for Coleridge, even more strikingly than for his contemporaries, the actual experience out of which such treasuring arose was one of fragmentation and splitting apart, and those wounds the doctrine of polar reconciliations was never satisfactorily able to heal.

CHAPTER SIX

The Psychic Economy and Cultural Meaning
of Coleridge's *Magnum Opus*

◊♦◊

In the E. J. Pratt Library of Victoria University in Toronto there are three clasped vellum manuscript volumes. They, along with a manuscript chapter in a commonplace book in the Huntington Library, and some data in the Berg Collection of the New York Public Library, are what remains of one of the most legendary works ever conceived: the *magnum opus* of Samuel Taylor Coleridge—or as he sometimes called it, "my Great Work." I say "legendary" advisedly, for by that adjective I mean to focus three aspects of the enterprise: first of all, its fame; secondly, its basis in fact; thirdly, its substantial non-existence along with its numinous or aura of fictional being.

The fictional aspect of the *magnum opus*, which derives from the discrepancy between the amount of discussion and hope Coleridge devoted to the work, on the one hand, and the fact on the other hand that neither he nor his literary executor published it, finds its most compelling analogue not in any title that may be discovered in such a standard reference source as *The Cambridge Bibliography of English Literature*, but rather in a title that can best be termed meta-fictional. For in important respects the thought of the *magnum opus* brings to mind Casaubon's vast *Key to All Mythologies* in George Eliot's *Middlemarch*. Coleridge's great work, like Casaubon's, is at least, and if nothing more, an unforgettable monument to ruined endeavor.

If the non-existence of the *magnum opus* as a published entity generates a considerable portion of its fictional aura, another portion arises from its role in Coleridge's mental life. For the work danced before him, as does heaven in the mind of mortals, from his early days to his latest. He pondered the project for more than twenty years before he wrote any of it at all, and he then worked on it intermittently for nearly two decades longer. In short, as he said in 1803, the plan for his *"last & great work"* was one he "always had in mind."[1]

The work was thus, to use Jasperian terminology, the great *Transzendenz* to which Coleridge's living *Existenz* was oriented. I invoke the Jasperian linkage specifically to indicate the paradox that the *magnum opus*, even in its non-existence, was not only a major and permanent goal of Coleridge's living thought but also incorporated much of the meaning of Coleridge's role as a cultural figure. As the hypothetical final justification of his life activity, the treatise, in both its non-existence and its partial existence, influenced and even dictated the form and the tone of what Coleridge otherwise did. In short, as I shall be arguing for the next several pages, the *magnum opus* radically affected both Coleridge's poetry and his prose, though in different ways. It tended to draw off his poetic energies and shut down his poetic productivity, and it tended to make his prose production both seem and be tentative and preliminary. As a commentator has pointed out, "There can be little doubt that philosophy was [Coleridge's] central activity, and that the criticism along with other journalistic enterprises was a digression from it. . . . It is clear that his criticism . . . is his astonishing substitute for hack-work; that while he undertook it earnestly in the hope of doing good, he regarded it as being of a lower order than the serious treatises to which he was devoting his life."[2]

Not only was the role of Coleridge's literary criticism depressed by the proleptic weight of the *magnum opus*, but also the shadows of that treatise's futurity darkened the very language and structure of his critical efforts. To quote Jackson once more, "the occasional nature of [Coleridge's] criticism accounts for most of the faults for which he is sometimes blamed. Charges of obscurity, lack of organization, plagiarism, and downright intellectual charlatanism, have all been levelled from time to time; most of them derive from the subsidiary place which the criticism occupied in his attention."[3] In truth, one may expand the judgment and say that the reflexive pressure of the *magnum opus* made the whole of Coleridge's actual prose achievement provisional in its nature.

Jackson's mention of that curious feature of Coleridge's productivity, "plagiarism," can also be expanded; it seems likely that the futurity of the *magnum opus* worked in Coleridge's mind to make the plagiarisms in his occasional work seem less serious. As I have

---

[1] *Notebooks*, I, 1646.   [2] Jackson, p. 15.
[3] *Ibid*.

said in another place, "A man may take raw material from other authors when he is confident of his ultimate ability to generate the flame necessary for a final transmutation of these materials into a *magnum opus*. Doubtless the *magnum opus* . . . was an important teleological rationalization, a psychic cover story, for Coleridge's borrowings."[4] In addition, the *magnum opus*'s systematic character tended to lessen the value of originality (which is in any case a culturally ambiguous idea).[5] As Coleridge said, "A System may have no new Truths for it's component Parts, yet having nothing but Truths may be for that very reason a new System."[6] As he elsewhere said, his "system" would attempt "to reduce all knowledges into harmony. It opposes no other system, but shows what was true in each. . . . I have endeavoured to unite the insulated fragments of truth, and therewith to frame a perfect mirror."[7] In such a conception, Coleridge exhibited the high credentials of a Romantic philosopher in the German manner. For a confirming illustration, one may pass by the apposite but expected quotation from Hegel, and substitute Novalis. "The philosopher," said Novalis, "who can transform all single philosophemes into one single one . . . achieves the maximum in his philosophy. He achieves the maximum as a philosopher if he unites all philosophies into a single philosophy."[8]

If the idea of the *magnum opus* explains important features of Coleridge's practice in his published prose writings, it also constituted part of the reason for his virtual abandonment of his poetic ambitions. One must speak with qualification here, for another and perhaps larger factor, as has been argued in previous chapters of this volume, was the combination of Coleridge's awareness of Wordsworth's greatness as a poet and Wordsworth's lack of generosity to Coleridge's aspirations in return.

But the pushing away from poetry effected by the proximity of Wordsworth was complemented by a pulling away from another source. "He is a great, a true Poet," wrote Coleridge of Wordsworth, "I am only a kind of a Metaphysician."[9] The statement, despite its self-disparagement, is revealing: Had Coleridge not had metaphysics into which to withdraw, the implication seems clear,

---

[4] *CPT*, p. 28.

[5] For comprehensive discussion, see my article, "The Originality Paradox," *New Literary History*, 5 (1974), 447-76. Cf. Novalis: "The search for originality is learned, crude egotism" (*Novalis*, III, 405).

[6] *Collected Letters*, II, 700.

[7] *Table Talk*, pp. 138-39 (Sept. 12, 1831).

[8] *Novalis*, II, 586.

[9] *Collected Letters*, I, 658.

he would not have been so docile in his forfeiture of his poetic ambitions. The metaphysical preoccupation tended to make the withdrawal from poetry much easier. Thus the abandonment of poetic activity is almost invariably linked in Coleridge's statements to a deepened commitment to the substitute activity of philosophy. "All my poetic genius," he wrote to Southey in 1802, "is gone— and I have been fool enough to suffer deeply in my mind, regretting the loss—which I attribute to my long & exceedingly severe Metaphysical Investigations."[10] To another correspondent, in the same year, he noted that, when he "wished to write a poem," he "beat up Game of far other kind—instead of a Covey of poetic Partridges with whirring wings of music . . . up came a metaphysical Bustard, urging it's slow, heavy, laborious, earth-skimming Flight over dreary & level Wastes."[11]

Though certain of Coleridge's statements at times seem to countenance a contrary interpretation, they are invariably statements made in a state of depression, and they seem, moreover, to be an attempt to oblige the prejudices of his English contemporaries. Those prejudices were vigorously and repeatedly expressed. Thus Hazlitt said in 1817,

> Mr. C., with great talents, has, by an ambition to be every thing, become nothing. His metaphysics have been a dead weight on the wings of his imagination—while his imagination has run away with his reason and common sense. He might, we seriously think, have been a very considerable poet—instead of which he has chosen to be a bad philosopher and a worse politician. [12]

Again, Byron's opinion as expressed to Medwin was that

> If [Coleridge] had never gone to Germany, nor spoilt his fine genius by the transcendental philosophy and German metaphysics, nor taken to write lay sermons, he would have been the greatest poet of the day. . . . Coleridge might have been any thing: as it is, he is a thing "that dreams are made of."[13]

Even Wordsworth shared this view as to the deleterious role of philosophy in Coleridge's commitment:

> Wordsworth, as a poet [reported an interlocutor] regretted that German metaphysics had so much captivated the taste of Cole-

---

[10] *Ibid.*, II, 831.
[12] *Hazlitt*, XVI, 137.
[11] *Ibid.*, p. 814.
[13] Medwin, pp. 121-22.

ridge, for he was frequently not intelligible on this subject; whereas, if his energy and his originality had been more exerted in the channel of poetry . . . he might have done more permanently to enrich the literature . . . than any man of the age.[14]

Despite the phalanx of adverse judgments on the part of his contemporaries, and despite an occasional subscription to such opinion on the part of Coleridge himself, the real situation, as we have repeatedly stressed in the preceding arguments of this book, was that Coleridge was ideally committed to an equilibrium—an interchangeability really—in the poetic and the philosophical functions. What he lamented was not his philosophical "abstruse Research" as such, but the fact that "that which suits a part infects the whole."[15] Actually, he could speak the same way when things were reversed and his poetic role threatened to overshadow his philosophical role. For instance, in 1803 he asked Godwin's advice about how to find a publisher for "a work which I consider as introductory to a *System*," and he comments that "Longman & Rees are very civil; but . . . they have no notion of me, except as of a Poet—nor any *sprinklings* of philosophical knowledge that could in the least enable them to judge of the value, or probable success, of such a Work."[16]

Thus Coleridge's ideal view of himself was neither as a poet nor as a philosopher, but as both. "Davy in the kindness of his heart," he says, obviously gratified, "calls me the Poet-philosopher." He identifies himself playfully in 1800 as "S. T. Coleridge, Esq. Gentleman-Poet & Philosopher in a mist." Still playful, he projects in another place a fantasy in which "I would write Odes & Sonnets Morning & Evening—& metaphysicize at Noon."[17]

What he wished for himself, he wished also for Wordsworth. Thus of a portrait of his friend done by Hazlitt, he writes to Wordsworth:

> Sir G. [George Beaumont] & his wife both say, that the Picture gives them an idea of you as a profound strong-minded Philosopher, not as a Poet—I answered (& I believe, truly—) that so it must needs do, if it were a good Portrait—for that you were a great Poet by inspirations, & in the Moments of revelation, but that you were a thinking feeling Philosopher habitually—that

---

[14] Grosart, III, 469.
[16] *Collected Letters*, II, 947, 948.
[15] Coleridge, *Poems*, I, 367.
[17] *Ibid.*, p. 668; I, 614, 223.

your Poetry was your Philosophy under the action of strong winds of Feeling—a sea rolling high.—[18]

In accordance with this view, Coleridge could elsewhere say, in words that indicate strongly that, though he gave up his own aspiration as a poet, he never gave up his allegiance to the ideal intermingling of poetry and philosophy, that

> Wordsworth is a Poet, and I feel myself a better Poet, in knowing how to honour *him*, than in all my own poetic Compositions, all I have done or hope to do—and I prophesy immortality to his *Recluse*, as the first & finest philosophical Poem.[19]

In short, however much Coleridge's English contemporaries reprobated his dual commitment to poetry and philosophy, that commitment was essential to his idea of his cultural role. In this orientation he was at one with his philosophical contemporaries in Germany. "To poeticize philosophy and to philosophize poetry," says Ernst Cassirer in summary of this important truth, "—such was the highest aim of all romantic thinkers."[20] (Because a representative portion of the abounding evidence that could be used to document this dictum has already been brought forward in earlier pages of this volume, we may content ourselves with only two additional illustrative statements, both by Novalis: "Die Trennung von Poët und Denker ist nur scheinbar—und zum *Nachtheil* beyder"—the separation of poet and thinker is only apparent—and to the disadvantage of both. *"Poet,"* says Novalis again, "is merely the highest grade of thinker.")[21]

So Coleridge lamented the pre-emption of the poet-philosopher role by that of philosopher merely. "I have almost wholly weaned myself from the habit of making Verses," he writes gloomily in 1802, "and for the last three years uninterruptedly devoted myself to studies only not *quite* incompatible with poetic composition. Poetic composition has become laborious & painful to me." "I have no heart for Poetry," he says in July 1801. "I found no comfort except in the driest speculations," he writes to Thomas Wedgwood on 20 October 1802; and the statement echoes one to Godwin in April 1801, where Coleridge says that his "exceeding skepticism

---

[18] *Ibid.*, II, 957.   [19] *Ibid.*, p. 1034.

[20] *Essay on Man*, p. 156.

[21] *Novalis*, III, 406. Again: "Philosophy is the *theory of poetry*. It shows us what poetry is, that it is the One and All" (II, 591).

respecting the sanity of my own Feelings & Tone of Intellect, relatively to a work of Sentiment & Imagination" has compelled him "to seek resources in austerest reasonings," by which he has "denaturalized my mind."[22]

The latter complaint is the same one that in the "Dejection Ode" erupts in the statement about "abstruse Research" stealing "From my own nature all the natural man—/ This was my sole resource, my only plan."[23] And though the depressive loss of his poetic abilities was somewhat tempered by the fact that Coleridge did manage to compose the great "Dejection Ode" itself, that poem did not restore him. At one point he finds that he cannot even copy it out, ceasing after these lines:

> But O! each Visitation
> Suspends what Nature gave me at my Birth,
> My Shaping Spirit of Imagination!

His comment as he does so is: "I am so weary of this doleful Poem that I must leave off."[24]

It seems clear, therefore, that Coleridge's dejected loss of his poetic imagination profoundly upset the equilibrium of his poet-philosopher commitment. Yet in this redistribution of the ideal direction of his energies, the *magnum opus* was crucial. A simple interest in metaphysics, taken as a kind of sideline or hobby, could never have justified an almost total transfer of intellectual attention away from his poetic endeavors, in which he had already realized achievement of a high order. The *magnum opus* alone was a project of sufficient weight to tip the plane toward philosophy and allow Coleridge's mental activity to roll down, as it were, almost exclusively to the philosophical side. Thus it is significant that the statement about *"My last & great work"* quoted above occurs in 1803, that is, more or less simultaneously with the statements about the demise of his poetic powers. When not directly lamenting the disequilibrium induced into his poet-philosopher conception of himself, moreover, Coleridge could speak proudly indeed—in what one might term his *"magnum opus* tone"—about his philosophical ambitions. For instance, in March 1801—the same month, we recall, that he asserted that his imagination was dead and said that by showing him what true poetry was, Wordsworth made him see that he himself was no poet—in March 1801, he writes to a correspondent about his purely philosophical

---

[22] *Collected Letters*, II, 903, 745, 875, 725.
[23] Coleridge, *Poems*, I, 367.   [24] *Collected Letters*, II, 972-73.

prospects, and the *magnum opus* tone is unmistakably present; for Coleridge talks of "the very important Researches & Studies, in which I have been lately immersed, & which have made all subjects of ordinary Interest appear to me *trifling* beyond measure."[25]

So poetry and philosophy shared a common plane of importance, one that in the first three years of the nineteenth century was tipped in philosophy's favor by the weight attached to the conception of the *magnum opus*. The prose actually published was ranged on a separate plane, one lower than that of poet-philosopher. We can see this in Coleridge's regretful statement, in 1817, that he had been "compelled" by journalistic enterprises "to give up all thought & hope of doing any thing of a permanent nature, either as a Poet or a Philosopher."[26] Such a grouping was constant and unchanging in his view of himself. Thus in 1796, two decades before, faced with the prospect of going to London to write for the *Morning Chronicle*, he had indicated the same ordering of concerns: "If I go, farewell Philosophy! Farewell, the Muse! Farewell, my literary Fame!"[27]

Because of the difference in his own mind between his vocation as a poet and that as a prose writer, Coleridge assigned different vectors of displacement to their relationship to the *magnum opus*. Curiously enough, and the point is crucial to our understanding of the dynamics of Coleridge's mental energy, the lower order of concern benefited more than did the higher. Because of Coleridge's very special neurotic situation, which entailed a substantial inability to work or to face any assigned duty, the provisional nature of his prose writing actually allowed him a certain achievement that the ultimate demands of his poetry did not. We have previously noted Leavis's judgment that Coleridge was "very much more brilliantly gifted than Arnold, but nothing of his deserves the classical status of Arnold's best work."[28] Paradoxically, it is only on the basis of the non-classical quality of Coleridge's critical prose that one can conclude that he was more brilliantly gifted than Arnold. Faced with the demand for classical polish, Coleridge would probably have done nothing at all. The choice for him was never between perfection and imperfection, but between imperfection and nothing. By displacing the hope of classical status onto the conception of *magnum opus*, he was enabled to produce casual and *ad hoc* writing that, imperfect though it is, is nevertheless among the treasures of our language. Surely no masterpiece has ever been

---

[25] *Ibid.*, p. 715.
[27] *Ibid.*, I, 227.

[26] *Ibid.*, IV, 737. Cf. V, 30.
[28] *Scrutiny*, 9 (1940), 69.

more flawed and disarrayed than the *Biographia Literaria*. As Leslie Stephen has said, "it was written at his very nadir, and published just after he had reached his asylum at Highgate. . . . The book, of course, is put together with a pitchfork. It is without form or proportion, and is finally eked out with a batch of the old letters from Germany which he had already used in the 'Friend,' and apparently kept as a last resource to stop the mouths of printers."[29]

Examination of the *Biographia* provides ample justification for Stephen's description. The book announces its pitchfork provenance on its very title page, for the subtitle is "Biographical Sketches of my Literary Life and Opinions"—and the words "Sketches" and "Opinions" bode well neither for perfection of form nor for rigor of content. Chapter headings still more anxiously reject any demand for classical status or perfected form. Chapter Ten bears a title that begins with these words: "A chapter of digression and anecdotes, as an interlude preceding. . . . " Chapter Twelve, again, exhibits the remarkable title of "A chapter of requests and premonitions concerning the perusal or omission of the chapter that follows." Yet this wild grab-bag is the most important single work of critical theory and practice in all of English literature.[30] The only conclusion to be drawn is that its provisional nature, or, if one wishes, its near-hackwork status, does not block the revelation of Coleridge's insights but is in fact the necessary condition under which they can be expressed. The provisional nature of the enterprise is dictated by the futurity of the *magnum opus*.[31]

A specific illustration should make this contention still more

[29] Stephen, III, 331. Despite its helter-skelter surface, however, the *Biographia* has a deep underlying cohesion—as indeed does all Coleridge's thought. See George Whalley, 'The Integrity of *Biographia Literaria*," *Essays and Studies*, collected for the English Association by Geoffrey Bullough, New Series, 6 (1953), 87-101. The characteristic of Coleridge's thought that makes its profound unity so difficult to discern is admirably stated by De Quincey: "Coleridge, to many people, and often I have heard the complaint, seemed to wander; and he seemed then to wander the most when in fact, his resistance to the wandering instinct was greatest—viz., when the compass and huge circuit by which his illustrations moved travelled farthest into remote regions before they began to revolve. Long before this coming round commenced most people had lost him, and naturally enough supposed he had lost himself. They continued to admire the separate beauty of the thoughts, but did not see their relations to the dominant theme" (*De Quincey*, II, 152-53).

[30] For instance, John Middleton Murry refers to the *Biographia*'s discussion of Wordsworth's poetry as "the most magnificent piece of critical writing in the English language" (Murry, *Style*, p. 18).

[31] As Coleridge says, "all my other writings (unless I except my poems, and these

clear. In the thirteenth chapter of the *Biographia*, Coleridge distinguishes primary imagination, secondary imagination, and fancy. The two paragraphs that constitute the distinction are surely among the most famous passages of prose in our literature, and the burden of theory they incorporate is by the same token one of our literature's most pregnant matrices. Yet, without the covering thought of the *magnum opus*, the passages could not have been presented at all. Coleridge has been arguing in Chapter Twelve toward a formal deduction for the imagination/fancy distinction, and the argument proceeds into Chapter Thirteen. At this point, he either runs out of energy, out of will, out of time, or possibly out of all three; at any rate, he finds himself unable to press forward. Instead of abandoning the argument, however, he calmly says that

> Thus far had the work been transcribed for the press, when I received the following letter from a friend

The friend, madly enough, is Coleridge himself, and the letter to himself commences to set forth something quite different from the expected deduction. "You ask my opinion concerning your Chapter on the Imagination," begins the letter, and eventually it says, "Be assured . . . that I look forward anxiously to your great book on the CONSTRUCTIVE PHILOSOPHY [that is, the *magnum opus*], which you have promised and announced: and that I will do my best to understand it." Having thus summoned up the futurity of the *magnum opus*, Coleridge coolly transfers the burden of proof to its supposed pages:

> But as for the PUBLIC, I do not hesitate a moment in advising and urging you to withdraw the Chapter from the present work, and to reserve it for your announced treatises on the Logos or communicative intellect in Man and Deity. . . . Be assured, if you do publish this Chapter in the present work, you will be reminded of Bishop Berkley's Siris, announced as an Essay on Tar-water, which beginning with Tar ends with the Trinity, the omne scibile forming the interspace. I say in the *present* work. In that greater work to which you have devoted so many years, and study so intense and various, it will be in its proper place.[32]

The tactic, however *outré*, is crudely effective; the invocation of the

---

I can exclude in part only) are introductory and preparative" to the *magnum opus* (*Collected Letters*, v, 28).

[32] *Biographia*, I, 198, 200, 200-201.

magnum opus neatly divests Coleridge of the onerous responsibility of formal deduction, and, so relieved, he is able simply to deposit—to dump, really—the distinction of primary imagination, secondary imagination, and fancy. The key point in the whole bizarre business, however, is that without such invocation, the distinction could not have appeared at all.

Nor is it only in this instance that the argument of the *Biographia* relies on the *magnum opus*. Earlier in Chapter Twelve, Coleridge has summoned that treatise, not as *magnum opus*, but as "my *Logosophia*," and used its magic invocation to help him through still another sticky place: "In the third treatise of my *Logosophia*," he says, "announced at the end of this volume, I shall give (deo volente) the demonstrations and constructions of the Dynamic Philosophy scientifically arranged. It is, according to my conviction, no other than the system of Pythagoras and of Plato revived and purified from impure mixtures."[33]

Thus the *Biographia Literaria* is a kind of antechamber to the *magnum opus*; indeed, the *Biographia*, which was finished, relates to the *magnum opus*, which was not, exactly as does Wordsworth's "Prelude," which was finished, to his "Recluse," which was not. It has long been recognized in fact that the *Biographia* is a counterpart, a kind of answer even, to the "Prelude."[34] Wordsworth talks in verse of the building up of his mind; Coleridge talks in prose of the building up of his. But the proportion is still more exact. For not only is the *Biographia* parallel to the "Prelude" but also the *magnum opus* is parallel to the "Recluse." We are faced here with a delicious irony. The twofold reason why Coleridge gave up major ambitions in poetry was on the one hand the call of the *magnum opus*, on the other, the sense of Wordsworth's superiority as a poet. When he announced that "I abandon Poetry altogether," he said in the same breath, as we have seen, that "I leave the higher & deeper kinds to Wordsworth."[35] In that bequest, however, he left also part of the intertwined poetic/philosophic aspiration that eventuated in its other part in his own *magnum opus*. For Wordsworth's "Recluse" is not only really Coleridge's poem in its origin, but also its content was to be virtually identical, although in verse, with that of the prose *magnum opus*. Coleridge said of the "Recluse" that the "plan" was "partly suggested by me," and Wordsworth was to use the poem "to deliver upon authority a sytem of philosophy," and,

[33] *Ibid.*, pp. 179-80.   [34] See above, Chapter One, note 2.
[35] See above, Chapter Four, note 32.

moreover, this activity was in substance "what I have been all my life doing in my [own] system of philosophy."[36] We have noted that Wordsworth was unable to proceed at all on his vast poem without the constant help of his friend—because the "Recluse" was in fact his friend's system of philosophy.[37]

The "Recluse," therefore, though nominally Wordsworth's philosophical poem, was actually the heir to Coleridge's earlier aspirations, revealed in projections such as "Hymns to the Elements" or "The Siege of Jerusalem," to write for himself a great philosophical poem. It was tied to the fortunes of the *magnum opus*, and, like the *magnum opus*, it remained a ruin.

So much for the effect of the *magnum opus* on the inner economy of Coleridge's mental life, as that life revealed itself in both poetry and prose. The question remains, however, what was the *magnum opus* in and of itself supposed to be? The answer can be divided into an intent of form and an intent of topic. As an intent of topic, the work was to discuss a question and to deny a probability that haunted Coleridge throughout his life. It was the one great question that in varying formulations and contexts occupied his impassioned concern from early to late; and as good a statement of it as any can be found in a Coleridgean locus of 1795 that he later entitled "Fragments of Theological Lectures":

> When Death shall have closed my eye-lids, must I then bid my last farewell to the streams whose murmurs have soothed me, to the fields and woodlands, where I have delighted to wander? Must yonder blue Region and all this goodly scene darken upon me and go out? . . . . Have I moved and loved and reasoned and all this that I may at last be compressed into a Clod of the Valley?[38]

The queries are posed in the context of what Coleridge further on calls "natural longings after Immortality" and an "ardent *desire* of a future state," and both here and in the ramified conceptions of the *magnum opus* they obsessed Coleridge for forty years and more.

In its intent of form, the *magnum opus* was to be the *systematic* terminus for all Coleridge's intellectual strivings to supply a positive answer to that great question; it was to demonstrate systematically that "Christianity is true Philosophy, & . . . that all true

---

[36] See above, Chapter One, note 139.
[37] See above, Chapters One and Four, pages 97-99, 222, 227.
[38] *Lectures 1795*, p. 349.

Philosophy is Christianity." As a system, it was to be as well the satisfaction of a craving that never left him, "an intense craving," as he says, "after a resting-place for my Thoughts in some *principle*, that was derived from Experience, but of which all other Knowleges should be but so many repetitions under various limitations, even as circles, squares, triangles, &c. are but so many positions of space."[39] In the attempt to satisfy this craving, Coleridge projected not one, but many *magna opera*. Or rather the same *magnum opus* appeared under various tentative titles and evolving schemes of content. It was, as we have already seen, called *Logosophia* around the time of the *Biographia Literaria*; in 1803 it was called *Eidoloclastes*; at one point in the 1820s it was called *Assertion of Religion*. It was called both *magnum opus* and *Opus Maximum* at various times by Coleridge himself. And it had still other names.

Throughout the protean progression of titles and emphases, one truth is apparent: the *magnum opus*, perhaps appropriately enough in an author to whom the doctrine of polarity was a vital commitment, was actually a double entity, one ideal, and one real. As a vast but chimerical composition, it was continually being raided to produce slighter works that Coleridge did in fact publish. Some years ago a scholar wrote an article suggesting that Coleridge's *Theory of Life* fit the requirements for the *magnum opus*; and the *Theory of Life* is in truth a compendium or syllepsis of at least the scientific portions of the great work.[40] To utilize an organic analogy that Coleridge himself might have found congenial, it was as though a stalk called *magnum opus* grew up out of the deepest concerns of Coleridge's life, but then kept dividing into subsidiary branches that bore blooms and foliage and were harvested before the trunk itself matured. The subsidiary flowering at the same time tended to deprive the parent plant of the sap needed for maturation. Coleridge's *Logic*, for instance, which Jackson has edited as a separate work in *The Collected Works of Samuel Taylor Coleridge*, was unquestionably in its first conception a part of the *magnum opus*; equally unquestionably, it was not included in later projections of the contents of that great work.

The *Biographia Literaria* itself originated as part of the *magnum opus*. It was called *Autobiographia Literaria* before the published title

[39] *Collected Letters*, iv, 592; v, 289. Again, Coleridge refers to the *magnum opus* as a "System of Truths respecting Nature, Man, and Deity, evolved from one Principle" (v, xli).

[40] Sam G. Barnes, "Was *Theory of Life* Coleridge's 'Opus Maximum'?" *Studies in Philology*, 55 (1958), 494-514.

was adopted,[41] and this earlier title points directly to one of the projections of the *magnum opus*. Speaking of that work on September 12, 1814, Coleridge mentions a "prefatory Essay on the Laws & Limits of Toleration & Liberality illustrated by fragments of *Auto*-biography."[42] The "fragments of *Auto*-biography" (we note without comment the diasparactive genesis of the work) seem to be indisputably an early form of the *Biographia Literaria*.[43]

So unclosable is the gap between the ideal and the real entities indicated by the term *magnum opus*, in fact, that scholars by mutual agreement now call only the ideal entity *magnum opus*; by the same agreement, the manuscript fragments in the libraries in New York, California, and Ontario are called by the name *Opus Maximum*.[44] By a further paradox, there is no particular reason for thinking that these fragments deserve even that name; though written with the idea of the larger whole in view, they are actually merely the residuum of Coleridge's conception, and, if one wishes to play fur-

[41] *Collected Letters*, iv, 578. [42] *Ibid.*, iii, 533.

[43] The seeds of the *Biographia Literaria* were planted very early in Coleridge's concern, and they grew from the two things most important to him: Wordsworth and the aspiration to do a great philosophical work. In 1800 the "works which I gird myself up to attack as soon as money-concerns will permit" include, "the Life of Lessing—& the Essay on Poetry. The latter is still more at my heart than the former—its Title would be an Essay on the Elements of Poetry/ it would in reality be a *disguised* System of Morals & Politics" (*Collected Letters*, i, 632). We are perhaps justified in regarding what Coleridge here calls "the latter"—"the Essay on Poetry"—as the earliest adumbration of the *Biographia Literaria*. We can see how much this kind of project was bound up with the idea of the *magnum opus* in a statement of 1801: "let me work as hard as I can, I shall not be able to do what my heart within me *burns* to do—that is, *concenter* my free mind to the affinities of the Feelings with Words & Ideas under the title of 'Concerning Poetry & the nature of the Pleasures derived from it.'—I have faith, that I do understand this subject/ and I am sure, that if I write what I ought to do on it, the Work would supersede all the Books of Metaphysics hitherto written/ and all the Books of Morals too" (ii, 671). This vast project began to concern itself specifically with Wordsworth's theory of poetry after the publication of the "Preface" to *Lyrical Ballads*. In 1802 Coleridge wrote that "I am far from going all lengths with Wordsworth," and that "I rather suspect that some where or other there is a radical Difference in our theoretical opinions respecting Poetry." "This," he adds significantly, "I shall endeavor to go to the Bottom of" (ii, 830). By October of 1802 we can clearly see the outline of the *Biographia* as it actually was written, because Coleridge says that "in point of poetic Diction I am not so well s[atisf]ied that you do not require a certain *Aloofness* from the language of real Life, which I think deadly to Poetry. Very shortly however, I shall present you . . . with my opinions in full on the subject of Style both in prose & verse" (ii, 877). Fifteen years later he did so.

[44] Cf. Walter Jackson Bate, *Coleridge* (New York: The Macmillan Company, 1968), p. 182n.

ther with paradox, it may be said that they actually have no greater claim to being thought of as elements in the *magnum opus* than does, say, the *Aids to Reflection*. As I have elsewhere argued, the *magnum opus* was "not merely a concrete plan dating from a certain period around the year 1815, but an omnipresent reality, even when imperfectly expressed."[45] In this respect, perhaps no more accurate description of the ideal entity exists than that provided in a statement by Coleridge in 1821, where he calls it "my Opus Magnum on Revelation & Christianity, the Reservoir of my Reflections & Reading for 25 years past."[46]

Although Coleridge is frequently inaccurate in the assigning of dates,[47] in this instance the period of twenty-five years appears to be quite correct. For it is in 1796 that we encounter the first adumbrations of the *magnum opus*—the topic of which, as we have just seen, was present to his consciousness at least as early as the preceding year. In 1796 Coleridge feels a necessity "to rescue this *enlightened age* from general Irreligion. The stream of Knowlege has diffused itself into shallows."[48] The statement, as will become apparent, defines two major and unchanging motives of the *magnum opus*: it was a work in the service of the Christian religion; secondly, it was a conservative venture, undertaken as a reaction against the Enlightenment—or as he here says, this *enlightened age*, and especially against the currents emanating from France. (However much the arguments of the preceding chapter may have made Coleridge seem similar to Hegel, a radical difference between the two was that Hegel's espousal of the Enlightenment was in direct opposition to Coleridge's rejection of it.)[49]

Earlier in 1796 Coleridge had entertained the scheme of having "Robinson, the great London Bookseller" pay his way to and from "Jena, a cheap German University where Schiller resides." "If I could realize this scheme," he continues,

> I should there study Chemistry & Anatomy, [and] bring over with me all the works of Semler & Michaelis, the German Theologians, & of Kant, the great german Metaphysician. On my return I would commence a School for 8 young men at 100

[45] *CPT*, p. 194.   [46] *Collected Letters*, v, 160.

[47] Cf. Schneider, e.g., p. 155: "Coleridge . . . was one of the very last persons to be relied upon for an accurate date."

[48] *Collected Letters*, I, 248.

[49] Cf. *Hegel's Werke*, IX, 526 ff., the chapter called "Die Aufklärung und Revolution."

guineas each—proposing to *perfect* them in the following studies in order as follows—

1. Man as Animal: including the complete knowlege of Anatomy, Chemistry, Mechanics & Optics.—

2. Man as an *Intellectual* Being: including the ancient Metaphysics, the systems of Locke & Hartley,—of the Scotch Philosophers—& the new Kantian S[ystem—]

3. Man as a Religious Being: including an historic summary of all Religions & the arguments for and against Natural & Revealed Religion.[50]

Though this is not a plan for a vast published philosophical system, but rather one for educating "8 young men at 100 guineas each," the difference is not historically so great as might at first glance seem. For as Jaeger has comprehensively demonstrated, not only the Socratic philosophy but the whole substance of Greek culture developed as *paideia*—the education of young men.[51] Indeed, the interchangeability of education and philosophy under the aegis of *paideia* is indicated by Coleridge some three years later after he has actually gone to Germany. He writes to Josiah Wedgwood in 1799—from Germany—that "I shall have bought 30 pounds worth of books (chiefly metaphysics/ & with a view to the one work, to which I hope to dedicate in silence the prime of my life)."[52] With the phrase, "the one work," we are perhaps justified in seeing the first appearance of a specific commitment to a *magnum opus*; for central to the conception of that work were always the twin attributes of uniqueness and comprehensiveness. The comprehensiveness of "the one work" of 1799, however, is clearly an outgrowth of the paideutic commitment of 1796. In fact, in the earlier projection, Coleridge's three divisions, "Man as Animal," "Man as an *Intellectual* Being," and "Man as a Religious Being," precisely denominate the idiosyncratic amalgam of scientific investigation, philosophy, and theology that characterizes both Coleridge's general commitment of thought and the detailed content of the *Opus Maximum* as we have it.

The emphasis on comprehensiveness that signalized the scheme of 1796 is also present in a ramified proposal of 1803, although now

[50] *Collected Letters*, I, 209.

[51] See Werner Jaeger, *Paideia; The Ideals of Greek Culture*, second edition, trans. Gilbert Highet (New York: Oxford University Press, 1969). The work is in three volumes.

[52] *Collected Letters*, I, 519.

the paideutic intent is wholly transformed into the plan for a philo-
sophical work. In a list of "names of Works that I have planned"
there appears

Eidoloclastes.———6th

Underneath this, placed within and emphasized by a rectangle,
there is the specification:

On Man, and the probable Destiny of the Human Race.—*My last
& great work*—always had in mind.

Underneath this, "The History of Logic with a Compendium of
Aristotelean Logic prefixed. 7th. History of Metaphysics in Ger-
many. 8th." Then underneath that, crossed out: "Organum vere
Organum." Then still further down:

Revolutionary Minds, Thomas Aquinas, Scotus, Luther, Baxter
as represent. of the English Presbyterians & as affording a place
for the Church of England—Socinus, G. Fox.—9th.
Giordano Bruno, Jacob Boehmen, Spinoza. 10th.
The work which I should wish to leave behind me or to publish
late in Life, that On Man, and the probable Destiny of the
Human Race, followed & illustrated by the Organum vere Or-
ganum, & philosophical Romance to explain the whole growth
of Language, and for these to be always collecting materials.[53]

This projection of 1803, all of it, is the *magnum opus*. By Septem-
ber 1815, "my most important work" was being referred to as con-
taining "six Treatises," and its plan had become so detailed as to
warrant quotation in its entirety. The plan appears in a letter to
John May on 27 September 1815:

My highest object in writing for the stage is to obtain the means
of devoting myself, *a whole and undistracted man*, to the bringing
forth a work, for which I have all the materials collected & ready
for use;

We interrupt Coleridge's statement here to call attention to this
choice example of a truth urged earlier—that his other writing took
on a provisional character because of the reflexive influence of the
magnum opus. Coleridge continues:

a work, which has employed all my best thoughts & efforts for
the last twelve years and more, and on which I would ground

[53] *Notebooks*, I, 1646.

my reputation, that is, the proof, that I have labored to be *useful*. This work will be entitled Logosophia: or on the Logos, divine and human, in six Treatises. The first, or preliminary treatise contains a philosophical History of Philosophy and it's revolutions from Pythagoras to Plato & to Aristotle—from Aristotle to Lord Bacon, including the scholastic metaphysicians of what are *called* the dark ages—from Bacon to Des Cartes and Locke—and from Locke to the revival of the eldest Philosophy, which I call *dynamic* or constructive as opposed to the material and mechanical systems still predominant. (A perspicuous Compendium of the Hist. of Phil. has been long wanted: for Enfield's is a mere Bookseller's *Job* Abridgement of Brucker, a man of great Learning & unwearied industry, but scantily gifted with the true philosophic insight.)

The second Treatise is (Λόγος κοινός) on the science of connected reasoning, containing a system of Logic purified from all pedantry & sophistication, & applied practically to the purposes of ordinary life, the Senate, Pulpit, Bar, &c—I flatter myself that I have not only brought together all the possible Forms of Deception and Delusion in Reasoning, from the grossest Bull which raises the laughter of a Taproom to the subtlest Sophism which has set nation against nation, illustrated by instances from writers of the highest name; but have likewise given some rules for the easy detection of false reasoning. I have labored to make it not so much a Novum Organum, as an Organum verè Organum. The III. (Logos Architectonicus) on the Dynamic or Constructive Philosophy—preparatory to the IV. or a detailed Commentary on the Gospel of St John—collating the *Word* of the Evangelist with the Christ crucified of St. Paul.—

The Vth. (Λόγος ἀγωνίότης) on the Pantheists and Mystics; with the Lives and Systems of Giordano Bruno, Jacob Behmen, George Fox, and Benedict Spinoza.—

The VIth. (Λόγος ἄλογος), on the Causes & Consequences of modern Unitarianism.—

Previously to its being sent to the Press I mean to submit the work to some one or more learned and dignified Divines of the Church of England, the defence of whose articles I have most at heart, next to that of the Gospel Truth, which in all but some inessential and comparatively trifling points I sincerely believe coincident with our Articles & Liturgy.[54]

[54] *Collected Letters*, iv, 589-90.

The "second Treatise" in this projection, which is "on the science of connected reasoning, containing a system of Logic," is evidently an expansion of the proposal of 1803 with regard to "The History of Logic with a Compendium of Aristotelean Logic prefixed." Its aim of being "not so much a Novum Organum, as an Organum verè Organum" repeats the rubric of the earlier scheme: "Organum vere Organum." The "first, or preliminary treatise" of the plan of 1815, which "contains a philosophical History of Philosophy" takes up the "8th" proposal of 1803: "History of metaphysics in Germany." The fifth section of the 1815 plan, "on the Pantheists and Mystics; with the Lives and Systems of Giordano Bruno, Jacob Behmen, George Fox, and Benedict Spinoza" expands the "10th" proposal of 1803: "Giordano Bruno, Jacob Boehmen, Spinoza."

Another aspect of the 1815 projection, the compendium of the history of philosophy, seems to maintain the paideutic commitment of the adumbrative version of 1796, for Coleridge notes that the compendium "has long been wanted." The same educational commitment seems to be implied in the statement that he has "labored to be *useful*."

The plan communicated to May, although it is perhaps the most comprehensive of all Coleridge's visions of the *magnum opus*, is only one of a spate of statements that occur about the same time. On 7 October 1815, Coleridge wrote to Daniel Stuart in much the same detail as he had to May. In this projection he speaks rather poignantly of "the Work, on which I would wish to ground my reputation with Posterity . . . a work, for which I have been collecting the materials for the last 15 years almost incessantly." The third of the treatises is here called "the Science of Premises, or transcendental Philosophy" and is introductory to the fourth, which is "a detailed Commentary on the Gospel of St. John." The fifth is on the Mystics and Pantheists, and here it is to include not only the lives of "Giordano Bruno, Jacob Behmen, George Fox, and Benedict Spinoza," but also "an analysis of their systems." Coleridge concludes by saying that the *magnum opus* "will comprize two large Octavo Volumes, 600 pages each."[55]

Earlier, on 27 August 1814, his first published plan for the *magnum opus* appeared in the essay called "On the Principles of Genial Criticism," in *Felix Farley's Bristol Journal*:

I am about to put to the press a large volume on the Logos, or the communicative intelligence in nature and in man, together

[55] *Ibid.*, 591-92.

with, and as preliminary to, a Commentary on the Gospel of St. John.[56]

In 1817 the *Biographia Literaria* came off the press, and it contained the second published notice of the *magnum opus*. Rejecting "materialism" because in order "to explain *thinking*, as a material phaenomenon, it is necessary to refine matter into a mere modification of intelligence," Coleridge says the subject

> will (if God grant health and permission), be treated of at large and systematically in a work, which I have for many years been preparing, on the PRODUCTIVE LOGOS human and divine; with, and as the introduction to, a full commentary on the Gospel of St. John.[57]

We are beginning to see the truth of what Coleridge had said in 1803, that the plan for his *"last & great work"* was one he "always had in mind." On December 1, 1812, for instance, he wrote to his benefactor Josiah Wedgwood and spoke of his hope of finding

> heart & spirits (still more necessary than time) to bring into shape the fruits of 20 years Study & observation.—[58]

On September 12, 1814, he wrote with great fullness to Stuart of the work, which he disingenuously announced as actually in the process of "printing at Bristol." In this lengthy projection, the title is not *Logosophia*, but "Christianity the one true Philosophy," and it is to contain, as the subtitle says, "5 Treatises on the Logos, or communicative Intelligence, Natural, Human, and Divine." Here the third treatise is to be "a full Commentary on the Gospel of St John, in development of St Paul's doctrine of preaching Christ alone, & him Crucified," and the "4th, on Spinoza, and Spinozism with a life of B. Spinoza—this entitled, Logos Agonistes." Coleridge concludes by saying that "The purpose of the whole is—a philosophical Defence of the Articles of the Church, as far as they respect Doctrine, or points of Faith.—If Originality be any merit, this work will have that at all events from the first page to the last."[59]

The plan, however, underwent gradual but continual metamorphosis. After Coleridge took up residence in the house of the physician James Gillman at Highgate, the work actually began to be written, and paradoxically its conceptions began to be fragmented into more limited vehicles. In March 1820 Coleridge writes

---

[56] *Biographia*, II, 230.
[58] *Collected Letters*, III, 421.

[57] *Ibid.*, I, 91-92.
[59] *Ibid.*, pp. 533-34.

to Allsop of "my GREAT WORK, to the preparation of which more than twenty years of my life have been devoted," and says that "of this work something more than a Volume has been dictated by me, so as to exist fit for the Press."[60] On 8 January 1821 he writes to another correspondent of an "Assertion of Religion as necessarily implying Revelation, and of Xtianity as the only Revelation of universal validity.—Of the latter some thing more than a Volume is written."[61] By 24 September 1821, the logical prolegomenon, which was so important a feature of the early projections of the *magnum opus*, is being spoken of as a work in its own right, one different from "the greater Work." The latter, as he says, will be an

> assertion of the ideal truth & the *a priori* probability and a posteriori internal and external evidence of the historic truth of the Christian Religion. . . . I entertain some hope too, that my Logic, which I could begin printing immediately if I could find a Publisher willing to undertake it on equitable terms, might prove an exception to the general fate of my publications.[62]

By 1824, the *magnum opus* had branched out into three works, one of them, the *Aids to Reflection*, actually soon to be published:

> As soon as this little Pioneer [i.e. *Aids to Reflection*] is out of hand, I go to the Press with the Elements of Discourse, or the Criteria of true & false Reasoning [i.e. the *Logic*]—and meantime shall devote myself to the completion of my great work, on the Philosophy of Religion.[63]

Subsequent descriptions of the great work become even more explicitly theological in their emphasis.[64]

I have quoted Coleridge's projections at such copious and possibly even wearisome length—and their number has by no means been exhausted—in order to indicate that the *magnum opus* was both more concrete and less hazy in its plan than the earlier part of this discussion might have suggested. On the contrary, it was the continuing focus of the most intense intellectual effort Coleridge could bring to it. Furthermore, not only do several hundreds of manuscript pages of it actually exist but also many hundreds of printed pages of its offshoots also exist. Having taken note of these facts, one may now go still further and suggest that on the evi-

---

[60] *Ibid.*, v, 27-28.   [61] *Ibid.*, p. 134.
[62] *Ibid.*, p. 177.   [63] *Ibid.*, p. 337.

[64] The most detailed of these projections is still in manuscript form and will be published in the concluding volume of the *Notebooks*.

dence of what the larger entity was to be, combined with testimony from the parts of the venture still in manuscript form, the *magnum opus* should be regarded as one of the most prophetic works of the nineteenth century, and in terms of the depth and power of the intellectual currents it stood against, one of the most heroic as well.

No exhaustive attempt to document such a contention will be made in the space remaining in this chapter; even the issues that are brought forward must be necessarily truncated, while other issues have to be omitted entirely. But perhaps by reference to five names in the forefront of the Western tradition, specifically Plato, Kant, Spinoza, Schopenhauer, and Darwin, one can at least indicate why Coleridge is so very much more than just another Christian conservative like Newman, Keble, Hurrell Froude and other members of the Oxford Movement. Though Coleridge can be seen as ranging himself with some of the goals of that movement, he also understood, in a way that none of its members did, what was really happening in the culture of his time. Indeed, the men of the Oxford Movement sometimes seemed to be equipped with a knowledge of Greek grammar and a high-minded devotion to the Church Fathers, and very little else;[65] certainly they were insulated against social and economic realities by wealth and upper-class privilege,[66] and they had little of Coleridge's awareness of the

[65] For instance, a commentator notes that "It was in a discussion over a few fragile lines of Greek poetry that Keble first met the man whose name was destined to be linked so closely to his own. . . . 'I never knew,' Keble observed later, 'how Pindar might be put into English until I heard Pusey construe him in his examination' " (O'Connell, p. 94). Again, "On October 24, 1831, the first term after Newman had ceased to be tutor, he received from his former pupils 'a very valuable present of books . . . consisting of thirty six volumes of the Fathers. . . . They are so fine in their outside,' he wrote to his mother, 'as to put my former ones to shame—and the editions are the best' " (Culler, p. 79). Comparing Darwin's eager voyage to the South Atlantic and the Pacific with Newman's attitude, Culler says of Newman that to "him the world of cities was little more than a busy and fretful dream, and the only voyage was that which he took in the silence of his own heart or among the works of his beloved Fathers" (Culler, p. 83).

[66] Thus Keble's father "was a Tory and a High Churchman. . . . Nor did he listen to those with fanciful ideas of social reconstruction. Some people are gentlemen, he would say, and some are not; and gentlemen are meant to rule and others to obey. . . . God loves all Englishmen, whatever their station. . . . And so a man must revere God's holy name, and all that he has made; and he must be good to the poor, loyal to his friends, his country and his king" (O'Connell, p. 90). Again, "Pusey, like Keble, was a member of the country gentry. . . . His father was the youngest son of a viscount, and his mother the daughter of an earl and the widow of a baronet. Edward, the second of their nine children, never lacked social connection or financial resources" (p. 94).

complex interactions of scientific, philosophical, and theological tides and currents.

Those tides and currents were comprehensively present to Coleridge's awareness, and accurately understood by him as leading toward the nihilism that Nietzsche later predicted must be the inevitable form of twentieth-century thought. Owen Chadwick has documented the gradual replacement, in the century and a half between Bossuet and Newman, of theological ideals of permanence by those of process;[67] Coleridge saw that such a change was endemic to all manifestations of European intellectual activity, and that it would eventuate in the destruction of all that gave assurance of meaning to life.[68] Thus he set against it a philosophy that I have elsewhere called Platonico-Christo-Kantism,[69] and that he called simply, to use one of the titles of the *magnum opus*, "Christianity the one true Philosophy";[70] and he espoused this philosophy with the realization that it was necessary to argue against the encroach-

[67] See Chadwick, *From Bossuet to Newman; The Idea of Doctrinal Development* (Cambridge: Cambridge University Press, 1957).

[68] Carlyle too realized that "Change is universal and inevitable"; but in accordance with his programmatic optimism he asserted that "the Present is the living sum-total of the whole Past," and that as a consequence "In change . . . there is nothing terrible, nothing supernatural: on the contrary, it lies in the very essence of our lot and life in this world." "[S]o much has become evident to every one, that this wondrous Mankind is advancing some whither; that at least all human things are, have been and forever will be, in Movement and Change;—"; "How often, in former ages, by eternal Creeds, eternal Forms of Government and the like, has it been attempted, fiercely enough, and with destructive violence, to chain the Future under the Past. . . . A wholly insane attempt." But even Carlyle's optimism occurred in the context of a recognition that "Belief, Faith has well-nigh vanished from the world"; "Not Godhead, but an iron, ignoble circle of Necessity embraces all things"; "Whither has Religion now fled?" (Carlyle, xxviii, 38, 39, 37, 29, 30, 22).

[69] For extended discussion, see *CPT*, pp. 202 ff. Although the rationalistic rigor of Kant's argument led some, both in his own day and later, to view him as an enemy of religion, Coleridge saw the deeper compatibility of Kantian doctrine with Christian conceiving. Compare Nietzsche's characterization of Kant's thought as "subterranean Christianity" (*Nietzsche*, iii, 502). As Kant himself said, "the ultimate aim to which the speculation of reason in its transcendental employment is directed concerns three objects: the freedom of the will, the immortality of the soul, and the existence of God" (*Gesammelte Schriften*, iii, 518). Compare Coleridge: "God created man in his own image . . . gave us REASON . . . gave us CONSCIENCE—that law of conscience, which . . . unconditionally *commands* us attribute *reality*, and actual *existence*, to those ideas and to those only, without which the conscience itself would be baseless and contradictory, to the ideas of Soul, of Free-will, of Immortality, and of God" (*Friend*, i, 112).

[70] *Collected Letters*, iii, 533.

ing changes in cognitive terms and not by a simple asseveration of faith—or exercise of the mechanism of denial.

Coleridge's own stake in Christianity was existential: if Christianity were true, then his own life, miserable and shattered though it was, could be seen as having the possibility of final meaning, and its sufferings could be accepted. If it were not true, then neither his life nor that of anyone else had meaning, and lives that were broken and deficient in happiness, such as his own, became intolerable.

To be able to see Christianity as true, it was necessary to conceive of its guarantees as real, not tentative, provisional, or mythological. "If in this life only," said Paul in a passage quoted by Coleridge, "we have hope in Christ, we are of all men most miserable."[71] "If there be no resurrection of the dead," said Paul bluntly, "then is Christ not risen: And if Christ be not risen, then is our preaching vain, and your faith is also vain." "I cannot conceive a supreme moral Intelligence," agreed Coleridge, "unless I believe in my own immortality."[72]

If the Christian religion and its guarantees of meaning and life were true, then they could not be conceived of as changing, or as subject to re-definition, after-thought, or historical vicissitude; for truth of necessity must be "One clear, unchanged, and universal light." Seven plus five equals twelve in the nineteenth century no less than in the fourth century. "The True Church," in Eliot's words, "can never fail/ For it is based upon a rock."[73] "The true simplicity of the Christian doctrine" wrote the far-seeing Bossuet to Leibniz, "consists principally and essentially forever in resolving matters, in that which regards faith, by this certain fact: Yesterday, it was believed thus; consequently, today it is necessary to believe the same." "Thus I say to you one more time, Sir," he wrote again, "that it is an unchanging maxim that in a matter of dogma of faith, that which has been believed one day has been and will always be;

---

[71] I. *Corinthians*, 15. 19.

[72] *Ibid.*, verses 13-14; *Inquiring Spirit*, p. 142. Paul's formulation goes to the heart of the matter; the postulate of immortality must always be the basis for any true meaning in life. Tennyson, for instance, realizes that "My own dim life should teach me this,/ That life should live for evermore,/ Else earth is darkness at the core,/ And dust and ashes all that is" (*Tennyson*, p. 171). "It has been said that the immortality of the soul," observes Byron, "is a 'grand peut-être'—but still it is a *grand* one. Every body clings to it—the stupidest, and dullest, and wickedest of human bipeds is still persuaded that he is immortal" (Byron, *Letters*, VIII, 35).

[73] Eliot, *Poems*, p. 57.

otherwise the succession would be broken, authority annulled, and the promise destroyed."[74]

By Coleridge's day, the fixities and definites of truth were crumbling ever more rapidly into the onrushing stream of process. To protect against this accelerating erosion, Coleridge looked to Plato and to Kant for girders of thought with which to shore his countervailing ruin.[75] This act of reinforcement, in fact, is the sum and simple substance of Coleridge's continuing obligation to both of those mighty thinkers.

Specifically, the whole philosophy of Plato is one that refers not to conceptions of growth, progress, and innovation, but to the conception of a timeless perfection from which all temporality is a form of lapse, and all change a mere eddying of phenomena. It is, if one wishes, in historical description a thought that binds the destructive flux of Heraclitus by forcing it into a reciprocal polarity with the unchanging One of Parmenides. In terms of the idea of man's historical development, Plato, as Eric Havelock has said,

> denied that there had been any significant development at all. To understand man, you fix your gaze on what he should be. For in a sense this is what he always has been—a species apart from the brutes, rational and moral, intelligent and just. If man's practice did not fit this theory, then man was to be corrected and educated till it did. For the norms by which his behaviour is governed, while they lie within the cosmos, lie outside history and process. They are as eternal as the cosmos itself. If the cosmos had a history, well and good. But it was always a history which exhibited a complete intelligence already present at the beginning.

On the other hand, a rival strain in ancient thought—and it was this strain that was swelling to an irresistible flood in the nineteenth century—tried, as Havelock says, "to imagine a pre-moral and pre-intellectual condition of man. They felt that what he was now could best be understood by building an historical bridge

[74] *Bossuet-Leibniz*, pp. 133, 144.

[75] Compare, for instance, Kant: "the argument of our Critique, taken as a whole, must have sufficiently convinced the reader that although metaphysics cannot be the foundation of religion, it must always continue to be a bulwark of it" (*Gesammelte Schriften*, III, 548-49). Compare also Plato: "we find soul to be prior to body, and body secondary and posterior. . . . And as soul thus controls and indwells in all things everywhere, must we not necessarily affirm that it controls Heaven also? . . . Plainly we must say that it is the supremely good soul that takes forethought for the universe and drives it on its course" (*Laws*, 896C-E, 897C).

between the present and the past; and between what man had been, and still was, not-man." As Havelock goes on to argue,

these competing conceptions rest upon competing doctrines of the origin and nature of man himself. According to the first, man . . . either . . . came into existence on the earth as a superior species with special prerogatives; or else he was created in the image of perfection by God. This can be called the anti-historical view of man. Civilizations may vary in their material forms, but man the human being has been a constant.

The second and non-metaphysical view of his morality and law is derived from an historical science which argues, first, that the human species emerged from non-human forms of life, by some evolutionary process, so that man's present body and brains represent the end-product of a long series of mutations; and second, that his moral and social codes have developed since he became intelligent, as a continuation of the evolutionary process.[76]

In the Romantic era and its prologue, the second of these competing traditions—that of "evolutionary process"—was gathering momentum, and was in due course, with the advent of Darwin's *On the Origin of Species* in 1859, to gain a decisive ascendancy.[77] Coleridge's *magnum opus* was, among other things, a brief on behalf of the first, or Platonic view of the nature and origin of man and his morality. Emerging as it did in the wake of such notable and cumulatively powerful arguments for the evolutionary view as those contained in Diderot's *Lettre sur les aveugles à l'usage de ceux qui voient* and his *Le Rêve de d'Alembert*, in Lessing's *Die Erziehung des Menschengeschlechts*, in Herder's *Ideen zur Philosophie der Geschichte der Menschheit*,[78] and pervasively in the work of Schelling

[76] Havelock, pp. 26-27, 27, 29-30.

[77] For evolutionary theory antecedent to Darwin see, e.g., *Forerunners of Darwin: 1745-1859*, ed. Bentley Glass *et al.* (Baltimore: The Johns Hopkins Press, 1959); also the book by Émile Guyénot, *Les Sciences de la vie aux XVIIᵉ et XVIIIᵉ siècles; l'idée d'évolution* (Paris: Albin Michel, 1941).

[78] How much of a ferment there was may be gauged from Goethe's testimony that his own evolutionary theorizing was helped by Herder's composition of the *Ideen*: "Our daily conversation was concerned with the earliest beginning of the water-earth and the organic creatures developing on it from the earliest times. The earliest beginning and its incessant, continual developing was constantly discussed, and our scientific possessions were daily enriched and clarified through alternate communication and attack" (As quoted and translated in Robert T. Clark, Jr., *Herder; His Life and Thought* [Berkeley: University of California Press, 1969], p. 303). It should be emphasized that in terms of the actual science of biology Herder cannot be seen as a

and Hegel, the *magnum opus* was from its inception not only con-
servative but backward-looking, not only traditional but even
anachronistic—in somewhat the same way that Milton's great
theodicy was anachronistic and actually archaic in terms of the cul-
tural realities that obtained in the latter part of the seventeenth cen-
tury. "The purpose of the whole," said Coleridge, "is—a philo-
sophical Defence of the Articles of the Church,"[79] and as a
subsidiary of this goal, it was intended to effect "a revolution of all
that has been called *Philosophy* or Metaphysics in England and
France since the aera of the commencing predominance of the me-
chanical system at the Restoration of our second Charles."[80] "What
is it," asks Coleridge elsewhere, in passionate defence of the first,
or Platonic hypothesis,

> that I employ my Metaphysics on? To perplex our clearest no-
> tions, & living moral Instincts? To extinguish the Light of Love &

strict precursor of Darwin (see, e.g., Max Rouché, *Herder précurseur de Darwin? his-
toire d'un mythe* [Paris: Publications de la faculté des lettres de l'université de Stras-
bourg, 1940]). In terms of the *meaning* of the Darwinian hypothesis for theological
and ethical concern, however, Herder is precisely such a precursor. As Pfleiderer
maintained, the "doctrine of development" is the "universal starting point" for
Darwin and his followers; but the "Urheber"—originator—of this doctrine was
"none other than Herder": "In his 'Ideas on the Philosophy of History,' he regarded
man as the final goal toward which earthly organization strove, as 'the form of or-
ganization evolved from stone to crystal . . . from crystal to vegetable creation. . .
from vegetable creation to man . . .' "; "Thus are 'the animals the older brothers of
man,' the preliminary steps on which forming nature represented transitorily in the
particular what she wanted to make real in man." (Pfleiderer, II, 341). Much the
same could be said of the contentions of Darwin's grandfather, Erasmus Darwin,
whose work Coleridge knew well, and who postulated that "Organic Life beneath
the shoreless waves/ Was born and nurs'd in Ocean's pearly caves." Those minute
forms then "New powers acquire, and larger limbs assume;/ Whence countless
groups of vegetation spring,/ And breathing realms of fin, and feet, and wing"
(*Erasmus Darwin*, pp. 90-91). As his modern commentator says, "Erasmus Darwin
propounded a theory of evolution that was more complete than any earlier ver-
sion"; "Erasmus had the right ideas, but failed to produce enough evidence to con-
vince the world"; "many of Charles Darwin's champions continued to suppress
Erasmus long after the need had passed, with the result that he has been consis-
tently under-rated as an evolutionist. A whole book could be written on the links
between Erasmus's and Charles's theories of evolution" (pp. 82-83). For an
enumeration of Erasmus Darwin's specific anticipations of Charles Darwin, see
Loren Eiseley, *Darwin's Century; Evolution and the Men Who Discovered It* (Garden
City, N.Y.: Doubleday Anchor Books, 1961), p. 47. For Coleridge's early knowledge
of the work of Erasmus Darwin, see John Beer, *Coleridge's Poetic Intelligence* (London
and Basingstoke: The Macmillan Press Ltd., 1977), pp. 50-57, 65-66, 74-77.

[79] *Collected Letters*, III, 534.   [80] *Ibid.*, V, 28.

of Conscience, . . . to make myself & others . . . *Worthless, Soul-less, God*less?—No! To expose the Folly & the Legerdemain of those, who have thus abused the blessed Organ of Language, to support all old & venerable Truths, to support, to kindle, to project, to make the Reason spread Light over our Feelings, to make our Feelings diffuse vital Warmth thro' our Reason—these are my Objects—& these my Subjects.[81]

How radically this stance differed from the intellectual attitudes of those contemporary German philosophers with whom Coleridge in other respects has much in common may be gauged by comparing the passage just quoted with summarizing statements by a commentator on Hegel's intellectual background:

A ceaseless, limitless activity, therefore, as the basis or groundwork of all, for ever crossing, arresting, and limiting it-self: an eternal war, which, however is always being led back to peace,—a process of differentiation which rests upon, is the product of, and is for ever forced back to integration, is the per-petual rhythm of the natural universe. . . . Even the tranquil rest of geometrical figures came to be explained as a meeting point and transition moment of opposite forces. But these ideas pro-duced an even greater effect on biology. . . .

The idea of Evolution or Development, thus introduced by Schelling into philosophy as a governing principle in the study of matter and of mind, is not to be confused either with the older use of these terms or with their current applications to-day. . . . [But] so far as Darwinism is an attempt to show that the classes of plants and animals are not a mere juxtaposition and aggrega-tion, but are to be explained by reference to a single genetic prin-ciple, it is in harmony with the Evolution taught by Schelling and Hegel. Both alike overthrow the hard and fast lines of divi-sion which semi-popular science insists upon, and restore the continuity of existence. Both regard Nature as an organic realm, developing by action and re-action within itself.[82]

In his attempt to "support all old & venerable Truths," Coleridge was concerned most centrally with the preservation of the "living moral Instincts," which depended on the Christian conception of God. In a "*God*less world," man would be "*Worthless, Soul*-less." So Coleridge summoned to the walls and crenellations of his de-

[81] *Notebooks*, I, 1623. Cf. *Friend*, I, 108-109.
[82] Wallace, pp. 115-19.

fense not only the strength of Plato but that of Kant as well; for Kant, as Richard Kroner says in his magisterial study of German philosophy from Kant to Hegel, attests to the same ultimate meaning as Plato:

> The Kantian philosophy, leaving aside all those contexts in which it relates to its immediate predecessors, can be regarded as a renewal of Platonic idealism from out of the German mind.[83]

This truth is as important as it is venerable; and it has been seen repeatedly by those who have penetrated most deeply into philosophical meanings. We shall content ourselves with presenting a single additional witness, but this one of the highest authority. For Schopenhauer says:

> If Kant's teaching, and since Kant's time, that of Plato, had ever been properly understood and grasped, if men had truly and earnestly reflected on the inner meaning and content . . . of the two great masters . . . they could not have failed long ago to discover how much the two great sages agree, and that the true significance, the aim, of both teachings is absolutely the same.[84]

Above all, both philosophies, and Coleridge's too, subscribe to the idea of a timeless permanence, indicated in Plato by the realm of ideas, in Kant by that of things-in-themselves, and in Coleridge by the idea of God. All three oppose the massive counter-philosophies of evolutionary change. "The Hegelians," as Schopenhauer affirms of the latter mode,

> who regard the philosophy of history as . . . the main purpose of all philosophy, should be referred to Plato, who untiringly repeats that the object of philosophy is the unchangeable and ever permanent, not that which now is thus and then otherwise. . . . This is what Plato means, this is what Kant means.[85]

But Coleridge could not simply assert a philosophy of Platonico-Christo-Kantism—the way, so to speak, one might decide to write a novel; he also had to *defend* against those counter-philosophies that threatened the Christian God. The undertaking of this defense, no less than the assertion of "Christianity the one true Philosophy," constitutes the task of the *magnum opus*. Specifically, Coleridge had to defend against two major forms of anti-

---

[83] Kroner, I, 35.
[84] Schopenhauer, II, 204.
[85] *Ibid.*, III, 506.

Christian implication endemic in his time: the first was Spinozism, which denied any God other than the world itself, and the second was the materialistic philosophy of process that eventuated in Darwinism, which denied any essential difference between man and beast and any ultimate purpose in human life. As he says in the *Opus Maximum*, he stood "at equi-distance from the opposite errors of the mechanic materialist and of the pantheist." He had to proceed across a "narrow isthmus" with "atheism on one side or a world without God, and Pantheism or a world that is itself God" on the other.

Coleridge was concerned to provide a cognitive, not a mystical, defense of God ("I distinctly disclaim all intention of explaining life into an occult quality"). He was accordingly forced to concede much to the gathering pertinence of evolutionary explanation. But on two issues, God as guarantor of human meaning and an essential difference between man and beast, he had to make a stand. To retreat further would be to concede the field entirely to the legions of atheism and hence of nihilism. "To *account* for Life is one thing; to explain Life another. . . . And to this, in the question of Life, I know no possible answer, but GOD." He was "Convinced—by revelation, by the consenting authority of all countries, and of all ages, by the imperative voice of my own conscience, and by that wide chasm between man and the noblest animals of the brute creation, which no perceivable or conceivable difference of organization is sufficient to overbridge—that I have a rational and responsible soul."[86] He was unwilling to "assign that soul which I believe to constitute the peculiar nature of man as the cause of functions and properties, which man possesses in common with the oyster and the mushroom."[87]

But all this was precisely what the proleptic force of Darwinism attacked. "The difference in mind between man and the higher animals, great as it is," said Darwin specifically, "certainly is one of degree and not of kind."[88] Coleridge's "wide chasm between man and the noblest animals," which no "conceivable difference of or-

---

[86] *Theory of Life*, pp. 33, 35, 33. Again, "Conscience" was "the great *Privilege* of our Nature by which alone we are contra-distinguished from the Brutes" (*Collected Letters*, IV, 958).

[87] *Theory of Life*, p. 33. But contrast Darwin: "Grant a simple Archetypal creature, like the Mud-fish or Lepidosiren, with the five senses and some vestige of mind, and I believe natural selection will account for the production of every vertebrate animal" (Darwin, *Life*, I, 528).

[88] Darwin, *Descent*, p. 128.

ganization is sufficient to overbridge," was contradicted by Darwin's postulate that "Every one who admits the principle of evolution, must see that the mental powers of the higher animals, which are the same in kind with those of man, though so different in degree, are capable of advancement."[89] As to the favored place of man as the unique creation of God, Darwin said that "The great principle of evolution stands up clear and firm. . . . He who is not content to look, like a savage, at the phenomena of nature as disconnected, cannot any longer believe that man is the work of a separate act of creation."[90] Irenic and desirous of avoiding conflict though he was, and sometimes perhaps not entirely ingenuous in declaring his beliefs, Darwin nevertheless confessed himself "aware that the conclusions arrived at" in his theory "will be denounced by some as highly irreligious."[91]

The philosophy of Spinoza, though lacking the Darwinian em-

[89] *Ibid.*, p. 624.

[90] *Ibid.*, p. 621. We can see another form of the unequivocal opposition between Coleridge and Darwin in Coleridge's wish to refute "all the countless Believers—even (strange to say) among Xtians of Man's having progressed from an Ouran Outang state—so contrary to all History, to all Religion, nay, to all Possibility" (*Collected Letters*, IV, 574-75). But contrast Darwin: "The main conclusion arrived at in this work, namely that man is descended from some lowly organised form, will, I regret to think, be highly distasteful to many. But there can hardly be a doubt that we are descended from barbarians. . . . He who has seen a savage in his native land will not feel shame, if forced to acknowledge that the blood of some more humble creature flows in his veins. For my own part, I would as soon be descended from that heroic little monkey, who braved his dreaded enemy in order to save the life of his keeper, or from that old baboon, who descended from the mountains, carried away in triumph his young comrade from a crowd of astonished dogs—as from a savage who delights to torture his enemies" (Darwin, *Descent*, pp. 633-34). For eighteenth-century adumbration of Darwin's position, compare Monboddo: "Now where-ever there is a progress, there must be a beginning; and the beginning in this case can be no other than the mere animal: for in tracing back the progress, where else can we stop? . . . From savage men we are naturally led to consider the condition of the brute; betwixt whom and the savages there is such a resemblance, that there are many who will hardly admit of any difference"; ". . . there is no *natural* difference betwixt our minds and theirs . . . the superiority we have over them is *adventitious*, and from *acquired habit*"; "Further, not only solitary savages but a whole nation . . . have been found without the use of speech. This is the case of the Ouran Outangs that are found in the kingdom of Angola in Africa"; "the Ouran Outangs, who . . . are proved to be of our species by marks of humanity that are incontestable. . . . They live in society, build huts, joined in companies attack elephants . . . but have not yet attained the use of speech" (Monboddo, pp. 134, 135, 174, 289). For still earlier adumbration see Edward Tyson, *Orang-Outang, sive Homo Sylvestris: or, the Anatomy of a Pygmie Compared with that of a Monkey, an Ape, and a Man* . . . (London, 1699).

[91] Darwin, *Descent*, p. 627.

phasis on process and evolution, conduced to the same view of a godless world.

Now the pantheism of Spinoza had virtually flooded European thought by Coleridge's time, and it continued to do so throughout the nineteenth century. All the post-Kantian German philosophers, despite declarations of allegiance to Kant, were Spinozists. As Schopenhauer acerbically but acutely pointed out,

> In consequence of Kant's criticism of all speculative theology, almost all the philosophizers in Germany cast themselves back on Spinoza, so that the whole series of bungled attempts known by the name of post-Kantian philosophy is simply Spinozism tastelessly got up, veiled in all kinds of unintelligible language, and otherwise twisted and distorted.[92]

Heine was aware of the same truth: "all our contemporary philosophers," he writes, "—perhaps often without knowing it—see through spectacles ground and polished by Baruch Spinoza."[93] Feuerbach realized it too: "Spinoza is the real originator of modern speculative philosophy, Schelling its re-stater, Hegel its completer."[94]

Indeed, Spinoza dominated not only formal philosophy but the entire intellectual presuppositions of the nineteenth-century milieu. Many logicians and psychologists, without direct reference to ontological problems, departed in their specialized researches from axioms that assumed the correctness of Spinozism. As Paul Ricoeur says of such a product of the late-nineteenth century as Freud, to take only one instance, "reality has the same meaning at the end of Freud's life as it did at the beginning: reality is the world shorn of God. . . . One can thus find in Freud the sketch of a Spinozistic meaning of reality."[95] For the century as a whole, to adopt Friedrich Schlegel's summing up, "Spinoza is everywhere in the background, like fate in Greek tragedy."[96]

The dominance of his thought can hardly be overestimated, and it increased rather than decreased as the century rolled on. "I knew the Ethics of Spinoza," exclaimed Flaubert in 1870, "but not the Tractatus theologico-politicus, which stuns me, dazzles me, transports me with admiration. My God, what a man! What a mind! What science and what spirit!" He noted again, in 1872, that "I am falling voraciously on my old and thrice-great Spinoza. What a ge-

[92] Schopenhauer, III, 741.
[94] *Feuerbach's Werke*, II, 244.
[96] *Friedrich Schlegel*, XVIII, 396.
[93] Heine, p. 176.
[95] Ricoeur, pp. 327-28.

nius! What a work his Ethics is."[97] For another example, Nietzsche wrote with rapture in 1881:

I am totally amazed, totally enchanted! I have a forerunner, and what a forerunner! I hardly knew Spinoza, that I should have turned to him just now was inspired by "instinct." Not only is his whole tendency like mine . . . but in five main points of his doctrine I recognize myself.[98]

The *magnum opus* resisted this current. To vary the metaphor of defense, it can be understood in philosophical perspective as an attempt to dam the flood of Spinozism in the nineteenth century.[99] "Spinozism," said Coleridge, "consists in the exclusion of intelligence and consciousness from Deity—therefore it is Atheism."[100] "Pantheism," he said again, "is equivalent to Atheism . . . there is no other Atheism actually existing, or speculatively conceivable, but Pantheism."[101]

Spinozism, as the speculative form of atheism, conjoined in its cultural effect with Darwinism, the scientific form. But though *On the Origin of Species* brought to historical focus all those evolutionary threats against which the *magnum opus*, a generation before, had been designed as safeguard, it presents nevertheless only a partial antithesis to Coleridge's endeavor. Darwin's work is neither religious nor philosophical in its overt statement, however much so it may be in its implication;[102] and it is neither systematic nor culturally inclusive in its structure and texture of discourse. The truest antithesis to Coleridge's *magnum opus* is provided instead by that *magnum opus* of Schopenhauer called *Die Welt als Wille und Vorstellung*.

Another reason why *On the Origin of Species* is not a full antithesis for Coleridge's "Great Work" is that the presentation of implications tends in Darwin's book to be veiled. He expresses himself somewhat more directly in letters and later publications; but in his

[97] *Flaubert*, VI, 113, 364.

[98] *Friedrich Nietzsches Briefwechsel mit Franz Overbeck*, ed. Richard Oehler and C. A. Bernouilli (Leipzig: Insel-Verlag, 1916), p. 149.

[99] For additional discussion of the rise of Spinozism see *CPT*, "The Spinozistic Crescendo," pp. 53-106.

[100] *Critical Annotations of S. T. Coleridge*, ed. William F. Taylor (Harrow, 1899), p. 32.

[101] *Complete Works*, V, 406. Compare Feuerbach: "Pantheism is theological atheism" (*Feuerbach's Werke*, II, 289).

[102] Nevertheless Darwin did say that "I do not believe that there ever has been any revelation. As for a future life, every man must judge for himself between conflicting vague probabilities" (Darwin, *Life*, I, 277).

chef d'oeuvre he speaks of the ominous "Struggle for Existence," or "universal struggle for life," in incongruously mild language:

> We behold the face of nature bright with gladness, we often see superabundance of food; we do not see, or we forget, that the birds which are idly singing round us mostly live on insects or seeds, and are thus constantly destroying life; or we forget how largely these songsters, or their eggs, or their nestlings, are destroyed by birds and beasts of prey; we do not always bear in mind, that though food may be now superabundant, it is not so at all seasons of each recurring year.[103]

Thus Darwin in 1859. But Schopenhauer's presentation of the same thought a decade and a half earlier confronts with almost poetic vividness the philosophical dimensions and moral consequences glossed over in Darwin's formulation; his own examples—not those of "songsters"—resound with diapasons from the abyss:

> There is nothing to show but the satisfaction of hunger and sexual passion, and in any case a little momentary gratification, such as falls to the lot of every individual animal, now and then, between its endless needs and exertions. . . . The futility and the fruitlessness of the struggle . . . are more readily grasped in the simple and easily observable life of animals. . . . We see only momentary gratification, fleeting pleasure conditioned by wants, much and long suffering, constant struggle, *bellum omnium*, everything a hunter and everything hunted, pressure, want, need, and anxiety, shrieking and howling; . . . Junghuhn relates that in Java he saw an immense field entirely covered with skeletons, and took it to be a battle-field. However, they were nothing but skeletons of large turtles five feet long, three feet broad, and of equal height. These turtles come this way from the sea, in order to lay their eggs, and are then seized by wild dogs . . . with their united strength, these dogs lay them on their backs, tear open their lower armour, the small scales of the belly, and devour them alive. But then a tiger often pounces on the dogs. Now all this misery is repeated thousands and thousands of times, year in and year out. For this, then, are these turtles born. What is the point of this whole scene of horror?[104]

Thus in the *magnum opus* of Schopenhauer the implications of evolution are confronted along all the lines of significance with which Coleridge is concerned, and confronted, as with Coleridge,

[103] Darwin, *Origin*, p. 116.   [104] Schopenhauer, III, 404-405.

before *On the Origin of Species* appeared.[105] Schopenhauer's great work, like Coleridge's, is deeply involved with final questions of religion and the structure of reality; like Coleridge's, it brings to the fore the question of the meaning of human existence; like Coleridge's, it sees will as philosophically central; like Coleridge's, it is based on extensive erudition, especially with regard to the legacy of Kant; like Coleridge's, it is comprehensively concerned with the state of science in its own time; like Coleridge's, it sees the relation of the individual to nature as decisive for human possibility; like Coleridge's, it is profoundly responsive to the tidal wave of Spinozistic influence; like Coleridge's, finally, it is ambitiously and definitively systematic. Indeed, like Coleridge's, it is haunted by the specter of incompleteness: Schopenhauer's first edition of 1819 was succeeded by a second edition in 1844 that, to an extent possibly unique in the annals of authorial afterthoughts, more than doubled the size of the treatise.

That Schopenhauer was able, by heroic augmentation, to replace partial statement by at least a formal completeness and that Coleridge was not indicates perhaps not merely temperamental differences between the two men but also the gradual swing of evidence away from Platonico-Christian ideals of permanence toward Darwinian-Atheistic ideals of process and change. In any event, Coleridge's *magnum opus*, as a ruin of hopeful assertion, and Schopenhauer's *Die Welt als Wille und Vorstellung*, as an erected edifice that despairingly sees life as containing no meaning,[106] are in powerful contrast throughout the entire range of their community of involvement. Coleridge, like Schopenhauer, understood the consequences of the Darwinian hypothesis before that hypothesis actually triumphed in 1859. Unlike Schopenhauer, Coleridge

---

[105] See further A. O. Lovejoy, "Schopenhauer as an Evolutionist," *Forerunners of Darwin: 1745-1859*, pp. 415-37. Lovejoy finds Schopenhauer "not only an evolutionist but also a mutationist; his speculations are prophetic of the theory of De Vries and Goldschmidt rather than that of Darwin" (p. 427). For our purposes here, however, it is plain that Schopenhauer encompasses all the implications of the Darwinian transformation of reality's meaning: "It is thus clear that by 1850 Schopenhauer had formulated his conception of the 'objectification of the Will' in thoroughly evolutionistic terms and had incorporated into his philosophy a complete system of cosmogony and phylogeny" (pp. 430-31).

[106] Compare a collage of judgments by Nietzsche: "Schopenhauer as a philosopher was the first declared and uncompromising atheist that we Germans have had" (*Nietzsche*, II, 227). He speaks of Schopenhauer's "terrible look into a world that has become de-Godded, dumb, blind, and questionable" (II, 229). He identifies the "Schopenhauerian question" as "does existence have any meaning at all?" (II, 228). And he says succinctly that "Schopenhauer was inimical to life" (II, 1169).

did not accept evolutionary meaning and its pessimistic consequence of loss of faith in the significance of life itself. All Coleridge's powers, and the whole conception of the *magnum opus*, were on the contrary devoted to a last ditch stand, at the innermost ramparts of Christianity, for the assurance of meaning in man's existence and action. As he said, "if dead, we cease to be" then we are "purposeless, unmeant"; if we are merely the "Surplus of Nature's dread activity," a "blank accident," then we are "rootless" and "substanceless," and the conclusion must be that it makes no difference whether we are sad, or glad, or neither.[107] If the world and man are, in his phrase, simply "the coagulation of Chaos," then all moral concerns collapse.[108]

But Coleridge lost, of course. The *magnum opus* was not completed. The enemy carried the day. Yet a journal entry by Carlyle in 1869, some ten years after the Darwinian triumph, allows us to gauge how prophetic had been Coleridge's forebodings about "the coagulation of Chaos":

The quantities of potential and even consciously increasing Atheism, sprouting out everywhere in these days, is enormous. . . . Not only all Christian churches but all Christian religion are nodding towards speedy downfall in this Europe that now is. Figure the residuum: man made chemically out of *Urschleim*, or a certain blubber called *protoplasm*. Man descended from the apes, or the shellfish. Virtue, duty, or utility an association of ideas, and the corollaries from all that. France is amazingly advanced in that career. England, America, are making still more passionate speed to come up with her, to pass her, and be the vanguard of progress.[109]

---

[107] Coleridge, *Poems*, I, 425-26.

[108] The coagulation of chaos is the only alternative to a God-ordained explanation of reality. Thus Plato identified his cosmological opponents in just such terms: "Let me put it more plainly still. Fire and water, earth and air—so they say—all owe their being to nature and chance, none of them to art; they, in turn, are the agents, and the absolutely soulless agents, in the production of the bodies of the next rank, the earth, sun, moon, and stars. They drifted casually, each in virtue of their several tendencies. As they came together in certain fitting and convenient dispositions— hot with cold, dry with moist, soft with hard, and so on in all the inevitable casual combinations which arise from blending of contraries—they gave birth to the whole heavens and all their contents, and, in due course, to all animals and plants . . . not, so they say, by the agency of mind, or any god, or art, but, as I tell you, by nature and chance" (*Laws*, 889B-C).

[109] Froude, II, 414. Carlyle's word "*Urschleim*" was given currency by Coleridge's contemporary, Oken.

Precisely a hundred years later, in 1969, Jacques Monod, Nobel Prizewinner in biochemistry and director of the Pasteur Institute in Paris, provided a signal validation for Carlyle's assessment. Saying that "I have done no more than summarize what are considered established ideas in contemporary science,"[110] and brushing aside the hopeful ameliorations that earlier thinkers such as Spencer and Bergson had sought to attach to the evolutionary model, Monod in a chilling series of lectures identified inanimate matter and blind chance as the sole building blocks of reality, human as well as natural:

> . . . chance *alone* is the source of every innovation, of all creation in the biosphere. Pure chance, absolutely free but blind, at the very root of the stupendous edifice of evolution: this central concept of modern biology is no longer one among other possible or even conceivable hypotheses. It is today the *sole* conceivable hypothesis, the only one compatible with observed and tested fact.[111]

He continues bleakly: "The universe was not pregnant with life nor the biosphere with man. Our number came up in the Monte Carlo game."[112]

As Coleridge foresaw, a world understood in this way will inevitably be a cosmos where traditional moralities are undermined, and substituted ones nullified in their ultimate authority. "Our societies," recognizes Monod, "are still trying to live by and to teach systems of values already blasted at the root by science itself." He speaks of "The 'liberal' societies of the West" that "still pay lip-service to, and present as a basis for morality, a disgusting farrago of Judeo-Christian religiosity, scientistic progressism, belief in the 'natural' rights of man, and utilitarian pragmatism"; and he acutely identifies the "sickness of the modern spirit" as stemming from "this lie at the root of man's moral and social nature." But if man "accepts this message in its full significance," continues Monod, he

> must at last wake out of his millenary dream and discover his total solitude, his fundamental isolation. He must realize that,

[110] Monod, p. 13.

[111] *Ibid.*, p. 110. This is even more bleak than Darwin himself, for Darwin's "inward conviction" was "that the Universe is not the result of chance" (Darwin, *Life,* I, 285).

[112] Monod, p. 137.

like a gypsy, he lives on the boundary of an alien world; a world that is deaf to his music, and as indifferent to his hopes as it is to his suffering or his crimes.

Who, then, is to define crime? Who decides what is good and what is evil? All the traditional systems placed ethics and values beyond man's reach. Values did not belong to him; they were imposed on him, and he belonged to them. Today he knows that they are his and his alone, but now he is master of them they seem to be dissolving in the uncaring emptiness of the universe.[113]

So much for the "amazingly advanced" atheist progress of France that Carlyle noted. Other countries supplied other voices in the gathering chorus of atheism. A "fundamental," said the German Karl Marx in 1844, is that *"man makes religion;* religion does not make man. . . . Religion [is] an *inverted consciousness of the world.* . . . It is the *opium* of the people."[114] "If he had decided that God and immortality did not exist," mused Alyosha Karamazov, a figure in the great novel by the Russian Dostoevsky in 1879, "he would at once have become an atheist and a socialist. For socialism is . . . before all things the atheistic question." "There is no virtue if there is no immortality," said Alyosha's brother Ivan. If there is no God, "nothing would be immoral, everything would be permitted." And Ivan projects a grimly jesting vision of atheist priests protecting the masses from the knowledge of an empty cosmos: "Peacefully they will die, peacefully they will expire in Thy name, and beyond the grave they will find nothing but death. But we shall keep the secret."[115] "God is dead," proclaimed the German Nietzsche in the fourth quarter of the nineteenth century[116] (he was echoing his predecessor, Hegel); and the Englishman Thomas Hardy in 1908 signalized the demise by a poem called "God's Funeral," which broached the sombre question, "who or what shall fill his place?"[117] Nietzsche's deranged epigone, Hitler, freed from God, joined the Russian Marxist Stalin in showing that everything was indeed permitted.

Hardy's poetic forerunner, Matthew Arnold, had earlier, in 1867, heard the "melancholy, long, withdrawing roar" of the "Sea of Faith," and he had concluded that

---

[113] *Ibid.,* pp. 159, 160, 160-61.   [114] *Marx,* I, 378.

[115] *The Brothers Karamazov,* Book One, Chapter Five, "Elders"; Book Two, Chapter Six, "Why is Such a Man Alive"; Part Two, Book Five, "The Grand Inquisitor."

[116] *Nietzsche,* II, 115.   [117] *Hardy,* p. 308.

the world, which seems
To lie before us like a land of dreams,
So various, so beautiful, so new,
Hath really neither joy, nor love, nor light,
Nor certitude, nor peace, nor help for pain.
And we are here as on a darkling plain.[118]

"The total character of the world," confirmed Nietzsche, "is in all eternity Chaos."[119]

Nor were these merely occasional statements. The death of God knelled no less insistently in the mind of Arnold's friend Clough than it did in Arnold and in Nietzsche himself:

I dreamt a dream; till morning light
A bell rang in my head all night.
Tinkling and tinkling first, and then
Tolling; and tinkling, tolling again.
So brisk and gay, and then so slow!
O joy, and terror! mirth, and woe!
Ting, ting, there is no God; ting, ting—
Dong, there is no God; dong,
There is no God; dong, dong!

The *leit-motiv* of Arnold's whole poetic performance, in fact, is depression at the thought of a world shorn of its meaning. He felt himself "Wandering between two worlds, one dead,/ The other powerless to be born" and said that "on earth I wait forlorn."[120] The "old is out of date,/ The new is not yet born,/ And who can be *alone* elate,/ While the world lies forlorn."[121] We are "Poor fragments of a broken world"—"That glow of central fire is done/ Which with its fusing flame/ Knit all your parts, and kept you one—"; "Your creeds are dead, your rites are dead." Most men "in a brazen prison live/ . . . Their lives to some unmeaning taskwork give"—"ye work and plan," he cries, "and know not ye are sever'd." In the "Scholar-Gipsy" he speaks of "this strange disease of modern life" with its concomitants: "the sick fatigue, the

---

[118] Arnold, *Poems*, pp. 211-12.

[119] *Nietzsche*, II, 115.

[120] *Clough*, p. 247; Arnold, *Poems*, p. 302.

[121] Arnold, *Poems*, p. 321. Cf. Carlyle: "The doom of the Old has long been pronounced, and irrevocable; the Old has passed away: but, alas, the New appears not in its stead; the Time is still in pangs of travail with the New" (*Carlyle*, XXVIII, 32).

languid doubt"; each of us "strives, nor knows for what he strives."[122]

"Do we hear nothing as yet of the noise of the grave-diggers who are burying God?" asked Nietzsche again. "Do we smell nothing as yet of the divine decomposition? Gods too decompose. God is dead. God remains dead. And we have killed him."[123] "There is no God, and man is his prophet," said Niels Lyhne, the protagonist of the great novel by the Danish writer Jens Peter Jacobsen.[124] Niels later taught his young bride that "all gods were the work of men, and like everything else made by men could not endure eternally, but must pass away. . . . He went on to teach her how the belief in a personal God . . . is a running away from the harsh realities of life."[125]

But even here, in the very keep of atheism, as it were, Coleridge's prophetic fears are realized; for though Niels "made his faith as beautiful and blessed as he could," still he "did not conceal from her how crushingly sad and comfortless the truth of atheism would seem in the hour of sorrow compared to the old, fair, happy dream of a Heavenly Father who guides and rules."[126] It was in the dedicated service of that old, fair, and happy dream that Coleridge planned, labored, and eventually foundered. The ruin and at the same time the monument of his striving is the legendary *magnum opus*.

[122] *Ibid.*, pp. 320, 243, 320, 261, 260.

[123] *Nietzsche*, II, 127.

[124] Jacobsen, p. 160. For the cultural centrality of Jacobsen compare Rilke: "Of all my books just a few are indispensable to me, and two even are always among my things, wherever I am. They are about me here, too: the Bible, and the books of the great Danish writer, Jens Peter Jacobsen." "If I am to say from whom I have learned something about creative work . . . there are but two names I can mention: that of Jacobsen, the great, great writer, and that of Auguste Rodin." "*Niels Lyhne* will open up before you, a book of glories and of the deeps . . . there seems to be everything in it from life's very faintest fragrance to the full big taste of the heaviest faults. There is nothing that does not seem to have been understood" (*Letters to a Young Poet*, trans. M. D. Herter Norton [New York: W. W. Norton & Company, Inc., 1954], pp. 24-25, 27).

[125] Jacobsen, pp. 266-67.

[126] *Ibid.*, p. 268.

The Place Beyond the Heavens: True Being, Transcendence, and the Symbolic Indication of Wholeness

◊ ◆ ◊

Iᴆ ᴛʜᴇ strivings of Coleridge and Wordsworth, as viewed from the shifting perspectives of the preceding chapters, all participate in that *ständige Unganzheit*—that continuing incompleteness—seen by Heidegger as an unavoidable limitation of life itself, we might expect the form and purpose of those strivings to reveal themselves, under inspection, as an attempt to overcome or at least to compensate for such fragmentation. We might expect to find that the ceaseless effort discharged into philosophical formulation, interchangeably with the continuously pulsating transformations of spirit into poetic statement, was somehow prompted by the diasparactive condition of our existence.

We shall commence such an inspection by considering the nature of artistic activity in its widest ramification, using that comprehensive specification to convey, as occasion requires, the sense either of poetic and other aesthetic endeavor or again that of philosophical endeavor, or still again that of all such endeavor taken together.

Artistic activity seems almost synonymous with culture itself. It is, furthermore, largely exempt from the kind of adverse criticism that accretes to scientific activity. Science, in both its theoretical and its applied functions, is greeted with fear and revulsion in virtually the same ratio as it is accorded respect and considered a necessity for the improvement of the human lot (we think immediately of such ambiguous aspects of scientific progress as nuclear fission, genetic manipulation, and industrial pollution). Art, on the other hand, is almost universally and unequivocally considered a good. One has only to witness the hordes descending on the museums of Europe and America, or call to mind the willingness of the more affluent to support opera, ballet, theater, or still again to think of the cachet accorded the decision on the part of the young to be "creative"—whether in painting, sculpture, music, dance, literature, or the stage—to realize that art draws to itself much of the ideal aspiration of our civilization. "At forty she was still ambitious to become a painter," muses Bellow's Tommy Wilhelm in somber reflection on his sister: "She worked very hard, but there were fifty thousand people in New York with paints and brushes, each practically a law unto himself. It was the Tower of Babel in paint."[1] And though art deals with and utters the motifs of *Unbehagen* that Freud found endemic to *Kultur*, it exists in itself as a haven from and palliative for those discontents.

Unlike science, however, artistic activity is shrouded in uncertainty. Just what it is and what it is doing, despite an enormous amount of explanatory conceptualization from antiquity to the present day, remain problematical and, to the vast majority of its acolytes, mysterious. The question as to why art is important is one that largely receives a circular answer; it is important because the more sophisticated members of society say it is important, and because the less sophisticated are blamed for not being aware of its importance. Tolstoy, in his *What is Art?*, can deliver fiercely heterodox censures on the artistic preoccupation; yet his entire life was devoted to its service, and his reputation stems from his achievement in its enterprise.

The two questions, what is art and why is it important, can hardly be separated. Without attempting here to adjudicate or even to ascertain the full range of subsidiary structures arising from those two primary questions, one may suggest that such topics become more tractable if we make ourselves aware of a fundamental distinction in the forms of artistic activity.

Although all art is involved with experienced reality—or, to adopt Auerbach's rubric, with the "representation of reality"—the way it is involved divides into two contrasted relationships. In the first, art imitates *what is there* in reality; in the second, it imitates *what is not there*. In deference to traditional usage, we might reserve the word "imitate" for the first relationship alone and call the tradition of theory and practice that has arisen in its service the *mimetic* mode. Perhaps the theorist who stands as most suitable godfather to this entire division of artistic activity is Aristotle; and from

[1] Saul Bellow, *Seize the Day*.

among the countless formulations presented in its behalf, perhaps the one that most fittingly emblemizes its perdurable dignity is Shakespeare's statement that the purpose of art, at least in its form as drama, is "to hold, as 'twere, the mirror up to nature." The *degré zéro*, so to speak, of such artistic mirroring may reside in such efforts as the Venetian scenes of Canaletto or Southey's "The Cataract of Lodore." In more ambitiously and complexly conceived creations, however, the mimetic mirror not only reproduces but in addition focuses experienced reality. "Poetry," says Shelley, "is a mirror which makes beautiful that which is distorted."[2]

It would be difficult to overestimate the currency of this single image of the mirror for formulations of literary function throughout the entire range of Western culture. A revealing book could be written simply on its incidence in the Middle Ages and the Renaissance, while the four most central documents in the theorizing of Romantic intent—Wordsworth's *Preface to Lyrical Ballads*, Schlegel's *Athenäums-Fragment 116*, Shelley's *Defence of Poetry*, and Hugo's *Préface de Cromwell*—all invoke the image of a mirror as an aid to their formulation. It is because in this world we see *per speculum in aenigmate* that the idea of mirroring seems so apposite to any description of artistic activity. As I have elsewhere said,

> Tragedy is the mirror of human existence. From our position amid the varied events of daily life, just as from our eyes looking out on the world, we can see much, but not our own selves. To see the events of the world, we look at the world; but to see ourselves, we need a mirror.
>
> We look into the tragic mirror, however, not only to view our full reality, but also to set at a remove its rending paradox.[3]

The second tradition of artistic activity, that in which the imitation is not of what is there, but of what is not there, may be called the *meontic* mode. The opposition of these two approaches, the mimetic and the meontic, can be illustrated in rudimentary terms by Keats's comparison of himself to Byron: "You speak of Lord Byron and me—There is this great difference between us. He describes what he sees—I describe what I imagine."[4] Indeed, the whole body of Romantic theorizing that was devoted to the apotheosis of imagination—in England alone we may point to Blake, Coleridge, Wordsworth, Keats, Hazlitt, and Shelley—is a

[2] Shelley, *Prose*, p. 10.
[3] *Tragic Meanings in Shakespeare* (New York: Random House, 1966), p. 3.
[4] Keats, *Letters*, ii, 200.

form of obeisance to the meontic mode. Blake, for instance, sets imaginative activity squarely in opposition to the hegemony of *what is there*: "Natural Objects always did & now do Weaken deaden & obliterate Imagination in me."[5]

Baudelaire, too, raises the banner of imagination in opposition to the mimetic mode. "In recent times," he says in the *Salon de 1859*, "we have heard it said in a thousand different ways: 'Copy nature, only copy nature. There is not a greater joy nor a more beautiful triumph than an excellent copy of nature.' "[6] But he himself brutally rejects this doctrine as "ennemie de l'art," and represents the adherent of the meontic mode—"un homme imaginatif"—as justifiably responding:

> I find it worthless and tedious to represent that which is, because nothing of that which is satisfies me. Nature is ugly, and I prefer the monsters of my fantasy to matter-of-fact (*positive*) triviality.[7]

Taking up the word *"positive,"* he proceeds to divide artists into "imaginatives" and "positivists":

> The immense class of artists, that is to say, of men who are devoted to the expression of art, can be divided into two quite distinct camps: one on this side who calls himself *realist*—word of double meaning and of which the sense is not properly determined, and that we may call, in order better to characterize his error, a *positivist*—says: 'I want to represent things as they are, or rather as they should be, supposing that I do not exist.' The universe without man. And the one over there, the imaginative, says: 'I want to illuminate things with my spirit and project the reflection of it upon other spirits.[8]

The mimetic and meontic modes, though contrasted, can intermingle in the work of a single practitioner, and indeed in a single artistic artifact; for as methods of artistic activity they form a continuum rather than an absolute opposition. At the extremes they can be represented on the purely meontic scale by, say, Mondrian or Kandinsky, or in poetry by, let us say, Ashbery; on the mimetic, by the painting of Ingres, or the novels of James T. Farrell. Most artistic representation, however, takes place somewhat nearer the meeting point of the two modes. An exquisite courtyard depiction

[5] *Blake*, p. 655.   [6] Baudelaire, II, 619-20.

[7] *Ibid.*, p. 620. Cf. Blake: "Why Are Copiers of Nature Incorrect while Copiers of Imagination Are Correct this is manifest to all" (*Blake*, p. 563).

[8] Baudelaire, II, 627.

by De Hooch in Washington's National Gallery is strongly on the mimetic side, but with an intermixture of meontic conception; Botticelli's "Venus and Mars" in London's National Gallery is strongly meontic (neither Venus nor Mars can be met in experienced reality) but with certain mimetic commitments also (males and females *are* met with in experienced reality).

Some of the greatest artists can utilize both modes simultaneously with extraordinary effect. Thus the magnificent self-portrait of Rembrandt in Washington's National Gallery—and much the same could be said of the great Rembrandt self-portrait in the Frick Collection—shapes its artistic being almost at the intersection of mimetic and meontic endeavor. The face is rendered with extreme naturalism. There is, for instance, an inspired realization of the aging cheek, with an awesomely real graininess of the skin between the cheekbone and neck, and an ever so slight slackening of skin over bone that occurs after the age of fifty. Other parts of the portrait, however—the shoulders, the breast, the background—are treated almost contemptuously in mimetic terms, with shadow for their coloring, and virtual abandonment of artistic attention. Except for the tension of the hands, everything is focused on the eyes, which are surrounded by mimetic evocations of wrinkled tiredness and age, but which in their uncanny depth become windows to that meontic wonder, the spirit. The portrait in truth is ultimately nothing less than the representation of soul itself.

In other configurations, what seems to be exclusive adherence to one mode becomes by adjustment of definition an adherence to the other. For instance, Chekhov seems to cast his lot unequivocally with the mimetic mode: "a writer should, above all, become a shrewd, and indefatigable observer, and should train himself in such a way that it becomes a habit, second nature with him. . . . A man of letters should be as objective as a chemist, he should abandon the subjectivity of everyday life." But in another place Chekhov autobiographically amends this prescription in a way that reveals his allegiance as belonging to the meontic mode: "I can only write from recollection and I have never described directly from nature. I need my memory to strain my theme and retain, as in the bottom of a filter, whatever is important and typical."[9] We recognize the conception here as virtually identical to Wordsworth's dictum that poetry "takes its origin from emotion recollected in tranquillity: the emotion is contemplated till, by a species

[9] *Chekhov*, pp. 17, 48.

of re-action, the tranquillity gradually disappears, and an emotion, kindred to that which was before the subject of contemplation, is gradually produced, and does itself actually exist in the mind."[10] Both formulations transform an initially mimetic emphasis into a meontic undertaking.

Not only individual artists and individual works of art but larger forms of art as well can be described in terms of the division of meontic and mimetic modes. Music, for instance, is for the most part a meontic mode, and is in fact the most meontic of all art forms; but even music, because it must hold commerce with the physical reality of sound, retains at least some possibilities in the mimetic realm—as, for instance, the storm in Beethoven's *Pastoral Symphony*. Painting, on the other hand, has a natural and proprietary interest in the mimetic. This interest was historically usurped—the claim was jumped, so to speak—by the rise of photography; but painting as an art was able to survive by sliding its base along the continuum from the mimetic to the meontic. In fact, one may see the advent of French Impressionism as at least in part the displacement of painting's mimetic function by photography, with a consequent movement of painting itself toward the meontic. When we call to mind characteristic canvases by Cézanne, we realize that his technique involves varying and partial divestitures of reality from experienced objects.

The historical dislocation of painting's aesthetic base from a combination of the mimetic and meontic to a larger proportion of the meontic eventuated in surrealism, where nothing *there in reality* was contemplated even at the outset. With Cézanne, however, this process had not yet been completed. The natural adhesion of painting to objective reality had not yet been entirely displaced. Cubism, too, though further along the continuum toward the purely meontic, kept at least a genetic relationship to objective reality. Later avatars of the meontic mode, however, such as the work of Pollock or De Kooning, abandoned all but the fictional nomenclature of mimetic genesis.[11]

[10] *Prose*, I, 149. Cf. Coleridge: "Examine nature accurately, but write from recollection: and trust more to your imagination than to your memory" (*Table Talk*, p. 109 [Sept. 22, 1830]).

[11] As I write this I am contemplating reproductions of "Fish Magic" by Klee and "Personages and a Blue Moon" by Miro. The former is a very great painting, a statement much less successful in copying fish than in evoking the depths of primal thalassic instinct—and by implication the depths of the universe itself. And the latter is a playful surrealism by which the title confers the representation rather than the other way around.

Something of the same process may be seen in the history of sculpture, although the parallelism is by no means exact. Sculpture, because of the inherent difficulty of working in stone or metal, has always been involved in the heroic and the ideal; and this commitment has existed side by side with its mimetic renderings. The David of Michelangelo is both naturalistically mimetic in its depiction of the male body, and meontically ideal in its heroic representation of human pride and dignity. Nevertheless, because of changes in our cultural situation—of which in this reference photography would be only one—sculpture has more and more tended to depress its mimetic function and elevate its meontic function. Sculptural mimesis somehow now suggests Civil War generals in parks, while living art resides, say, in the meontic abstraction of the Henry Moore pieces in the pool of the Beaumont Theater in New York's Lincoln Center.

The mimetic mode derives much of its enduring and indeed irrefragable power from the fact that it blocks the dispersal of human experience by time. There is a very special wonder in becoming aware that something in time gone by was exactly like the representation we see at the present. For instance, in Washington's National Gallery, after experiencing the meontic glories of St. George and the Dragon, as conceived in the differing presentations of Van der Weyden and Raphael, we turn to two mimetic paintings of homely seventeenth-century tavern scenes by Teniers, and there find ourselves almost intoxicated by the realization that this is the way it really was in a seventeenth-century tavern. Likewise, the evanescence of sunlight on a shabby brick building, as rendered by Edward Hopper, seizes our souls with the peculiarly affecting apprehension that a fleeting moment in 1910 is now forever there. A painting, currently in the National Gallery of Scotland, that depicts an unruly schoolroom, with the children tussling with one another and mocking their harried teacher, achieves under the master hand of Jan Steen an eternal *mimesis* of childhood.

Because of the palpable thereness of our relation to perceived reality—to live is to kick Dr. Johnson's stone, and to do so constantly—and because of our universal experience of the dispersal of that thereness by time, the mimetic mode of art is directly grounded upon ontological bedrock. Our awareness of that grounding is immediate and continually renewed. Probably no one able to read and write has not at least on one occasion started a diary, and the gesture, even if not pursued, renders homage to the ontological permanence and necessity of the mimetic mode.

The ontological basis of the meontic mode, though equally impregnable, is not so directly or palpably thrust upon our awareness. Indeed, because of the priority of our experience of what is there to what is not there, conceptualizations of meontic ontology often seem to have been evicted, as it were, from the theory of art. When they make a re-entrance into the discourse of culture, they tend to appear as the exclusive concern of philosophers. Actually, the evictions are reciprocal, and the most famous of them, that in which the philosopher Plato evicts the mimetic poets from his ideal state, involves in its complex of historical factors the ontologies both of mimetic and of meontic art.

Mimetic and meontic art are in one sense polar opposites. But as we have stressed, in another sense they constitute the two extensions in a continuum and subsume themselves in common under a larger conception of *mimesis*. This ambiguous possibility of their relation generates the paradoxes that commentators have repeatedly noted as inhering in Plato's attitude toward poetry. Thus Sidney asserts a primary paradox when he says that "truly even *Plato* who so ever well considereth, shall finde that in the body of his worke though the inside & strength were Philosophie, the skin as it were and beautie, depended most of Poetrie."[12] This constellation, however, then becomes the thesis for another antithesis; for Sidney, in defending poetry, must come to terms with the weighty fact that its denigrators urge Plato's eviction of the poets as one of their strongest arguments: "And lastly and chiefly, they cry out with open mouth as if they had overshot *Robinhood*, that *Plato* banished them out of his Commonwealth. Truly this is much, if there be much truth in it."[13]

Sidney's own method of reconciling the paradox is to abuse the "Poet-whippers" and assert their misunderstanding of Plato: "For indeed, I had much rather . . . shew their mistaking of *Plato*, under whose Lyons skinne, they would make an Aslike braying against *Poesie*, then go about to overthrow his authoritie."[14] The motive for reverencing the authority of Plato, however, is itself the product of paradox. The philosopher and the evicter of poets is—improbably—the greatest friend of poetry: "But now indeede my burthen is great, that *Plato* his name is laide uppon mee, whom I must confesse of all *Philosophers*, I have ever esteemed most worthie of reverence; and with good reason, since of all *Philosophers* hee is the most *Poeticall*."[15] To bulwark this claim, Sidney cites against the

[12] *Sidney*, iii, 5.
[14] *Ibid.*, p. 34.
[13] *Ibid.*, p. 28.
[15] *Ibid.*, pp. 32-33.

statements in the *Republic* the contrary statements of the *Ion*: "Plato
. . . in his Dialogue called *Ion*, giveth high, and rightly divine com-
mendation unto *Poetrie*. So as *Plato* banishing the abuse, not the
thing, not banishing it, but giving due honour to it, shall be our
Patron, and not our adversarie."[16]

The same kinds of paradox cluster about the common use by
Plato and Aristotle of the term *mimesis*. As a commentator, Gerald
Else, has noted:

> There can be no doubt that Aristotle took this concept of μίμησις
> as the common character of Ποιητική from Plato. . . . Neverthe-
> less we ought to notice even at this stage that there is a potential
> discrepancy, or at least an ambiguity, between the concepts of
> the poetic art as "making" and as "imitating." The two terms
> glance past each other; and this asymmetry is grounded in their
> history.

"Making" and "imitating" readily subsume themselves under the
division between meontic and mimetic, and the paradoxes in the
relationship of the generic terms of poetic function extend also to
the use of these terms by Aristotle as contrasted to Plato. "But al-
though Aristotle borrowed the scheme" from Plato, says Else, "he
revised its inner meaning, and therewith its practical application,
so decisively as to make it in effect a new theory. This drastic revi-
sion is in the concept of imitation itself." He continues: "For both
Plato and Aristotle the dramatic mode is imitation *par excellence*";
nevertheless, "Aristotle puts highest what Plato put lowest. . . . It
is the same scheme, but upside down."

In the course of his commentary, Else speaks of Aristotle's em-
phasis in a way that removes it from any flatly naturalistic repro-
duction of present reality, and indeed might make it seem more
meontic than mimetic:

> A poet, then, is an *imitator* in so far as he is a *maker*, viz. of plots.
> The paradox is obvious. Aristotle has developed and changed
> the bearing of a concept which originally meant a faithful *copying*
> of preëxistent things, to make it mean a *creation* of things which
> have never existed or whose existence, if they did exist, is acci-
> dental to the poetic process. Copying is after the fact; Aristotle's
> μίμησις creates the fact. . . . Without Plato especially, and a con-
> siderable development of the idea in him, Aristotle's use of
> μίμησις would be inconceivable.

[16] *Ibid.*, p. 34.

Yet such an emphasis arises from the special requirements of the dramatic topics addressed by Aristotle; it represents the action of Shelley's focusing mirror rather than a truly meontic mode. For as Else concedes:

Aristotle is a Greek, for whom creation means discovery (εὕρεσις), the uncovering of a true relation which already exists somehow in the scheme of things. The poet is not a creator in the irresponsible sense that the whole construct is made out of his own unregulated sensibility. He is not invited to study his own soul and express things that never existed before, but to apprehend true types of human character and represent what they will do or say under given circumstances. [17]

The way in which Aristotle's *mimesis* "creates the fact" does not, therefore, participate in the meontic mode. When Stevens, on the other hand, hails the poet's "Blessed rage for order," he both produces and theorizes about meontic art:

> The maker's rage to order words of the sea,
> Words of the fragrant portals, dimly-starred,
> And of ourselves and of our origins,
> In ghostlier demarcations, keener sounds [18]

Santayana, again, points to meontic art when he says that "the great function of poetry" is

to repair to the material of experience, seizing hold of the reality of sensation and fancy beneath the surface of conventional ideas, and then out of that living but indefinite material to build new structures, richer, finer, fitter to the primary tendencies of our nature, truer to the ultimate possibilities of the soul. [19]

But Santayana does not reveal just what are "the primary tendencies of our nature," nor does he elucidate the structure of "the ultimate possibilities of the soul." Nor does Stevens specify the words that speak "of ourselves and of our origins." He does not show us the place of "the fragrant portals."

The ontological basis of meontic art, in other words, remains veiled—dimly-starred—in such statements. To penetrate to that ground we must return to the Platonic collocation of attitudes and look more closely at the structures inhering in Plato's attitudes to-

---

[17] Else, pp. 12-13, 97, 97-98, 322, 320.
[18] *Stevens*, p. 130.   [19] *Santayana*, I, 77.

ward philosophy and poetry; for Platonic thought provides a paradigm for the understanding of what meontic art is.

Eric Havelock, in *Preface to Plato*,[20] has argued that the historical background and motivation of Plato's attack on the mimetic poets was the need to replace tribal knowledge, which in preliterate periods had been imbedded in epic memory, by a new and deliberately rational kind of knowing (Havelock's contention as to the encyclopedic social use of epic in preliterate thought was adumbrated as early as the seventeenth century—I have seen it in Bossuet—and repeatedly throughout the eighteenth). Yet, without contesting the historical validity of this analysis, we may invoke the philosophical authority of the Marburg School (viz. Hermann Cohen and Paul Natorp) and transpose our consideration of the meaning of Plato's rejection of the mimetic poets into epistemological matrices.

We note at the outset that Plato's exclusion of poetry is confined to the mimetic; he refuses "to admit at all" so much of poetry "as is mimetic."[21] Secondly, his rejection is based not on a dislike of such poetry—which he expressly says that he finds moving—but on the claim that it misrepresents reality. In other words, he attacks the ontological basis of the mimetic mode. The imitative poet (μιμητικός ποιητής) imitates a phantasm (φάντασμα) and not the truth (ἀλήθεια); and in fact "mimetic art is far removed from the truth" (598B). Plato is undeviating in this insistence: the poets he rejects are "imitators of images of excellence" (μιμητὰς εἰδώλων ἀρετῆς) and "do not lay hold of the truth" (τῆς δὲ ἀληθείας οὐχ ἅπτεσθαι) (600E). They are—he uses the formula for the second time—"far removed from the truth" (πόρρω μὲν τῆς ἀληθείας) (603A). We must not, he says, "take poetry seriously as a serious thing that lays hold on truth" (608A). In the *Republic*, moreover, Plato speaks of a "quarrel between philosophy and poetry" (607B); and it is evident that philosophy, unlike the poetry he is rejecting, is a serious thing and does lay hold on truth.

If, as Else says of Aristotle, Plato as a Greek must conceive of "creation" as a "discovery (εὕρεσις), the uncovering of a true relation which already exists somehow in the scheme of things," and if the truth is not in the things that the mimetic mode reproduces, then we are logically led to posit a discoverable "true relation" that somehow exists outside the realm of the given things that surround us and that also constitutes final truth. We take as our entry

[20] (Cambridge, Mass.: Harvard University Press, 1963).
[21] *Republic* 595A.

into the portals of such a realm an argument in the *Theaetetus* where Socrates, in a memorable discussion of the superiority of the philosophical training and life over a worldly training and life, concludes by saying that the philosopher disdains a world too much with us and a life of daily chatter and mundane concerns—what Heidegger in a different schematism stigmatizes as *Gerede* and *durchschnittliche Alltäglichkeit*. The philosopher instead looks both "below the earth" and "beyond the heavens"; he investigates "the being of everything that is."[22]

The phrase "beyond the heavens" (οὐρανοῦ τε ὕπερ) accords exactly with what we have posited as the necessary *topos* for a realm outside of that copied by the mimetic artist; it becomes still more worthy of our attention by its linkage to the philosophical responsibility to investigate "the being of everything that is" (a literal rendering of the Greek is even more emphatic about the investigative function that must extend beyond the heavens: "investigating all nature in every aspect, the things that exist, each one in its entirety"). Still further, Plato does not coin the phrase "beyond the heavens," but quotes it, not from another philosopher, but—and he admits the fact—from Pindar, a poet. Clearly we are in the presence of a different concatenation of poetic activity, and a different conception of the relationship and respective tasks of poetry and philosophy, from the one that obtains in the *Republic*.

The specified objectivity of the "beyond the heavens" where the philosopher looks is, as we shall presently see, essential to the foundation of the meontic mode. Without such a noematic correlate, it is impossible to conceive any genuine basis for Plato's repeated judgment that the mimetic poets are far removed from the truth.

Thus Sidney, positing no such specified objectivity, attempts to justify poetry against history, which in his tract is given the role of mimetic standard bearer. To those who urge Plato's opinion that poets are "the principall lyers," he retorts: "I answere *Paradoxically*, but truly, I think truly: that of all writers under the Sunne, the *Poet* is the least lyer: and though he wold, as a *Poet* can scarcely be a lyer."

Sidney then buttresses this claim by a possibly somewhat sophistic distinction between the historian and the poet:

Now for the *Poet*, he nothing affirmeth, and therefore never lieth: for as I take it, to lie, is to affirme that to bee true, which is

[22] *Theaetetus* 173E.

false. So as the other *Artistes*, and especially the *Historian*, affirm-
ing manie things, can in the clowdie knowledge of mankinde,
hardly escape from manie lies. But the *Poet* as I said before, never
affirmeth, the *Poet* never maketh any Circles about your imagina-
tion, to conjure you to beleeve for true, what he writeth. [23]

Though one may applaud the shrewd hit against the historian and
the limitations of his practice, the claim that the poet "nothing
affirmeth" is perhaps not entirely true; and if it is in fact true, it
relinquishes reality, however faultily cognized, to the historian. In
doing so, it leaves the poet dangling in his own fantasy, without
ontological grounding. It was apparently to avoid this outcome
that Baudelaire refused to allow the mimetic poet to pre-empt the
name of "réaliste," but substituted "positiviste."

So it seems that at this critical juncture Sidney's argument takes
a false turning into a philosophical cul-de-sac. In his eagerness to
escape the rejections of the *Republic*, he perhaps bursts too pre-
cipitously into the precincts of the *Ion*. For though the *Ion* contains
an historically influential metaphor for the conception of poetry as
divinely inspired, the dialogue itself is not a major formulation of
Platonic thought and does not possess the philosophical weight to
be used as an effective counterbalance to the *Republic*. It does not
provide access to any cognitively firm basis for understanding the
nature and necessity of meontic art.

But the *Phaedrus* does provide such access. The hyperouranic
realm invoked by the words of Pindar in the *Theaetetus* is in the
Phaedrus described in more ramified philosophical reference; and
the reason why the mimetic poets do not reveal the truth is
explicitly set forth. The mimetic poets imitate what is in this world,
and the truth—true being—is not in this world:

> Of the place beyond the heavens (ὑπερουράνιον τόπον) none of
> our earthly poets has yet sung, and none shall sing worthily. It is,
> however, as I shall tell; for I must dare to speak the truth, espe-
> cially as truth is my theme. It is there that true being (οὐσία
> ὄντως οὖσα) dwells . . . mind alone, the steersman of the soul,
> can behold it, and all true knowledge is knowledge of it (247C).

The great thinker continues: the "soul which has never seen the
truth can never pass into human form" (249B); "every human soul
has, by reason of its nature, had contemplation of true being; else it
would not have entered into this human creature" (249E). Those

[23] *Sidney*, III, 28, 29.

that remember most of what existed in the place beyond the heavens function in this life at the apex of human possibility:

> the soul that has seen the most of being shall enter into the human child that shall grow into a philosopher or a beauty-seeker or a follower of the Muses, and a lover (248D).

The highest achievement of human activity, in other words, whether it takes form in philosopher, artist, poet, or impassioned lover, is to regain awareness of this "place beyond the heavens," where "true being" dwells.

The hyperouranic grounding of true being is at the same time the ontological foundation for the meontic mode. The impregnability of such a foundation is guaranteed both by its gravely serious philosophical specification as "true being," and by its coherence with the deepest motifs of Plato's architecture of thought. For Plato is everywhere divided in a dual allegiance. "Looking back at this edifice," says Popper of the whole of Plato,

> we may briefly consider its ground-plan. This ground-plan, conceived by a great architect, exhibits a fundamental metaphysical dualism in Plato's thought. In the field of logic, this dualism presents itself as the opposition between the universal and the particular. In the field of mathematical speculation, it presents itself as the opposition between the One and the Many. In the field of epistemology, it is the opposition between rational knowledge based on pure thought, and opinion based on particular experiences. In the field of ontology, it is the opposition between the one, original, invariable, and true, reality, and the many, varying, and delusive, appearances; between pure being and becoming, or more precisely, changing. In the field of cosmology, it is the opposition between that which generates and that which is generated, and which must decay.[24]

Jaspers summarizes the same truth more briefly: "Thus Plato knows two worlds: the world of Ideas and that of the senses, the world of being and that of becoming, the noetic (intelligible) world and the world of appearances."[25]

The cognizance of "two worlds," with the second as the dwelling place of "true being," generates the meontic mode in art. The "place beyond the heavens" relates to our concerns here and at the

[24] Popper, *Open Society*, I, 84-85.
[25] Jaspers, *Plato*, p. 30.

same time transcends them. But it must be understood as no less real than the things that surround us; otherwise, the realm of meontic art becomes a pure fiction. Thus Sidney realizes that meontic poetry must refer to a second world, but he does not think of that world as grounded in true being:

> Nature never set foorth the earth in so rich Tapistry as diverse Poets have done, neither with so pleasaunt rivers, fruitfull trees, sweete smelling flowers, nor whatsoever els may make the too much loved earth more lovely: her world is brasen, the Poets only deliver a golden.[26]

Though Sidney, by his phrase "the too much loved earth" indicates his allegiance as hyperouranic, his fealty to that realm is finally offered in terms of Christianity rather than in those of literature; and for him the second world delivered by literature is only a golden construct of the poet's fancy.

It is quite otherwise with Baudelaire. Not only does he avoid the cul-de-sac of Sidney's "nothing affirmeth" argument, but he restates the conception of the "place beyond the heavens" in a way that changes the meontic mode from a form of fanciful play to the pursuit of true being:

> It is this admirable, this immortal instinct for beauty that makes us regard the earth and its sights as an *aperçu*, as a *correspondence* of Heaven. The insatiable thirst for all that which lies beyond, and that reveals life, is the most living proof of our immortality. It is at once by poetry and *through* poetry, by and *through* music, that the soul glimpses the splendors situated behind the tomb; and when an exquisite poem brings tears to the rim of the eyes, the tears are not proof of an excess of pleasure, they are rather the witness of an irritated melancholy, of a postulation of nerves, of a nature exiled in the imperfect that would like to take possession immediately, on this very earth, of a paradise revealed.[27]

"Exiled in the imperfect," and with an "insatiable thirst for that which lies beyond," Baudelaire, though here historically utilizing the thought of Swedenborg rather than that of Plato specifically, comes into congruence with Plato in witnessing the hyperouranic rationale of the meontic mode.[28]

It is interesting to note that a greater emotion is generated by

[26] *Sidney*, III, 8.   [27] Baudelaire, II, 334.

[28] In fact, Baudelaire's next sentence runs as follows: "Thus the principle of poetry is strictly and simply human aspiration toward a higher beauty."

Baudelaire's postulation of a second world of "true being" than by Sidney's second world of golden fiction. Such conviction as to "les splendeurs" that can be found "au delà" is always the motive condition for the greatest achievements of meontic art. We stand in the Sistine Chapel and turn our gaze upwards to view the flaming kinesis of Michelangelo's imitation of things that no man has ever seen in this world, but which none the less partake of the "true being" of Christian faith: we see in meontic splendor God and Adam and saints and angels and souls; and in this glimpse we are able "s'emparer immédiatement, sur cette terre même, d'un paradis révélé."

Proust, again, was motivated to his titanic novel by the need to find again something that was no longer present in the world of surrounding experience. For him, as for Plato and Baudelaire, "les splendeurs" were "au delà." As Painter says:

> Unconscious memory was linked with other feelings of inexplicable delight in which memory had no part, such as the ecstasies he owed to the moving spires, or the "little phrase" in what became the Vinteuil Sonata. They revealed the existence, somewhere deep within him, of a region in which beauty was real and eternal, uncontaminated by disappointment, sin and death. Later in life these feelings became more important than anything else in the world, more valuable than the false enchantments of love or society: they were signposts, marked with an unexpectedly short distance, to the only true reality.[29]

Such a formulation indicates the genuineness and unequivocal seriousness of meontic art's commitment to the place beyond the heavens. The "only true reality" is not here but "au delà."

But that reality cannot be comprehended; it can only be discerned through momentary epiphanies or intuited in elusive complexes of experience. Baudelaire says that the soul "glimpses" (*entrevoit*) the splendors situated behind the tomb. And Plato says that only a very few of those who had contemplation of true being "can still remember much, but when these discern some likeness of the things yonder, they are amazed, and no longer masters of themselves, and know not what is come upon them by reason of their perception being dim."[30] Proust's "ecstasies" that he owed to the moving spires or the musical phrase are precisely the dimly descried Platonic "likeness of the things yonder."

[29] Painter, I, 38.　　　　　[30] *Phaedrus* 250A.

It is necessary to elucidate more clearly the reasons for the emotional intensity of meontic art as well as those for asserting its ontological ground to exist as irrefutably as that of mimetic art. To do so we shall more and more in this chapter interweave the language and conclusions of phenomenological analysis with those of historical illustration. Plato speaks of "yearning for that other time" (δι' ἥν πόθῳ τῶν τότε).[31] The functions of yearning or longing, combined with those of glimpsing or indistinctly cognizing, generate the characteristic movement of meontic art. Because true being is not here, in surrounding things, but there, in the hyperouranic place, it cannot be appropriated by clear and distinct ideas; it exists "beyond substance" (ἐπέκεινα τῆς οὐσίας)[32] and thus does not for us have possibility of epistemic form at all (Plato says that it is "colorless, formless, and intangible").[33] In other words, it exists for cognition as a *void*. It is a realm simultaneously *present as home and origin* and *empty of all content*. This double emphasis is admirably stated by Wordsworth:

> The Soul that rises with us, our life's Star,
> Hath had elsewhere its setting,
> And cometh from afar:
> Not in entire forgetfulness,
> And not in utter nakedness,
> But trailing clouds of glory do we come
> From God, who is our home;[34]

Except for our glimpses and presentiments, however, Wordsworth's "forgetfulness" is a mental state that correlates with the meontic void. "I cannot paint/ what then I was," he laments. Like Plato "yearning for that other time," Wordsworth finds that "That time is past,/ And all its aching joys are now no more."[35] He cannot locate in the world that surrounds him the true being of which he has presentiment:

> It is not now as it hath been of yore;—
> Turn wheresoe'er I may,
> By night or day,
> The things which I have seen I now can see no more.

He may experience many things,

---

[31] *Ibid.*, 250D.
[33] *Phaedrus* 247C.
[35] *Ibid.*, II, 261.

[32] *Republic* 509B.
[34] Wordsworth, *Poems*, IV, 281.

> But yet I know, where'er I go,
> That there hath past away a glory from the earth.[36]

The yearning of the here and now is thus a yearning for something not in the here and now. It is to penetrate this void that meontic activity, in its joint artistic and philosophical enterprise, erects its structures.[37] "Do our pleasures, and knowleges leave a craving?" asks Coleridge: "a Sense of a Plus Ultra?—an aching Void? The complement of this Void would needs be *Sophia*, the earnest seeking after it for its own sake *Philo*sophia."[38] But the sense of the void is also the sense of origin: we are, as Baudelaire says, *exiled* in the imperfect; we do not really belong here. The lover, says Plato,

> as soon as he beholds the beauty of this world, is reminded of true beauty, and his wings begin to grow; then he desires to lift his wings and fly upward; yet he has not the power . . . he gazes upward like a bird, and cares nothing for the world beneath.[39]

This is the respect in which Novalis can say that "philosophy is really homesickness," or that Heidegger can say that "All the poems of the poet who has entered into his poethood, are poems of homecoming."[40]

The need to return home, to true being, acts as an attracting accelerator toward the hyperouranic realm, while the absence of objective content in that realm removes all sense of obstacle. Thus, for instance, surrealist painting can do whatever it wishes—the idlest whim can substitute for serious intent, because there is no obligation to render any aspect of experienced reality. There are no obstacles. The mimetic portrait painter, on the other hand, is always held back by the need to render a likeness of an experienced object. Of course one often wishes there were as many obstacles as

---

[36] *Ibid.*, IV, 279.

[37] Just as poetry is subsumed under philosophy in the *Phaedrus*, so in the *Symposium* does a larger conception of *"poiesis"* subsume all activities by which anything passes "from not being into being" (ἐκ τοῦ μὴ ὄντος εἰς τὸ ὂν ἰόντι ὁτῳοῦν). Though a single portion of the multiple whole of *poiesis*—namely that portion that is "merely the business of music and meters"—has usurped the name "poetry," in fact the productions of all crafting artistries (τέχναις) are "kinds of poetry, and their craftsmen are all poets" (*Symposium* 205B-C).

[38] *Collected Letters*, IV, 848.

[39] *Phaedrus* 249D.

[40] *Novalis*, III, 434; Heidegger, *Existence and Being*, p. 253. As an observer comments: "The Homecoming of Hölderlin is revealed as the homecoming to the neighborhood of being" (Allemann, p. 122).

possible to many of the paintings, sculptures, novels, poems and other cultural effluvia that waft into modern life—one would welcome some check on the fanciful self-indulgence of, say, Pynchon; the point, however, is not to defend bad art but to insist on the absence of obstacles in the meontic situation.

The combination of the sense of attraction from the home and origin, and of no obstacles in the void, allows meontic art to *rush toward* its glimpsed realm. It is this rushing, this accelerating eagerness, that generates the characteristically rapturous or singing tone one repeatedly encounters in great meontic statements:

> Weave a circle round him thrice,
> And close your eyes with holy dread,
> For he on honey-dew hath fed,
> And drunk the milk of Paradise.[41]

Or

> There entertain him all the Saints above,
> In solemn troops, and sweet Societies
> That sing, and singing in their glory move,
> And wipe the tears for ever from his eyes.[42]

Or

> Now walk the angels on the walls of heaven,
> As sentinels to warn th' immortal souls
> To entertain divine Zenocrate.
> Apollo, Cynthia, and the ceaseless lamps
> That gently looked upon this loathsome earth
> Shine downwards now no more, but deck the heavens
> To entertain divine Zenocrate.
> The crystal springs, whose taste illuminates
> Refinèd eyes with an eternal sight,
> Like trièd silver runs through Paradise
> To entertain divine Zenocrate.
> The cherubins and holy seraphins,
> That sing and play before the King of Kings,
> Use all their voices and their instruments
> To entertain divine Zenocrate. . . .
> Then let some holy trance convey my thoughts
> Up to the place of th' imperial heaven,
> That this my life may be as short to me
> As are the days of sweet Zenocrate.[43]

[41] Coleridge, *Poems*, ı, 298.   [42] Milton, *Poems*, p. 296.
[43] *Marlowe*, pp. 131-32.

In rushing toward the void that is also the home of true being, meontic art has no other forms of representation available to it than those it draws from daily experience. The meontic artist, like the mimetic artist, is in his representations bound by the sensible forms of psychological perception. Unlike the mimetic artist, however, he uses those forms to bridge the *chorismos* between his own imperfect existence and the realm of true being. The artistic projection of elements of cognized reality into the meontic void toward the apprehension of true being is the process subsumed by the literary term *symbol*.

To conceive of such an artistic projection as a *bridging*, on the other hand, is a mental act subsumed by the philosophical term *transcendence*. "La transcendence," says Sartre simply, is "projet de soi par delà."[44] It is also a central concern in the phenomenological analysis of human existence and of being itself. "*Sein*," asserts Heidegger comprehensively, "*ist das transcendens schlechthin. . . . Phänomenologische Wahrheit (Erschlossenheit von Sein) ist veritas transcendentalis.*"[45] It is in examining the relationship between symbol and transcendence that we can arrive at a cognitive understanding of the process otherwise accepted as merely historical occurrence or intuitive cluster.

We must at the outset recognize that the conception of symbol can take more than one form. Indeed, it is this that caused Romantic theorists frequently to insist on a distinction between symbol and allegory. Both symbol and allegory are noematic presentations by which a given meaning is understood to entail also one not given. In this discussion, however, we shall insist on symbol as denoting exclusively the bridging of the chorismos between experienced reality and hyperouranic being; all other multiple tenors for a single vehicle we shall relegate to the function of allegory.

The exclusivity of our understanding of symbol does not do violence, however, to the historical currency of the term; it merely separates the historically central usage from irrelevant accretions. Thus symbol as we use it, or if one wishes, true symbol, always testifies to an ontological duality. There is no true symbol if there are not two worlds. We urge with Ingarden that

> The symbolizing function undoubtedly has its ontic source in represented states of affairs or in sentence meanings. But it is performed only by represented objectivities. . . .
>
> [W]hereas manifested metaphysical qualities attain *self-revelation* on the basis of represented situations and appear as

---

[44] Sartre, *L'Être et le néant*, p. 54. [45] Heidegger, *Sein und Zeit*, p. 38.

already revealed qualities [i.e. in a concretization] in precisely the same sense as does the objective world, it is part of the essence of the symbolizing function that (1) what is symbolized and that which symbolizes it belong to *different* worlds.[46]

Secondly, there is no true symbol if the second world is accessible by other means. Indeed, in a true symbol, the symbolic projection itself is always swallowed by the void. Thus Jaspers speaks of "the vanishing mediation of ciphers [symbols]."[47] And Goethe describes true symbol as transferring "the idea into the image" in such a way that the idea remains "unattainable" (*unerreichbar*), and, even if expressed in all languages, "inexpressible" (*unaussprechlich*); the truly symbolic is "a living and momentary revelation of the impenetrable."[48] Goethe's "impenetrable" (*das Unerforschliche*) is precisely the meontic void; his "living and momentary revelation" (*lebendigaugenblickliche Offenbarung*) precisely Baudelaire's "glimpse." Thus Ingarden proceeds to a second specification of the symbolizing function:

> (2) what is symbolized is in fact only "symbolized" and *cannot* attain self-presentation. As something symbolized, it is, according to its essence *directly* inaccessible, it is that which does not show itself. . . . And symbols or symbolizings are indispensable precisely whenever, for one reason or another, we cannot originally know the symbolized object or at least at a given moment are not in the position to do so. It is for this reason that symbols are used most frequently in religious life and, for that matter, in all things mysterious and inaccessible.[49]

If the approach to "true being" can only be through the symbol, it is also the case that the gap between phenomenal existence and true being is bridged by human awareness of transcendence. "Man," says Jaspers in an epitome of his entire philosophy, "is possible existence who orients himself in the world as consciousness in general, and is drawn through the world to transcendence."[50] Transcendence, however, is not a delimited content of consciousness, but rather a horizon of consciousness,[51] and with

---

[46] Ingarden, p. 299.

[47] Jaspers, *Wahrheit*, p. 1051.

[48] *Gedenkausgabe*, IX, 532.

[49] Ingarden, pp. 299-300.

[50] Jaspers, *Philosophie*, I, 52.

[51] Cf. Jaspers: "the reality of transcendence is neither empirical existence as materialized transcendence, nor on the other side another world. . . . The place of transcendence is neither this side nor the other side, but boundary; boundary, however, that I stand before if I am authentic" (*Philosophie*, III, 12-13).

it, as with horizon in general, any attainability is precluded by a melting into new horizon.[52] To approach a horizon is to supplant it with another horizon. "Our astonishment," says Jaspers, ringing changes on the opinions of Plato and Aristotle by which all philosophizing begins in wonder, "carries us rushing and plunging through the world into transcendence. But we remain in the world and find ourselves again, not in transcendence but in heightened awareness."[53] It is because of the necessary orientation of every *Existenz* to *Transzendenz* that we are launched on the highway to hyperouranic being. What we can carry with us onto that highway is restricted to the symbol.

Even when no symbolic reaching for hyperouranic being is present, however, even in a debased or unfulfilled meontic form such as is frequently rendered by the efforts of surrealism, the horizon of transcendence is palpably present. As Alquié says in summary, after investigating the theory and practice of surrealism as a whole,

> I believe . . . that it is in the metaphysical affirmation of transcendence that man finds his most authentic truth. And I know that sheltered from all superstition and from all dogmatism this affirmation can be integrally founded in reason: the eternal philosophical critique, demonstrating that every object known only has sense and reality relative to our knowledge, suffices to lay claim for the transcendence of being the title of supreme certitude. But surrealist evidence is not metaphysical: it wants to remain human and thus poetic. Nevertheless, among poets, the surrealists seem the nearest to metaphysics. More precisely it reveals that, setting aside metaphysics, poetry is for man the path that leads closest to truth, provided that its language remains scrupulously faithful to the truth of man. Of this scrupulous fidelity, the work of André Breton is without doubt the most perfect example in this century, and the most admirable. That is why Breton seems, in spite of himself, like a messenger from transcendence. He is inspired by Engels, but returns to Plato.[54]

There is, nevertheless, an inherent weakness in all surrealistic practice. However much it may launch us onto "le chemin qui conduit le plus près de la vérité," it tends to abandon the reality of this world. Greater configurations of meontic art, on the other hand, honor this world while pointing us to the place beyond the

[52] Cf. Jaspers, "*Objectivity* that is appearance of transcendence must be *disappearing* for the consciousness" (*Philosophie*, III, 15).

[53] Jaspers, *Wahrheit*, p. 1031.   [54] Alquié, pp. 211-12.

heavens. Though we see on the ceiling of the Sistine Chapel things never seen by man, in another sense we see forms quite familiar from daily experience. Though the frieze of Phidias on the Parthenon moves us toward a sacred transcendence, the figures themselves correspond to objects familiar to our eyes—no horses have ever been more equine than those we view in the Elgin Marbles.

The greatest meontic art does not abandon the forms of this world in its quest for the place beyond the heavens. Rather it unfolds, as it were, from those forms to point toward hyperouranic being. The process, to use a homely metaphor, might be compared to the unfolding of a carpenter's rule toward a lengthened measurement. The unfolding of the extension from the initial mass is, so to speak, a cantilevering of meaning that resists surrealism's immediate dissipation in the meontic void. The meaning is not there, in the void, but is the act of extension; it is only on the rule itself that measurements are marked.[55] "The object which is a symbol," says Jaspers, "is *not* to be grasped *as* existing being-real of *Transzendenz*, but *only as* hearing *its language*. Being-there (*Dasein*) and being-symbol (*Symbolsein*) are like two aspects in one world that reveal themselves either for consciousness in general or for possible existence."[56]

Symbolic extensions are thus hinged, inextricably involved with the objects presented in an artistic discourse. "The natural object," insists Pound, "is always the *adequate* symbol."[57] It is this inextricable involvement that Coleridge recognizes when he states that every symbol must be a part of the larger whole of its extended meaning:

> Now an Allegory is but a translation of abstract notions into a picture-language which is itself nothing but an abstraction from objects of the senses; the principal being more worthless even than its phantom proxy, both alike unsubstantial, and the former shapeless to boot. On the other hand a Symbol . . . is characterized by a translucence of the Special in the Individual or of the General in the Especial or of the Universal in the General. Above all by the translucence of the Eternal through and in the Temporal. It always partakes of the Reality which it renders intelligi-

[55] Cf. Heidegger: "Poetry is a measuring. But what is it to measure? . . . Hölderlin sees the nature of the 'poetic' in the taking of the measure by which the measure-taking of human being is accomplished. . . . The poet makes poetry only when he takes the measure, by saying the sights of heaven in such a way that he submits to its appearances as to the alien element to which the unknown god has 'yielded' " (Heidegger, *Vorträge*, pp. 196, 200).

[56] Jaspers, *Philosophie*, III, 16.   [57] Kenner, p. 181.

ble; and while it enunciates the whole, abides itself as a living part in that Unity, of which it is the representative.[58]

Coleridge's understanding that the symbol is a part that enunciates a whole points us toward a phenomenological apprehension of the emotional intensity of meontic art. For the Platonic yearning (πόθος) toward the hyperouranic realm is phenomenologically describable as the need for a part to reconstitute itself into wholeness, or more precisely, for a part to define itself by reference to its wholeness.[59] Because of the discrepancy between our being at any given moment of our life and our sense of a personal identity spanning years before and after that are not present to us, we must necessarily and at all moments feel our existence as a part of a whole; and all phenomenological analysis of what we are must report this truth.[60] Thus any consistent accounting must utilize terms to indicate our self-surpassing from our being of the moment to our being that lies on horizons of temporality, as for instance, Heidegger's *sich überholen*, or Sartre's *se dépasser*, or Jaspers's polarity of *Dasein* and *Existenz*. It is the essential phenomenon of self-surpassing that impels us into transcendence.

But the need for a transcendent realm is generated wholly by our subjectivity in the present. "Transcendence," states Heidegger,

> denotes the essence (*Wesen*) of the subject; it is the foundation of subjectivity. The subject never exists beforehand as "subject," in order then *in case* any objects are at hand, *also* to transcend; rather to be a subject (Subjekt*sein*) means: to exist in and as transcendence.[61]

Jaspers, indeed, even cautions against thinking of transcendence

---

[58] *Lay Sermons*, p. 30.

[59] In line with this truth, Plato specifically says that "Thine own being, foolish man, is a fragment, and so, for all its littleness, its striving is ever directed toward the whole . . . to win bliss for the life of the whole; the life of the whole is not made for thee, but thou for it. For every physician and every craftsman does all his work for the sake of some whole, and he produces a part for the sake of a whole, to contribute to the general good, and not a whole for the sake of part" (*Laws*, 903C-D).

[60] And in fact any true account of any kind must report it. Schiller, for instance, says that "every individual man . . . carries . . . a pure ideal man within himself, with whose unalterable unity it is the great task of his existence . . . to harmonize" (Schiller, *Werke*, xii, 11). Cf. Hegel: "Das Selbst is nur als *aufgehobenes* wirklich."

[61] Heidegger, *Wegmarken*, p. 34. Again, Heidegger notes that "Transcendence in its elucidated terminological significance means that which belongs to *human existence*, and indeed not as a posited mode of conduct among other possible modes occasionally accomplished but rather as a *fundamental constituent of this existing being occurring before all conduct*" (p. 33).

in two-world terms at all if the second world is conceived as a
doubling of this one (*Weltverdoppelung*).[62] Instead of a second world
furnished as is this one, what we can describe phenomenologically
is a *way toward*, a *need for*, an *attraction to*. The logically implied ter-
minus of such phenomenological directings can be experienced in
two ways, neither of which excludes the other. The first is as an
emotional complex, and the second as a cognitive structure. The
first is the evocation, in varied symbolisms, of a paradisal longing,
and is aptly illustrated by the poetries of Stevens, Wordsworth,
Coleridge, Milton, and Marlowe quoted earlier in this discussion.
It is the vision reported by Diotima:

> And if, my dear Socrates, man's life is ever worth the living, it is
> when he has attained this vision of the very soul of beauty. . . . If
> it were given to man to gaze on beauty's very self—unsullied,
> unalloyed, and freed from the mortal taint that haunts the frailer
> loveliness of flesh and blood—if, I say, it were given to man to
> see the heavenly beauty face to face, would you call *his* an unen-
> viable life?[63]

It is, again, the soaring affirmation of Marlowe's testament to
beauty—a poetry in which the mimetic image of the mirror, even in
its highest use, is surpassed by the meontic rush toward transcend-
ence:

> What is beauty, saith my sufferings, then?
> If all the pens that every poets held
> Had fed the feeling of their masters' thoughts
> And every sweetness that inspired their hearts,
> Their minds, and muses on admirèd themes;
> If all the heavenly quintessence they still
> From their immortal flowers of poesy,
> Wherein, as in a mirror, we perceive
> The highest reaches of a human wit;

[62] Cf. Jaspers, "If transcendent reality does not occur as empirical and is not *Exist-
ence*, one might conclude that it is therefore a reality *beyond*. Metaphysics would be
the knowledge of a world behind this one, which exists beyond the real world,
elsewhere, inaccessible. If I transcended, I would walk a path into this other world.
With luck someone might someday be able to give a report of it.

"This world-doubling proves itself deceptive. In the other world there would be
merely things and events transplanted from this world, fantastically magnified, di-
minished and combined. . . . The beyond as a merely other reality must collapse as
illusion" (*Philosophie*, III, 9).

[63] *Symposium* 211D-E.

If these had made one poem's period,
And all combined in beauty's worthiness,
Yet should there hover in their restless heads
One thought, one grace, one wonder, at the least,
Which into words no virtue can digest.[64]

The lines are poetic verification for Jaspers's dicta that "The symbol is *infinite*. In pursuing the symbol, and with it the experience of essential reality, thought stands still. No thought is adequate to the symbol"; "Being is revealed through the symbol. The symbol is suspended when I grasp essential reality in it. If it becomes fixed and definite and turns into an object in the world, then it loses its essential reality. It collapses into a sign, a signification, into a metaphor."[65]

The implied second, or cognitive, terminus is the concept of wholeness. The hyperouranic realm for which Proust longed, and which he attempted to approach by means of his novel, was not only something of intricate and cherished sweetness and evanescence, but also a realm of wholeness. As Painter says,

> though he invented nothing, he altered everything. His places and people are composite in space and time, constructed from various sources and from widely separate periods of his life. His purpose in so doing was not to falsify reality, but, on the contrary, to induce it to reveal the truths it so successfully hides in this world. Behind the diversity of the originals is an underlying unity, the quality which, he felt, they had in common, the Platonic ideal of which they were the obscure earthly symbols. He fused each group of particular cases into a complex, universal whole, and so disengaged the truth about the poetry of places, or love and jealousy, or the nature of duchesses, and, most of all, the meaning of the mystery of his own life.[66]

In short, in every emotional longing for the absent then (πόθος τῶν τότε), there is also a longing for wholeness. "The utmost," says Coleridge, in a passage that we may take as summary of this entire melding of emotional and cognitive longing, "is only an approximation to that absolute *Union*, which the soul sensible of its imperfection in itself, of its *Halfness*, yearns after."[67]

---

[64] *Marlowe*, p. 102.   [65] Jaspers, *Wahrheit*, pp. 1032, 1036.
[66] Painter, I, xiii.
[67] *Notebooks*, III, 3325. Compare Sartre: "The for-itself cannot sustain nihilation without determining itself as a *lack of being*. . . . The concrete, real in-itself is wholly

Although Coleridge's formula was amply grounded in and no doubt derived from this own experience of existence, it coincides with the structure of Plato's hyperouranic tropism. We recall that for Plato those souls who had seen most of being would grow into philosophers or beauty-seekers or followers of the muses—and lovers. Up to this point we have been mainly concerned with the equation by which those who engage in philosophical activity and those who engage in artistic activity become seekers after the same being, with a consequent healing of the age-old rift between philosophy and poetry. If we now, however, direct our attention to the final term of that equation—the *and of a lover* (καὶ ἐρωτικοῦ)— we shall be able to understand the cognitive as well as the emotional aspect of hyperouranic tropism.[68]

In the equation as just presented, Plato seems to insert erotic activity almost as an afterthought to philosophical and artistic activity. Shortly further on, though, he speaks more emphatically of erotic activity, extending to it the appellation of beauty-seeking originally invoked for philosophical activity: "this is the best of all forms of divine possession, both in itself and in its sources, both for him that has it and for him that shares it—and he that loves beauty, partaking of such madness, is called a lover."[69]

But it is in the *Symposium* more than in the *Phaedrus* that the cognitive as distinguished from the emotional features of the lover's relation to being become clear. Indeed, in the myth there ascribed to Aristophanes, it seems that Plato deliberately depresses the emotionally soaring metaphors of his characteristic discourse about true being, and substitutes instead a comically playful series of images. Thus Aristophanes speaks of the originative human in terms of merry grotesquerie:

> each of these beings was globular in shape, with rounded back and sides, four arms and four legs, and two faces. . . . They walked erect . . . but when they broke into a run they simply stuck their legs straight out and went whirling round and round like a clown turning cartwheels.[70]

---

present to the heart of consciousness as that which consciousness determines itself not to be. The cogito must necessarily lead us to discover this total and out-of-reach presence of the in-itself. And, without doubt, the fact of this presence will be the very transcendence of the for-itself. But it is precisely the nihilation that is the origin of transcendence conceived as the original bond of the for-itself with the in-itself" (Sartre, *L'Être et le néant*, p. 128).

[68] *Phaedrus* 248D. [69] *Ibid.*, 249D-E.
[70] *Symposium* 189E-190A.

The comic aura is sustained as Aristophanes proceeds to a description of the etiology of human incompleteness:

> Zeus offered a solution. I think I can see my way, he said, to put an end to this disturbance by weakening these people without destroying them. What I propose to do is to cut them all in half.
> . . . They can walk about, upright, on their two legs, and if I have any more trouble with them, I shall split them up again, and they'll have to hop about on one.[71]

The tone adopted in this report of how our sense of "halfness" originated has none of Coleridge's yearning (nor of Plato's either). But we have none the less arrived, under cover of myth, irony, and simple frolic, at that same point. Each of us, says Plato, signalizing the relation of our existence to its symbolic quest, is merely "the symbol of a man" (ἀνθρώπου σύμβολον). Each of us is always striving to convert fragments into wholes—or as Plato says from the perspective of *eros*, to "make one from two" (ποιῆσαι ἕν ἐκ δυοῖν). And the absolute character of our longing—that which we name *eros*—is nothing less than "the desire and pursuit of the whole" (τοῦ ὅλου οὖν τῇ ἐπιθυμίᾳ καὶ διώξει ἔρως ὄνομα).[72]

The desire and pursuit of the whole. With this phrase we arrive at full justification of our programmatic assertion that the ontological grounding of the meontic mode is no less impregnable than that of the mimetic. With this phrase the holocleric foundation of meontic striving emerges from the background into cognitive relief.

The whole thus striven for is a *transcendently constituted whole*. It is also the one true whole. We achieve it only in epiphanies[73]— those of art or those of philosophy and love—and as a consequence the consciousness of the actual life we lead is irrevocably, in Hegel's pregnant phrase, an unhappy consciousness. As was argued in the introduction to this volume, the only wholes encountered in experience are themselves fragments and can all be subsumed under the categories of *nominal wholes, contingent wholes,* and *wholes of faith*. The only true whole is a transcendently constituted whole. Husserl understands the philosophical importance of the relations of parts to wholes, but his lengthy attempt in the *Logische Untersuchungen* to establish the logical forms of such rela-

[71] *Ibid.*, 190C-D.

[72] *Ibid.*, 191D, 192E-193A.

[73] Thus Jaspers: "Plato created a written work which for depth and greatness has no equal in all the history of philosophy. . . . And yet in his own judgment this lifework consisted merely of intimations and reminiscences" (Jaspers, *Plato*, p. 20).

tion founders because he does not seem—at least there—to see the provisional nature of the wholes he invokes for examination.[74]

More pertinently for our present argument, the logical considerations that require a true whole to be transcendently constituted are sketched in a jotting by Coleridge:

> Now it is absolutely impossible to think of a material Universe, or even of a world of spirits, as an aggregate of separate Finites, under the idea of *a Whole*—we might say, These are all that there are—but never these are all that there *can* be—and why not more? If in basic attempts to answer this latter question, the imagination goes on adding and adding, and if to hide from itself its perpetual failure, & to evade the perpetual recurrence of the same question, why not more yet?—it takes the salto mortale, and vaults at once into the transcendental Idea, of Infinity—yet still how can this Infinity of Finites be *a whole*? To be *a Whole* it must in some sense or other *be one*. Totality is Multitude participating of Unity. *A world* therefore in order to be a World (κοσμος, *Uni*versum) supposes a god—an infinite *one*—*one* not by participation, or union, but one essentially—and infinite not by an infinity of finite parts, but absolutely infinite.—Now to *conceive* this is impossible—but to assume it is necessary.[75]

That the transcendently constituted whole is the only true whole, and that the desire and pursuit of the whole is a hallmark of existence, and by extension the invulnerable ontological ground of meontic art, are, however, propositions that can also be confirmed by phenomenological analyses supplied by our own era and cultural milieu. It would be easy to parallel the holocleric argumentation of Plato by detailed progressions from the thought of Jaspers. But it might be even more instructive for our present purposes not

---

[74] Every whole is actually a part in a phenomenological field. As Gurwitsch points out: "When we deal with an object and choose it as theme of our mental activity—of whatever kind our mental activity may be—our conscious life is never confined to the exclusive experience of our theme. At the time of our dealing with the theme, we are aware, in varying degrees of clarity and explicitness, of other objects and events. Our theme presents itself in a total field of consciousness"; hence Gurwitsch speaks of a *"thematic field"* and of a *"partial domain"* in reference to the objects of attention (Gurwitsch, pp. 123, 202). Husserl of course is quite aware of these truths, e.g.: "From our observations we can also draw the eidetically valid and self-evident proposition; that *no concrete experience* can be accepted *as independent in the full sense of the term*. Each 'stands in need of completion' with respect to some connected whole, which in kind and form is not our own choice" (*Ideen*, p. 202).

[75] *Notebooks*, III, 4047.

to levy the contribution of such a Platonic epigone as Jaspers, but to tax instead Sartre, a thinker antipathetic to all platonisms of attitude or temperament, and most especially antipathetic to the thought of Jaspers (he falls on Jaspers with a Marxist fury reminiscent of Engel's attack on Schelling: "Philosophically," says Sartre in unseeing dismissal of his great contemporary, "this flabby and underhanded thought is only a survival, it offers no great interest").[76]

Atheist and Marxist, not Platonist and Christian like Coleridge, Sartre in his analysis discloses the holocleric need and its dispersal in transcendence to belong to the bedrock of human reality no less urgently than does Plato himself. Sartre sets out from the starting point of his countryman, Descartes: a study of human reality should begin with the *cogito*.[77] Sartre then suggests that the deep sense of the *cogito* is to refer outside itself.[78] In so doing, the *cogito* moves toward a totality founded on "lack" (*manque*); and the Sartrean understanding of lack reveals itself as exactly parallel to the conceptions marshaled by Plato's "symbol-man" and Coleridge's "*Halfness*":

> of all internal negations, the one that penetrates most profoundly into being . . . is *lack*. This lack does not belong to the nature of the in-itself, which is all positivity. It appears in the world only with the upsurge of human reality. It is only in the human world that there can be lacks.[79]

The line of Sartre's analysis leads him to the conclusion that "the human reality by which lack appears in the world must itself be a lack," and from this point his reasoning flows into a Platonic convergence almost indistinguishable with what we have seen to be the nature of *eros*: "that human reality is lack, the existence of desire as a human fact suffices to prove."[80]

Without any reference to Baudelaire's "soif insatiable de tout ce qui est au delà,"[81] and doubtless without even any knowledge of

[76] Sartre, *Critique*, p. 22.

[77] Sartre, *L'Être et le néant*, p. 127: "Une étude de la réalité humaine doit commence par le cogito."

[78] *Ibid.*, p. 128: "Le sens profond du cogito c'est de rejeter par essence hors de soi."

[79] *Ibid.*, p. 129. How deep a personal lode Sartre is here mining may be gauged by the fact that his virtuoso analysis of *manque* in the individual is complemented, in the later *Critique de la raison dialectique*, by analysis of *rareté* in the social group.

[80] *Ibid.*, p. 130.

[81] Sartre does refer to the passage, however, in his study of Baudelaire. In fact he

Coleridge's characterization of the *leit-motiv* of Platonic thought as a "thirst for something not attained, to which nothing in life is found commensurate and which still impels the soul to pursue"[82]—without reference to these usages, Sartre begins to analyze the structure of incomplete circles, hunger, and above all thirst (*soif*) to demonstrate the way in which lack becomes *desire toward*:

> A being that is what it is . . . summons nothing to itself in order to complete itself. An incomplete circle does not call for completion unless it is surpassed by human transcendence. In itself it is complete and perfectly positive as an open curve. A psychic state that existed with the sufficiency of this curve could not possess in addition the slightest "appeal to" something else; it would be itself without any relation to what is not it. In order to constitute it as hunger or thirst, an external transcendence surpassing it toward the totality "satisfied hunger" would be necessary.[83]

If hunger is hunger only by external transcendence toward the totality of "hunger satisfied," the same holds true for thirst. Thirst cannot be derived from the conception of the organism itself, but only by that conception and an added conception of transcendence:

> Thirst as an organic phenomenon, as a "physiological" need of water, does not exist. An organism deprived of water presents certain positive phenomena: for example, a certain coagulating thickening of the blood, which provokes in turn certain other phenomena. . . . Consequently, the being of psychic thirst will be the being in itself of a *state*, and we are referred once again to a transcendent witness (pp. 130-31).

From the analysis of thirst, Sartre proceeds to a general formulation that is hardly distinguishable from the meaning of Plato:

> If desire is to be able to be desire to itself, it must necessarily be itself transcendence; that is, it must by nature be an escape from itself toward the desired object. In other words, it must be a lack, a lack undergone, created by the surpassing which it is not; it must be its own lack of—. *Desire is a lack of being* [italics mine]. It is haunted in its inmost being by the being of which it is desire.

---

analyzes it and its surrounding complex with keenness and distaste, commenting that "The whole of Baudelaire is in this passage" (Sartre, *Baudelaire*, p. 180).

[82] *Philosophical Lectures*, p. 158.   [83] *L'Être et le néant*, p. 130.

Thus it bears witness to the existence of lack in the being of human reality (p. 131).

Although the "soif" addressed by *L'Être et le néant*, unlike Baudelaire's "soif insatiable" for the "au delà," transcends merely toward totality, the very prosaism of Sartre's depression of the emotional expansions of hyperouranic tropism makes more prominent the whole that is desired and pursued. Thus in two climactic passages Sartre hammers home the wholeness that underlies all directings to transcendence:

Human reality is its own surpassing toward what it lacks; it surpasses itself toward the particular being which it would be if it were what it is. Human reality is not something that exists first in order afterwards to lack this or that; it exists first as lack and in immediate, synthetic connection what what it lacks. Thus the pure event by which human reality rises as a presence in the world is apprehended by itself as its own lack. In its coming into existence *human reality grasps itself as incomplete being* [italics mine]. It apprehends itself as being in so far as it is not, in the presence of the particular totality that it lacks (p. 132).

If human reality apprehends itself only in the presence of the particular totality that it lacks, a corollary must be, concludes Sartre, that

Imperfect being surpasses itself toward perfect being; the being that is the foundation only of its nothingness surpasses itself toward the being that is the foundation of its being. But the being toward which human reality surpasses itself is not a transcendent God; it is at the heart of human reality; it is only human reality itself as totality (p. 133).

After this glimpse of the transcendently constituted whole for which we yearn, even Sartre becomes almost poetical:

Human reality is suffering in its very being, because it rises in being as perpetually haunted by a totality which it is without being able to be it, precisely because it could not attain the in-itself without losing itself as for-itself. Human reality therefore is by nature an unhappy consciousness without possibility of surpassing its unhappy state (p. 134).

Schiller, too, was haunted by totality, but his more aesthetic nature made him more hopeful: "It must be false that the cultivation of individual powers necessitates the sacrifice of their totality; or however much the law of nature did have that tendency, we must be at liberty to restore by means of a higher art this wholeness in our nature (*diese Totalität in unserer Natur*) which art has destroyed."[84]

So the meontic mode of poetry and art is as essential to human life as is the mimetic. Meontic poetry is, to adopt Sidney's words, not "an Art of lyes, but of true doctrine"; it is "not banished, but honored by Plato."[85] The meontic and the mimetic modes conjoin in their human function. The mimetic *arrests* the flow and dispersal of existence. "To arrest, for the space of a breath, the hands busy about the work of the earth," writes Conrad, "and compel men entranced by the sight of distant goals to glance for a moment at the surrounding vision of form and color, of sunshine and shadows; to make them pause for a look, for a sigh, for a smile—such is the aim, difficult and evanescent, and reserved only for a very few to achieve."[86] Poetry, says Shelley, "arrests the vanishing apparitions which haunt the interlunations of life, and veiling them, or in language or in form, sends them forth among mankind."[87]

Meontic activity, on the other hand, *restores* the wholeness of existence; that is the highest common *topos* for all such art. It restores this wholeness even though daily experience supplies only an awareness of fragmentation and incompleteness. Its tactic of restoration is as protean as are the triumphal visions of great artists. It can be by the language and meaning of the "Epithalamion," of Spenser; it can also be by the different language and different statement of Spenser's "Fowre Hymnes." Both poetries are illustrations of what we may call the *holocleric* way. That way presents itself in epitome in these lines from "Sailing to Byzantium":

> An aged man is but a paltry thing,
> A tattered coat upon a stick, unless
> Soul clap its hands and sing, and louder sing
> For every tatter in its mortal dress.
> Nor is there singing school but studying
> Monuments of its own magnificence.[88]

The way of restoration, again, can be by the deep remembering of Proust and of Wordsworth—the *anamnetic* way.

The meontic restoration to wholeness, in still a third major proc-

---

[84] *Schillers Werke*, XII, 24.   [85] *Sidney*, III, 35.
[86] Joseph Conrad, "Preface" to *The Nigger of the Narcissus*.
[87] Shelley, *Prose*, p. 32.   [88] *Yeats*, p. 191.

ess of art, can occur by what we may term the *thaliatic* way, as in these lines:

> Deer walk upon our mountains, and the quail
> Whistle about us their spontaneous cries;
> Sweet berries ripen in the wilderness;
> And, in the isolation of the sky,
> At evening, casual flocks of pigeons make
> Ambiguous undulations as they sink,
> Downward to darkness, on extended wings.[89]

Though the lines conclude with an image of descent, their tone and truth are celebratory ascent and blooming abundance. To cite a single further example, the thaliatic way is exemplified in the opulent fullness of Marvell's garden:

> What wond'rous Life in this I lead!
> Ripe Apples drop about my head;
> The Luscious Clusters of the Vine
> Upon my Mouth do crush their Wine;
> The Nectaren, and curious Peach,
> Into my hands themselves do reach;
> Stumbling on Melons, as I pass,
> Insnar'd with Flow'rs, I fall on Grass.[90]

Just as any work of art, however, can and frequently does develop itself in both the mimetic and meontic modes, so too in the special sphere of meontic poetry do the three major tactics of restoration frequently and in fact characteristically intermingle. This effect is not accidental, but essential to the being of a great poem in the meontic mode. Such a poem is in its nature an *iridescence*. Its various colorations pulsate and shade into one another; its kinetic reaching toward the hyperouranic realm, because of the indefiniteness of that realm, becomes a *shimmering*. Thus, to bring forward merely two examples from poems just noticed, the almost perfectly thaliatic stanza from Marvell's "The Garden" is iridescently complemented, in that same poem, by an equally perfect holocleric stanza that shimmers both in itself and with the other stanza in hyperouranic longing:

> Here at the Fountains sliding foot,
> Or at some Fruit-trees mossy root,
> Casting the Bodies Vest aside,

---

[89] *Stevens*, p. 70.   [90] *Marvell*, I, 149.

My Soul into the boughs does glide:
There like a Bird it sits, and sings,
Then whets, and combs its silver Wings;
And, till prepar'd for longer flight,
Waves in its Plumes the various Light.[91]

On the other hand, but by the same token, the holocleric stanza about the aged man, which we quoted from "Sailing to Byzantium," merges into iridescence with the thaliatic fullness of that same poem's last stanza:

Once out of nature I shall never take
My bodily form from any natural thing,
But such a form as Grecian goldsmiths make
Of hammered gold and gold enameling
To keep a drowsy Emperor awake;
Or set upon a golden bough to sing
To lords and ladies of Byzantium
Of what is past, or passing, or to come.[92]

Shimmering is started by the repeated invocations of goldenness, and the discrete nominations fuse to a perfect wholeness in the final gathering together of "what is past, or passing, or to come."

From another perspective, we may think of the shimmering of great meontic poetry as the breaking of linear bounds by the tidal attraction of the hyperouranic realm. Indeed, the very existence of poetic cadence and rhythm—and specifically of poetic meter and rhyme—constitutes a wavelike pulsation that both shimmers within the poem and prepares for iridescent lengthening and breaking toward the place beyond the heavens:

From this the poem springs: that we live in a place
That is not our own and, much more, not ourselves
And hard it is in spite of blazoned days.

We are the mimics. Clouds are pedagogues
The air is not a mirror but bare board,
Coulisse bright-dark, tragic chiaroscuro

And comic color of the rose, in which
Abysmal instruments make sounds like pips
Of the sweeping meanings that we add to them.[93]

[91] *Ibid.*

[92] *Yeats,* p. 192.

[93] *Stevens,* pp. 383-84.

All poets of the first rank arrive at some version of the realization that "the poem springs" from the fact that "we live in a place that is not our own." Their paths of approach are varied, but the essence of their recognitions is identical. Wordsworth, for instance, says that the "appropriate business of poetry" is "not to treat of things as they *are*." In the "higher poetry" we look for "a reflection of the wisdom of the heart and the grandeur of the imagination." He then says that "Poetry is most just to its own divine origin when . . . it breathes the spirit of religion." The mind, he notes, rests part of its religious burden upon "words and symbols"; and he then speaks of "the affinity between religion and poetry . . . between religion—whose element is infinitude . . . and poetry— ethereal and transcendent, yet incapable to sustain her existence without sensuous incarnation."[94]

Poets quite different from Wordsworth reach similar understandings. Symbol and transcendence—the referents of the fact that "we live in a place that is not our own"—permeate, to take an additional example virtually at random, a poem by Rubén Darío that Octavio Paz called the "greatest poem" in a culled collection. To Paz it contained not only "the desire to grasp the infinite" but also "all of Symbolism." Hailed as master by Lorca and Neruda (". . . that great shadow who sang more loftily than ourselves"), Darío wrote in his *Prosas profanas y otros poemas*:

> I seek a form that my style cannot discover,
> a bud of thought that wants to be a rose;
>
> . . . . . .
>
> the stars have predicted that I will see the goddess;
> and the light reposes within my soul like the bird
> of the moon reposing on a tranquil lake.
>
> And I only find the word that runs away,
> the melodious introduction that flows from the flute.[95]

In whatever combinations of holocleric, anamnetic, and thaliatic statement the subtleties of great art may dictate, however, the meontic mode, like the mimetic mode, responds to the phenomenon of mortal loss. The mimetic *arrests* the loss of being, the meontic *restores* the loss of being. That startlingly proliferated type and theme of Renaissance painting, visible in all the great museums of Europe and America and called "The Annunciation," in which an angel appears to Mary to announce her role in the redemptive

[94] *Prose*, III, 64-65.   [95] *Darío*, pp. 14, 141, 60.

process, is also the archetype, as it were, of meontic art. The hyperouranic realm is represented by the angel, the autochthonic by the prospective mother, the necessary commerce between them by the annunciation itself. And the presence of the angel, the emissary of *what is not there*—winged, too, like Plato's souls that have seen true being—no less than that of the angel's prophecy, which is also *not there*, authenticates the sublimely meontic hope of human restoration.

Yet perhaps not even in that high *topos* is the symbolizing of wholeness more exalted than in the holocleric vision of Plato:

> then were we all initiated into the mystery which is rightly accounted blessed beyond all others; whole and unblemished (ὁλόκληροι) were we that did celebrate it, untouched by the evils that awaited us in days to come; whole and unblemished (ὁλόκληροι) too, steadfast and calm and happy were the spectacles we beheld; pure was the light that shone around us, and pure were we, without taint of that prison house in which we are now enclosed, and call body, bound there like an oyster in its shell.[96]

The realm to which the initiate bore witness is the *topos* to which all meontic art aspires. It is a wholeness and a transcendence, shimmering before us as the goal of all strivings. It alleviates the burden of incompleteness, fragmentation, and ruin. And if we could enter rather than glimpse it, all strivings would cease; for there could be no need of art in paradise.[97]

[96] *Phaedrus* 250B-C. The passage well illustrates by its objectifying of the transcendent terminus the necessity of a positive conception—as opposed to a fictional or negative conception—of such a realm. Cf. Levinas: "The idea of the perfect and of infinity is not reducible to the negation of the imperfect; negativity is incapable of transcendence. Transcendence designates a relation with a reality infinitely distant from my own reality, yet without this distance destroying this relation and without this relation destroying this distance" (Levinas, p. 41).

[97] Compare Gide in 1891: "The poet is he who looks. And what does he see?—Paradise. For Paradise is everywhere; not in trusting to appearances. Appearances are imperfect: they stammer out the truths they conceal. . . . The poet piously contemplates; he leans upon symbols, and in silence descends deeply into the heart of things—and when he, visionary, has pierced to the idea, the intimate number harmonious of his being, which sustains the imperfect form, he seizes it; then, careless of this transitory form that clothes the idea in time, he knows how to restore to it a form eternal, *its* form at last true, and fatal—paradisaical and crystalline" (Michaud, pp. 730-31). Compare further Edward Young in 1759: "so boundless are the bold excursions of the human mind, that in the vast void beyond real existence, it can call forth shadowy beings, and unknown worlds, as numerous, as bright, and, perhaps, as lasting, as the stars; such quite-original beauties we may call Paradisaical" (*Conjectures*, p. 70).

Index

◊ ♦ ◊

Index compiled by Annette Cafarelli

Library of Congress Cataloging in Publication Data

McFarland, Thomas.
Romanticism and the forms of ruin.

Bibliography: p.
Includes index.
1. English poetry—19th century—History and criticism.
2. Romanticism.
3. Wordsworth, William, 1770-1850—Criticism and interpretation.
4. Coleridge, Samuel Taylor, 1772-1834—Criticism and interpretation.
5. Poetry.   I. Title.
PR590.M25   821'.7'09   80-7546
ISBN 0-691-06437-7
ISBN 0-691-01373-X (pbk.)